Punishment and Social Control

Enlarged second edition

NEW LINES IN CRIMINOLOGY
An Aldine de Gruyter Series of Texts and Monographs

SERIES EDITOR

Thomas G. Blomberg, *Florida State University*

Thomas G. Blomberg and Stanley Cohen
Punishment and Social Control (*Enlarged Second Edition*)

Thomas G. Blomberg and Karl Lucken
American Penology
A History of Control

Bruce A. Jacobs
Robbing Drug Dealers
Violence Beyond the Law

David J. Rothman
Conscience and Convenience
The Asylum and Its Alternatives in Progressive America

David J. Rothman
The Discovery of the Asylum
Social Order and Disorder in the New Republic

Sandro Segre
Controlling Illegal Drugs
A Comparative Study

Pamela Wilcox, Kenneth C. Land, and Scott A. Hunt
Criminal Circumstance
A Dynamic Multicontextual Criminal Opportunity Theory

Punishment and Social Control

Enlarged Second Edition

Thomas G. Blomberg and Stanley Cohen

Editors

ALDINE DE GRUYTER
New York

About the Editors

Thomas G. Blomberg is Sheldon L. Messinger Professor of Criminology at the School of Criminology and Criminal Justice at Florida State University.

Stanley Cohen is Martin White Professor of Sociology at the London School of Economics.

Copyright © 2003 Walter de Gruyter, Inc., New York

All rights reserved. No part of this publication may be reproduced or transmitted in any form or by any means, electronic or mechanical, including photocopy, recording, or any information storage or retrieval system, without permission in writing from the publisher.

ALDINE DE GRUYTER
A division of Walter de Gruyter, Inc.
200 Saw Mill River Road
Hawthorne, New York 10532

This publication is printed on acid free paper ∞

Library of Congress Cataloging-in-Publication Data

Punishment and social control / edited by Thomas G. Blomberg and Stanley Cohen. — Enlarged 2nd ed.
    p. cm. — (New lines in criminology)
Includes bibliographical references and index.
  ISBN 0-202-30701-8 (pbk. : alk. paper)
  1. Prisons—Government policy—United States. 2. Punishment—
Government policy—United States. 3. Social control—United
States. 4. Criminal justice, Administration of—United States.
5. Alternatives to imprisonment—United States. 6. United States—
Social policy. I. Blomberg, Thomas G. II. Cohen, Stanley. III. Series.

  HV9469.P86 2003
  364.6'0973—dc21
                                2003001948

Manufactured in the United States of America

10 9 8 7 6 5 4 3 2 1

Contents

In Memoriam
Sheldon L. Messinger

1925–2003

Sheldon L. Messinger passed away on March 6, 2003, following a re-markable career in which he had a major influence upon the disciplines of sociology and criminology and the lives of many colleagues, students, and others who knew him. Better known within his academic communities than in the public world, Shelly was the sociologist's sociologist, the crim-inologist's criminologist. And rather than make statements about his val-ues or devise theories about his work, he simply transferred to those whom he studied, the same kindness, respect and humanity shown towards his friends, colleagues, and students.

Shelly Messinger was born in Chicago in 1925 and went to Hyde Park High School. He was an undergraduate at the University of Chicago and UCLA, and then completed his Master's and Ph.D. in sociology from UCLA. He began his long affiliation with the University of California at Berkeley in 1961, when he joined Philip Selznick in founding the Center for the Study of Law and Society. His subsequent positions at Berkeley in-cluded Professor and Dean of the School of Criminology (during its tur-bulent years), Professor of Law, and Chair of the Jurisprudence and Social Policy program. At the time of his retirement in 1991, he was the Elizabeth Josselyn Boalt Professor of Law.

From the beginning of his long academic career Shelly was an inspiring and ever-helpful colleague and teacher. You could never doubt that his in-terest in your work was genuine; he would praise what you had done, but knew exactly how to challenge you to go further. He was famous for his writ-ten comments on manuscripts (however crude their stage of drafting). Meticulous, long and carefully organized, these responses were more like re-views than "comments." Shelly's invariable introduction would be: "I think what you are trying to say is . . . ." He would proceed gently to refine the way you had formulated the problem, to remind you about the empirical ev-idence you so obviously lacked and to spot the missing links with broader theoretical arguments and social issues. This help went far beyond the norms of academic review. Moreover, his normal, unselfish contributions were vis-ible only in the hundreds of unnoticed footnotes and acknowledgments thanking Shelly for his help. And this help was uniquely empowering.

In criminology, the name of Messinger is invariably associated with the classic 1960 paper he wrote with Gresham Sykes, "The Inmate Social System." Shelly's early research interests and publications covered a range of topics besides inmate social life, including the transformation of social movements, dramaturgical aspects of social life, civil justice and the poor, and family normalization of schizophrenia. His later research was focused upon the sociology and history of parole, the context of parole decisions and the control of coercive justice institutions. Throughout this work, he retained his sense of macro- and critical theory but always stayed with the empirically concrete. In the seventies and eighties, Shelly was in a recognizably unique position in the emerging new discourse of punishment, law, crime, and social control. He seemed equally at home in the mainstream criminology world; in the "law in action" and "law and society" movements; and in the new sociology of deviance (associated with such friends of his as Howard Becker, Erving Goffman, and John Kitsuse). His easy combination of Chicago and West Coast intellectual styles, alongside his gentle (but permanent) irony, virtually personified what his friend David Matza termed the "central irony" of the "neo-Chicagoan" idea of labeling theory.

The volume of essays that we edited, *Punishment and Social Control* (1995), was meant to celebrate Shelly's retirement as well as reflect his research and theoretical interests. All the contributors—old colleagues and students from different cohorts and traditions—were delighted to participate in this project. We received the same enthusiastic response to this enlarged second edition, which Shelly did not live to see. A living tribute, alas, has turned into a memorial. If Shelly treated sociology as no different from other parts of his life, so—even after his retirement—he treated parts of his life as if they were opportunities to do sociology. After the devastating fires of 1992 in Berkeley and Oakland, Shelly initiated an "action research" project to investigate and improve the methods of insurance compensation for the victims. When he discovered how little was known about the rare form of leukemia he had developed, he organized a sophisticated e-mail survey to collect basic epidemiological data. A few days after Shelly's death, his younger son, Eli, wrote (to one of Shelly's London friends, the criminologist Malcolm Davies) ". . . a personal note I think you'll enjoy: One of the last conversations he and I had while he was in the hospital began with his observation 'This is an unusual life.' When I asked him what he meant, he talked briefly about the life of one living in the hospital—being ill, dealing with doctors and nurses, etc. Obviously he was applying his sociological powers of observation to the very end."

We are saddened by Shelly's passing, but grateful for the years of his friendship and support.

Thomas G. Blomberg
Stanley Cohen

Introduction

The first edition of this book was published in 1995 to mark the retirement of Sheldon L. Messinger from the Center for the Study of Law and Society at the University of California, Berkeley. The scope and orientation of this Enlarged Second Edition remain the same, but we have excluded all personal tributes and references to Messinger's own contribution to the study of punishment and social control.[1] In recognition of the continued growth and diversity of interest in this field, seven completely new chapters have been added[2] and seven of the original chapters have been updated and revised.

Virtually all these additions and revisions reflect (and reflect on) two notable changes over these years. The first, paradoxically, is a declining use of the broader concept of social control, in favor of a more exclusive focus on punishment. Some reasons for this concentration lie in the second change: not a mere numerical rise in rates of imprisonment, but the emergence (notably in the United States) of the distinctive phenomenon of mass imprisonment (Garland 2001a, 2001b).

The "mass imprisonment thesis" is directly addressed by several papers; in this Introduction we pay more attention to the origins and fate of the concept of social control.

ORIGINS

While "crime," "law," and "punishment" are subjects that have everyday meanings not very far from their academic representations; "social control" is one of those terms that appear in the sociological discourse without any corresponding everyday usage. This concept has a rather mixed lineage.

Political

The oldest branch goes back to the tradition of classic political and social theory associated with the emergence of the liberal democratic state.

1

Here the *political* problem was how a government could achieve a degree of control over its citizens that did not infringe on their rights and liberties. The *conceptual* problem was how to understand the social space that was created between the individual and the state. In both political and conceptual terms, the problem of social control was part of a broader discourse about individual freedom, regulation, citizenship, and the social order.

This connotation of the term "social control" all but disappeared within the public discourse of Western democratic societies. When it did reappear, the meaning was always pejorative—as in standard futuristic and dystopian imagery (such as *1984* and *Brave New World*) about overcontrolled societies. Or else it was used to characterize real totalitarian regimes as in, "Saddam Hussein controls the Iraqi population through fear." Punishment and fear of punishment were the means toward total control.

The utopia of Skinner's behaviorist psychology, *Walden Two*—published in 1948 and now virtually forgotten—promised a synchronized, but "non-punitive" society, a world where people would naturally behave well, but *without* punishment. This is obviously opposed to the "pure" punishment of retributive and just deserts theories. Less obviously, Skinnerian operant conditioning is also quite different from the version of behaviorism found in utilitarian theories, notably deterrence. As Kleck shows (Chapter 13), the doctrine of general deterrence depends on a "limited rationality": informed by something like the pleasure-pain principle and attuned to the risks of punishment. Operant reinforcement, on the other hand, is the proper arrangement of environmental contingencies and conditioning. In this respect it resembles today's "managerial criminology" and "new penology": preemptive, preventive and depoliticized.

The component parts of this package—situational crime prevention, environmental criminology, risk analysis, surveillance etc.—have been well documented. There is, however, much controversy (see Chapters 1–3, by Sparks, Garland, and Simon and Feeley) about whether these models have indeed become dominant and their supposed relationship with more traditional moralistic and punitive methods. Their political success lies precisely in their claim to be nonpolitical, that is, technological solutions to problems (insecurity, victimization, fear of crime) that are beyond political dissent.

There are, however, some important signals of a return to the political. The techniques of surveillance, covert tricks, and invisible deceptions described by Marx (Chapter 8) and Staples (Chapter 9) raise traditional liberal concerns about privacy and the protection of negative liberties (that is, freedom from unnecessary state intervention). Debates about civil society and "governance," both in the West and in post-Communist societies, have revived earlier political interests. And one of the most influential ideas in modern criminology, Braithwaite's neo-Durkheimian theory of reintegrative shaming, is seen by its advocates as allied to communitarian visions and as belonging to the political ideal of "republicanism."

Anthropological

Another quite different lineage goes back to the twentieth-century academic institutionalization of sociology in the United States. Here, the political dimension gives way to a concern with the *universal* social processes by which societies were integrated and social conformity induced. Integration, in functionalist theory, was explained in terms of the interdependency between different social institutions. Conformity was explained at the family or cultural level ("informal social control") and in terms of the Freudian metapsychology of internalization, socialization, and conscience formation. The superego was the "policemen in the head." This tradition is "anthropological" in the sense of looking for universal forms and patterns.

Social control was very much a central concept in the sociology of the Chicago School, but social control and its breakdown (social disorganization) were not macropolitical issues; they were to be observed in the more immediate settings of city, neighborhood, slum, peer group, and gang. The process of learning is a matter of cultural transmission; the content of what is learned depends on the social ecology of the community.

Despite such differences between schools of sociology, the assumption—still to be found in some introductory sociology textbooks—was that the "informal" and universal processes of inducing conformity normally worked. Only when they "failed" through some breakdown, disintegration, or pathology (whether at societal or community levels) were the "formal" methods of social control—the police, criminal law, and justice system—brought into play. These formal methods themselves were the proprietary subject matter of disciplines such as criminology that were intellectually marginalized precisely because they were not concerned with the normal.

"Anthropological" thinking (in the vernacular, nonacademic sense) allows for a typology of social control practices: formal versus informal, state versus market, coercive versus voluntary, public versus private, etc. There should also be measures of social control that are more refined than statistical normality versus abnormality, thus allowing for comparisons within one society over time or across different societies.

All this is only a prelude to interesting matters. Consider, for example, Carlen's (Chapter 4) question about how the informal ("antisocial") social control of women "preempts and buttresses" women's relatively infrequent criminalization and imprisonment.

Sociology of Crime, Deviance, and Control

The original conceptual source of this volume seldom addressed either political and anthropological interests. In the 1960s, social movements calling for decriminalization (especially of "crimes without victims," such as homosexuality, gambling, and recreational drug use) did indeed appeal to the political ideals of protecting privacy and individual rights against an overreaching state. But this impetus was not followed through. The concept of social control was grounded in the new sociology of deviance of the same period—often called "labeling theory." It derived from the symbolic interactionist and ethnographic strands of the Chicago school (and hence labeled by David Matza as "neo-Chicagoan"). Its contribution was to place the microsociology of social control—the construction of deviance, deviant identities, and stigma—onto the sociological agenda. It concentrated on the paradoxical and ironical relationships between deviance and social control (many illustrated in Marx's Chapter 7 on undercover policing). The most intriguing irony of all was the causal reversal: not that deviance leads to social control, but that social control creates deviance.

These ideas have lost their original fascination. But for a while they opened up the restricted domains of criminology and the criminal justice system to the resonant subjects of the wider 1960s culture: drugs, sexuality, madness, political protest, and a celebration of cultural diversity. This gave rise to facile dichotomies—control and repression on the one hand, diversity, freedom, and tolerance on the other. It also left behind a distinctive vision of ideal social control (Cohen 1985): informal, decentralized, inclusive, and nonstigmatic—lying somewhere outside the tentacles of the organized state systems of law, criminal justice, imprisonment, and punishment. In a more conventional sense, it left behind the pragmatic definition of social control as the repertoire of institutional responses to deviance.

Sociologists of deviance and crime began to apply this notion of social control at three levels. First, the micro-, interpersonal, or face-to-face level: how stigmatic meanings, identities, and roles were constructed and negotiated. Second, the organizational level: how formal bureaucracies and professions (the police, courts, corrections, welfare and treatment agencies) went about their business of deviance-processing. Third, the macro- or historical level: how particular deviant categories (such as drug abuse) or laws (such as prohibition) or institutions (such as the juvenile court) were established in the first place.

Whatever conceptual or substantive unity held all this together—in truth, not very much—was breaking up at the beginning of the 1970s. The dominant frame was now the state's power to criminalize. The heavyweight subjects of law, punishment, and criminal justice came to dominate social policy and academic study. Other forms of social control were misleadingly referred to (with either romantic envy or else lack of interest) as "alternatives." At the same time, the legal gaze widened to include soci-olegal studies, sociology of law, critical legal studies, and "law and soci-ety." A distinctive policy-driven agenda emerged around such issues as the critique of imprisonment, skepticism about rehabilitation, the search for "alternatives," the emergence of the "back to justice" model, and the implementation of determinate sentencing reforms.

In the meantime, the residues of labeling theory still influenced the more amorphous areas of deviance and social problems. The theory of social problems as claims-making (Spector and Kitsuse 1977) led today's influ-ential "social constructionist" model of social problems (Holstein and Mil-ler 1993).

The British version of the original deviance-control paradigm had, from the outset, taken on a committed political character missing in the United States. By focusing on the political origins and enforcement of the criminal law, it also returned to a more state-centered view of social control and re-stored some connections with classical European social theory. All this re-quired a rather delicate balancing act between immediate public demands for the criminal justice system to "do something," and the long-term agenda of critical theory.

By the end of the 1970s, this literature had become enriched by contri-butions from outside its original theoretical sources. Most notably there was the first wave of "revisionist" histories about the origins of the asylum or total institution: prisons, mental hospitals, and juvenile correctional in-stitutions. The historical accounts by Rothman (on the early-nineteenth-century American penitentiary), Ignatieff (on the equivalent developments in England), and—more complicatedly—Foucault, all opened the theoret-ical landscape well beyond this apparently specialized subject matter.

Research on the historical roots of the prison in the early nineteenth century should have signaled a return to the original wider meaning of the concept of social control. The early "discoverers of the asylum," in Rothman's influential account, were Durkheimians before Durkheim. The cause of deviance, they thought, was an anomic normlessness; the solu-tion was for the state to compensate for this breakdown of traditional con-trol; the penitentiary not only had to segregate deviants (from outside and within the walls) but also had to stand as a model or microcosm of what a well-ordered society should look like. Much of this quite explicit *causal* thinking is lost by an exaggerated use of the prison as a *metaphor* for so-cial control. While Blomberg (Chapter 19) questions the use of control metaphors such as net-widening, Wacquant (Chapter 21) uses the ghetto and Christie (2000) the gulag to depict the human geography of mass imprisonment.

By this time, Foucault had become the dominating presence. His work became (as he wanted it to be) a series of open texts that allowed quite dif-ferent readings and directions. Versions of radical, feminist, and critical theory began to find resonant message in his gnomic writings about power, discipline, and control; social constructionists adapted concepts such as "normalization," "power/knowledge," "regimes of truth;" subjects such as mental illness, the self, the body, and sexuality reappeared at the center of the theoretical stage.

Academic work continued in theoretical and historical directions: the continued attempt to explain changes in state-organized systems of social control: ideologies, master patterns, strategies, tactics, alliances. Various systems of punishment, treatment, welfare, and rehabilitation became the subjects of a new style of sociological enquiry best exemplified by Garland's (1985) study of the emerging juvenile justice system in late-nineteenth-century Britain. The three requirements for an ideal study of social control were becoming clearer:

1.   A historical explanation of correctional change (whether conventionally historical or more like either of Foucault's "archeology" or "genealogy").

2.   Close familiarity with the actual strategies deployed by correctional agencies as they go about their business of segregating, housing, controlling, classifying, and disposing of deviant populations.

3.   The element that unfortunately became more and more marginal: a sense of the subjective experience of those people who become the objects of control.

Policy interests, at the same time, were driven by the continued escalation of crime rates and the continued looming presence of the prison. Here came yet another round in the historical quest for "alternatives." And yet again as the critique of imprisonment became more obvious and the implementation of alternatives more frenzied, so the prison came even more to dominate the punitive landscape. Strategies such as diversion, community corrections, and intermediate punishment were implemented (Blomberg, Chapter 20) analyzes a typical set of examples) without lowering the rates of either crime or imprisonment. This led to the net-widening critique: that alternatives were really becoming supplements, the system was increasing its reach. Particular attention was paid to newsworthy innovations such as tagging, electronic monitoring, or house arrest, rather than the traditional noncustodial alternatives within the old system, such as probation and parole.

This is the point—at the beginning of the 1990s—when most stories in this volume start. From a distance these stories are similar; at close glance, we see that the same themes—spiraling rates of imprisonment, public punitiveness, the managerial ethos—are woven together rather differently. Christie's disturbing thesis about the apparently infinite expansion of the American crime control industry was originally published in 1993 and becomes more plausible with each updated edition (Christie 2000). This invokes as causes populist punitiveness, financial entrepreneurship, and amoral bureaucratic inertia. This mixture is rather different from Feeley and Simon's "new penology" (Feeley and Simon 1992) as updated in Chapter 3. Echoes of both these versions appear in Garland's original 1995 account (Chapter 2) of the oscillations within modernist penality and his further elaboration of the "culture of control"(Garland 2001b).

In his guide to trends and literature in the sociology of punishment, Sparks (Chapter 1) warns us that punishment "is pervaded by history, porous to culture, buffeted by the contingencies of politics and economy." Punishment and social control, far from being residual or marginal, are exemplary sites for observing such grand trends as managerialism, the proclaimed end of history, actuarial prediction, neoliberal rationality, privatization, and the rolling back of welfare states. The correctional system is not driven by its surface utilitarian justification ("what works") but by those wider social trends it also mimics so well. In the United States especially, the political signifiers of crime control are self-evident: public talk about fear and insecurity; new laws; the populist symbiosis between resentment and punitiveness; massive budgetary allocations; and electoral politics. If only in this sense, the social control literature has begun to register its original political lineage.

There may also be a more subtle return to the more generic ("anthropological") meaning of social control; this comes from two directions.

First, as the European abolitionists have always said in their visionary style, the punitive/criminal law model must be seen as only one form of social control. The misleading notion of "alternatives" to punishment implies that punishment through the criminal law is the normal method of social control. In fact, it is this mode of social control that is really the "alternative." This point is self-evident in anthropological typologies of the social control repertoire (Black 1991; Horwitz 1990). These place the punitive criminal law model alongside other forms of control such as therapy, mediation, restitution, compensation, tolerance, and avoidance. Most importantly, these are lists not only of "how to control deviance" but also "how to deal with conflict."

A second direction comes from feminism—both in the wider sense of understanding gender as a form of social control and in the narrower sense of uncovering the gender-base of decision-making within the formal social control system. Both senses are covered by Pat Carlen (Chapter 4), who shows how concerns that seem specific to feminism raise broader issues about inclusive and exclusive forms of control. For example, institutions for the treatment of such problems as anorexia and eating disorders are sensitive to wider social processes—in this case, not just the control over the (female) body, but the commodification of "social control" as a property to be bought and sold (Ewick 1993).

CONTENTS AND THEMES

Part I of this volume offers some guides to the theoretical interface be-tween the narrow field of correctional punishment and the broader socio-logical study of social control. Part II deals with selected modes of surveillance, policing, and law enforcement—subjects of interest in them-selves, but also as "entry points" or filters leading into the correctional sys-tem. Part III refocuses on punishment: how it may be measured, its supposed "stability" over time, how it has been justified in principle and allocated in practice. Part IV deals with the prison: its history and sociol-ogy, the attempts to reform it from within, the search for alternatives, and above all, the unrelenting increase in the sheer numbers of people incar-cerated.

The origins of "punishment and social control" as a field of study raise some common questions.

Master Shifts

The original features of deviancy control systems associated with the birth of the modern democratic state were (1) the consolidation of state power through the criminal law, (2) the segregation of deviants in closed institutions such as the prison, and (3) the foundation of expert, profes-sional, and academic classificatory systems (like criminology itself). A number of our chapters keep returning to these original traces before try-ing to detect later shifts in thinking about and carrying out social control policy.

These chapters are preoccupied (perhaps too much) with what is new, different, or continuous with what went before: are these "new" forms of surveillance and control, and are they "more" intrusive, technical, and penetrating than before? What is "new" about the "new penology"? More ambitiously, Garland asks whether the seismic shifts of modernism and postmodernism have any bearing on the changing ideas and practice of punishment. How do we explain such changes, and are these indeed, in Foucault's sense, instances of "strategies without a strategist"? What effect do these changes have?

Ideas and Policy

Any study of these overall changes, real or putative, raises the vexed question of the relationship between ideas and policy. Putative reforms or policy shifts—for example, in parole, policing, fixed sentencing guidelines, prison architecture—may be viewed as three phases. First, there are the visions, intentions, ideas, concepts, theory, ideologies, and knowledge (or knowledge-claims), which are supposed to have informed this policy. Second, there are the programs, plans, projects, and blueprints in which the theories are supposedly embedded. Third, there are the observable, ground-level ways in which the policy is set up, practiced, or implemented. These phases of social policy—theory and practice, ideas and implementation, knowledge and power—are related, but they are not the "same." As Foucault sardonically remarked, if knowledge and power were the same—the claim that some of his readers attribute to him—then he would have wasted all his intellectual life trying to understand the relationship between them.

Ideas/policy, knowledge/power, and theory/practice—these might also be seen, as many of our contributions do, as a relationship between intentions and consequences. For many observers, the entire history of social control over crime and deviance is a story of good intentions leading to bad consequences. But what keeps going wrong? What accounts for this apparently permanent gap? This question is central—because without this gap, neither criticism nor empirical research on correctional policy would ever be needed. One answer is that things go wrong at the implementation stage: the original intentions are not understood, there are not enough resources or appropriate staff, the mistakes are technical. Another theory is that intentions are undermined by bureaucratic convenience or professional self-interest. In yet other versions, the original intentions are themselves suspect—riddled by ideological contradictions or mere masks for political economic interest and other historical imperatives.

Virtually all our contributors work at this interface between ideas and policy. The various discussions about prison reform, alternatives to imprisonment and determinate sentencing are all obvious examples. Our contributors do not always agree with each other; thus Rothman (Chapter 18), for example, applies the "good intentions–bad consequences" model to the link between the ideal of proportional sentencing and the escalation of imprisonment rates; for von Hirsch (Chapter 12), current policy does not result from the logic of proportionality, but from external political changes.

The theoretical problem of conceptualizing the link between knowledge and power bears directly on the question of evaluation: how do we judge whether a policy has succeeded or failed? The logic of standard criminological research about "what works" tends to lead to a ritual confirmation of the null hypothesis: policy X works sometimes with some offenders in some places, but it cannot be proven to have worked better than policy Y. Instead of technical solutions to this nihilism—more sophisticated statistics, larger samples—evaluation needs to be studied in a more historical and contextualized way. The question raised by Matza and Morgan (Chapter 5) on the prohibition of drug use—how can such a massive project of social engineering continue despite a widely shared sense of total failure?—can be projected onto many other policies. So too could Jacobs's question (Chapter 17) about the impact of judicial reform on prison: what would count as a significant social reform?

In Waldo and Paternoster's detailed story (Chapter 14), recent attempts to reform the discredited and "broken" institution of the death penalty are merely "tinkerings with the machinery of death." Their conclusions about the "failure of a social experiment" have wider implications—especially if we take failure to refer not only to the "tinkering" but to the policy itself.

Deviance and Control, Crime and Punishment

Another more theoretically subtle theme runs through some other contributions. The problem began with Durkheim's original formulations about the relativity of deviance and the positive functions of control. It reappeared more than half a century later in labeling theory's speculations about deviance and control. The point is to understand the relationship between the raw phenomena—street crime, victimization, corporate crime, family violence, drug abuse—and the *social control filter* that (1) selects out some of these events and not others, then (2) does different things to each of the selected events.

There are at least five theoretical possibilities.

The commonsense model looks for *rationality* and *correspondence:* the response to crime is first, appropriate to its character; second, proportionate to its extent; and third, sequentially related (that is, the crime comes first, then the control system reacts). The seriousness of the crime problem (and each of its components, visible or not) is exactly "matched" by the responses of crime control institutions. This is analogous to supposing that the selection and coverage of crime by the mass media could and should exactly replicate its occurrence "out there." Needless to say, such expectations about the filters of both social control or mass media are ludicrous.

The polar opposite model suggests a sheer *randomness* and *unpredictability.* This is just as unlikely. We cannot assume (although it often looks like this!) that the control system acts without any internal logic, order, or priorities—and touches the worlds of crime and deviance only by chance.

A third model also assumes that social control is not simply a congruent reaction to deviance. Neither is it random. Modes of control and punishment are transformed almost entirely by "external" social, political, and economic forces.

Another possibility is that any real or putative rationality is a property of crime control organizations; these organizations are "self-regulated" rather than responsive to changes in patterns of crime. Rates of crime are artifacts of social control.

Finally, there is the Durkheimian derived "stability of punishment" hypothesis. Blumstein, a leading contributor to this debate considers (Chapter 10) how the hypothesis makes sense of continually rising prison rates.

The real objection to the correspondence model questions the very possibility of distinguishing the substance of crime, deviance, and social problems as raw phenomena "waiting" for a response. The form taken by the substance is socially constructed from the outset. This construction is produced by such forces as criminalization or the invention of new diagnostic categories.

At the theoretical level, these issues are even more subtle than they appear. But one hardly requires much subtlety to see the complete lack of correspondence and rationality at the policy level. Just living in the contemporary United States should be enough to know that current systems of punishment and control do not work, and are themselves out of control. How else to explain Austin, Irwin, and Kubrin's estimate (Chapter 19) that seven million Americans are under the control of one of several adult and juvenile correctional systems? It is tempting to dismiss these policies as thoughtless but, as Foucault reminds us about the prison system—even the most stupid institutions do have ideas.

No conventional or even innovative ideas, however, can match the policy challenge about to face the "correctional industrial complex" and the theoretical challenge to those who study these policies. "After September 11" has become a slogan that conveys all things to all people but carries some very specific implications (hinted at only by Skolnick's [Chapter 9] on interrogation) for the future of punishment and social control. The already labile boundaries between "ordinary" and political crime will become more unstable; national and global considerations will come closer together; domestic crime control policies will be more influenced by interests of national security; measures to prevent and control international terrorism will cast their reach wider (to financial structures and ideological support); the movements of immigrants, refugees, and asylum seekers will be curtailed and criminalized; taken-for-granted human rights and civil liberties will be restricted.

In the midst of these dramatic social changes, hardly anyone will notice the academic field of "punishment and social control" being drawn closer to political matters. Criminology occupies an uneasy place among the disciplines concerned with systems of punishment and social control. Sociology, as much as it may be drawn into public controversy and internal debates about "value-freedom," can always fall back on its academic identity in the social sciences. Law is secure in its prestige and professional identity.

Criminology, however, is neither a "pure" academic discipline nor a

12   Introduction

profession that offers an applied body of knowledge to solve the crime problem. Its historical lineage has left an insistent tension between the drive to understand and the drive to be relevant. A radical resolution of this tension is the splitting away of applied interests into such areas as "criminal justice studies." This resolution, however, perpetuates rather than solves the tension. The turmoil in American society in the mid-1960s—the anti–Vietnam War protest, campus radicalism, distrust of authority, social unrest, violence in the ghettoes—added a different tension: Should the connection between criminology and crime control agencies (police, courts, prisons) be used neither for "pure" knowledge nor to help these practitioners, but to support a wider program of social justice, even at the expense of antagonizing the dominant political powers?

Such questions soon slipped off the agenda. Now, four decades later, they are returning with greater force. Standard items in a glossary of social control—law and order, private and public security, surveillance and privacy, punishment and intervention—will not look the same.

NOTES

1. For these, see Blomberg and Cohen (1995) especially: Philip Selznick's Forward; our Editorial Introduction; Chapter 2 by Jerome Skolnick (about Messinger's work), and Chapter 16 by Gilbert Geiss (about the Berkeley School of Criminology).
2. Sparks; Skolnick; Staples; Kleck; Waldo and Paternoster; Gartner and Krutschnitt; Austin and Irwin; Wacquant; and Currie.

REFERENCES

Black, Donald. 1991. "The Elementary Forms of Conflict Management." Pp. 43–69 in *New Directions in the Study of Justice, Law and Social Control*, edited by School of Justice Studies. New York: Plenum.
Blomberg and Cohen. 1995. *Punishment and Social Control* (1st ed.). Hawthorne, NY: Aldine de Gruyter.
Christie, Nils. 2000. *Crime Control as Industry: Towards Gulags, Western Style.* London: Routledge.
Cohen, Stanley. 1985. *Visions of Social Control.* Cambridge: Polity.
Cohen, Stanley. 1998. "The Revenge of the Null Hypothesis." *The Critical Criminologist* 8(1):21–25.
Ewick, Patricia. 1993, "Corporate Cures: the Commodification of Social Control." *Studies in Law, Politics and Society* 13:137–57.
Feeley, Malcolm and Jonathan Simon. 1992 "Reflections on the New Penology." *Criminology* 30:449–74.
Garland, David. 1985. *Punishment and Welfare.* Aldershot: Gower.

Garland, David (Ed.). 2001a. "Mass Imprisonment in the USA." *Punishment and Society* 3(1, Special Issue).

Garland, David. 2001b. *The Culture of Control: Crime and Social Order in Contemporary Society.* New York: Oxford University Press.

Holstein, J. A. and G. Miller (Eds.). 1993. *Constructionist Controversies: Issues in Social Problems Theory.* Hawthorne, NY: Aldine de Gruyter.

Horwitz, Alan. 1990. *The Logic of Social Control.* New York: Plenum.

Spector, Malcolm and John Kitsuse. 1977. *Constructing Social Problems.* Hawthorne, NY: Aldine de Gruyter.

I

Punishment and Social Control:
Theories and Trends

Introduction to Part I

Besides being wider in scope than traditional criminology or criminal justice studies, the subjects of "punishment" and "social control" are free of the constraints of immediate policy relevance. Very practical matters can be studied—how courts reach decisions, what goes on in prisons, how drug laws are enforced—but (1) through the lens of "theory,"(2) over a time span that moves in "trends," and (3) always linked to "society." These requirements are met exactly by the journal started in 1999, *Punishment and Society* (edited by David Garland until 2002, and now by Richard Sparks).

In Chapter 1, Sparks shows how the new sociology of punishment reflects the changes and uncertainties of a runaway world as well as the "primordial and unchanging" aspects of punishment. Garland, in Chapter 2, is also careful about identifying the "new." He moves to a broader sociological canvas—the much-proclaimed era of postmodern society—only to find the residues of modernism in penal practice. Jonathan Simon and Malcolm Feeley (Chapter 3) summarize their 1992 paper and look back now on their unambiguous announcement that a "new penology" was emerging. They also discuss the lack of congruence between the internal professional-academic discourse and general public opinion.

Feminist theories and movements continue to make a major impact on law and the social sciences. In the control and punishment area, this work soon moved beyond showing the distorting results of leaving half the population out of the deviance-control equation. The next phase of work—in which Pat Carlen belongs—was to show how the social control of women points to more general issues. Her subject in Chapter 4 is the social control of women, but her object is the dichotomies that run through all strategies and meanings of social control: formal/informal, public/private, and exclusion/inclusion.

In a different way, Chapter 5 by David Matza and Patricia Morgan also moves from the specific to the general. The character and size of today's correctional systems are impossible to explain without referring to the subject of drug control. We have numbly accepted these facts as normal: the massive government resources devoted to the "war against drugs;" its costs in human misery; its impact on the criminal justice system (accounting for some two-thirds of the entire prison population); and the brutal indices of failure. Is this all inevitable? The allusion to "prohibition" in Matza and Morgan's subtitle is not just a historical reference to the failed American experiment with controlling alcohol use, but an invitation to think about the whole logic of all social control based on prohibition and "ban."

1

State Punishment in Advanced Capitalist Countries

RICHARD SPARKS

> *Ariel*   Just as you left them; all prisoners, sir,
>   ... They cannot budge till your release ...
>   ... if you now beheld them, your affections
>   Would become tender.
> *Prospero* Dost thou think so, spirit?
> *Ariel*   I would sir, were I human.
>   —Shakespeare, *The Tempest*

PROLOGUE

Punishment is among the most Janus-faced of our social practices. In some of its aspects punishment appears primordial and unchanging. It appeals to passions and intuitions in us that reach back into the remote past—the yearning for justice, the desire for retribution, the fear of chaos and disorder. In other respects punishment seems entirely contemporary. It is a quite technical matter, administered by professional people in settings (offices, hostels, day-centers, busy courthouses) that seem resolutely mundane, and whose activities are governed by volumes—frequently revised—of statutes, standing orders, circular instructions, rules for reporting, requisitioning and accounting, and so on that are essentially similar to those of almost any other administrative body. Lately, these institutions have in many cases increasingly adopted certain vocabularies and practices that are also current in other organizations both public and private. They begin to feature the language of auditing, operations research, and risk management. Certain of their functions and activities have in some countries, notably in the United States, the United Kingdom, and Australia, been delegated or "contracted out" to private sector businesses. In some places—most drastically and obviously in the case of the prison population in the United States, but not just in that respect and not just there—the scale of their operations would seem to have increased, sometimes abruptly so. But are these shifts primarily owing to a reawakening of the antique will to punish, or does their explanation rather lie mainly within the logics or "rationalities" of the contemporary institutions themselves?

I want here to begin to explore some of the implications of such paradoxes, and their consequences for the practitioners, recipients, and onlookers of contemporary penal processes. In exploring these we find ourselves facing some of the larger and more challenging questions that encircle our current systems and practices of punishment. What are the primary dimensions of those systems—their scope, scale, and ambitions? How have those ambitions extended or retrenched in recent times? Which of their features are common across Western societies and which variable or particular? How far, therefore, do they fall under willed political control? To the extent that they escape such control what are the sources of their intractability? How then do penal practices intersect with other spheres of the culture, politics, or economic structures of the social formations in which they arise? Is it fanciful to suggest that we can interpret some wider features of our contemporary social and political predicaments through the prism of the penal?

Yet much twentieth-century social science addressed problems of punishment in ways that tended to relegate such questions to the periphery of its concerns, or to treat them as altogether unanswerable—and hence in effect to suppress them. Conventionally much of criminology and penology only gestures at the political. Some decidedly thin and unilluminating conceptions of political "distortion" or "interference" (a skimpily drawn idea of "populism," for example) are introduced when explanation fails. These notions are not themselves explanations—rather they are often little more than the groans of complaint that intellectuals make when penal politics appears to them to turn sour and irrational. Yet unless we make a serious attempt to understand how often and how powerfully this occurs, we are left tinkering at the edges of the topic. This essay will argue, conversely, that punishment is ineluctably both a political and a cultural matter. If we want to develop a tough-minded and critical approach to the ways of punishing that happen to be dominant now, we have to pose two distinct kinds of questions. The first is the kind that orthodox criminology and penology are quite good at. Does this work as it claims? Is it coherent? The second, which is more my topic here, is more demanding in terms of sociological and political insight. Where does this come from, and why now? Where does it lead, and do we wish to go there? What models of human motivation, state capacity and political community does it imply?

TWO FACES OF PUNISHMENT

I have spoken of punishment as Janus-faced in its capacity simultaneously to invoke antique forms of rage and desire and to spin novel techniques and managerial styles. Various contemporary penal innovations—electronic monitoring or "tagging" and random drug-testing perhaps *par excellence*—were undreamed of except as dystopian science fictions only twenty years ago. What currently fictive prospects, from fields such as genetic modification, will find practical realization in coming decades can only be guessed at (though one suspects, for reasons outlined below, that markets for such experimentation will readily be found). Yet such novelties neither displace nor in any practical sense contradict such equally contemporary phenomena as the persistence of capital punishment in the United States or the apparent vitality of prison populations across most of the advanced capitalist world. Sightings of this kind bear witness both to the scale and durability of the penal enterprise (an embedded feature in the governance of every modern nation-state of which we are aware) and to its mutability and inventiveness.

By the same token, punishment is both a severely *practical* matter and a thoroughly *expressive* one. It is used in attempts to intervene in and to control many forms of undesired behavior. In punishing we threaten, detain, deprive, immobilize, supervise, watch, guard, enjoin, entreat, cajole, and educate. Yet we also, in punishing, act out anger, voice pain, exclude, reject, tell stories, vindicate the authority of law, defend the state from external threat or internal subversion—real or imagined, invoke the divine, cherish, and occasionally forgive. It seems unwise now to suppose that one of these faces necessarily takes precedence over the other, or even that we can know with confidence how the tension between them will be resolved in any given place and time. Some theories of modernity have proposed teleologies that now seem suspect. For example, Emile Durkheim once suggested that restitution would at length supersede revenge. In the present it seems less tempting to view penal change as a one-way street. Instead we seem beset by variety, contradiction, and local circumstance. Even in the face of continual skeptical challenges, disproofs, and failures punishment cycles through its repertoire of golden oldies and one-hit wonders like an untended jukebox.

Let us now begin to impose some form on this confusing picture (albeit that *coherence* may be too much to seek). David Garland has argued that we are today living out the consequences of a "crisis of penal modernism." Whereas some intellectuals and *fonctionnaires* have thought it possible to subject punishment entirely to the demands of rational administration, it has in part escaped such domestication. What results its a chronic tension. For Garland:

> There are two contrasting visions at work in contemporary criminal justice—
> the passionate, morally-toned desire to punish and the administrative, ra-
> tionalistic, normalizing concern to manage. These visions clash in many
> important respects, but both are deeply embedded within the [modern] so-
> cial practice of punishing.

This seems a good starting point. It acknowledges what some critical
perspectives too readily deny, namely that punishment really is practically
involved, however failingly, in attempts to control crime and govern social
existence. But at the same time Garland gives full recognition to the tendency of punishment to exceed the bounds of the practical and to become
enmeshed in the flux of culture and politics, including sometimes in the
most exorbitantly emotive forms of demagogic posturing. Such a position
suggests the possibility at least of unpicking some important puzzles. Principal among these is that while in broad terms all advanced capitalist countries (including that outlier of penal severity the United States) have
developed recognizably similar arrays of penal measures and techniques,
they differ markedly in terms of penal range (a term that I explore further
below) and in the centrality of questions of punishment to their electoral
politics and cultural conflicts. If we begin to examine such questions empirically we may thereby start to clarify a central paradox, namely that
whereas some features of the penal realm seem both rather durable and
quite widely diffused across national boundaries, others are currently
highly unstable and prone to sudden and often quite jagged changes of direction. Garland again anticipates this issue pointedly when he distin-
guishes between the "relatively fixed infrastructure of penal techniques
and apparatuses" on the one hand and on the other those "mobile strategies that determine aims and priorities."

In the remainder of this essay I will set out some of the main ways in
which students of contemporary penal systems and institutions try to
make sense of the continuities and changes in state punishment in the advanced capitalist countries. Throughout, the ambiguity implied in the image of the two faces of punishment is a besetting issue. If punishment is a
matter both of government (in the sense of the regulation and ordering of
activity) and of the passions (in the sense of the mobilization of anger or
fear that may underpin demands for penal stringency) then its political importance is likely to consist in the interaction between these properties. I
will attempt to clarify this conjunction, and its particular manifestations in
the often febrile penal politics of the advanced capitalist societies today, in
the following way;

Changes in the "Mode of Calculation"

Here we encounter debates about risk and prediction, and the uses of
cost-benefit arithmetic to argue the utility of particular penal strategies.

One important possibility is that the current prominence of *incapacitation* as a rationale for imprisonment in the advanced liberal societies (and for more intensive forms of noncustodial supervision) stems rather directly from the invention of new techniques for calculating the frequency and prevalence of offending. The implication is that the penal system is entirely a regulatory instrument—a kind of social sluice gate whose optimal rate of flow can in principle be rationally determined. This perspective has certainly had its influential intellectual proponents in recent years. A related question concerns how the state itself has shifted its posture with respect to punishment. Is it the case that the state has on the one hand divested itself of some of its former obligations toward its offending citizens (specifically the expectation that it will "treat," "rehabilitate," or "resettle") and on the other undertaken an enhanced role in the management of the risks presented by that fraction of its subjects regarded as inherently and incorrigibly troublesome? If so, in what sense do these shifts flow from larger changes in the dominant economic and political principles of those societies?

Changes in the "Mode of Representation"

How and why, in some countries much more than in others, is punishment invoked in response to allegations of social crisis or emergency? Under what conditions does it take a central position in political rhetoric, and what kinds of rhetorics are these? Are there special moments (when certain kinds of anxiety or resentment are felt especially acutely, or the tolerance of the public is especially strained) when the time is ripe for politicians and demagogues to turn the penal question to their own advantage?

Although these two sets of issues look very distinct they are rarely encountered separately in empirical reality. Rather they are two aspects of a complex formation—a duality rather than a dualism. Thus, for example, even if a certain set of bloodless and dispassionate calculations in some sense underpins the increasing frequency and length of prison sentences for drug offenses in several Western countries in recent years, it is also true that in its public aspect that strategy comes vested in all the ancient, drastic, and dramatic language of warfare—the "war on drugs." If we wish to understand precisely why the attempt to intervene in illegal drug markets so often, and increasingly, terminates in imprisonment *rather than in other varieties of risk management or "harm reduction"* then it would seem important to grasp what it means to be at war—wars are special times and they call for special measures.

In other words, even if risk calculations become predominant within the procedures and decisions of the agents of the penal apparatus, there is no morally neutral or politically anodyne position from which to begin.

Disputes between *antiqui* and *moderni* have been fought and refought many times in the development of our ways of punishing but never decisively resolved. Today those battles take place predominantly on the terrain of *risk*. In looking more closely at the ambiguities implied in that term we edge closer again to the central perplexities of the contemporary penal realm. First, however, we need some sense of the *scale* of that domain and of the historical and international dimensions on which it has varied. Only then can we begin to reach toward explanation (what features of the contemporary scene seem to produce penal populations and regimes of these kinds?) or intervention (are we fated to go on in this way or can we plausibly imagine and create other futures for punishment?). Can we indeed envision a society in which punishment as we now know it ceased to be necessary to us and in which the prison, the probation hostel, and the electric chair could be consigned to the museum of antique curiosities alongside the ducking stool and the executioner's axe?

A NOTE ON COMPARATIVE PENOLOGY

It is commonly agreed in the social sciences that thinking comparatively about problems is a good thing. There is rather less agreement about how to go about it or indeed about precisely what comparison is for. (There are even fewer examples of really worthwhile comparative work actually being done.) It can indeed be argued that *all* serious and imaginative social inquiry is in a broad sense comparative—whether the terms of comparison involve placing our present local circumstances in a longer *historical* perspective (how differently did our own predecessors think about this?) or whether they involve a similar displacement in terms of *contemporary* differences of place and culture.

There may be pressing reasons why we should wish to subject our experience of penality to this kind of intellectual discipline. The penal practices characteristic of our own current contexts confront us as obdurate and embedded realities. Yet these are also dynamic systems, subject at times to rapid and seemingly uncontrolled growth and change and to the push and pull of successive fashions and projects. Our politicians and newspaper headlines often urgently insist that there is no morally or practically viable alternative to this or that course of action with regard to the sentencing, supervision, or release of offenders. Even if we have vague misgivings about this, without a more cosmopolitan perspective we have little prospect of rationally appraising these assertions, let alone of contesting their claims or arguing for other possibilities.

However, comparative penology ain't what it used to be. Punishment is among the defining activities of the nation-state. It is a core feature of the state's sovereign power and stands close to the heart of its claim to exercise legitimate authority; and the political and cultural dynamics of punishment remain sharply different in distinct national contexts. In advanced capitalism we can no longer presume that nation-states are sharply bounded and separate entities that we can simply line up and compare one with another. Contemporary states are intrinsically permeable to the movement of capital and technology. Both the problems of economic management and those of social regulation and ordering that confront them with their most acute political difficulties increasingly exceed their capacity to control. In particular, the very crime problems that demand visible and authoritative action from national governments either literally transgress their borders (as is the case with drug markets or the illegal movement of people, money, arms, and other commodities) or else seem so deeply woven into the opportunity structures, the routine activities and transactions, and the ceaseless consumption and flows of popular culture of their citizens as to escape them from below. In this sense the nation-state is doubly in jeopardy—"hollowed out" from without by economic globalization and from within by the barely controllable complexity of the social formations over which they preside in their increasingly impotent magnificence.

All of this has profound and complicated consequences for the politics of punishment in the advanced capitalist countries. In the first place, globalization does not produce homogeneity. The penal cultures of the different nation-states remain in some degree distinctive, structured by their diverse legal and political traditions and the exigencies of their domestic crime problems and priorities. Furthermore, the clamor from anxious and uneasy citizens for reassurance and protection by the state arises with differing degrees of insistence; and this seems more prone to being translated into a demand for reassurance *through state punishment* in some national contexts than in others. It remains essential to grasp these differences and to think through their implications.

Yet nowhere is immune. At the level of the individual, it may be argued, concerns about crime take their place among what Anthony Giddens terms the "anxieties that press in on everyone" in late modernity. For Giddens, "The risk climate of modernity is unsettling for everyone; no-one escapes," and one response to the disruptions and uncertainties of the modern world is the growth of moral fundamentalisms—of which the demand for traditional and stringent forms of punishment may be one form. At the level of the nation-state the picture is also complex.

Contemporary states are subject to penal trends and influences of diverse kinds:

First, they are signatories to international treaties and agreements on human rights, migration, extradition, and other matters. Some of these, for example, the European Convention on Human Rights and (although its legal force is less clear) the Council of Europe's European Prison Rules, expressly seek to regulate and in some degree harmonize penal practice. The performance of national governments in these matters is also monitored by nongovernmental organizations of various kinds, some of which (such as Amnesty International and Human Rights Watch) are themselves transnational in scope.

Second, there is routine exchange of information and expertise through governmental, commercial, and intellectual networks. One key sphere in which this applies is the growth of an international market in private correctional services, whose major players increasingly have global reach and interests. Yet something similar also applies to the transfer of criminological and penological *knowledge* as such. Ideas, techniques, slogans, and catchwords (such as "risk assessment," "selective incapacitation," "truth in sentencing," and "zero tolerance") scurry around the world with accelerating rapidity. This has some curious and as yet uncertain consequences. An appealing idea adapted from Maori traditional practices (the family group conference pioneered in New Zealand, the central totem of the "restorative justice" movement) is abruptly wrenched away from its original context and experimentally applied in Oxfordshire or Manitoba. Global mass media ensure that instantaneous exchange of news and imagery infiltrates popular culture and everyday life as well. The grainy image of tiny James Bulger being led to his death from a shopping mall at the impoverished edge of an English conurbation sends an icy shard of terror through the hearts of parents in New Jersey and New South Wales. Unsuccessful eleventh-hour pleas for a stay of execution in the southern United States arouse more outrage and sorrow in Italy and in Britain than in the communities clustering around the prison walls. The effect of these borrowings and influences is by no means uniform, as this ad hoc list suggests. They compound the feeling that punishment is a major political question, but that its forms may be varied if not outrightly contradictory.

Third, therefore, the receptiveness of both policymakers and publics to some of these globally available themes and images varies widely but probably not in accidental ways. One dimension of this variation in recent decades may be the degree of exposure of the political cultures and policy networks of different states to the influence of New Right political thought. Until very recently the primary laboratories for this political experiment have been the United Kingdom and the United States, and here penal politics since the late 1970s have been especially volatile and expansive in nature. Before exploring this ideological influence further we need some basic factual resources on penal comparisons between contemporary advanced capitalist countries and some of the ways in which variations in their systemic behavior may be understood.

The Penal Range and the Choice of Punishments

With the notable exception of the United States, the Western liberal democracies have abandoned the use of capital punishment. In other respects the "penal range" (the variety of available penalties) in all such societies is broadly comparable, albeit organized and applied in very different ways. It extends from various forms of token penalty and conditional release (for instance in Britain absolute and conditional discharges, binding over) through financial penalties (fines, compensation orders) and varieties of noncustodial or "community" supervision (probation, community service, in some cases "curfew orders") to imprisonment. In most systems financial penalties are by some margin the most commonly used. This has led some commentators to argue that in fact it is the "cash nexus" of the fine that is the most characteristic form of contemporary punishment rather than the more drastic but more rarely used sanction of imprisonment.

Of course, it is imprisonment that continues to attract the lion's share of media debate, academic attention, and political controversy. The reasons for this preoccupation are perhaps not too difficult to detect. The scale of punishment is organized hierarchically in the form of a "tariff" and the prison stands at the apex of this rising series of values. Although it is by no means the case that everyone who goes to prison has been convicted of grave offenses, ordinary language (and judicial reasoning) generally sees a powerful connection between the severity of an offense and the likelihood or appropriateness of imprisonment. Imprisonment involves the deprivation of something on which most societies, and certainly ones in which liberalism is a dominant ideology, set a special value: liberty, freedom of movement and association. For this reason the general problems of justifying punishments are seen to apply in especially acute ways to imprisonment. At the same time the prison looms quite large in popular culture and imaginative fiction: consider its prominence in Hollywood films from the days of James Cagney, Spencer Tracey, or Burt Lancaster to those of Clint Eastwood, Tom Hanks, and Jodie Foster. This cultural fertility leads some authorities to argue that the prison is in some sense a "basic metaphor"; but if so it is one whose resonances can range from images of outright repression and heroic resistance to depictions of wholly just retribution.

Plainly, sanctions other than imprisonment ("community" and "intermediate" penalties of various kinds) also restrict liberty, but not in so obvious or readily understood a fashion. This leads to a number of ambiguities in the interpretation of such penalties. In much "commonsense" discussion and in popular press imagery, noncustodial penalties are not regarded as "proper" punishments at all. The equation between punishment and imprisonment for many people is so strong that for the offender to remain "in the community" is for them to be "let off." It is common for such measures to be described as "alternatives to" imprisonment, implying that incarceration remains the central, perhaps the only "real," sort of punishment. This is one reason why in several countries now so much effort is devoted to convincing people that "noncustodial" or "community" penalties really are "tough," "demanding," and "effective." We can therefore only really understand the uses of imprisonment within any particular criminal justice system in the context of the range of other measures that that system also applies. The relation between imprisonment and its alternatives is thus a complicated one. The history of attempts to introduce additional sentencing options, especially where these are meant to divert offenders from prison is littered with unintended (and sometimes actively "perverse") consequences.

Comparing Imprisonment in Europe and North America

Consider Table 1.1, which shows trends within and between the prison populations of various countries for the ten years between 1985 and 1995. The picture here is complex, and all such raw numbers must be treated with caution. They mask many differences in counting procedures, for example, in such matters as the inclusion or exclusion of young offenders or those offenders confined following a diagnosis of mental disorder. Neither do these blunt figures include any indication of the proportionate relationship between imprisonment and recorded crime; and this often tends to moderate some of the very large disparities shown here. Many of the highest rates of imprisonment, and the most violent fluctuations, are in the countries of the former Soviet bloc. These would require separate and detailed analysis in terms of the social and political transitions and instabilities of those societies (Russia in particular remains an outlier by any standard): but this exceeds our scope here. Yet even if we confine our attention to the countries of Western Europe, certain distinctions stand out. First, in many but not all of those countries prison populations have risen, in some cases (the Netherlands, Greece, Portugal, Spain) sharply so. Second, the gap between the lower and higher groups of countries (Ireland, the Scandinavian countries versus the three United Kingdom jurisdictions and France) nevertheless remains wide.

There are a number of other aspects of the issue that such simple lists tend to conceal. The "rate of detention" as recorded in Table 1.1 is a measure of the "stock" of prisoners on a given day. It gives no indication of the "flow" of prisoners through the system. Such "flow" data include the numbers of committals to prison. This is known as the "rate of imprisonments" (i.e., how many individuals are received into prison in the course of a year). We also need to consider the lengths of time spent in prison. It is only when we know all these things (rate of detention, rate of imprisonments, duration of imprisonment) that we can really claim to describe how each system behaves. Such more detailed comparisons reveal some surprising discoveries. For example, Norway actually has a comparatively high rate of imprisonments but the average duration of imprisonment there is rather

Table 1.1. Trends in the Prison Population 1985–1995 Approximate Rates (per 100,000 of the general population) at 1 September 1985 and 1995 (or nearest available date)

	Prison popn rate 1985	Prison popn rate 1995
Australia	120	85
Belgium	65	75
Cyprus (Republic of)	30	30
Czech Republic	270	190
Denmark	65	65
Estonia	455	270
Finland	80	60
France	75	95
Germany	90*	85
Greece	5	55
Hungary	220	120
Iceland	Not available	40
Ireland	55	55
Italy	Not available	85
Latvia	640	375
Lithuania	405	360
Malta	Not available	55
Netherlands	35	65
Norway	45	55
Poland	270	170
Portugal	90	125
Romania	260	200
Russia	Not available	690
Slovakia	225	150
Slovenia	70	30
Spain	60	105
Sweden	50	65
Turkey	90	80
United Kingdom		
England and Wales	90	100
Northern Ireland	Not available	105
Scotland	100	110
Canada	Not available	115***
USA	315	600

*Figures relate to Federal Republic of Germany (West Germany only)
***Figures are for year to 31.3.95
Adapted from R. Walmsley (1997), *Prison Populations in Europe and North America, Helsinki: The European Institute for Crime Prevention and Control*

short. The "flow" is quick, so the "stock" remains comparatively low. In this respect some Scandinavian countries today continue to act much as Britain, and to some extent the United States, did in earlier decades when their prison populations too were lower and more stable, partly for the same reason.

All of this complicates our understanding of which countries are "lenient" and which "punitive" rather sharply, although it does suggest that restricting average sentence lengths is one of the most effective ways of keeping overall prison populations in check (though this in turn raises some equally difficult questions about whether short prison sentences are ever particularly useful either for the protection of the public or for the correction or rehabilitation of the offender). The "exceptional" nature of the British prison populations now appears in clearer relief. The high rate of detention in England and Wales results from the combination of a rather high (though not the highest) rate of imprisonments with a rather long (though not the longest) average duration (though this discovery still begs the question as to why the English system acts in this particular fashion). Its "flow" is both strong and slow, so its "stock" is high. Since both the number and average duration of imprisonments in England and Wales have increased in recent years the prospects for restraining the growth in the English prison population do not look very bright.

There is, however, one Western society that makes the British or Spanish prison populations look positively minute. In the United States the number of persons confined in federal and state prisons has increased at an unprecedented rate since 1980 (from around 330,000 in 1980 to over one million by the mid-1990s). When one includes the many thousands of persons held in local jails (usually for less than one year) the total number incarcerated in the United States has exceeded 1.5 million since 1994 and topped 2 million at the century's end. This mean there are around 650 inmates for each 100,000 inhabitants in the United States. To consider these trends against European comparisons is to invite incredulity. Even after several years of rapidly rising prison numbers in England and Wales (one of the nearer comparators) the United States nevertheless confines around five times as many people in proportion to its total population, or about ten times as many of its inhabitants as any of the Scandinavian countries.

This picture is by no means uniform within the United States. Some states (for example Minnesota) continue to imprison on "European" levels. But this merely underlines the fact that certain other states, including some of the largest such as California and Texas, have behaved in an even more discrepant fashion.

Such figures have no parallel in the modern history of liberal democratic societies. They cry out for explanation. Yet some of the most temptingly obvious "explanations" fail to hold water. Principal among these is that the United States must have an exceptionally high and ever spiraling crime rate. This is certainly a commonly held view both within the United

States itself and elsewhere. Many American citizens and policymakers share the perception that the country's crime problem is now out of control. It is true that rates of many crimes in the United States (both officially recorded and as measured by victimization surveys) are quite high in international terms, but not to anything like the exceptional degree that is often asserted. It is really only in the crucially important but numerically quite small category of firearms-related violence that the United States is truly in a class of its own. The United States is indeed unusual among Western countries in that its recorded crime rates remained rather static during the 1980s and have since gone into a sustained decline. This confirms what we have already seen in Europe, namely that overall crime rates and imprisonment rates show no simple correspondence. The same is true over longer time scales for the United States in the 1960s (crime rose, imprisonment fell) and for Australia in the 1970s (the same). As Zimring and Hawkins report for California (a state whose incarcerated population tripled during the 1980s),

> most of the increased imprisonment in California was not directly related to either increases in crime or changes in population. Most crime levels in 1990 were close to their 1980 rates. And the kinds of crime associated with the largest share in California's prison expansion—drug offences, housebreaking and theft—are precisely the offences that flood the criminal justice systems of every major Western democracy. We think that the sorts of policy shifts observed in California could double the prison population of any country in Western Europe experiencing no change in the volume or character of crime.

The "policy shifts" that Zimring and Hawkins have in mind here are changes in discretionary law enforcement and sentencing rather than being centrally directed or statutorily required. They are, as Zimring and Hawkins put it, "more a matter of sentiment than legislation." The shifts in question include a disproportionate increase in the numbers imprisoned for lesser property offenses (they report a 565 percent increase in the number of persons imprisoned for the various categories of theft). Meanwhile, although there is some evidence from survey data of a *decline* in illicit drug use in the United States throughout the 1980s, the numbers of persons arrested for drugs offenses increased sharply and so did the proportion of those imprisoned following conviction. In fact the numbers of males in Californian prisons for drugs offenses increased by *fifteen times* during the 1980s. This followed the national shift in the mid-1980s toward a widely publicized, symbolically powerful, and punitively oriented "war on drugs" as a primary way in which the United States was to address its problems of addiction. Such accelerations in imprisonment do not now have, and have never had, equal impacts throughout the population. In the United States (and elsewhere) the "war" has primarily been directed at street-level drug markets, and it has drawn its combatants from among particular people and places. For this reason among others, the prison population, like the "ghetto underclass" that supplies so many of its personnel, consists increasingly and disproportionately of black and Hispanic people.

As Zimring and Hawkins comment, it would appear that given sufficiently great changes in the "penal climate" or political culture of a society its prison population may have an "open ended capacity for change." That is, marked changes in penal practice can occur without corresponding changes in crime rates, nor even radical changes in the statutory basis of sentencing. They seem to result rather from external pressures in the crime control culture more broadly conceived and the priorities that emerge there for the stringent suppression of certain kinds of activity in particular, in this case especially drug offenses. Thus while it is true that recent American penal developments have no precedent *in peacetime,* perhaps the United States is strictly speaking not "at peace" but rather has "declared war": the "war on crime." To the extent that the motives and occasions for such shifts of penal gear lie not just in crime rates as such but rather in the rhetoric, culture, and practice of crime control, and insofar as these movements have been most marked in the United States (and latterly, especially since 1993, in the United Kingdom) there is a significant puzzle for political sociology here. At this point, though it is far from the only issue involved, we rejoin the question of the influence of New Right social philosophy.

PUNISHMENT AND THE NEW RIGHT

The term New Right is an umbrella that encompasses a broad and internally differentiated social movement. Under that umbrella have marched libertarians, free-market liberals, conservatives, and outright reactionaries of many stripes. What unites these diverse strands of opinion is a vigorous critique of the outcomes of the economic interventionism and welfare provision that characterized the post-World War II "settlements" of many Western countries. For some, whom we may see as being primarily *neoliberals,* the key result has been economic inefficiency. The suppression of market freedoms for political purposes diminishes competitiveness, multiplies tax burdens, and discourages entrepreneurship—all perverse outcomes of good intentions. For others, primarily *neoconservative* in orientation, the greatest detriment has been moral. The interventionism of the "nanny state" promotes dependency rather than personal responsibility, and engages in a wrongful transfer of authority from families and local communities to the state. The result is again perverse—a moral climate of permissiveness, agnosticism, mushy pluralism, and hedonism. Where these streams of thinking primarily flow together, therefore, is in the critique of the overambition of the state and the resulting inflation of the public sector.

Space entirely precludes an adequate summary of these positions, which have generated a massive literature of both advocacy and criticism. These are, after all, initially in the United States and United Kingdom and latterly in varying degrees across the developed and developing worlds, the most influential political and economic intellectual movements of our times. Here we can deal only with their strictly *penological* consequences. These are themselves complex and can be rendered here only in summary, and doubtless contentious, form.

The New Right and the Restoration of State Authority

Governments influenced by the New Right have characteristically assumed power partly on the strength of an allegation of social and economic "crisis" of the "welfare state." In the United Kingdom in 1979 Margaret Thatcher successfully seized the initiative by representing the accumulation of problems of the Keynesian welfare state as a twin crisis of "ungovernability" and uncompetitiveness. "Law and order" was a key token of ungovernability, and her project promised nothing less than the "restoration of freedom under law." The state was to withdraw from those tasks that it performed badly (micromanaging economic and social activity while profligately wasting public monies) in order to focus on its essential and legitimate tasks—sound money, free trade, defense, and the maintenance of "law and order." Countries in which governments have adopted similar positions have in this sense experienced a hiatus—a self-conscious discontinuity from a discredited past—in their recent history. The politics of law and order, and the associated naming of enemies, have been part and parcel of representing that moment as a quasi-revolutionary one. Among Western countries the United States and United Kingdom have perhaps experienced this revivalism of state authority (what Thatcher memorably called the "smack of firm government") in combination with a neoliberal emphasis on the free play of market forces most forcefully, especially during the 1980s and early 1990s. Elsewhere in the world, perhaps especially in the countries of the former Soviet bloc—most obviously Russia itself—other and more drastic social and political transformations have also had far-reaching penological effects. The picture is complex. Suffice to note that the advent of liberal free-market economic reforms has by no means automatically heralded a new liberalism in the penal realm, especially in those countries where the state itself seems menaced by the very disorders and upheavals that the political transitions have unleashed. These have in some cases included alarm about newly virulent forms of criminality (the rise of the Russian "mafia," the extraordinary murder rates in parts of South Africa); and such alarm frequently finds its political expression in nationalist and fundamentalist political movements and in nostalgia for the ordered world of the *ancien regimes*. In many of these very different circumstances an association can be seen between an allegation of political or social crisis and the demand for "law and order," crystallized in the intensification of state punishment.

The "Grain of Human Nature"

Among the mistakes of social democracy, for thinkers of the New Right, was its tendency to assume the malleability and even perfectibility of human nature. Neoliberalism, by contrast, is a "politics of imperfection." People's behavior can be guided (by the early inculcation of a proper respect for authority and a love of family and country) and they have a legitimate and socially necessary desire to enrich themselves. But they cannot fundamentally be changed. They are whatever their upbringing and personal dispositions make them. It follows that it makes little sense (other than with the partial exception of the very young) to counsel, treat, coddle, or blandish those who misbehave. In order that people learn to govern their own conduct they must be treated as personally responsible for it (hence eligible for retributive punishment). At the same time, insofar as their motivations (and certainly those of the less respectable) are fundamentally economic and self-interested, the law must ensure that the incentives to compliant behavior outweigh the attractions of offending. Since only the latter is directly under its control, its proper business focuses on setting the level of sanctions sufficiently high (hence a principle of rational deterrence). Those who demonstrate a persistent failure to comply must be incapacitated or effectively supervised. There is thus a preference not only for robustness in determining *levels* of penalties, but also for those *justifications* for punishing that favor a certain implied account of human motivation.

The Tolerance of Inequality and the Emergence of the "Underclass"

"Good governance" is a key theme of neoliberalism, but the best government, according to the worldview of the New Right, is limited in its scale and objectives. We do not live in state-governed societies. The overreach of government during the era of welfarism encroached upon personal freedom and inhibited responsibility, impeded competitiveness, and perversely undermined the authority of the state. The attempt to use taxation and state institutions for redistributive purposes—and thereby to impose artificial egalitarian restraints on natural hierarchies of talent and application—is the single most foolish, and ultimately immoral, of these errors. Redistributive social policy illegitimately transfers wealth from its creators to the unproductive, noncontributing members of society. Not only is this wrongful in itself but it may also constrain the performance of the economy as a whole and, moreover, let those at the bottom off the hook of attempting to better their own lot; and anyway, the intensifying demands of international competition in a globalizing economy make the strategy unsustainable. International capital will simply flee those countries in which tax burdens are aversive; entrepreneurs will not take risks without the possibility of sufficient dividends; and the prize of prosperity flows toward those economies whose social costs are kept in check.

For all these reasons neoliberal economic and political strategy is more tolerant of inequality than were its predecessor *state regimes*. Ultimately, it is asserted, the bloat and inefficiency of welfarism has its most detrimental consequences on those at the bottom of the heap. In softening the impact of inequality it tends to maintain the poor in their poverty: it provides a "handout" where it should at most offer a "hand up." In so doing it transfers responsibility away from individuals and families and onto state agencies. The perverse result is an undermining of the personal virtues of thrift and prudence and the preparedness to accept the burden and challenge of responsibility for shaping one's own destiny. In place of these we get "dependency," apathy, fecklessness, and the assumption that the world "owes us a living," which in turn sap the very forms of individual self-government and familial solidarity that provide the basis for social order and the restraint of crime. In certain locations, it is asserted, this decadence has taken hold. Young women see no moral or practical inhibition against single motherhood. Young men lose sight of the notion of the dignity of labor or the pride of supporting their family. Instead they become feral, wayward, hedonistic, and impulsive. They serially father children and then abandon them. They mistreat their women; but they are in any case unmarriageable. Their lives are a mixture of swagger and drift. They do little well, not even crime. They use and deal drugs, joy-ride, burgle, and rob with the same intermittent abandon that they do everything else. They are not in the classic sense "underprivileged," and their lifestyle is a mockery of the term "working class." They have become "the underclass."

In New Right political thought, the misguided generosity of the welfare state and the moral vapidity of liberal "permissiveness," with its refusal to countenance the necessity of social discipline, condemnation, and punishment, have conspired to produce this disaster. Meanwhile, law-abiding citizens, fearing victimization or hearing disturbing rumors through the mass media about the alien and predatory free-riders in their midst, look upon this spectacle with understandable dismay. The idea of a social, and more especially a redistributive, approach to the problem has become threadbare and politically unsayable—the degrees of sympathy, fraternalism, or confidence that would make it plausible are ideologically precluded. Yet at the same time there is the assurance, both in political rhetoric and from certain serviceable quarters of criminological knowledge, that the threat resides in persons and places that can be identified. Perhaps then those who stand beyond the pale of recuperation can at least be *known,* and their behavior predicted. To this extent the political demands upon the state become simpler and clearer and they focus more sharply on its specifically *penal* capacities. The state must use its knowledge to predict effectively. It must manage the risks it discovers (preferably without overburdening taxpayers) in ways that do not reflect badly on its competence. It must be unambiguous in its allocation of punishments and rewards, or face the damage to its own legitimacy. It must therefore be plausible in its "vocabulary of motives," speaking over the heads of skeptics, doubters, liberals, and permissives directly to the motivations and dispositions of offenders themselves. It may correct where it can, deter whom it cannot otherwise correct, and incapacitate all who show themselves impervious. Only under these conditions will it ride the tiger of its crime problems without severe damage to its authority. In these respects the two faces of punishment (the managerial and the punitive) and the two dimensions of risk (the mode of calculation and the mode of representation) remain integral to the position of the state in advanced capitalism, whatever other roles and responsibilities it divests, delegates, or denies.

TWO FACES OF RISK: CALCULATION AND REPRESENTATION

The problem of risk arises wherever institutions and individuals encounter a need to weigh the possibility of harm or loss against desired outcomes and thus to institute practices that will manage or reduce their risks. Put in this way the question of risk sounds like a very rational, calculable, and practical matter. Indeed for many purposes it is. In many organizations and systems (and in the bodies of knowledge that inform how those organizations work) planning for and predicting risk are core activities. We can easily think of a list of such activities that are integral to contemporary social organization—weather forecasting, insurance, road safety, air traffic control, immunization, routine health screening for common cancers or circulatory illnesses, water purity, cashless transactions and "smart cards," expiration dates on food packaging, the inspection of restaurant premises by environmental health officers, fire safety regulations, and so on. The list could be extended almost indefinitely. In many contemporary intellectual disciplines (in economics and in some branches of psychology, for example) behavior under risk has become the very criterion of what it means to act rationally. Risk in this sense refers not simply to an "amount" of danger to which one is exposed but rather to ways of assessing and deciding about undesirable things. One of the distinctive features of the late twentieth century is that as well as creating or discovering many risks (from the management of nuclear waste to the carcinogenic properties of sunshine) it has invented and institutionalized many ingenious and refined ways of predicting and coping with them (actuarial tables, psychological profiles, manuals of professional good practice, and so on). The "best" systems are for us those which build in the "smartest" ways of anticipating and rectifying their own possible failures. These combinations of risk-generation and risk-management lead some social commentators to characterize our contemporary social reality as a "risk society."

It would be amazing if the domain of crime and punishment were untouched by such developments, and there are indeed grounds for thinking that this is not the case. But what would be the signs of such influence, and what consequences ought we to expect? One of the more provocative responses to such questions is offered by Malcolm Feeley and Jonathan Simon, who argue that we are witnessing the emergence of a "new penology," one that is less concerned either to "do justice" as traditionally understood or indeed to look to the welfare and correction of the erring citizen, but rather one that confines itself to managing the degrees of risk that certain *categories* of offender present. Feeley and Simon argue that although these changes are "incremental" and "emergent" they herald a shift in the very aims and purposes of penality. Whereas older penologies were concerned with individual culpability, specific deterrence, or clinical dangerousness,

> in contrast the new penology is markedly less concerned with responsibility, fault, moral sensibility, diagnosis, or intervention and treatment of the individual offender. Rather it is concerned with techniques to identify, classify and manage groupings sorted by dangerousness. The task is managerial, not transformative.

Among the contemporary developments indicative of such a transition would be the growth of selective incapacitation as a sentencing rationale (especially in the United States), the increased technical complexity of parole, and other release mechanisms, and the expansion of probation and other kinds of extracustodial (or "transcarceral") supervision (for example, the introduction of "smart" or "intermediate" sentencing, such as intensive probation and electronic monitoring).

Perhaps it is possible to overstate the newness of some of these sightings. Utilitarian calculation has played a prominent role in penal practice at least since Jeremy Bentham formulated the principles of rational deterrence in the late eighteenth century. Conversely it is hard to argue that the impassioned reactions of anger, resentment, censure, and fear have actually departed the field of penal politics. Nor have they; and here our argument starts to draw toward completion. We have spoken above of the Janus-faced nature of punishment, in its governmental and passionate aspects. We have pointed to some influences from contemporary social and political ideology (especially those views associated with the New Right) in accentuating the prominence of the penal in the maintenance of social order. Now we have briefly alluded to the ways in which risk-based reasoning increasingly pervades our institutions including, it is argued, those of the penal system. The outstanding question is: What sort of hybrids arise when these diverse and ostensibly disparate influences conjoin?

First, we should simply expect to continue to see a certain amount of diversity. In any given period, certain sets of ideas may predominate, but other and sometimes incompatible views (survivals from the past, or else intimations of a somewhat different possible future) also circulate. So, for example, in the present penal practices centering on the anticipation of future risk seem ascendant; but they are accompanied by a different emphasis—to some extent a countermovement—that favors a language of "shaming," "reintegration," and "restoration." Second, the risk arithmetic is also very much accompanied by the emotionally vivid rhetoric of politicians promising firmness, protectiveness, and the old-fashioned satisfactions of justice, as well as by the dramatic and sometimes harrowing stories of newspapers and "reality television" shows detailing the latest horror to befall somebody's daughter, son, spouse, parent. So far as crime and punishment are concerned, the professional practice of the criminal justice process may increasingly tend to prioritize risk-management, but we the public continue to inhabit an environment of story and symbol. As Mary Douglas has argued, risk does not "unload its ancient moral freight." Instead this ostensibly very modern diction has "fallen into antique mode." It is for this reason that I have argued throughout this essay that we need to understand punishment both in terms of *calculation* and of *representation*. This may strike some people as unduly abstract. But is not. It is real in its consequences. It means that how we picture to ourselves those whose past actions we deplore or whose future ones we fear determines what we feel entitled to do to them.

Here we rejoin the question of how risk-calculation and New Right political thinking meet and cross-fertilize. Increasingly, I suggest, we are encouraged to hold two convictions, somewhat in tension with one another but both very current. The first is that we have the ability to predict what people will do. The second is that we each make our own luck. The first conviction gives us permission to hold or supervise people not primarily on grounds of justice or censure but against the expectation that they will incorrigibly reoffend. The second conviction allows us to disclaim interest in the personal or social circumstances that preceded the offense and licenses us to feel that whatever hardships they incur as a result are ones that they have brought on their own heads. Insofar as our ways of calculating about and of representing the offender tend to reduce him or her to a cipher, a mere bearer of a certain quotient of risk, it is unsurprising if our characteristic disposition toward him or her comprises some combination of fear, contempt, and indifference. As McConville pithily puts it:

> The essence of incapacitation is that the offender lies beyond human intervention and influence, whether measured by susceptibility to deterrence or reform, or expiation through suffering . . .

... Containment means that we can't be bothered to engage the offender: "It is too much trouble, too unreliable, and might make civic demands which I have neither the time nor the inclination to meet." The offender becomes a commodity or waste product.

In this respect, and others, the state of the penal realm reflects a rather dismal picture of the way we live now. There is a certain moral flatness, punctuated by bursts of emotionalism; an uneasy oscillation between the technocracy of risk management and the archaism of the mass media hue and cry.

Are these the best visions of social order that market society offers? There is no shortage of evidence that urges this gloomy conclusion, but many reasons for wishing to resist its inevitability. In the United States the "natural experiment" in prison expansion has been running now for some twenty years. With approaching two million Americans behind bars and several times that number under probation or parole supervision, America has at best stabilized its recorded crime rate at unacceptably high levels (and even this, and the reasons for it, are sharply in dispute). In California where, as we have seen, the prison population now runs at three times its 1980 level the costs of imprisonment now directly compete with higher education and all other public services that are not expressly ring-fenced. As the "three strikes and you're out" provisions take their effect in many states these levels of imprisonment and their associated costs seem destined to increase further. And some at least of the rationales behind this are the same as in the slogan "Prison Works!" which was so ably canvassed by the Conservative government in Britain during the mid-1990s. There is a similar conjunction of a technocratic assertion of the capacity of imprisonment to deliver increased public safety through incapacitation and deterrence, alongside a profound *irrationalism* in many media and popular cultural responses to crime—this is, as the American criminologist Barry Krisberg has put it, penal policy "fashioned on an anvil of fear" in which a symbolism of strength covers what is at a deeper level a failure of politics.

Some of the tokens of that failure have been documented most forcefully by Jonathan Simon in his book *Poor Discipline*. In the face of the hardening and geographical concentration of poverty in America, those who inhabit the "poverty zones" of the deindustrialized urban core become progressively more separate from the rest of society. Their connection with the legitimate labor market, the education system, and other resources of social support and integration becomes attenuated. In this vacuum of social control the denizens of the poverty zones are left "unsecured and unregulated." The criminal justice system becomes almost their only point of contact with the institutions of mainstream society. But whereas at times in the past the functions of criminal justice have included the attempts to resettle and to reconnect the offender with the disciplines and opportunities of work and family, now they reduce to the management of a permanently marginal (and demonized and feared) "underclass." Such "communities" (and one has to use this word under advisement) cease to be, in Simon's phrase, a "coherent target for intervention." Nothing remains for criminal justice except to act as a form of "toxic waste management."

A KIND OF CONCLUSION

There is much more that might be said. I have tried to show why the twin faces of punishment remain with us and to sharpen our perception of some of the paradoxes of punishment in the era of globalization. However clever the new penologists and other technocrats become (and I have only scratched the surface of their ingenuity) there are also antique features of the penal realm that refuse to go away. Indeed the anxieties and dangers of our uncertain world, and especially the fear and distaste in which we hold a fraction of our fellow citizens, create new opportunities and demands for punishment. The more alien and threatening they become in our eyes the more disposed we become to accept and even welcome the development of measures for their containment. The less we believe in the possibility of their recuperation or correction the more we wish that containment to be hermetic and permanent. The more we deny their shared humanity with us the more we tolerate encroachments on our own. In insisting upon their intrinsic and incorrigible difference from us we are also changed. The more the state retreats from the obligation to provide for the welfare of all its citizens the more its claims to authority may be staked upon its capacity to influence behavior specifically by penal means. As Zygmunt Bauman proposes:

> Given the nature of the game now played, the hardships and misery of those left out of it, once treated as a *collectively caused blight* which needs to be dealt with by *collective means,* can be only redefined as *individual crime.* . . . And so the prisons now fully and truly deputize for the fading welfare institutions.

In the era of globalization we have reason to suspect the state of hollowness. Yet at some level of our being we want it to be strong; and its power-holders, menaced by our suspicion and sensitive to our desire, are ready enough to provide displays of their strength. Is the political duality of managerialism and populist demonstrations of punitive power the best future we are capable of imagining for punishment?

The English political philosopher John Gray, himself an angry refugee from the New Right, expresses some aspects of our contemporary condition acutely when he writes that the "market freedoms" so beloved of the New Right can and do coexist with an "authoritarian individualism resting on the political foundations of a centralist state":

Macaulay's observation that the gallows and the hangman stand at the back of James Mill's utilitarian state seems premonitory of the neo-liberal minimum state, in which the privatized prison and the . . . accountants fulfil similar functions.

Is that it then? It is admittedly a bleak conclusion, and I have admittedly, for the sake of the argument, left much out. But I think it as well that those who wish to press the debate on penal questions in other and more constructive directions acknowledge the scale of the challenge that confronts them. The manipulations of politicians and some commercial interests may be contemptibly exploitative at times but they are not, as Gray further puts it, "mistakes." There are structural reasons for their appeal. Neither are the fears and worries on which they play, which are in any case not wholly illusory, imminently likely to diminish. There may be little enough that academic criminology can contribute here. It can lend support to those many penal professionals and rather fewer politicians who wish to develop more thoughtful and morally responsible responses to lawbreaking. It can certainly do its best, as Stanley Cohen once put it, to "forbid facile gestures." But in so doing it needs to recognize that the pressures that drive penal politics do not originate *within* the criminal justice system alone. Rather they concern the very character of our political culture, of which our choices about punishment are among the most telling and consequential expressions. If, as the Brazilian political theorist Roberto Mangabeira Unger puts it, society is both "made and imagined," we must first face up to what we have made in order to imagine acting otherwise: "We must be realists in order to become visionaries."

BIBLIOGRAPHICAL NOTE

The literatures that deal with the historical development and other social and political aspects of punishment are large and diverse. For the benefit of the interested reader I list here the sources on which I have drawn directly in preparing this essay and some other more general ones that are of special current relevance. For ease of use I arrange these by topic, roughly in the order in which they appear in the essay. Where possible I refer to material that is widely available in book form rather than in specialist journals (but this is not always possible).

On the historical development of imprisonment.   The references I make come from Thorsten Sellin's edition of Beaumont and de Tocqueville's *On the Penitentiary System in the United States and its Application in France* [1833] (Southern Illinois University Press, 1964). Extracts from John Howard's writings (and from some previously published accounts by historians and sociologists of punishment) are included in John Muncie and Richard

Sparks (eds.), *Imprisonment: European Perspectives* (Harvester Wheatsheaf, 1991). Probably the most celebrated of all historical treatments of imprisonment, but also most contentious and hotly debated, is the ambitious account of the emergence of modern ways of punishing in the context of the industrial and political revolutions of the later eighteenth century by Michel Foucault in his *Discipline and Punish* (Allen Lane, 1977). It is through Foucault's influence that the term *penality* (denoting the interlocking of a range of practices, institutions, and cultural forms involved in the punishment and regulation of offenders) is now sometimes preferred to the more orthodox "punishment." A synoptic account of the views of Foucault and other penal theorists is provided by David Garland, in his influential *Punishment and Modern Society* (Oxford University Press, 1990). Overall, the most accessible introduction to the historical development of the prison is Norval Morris and David Rothman (eds.), *The Oxford History of the Prison* (Oxford University Press, 1995).

On the "crisis of penal modernism" (or what I call the "Janus-faced" nature of punishment). I draw fairly extensively on David Garland (op. cit.). See also the important essays by Garland and by Jonathan Simon and Malcolm Feeley in T. Blomberg and S. Cohen (eds.), *Punishment and Social Control* (Aldine de Gruyter, 1995). A very thoughtful and clear overview of current tendencies is provided by Anthony Bottoms in his essay "The Philosophy and Politics of Punishment and Sentencing," in C. Clarkson and R. Morgan (eds.), *The Politics of Sentencing Reform* (Oxford University Press, 1995). For more specific treatments of certain developments in particular national contexts (and in particular the influence of political slogans such as "Prison Works!" and "Three Strikes" see especially Lord Windlesham, *Responses to Crime,* Volume 3: *Legislating with the Tide* (Oxford University Press, 1996); Richard Sparks "Penal Austerity: The Doctrine of Less Eligibility Reborn?" in R. Matthews and P. Francis (eds.), *Prisons 2000* (Macmillan, 1996), and the essays collected in D. Shichor and D. Sechrest (eds.), *Three Strikes and You're Out* (Sage Publications, 1996) (especially the contributions by Jonathan Simon, Peter Greenwood et al., and James Austin).

On comparative penology and the state. For a challenging elaboration of the thesis that the prominence of penal severity in the recent politics of advanced capitalist countries is a reaction against the threats to their sovereign power posed by globalization, see David Garland "The Limits of the Sovereign State: Strategies of Crime Control in Contemporary Society" (*British Journal of Criminology,* 36(4):445–471, 1996). More generally for a thorough overview of the state-of-the-art in the social analysis of punishment see Dario Melossi (ed.), *The Sociology of Punishment* (Dartmouth, 1998). For substantial research-based discussions of comparative penal issues see V. Ruggiero, M. Ryan, and J. Sim (eds.), *Western European Penal Systems* (Sage Publications, 1993); F. Dunkel and D. van zyl Smit (eds.), *Imprisonment*

Today and Tomorrow (Gouda Quint, 1992). My discussion here of comparative prison populations condenses and updates earlier work by John Muncie and myself in Muncie and Sparks (op. cit.). The extracts on the Californian experience used in this essay are taken from Franklin Zimring and Gordon Hawkins, "The Growth of Imprisonment in California," in R. King and M. Maguire (eds.), *Prisons in Context* (Oxford University Press, 1994). See also their books *The Scale of Imprisonment* (University of Chicago Press, 1991), and, most recently, *Crime Is Not the Problem* (Oxford University Press, 1998).

For an influential account of the more general psychosocial consequences of living in the runaway world of what he calls "late modernity," including the growth of moral fundamentalisms, see Anthony Giddens, *Modernity and Self-Identity*, pp. 123–24 (Polity Press, 1991). For some further discussion of the relevance of Giddens's social theory to this field see my "Recent Social Theory and the Study of Crime and Punishment," in M. Maguire, R. Morgan, and R. Reiner (eds.), *The Oxford Handbook of Criminology* (Oxford University Press, 1997).

On the international growth and reach of private prison and security industries. See (for perhaps the most challenging and oppositional summary) Nils Christie's *Crime Control as Industry* (Routledge, 1993). But see also Robert Lilly and Paul Knepper, "An International Perspective on the Privatization of Corrections" (*Howard Journal*, 31(3):174–91, 1992). Lilly and Knepper use the term "corrections-commercial complex" (by analogy with Eisenhower's "military-industrial complex") to denote the transnational reach and political influence of the private prisons business.

On crime, punishment, and the "underclass." This is a major debate and a heated one. Among the most articulate proponents of the "underclass" thesis, from a perspective broadly in sympathy with the "New Right," is Charles Murray in a series of books and articles including *Losing Ground* (Basic Books, 1986), *The Emerging British Underclass* (Institute of Economic Affairs, 1990), and *Does Prison Work?* (Institute of Economic Affairs, 1997). For alternative prospectuses see John Hagan and Ruth Petersen (eds.), *Crime and Inequality* (Stanford University Press, 1995), and Michael Tonry, *Malign Neglect: Race, Crime and Politics in America* (Oxford University Press, 1995). For the latter authors and for Christie, the racial disparities in both "underclass" membership and imprisonment are major causes for concern. For Tonry in particular the language and prosecution of the "war on drugs" has been primarily responsible both for the acceleration of the growth of imprisonment in the United States and for the racial disproportions therein. A persuasive and readable recent overview of this territory, with special reference to political campaigns and mass media influences is provided by Katherine Beckett in her *Making Crime Pay: Law and Order in Contemporary American Politics* (Oxford University Press, 1997). For me, however, the key source and the book that makes most clear the relationship between incarceration and risk-based reasoning is Jonathan Simon's *Poor Discipline* (University of Chicago Press, 1993). Meanwhile, I borrow the expression "vocabulary of motives," and much else, from Dario Melossi. See in particular his article "Gazette of Morality and Social Whip" (*Social and Legal Studies*, 2:259–79, 1993).

On risk and the "new penology."   Feeley and Simon's trenchant opening position statement is their paper "The New Penology: Notes on the Emerging Strategy of Corrections and Its Implications" (*Criminology*, 30(4):449–75, 1992). They revise their position in some important ways in a subsequent paper: J, Simon and M. Feeley, "True Crime: The New Penology and Public Discourse on Crime," in T. Blomberg and S. Cohen (eds.), *Punishment and Social Control* (Aldine de Gruyter, 1995), where they acknowledge the continuing significance of broader cultural and political influences. Simon's witty and insightful skewering of the ideological basis of the "boot camp" movement in his paper "They Died with Their Boots On: The Boot Camp and the Limits of Modern Penality" (*Social Justice*, 22(2):25–48, 1995), is an excellent example of the latter. Simon suggests that the popular credibility of the boot camp relies upon an iconography of wholesome, masculine military discipline that provides "an infusion of meaningfulness through nostalgia." The idea of a penal "hybrid" is one that I develop from Mary Douglas's brilliant but difficult book *Risk and Blame* (Routledge, 1992). Meanwhile Sean McConville's succinct and powerful critique of the implicit political morality of incapacitation comes from his short paper "An Historic Folly?" in *Criminal Justice Matters* (30:4–5, Winter 1997/98). The expression "fashioned on an anvil of fear" is from Barry Krisberg, "Distorted by Fear: The Make-Believe War on Crime" (*Social Justice*, 21(3):38–49, 1994).

The sources quoted in the conclusion attempt to make the link back from penology to normative political theory. Zygmunt Bauman's remarks come from his paper, "The Strangers of the Consumer Era," in his *Postmodernity and Its Discontents* (Polity Press, 1997). John Gray's controlled anti-New Right polemic is in his book *Endgames: Questions in Late Modern Political Thought* (Polity Press, 1997). Roberto Unger's rallying call (not directed specifically toward penal politics but nonetheless relevant in my view) comes from his *Social Theory: Its Situation and Its Task* (Cambridge University Press, 1987). Having traversed some dispiriting ground let us end on a positive note. The counterprogram of "restorative justice" finds its most influential expression in John Braithwaite's book, *Crime, Shame, and Reintegration* (Cambridge University Press, 1989), a flawed but invigorating text. If you follow up only one of these references let it be this one. For Braithwaite retains the aspiration toward a qualitatively better future for the penal realm. As Antonio Gramsci urged us: "Pessimism of the intellect, optimism of the will."

2

Penal Modernism and Postmodernism

DAVID GARLAND

One of the most harmful habits in contemporary thought is the analysis of the present as being precisely, in history, a present of rupture, of high point, of completion, or of a returning dawn. The solemnity with which everyone who engages in philosophical discourse reflects on his own time strikes me as a flaw. . . . I think we should have the modesty to say to ourselves that . . . the time we live in is not the unique or fundamental irruptive point in history where everything is completed and begun again. . . . [O]n the other hand, the time we live in is very interesting; it needs to be analysed and broken down, and that we would do well to ask ourselves, "What is the nature of our present?"

—Michel Foucault, *Structuralism and Poststructuralism*

INTRODUCTION

There is a widespread sense today that contemporary penality is undergoing some kind of transformation. Until quite recently, accounts of contemporary penal transformations tended to be quite narrow in their focus and quite modest in their claims. In the last year or two, however, a new and stronger thesis is beginning to emerge, one that is much broader in its scope and much deeper in its implications. The new suggestion is that the penal realm, like other areas of social and cultural life, is becoming in some sense "postmodern," and that this historic shift forms the broad explanatory framework within which the diverse trends of contemporary penality can best be understood.

Postmodernism is, of course, very old news in cultural studies, social theory, and some branches of philosophy, where the term has been a hot topic of debate for the last fifteen years. Once the term *postmodern* escaped from the lexicon of artistic styles into broader debates about the nature of contemporary experience, it rapidly became a kind of catchall adjective to describe the various intellectual and political predicaments of an age in which foundational claims (in respect of knowledge, value, truth, and so on) are viewed as "mere" conventions.[1] Now, a decade and a half later, when the word has begun to lose its initial incendiary appeal, and has started to settle down as a more or less defined position in a number of well-worn debates, it has at last reached the distant shores of criminology and penology, where its precise implications have yet to be worked out.

The importation of modish intellectual terms is often dismissed as the product of an academic fashion industry, driven by the marketing strategies of publishers and the status concerns of writers who hope to impress by their taste in terminology. But it is also the case that writers who are seeking to develop new perspectives in their field do so using the language and concerns of contemporary intellectual life. Consequently, the appearance of the vocabulary of postmodernism in this latest field is liable to produce original insights and radical perspectives as well as the slavish repetition of fashionable postures developed elsewhere. One can only judge the matter in terms of the substantive analyses actually produced, and seek to avoid the polarized "love it or hate it" response that the mere mention of the term *postmodernism* now frequently provokes.

The claim that penality is becoming postmodern takes a number of forms and has been put forward by a number of writers, but the precise meaning of the claim is still rather inchoate. Writers such as Stanley Cohen (1990) and Jan van Dijk (1989) have used the term *postmodern* to refer to certain aspects of contemporary criminological discourse. Others such as Carol Smart (1990), and John-Paul Brodeur (1993) have proposed postmodernism as an intellectual and political stance relevant to thinking about crime and punishment (and especially to thinking about that thinking). Robert Reiner (1992) has discussed the problems of policing what he terms a "postmodern society." However the postmodernist thesis has been put forward in its strongest form by Jonathan Simon, first of all in an article entitled "The New Penology" (coauthored with Malcolm Feeley [Feeley and Simon 1992]) and more recently in his 1993 book *Poor Discipline*, where he titles one chapter "Penal Postmodernism: Power without Narrative" and explicitly raises the question, Are we postmodern? (see also Simon 1991; Howe 1994; Schwartz and Friedrichs 1994; Henry and Milovanovic 1994).

A common feature of these references to the postmodern is that they all have something of a *gestural* character. Their use of the term evokes a whole range of new attitudes, discourses, and practices, against the broad background of a new social and cultural configuration, but the precise meaning of the postmodern *in criminology or penology* is rarely specified in any detail. Even Simon's writings, which are by far the most substantive and interesting, are disappointingly thin when it comes to a positive characterization of what is postmodern about the present. (He is much better on what has become problematic about the modernist past.)

Since most readers of criminological theory have some understanding of what postmodernism has come to mean in other fields, it has been possible to use the term in an ill-defined way and yet still succeed in communicating something (though that something is often very imprecise). At a minimum, the suggestion is that penality now increasingly exhibits certain new characteristics, which are distinguishable from those of the recent past (i.e., from penal "modernity") and which resemble the kinds of postmodern phenomena that analysts have identified elsewhere in contemporary culture and society. The task of specifying precisely what the postmodern elements of penality might be is an important exercise that has not yet been undertaken. I hope that the analyses developed in the following pages may succeed in provoking further work in this direction.

If the notion of a postmodern penality could be shown to be a plausible description of the present this would have a far-reaching significance. It would, for example, imply that the sociology of modernity was an increasingly inappropriate framework for understanding punishment and penal history. Our interpretation of penality would no longer be set within the long-term processes of rationalization, differentiation, commodification, and civilization that the sociology of modernity has established as the configurational setting in which modern penal institutions developed (see Garland 1990). Recent work by sociologists and historians of punishment has extended that analysis of modernity into the field of penality and described the contours of "the modern" in this area of social life: such work would cease to be a history of the present and become instead the history of a past that is now disappearing before our eyes.

The coming of postmodernity might also suggest that the *politics* of penality—with its characteristic conflicts, interest groups, structural constraints, cultural sensibilities, etc.—are no longer as we have come to understand them. The plausibility of current political objectives, the appropriateness of particular values, the possibility of desired social arrangements, and the viability of specific reform strategies would all be put in question if we have indeed entered upon a new historical era in which the assumptions of modernity no longer hold.

Following a discussion of the issues and an extended attempt to set out a postmodern interpretation of current penal trends, my argument will be that the concept of the postmodern is not particularly persuasive or powerful as a means of understanding contemporary penal developments. I will suggest instead that the various changes taking place are better understood in terms of concepts derived from the sociology of modernity, and I will briefly sketch out an analysis that attempts to make such an interpretation. My claim will be that these changes are the outcome of certain long-term modernizing dynamics operating in combination with a set of conjunctural political and cultural shifts. To the extent that important changes have occurred and indeed they have—these need to be understood at a level of specificity that is less global and less world-historic than the notion of postmodernity tends to imply. They need to be understood in relation to the specific social and penal settings in which they occur—globalizing tendencies have not altogether erased the importance of national differences in this respect, as comparative research has shown (e.g., Downes 1988)—and in relation to the shifting political and professional balances of power in these locales.

That I come to a negative conclusion on the question of postmodern penality does not, I think, make the discussion of these matters any less valuable. The attempt to come to terms with the idea of the postmodern in social and cultural studies has had the immense value of sharpening our sense of the historical and cultural configuration in which we live. In debating the postmodern, social theorists have improved our understanding of modernity and the ways in which it is and is not subject to change. The discussion now under way in respect of penality has the potential to do the same in this corner of social inquiry.

PENAL MODERNITY

The concept of the postmodern (and its derivatives, postmodernism and postmodernity) is, of course, defined in terms of a contrast with the modern (and with modernism and modernity), although the precise referents of these generic terms will vary according to the field in which they operate. The contrasts between the modern and the postmodern in the conventions that govern the production and reception of artistic, architectural, or literary works are rather different from the contrasts drawn by sociologists between modern and postmodern social forms, cultural experiences, or political interventions. Consequently, it is necessary to begin by describing how terms such as modern and modernism have come to be used in the sociology of punishment and penal history. In setting out the key features of penal modernity I also provide a basis from which to gauge the extent to which current trends depart from the modern configuration.

The modern system for managing, supervising, and punishing violators of the criminal law is a specialized differentiated one, formally independent of other normative systems, and increasingly distinct from other forms of legal regulation. It is largely state controlled and administered by professional bureaucracies that exercise legally sanctioned powers over individual offenders, utilizing institutions and sanctions specially designed for that purpose. Historical work makes it clear that these modern arrangements were put in place comparatively recently, and in fact the movement toward system differentiation and professionalization continues today. In that respect, modernity is best thought of as a dynamic and continuing historical process rather than a static social type.

As the nation-state gradually wrestled control of the power to punish away from competing secular and spiritual authorities and concentrated it in the institutions of criminal justice, so too did the forms of punishment take on their distinctive modern character. The traditional repertoire of corporal and symbolic punishments, carried out in public, together with banishment and exile and public works, slowly gave way to the deprivation of liberty, the use of institutional enclosures, and a quiet penal discipline that took place largely behind the scenes.

The prison and the reformatory have come to be seen as the characteristic inventions of the nineteenth century, although it is probably more accurate to regard that period as the point at which such institutions became the standard and accepted response to crime. In fact, penal institutions based on work and reformatory discipline had been evolving in Europe since the mid-sixteenth century, and may be regarded as one of the institutional features of the early modern social landscape that began to emerge in Europe at that time (Spierenburg 1991; Beattie 1986). Similarly, monetary penalties slowly became a standardized means of punishing offenders. Fines payable to the state came to replace the traditional practice of private restitutive settlements between the parties, and, with the monetarization of the economy, it gradually became possible to use the fine to punish the mass of common offenders and not just the wealthy minority. To this penal repertoire, the twentieth century added a lighter, more dispersed network of supervisory practices, variously known as probation, suspended sentences, parole, or community supervision. In the perspective of the long term, these were new forms of punishment and control, adapted to the conditions of modernity, and substituting for traditional modes of control, which had become either ineffective or intolerable.

These new institutions emerged correlatively with groups of functionaries that, over time, became increasingly differentiated and professionalized, developing distinctive identities, ideologies, and interests. And alongside this developing industry there emerged a profession of criminologists whose task it was to supply the new forms of knowledge upon which the system increasingly depends: knowledge about individual offenders and their antecedents, but also the reflexive, self-monitoring knowledge that has become such a necessary aspect of all modern institutions. Modern organizations strive to become transparent to themselves, scrutinizing their own practices, tracing their own effects, and it is this reflexive function—rather than their more ambitious efforts to uncover the causes of crime—that increasingly provides criminologists with their professional raison d'être.

THE CULTURE OF MODERN PENALITY

The apparatus of modern penality has, over the past two centuries and more, slowly displaced the penal arrangements of traditional society. Where traces of these remain, as with the death penalty, their forms and representations have been thoroughly "modernized."[2] For most of that two-hundred-year period, a powerful reforming tradition of Enlightenment rationalism has been the leading current of penal culture. Against the "harsh" methods and "terroristic" objectives of absolutist penal regimes, this liberal reforming movement counterposed utility, rationality, the rights of man, and the rule of law. Punishments were to be regulated by law and by reason, carefully calibrated to ensure the maximum effect from the minimum of pain, put to good use rather than striking out destructively and at random. From Montesquieu, Voltaire, and Beccaria to Howard, Bentham, and Mill, punishments were to be rationally administered and made positive in their results. According to this way of thinking, punishment should be preventative. It should deter, reform, and, if necessary, restrain. Hence, it should be measured, parsimonious, temperate, not destructive of the offender's capacities, and not neglectful of his or her rights. A reformed criminal law was to be the first step toward realizing this liberal program. The well-run penitentiary would be its showpiece institution. The fine, especially the modern system of adjusted installments and day-fines, would be its most authentic expression.

From around the 1890s a different cultural theme began to emerge in the penal realm. This new current was a legitimate child of Enlightenment tradition; indeed, in many ways it was the highest expression of that tradition's rationalist and utilitarian ambitions. But the new current opposed itself to the penological program of Beccaria and Bentham and viewed itself as an antidote to that program rather than a development of it. This new approach is usually known as the treatment model, correctionalism, or else the rehabilitative ideal, and is closely associated with the new science of criminology (or "criminological positivism" as the latter is often termed). I think, however, that these terms tend to narrow the phenomenon, reducing a whole way of thinking and acting to the particular forms of policy to which it gave rise. I would prefer to describe the new approach as a new penal rationality that might best be known as *penological modernism*. This term will, I hope, capture the scope and historic importance of this new approach, as well as suggest the links between this specifically penal culture and the trends that dominated other areas of cultural and intellectual life from the 1890s onward. It describes not just a particular policy but a whole style of reasoning, together with the broad program of criminological thought and penological action to which it gave rise.

Penological modernism took the Enlightenment rationalist framework to its logical conclusion and, in so doing, threw out many of its liberal principles and assumptions about how to govern the social realm. Punishment in general, and retributive punishment in particular, is viewed by modernists as an irrational disutility, a remnant of premodern traditions based upon emotion, instinct, and superstition. Even the liberal principles of proportionality and uniformity are tainted by archaic thinking. The proper management of crime and criminals requires individualized, corrective measures adapted to the specific case or the particular problem. To this end, one needs expert knowledge, scientific research, and flexible instruments of intervention, as well as a willingness to regulate aspects of life that had previously been deemed beyond the reach of government. The normative system of law must give way to that of science. Punishment must be replaced by treatment. Good government and social utility should become the overriding aims of criminal justice.

For penal modernism, the phenomena of crime are symptoms of deeper problems. They speak of maladjusted individuals and social pathologies. Good government can address these underlying problems, given the proper know-how and the political will. Penality need no longer be a tragic realm in which bad things happen. In this new reforming culture, knowledge, transparency, the understanding of action, and the in-depth control of conduct become the key considerations. Moral concerns give way to technical issues. The more complex and layered image of psychological man, with its social determinants and precarious stability, replaces the robust rational hedonist that Bentham had described. Welfarism and social defense, in-depth knowledge and in-depth intervention, individual investigation, and customized treatment regimes are the hallmarks of the modernist program.

It seems to me that this program can properly be described as modernist in respect of its technicist, social engineering, positivist style; because of its statism and its explicit linking of penality with distinctively modern strategies of rule; because of its utter confidence that human reason can penetrate to the essential truth of social conditions, making them fully amenable to social control; and above all because the criminologists and reformers of the early twentieth century were self-consciously aligning themselves with the culture of scientific modernism that they saw all around them. It is also modernist in that it reflects the interests and experience of key actors and social groups who owe their existence to the new functional positions that emerged in the modern system. Penal modernism is the product and working ideology of the new professional groupings in the modern penal system, the new class of criminological experts and knowledge professionals who increasingly challenged the hold that lawyers and moralists once had on this field.

From the 1890s onward, penal modernism increasingly became the leading *critical* discourse in the penal realm, and was widely supported by criminologists, psychiatrists, social workers, and penal reformers. During the course of the twentieth century, this critical vision began to make a serious impression, as social inquiries, reformatory regimes, individual classification, and indeterminate sentences became routine aspects of the system. The practical success of the new movement was always uneven and rarely satisfied its most enthusiastic proponents. There was always resistance to its efforts, either from the liberal legalism of the Enlightenment tradition, which insisted upon proportionality and just deserts, or else from an older, premodern tradition, which saw punishment either as an important end in itself or else as a necessary manifestation of sovereign power. But the modernist movement did succeed in transforming the character of penality to some extent and it was able to do so because the ideologies and interests of the new penal professionals articulated smoothly with the developing strategies of rule of the welfare state (see Garland 1985). "Reform," "rehabilitation," "treatment and training," "the best interests of the child"—all of these objectives meshed effectively with the ideological stress upon universal citizenship and social integration that characterized social politics in the postwar period. So too did the concern to utilize science for social purposes and to extend the capacity of the state to govern more and more aspects of individual and social life.

Above all, the modernist reformers succeeded in the establishment of a new apparatus of investigation, assessment, record keeping, classification, and prediction. And while this apparatus was initially justified in the name of rehabilitation and welfarism, its uses were not, and are not, restricted to those of that particular version of the modernist program. Penal modernism insists upon an apparatus of investigation, upon expert authority, upon self-reflexive, rationalized practices, and upon a utilitarian, rationalist orientation. But the substantive ends to which this apparatus is put remain indeterminate. It is, and always has been, an apparatus capable of supporting strategies other than the rehabilitative, correctionalist one that accompanied its construction.

The politics of penal modernism are deeply ambivalent. They depend upon the ideological orientation of those who staff the institutions, and upon the political and legal context in which they operate. They can range from the Fabian reformism that has dominated British criminology and the British social work establishment to the crude authoritarianism of many fascist and communist regimes. Moreover, one cannot read off the effects of these programs from the declared objectives of the reformers' programs, as critical analyses sometimes do, since these aims have frequently been undermined or transformed in the process of implementation (cf. Rothman 1980; Allen 1981). Like the Enlightenment tradition from which it stems, penal modernism is capable of progressive and humane applications, but also of reactionary and dehumanizing ones.

Much of the revisionist penal history of the last twenty-five years has been concerned to bring the repressive aspect of the Enlightenment to our attention, sometimes in a very dramatic and disconcerting way. As we will see, the relatively rapid transformation of modernism from being a critical, reforming program, to being an element of the established regime and the focus of a newly critical self-consciousness, is one of the causes of what I have elsewhere termed the current "crisis of penal modernism" (Garland 1990:7). The question to be addressed is whether that crisis is a terminal one, which now points to the death of modernism and the emergence of a postmodern penality, or whether it will be recuperated in a modernism that survives despite its chronic weaknesses and self-doubt. To better approach that question, we need to consider the accounts of penal change that are currently in circulation. As we will see, the postmodern thesis does not deny these existing accounts, so much as subsume them within a broader characterization of penal and social change.

THEORIES OF TRANSFORMATION

One of the most interesting characteristics of commentary on penality today is that everyone agrees the field is changing, and in fundamental ways. However, there is surprisingly little agreement about the precise nature of this transformation, or about the causes that are bringing it about.

Francis Allen (1981) has described the "decline of the rehabilitative ideal" during the 1970s, and has attributed this ideological shift to a series of converging circumstances, including the failure of correctional efforts, abuses of implementation, and a changed cultural climate in which value consensus and faith in state institutions are no longer widespread. Others have taken up this story and described the subsequent movement toward determinate sentencing laws that took place in the United States and elsewhere, as well as the broader influence of the just-deserts model upon sentencing, prison regimes, and even probation practice (see von Hirsch 1983; Bottoms and Preston 1980; Hudson 1987; Cavadino and Dignan 1992).

While acknowledging the ideological changes noted by Allen, sociologists such as Andrew Scull and Stanley Cohen have identified the expansion of "community corrections" as the major developmental tendency. Scull (1977) initially suggested there had been a shift from custody to community prompted by fiscal considerations and the critique of "total institutions," but later acknowledged that "decarceration" was less evident in the penal sphere than it was in the control of treatment of the mentally ill (see Scull 1984). Cohen (1985) argued that, despite the apparent intentions of reformers, no transfer of the penal population from institutional confinement to community supervision had actually occurred, but rather that there had been an overall expansion in "the net of penal control," with both prisons and community "alternatives" undergoing a massive expansion and elaboration (see also Gordon 1991; Marx 1988). Cohen's net-widening thesis has been very influential, among practitioners as well as academics, but it has been recently been subjected to criticism. Maeve McMahon (1990) has questioned the empirical and methodological basis of Cohen's claim, suggesting that some of the evidence for the proposition may be unreliable and pointing to the fact that policymakers and practitioners have begun to take steps to prevent the occurrence of this unintended consequence.[3] Tony Bottoms (1983) has also argued that the most significant development of the last twenty years is not the expansion of the net of penal control, and certainly not "the dispersal of discipline" in any Foucauldian sense, but rather the increased use of sanctions such as the fine, compensation, and suspended sentences, which involve little in the way of "normalization." Bottoms places this development in parallel with a trend toward more severe custodial sentencing for offenders who are deemed to be "dangerous," and suggests that this "bifurcated" penal strategy is designed to deal with two different populations of offender. For those offenders who are viewed as largely self-controlled and integrated into mainstream society through work, family, respectability, and so on, a light form of penalty is all that is required. For those offenders who are deemed more marginal or more threatening, the emphasis continues to be upon punitive discipline and incapacitation.

Bottoms is also one of several commentators (see also Peters 1988; Feeley and Simon 1992; Tuck 1991) who have pointed to the growth of what he terms "managerialism" in the penal system—a new and pronounced concern with system management, resource allocation, cost-benefit considerations, and organizational efficiency. This theme is given its fullest elaboration by Malcolm Feeley and Jonathan Simon (1992), who argue that the managerial approach forms a part of a "new penology," which is beginning to emerge as an important framework of thought and action.

According to Feeley and Simon, the social-psychological criminology of the mid-twentieth century—and the normalizing, rehabilitative penal practice that it supported—is now being displaced by a framework that no longer focuses upon the individual offender and no longer aims to produce behavioral change. Instead, the new approach addresses itself to aggregate populations and large groups of offenders, which it seeks to manage by reference to actuarial inferences from statistical data sets. The calculation of risks is now a matter of viewing each individual as a member of a calculable group, whose profile can be derived from actuarial tables compiled from large-scale data sets that condense the details of large numbers of offenders, rather than seeking to develop a direct clinical knowledge of the particular individual. The primary goal of prediction is now to ensure the proper allocation of resources and the efficient management of risk, not to secure the best treatment for the purpose of individual reform.

As Simon discovered in his own research, field workers in probation and parole (at least in parts of the United States) are ceasing to be social work counselors and are becoming risk management technicians, whose task it is to monitor offenders by means of urinalysis and electronic checks, measuring them the whole time against an actuarial profile of high and low risk. Professional, clinical discretion is increasingly limited by centralized system monitoring in which the key decision is whether to return the offender to custody or not. And where returning a client to court was previously regarded as a failure to rehabilitate, it is now seen as an index of the efficient and effective management of risk (see Simon 1993).

For Feeley and Simon, this new penology is the outcome of a number of forces. The resource pressures upon penal systems, the failures of penal-welfare strategies, the logic of modern power-knowledge, the decline of industrial work, the erosion of the community resources and solidarities upon which the old penology relied, and the willingness of governments to accept the existence of an underclass that is to be contained and controlled without any serious prospect of integration into the social and economic mainstream all combine to render the old penology archaic and produce conditions in which the new one can thrive.

One of the characteristics of this new penology is that criminological discourse becomes more statistical, more actuarial, ever more concerned with aggregate groups and populations, and decreasingly interested in the individual offender as a clinical case. This point registers one aspect of a broader shift that has affected criminological thinking since the 1970s. Starting with the influential work of James Q. Wilson in the United States, and of Ron Clarke in the United Kingdom, the idea of the offender as a maladapted or undersocialized individual with a criminal disposition has been challenged by a conception of the offender as a rational economic actor. This new pragmatic approach argues that, whatever the truth of the matter, offenders can, for policy purposes, be regarded as if they are fully rational agents, responding to incentives and disincentives, seizing opportunities where they exist, and desisting from crime wherever situational deterrents or preventatives are set in place. The criminal is thus viewed as a kind of consumer, though one who must be repelled rather than seduced (see Wilson 1983; Clarke 1983; Cornish and Clarke 1986; Mayhew, Clarke, Sturman, and Hough 1976; Felson 1994).

A similar emphasis on the rational, "responsible" actor now features in, of all places, the policy statements of prison regimes, which declare that the prisoner must be viewed as a customer who is capable of making choices and must be "made to take responsibility" for such things as sentence planning and personal development (Scottish Prison Service 1990). It has echoes as well in the philosophy of punishment, which has also undergone significant shifts in the last two decades. Here one sees a forceful reemergence of a deontological discourse, emphasizing the autonomy of the individual but also the necessity of punishment as a social duty and thus an end in itself. The intellectual focus is now much more upon retribution—whether as a Kantian requirement of justice or as a means of communicating community values. Utilitarian argument and reformative purposes have given way to an emphasis upon desert, denunciation, and punishment (see Duff and Garland 1994). And although much of this retributive theorizing emerged as a liberal reaction to the excesses of the therapeutic state, the new respectability it has lent to "punishment" would seem to have encouraged more punitive government discourses and policies (see Home Office 1988). What was originally intended as a liberal critique of modernist reasoning in favor of classic Enlightenment restraints has been taken up by a more punitive antimodernism, which emphasizes the importance of punishment as a symbol of sovereign power and social authority.

A POSTMODERN PENALITY?

We have, then, a cluster of historical theses. Each one highlights a transforming dynamic, each draws distinctions between a before and an after, and each characterizes the present as somehow different from the arrangements that prevailed in the past. Penality is variously described, in effect, as "postrehabilitative," "postdisciplinary," "postcriminological," "postindustrial," "postutilitarian." No wonder that the term *postmodern* so easily suggests itself to many analysts as a way of summing up the present. Penality is a social field in flux. It is eclectic; host to a hotchpotch of different discourses and programs; devoid of any coherent, overall direction. The fleeting, fragmentary, recursive quality of postmodern culture seems to have displaced what was once a strong sense of penality's historic mission and progressive reforming program. One of the few constant themes to emerge is a negative one, namely, that all of these diverse developments tend to define themselves in opposition to the framework of penal modernism.

Postmodern is the term that most readily suggests itself as a way of characterizing—however vaguely—the dynamics and discontents of the present. And as we have seen, postmodernism is beginning to enter the discourse as a shorthand, catchall term that conveys the sense of one era ending and another getting under way. But despite the attractions of this way of conceiving things—particularly its implication that nothing is settled and that the future of penality is once more "up for grabs"—there is reason to avoid the casual use of such powerful terms, especially if their tendency is to overstate the novelty of the present and to imply a qualitative break with the past. In the pages that follow, I have sought to go beyond the fragmentary suggestions made by other commentators, and to set out a more elaborated account of postmodernity in the penal realm. This account is my attempt to explore the possibility that the phenomena and developments described as postmodern in the wider sociological and philosophical literature might have a number of direct analogies in the field of penality. Other theorists may subsequently construct a different and more persuasive account, in which case my conclusions will need to be revised. However, I have sought to make the postmodernist case in its strongest form, given my own, no doubt limited understanding of both the literature of postmodernism and the contemporary character of penal developments.

What follows, then, is an inventory of postmodern sightings in the penal field—glimpses of what might conceivably be postmodern phenomena, whether these be forms of consciousness, discursive formations, or policies and practices. First, I will present these observations in a way that highlights their postmodern affiliations. Thereafter I will consider whether this is the most plausible way of interpreting them.

Most strikingly, one can point to a collapse of the grand narrative of penal reform and penal progress as a characteristic sign of the postmodern.[4] In the penal context, this collapse has a number of aspects. The Enlightenment ideal of a rational, utilitarian penal policy has been subjected to a thoroughgoing critique. Revisionist histories have changed our relationship to the Enlightenment project. Where we once saw the advance of reason and humanity, we now see a darker side. The monstrous aspects of modernity—its disciplines, its dehumanization, its well-administered Holocausts—are now never far from our thoughts when considering policies of "correctional intervention" or "social defense" (see Foucault 1977; Christie 1993; Bauman 1989). This disavowal of Enlightenment rationalism is most forcefully expressed in contemporary reactions to the treatment or rehabilitative model or, more broadly, to what I have termed penal modernism. The modernist project is now regarded not just as a failure, but as a positive danger—an intrusive, authoritarian program, blind to the importance of individual autonomy and human worth. After a century of tirelessly pursuing the modernist vision, criminologists and penologists now increasingly distance themselves from its aims.

The intellectual climate and penal policy culture of the 1970s and 1980s took on a disillusioned, cynical, nihilistic character. For the first time in two hundred years there was no guiding vision, no coherent philosophy of progress. Instead, there was the sense of the exhaustion of a tradition, the end of an era. The view that "nothing works" quickly became widespread, particularly among academics, and even the most optimistic of practitioners lacked general solutions. The best one could hope for became small-scale, local initiatives with a markedly low level of ambition (see Palmer 1992). The broad consensus of the correctionalist era quickly fragmented, and in its place there emerged an eclectic mixture of competing perspectives and politics. The old paradigm was dead, but no new one rose up to replace it. The leading historian of the age of penal progress—Sir Leon Radzinowicz—set his judgment on the new era, when he gave his review of recent history the title "Penal Regressions" (Radzinowicz 1991).

In criminological discourse, and indeed in crime control policies, there is evidence of what one might term a shift from depth to surface.[5] it was an article of faith for criminological modernism that crime is a symptom of deeper psychological and social problems that must be investigated and treated; that the truth of crime lay deep in the offender's biography and circumstances. Nowadays prominent criminologists are losing interest in criminological depth, and indeed, in criminological truth (cf. Wilson 1983; Clarke 1983). Pragmatic considerations prompt a return to surface phenomena—to choices and opportunities and rational calculations. Whatever one thinks about causation, offenders can be treated "as if" they are free, rational, responsible individuals, responsive to penalties and prices. Crime can be addressed by manipulating situations rather than changing dispositions. The fact that such policies do not address the "root causes" or deep-lying problems is not perceived as a failing. Pragmatic considerations prefer available, manipulable surface to hard-to-reach depth. In any case, the critique of the treatment model has made in-depth approaches problematic in principle as well as in practice. In these perspectives, the category of the criminal shifts from deep subject to shallow opportunist, from psychological man to situational actor, from a specific individual with a history that has to be explored to a universalized decision-maker whose behavior can be statistically predicted.

These shallow conceptions of the offender, though important for policy, are by no means the only current conceptions. Indeed, the criminological field has never been more diverse, fragmented, and eclectic (see Ericson and Carriere 1994). Genetic, neurological, and biological perspectives that were once considered archaic are now back in the repertoire (see Nelkin 1995) as are econometric models, so that there is hardly any human science approach that is not present in the criminological domain. The field is divided into dozens of competing perspectives, none of which can claim to be the orthodox position. This endemic eclecticism and pluralism has given rise to a sense that the "truth" of crime is unattainable. All that we have is a repertoire of accounts that can be selectively drawn upon depending on one's purposes. The self-conscious sense that truth-claims, in this field, are merely strategic rhetorics—that one describes offenders in ways that suit one's purposes rather as lawyers do in court—echoes a broader sense that postmodern pragmatism has replaced modernist hopes of scientific objectivity.

The relativization (and thus the abolition) of criminological truth has its parallel in the relativization of morals in the penal realm. Despite its claim to be a form of social hygiene or social medicine, the rehabilitative approach confidently endorsed a definite moral code with which offenders were to be realigned. Values such as work, respectability, domesticity, sociability, and self-knowledge were at least as important in the process as respect for law or the prevention of recidivism. The postmodern decline of moral codes and the erosion of state authority have destroyed the easy moral confidence upon which rehabilitation was based. Using the penal process to impose values upon inmates and clients is now viewed as morally suspect. The moral authority of the system is contested and uncertain. The idea of a mainstream moral community into which offenders must be integrated appears dangerously outmoded in the age of multiculturalism, moral disestablishment, and the deification of "difference."

Crime control has likewise become increasingly amoral or demoralized. Policies such as situational crime prevention, target-hardening, and general deterrence seek to manage criminal risks, not to reform criminal attitudes. Similarly, the displacement of rehabilitation by just deserts and incapacitation makes punishment a matter of costs and constraints, not moral education. Punishment becomes a system of inputs and outputs, risks and resources, and the impact of moral sentiments (whether these are compassionate or punitive) are viewed by the professionals as a kind of unwanted noise in the system.[6]

Systems of crime control have become increasingly self-referential and self-serving, increasingly "autopoietic."[7] The aim is no longer to respond to external social demands for the control of crime and the reform of offenders. Instead the aim is to develop an immunity from outside demands of this kind by setting up internal aims and self-generated criteria of success. If the system cannot influence crime rates, then perhaps it can at least control punishment rates. If it fails in its social task, perhaps it needs to redefine its mission in terms of goals it can achieve—hence the focus on system management, new performance indicators, and the repeated refrain that police and prisons cannot control crime by themselves. The waning of penal modernism, and the widespread cynicism about penality's capacity to produce real social benefits, has been accompanied by a much more explicit commercialization of the penal process. The monetary costs of doing justice are no longer a background consideration. Instead they are foregrounded and explicitly made part of the process. They become a value consideration on the same plane as other values (such as justice and humanity) and in direct competition with them. So, for example, the British police were recently advised by the government's Audit Commission to classify reported offenses into those which would be investigated and those which would not, in order to avoid wasting resources on inquiries that are likely to be fruitless (reported in the *Manchester Guardian*, 20 September 1993).

In much the same way, crime control and punishment have become much more explicitly politicized. Issues that were once a matter for expert discretion—such as sentencing decisions, regime design, and the content of supervision—are no longer left to the professionals and their established canon of accepted practices. Instead these have become the subject of political debate and public controversy. The widespread fear of crime and the sense of urban insecurity have prompted politicians to reclaim the issue and to make it a core symbol in debates about social order and political authority (see Scheingold 1991; Hall, Critcher, Jefferson, Clarke, and Roberts 1978). And in these debates, the findings of criminologists and the common sense of penal functionaries are not regarded as authoritative.

Finally, one might mention the tendency of philosophical writing in this area to focus more and more upon the signs and symbols of punishment. The new philosophical work privileges the expressive over the instrumental, characterizing punishment not as a form of violence or material deprivation, but as a special form of communication. Punishment is increasingly seen as a system of signs and images, a semiotic conductor, a way of "saying things with walls" (see Duff and Garland 1994). At a time when theorists of postmodernity are increasingly intent on rethinking the social world as an economy of signs, an information society, a universe of free-floating images and *simulacra* (cf. Baudrillard 1983), we begin to see the materiality of punishment dissolved into one more set of ethereal signs and representations.

THE PERSISTENCE OF THE MODERN

The collapse of grand narratives and Enlightenment ideals, the preference for surface over depth, the fragmentation of discourse and moral code, the self-conscious pragmatism and eclecticism, the waning of affect and of a sense of history, the dominance of signs and images, the turn to nihilism, localism, commercialism, politicization.[8] These are, of course, the well-known thematics and motifs of the postmodern, and the fact that penality can be represented in these terms indicates that the thesis of an emerging postmodernity has a certain plausibility.

Such a thesis would have considerable appeal. If penal trends could be shown to be local instances or analogs of broader social and cultural trends, then this might provide a powerful means of explaining the causes and character of the contemporary penal changes. Explaining the particular by reference to the general, the penal by reference to the social and cultural, is, after all, a favored explanatory trope in the sociology of punishment. Similarly, it would be a nice paradox (and sociologists are notoriously susceptible to paradoxical accounts) if a system that is often seen as archaic, uncivilized, even premodern, were to be shown to be at the forefront of cultural and social change. But despite these attractions, I want to argue that the developments that are affecting contemporary penality are occurring *within* the contours of modernity and modernism, rather than representing some kind of break with them. Therefore, if the notion of the postmodern implies such a break, as I believe it does, if it involves a movement beyond the contours of the modern into some new and distinctive social and cultural configuration, then it would be misleading to talk of a postmodern penality in any empirically descriptive sense.[9] I will argue that we should think instead in terms of a penality that has entered a phase of "high modernity" (cf. Giddens 1990) or, as I might less elegantly put it, a self-conscious and hence self-doubting phase of modernity. Such descriptions place the phenomena within the long-term processes of modernization, which I will argue to be their proper analytical location, and suggest the continued relevance of the sociology of modernity as a framework for their explanation.

I would argue, against my own effort to represent penality as postmodern—and, by implication, against other attempts to do the same—that the postmodernist interpretation is undermined by three interrelated problems: first of all, the indeterminacy and ambiguity of some of the key concepts involved; second, the fact that certain purportedly postmodern characteristics are actually typical of modernity rather than distinct from it; third, that the thesis of a distinctive postmodern social configuration depends upon a caricature of modernity and its sociological referents.

Some of these "postmodern sightings" fail to carry much evidentiary weight because the motifs of postmodern identification are so abstract and empirically indeterminate that facts can easily be made to fit. For example, claims about the decline of grand narratives could have been made at any time in history. Grand narratives are always collapsing, only to be replaced by others. (Ironically enough, postmodernism has become such an all-encompassing account of historical and cultural change that it is often presented as if it were a candidate for such a status, to the embarrassment of theorists like Lyotard, who are thus caught in a contradiction.) *Penal modernism*—like the modernisms that prevailed in architecture, or art, or literature—has always had its critics and dissenters, just as the rationalism of the Enlightenment has long been challenged by romantics, conservatives, and traditionalists of all kinds. As I argued above, the narrative of penal modernism was always compromised and challenged by these alternative narratives. Today, opposition to modernism still takes the dual form of a liberal "just deserts" critique, and a more conservative drive toward a form of punitiveness that operates as an archaic symbol of sovereignty. All that has changed is the balance of power in the struggle to define what punishment should mean. And even then, the basic Enlightenment notion that punishment should be made to be useful—that it should aim to control crime and reform criminals—continues to be the central assumption of most penal policy, despite the skepticism of academic critics. Moreover, although the critique of penal modernism has clearly had an international impact, it is by no means clear that the "decline of rehabilitation" or the critique of positivist criminology has meant the same thing in different national contexts.

Other aspects of my account suffer from a similar imprecision and looseness of fit. Metaphors of surface and depth are just that—metaphors—which are too vague and too loose in their application to be very useful analytical tools. This is especially true when such terms are applied to discursive fields where they have no settled meaning or controlled connotations. In the field of aesthetics, the concepts of surface and depth are well defined and capable of precise and well-understood usage. But when one uses these terms out of context, they become metaphors rather than concepts, and can be used to gloss very different phenomena with spurious and superficial resemblances. Criminology's supposed relinquishment of "depth" and new concentration upon "surface" is probably a gloss of this kind, which simplifies a complex discursive phenomenon and overstates the resemblances between developments in criminology and broader cultural trends. We should remind ourselves, for instance, that J. Q. Wilson is also the author of *Crime and Human Nature: The Definitive Study of the Causes of Crime* (Wilson and Herrnstein 1985), which suggests that the concern for etiological inquiry has not entirely faded. Similarly, we should note that perhaps the most influential criminological work of the 1980s and early 1990s was that of Travis Hirschi and his coworkers, whose concern is precisely to produce a general theory of crime (see Gottfredson and Hirschi 1990). We should also remember that the rejection of causal inquiry in favor of a more pragmatic type of analysis is no new development of the 1970s and 1980s. In the immediate postwar period, at the height of enthusiasm for penal modernism and positivist criminology, leading figures, such as Walter Reckless, Mannheim and Wilkins, and Leon Radzinowicz all argued for the pragmatic, administrative approach that J. Q. Wilson is now assumed to have invented (see Garland 1994). More importantly, the depth/surface distinction breaks down when one recalls that, however familiar they have become, notions such as reason and the calculation of economic interest involve a definite psychology and conceptions of subjectivity that are hardly behaviorist. And to describe rational choice criminology as postmodern would be to suggest that neoclassical economics and Benthamite utilitarianism must also be included in postmodernism.

There are, at present, interesting changes taking place in the ways in which the figure of "the criminal" is represented in official and policy-oriented criminology. These changes are important and are influenced by wider political and ideological trends, as well as by pragmatic considerations. (The now-popular image of the offender as situationally induced actor seems closer to the modern figure of the consumer than to the

Enlightenment ideal of the rational man.) But changing styles of criminological representation are just glossed over and explained away if we take
them to be merely one more example of a general stylistic shift that first
occurred in architecture and aesthetics and now purportedly defines the
whole cultural domain.

Similar points can be made about criminology's eclecticism, which I
would claim is a constitutive part of the discipline, rather than a new development (see Garland 1994; Ericson and Carriere 1994), and about the
demoralization of policy, commercialism, politicization, and so on. Each of
these claims is easier to assert than to demonstrate, because they all rely
upon a version of the past (and of the present) that derives from critical
purposes rather than from historical research. It may be the case that commercial and political concerns have become more prominent recently, if the
contrast is with the immediate past, but a longer-term comparison would
show no great change in this respect (see Rusche and Kirchheimer 1968;
Wiener 1990). And alongside the "demoralization" of some policy developments one would have to place the "remoralization" of penal measures,
which has been a theme of recent governmental rhetoric in both the United
States and the United Kingdom. To assert the coming of postmodernity in
the penal realm is to rely upon spurious contrasts and pseudohistorical
periodizations. As an interpretation it depends upon our willingness to accept very simplified accounts of how things used to be as a basis for differ-
entiating how they are today (cf. Calhoun 1993).

If the concept of the postmodern does not advance our understanding
of contemporary trends in penality, what will? In the remainder of this
chapter, I present a number of points that suggest that the rumblings of
contemporary change need to be placed within a long-term process of
modernity and modernization, rather than mistaken for signs of a great
postmodern upheaval. And to the extent that institutional changes and
shifts of direction are occurring, these should be attributed to political
forces that are local, contingent, and reversible, rather than to the stirrings
of a new historical epoch (cf. O'Malley 1991). Precisely because the changes
affecting contemporary penality do not involve a break with the broad so-
ciohistoric configuration of modernity, any analysis of these developments will have to proceed at a much lower and more concrete level
of analysis.

The first thing to notice is that the *apparatus* of penal practice is not undergoing any major change of form or any radical shift of emphasis. When
we move from the rather impressionistic analysis of discourse to the more
quantifiable examination of institutional practice, we do not see the same
glimmers of a major realignment. Imprisonment, supervision, and monetary penalties continue to be the mainstay of penal practice, and there is no
sign that any one of these sectors will soon disappear or that a new one
will emerge to augment them. There are, of course, new technologies of

surveillance, new forms of custody, and new financial sanctions (see Gordon 1991; Marx 1988). And the balance between the different sectors is continually shifting as the whole system expands in an uneven and usually unplanned way. But this is not an era in which new institutions and practices are being legislated into existence. It is not, in that sense, comparable with the late eighteenth century or with the period between the 1890s and the First World War. If the apparatus of penality is changing, it is in its objectives and orientation, not in its institutional forms.

Once in place, the infrastructure of penality attains a certain resilience and inertia, and major changes in that apparatus tend to occur slowly and against a great deal of resistance. But these institutions and practices are always capable of being deployed in a number of different ways and supporting quite distinct strategies, so that change at the level of strategy can be much more rapid and much more frequent. Thus, for example, the procedures of examination, assessment, and classification—which were gradually introduced during the course of the twentieth century as part of the strategy of penal-welfarism (see Garland 1985)—were not suddenly dismantled when the policy of rehabilitation fell into disrepute. On the contrary, they were simply put to different uses, such as measuring security risk or crime career profiles. Consequently, the normalizing apparatus continues to grow more extensive and more sophisticated, even if the aims that guide it now seem somewhat different (see Cohen 1985).

Similarly, the professional groups that staff the penal apparatus are essentially the same ones that have been developing throughout the twentieth century, albeit that each individual sector has expanded and differentiated, and the balance of power between and within groups has been subject to frequent change. The working patterns and official objectives of probation officers, prison governors, parole agents, and others are currently undergoing important changes, partly in response to new social environments, partly at the behest of political masters with specific agendas (see Simon 1993; Hudson 1993). But there is nothing to suggest the diminishing importance of the utilitarian forms of knowledge and knowledge-based intervention that have come to define modern penality and the contribution that these professional groups make to it. Nor is it clear that the forces bringing about these changes are identical on either side of the Atlantic. (Compare the analyses in Rees and Hall-Williams [1989] with those of Simon [1993].)

The rise of managerialism in the penal sphere is a new and important development, and analysts such as Feeley and Simon have made a valuable contribution by highlighting this trend and its potential consequences. But managerialism is a phenomenon that is largely explicable in terms of the dynamics of organizational growth and the new possibilities for control generated by advances in information technology. Organizational sociology, building largely upon the work of Max Weber, has long since charted this developmental tendency and identified its operation in a variety of organizational settings (see Heydebrand 1979; Heydebrand and Seron 1990). Far from being a postmodern phenomenon, the penal system is only now, somewhat belatedly, experiencing a form of management that has long been taken for granted elsewhere.

This is not to downplay the significance of these changes. Recent government initiatives accelerate this tendency by imposing strict auditing mechanisms and fiscal controls, and by requiring criminal justice agencies to monitor their performance by reference to government-specified criteria. These initiatives change the balance of power between field staff and management, subject agencies to closer governmental control, and bring about changes in the day-to-day activities of the organization and its treatment of offenders. But however significant these changes may prove to be, they fall squarely within the analytical framework of modernity rather than postmodernity.

I think the same may be said about Feeley and Simon's claim that an actuarial style of analysis is replacing the older concern for an in-depth, reformative knowledge of the individual offender (Feeley and Simon 1992). I am not convinced that this development is either as novel or as extensive as they suggest. A focus upon the differential risks posed by classes and categories, a notion of criminality as an aggregate phenomenon, and a concern to manage populations were all characteristic of the eugenics movement at the turn of the century, a movement that influenced both criminological discourse and penal policy at that time (see Garland 1985). And even today, with all the clamor about career criminals and actuarial prediction, this remains a rather marginal aspect of penal practice, particularly outside the United States. (As Diana Gordon suggests, sometimes "the more hotly debated the policy shift, the fewer people it directly affects" [1991:34].) But even if we grant that some such shift is beginning to occur, it would be entirely in keeping with the administrative logic of modern management, and suggests the deepening importance of modernist practices rather than their supersession by something quite different.

The "decline of the rehabilitative ideal" and the "crisis of penal modernism" also need to be understood as something other than the end of an era, or one more example of the collapse of grand narrative. To begin with, the critique of penal modernism has not made it possible to think and act in ways that are postmodernist. As I noted above, the leading alternative to penal modernism is actually an Enlightenment liberalism, which is also committed to making punishment useful, but is unwilling to abandon individual rights or the rule of law in pursuit of utilitarian goals. At most, one might say that an antimodernist moralism has been resurgent since the 1970s, pressing for punishment as a ritualistic end in itself. But as I have argued at length elsewhere, modern penality has always been characterized by this struggle between the modern and the antimodern: "There are two contrasting visions at work in contemporary criminal justice—the passionate, morally toned desire to punish and the administrative, rationalistic, normalizing concern to manage. These visions clash in many important respects, but both are deeply embedded within the [modern] social practice of punishing" (Garland 1990:180).

Nor has this critique produced a lasting mood of nihilism or an abandonment of all Enlightenment ambition. It is true that a certain 1970s literature made heavy use of the rhetoric of reaction (Hirschman 1991), claiming that the correctionalist approach produced perverse results, or was altogether futile, or jeopardized the very values that it claimed to support. But this moment of intransigent opposition quickly gave way to a more positive policy climate (see Palmer 1992). The past two decades have witnessed a positive deluge of new schemes for making punishment useful again: whether through deterrence, or incapacitation, or denunciation, or punishment in the community, or through some revised form of rehabilitation. Rather than seeing the development of a postmodern consciousness on the part of penal agents, we see instead the beginnings of yet another version of a project that, in its general orientation, would be familiar to penal reformers from any time in the last two centuries.

As for the claim that the modernist penal project cannot prosper in an age of multiculturalism and moral disestablishment—that it depends upon some kind of value consensus that once existed but is now no more— this seems to misunderstand the way that normalizing practices actually work. Normalizing strategies do not require a public moral consensus because they delegate the specification of norms and values to professional agencies that develop these in the context of their local practices. Such a strategy is, in fact, characteristically found in pluralistic societies where moral standards are contested, because in these settings, more traditional sources of moral authority have been undermined and replaced by the kind of behavioral expert promoted by modernist penal policy. Typically, these experts seek to adjust conduct in pragmatic and adaptive ways, rather than to preach a moral code, and it is precisely this reliance upon "floating norms" and upon mutual, pragmatic adjustment that is best suited to modern society. The modernist penal project is not defeated by the fact of moral diversity—it was actually designed to deal with it (see Donzelot 1979). And while the critique of rehabilitation may have exposed the covert moralizing of penal professionals, it has done little to interrupt their task of seeking to impress different standards of conduct upon individual offenders.

The age of penal modernism is not yet over. Nor is penal modernity about to fade. Instead, what we have been witnessing since the late 1960s is the transformation of penal modernism from being a critical, reforming program to being itself a part of the fabric of modern penality, and hence a target for other critical, reforming movements. With this shift, one sees the closing of a long period of naive enthusiasm and optimism regarding the modernist project and the emergence of a more mature, more informed, more ambivalent understanding of what it entails. Modernism has come to understand itself better, and to appreciate that the program of modernist penality has serious limitations and is riven with a deep moral ambiguity.

This process of disillusionment and adjustment was always destined to happen. So long as modernism was a critical, reforming program, battling against a more traditional penal establishment, the likelihood of achieving successful results could be grossly overstated. Even when the system slowly began to adopt modernist practices, and the new experts and professionals struggled to lay claim to their new territory, it still made political sense to talk up the potential of this new approach. But the fact is that *reflexivity* is a crucial part of modern institutions, and as the penal system gradually modernized its approach, so too did it develop procedures for monitoring its own practices and examining their outcomes. Indeed, the new discipline of academic criminology made this monitoring and evaluating process a central part of its raison d'être, and put the scrutiny of penal practice onto a new, scientific, footing. The ironic result was that penal agencies soon learned about their own limitations and have had to face up to their failures. The accumulation of negative evidence, especially by the 1970s, has prompted these organizations to adjust to their failures—either by changing their practices, or, more usually, by altering their declared objectives and the terms by which they ask to be judged. One sees this process not just in relation to penal rehabilitation—though this has been the most dramatic example—but also, in the United Kingdom, to policing and to the government's overall policies of crime control.

This process may also help us to explain a number of important trends that are often noted but have not yet been theorized or explained in sociological terms. These include the growth of mediation and reparation schemes, the increased use of diversion, and especially the reemergence of the victim as a more active and more valued participant in the penal process.[10] To some extent, these developments might be described as a kind of controlled disinvestment by the state of certain minor aspects of criminal justice: a willingness, often prompted by resource constraints, to allow other parties into what had become a state monopoly. Similar considerations may well be involved in the development of a small commercial sector in the prison industry, and of the much larger private security industry. The new emphasis upon enlisting the help of the community in policing and preventing crime—through neighborhood watch, multiagency policing, target hardening, etc.—might also be viewed as a de facto breakup of an unsuccessful state monopoly and an attempt to enlist the aid of civil society in the business of crime control.

Precisely because modern institutions are self-reflexive and self-monitoring, they are necessarily also self-critical and self-reforming. Foucault singled out the prison and made a scandal of the fact that this institution is always in crisis and always undergoing reform. But he might more accurately have noted that all modern institutions share this characteristic, be they schools, or hospitals, or even government itself. All modern institutions are forced to constantly reinvent themselves because they are all increasingly caught in the tyranny of self-knowledge. Only unrealized programs and their reforming supporters can enjoy the luxury of unchallenged optimism.

The relative (and perhaps temporary) decline of the rehabilitative ideal and of research on the causes of crime does not signal the collapse of grand narratives nor the dawn of postmodernism in the penal realm. It is merely the historical moment when a program of government has become sufficiently established to allow its limitations and unintended consequences to be made clearly visible. As it happens, that moment of institutional disillusionment coincided with a powerful shift in the political orientation of several Western governments, with the result that penal organizations have been more vulnerable to external political pressures than they might otherwise have been. Indeed, if one were writing a history of penality's present, it is probably here that one would begin. But that is another story, and one that takes as its central theme the distinctively modern arrangement whereby strategies of punishment are articulated with strategies of rule.

To tell that story is to engage the issues with greater empirical specificity and more finely grained analytical instruments. Temporary and reversible conjunctural shifts must be distinguished from long-term structural transformations, just as changes in discursive style and emphasis must be distinguished from more profound transformations in the problematics and rationalities that structure criminological discourse and penal policy. The rapid changes manifest at the level of government representations and rhetoric must not be mistaken for alterations in working practices and professional ideologies, nor should it be assumed that the discrediting of a particular vocabulary (such as "rehabilitation") means that the practices that it once described have altogether disappeared. The relatively fixed infrastructure of penal techniques and apparatuses must be viewed separately from the more mobile strategies that determine aims and priorities and dictate how penal resources are deployed. The distribution of activity between penal agencies, shifts in power between professional groups, the relative and absolute rates of sanctioning, the forms adopted by penal measures, and their instrumental and symbolic functioning are all analytically distinct questions requiring quite different methodologies and data if they are to be properly addressed and answered. And analyses that wish to make international generalizations must ensure that they rest upon solid comparative analysis, rather than the looseness and ambiguity of catchall conceptual terms. These more modest and more mundane forms of analysis may have less intellectual cachet than the high-flown theory of the modernity/postmodernity debate, but they are liable, in the end, to be of more assistance in the struggle to understand the present.

ACKNOWLEDGMENTS

I am grateful to the following friends and colleagues for their help with this chapter: Colin Bell, Tony Bottoms, Stanley Cohen, James B. Jacobs, Russell Keat, Jonathan Simon, and Andrew von Hirsch.

NOTES

1. Philip Yenawine provides a good description of the artistic postmodern: "This term is used to reflect the diversity of styles and mediums that proliferated beginning in the 1970s, mostly reactive to modernism. . . . It is usefully defined by a set of contrasts. Where modernism was seen as elemental and formal, Post-Modern art is often ornamental, even to the point of excess. While modernists attempted to throw off the past and strove for individual innovations, Post-Modernists appropriated liberally from the past, putting old information into new contexts. Post-Modern art is blatantly emblematic and eclectic, collecting imagery, techniques, and ideas from diverse sources, some recent, some far back in history. Where modernism tried to invent universal languages that captured the 'now' and were self-evidently "true" (and therefore readable by people everywhere), Post-Modernists tend to be realistic about the fact that understanding modernism helped create an elite of experts and that Post-Modernism is also difficult for many people. While modernism was metaphoric, sometimes hermetic, and enthusiastic about the potential of the times, Post-Modernists are more likely to be socially engaged in a direct sense, often skeptical, critical, and/or overtly political. While modernists tended to create signature styles and usually stuck to a single medium, Post-Modernists often change from one style to another, from one medium to another, and/or combine mediums in bold and fearless ways. . . . While modernism tenets proclaimed a hegemony that established an artistic mainstream, Post-Modernist eclecticism embraces great diversity, welcoming artists and styles which were relegated to modernism's margins." (Yenawine 1991:153–54). Jean-Francois Lyotard gives a definition of the term's broader use: "The word *postmodern* . . . designates the state of our culture following the transformations which, since the end of the 19th century, have altered the game rules for science, literature and the arts. . . . Simplifying to the extreme, I define postmodern as incredulity toward metanarratives" (Lyotard 1984:xxiii–xxiv).

2. Thus although the death penalty is still employed by some modern Western states (see Hood 1989), it is nowadays represented as a technical, quasi-medical operation, which seeks to sanitize the violence involved, deny the gruesome bodily aspects of the killing, and turn the event into a symbol rather than a spectacle (see Garland 1990:Ch. 10).

3. There seems little doubt that the size of the population undergoing some form of penal control has markedly increased. The question at issue is whether this expansion can be explained by the fact of higher rates of crime, or whether the development of "alternative" sanctions has played a part in bringing about the overall expansion.

4. Compare Lyotard: "Simplifying to the extreme, I define postmodern as incredulity toward metanarratives" (1984:xxiv).

5. Compare Jameson: "The emergence of a new kind of flatness or depthlessness, a new kind of superficiality in the most literal sense [is] perhaps the supreme formal feature of all postmodernisms" (1991:59). See also Harvey (1989).

6. This is not true of all the advocates of just deserts: von Hirsch (1993) argues for a policy that combines proportionate sanctioning with moral censure.

7. Simon (1993:248) gives this as an example of contemporary penality's postmodern character. On autopoiesis, see Teubner (1992).

8. One might extend the list by referring to the tendency of current penal policy to "quote" from the penal styles of the past, producing a kind of pastiche effect, in which older practices are revived not because they are functional, but because they evoke the sense of a past era. Jonathan Simon (1993:248) refers to this as "nostalgia" and cites the current popularity of boot camps in the United States as an example.

9. The notion of a postmodern penality could certainly be used as a normative concept, or as a kind of utopian desideratum for the future. My discussion here is limited to its use as a sociological description.

10. At present, these developments have the character of radical innovations on the margins of criminal justice. Were they to develop into mainstream characteristics of the system they might well entail an important break with the structures of penal modernity.

REFERENCES

Allen, F. A. 1981. *The Decline of the Rehabilitative Ideal.* New Haven, CT: Yale University Press.

Baudrillard, J. 1983. *Simulations.* New York: Semiotext(e).

Bauman, Z. 1989. *Modernity and the Holocaust.* Cambridge: Polity.

Beattie, J. 1986. *Crime and the Courts in England 1660–1800.* Princeton, NJ: Princeton University Press.

Bottoms, A. E. 1983. "Neglected Features of Contemporary Penal Systems." Pp. 166–202 in *The Power to Punish,* edited by D. Garland and P. Young. London: Heinemann.

Bottoms, A. E. and R. Preston (eds.). 1980. *The Coming Penal Crisis.* Edinburgh: Scottish Academic Press.

Brodeur, J. P. 1993. "La Pensee Postmoderne et la Criminologie." *Criminologie* 26(1):73–121.

Calhoun, C. 1993. "Postmodernism as Pseudohistory." *Theory, Culture and Society* 10:75–96.

Cavadino, M. and J. Dignan. 1992. *The Penal System: An Introduction.* London: Sage.

Christie, N. 1993. *Crime Control as Industry.* London: Routledge.

Clarke, R. V. 1983. "Situational Crime Prevention: Its Theoretical Basis and Practical Scope." *Crime and Justice: An Annual Review of Research* 4:225–56, edited by M. Tonry and N. Morris.

Cohen, S. 1985. *Visions of Social Control.* Cambridge: Polity.

———. 1990. "Intellectual Scepticism and Political Commitment: The Case of Radical Criminology." Bonger Institute, University of Amsterdam.

Cornish, D. and R. V. Clarke (Eds.). 1986. *The Reasoning Criminal.* New York: Springer-Verlag.

Donzelot, J. 1979. *The Policing of Families: Welfare Versus the State.* London: Hutchinson.

Downes, D. 1988. *Contrasts in Tolerance: Post-War Penal Policy in the Netherlands and England and Wales.* Oxford: Clarendon.

Duff, R. A. and D. Garland. 1994. "Thinking about Punishment." Pp. 1–43 in *A Reader on Punishment,* edited by R. A. Duff and D. Garland. Oxford: Clarendon.

Ericson, R. V. and K. D. Carriere. 1994. "The Fragmentation of Criminology." Pp. 89–109 in *The Futures of Criminology,* edited by D. Neiken. London: Sage.

Feeley, M. and J. Simon. 1992. "The New Penology." *Criminology* 39(4):449–74.

Felson, M. 1994. *Crime and Everyday Life.* London: Pine Forge.

Foucault, M. 1977. *Discipline and Punish: The Birth of the Prison.* London: Allen Unwin.

———. 1983. "Structuralism and Post-Structuralism: An Interview with Michel Foucault" (with G. Raulet) *Telos* 55(Spring):195–211.

Garland, D. 1985. *Punishment and Welfare: A History of Penal Strategies.* Aldershot: Gower.

———. 1990. *Punishment and Modern Society: A Study in Social Theory.* Oxford: Clarendon.

———. 1994. "Of Crimes and Criminals: The Development of Criminology in Britain." Pp. 17–68 in *The Oxford Handbook of Criminology,* edited by M. Maguire, R. Morgan, and R. Reiner. Oxford: Clarendon.

Giddens, A. 1990. The *Consequences of Modernity.* Cambridge: Polity.

Gordon, D. 1991. *The Justice Juggernaut: Combatting Street Crime, Controlling Citizens.* New Brunswick, NJ: Rutgers University Press.

Gottfredson, M. and T. Hirschi. 1990. *A General Theory of Crime.* Stanford, CA: Stanford University Press.

Hall, S., C. Critcher, T. Jefferson, J. Clarke, and B. Roberts. 1978. *Policing the Crisis: Mugging, the State, and Law and Order.* London: MacMillan.

Harvey, D. 1989. *The Condition of Postmodernity.* London: Routledge.

Henry, S. and D. Milovanovic. 1994. "The Constitution of Constitutive Criminology: A Postmodern Approach to Criminological Theory." Pp. 110–83 in *The Future of Criminology,* edited by D. Neiken. London: Sage.

Heydebrand, W. 1979. "The Technocratic Administration of Justice." *Research in Law and Society* 2:29–64.

Heydebrand, W. and C. Seron. 1990. *Rationalizing Justice: The Political Economy of the Federal District Courts.* Albany: SUNY Press.

Hirschman, A. 1991. *The Rhetoric of Reaction.* Cambridge, MA: Harvard University Press.

Home Office. 1988. *Punishment, Justice and the Community.* London: HMSO.

Hood, R. 1989. *The Death Penalty: A World-Wide Perspective.* Oxford: Clarendon.

Howe, A. 1994. *Punish and Critique.* London: Routledge.

Hudson, B. A. 1987. *Justice Through Punishment: A Critique of the "Justice" Model of Corrections.* Basingstoke: MacMillan.

Hudson, B. A. 1993. *Penal Policy and Social Justice.* Basingstoke: MacMillan.

Jameson, F. 1991. *Postmodernism, or the Cultural Logic of Late Capitalism.* London: Verso.

Lyotard, J. F. 1984. *The Postmodern Condition: A Report on Knowledge.* Manchester: Manchester University Press.

Marx, G. 1988. *Undercover: Police Surveillance in America.* Berkeley: University of California Press.

Mayhew, P., R. V. Clarke, A. Sturman, and J. M. Hough. 1976. *Crime as Opportunity.* Home Office Research Study No. 34. London: HMSO.

McMahon M. 1990. "Netwidening: Vagaries in the use of a Concept." *British Journal of Criminology* 30(2):121–49.

Nelkin, D. 1995. *The Power of the Gene.* New York: Basic Books.

O'Malley, P. 1991. "After Discipline? Crime Prevention, the Strong State and a Free Market." Unpublished manuscript.

Palmer, T. 1992. *The Re-Emergence of Correctional Intervention.* London: Sage.

Peters, A. 1988. "Main Currents in Criminal Law Theory." Pp. 19–36 in *Criminal Law in Action,* edited by J. J. M. van Dijk. Deventer: Kluwer.

Radzinowicz, Sir L. 1991. "Penal Regressions." *Cambridge Law Journal* 50(930):422–44.

Rees, H. and E. Hall-Williams. 1989. *Punishment, Custody and the Community.* London: L.S.E.

Reiner, R. 1992. "Policing a Postmodern Society." *Modern Law Review* 55:761–81.

Rothman, D. 1980 (2002). *Conscience and Convenience: The Asylum and Its Alternatives in Progressive America.* Hawthorne, NY: Aldine de Gruyter.

Rusche, G. and O. Kirchheimer. 1968. *Punishment and Social Structure.* New York: Russell and Russell.

Scheingold, S. 1991. *The Politics of Street Crime.* Philadelphia: Temple University Press.

Schwartz, M. D. and D. O. Friedrichs. 1994. "Postmodern Thought and Criminological Discontent: New Metaphors for Understanding Violence." *Criminology* 32(2):221–46.

Scottish Prison Service. 1990. *Opportunity and Responsibility: Developing New Approaches to the Management of the Long Term Prison System in Scotland.* Edinburgh: Author.

Scull, A. 1977. *Decarceration: Community Treatment and the Deviant—A Radical View.* Englewood, NJ: Prentice Hall.

———. 1984. "Afterword 1983." Pp. 161–89 in *Decarceration,* 2nd ed. Cambridge: Polity.

Simon, J. 1991. "Doing Time: Postmodernity and the Crisis of Penal Reform." Unpublished manuscript.

———. 1993. *Poor Discipline: Parole and the Social Control of the Underclass, 1890–1990.* Chicago: University of Chicago Press.

Smart, C. 1990. "Feminist Approaches to Criminology or Postmodern Woman Meets Atavistic Man." Pp. 70–84 in *Feminist Perspectives in Criminology,* edited by L. Gelsthorpe and A. Morris. Milton Keynes: Open University Press.

Spierenburg, P. 1991. *The Prison Experience: Disciplinary Institutions and Their Inmates in Early Modern Europe.* New Brunswick, NJ: Rutgers University Press.

Teubner, G. 1992. *Law as an Autopoietic System.* Oxford: Blackwell.

Tuck, M. 1991. "Community and the Criminal Justice System." *Policy Studies* 12(3):22–37.

van Dijk, J. J. M. 1989. "Penal Sanctions and the Process of Civilization." Pp. 191–204 in *International Annals of Criminology,* Vol. 27. Liege.

von Hirsch, A. 1983. "Recent Trends in American Sentencing Theory." *Maryland Law Review* 42(6):6–36.

———. 1993. *Censure and Sanctions.* Oxford: Clarendon.

Wiener, M. 1990. *Reconstructing the Criminal.* Cambridge: Cambridge University Press.

Wilson, J. Q. 1983. *Thinking About Crime,* 2nd ed. New York: Basic Books.

Wilson, J. Q. and R. J. Herrnstein. 1985. *Crime and Human Nature: The Definitive Study of the Causes of Crime.* New York: Simon and Schuster.

Yenawine, P. 1991. *How to Look at Modern Art.* New York: Harry N. Abrams.

3

The Form and Limits
of the New Penology

JONATHAN SIMON AND MALCOLM M. FEELEY

INTRODUCTION

In "The New Penology: Notes on the Emerging Strategy of Corrections and Its Implications" (Feeley and Simon 1992) and again in "Actuarial Justice" (1994), we identified three emerging features of the criminal process that together we termed the *new penology*. This chapter summarizes our account of these new developments, briefly examines some of the responses to the new penology, and then explores one of its anomalies—the growing gulf between penology on the one hand and public discourse about crime and crime policy on the other. Despite the rise of the new penology, contemporary crime policy, in the words of one perceptive observer, has "embraced . . . the reliance of retribution as an articulated purpose of criminal punishment . . . with a vengeance" (Cotton 2000:1313). Our purpose here is to reassess our claims about the rise of a new penology in light of this hypermoralistic, retributive movement that on the surface appears to conflict with the idea of the new penology.

There is a growing body of work that builds on it in just the ways we invited in our initial presentations, using it as a grid to identify both sameness and difference in particular areas of criminal justice discourse and practice. Some have located elements of the new penology and actuarial justice in various settings, often in places and ways we had not anticipated, and then applied it (O'Malley 1998). And others have found it applicable to interpreting change outside the U.S. context that was its focus, including Europe (Ruggiero et al. 1998; Young 1999), Australia (O'Malley 1996), and Latin America.

All this work is part of a growing and more general shift in the effort to understand the ways late modern, advanced liberal, or neoliberal societies deal both with crime (Cohen 1985; Reichman 1986; Ericson and Haggerty 1997; Beckett 1997); and the problem of governance more generally (Foucault 1977; Ewald 1986; Lowi 1990; Burchell, Gordon, and Miller 1991; Baker and Simon 2001; Douglas and Wildavsky 1982; Beck 1992; Giddens 1999; Hacking 1990). In this sense the new penology is part of the broad shift in the understanding of contemporary developments in governing. Recent works in this vein include George Pavlich's *Critique and Radical Discourses on Crime* (2000), Nikolas Rose's *Powers of Freedom* (1999), David Garland's *The Culture of Control* (2001), and Baker and Simon's *Embracing Risk* (2001). This response to our work reinforces our belief that we have identified important new features of the criminal process and that they are linked to even broader and more general strategies of governance.

The new penology has also had a number of thoughtful critics, who claim that we have not identified such profound changes as we have imagined. David Garland, for instance, has argued that the new penology is "not as novel or as extensive as they suggest" (1995:201), that "managerialism is a phenomenon that is largely explicable in terms of the dynamics of organizational growth and the new possibilities for control generated by advances in information technology," and that ". . . the penal system is only now, somewhat belatedly, experiencing a form of management that has long been taken for granted elsewhere"(ibid.). More recently, he has argued that a significant shift in crime policy has taken place since the mid-1970s. It is, he maintains, a shift away from penal-welfarism to a strident and vindictive "culture of control" (Garland 2001). Still others argue that if one looks at conventional criminology, as indicated by methods and topics of articles in leading criminology journals, the new penology has barely registered (Savelsberg, King, and Cleveland 2002), that at the micro-and local levels, public officials continue to follow traditional practices anchored in concerns about rehabilitation and deterrence (Miller 2001; Lynch 1998; Bayens, Manske, and Smykla 1998; Walters 1994).

Had we framed the issues as starkly as these critics suggest, we would have to agree with them. However, in our previous articles we tried to make clear that the new penology was to some extent a belated application of standard forms of risk management, actuarial thinking, and systems analysis to the criminal process, an area of law that is resistant to innovation, and that elements of it had long been incorporated into discourse and policy. We also emphasized that it was an emergent phenomenon and not a fully realized policy or set of institutions. Additionally, we pointed out that actuarial thinking was not distinct to the criminal process, that it indeed had already deeply penetrated other areas of law as well, most notably tort law (Calabresi 1970 Steiner 1987) and employment discrimination law. In many respects, with the new penology the criminal process is catching up with modern management practices firmly ensconced in most other areas of modern bureaucratic life and law. Furthermore, we noted that many of its concepts—from the "habitual offender" to the "dangerous classes" to strict liability—had long pedigrees. In short, in putting forward the concepts the new penology and "actuarial justice," we did not claim, or mean to claim, that it was wholly new or that it had become the dominant or even a major paradigm in contemporary criminology. More modestly, however, we did suggest that there were enough instances of discourse, policies, and programs that reflected these concerns that these developments should be treated as something more than idiosyncratic anomalies in an otherwise unchanging process. In this we think we succeeded.

To the extent that we were read as trying to predict a new "stage" of development in crime control techniques to identify a fully realized vision of an alternative to the dominant penal strategies of the twentieth century (anchored in a now old penology of penal welfarism), or to provide a description of and an explanation for a dramatic transformation that had not yet been fully documented let along understood, the new penology fails. Certainly the most salient changes in American and English crime policy since the mid-1970s cannot be characterized as instances of the new penology-in-action. Indeed, what is widely seen as the most important development, the enormous expansion of punitive control measures may even have stymied the expansion of the new penology, since it seems to flow from Durkheimian-like impulses for retribution and vengeance rather than rational, technocratic management of risk. Developments in crime policy since the 1970s have been animated not by careful calculation, but by near-primitive public anger (Scheingold 1984; Simon 1997; Garland 2001) or the frustrations of late modernity (Tyler and Boeckman 1997). They have resulted in policies that are better explained by the familiar motivations and ways of thinking of long-standing in crime analysis—volitional theories of crime, guilt, retribution, fear, morality, the assertion of authority—than by any new discourses embraced largely by experts. The expected triumph of risk management has been stillborn in favor of a return to what Nonet and Selznick (1978) would term "repressive" law. With the new penology, penal law seemed to be proclaiming its (relative) autonomy, but that voice if it ever sounded has been silenced by an undeniable populist backlash and a demand that penal practices be comprehensible, useful, and meaningful to the "people" as manifested in elections and the permanent polling/permanent news reporting cycle that now encompasses American politics. Still, as we point out below, these two trends are by no means mutually exclusive; we will comment on the surprising cohabitation of *both* developments in recent years.

Perhaps it is best to focus on the new penology not as general change in social and political order (like Garland's "culture of control") or a fundamental shift in the way governance is rationalized (like Simon's "governing through crime"), but rather a shift in the way crime is governed (known about and acted on). It is not surprising that a political culture enamored of crime as a privileged problem, or victims as privileged subjects, produces punitive crime policies that drive a high prison population and much else. But when the state, and private actors (who are increasingly part of the response to crime), find themselves having to govern crime in new ways (whether notifying potential victims of sex offenders, protecting grade school students from "bullying," or executing condemned aggravated murderers) they draw on technologies, discourses, and forms of expertise that look and sound a lot like the new penology.

When seen from this perspective it is not the new penology that has failed, but rather those of us who labor in its vineyards, producing new ways of knowing and acting on crime for the growing penal governance market, have failed to go beyond the new penology, to a new way of narrating the power to punish that can help shape the public and political exercise of the power to punish. Only then will we be able to talk about something comparable to the paradigm shift that David Garland (1985) has described in his account of the transformation of crime policy in Edwardian England, from punitive practices to "penal-welfarism" or to what in the discussion below we link to Progressive Era penology (Rothman 1980).

Distinctive Features of the New Penology and their Implications

Below we review the central elements of three features of the new penology. The balance of the article then examines a number of reasons why it has not led to the kind of takeoff in the public imagination of crime that was true of an earlier movement of new scientific discourses into criminal law in the Progressive Era.

Discourses

The discourses of modern punishment have varied widely over time, from the language of religion and economics to psychology and social work, and more recently sociology. Despite significant differences among them, each of these discourses portrays crime primarily as a relationship between individuals and their communities. In contrast, we have argued, the language of the new penology is anchored in the discourse of systems analysis and operations research. It conceives of crime as a systemic phenomenon and crime policy as a problem of actuarial risk management (Messinger 1969; Messinger and Berk 1987). While traditional divisions within the penal field, like that between academics and professionals, remain relevant, the dispersal of new penology discourses cuts across this and many other traditional divides.

Objectives

The objectives of modern punishment have also varied over time. Early eighteenth-century reformers stressed certainty and proportionality of sanction as a way of steering people away from crime. Nineteenth-century reformers developed penitentiaries for the purpose of reforming wayward souls. And in the early twentieth century, Progressive reformers produced a high modernist version of both these latter objectives, which aimed at adjusting the individual offender in his community. Our purpose here is not to argue that these objectives were achieved, but that as objectives they were widely shared by intellectuals, criminal justice policymakers, and the "public;" that there was—at least in broad outline—something of a consensus about objectives among the various interested communities.

In contrast, the new penology reveals a shift away from the objective of transforming individuals. It embraces a new objective, risk management and the management of the system itself. To use David Rothman's (1980) enduring phrase out of context, in the new penology convenience has become the primary form of conscience.

Techniques

Penology may have once been an incubator for general social technologies like the disciplines (Foucault 1977), but that is not true of the new penology. Much of what is new here is the movement of administrative techniques from the world insurance, financial management, and even retailing into a field that had long enjoyed considerable isolation from general administrative trends (an isolation abetted by criminal law's own monopoly over the field). Mostly these techniques (profiling, auditing, screening, etc.) were introduced as ways of improving administrative knowledge of and control over penal agents and subjects as if they would simply supplement the existing substantive penal policies (mostly penal correctionalism at the time they were introduced, today something else). But what makes it a new penology is how much these mundane techniques have in fact become the substantive program if not the policy. At the same time we see an almost endless recycling of modern penal techniques, ranging from the "silent system" in the new prisons of the early nineteenth century, to heavy reliance on imprisonment in the late nineteenth century, to the invention of the indeterminate sentence, juvenile justice, parole, and probation in the Progressive Era (Rothman 1980; Simon 1993). Many recent innovations in technique build on this heritage. Boot camps, for example, are defended in moral terms reminiscent of the justification of the silent isolation in the cell one hundred and sixty years ago. And intensive probation and parole seek in some ways to do with new technologies (electronic surveillance and drug testing) what Progressives sought to do through good casework. This gives the overall texture of the postmodern penality a heterodoxy that Pat O'Malley (2000) has aptly described as "contradictory and volatile." This does not contradict the dominance of the new penology so much as demonstrate its indifference to the end points of the penal process, the suffering of victims and punished criminals, and the level of crime in society.

Although we acknowledge that institutions are always in flux, in our earlier article we argued that these changes identified above, which have emerged over the last thirty or so years, represent the beginning of "a marked break with the past."[1] The new penology provides a useful analytic grid in which to interpret the emerging set of practices, discourses, and objectives in the criminal process. This new formation (and not our interpretation of it) offers a way of thinking about and working within the criminal process, which has important, if as yet unclear, implications. The historical weakness of our "model" is not likely to prove fatal if it nevertheless serves as a heuristic device for interpreting emerging changes in discourse and practice,[2] and for that matter providing a new look at some of its features of the past. For us the relevant questions are: Does the analytic grid suggested by the new penology help link, and therefore interpret, a variety of practices? Does it provide a means for imposing even quasi-coherence on a wide variety of disparate new practices? Does it help identify emerging strategies or possibilities for strategic action within the present situation?

A New Kind of Gap Problem

Although there has always been a gap between professional and public discourse, the gap has rarely been so great as it seems today, and at times a consensus among scholars, reformers, and public opinion leaders has facilitated significant reforms (Scheingold 1984, 1991). For example, during the consolidation of the welfare state in Edwardian England and the Progressive Era in the United States, which we consider below, the media, political leaders, and criminal justice professionals shared common assumptions and a mutual interest in diagnosing problems and presenting reforms. Ideas like the indeterminate sentence and juvenile justice were lauded not only by professionals in their journals, but in the writings of journalists and crusading community leaders who drew on professional penology to offer the public compelling portraits of crime and programs to deal with it.

Of course, there have always been policies and institutions that have been greeted skeptically by the public (e.g., parole), and there have been periods of widespread criticism of corrections and the criminal process. Still, these criticisms must be seen in the context of a broader influence of penology through narratives of crime and its control that helped guide institutional innovation and helped foster a reserve of political legitimacy for crime policies even in periods of strain.

An essential ingredient in that earlier relationship in the Progressive Era is representations of crime and criminals that link "scientific" theories and popular treatments of the problem.[3] Like "the recidivist," which has haunted the public imagination for over a century, the best of these representations allowed professional discourses, practices, and objectives to be inserted in the political process. That is, professional representations helped shape public understanding and pubic debate about crime and crime policy.

What seems striking today is the virtual absence of successful new representations of crime. Current penology provides neither "policies that succeed nor words that succeed" (Edelman 1964). It not only does not "solve" the crime problem, it does not even provide reassurances that something significant is being done. Indeed, the successful advancement of a new program for managing crime and criminals must be accompanied by a compelling account of the crime problem, its measure, and what can be done about it (Simon 1993:9).[4] As David Garland (1990:257) has argued, penality provides an inevitable cultural and narrative side, and if so, one function of policy discourse is to provide a culturally satisfying account of social problems, and assurances that they are "being taken care of." To date, however, the new penology has not provided such a compelling or culturally satisfying story about crime and how to deal with it. It has not (yet) succeeded in producing a viable "truth" about crime. Instead contemporary policy discourse is a recirculation of older representations that oscillate between what Stuart Scheingold (1984) calls "structural" accounts of crime and "volitional" accounts. The former, he says, tend to account for crime in terms of social factors—inequality, opportunity, structural unemployment—and the latter tend to account for crime in terms of individual attributes, character, will, the ability to defer gratification, deterrence, and the like. Drawing on this same theme, David Garland (2001) identifies what he calls a newly consolidated "culture of control" rising in the 1970s and 1980s that embraces a volitional understanding of crime and accordingly responds with harshness both as deterrence and retribution. The new penology does not fit very well within the language or concepts of either structural or volitional theories. Representations produced by the new penology probably heighten anxiety about crime, since they focus on system management and offer no compelling moral vision with which to come to terms with problems. Indeed they often call attention to the problems of the system itself.

THE NEW PENOLOGY AND THE PROBLEM OF PUBIC OPINION

In the United States, it is generally conceded that public opinion, stoked by "moral entrepreneurs," drives much public policy, crime policy included (Gusfield 1963; Scheingold 1991). Thus "moral panics" and strong pressures to "do something" are often thought to be the proximate causes of increases in sentence severity, increases in prison size and population, additional mandatory minimum sentences, calls for reintroduction of the death penalty, "three strikes and you're out" laws, and the like (Hall et al. 1979; Scheingold 1991; Gordon 1990; Currie 1987). Still, the programs of insiders—their discourses, techniques, and objectives—have always had a relationship to such moral panics.

Experts and the New Penology

It is no surprise that public discourse about crime differs from expert discourse—the two diverge in most areas of policy. In virtually every aspect of public policy, public discourse stresses values and emotional appeals, while expert discourse emphasizes operational questions that public discourse ignores. Being attentive to these distinctions illuminates the process of policy formation and implementation, as David J. Rothman's seminal analysis of "conscience" and "convenience" in the Progressive Era revealed (1980). But the same analysis makes clear that the key to mobilizing resources and power for policy institutions is the ability of players in both professional and public discourse to formulate common or at least complementary positions. As Murray Edelman (1967, 1977) has argued, one of the major functions of discourse about public policies, and indeed the policies themselves, is to present a coherent "understanding" of a social problem that provides a satisfactory diagnosis and a comforting solution. In Edelman's phrase, "words can succeed even though policies fail" (1977)—images generated by public policies can generate a sense of confidence that problems are being attended to even when little or no concrete progress is made.

In several important studies, Scheingold (1984, 1991) has employed Edelman's framework to understand not only the disjuncture in discourse between criminal justice administrators and politicians, but also between national-level politicians who are the most ardent champions of the war against crime, and state and local, and especially local, elected officials who must actually oversee the administration of whatever policies that are adopted. He finds that the further removed from administrative accountability an official is, the greater the likelihood of embracing successful words but questionable policies.

In the United States, it is generally conceded that public opinion, stoked by moral entrepreneurs, drives much public policy, including crime policy (Gusfield 1963; Scheingold 1991). Thus moral panics and strong pressures to do something are often thought to be the proximate causes of increases in sentence severity, increases in prison size and population, additional mandatory minimum sentences, calls for reintroduction of the death penalty, three-strikes laws, and the like (Hall et al. 1979; Scheingold 1991; Gordon 1990; Currie 1987). Still, the programs of insiders—their discourses, techniques and objectives—have always had a relationship to such moral panics. David Garland has made a similar observation:

> The success of the penal-welfare strategy—a success that has allowed its persistence for nearly a century—is not, then, the reform of offenders or the prevention of crime. It is its ability to administer and manage criminality in an efficient and extensive manner while portraying that process in terms that make it acceptable to the public and penal agents alike. (1985:260)

Perhaps the most important feature of our present internal discourse of crime is that the penal system has grown dramatically over the last decade and a half despite the failure of the insider discourse to influence public discourse in ways that it had in earlier eras. This gap between insiders and the public—or, put another way, the failure of the new penology to influence popular discourse—was highlighted in the mid-1990s by the rapid success across the United States of a variety of three-strikes laws, which imposed life sentences on repeat offenders.

The attachment of the baseball slogan to the long-standing idea of life sentences for repeat offenders was conceived by Mike Reynolds, a Southern California businessman whose daughter was brutally murdered by a man with a long string of prior convictions. The movement received massive press attention in 1991 after another murder, that of Polly Klaas of Sonoma County, California. The claim was that many violent crimes were committed by a handful of repeat offenders who continued to receive light sentences and premature release, and that it made sense to crack down on them. Within months of the Klaas murder a number of states and the federal government had embraced some version of a three-strikes law.[5]

Although police officials and prosecutors felt they had to support these measures, criminal justice insiders—criminologists, policy analysts, and administrators—categorically opposed them. They pointed out that these new laws would have little impact on serious repeat offenders since they were already subject to harsh penalties, but that the new laws would impose draconian sentences on large numbers of marginal offenders and require massive new expenditures, just as the ill-fated Rockefeller drug laws had two decades earlier (Feeley and Kamin 1996). Despite these warnings, three-strikes laws were adopted in virtually all the states. Their adoption within the space of a few months of each other can accurately be characterized as a moral panic and a mindless "spending spree," which "threw money at a problem" without likelihood of any real benefit. Indeed, the voices of those who expressed reservations did not even rise to the volume of a whisper in public discourse about crime and corrections.

Much crime policy, and certainly much public discourse about crime policy, is framed in moralistic terms that has almost no connection with the internal discourse of criminal justice actors. Unlike earlier eras in which they took an active role in articulating and shaping public opinion on crime policy, criminal justice professionals now seem to be on the fringes. Their discourse—expressed in varying degrees in terms of the new penology— has barely penetrated, and has not even begun to shape public debate. And when upon occasion the discourse is heard, it is usually ignored, resented, or ridiculed. Or it is rephrased within the language of the old penology. Penal reform has never proceeded by advancing proven solutions for crime. But at times it has succeeded in producing culturally satisfying accounts that have gained widespread public acceptance, and have legitimated crime policy and helped shape its formulation. The language of the new penology has not done even this. Below we provide a summary description of the Progressive Era's crime policy, a policy that in the United States held sway until well into the 1970s. It stands in sharp contrast to the new penology in at least two respects: it provides a fully realized vision of crime, crime policy, and what to do about it, and it is a vision that is generally shared by criminal justice professionals, criminologists, opinion leaders, and members of the public.

It is of course problematic to divide history into precise periods. History flows continuously, and it is impossible to provide a wholly convincing account of why it should be broken up into distinct periods. Still, it is useful to distinguish four periods in American history during which "professional" penology succeeded in capturing the public imagination: the Jacksonian era (1830s), the Progressive Era (1880–1920), the Great Society period of the 1960s and early 1970s, which embraced a modified version of Progressive penology, and a new period that began in the mid-1970s and that David Garland has termed the "culture of control" in late modernity. Each of these periods has been characterized by the emergence of new and powerful representations of crime and its solutions, which understood crime policy as a quest for national destiny. There is rich historical work on the first two of these eras, both for the United States (Rothman 1971; Melossi and Pavarini 1981; Rafter 1990) and for parallel movements in Europe (Foucault 1977; Ignatieff 1978; Garland 1985). However the third, postwar era is just now beginning to be the subject of scholarly analysis (Cohen 1985; Scheingold 1991; Walker 1993; Simon 1993), and the fourth is still in its formative stages and perhaps too close in time to allow for distanced assessment (for an effort, however, see Garland 2001). It is not our purpose to summarize this work here, but we do want to emphasize one of its central lessons: penal reform has a politics, a politics of cultural imagery and national identity (Scheingold 1991) just as much as it has a politics of coalitions built on conscience and convenience (Rothman 1980). Below we briefly survey the cultural imagery of the Progressive Era, and contrast it with the imagery of the current era. This contrast is useful, we think, because the scope of the Progressives' success and its institutional legacy remains potent today.[6]

Progressive Representations of Crime

There is broad agreement that the last two decades of the nineteenth century and the first two decades of the twentieth constituted a distinctive period of self-conscious social reforms, both in the United States, where the period is known as the Progressive Era, and in Europe, where the foundations for the modern welfare state were laid.[7] One measure of the success of the Progressives' agenda is that it developed representations that captured the essence of its policies and as well permeated and affected popular discourse. David Rothman (1980) has identified three of its most successful representations, and argued that their popularity helped facilitate acceptance of its criminal justice reform policies. They are the ideas of (1) a "delinquency area," (2) the "individual" delinquent, and (3) the "born criminal." We explore the significance of each.

Delinquency Areas

One of the most enduring representations of the crime problem to emerge from Progressive penology was the criminogenic neighborhood. If one had to give a name to the picture that was drawn, it might be "delinquency area," a phrase coined by Chicago school sociologists and Progressive intellectuals Robert Park and Ernest Burgess, who used it to describe certain urban neighborhoods with different waves of ethnic composition and high levels of crime (Shaw 1929). This was more than just a theory about crime causation, although it borrowed and extended environmental theories of criminogenesis that extends back into the nineteenth century. This potent representation centered on the ghetto or slum, which at the turn of the century was just beginning to be viewed as an endemic feature of American cities, swollen as they were with new immigrants from Southern and Eastern Europe. The representation was of an infected environment physically shaped by pathological forces (brought over from Southern and Eastern Europe in part), which in turn reinfected its denizens (Rothman 1980:52).

Although frightening, this representation was also optimistic. As Rothman observes:

The problem was manageable: it could be located spatially in the ghetto and it could be solved, given the right programs. The bad news all related to the immigrant slums. The good news was that the rest of American society was strong, prosperous, and stable. (ibid.)

In addition to the social scientists who coined the expression "delinquency area," journalists, novelists, and politicians all borrowed the image to make their own cases for national action. This idea—and the solution it implied—came to shape public perception of both the diagnosis of the problem of crime and its solution. The goal was to inoculate the new immigrant as it were, to educate him, to turn him into a new American, and thus to remove and to immunize him from the diseases of the delinquency areas.

Individual Delinquents

A second important metaphor Rothman (1980) identifies is that of the "individual delinquent." In his conception (the term comes from the title of an important book by William Healy, which David Rothman sees as a near-perfect exemplar of Progressive penality), the criminal is understood as the product of a specific developmental history, which leads to deviance and eventually lawbreaking (Rothman 1980:55; Simon 1994). Popular acceptance of this notion helped facilitate support for new programs, which would diagnose and treat individuals with abnormalities in order to transform them into healthy productive citizens.

Born Criminals

A third metaphor used in Progressive criminology was the "born criminal." This idea was first expounded by the Italian criminologist Cesare Lombroso to describe an inherently and permanently crime-prone individual, but it gained its strongest following in the United States (Rothman 1980:58), where it was used successfully to justify lengthy prison terms. Through education a new community of immigrants could be taught to lose the bad habits of the Old World. Through treatment the pathologies of the maladjusted individual could be cured. But for the born criminal, a lengthy prison term was the only solution. This representation of the born criminal was not an isolated concept; it was compatible with the then-powerful eugenics movement, which was so concerned about the racial make-up of the United States. Lengthy indeterminate sentences for born criminals promised to interrupt the biological reproduction of a criminal class.

Each of these three representations of crime was closely matched with prototypical stories, which reformers used to describe problems and promote new programs. Each borrowed from the discourses of medicine, social work, and the emerging new human sciences. Each implied a diagnosis of a problem as well as a solution to it. As Rothman (1980) pointed out, these representations accommodated a host of different stories about crime. The criminal as victim of the rotten environment could receive the necessary change of conditions so that he could escape these conditions. The criminal as psychologically maladjusted could be treated and cured. And the biologically doomed born criminal could be locked away for life. The widespread appeal and acceptance of these representations go a long way toward explaining the successes of the Progressive reformers.

The Progressive vision was anchored in a belief in individualization. Each built upon earlier eighteenth-century penal reforms, which also celebrated the individual in their press for uniform and transparent penalties (Ignatieff 1978; Garland 1985). And each reinforced reliance on the prison, which marked the individual as the central target of sanctions with its cellular structure and policies of penitent isolation and regimes of silence. However, these Progressive ideas reformulated the functions of the prison. As Garland (1985) has suggested, the eighteenth-century prisoner was conceived as a black box, targeted, but not necessarily penetrated, by penal ideologies. The distinctive contribution of the Progressives was in penetrating the black box, and in so doing endowing the criminal offender with social and psychological features—educatable, treatable, and at times incurable. With imprisonment, they sought to counteract the influences of bad environment, correct the maladjusted psyche, and when necessary permanently incarcerate the incorrigible. Such strategies required a strong and positive defense of discretion and a belief in professional expertise (Rothman 1980:45). Progressive penology vigorously sought both, and for the most part obtained them. The representations advanced by its professionals were widely embraced by the politicians and the public, and the policies that flowed from them were also embraced.

Progressive penology also implied a distinct methodology and epistemology, and it too was embraced. One of the most important methods in these new sciences was case analysis, a potpourri of observation and interview developed in social work and medicine, and embraced in penology as well. Another was the ethnographic community study made famous by the Chicago school sociologists, whose environmental accounts of crime constituted a plausible account of invisible networks of norms that shape life in definable communities. A third was the statistical study of inmates and parolees, also pioneered by Chicago sociologists, which measured recidivism and thus provided a basis for determining success or failure of new rehabilitative techniques. This epistemic base for Progressive penology was critical to winning support from the influential class of college-educated journalists and professionals who helped shape public opinion. The new human sciences represented modernity, and in their own way representations, portraits of power that had great cultural resonance for the new professional class that emerged as a major power in American institutions in the early twentieth century. Finally, and perhaps most important, Progressive penology "fit" within the larger Progressive political vision generally. Its penology was a natural and not a distorted feature of its general social aims for the poor, the growing urban masses, and new immigrants.

What Worked?

David J. Rothman (1980), David Garland (1985), and others have documented the ideological success of Progressives in the United States and like-minded reformers in England, in both generating a compelling account of crime and punishment, and in effecting a successful agenda for action. Both these scholars have shown how reform proposals were carefully crafted to reflect the distinct concerns of quite different factions within reform coalitions and to blur their many differences. Yet many ideological systems, ranging from Marxism-Leninism to Hare Krishna, have offered coherence and practical application without becoming successful programs of institutional power. A distinctive feature of Progressive penology was that it not only provided a more-or-less coherent view, it was successful in shaping public discourse about crime and thus crime policy itself. It offered a narrative that appealed to widely varying segments of society. The Progressive alliance, both in the United States and its equivalent in Europe, was based on class, religion and social status (Hofstadter 1955). Two factors in particular are significant, in light of our concern with the contemporary situation and the new penology: the rise of the working class, and the use of penality to emphasize a form of nationalism based on the problem of the social.

Normalizing the Working Classes

While the Jacksonians formulated their penology largely out of repugnance for the urban poor whose ranks had been growing since colonial days (Dumm 1987), the Progressives responded to the rising tide of working-class political power. This new power was expressed in labor militancy and in the voting power of the white working class. Historians have long stressed the roots of the Progressive movement, its humanistic principles and its basis in the growing power of the working class, and the interaction of the two. But the two are not exclusive of one another. U.S. Progressives and similarly situated Europeans recognized the task of creating social institutions capable of granting the working classes a measure of stability and a tangible (if limited) sense of entitlement to solutions to their problems from the government. In penology, as Garland (1985) emphasizes, Progressive reforms were from the outset understood as part of the formulation of a comprehensive system of social welfare, one that sought to separate the "social" from "socialism" and one that brought about a modus vivendi between classes based on a system of social welfare and not socialism. A whole set of measures aimed at securing the worker at work—rudimentary health and safety regulations, liability law reforms, worker's compensation, and the like—were adopted in the first two decades of the twentieth century. Progressive penal reform was but one component of this comprehensive agenda, and flowed directly from its central premises.

Penology and Social Solidarity

Since Durkheim ([1893] 1947), students of social control have argued that crime and crime policy foster social solidarity, that the process of creating deviance and labeling the deviant reinforces social solidarity (Erickson 1966). Yet Durkheim and his followers took such social response to crime as a manifestation of an underlying natural reality, the collective conscience. More recently a number of historians and political scientists have reformulated this understanding of crime and identified a variety of collective identities that can be reinforced by representations of crime and criminality (Hall et al. 1979; Garland 1990; Scheingold 1991).

In his recent study of Southeast Asia, Anderson has explored the unifying power of nationalism, showing how it helps construct "imaginary communities" (1986) and reinforce group solidarity. He argues that in contrast to other forms of collective identification, and especially race, nationalism is a powerful unifying force. While nationalist regimes have fomented great violence, nationalist movements also stress art, literature, and other forms of positive self-expression in ways that foster an intense sense of unity (ibid.:146–50).

Others have shown how crime and crime policy can play a role in fostering nationalism and hence collective solidarity. Social historians in both the United States and Europe have long pointed out how crime—as well as other social problems—was something that not only affected individual citizens, but threatened the very well being of the nation as well. Indeed, some argued that it revealed deep truths about the nation's flaws and potential. The combination of the latter two themes—the challenge of crime and the sources of national salvation—offered a compelling vision of national destiny that captured the public imagination and was expressed in a wide variety of forms.[8]

In both the United States and the United Kingdom, reformers were deeply concerned with the threat immigration posed for a coherent national identity (Painter 1987; Rothman 1980; Garland 1985:177). Crime was one of many pathologies spawned by the poverty and ignorance of immigrants. But, as we noted earlier, even though the Progressives embraced this view, they were also confident that the virtues of American political culture would not only be saved, but could be harnessed to attack these pathologies and absorb the immigrants into their new culture (Rothman 1980:48).

THE GREAT SOCIETY AND CRIME:
UPDATING PROGRESSIVE PENOLOGY

After World War II the Progressive penal agenda was revived. Younger politicians joined with older Progressives like California's Earl Warren to attack the problems of crime, but they were able to do so with a level of funding and a degree of public confidence that were unimaginable in the pre-war years (Simon 1993). And in the 1950s and 1960s, penological discourse became even more sociologically informed (Cloward and Ohlin 1960). As in the Progressive Era, criminological ideas became the locus for a mobilization of experts, politicians, and journalists, and many of the earlier representations reappeared in another guise, as discourse continued to reflect advances in the social and technological sciences.

Although the Great Society rekindled the Progressive New Deal agendas, it also added important new issues. The nation was vastly larger and wealthier and more centralized, and so its projects were bigger and more nationally centered. Perhaps most important, the Great Society was shaped in part by the moral vision of the civil rights movement, and thus it was more inclusive, more participatory, less enamored of expertise, more sensitive to issues of racial discrimination, and above all more rights-conscious than was the Progressive–New Deal agenda. These values were very much reflected in early efforts like the Kennedy administration's focus on juvenile delinquency.

The crime control strategy of the Great Society, however, was vintage Progressive: more expertise and more knowledge. This is reflected in its two most enduring legacies, the reports of the President's Commission on Law Enforcement and Criminal Justice (known as the President's Crime Commission) published in 1967, and the establishment of the Law Enforcement Assistance Administration in 1968.[9]

Despite the fact that the federal crime effort was anchored in the past, it did contribute two important new responses that flourished. By focusing on the "system" of law enforcement and criminal justice, the reports introduced new issues and new ways of thinking about the administration of criminal justice, and a new objective: the transformation of a "non-system" into a functioning "system." And by endorsing the idea of a "modest" role for the federal government in funding crime programs (and the eventual establishment of LEAA), it helped set the scene for a national discussion of crime and what do about it, a discussion that hitherto been conducted almost exclusively at the state and local level (Scheingold 1991). We explore the first of these two contributions below.[10]

Taming the System

In his important book, *Taming the System (1993)*, Samuel Walker takes a close look at national crime policy of the 1960s, and argues that the most enduring contribution of the criminal justice reform movement of the 1960s was the attack on unfettered discretion, and the success of the idea of subjecting decision-making to structure, rule, and oversight. One component of this effort was generated by the due process revolution precipitated by the U.S. Supreme Court, which extended rights to the criminally accused and sought to place limits on the discretion of police officer. The Court sought to tame the system by adjusting the balance of advantage in the adversary system in order to guarantee that state power would be offset by guarantees to protect the accused.

But Walker shows that the move to "tame the system" also had another and perhaps more important source: an administrative effort to professionalize law enforcement officials, impose modern management techniques on criminal justice agencies, and more generally establish the idea of a criminal justice *system*. Fostered by the pioneering earlier work undertaken at the American Bar Foundation and sponsored by the Ford Foundation in the 1950s, the creation of a criminal justice *system* became a central focus for some staff members on the Presidential Commission, and especially on its task forces on courts, and on sciences and technology. The recommendations coming from these reports sought to "tame the system" by controlling discretion, improving efficiency, and fostering systemic thinking about the operations of criminal justice agencies. Walker argues that this represented a watershed in thinking about the criminal process, and led to a host of new controls on police behavior and ways of thinking about pretrial detention and sentencing (Walker 1993). There is no doubt that he is correct, and that he has identified a profound change in thinking about crime and the problems of crime.

In our two articles (Feeley and Simon 1992, 1994) we suggested that this trend was a central feature of the new penology, and indeed linked it to another feature of the new penology, the move from an individualized criminal process to an actuarial system. Walker's analysis captures some of this shift, and reveals how potent this new idea of a system became. He is correct to insist that this is the central organizing metaphor for thinking about crime and crime policies since the 1960s.[11]

This constituted a radical departure from the past. Discretion—the exercise of professional judgment—was also at the heart of Progressives' clinical models of individualized penality or in Garland's (1985) phrase referring to English crime policy of the same time period, "penal welfarism." Under Progressive penology discretion was part—indeed, the central component—of the solution to the problem, discretionary authority to make important clinical judgments delegated to trained professionals. Although Progressive thinking was in many ways opposed to the adversary process and expanded conceptions of due process,[12] it had accommodated itself to the concerns raised by both Packer's (1968) due process and crime control models. Both these conceptions of the criminal process placed considerable faith in discretion, and thus did not run counter to the idea of professional expertise that underlay the Progressive vision. The difference was that the advocates of due process placed less trust in government officials and wanted to curb them through more rights, more due process, and a stronger defense. In contrast, the move to create and then establish a "real" system constituted a substantial change in thinking. It fostered bureaucratic accountability and thus sought to limit professional discretion.

One measure of the impact of this new development is that in short order operations research came to replace sociology as the frame of reference for crime policy analysts. The language of rights gave way to the language of administration; the language of social work was replaced by flowcharts. Situational crime prevention analysis emerged. In all this the quest for individual-focused justice was superseded by a concern with the management of risk-segregated populations. The new penology was embraced. No doubt we overstate. The old language did not wholly wither away, the new language did not emerge overnight, let alone immediately translate into fully realized new conception of the criminal process, and the new is not wholly new. Features of the new penology share a great deal with Colquhoun's (1796) late-eighteenth-century observations about the nature and functions of the police. New institutions did not sweep away traditional practices. Still, a new managerial orientation has emerged, even if orientation of old-line staff remains rooted in traditional concerns (Lynch 1998).

The basic outlines of Progressive penology remained in force throughout the 1960s and 1970s. But an important new language and perspective—and an emerging set of practices—began to grow up, grafted onto old institutions or standing side by side with the old. This represented much more than an effort to "tame" dysfunctional features of the adversary process or establish a new balance of advantage among contestants or enhance professionalization in laggard public agencies. It represented a serious and sustained effort to reframe issues, to replace a " nonsystem" with a new, integrated system. In so doing, it went some way toward decentering the individual as the focus of concern in the criminal process. It is in this sense that we criticize Samuel Walker for not working through the two quite different sets of implications of the efforts to tame the nonsystem that he otherwise recounts so ably in his important book. Below we examine some of the features of this new systems approach.

THE NEW PENOLOGY AND THE NEW CRIMINAL JUSTICE SYSTEM

The history of post-1960s penality is now only being written, and its first major analytic study was published only in 2001 (Scheingold 1991; Beckett 1997; Gest 2001; Garland 2001). Those who offer cultural analysis of the present are necessarily parasitical of such work and the emergence of the new penology in this period requires a far more detailed and contextualized analysis.[13] Still it is possible to see in the victory of the system and its logics over those of "penal welfarism" a decisive step away from Progressive penology. The new discourses and practices showcased in the recommendations of the President's Crime Commission, and widely embraced since, have fundamentally transformed the thinking and work of academics and criminal justice professionals.

But this new discourse has not become the language of the public, the media, or the politicians. Instead, it has created a chasm between those professionals and academics who have embraced it, and politicians and the public who have not. This development has not only created a gap between these two sets of communities, it has contributed to increased ambivalence among the public. For many, criminal justice agencies—the "system" itself—is now seen as the problem, and confidence in the criminal process has plummeted. This gap stands in marked contrast to the consensus and shared confidence among academics, professionals, the media, and opinion makers during the Progressive Era.

The Limited Appeals of the New Penology

In our previous work we examined a number of ideas and programs that exemplified the new penology. Foremost of course is the very idea of a criminal justice *system* itself. Other new concepts include selective incapacitation, preventive detention, and drug courier profiles. Below we revisit some of these programs in order to explore their links with public discourse about crime, links that may be illustrated by shifts in ways the problem of crime is portrayed in the media. What this examination reveals is that although these new ideas have gained a considerable foothold among criminal justice professionals and as concrete programs, they do not constitute a fully realized vision of criminal justice or even a significant part of it.

Career Criminals, Criminal Careers, and Selective Incapacitation

The idea of the "career criminal" is one of the most appealing representations proffered by the producers of the new penology. It offers a picture of the crime problem as rooted in the conduct of a small and specifiable subpopulation. Moreover, the idea of the career criminal promises that measures aimed at such offenders will lower crime with better management, and without the need for massive new programs or funds or even significant changes in crime-fighting strategies. In their two-volume compendium, *Criminal Careers and "Career Criminals"* (1981), Alfred Blumstein and Jacqueline Cohen review research on this topic for the National Research Council. The studies reported in these volumes document the emerging importance of these new ideas about crime and criminals. The career criminal is, of course, the contemporary cousin of the older "habitual offender" and the "born criminal," but this most recent offspring is also quite different. The career criminal represents a shift away from a eugenics-based explanation of crime, or any other type of sociological explanation that seeks to identify the causes of crime. Instead, it is agnostic about the causes of crime; it is preoccupied, not with an explanation of crime as a prelude to diagnosis and response, but with the identification of high-risk offenders in order to incapacitate and manage.

The new and distinctive feature of the concept of career criminal is that it purports to show that a small handful of people account for a vast share of all serious crime. Its policy implications are obvious: we achieve both crime control and fiscal restraint by focusing on and incapacitating the handful of high-rate offenders. The new criminal career research is overwhelming actuarial and managerial. Its aim is to identify patterns of behavior in whole cohorts in order to promote public safety by incapacitating high-risk offenders for lengthy periods.[14] Research on this topic contrasts sharply with earlier research on the professional or habitual criminal (e.g., Sutherland's *The Professional Thief* [1937] and Irwin's *The Felon* [1970]), which was undertaken with the aim of "understanding" offenders as a first diagnostic step toward treatment or deterrence. Here, the quest is to identify good predictors of dangerousness and assemble data bases to rapid detection of high-rate offenders.

This idea has entered public discourse. In the 1970s, the U.S. Department of Justice launched a major campaign of pilot grants and research to convince local police and prosecutors to concentrate on career criminals. In 1987, the United States Sentencing Commission cited career criminals as deserving of special targeting of resources. More recently, the idea received widespread attention in the media and in political discourse in connection with the spate of three-strikes laws adopted by a number of states. In California, for instance, supporters of three-strikes legislation to imprison violent repeat offenders for life repeatedly invoked the term "career criminal" and repeatedly cited Wolfgang, Figlio, and Sellin's (1972) work.

Even one of the more radical versions of the idea of career criminal, the idea of selective incapacitation that we examined in "The New Penology" (Feeley and Simon 1992) has made some gains in public discourse. First put forward by the Rand Corporation (Greenwood 1982) and later embraced in a book by Harvard University scholars (Moore et al. 1984), many thought that it was a political nonstarter because it broke so dramatically with conventional theory's principles of sentencing. Although its central image—of a handful of dangerous predatory offenders committing a disproportionate amount of the most serious crimes—is popular, the idea of selectively targeting a small group of high-risk offenders and singling them out for disproportionate punishment is not. In the California legislative battle over three-strikes laws, for instance, a moderate bill that would have concentrated on "predatory career criminals" lost out to a much more inclusive bill, which included all those—high risk or not—who had three strikes against them. This provision greatly expanded the scope and cost of the new law, and from the perspective of proponents of selective incapacitation was a colossal waste of resources. However other states adopted more moderate three-strikes statutes, most closely in tune with the idea of career criminals.

Furthermore, in the early 1990s, in an expansive legislative act that restructured that state's sentencing laws, the state of Virginia explicitly embraced the idea of selective incapacitation as its goal for sentencing policy (Ostrom et al. 1999). The new legislation also authorized the state's sentencing commission to conduct research designed to establish reliable predictors of future dangerousness and design a sentencing scheme to implement it. Unlike almost all three-strikes laws, it specifically embraced one of the key features of and ostensible appeals of the RAND Corporation's original idea, that those with low likelihood of future serious criminal behavior should receive substantially shorter sentences than those the model found to be high risk. The Virginia scheme modifies the "pure theory" of selective incapacitation in a number of ways, most particularly in allowing judges discretion to override sentences prescribed by the predictive model, and like the original scheme holding that some personal characteristics, most notably race, cannot be used in the model. Nevertheless, the new statute does fully embrace selective incapacitation as the state's rationale for sentencing, and to this end provides for the continuous refinement of its sentencing model.

The Underclass

The concept of the underclass is not new. Nor was it coined by criminologists or even first used within penological discourse (Wilson 1987; Katz 1992). Yet in recent years it has been revised and widely embraced, both within criminology and in broader public discourse, as a metaphor that captures the idea of a permanent subpopulation that is dangerous and in need of management. Elsewhere we have argued that it is a convenient term to convey the idea of a group of persons permanently trapped in poverty and social marginality and who pose a high danger risk for society (Jackson 1989; Feeley and Simon 1992). The idea invites an aggregate response; techniques like preventive detention and drug courier profiles are coherent risk management strategies directed at such a population.

The exploration of the relationship between disorder and fear of crime developed by Wilson and Kelling (1982), Skogan (1990), and others is another effort to develop a coherent response to the underclass. In some ways this work is an extension of the older environmental studies of crime, especially the social disorganization perspective of the Chicago school, in which crime is understood as a product of fears generated by an underclass and by concerns that the neighborhood is changing and becoming more underclass.

This picture of crime suggests a number of policy responses. One is to attack the disorder, no doubt because it is more visible and routine than criminal behavior. Another is that the fear of crime is itself a cause of crime, and thus crime can be attacked successfully by measures that bolster confidence. Such ideas have gained considerable popular acceptance. A number of mayors beginning in the 1990s, including Rudolph Giuliani in New York City, have adopted programs that attack visible traits of disorder such as begging, public drunkenness, and windshield washing, arguing that they are effective crime-fighting measures. Thus what was proposed in the early 1980s, was embraced and institutionalized over the next decade, and was proclaimed to be a success in the late 1990s. One of the most positive assessments was offered by George Kelling, one of the original architects of the "broken windows" strategy, and Catherine Coles, in their book *Fixing Broken Windows* (1999). Not surprisingly, it reports glowing successes. However, others are more skeptical (Harcourt 2001).

Another policy manifestation of the idea of the underclass is "community policing" (Skolnick and Bayley 1986). It promises that the focus of policing should shift from making arrests to addressing community fears of disorder by being more responsive to community calls for maintaining order. This policy draws on nostalgic representations of earlier American communities (Scheingold 1991:170), but also fits within the strategies of the new penology to the extent that it aims at establishing managerial control over disorderly populations. The 1994 Federal Crime Act may be an indication of the strength of public acceptance of this form of controlling the underclass; it provided funding for one hundred thousand new police officers. Although supporters are vague as to what these police will do, the act was defended in terms of the values of community policing.

A variety of other "new" programs such as "intensive" parole and probation, boot camps, and police-prosecutor partnerships also tie into the belief (Petersilia 1987; Feeley and Simon 1992) that there is an entire class that is no longer capable of maintaining basic order among its members, and needs police and other agents of the state to intervene not just to deal with crime, but to maintain order. Yet despite some limited successes, none of these programs has emerged as an alternative to traditional sanctions.

Drugs and Drug Testing

Since the early 1980s, for reasons largely independent of penology, drugs became a central focus in the political response to crime. Presidents from Reagan to George W. Bush have seen illegal drug use as signifying a deep moral decline in certain portions of American society, and have mounted the moral equivalent of war on it. Spectacular media coverage of the violence associated with drugs has helped build a public conception of drugs as a catalyst for violence. Furthermore, research has revealed the presence of drugs among a high proportion of arrestees, and this in turn has contributed to a continuous expansion of penalties for drug possession and tests for drug use. In light of all this, extraordinarily harsh sentences for drug use and widespread reliance on drug testing have come to be seen as sensible strategies to protect public safety (Gordon 1993). But even though drug use is identified as a reliable indicator of membership in a high-risk population, efforts to construct penal strategies to control drugs have not been embraced by the public. Although the 1994 Federal Crime Act does provide some funding for drug treatment programs, to date the response to drugs remains largely punitive.

Part of the problem lies in the distinctive way in which the new penology views drugs. The old penology understood drug use as an explanation for why some individuals became criminals, and thus it provided a story about how to control crime. In contrast the new penology regards drug use primarily in risk management terms, as an indicator of dangerousness. To the extent that the public also views drugs primarily as a measure of risk, evidence revealing high levels of drug use among arrestees may only solidify a belief in the need to manage a permanent high-risk underclass rather than punish use or treat users. Proponents of the new penology have not even been successful in meeting traditionalist halfway. The public stance on drug use since the 1970s has been "zero tolerance," and no important public officials have even dared to challenge the slogan, "Just Say No," coined in President Reagan's antidrug campaign in order to advocate a more cost-effective policy based on the principle of "harm reduction."

Racial Profiling

Law Enforcement officials have long relied on stereotypes to help them sort out vast amounts of information in short order. But in the 1990s some of these long-standing practices were vigorously challenged by various civil rights groups, who maintained that in many jurisdictions it appeared to be an unwritten offense to "drive while black."[15] As criticism mounted about police officers' selectivity in stop and frisk settings or in simply stopping cars on the freeway for allegedly speeding, systematic studies lent considerable credence to the complaints. After a number of police departments and state highway patrol agencies lost several highly publicized lawsuits, law enforcement officials adopted formal nonprofile policies. This movement has been gaining momentum for years, but in the aftermath of the attack on the World Trade Center on September 11, 2001, this momentum has slowed down and the value of profiling is again being debated. Profiling, at least for possible terrorist activities, took on a new respectability and a new urgency. As Americans grew to accept the idea of the inevitability if not desirability of trading some privacy and individual freedom for a bit more security, profiling came to be seen in a different light. It appears that since September 11 profiling has gained a new legitimacy, although of course there are significant differences between developing terrorist profiles in the search for suspicious foreign nationals and the practice of disproportionately stopping African-Americans for speeding on freeways. Profiling is one feature of the new penology that is easily understood, and perhaps for this reason, it is one area where the idea of efficiency is appreciated and the problem of effectiveness overlooked.

Sexual Predators

High-profile sexual assaults on girls by recidivist offenders have in recent years led to a variety of responses. They were one of the central features in the campaign for three-strikes and other tough sentencing laws. But they have led to still other responses that are part both of the popular discourse for greater severity, as well as actuarial in their conception. A number of states have enacted high profile and highly popular sexual predator laws that attempt to manage the risk of releasing those convicted of molesting children. These laws take various forms. Some require ex-offenders to register with local police departments when they move into an area. Others require notification of neighbors. And in some instances the courts have held that those convicted of sexual assaults can be detained in a type of civil confinement beyond the limits of their criminal detention on the grounds they continue to pose a high risk to society. One can easily interpret such provisions as "an exercise in scapegoating by people who are desperately trying to forge a greater sense of solidarity in a time of unprecedented change and division" (Kennedy 1995), and we would agree that they are certainly this (see e.g. Tyler and Boeckman 1997). But such provisions can also be understood in terms of risk assessment. Because of the nature of the offense, the history of the offender, and the availability of technologies, continued surveillance of those released (and at least in some instances in some jurisdictions, continued civil-like detention for those who have completed their sentences) can be framed as a rational response to an assessed risk. Clearly, one of the reasons that the idea of risk assessment in such situations is so widely embraced in the mass media and popular opinion is that invariably the risk analysis leads to more and more stringent controls, not fewer. Megan's Law-like provisions are one-way streets, leading to more stringent controls. Rarely if ever will offenders be assessed as low risks, and thus escape these "additional" notification and reporting requirements. As Simon (1998a) has noted, such provisions these laws contain a mixture of "risk talk" and practice with an image that has its origins in the Victorian era, even before the emergence of the old penology—the criminal "monster," beyond volition and in need of constant control.

Immigration Law and Deportation

Still another set of new policies that have struck a chord with the public and embrace actuarial-like form are the "aggravated felony" provisions in recent immigration law. The new laws justify the mandatory detention of resident aliens under new penological principles that are fully actuarial in form and content in that their justification and practice rest upon risk selection and removal with no due process (Simon 1998b). Here too these laws represent a hybrid blend of the new penology with premodernist penologies of fear and loathing of the "foreigner."

Situational Crime Prevention and Defensible Space

In our discussion of the new penology, we have emphasized the institutional arrangements in the criminal process itself. But the conception of risk management embraced in the new penology makes no hard and fast distinction between the criminal process and other forms of social control. Indeed, danger management must be understood as a complex of risk strategies directed at various institutions. Actuarial concerns have informed a host of other institutions that at first glance are not directly related to criminal justice concerns. Situational crime control fosters various new forms of surveillance—closed-circuit TV cameras, the explosive growth of these cameras and the rise of the private security industry, which can transform social control into a form of "waste management" (Feeley and Simon 1992; Lynch 1998; von Hirsch et al. 2000).

Defensible space (Newman 1972; Katyal 2002) can also redefine our understanding of the distinction between private and public. By privatizing space we heretofore have though of as public, unobtrusive risk-based danger management can be pursued with ease. Consider shopping malls, airports, condominium complexes, mega-amusement parks. In contrast to managers of public spaces, owners of private spaces have considerable freedom to specify their criteria for entrance, admission, or membership (Wakefield 2000). Perhaps most important, unobtrusive social controls can be embedded more easily in private than public space. Consider the proliferation of large-scale malls in the United States and elsewhere; indeed, the self-enclosed mall has literally come to replace the public square in some communities.[16] As malls take on features of the public square, consider the differences: No Shoes, No Shirt, No Service; No Clusters of Teenagers; Check Your Bags at the Door; suspected shoplifters detained on hunch or suspicion rather than probable cause. Indeed, the very entrances to such spaces serve as deterrents for the shoddily dressed, and thus alert officials to those who appear to have no legitimate business inside the area.

Restorative Justice

Since the late 1980s, John Braithwaite (1989; 1999) has almost single-handedly created a revolution in sentencing theory. As harsh retribution has been embraced with a vengeance in public discourse about criminal punishment, Braithwaite has patiently and persuasively argued for an alternative vision for at least some types of offenses and some types of offenders. In a series of books and articles beginning with *Crime, Shame, and Reintegration* (1989), Braithwaite has argued for an alternative (as well as a supplement) to retribution. It is a two-part ceremony: the first seeks to extract a sense of shame and remorse from the offender, and the second extends the embrace of the community to the remorseful offender in a way that communicates it desire to reintegrate the truly remorseful back into its bosom.

Braithwaite and other supporters of restorative justice argue that as simple as this idea is, it has been ignored in traditional theories of punishment and sentencing. Although it contains elements of rehabilitation, it does not rest upon a medical model or the belief that the offender is in some way pathological or in need of treatment. Similarly, nothing in it precludes the imposition of severe sanctions, although its ultimate aim is to reintegrate the errant persons back into their community, not to set them further apart. To this end, it seeks to confront the offenders with the consequences of their actions by having them listen to and respond to the reactions of those c-losest to them, family members, friends, teachers, coworkers, and the like.

Braithwaite's idea has been picked up around the world. And its popularity is often cited as evidence that unmitigated vengeful retribution is not wholly dominant in operational theories of punishment and that restorative justice and the rehabilitative-like ideals still have some purchase in the criminal process.

Restorative justice is often treated as a feature of what we have labeled the old penology. No doubt it is, but it may not be wholly at odds with the sort of risk management associated with the new penology. When it is employed, and indeed in the circumstances in which its use is usually envisioned, restorative or reintegrative justice is understood as an approach most suitable for relatively minor offenses and relatively "safe" offenders. As such it may be near one end of the surveillance to incapacitation continuum, and understood as a particularly appropriate form of response for a set of offenders along this continuum. Like many other forms of "community corrections," it may end up serving a variety of functions, some of which were not embraced by or envisioned by its proponents (Scull 1977; Cohen 1985; Blomberg and Lucken1993; Austin and Krisberg 1982).

THE ENDURANCE OF THE OLD PENOLOGY

In our original article, we argued that the new penology is more than just a set of ideas, or an integrated system of practices (Feeley and Simon 1992). Rather, it is an interpretive construct that we as observers cast over a complex set of ideologies and practices in order to help identify and interpret emerging relationships among them. Neither deep structure nor mentality, the new penology offers room for maneuver and adaptation. The question is, can it provide a successful set of narratives to guide public discourse and will it contribute to the acceptance of a new type of crime policy? To date, we argue here, it has not. Although it forms an important basis for professional and academic discourse about crime and crime policy, the new penology has not (yet) permeated public and political discourse. Public discussion of crime remains rooted in the moralism of the oldest penologies. In the discussion above we have explored why this is the case, why professional and academic discourse has not become public discourse as well. In doing so we have identified and begun to diagnose what may be a fatal weakness in the new penology, i.e., its failure to present a narrative of crime and its control and a representation of crime and its control that resonates with the public, and we have begun to explore why this is the case.

Still as suggested above, the new penology has produced significant new policy proposals that have considerable resonance with the public, and still more that are being quietly institutionalized. Some have been embraced widely and enthusiastically, and others are gaining ground. The language of the new penology is heard with some frequency in state and national debates about crime policy, but it remains a minor theme. The 1994 Crime Act included several measures that embody new penology themes about career criminals, the underclass, and drugs. Post-September 11 policies that spill over from national defense to domestic crime control significantly expand the embrace of preventive detention and the value of profiling is consistent with the new penology. Risk analysis of all sorts has grown by leaps and bounds. Selective incapacitation—the exemplar of the new penology—has been directly and officially embraced by at least one state and features of it enacted elsewhere. Drug testing has expanded exponentially over the past ten years and is now a routine condition for pre-trial release, probation, parole, as well as participation in extracurricular activities as diverse as choir and football. Since September 11, risk profiling has not only gained a new sense of legitimacy but a sense of urgency.

Despite all this, the new penology, with notably exceptions identified above, remains something of a stealth policy, and has not captured the imagination of either law enforcement professionals or the public. It has not been successful in presenting a fully realized "vision of social control." Despite the importance of these new policies anchored in new penology thinking, they are eclipsed by still other policies and programs that are anchored in traditional notions and narratives. In the discussion below we identify some of the reasons this failure, if that is what it is, of the new penology to play a larger role in the imaginations of criminal justice officials and the public. In particular we examine four different factors.

The Endurance of Volitional

One possible explanation for the limited success of the new penology in penetrating public discourse is the general distaste of the public for discourses that emphasize social and institutional circumstances and ignore willful individuals. As Stuart Scheingold (1991) has observed, volitional theories of crime have long dominated both professional and public discourse about crime in America. In contrast, he continues, structural accounts of crime, which seek to understand crime in terms of social conditions and social structures, are virtually absent in American policy discussions. The policy implications of these two perspectives are strikingly different: volitional theories imply alteration of factors that affect calculating individuals. Structural analysis of crime tells us that the causes and hence most important factors contributing to crime lie outside the purview of the criminal process and thus we should attack them if we really want to reduce crime.

Although structural analysis has some support in scholarly circles (Currie 1987), it has not even gained a precarious foothold in public discussions of crime. No doubt one important reason for this failure is that Americans are firmly anchored in a tradition of individualism and are skeptical about authority. Indeed, almost all American policy discourse—

both public and professional—is expressed in language that emphasizes volitional and eschews structural analysis. The new penology may fail for this same reason. Neither fully volitional nor fully structural—in Scheingold's dichotomy—the new penology falls some place in between. It is not fully structural since it focuses on crime. Nor is it fully volitional since it shifts attention away from affecting individual behavior to managing aggregates. Neither is it visionary; it does not depend upon the transformation of individuals or of society. Rather it seeks a more efficient and a more strategic management of dangerousness. Above all, it does not embrace traditional volitional notions of crime and criminality, and thus it remains somewhat distinct from established public and political discourse. Although it has come to be the language of choice among many academics and professionals, to date it has not caught on with the public.

The Popularization of Crime Politics

The politics of reform in the Progressive Era was largely a politics of elites. Apart from occasional highly salient issues (e.g., prohibition, the Mann Act), transformations in the objectives and techniques of punishment were rarely the subject of broad public debate. Even in legislative bodies there was little substantive political debate; most of the key conflicts were sorted out in the process of program formation internal to elite professional groups (Garland 1985). However, since the 1950s, and particularly since the late 1960s, crime policy has been an integral part of general political debate in popular forums and in the electoral process, a phenomenon that intensified in the 1980s (Scheingold 1991; Simon 1993).[17]

Although crime is a potent ideological issue in modern societies (Hall et al. 1979), until the 1970s its most popularized forms remained somewhat removed from the actual formation of penal institutions. As penal reform questions become a central issue in electoral politics, however, ideological appeals have come to dominate both cultural influence and system effects. By way of example, in the 1980s and 1990s, the California prison guards' union came to be a heavy contributor to political campaigns in the state; in 2000 it surpassed the California Teacher's Association as the single largest source of contributions.

Crime as a National Problem

Stuart Scheingold (1991; see also Humphries 1981; Heath 1984; Barak 1994; Beckett 1997) has argued that in recent years, crime and punishment have become increasingly defined as "national" problems, and that this tendency exacerbates the emotionalism already endemic to discussions of crime). Local crime politics are more pragmatic, because local public figures have to cope more directly with the problems of managing the policies that are put into place, and they have to answer for failure. We think, however, that it is more than the distance involved in national politics that has changed. Progressive discourse also defined crime as an issue of national significance, but it reflected elite fears and aspirations. Today national discourse on crime is populist and centered on fear. Moreover, the nationalism of the Progressive Era was expansive and at least partially (if grudgingly) inclusive of the new immigrants. Today's national crime discourse is defensive and exclusive. Some observers have noted a significant change in political discourse, a shift away from language that reinforces traditional group loyalties linked to ethnicity and locality to one based on more generalized appeals to policies and the nation (Simon 1987; Dionne 1991). This may have facilitated new types of political appeals:

> [In the past] political loyalties were reinforced by other forms of group solidarity. Now, insofar as voters identify with groups, it is often with abstract national groups rather than concrete local ones. An Italian machinist in a Detroit suburb may identify himself more with his fellow gun owners than with his ethnic group, his neighborhood, or his fellow workers. (Dionne 1991:17)

The General Crisis of Governmental Power

In the early twentieth century the problem of crime[18] constituted a powerful reason to expand the role of government in fostering welfare, in order to integrate marginal members of society into the mainstream. But by the end of the century it had become an alternative vehicle for expanding and mobilizing government (Simon 1997). The new penology divorces crime policy from concern with social welfare.[19] Increasingly, crime policy is conceived of as a process for classification and management of populations ranked by risk, in need of segregation not integration. Indeed, this new direction may reflect what E. J. Dionne, Jr. (1991:17) calls "the decline of a 'politics of remedy.'"

Since the 1960s, the key to winning national elections has been to reopen the same divisive issues over and over again. The issues themselves are not reargued. No new light is shed. Rather, old resentments and angers are stirred up in an effort to get voters to cast yet one more ballot of angry protest. Political consultants have been truly ingenious in devising creative ways to tap into popular anger about crime. And the rise of powerful victims' rights groups has added fuel to the fire of single-issue politics.

David Garland's important book, *The Culture of Control* (2001), examines these and other factors that have shaped contemporary crime policies. We are in basic agreement with him, although we would emphasize the political dimension more than he does. We would do so because among advanced capitalist societies, only two stand out—England and the United States—as having significantly developed "cultures of control" that rely so extensively on the criminal process to cope with the strains of contemporary societies. This, as we suggested above, is likely to be due to the "thinness" of support for the welfare state in these countries in contrast to most other advanced capitalist societies in Western Europe. Still, Garland's long list of factors must all be considered in any comprehensive treatment of the problem of the decline of penal welfarism, the inability of the new penology to fully "take," and the rise of hyperpunitive policies and the "culture of control." In this chapter, we have held such issues in the background, and concentrated instead on the internal features of the new penology, which have limited its success.

CONCLUSION

From the struggle against widespread use of capital and corporal punishment in the eighteenth and nineteenth centuries to the Progressive establishment of a separate juvenile justice process, the development of parole and probation, and other similar measures, new forms of penality have always had to deal with the traditional cultural meaning associated with crime and punishment. As Garland (1990), following Elias (1982), Spierenberg (1984), and others, has argued, these developments eventually came to be seen as part of a "civilizing process" by which Western societies have steadily denounced public displays of violence and pleasure in the suffering of others. But at the same time, these techniques and discourses have produced their own cultural effects (Garland 1990). As we argued above, one dimension of the Progressive effort was the production of potent representations of crime that achieved broad resonance in public discourse (see also Garland 1985; 1990:257). While these representations were very much rooted in the new human sciences and other modernist cultural developments, they also reached back to and incorporated much of the cultural meaning invested in the figure of the criminal by early and premodern society. Progressive penology transformed this figure of the dangerous felon into a site of humanity and thereby channeled the investment of new cultural meanings. The apparent failure of the old Progressive penology to sustain itself beyond the 1970s should not lead us to assume that the immense "deposits of power" (Cohen 1985) left behind no longer have any resonance or power.[20] Indeed, one weakness of the new penology is its failure to tap into these layers of meaning (and hence power) associated with the figure of the criminal and the Progressives' strategies for coping with crime.

Although the new penology has offered some representations by which to understand its central concerns—"underclass," "actuarial methods," "the funnel of justice," "system"—these terms do not constitute a fully realized, let alone satisfying vision of the criminal process, as did the Progressives' ideas on "penal-welfarism" that they have sought to displace. Nor are these new representations easily compatible with the moralism and individualism of the American national character. Thus despite its substantial development during the past thirty years, the new penology has not provided a comprehensive popular account of the *truth* of crime.

One reason for this is surely the very blindness of the new penology to the cultural effects of penality itself. The systems logic that pervades the new penology is based squarely on a denial of the very specialness of crime. It assumes that the problems of penality are no different than the problems of managing other types of large systems, whether they are transportation networks or military logistics. It fails to appreciate that the "irrational" division of the world through categories is near the heart of any adequate definition of culture (Douglas 1966), and as a consequence it fails to provide satisfying cultural representations of crime and the criminal.

Another problem is the failure of the new penology to join in public discourse at all. The tendency of penal practices to generate their own internal expert discourse has been developing for some time.[21] The Jacksonians and the Progressives had their own versions of specialized discourse, with a definite secular trend toward less overlap with popular discourses (like religion). Still, the new penology probably represents a quantum leap toward a more technical and internal discourse that cannot offer a plausible and culturally satisfying accounts of crime and its control.

While the new penology is formally neutral as to the specific objectives of the criminal process, its tendency to translate all issues into system flow questions ultimately influences the normative effects of penality. As Garland has noted:

> The internal regimes of most modern prisons are remarkably deficient in "moral tone" and rarely adopt any serious attempt to instill virtue or morality beyond the basic demands of obedience and discipline. (1990:261)

No doubt this reflects the long-term failure (and autocritique) that Foucault noted in modern punishment. Substantive studies of modern penal institutions (Messinger et al., 1972; Jacobs 1978; Rafter 1990; Simon 1993; Feeley and Rubin 1998) have all documented the gap between the programmatic aspirations behind the institutions and the reality of practice. Our current practices are even further removed. This is consistent with the political triumphs of incapacitation and deterrence, and the decline of the rehabilitative ideal. But the lines of causation may be more complex. The new penology has abetted these trends by producing representations of the system, which facilitate objectives like deterrence (which demands only efficiently produced punishment) and incapacitation. The traditional appeal of penal correctionalism was its emphasis on the humanity of offenders and the cruelty of current penal practices. These became more than minor themes in the general political culture in part because of the production of new forms of knowledge; Progressive social science made these issues visible to new publics in ways that made them politically active and effective. The new penology has trouble recognizing the cultural investment in the figure of the criminal; it has trouble with the concept of humanity. At just the moment when huge populations are being brought under correctional management, that management has ceased to be a source of producing meaningful representations of criminal subjectivity of the sort that engaged the public in dialogues on rehabilitation and prison reform (Simon 2000).

Ultimately the new penology fails to engage the public because it has abandoned goals that remain central to the whole notion of a public policy, those of reducing crime while controlling those whose crimes pose a serious threat to personal security and property. While pledging allegiance to those goals, the new penology has almost always moved instead into a focus on system performance and rationality that ultimately excludes the public. This trend was noted forcefully twenty-five years ago by political scientists Susan White and Samuel Krislov in their report on federally sponsored criminal justice research from 1968 to 1975, produced through the LEAA and its Institute:

> Unfortunately, the Institute's most recent response has been to deny its capacity to produce useful knowledge about crime problems at all and to substitute as its focus of concern the operation of the criminal justice system. . . . The danger we see is an Institute that avoids the hard questions of knowledge about crime and criminal behaviors in favor of easier but relatively trivial studies of system operations. . . . The goal of controlling crime for which LEAA and the Institute were originally established remains a valid objective, although a complex and difficult one. (1977:46)

The failure of modern criminal justice professionals to engage with the public is clearly not limited to crime policy. Somewhere between the Progressive Era and the Great Society, notwithstanding the goal of "maximum feasible participation" of the Johnson administration, professionals in government became more detached from the public and more specialized. Politics became "policies," administrators became "experts," and giant size came to dwarf individual experience. Bureaucracy often trumped professionalism. Throughout political life since the 1970s, at least in the United States, there has been a growing distrust of government and consequently a reluctance to embrace public solutions to pressing problems.[22] There are of course efforts to counter this: the "third way" and the "new public administration," which seeks to turn clients into customers, and the move to privatize, which seeks to turn citizens into consumers. More ambitious are ideas to foster deliberative democracy and foster the lost ethic of civic republicanism. At their worst, some of these ideas are gimmicks and rest upon a thin conception of the public sphere. At best, they represent ambitious efforts to rethink the meaning of democracy in the administrative state, though many seem to be built upon a recollection of a nonexistent yesterday. Within the crime policy sphere, few of these ideas suggest paths that might lead us away from the hypermoralism and vindictiveness that have characterized so much of contemporary crime policy since the mid-1970s. Until they do, we might reasonably expect more of the same.

In *The Culture of Control*, David Garland (2001) argues that there are complex and deep connections between features of late modernity and the emergence of a strident and vindictive "culture of control." Indeed, his argument is in some small part a sustained critique of the new penology and our claims that it represents an important new development. Echoing themes explored by Emile Durkheim one hundred years ago about the moral function of penality in sustaining social solidarity, Garland argues in effect that the many dislocations brought about by late modernity foster a quest for security that in turn leads to draconian and spiteful penal policies. Under the circumstances these penal policies may be a crutch, but if the patient is injured, their use may be inevitable.

Alternatively, as Simon (1997) has argued elsewhere, the contemporary American (at least) policy of "governing through crime" reflects a dramatic decline in confidence in the welfare state, the abandonment of responsive law, and a return to basics with a vengeance; if government can do nothing else it should be able to maintain order. If any of these theories are even close to being correct, a new direction in crime policy must await a new politics and a renewed confidence in the state. In the meantime, it appears that vindictive penality will maintain its public salience and the new penology will continue to expand on the margins. The new penology provides an emerging new framework for organizing the "governing of crime," while the politics of vengeance continues to provide a means of "governing through crime."

ACKNOWLEDGMENTS

We wish to thank Stan Cohen and Tom Blomberg for helpful comments on an earlier draft of this chapter.

NOTES

1. As we stressed in "The New Penology" (Feeley and Simon 1992), the distinction between discourses, techniques, and objectives is for analytic purposes only (we do not assume the world comes carved up into such pieces). Any particular

practice, e.g., house arrests, with electronic monitoring, may draw on and support a variety of discourses; it may deploy any number of new and old techniques; it may be aimed at any number of objectives (explicit and implicit).

2. Michel Foucault sometimes described his research that way, and while we do not lay claim to his powers of observation or description, we share his sense that those of us who comment on contemporary affairs must use the tools of historians without necessarily accepting their self-imposed disciplinary standards.

3. The role of metaphors in the operation of law more generally has been explored by Steven L. Winter (1989).

4. As David Garland puts it: "New sanctions or practices had to be argued for effectively in the political domain and had to be capable of being represented within the legitimate discourses that overlay penal relations and represented them to the public" (1985:171).

5. For a good collection that surveys the rise and rapid spread of three strikes laws, see David Shichor and Dale Sechrest (1996).

6. England developed policies similar to those in the United States. For a magnificent history of the development of penal-welfarism in Edwardian England, see David Garland (1985).

7. For purposes of convenience we use the term Progressive Era and Progressives to characterize these developments both in the United States and in Great Britain. For general discussions of politics and society in the Progressive Era see Hofstadter (1955), Weibe (1967), and Painter (1987).

8. Marie-Christine Leps has pursued this theme in her study of popular culture and criminology in the late nineteenth century (1992). She argues that crime policy and public perceptions of crime are important means of mobilizing concern around the problem of national identity: "The exclusion of the criminal served not only to contain certain segments of the population, but also, more importantly, to discern the limits of a consensual 'we,' identified with 'the people of the nation' or that well known character, 'the public'" (ibid.:69).

9. Established in 1965, the President's Crime Commission issued a series of widely heralded final reports in 1967. In retrospect what is most striking about these reports was that they were anchored so firmly in Progressive Era thinking. They represent simultaneously the high-water mark of this way of thinking and an unintended elegy for a way of thinking that was on the brink of annihilation. Created by the Safe Streets Act of 1968, the Law Enforcement Assistance Administration provided a mechanism for distributing federal funding to state and local law enforcement and criminal justice agencies, and thus paved the way for a substantial federal presence in the criminal process. Although LEAA was widely criticized and once thought to be dead, federal funding for state and local law enforcement and criminal justice agencies and federalization of the criminal process have expanded dramatically even during periods of government contraction and devolution. For an account of national crime policy in the mid-1960s and the establishment and operations of the LEAA, see Feeley and Sarat (1980).

10. The history of the nationalization of crime policy is still taking place. No comprehensive account of it, akin to Radzinowicz's (1948–1972) account of the creation of a national response to crime in England in the eighteenth and early nineteenth centuries in England, has been written. But partial efforts have begun (Feeley and Sarat 1980; Windlesham 1993, 1996, 1998).

11. This shift may be symbolized by the shift in iconography in the criminal

The Form and Limits of the New Penology

process; the flowchart of the funnel of justice that was published as a centerfold in the commission's Task Force Report on Science and Technology has subsequently come to replace the traditional representation of justice as a blindfolded woman holding a set of scales. American criminal justice texts published in the past twenty-five years, for example, are more likely to reprint the commission's funnel of justice chart than a representation of justice. The commission's reports are in sharp contrast with those of its predecessor, the Wickersham Commission, which issued its findings in 1931. The latter's reports emphasized corruption and lack of proper qualifications for personnel—failings of individuals—and not systemic factors.

12. Consider the differences between the juvenile court's search for what was "best" for a child, and a strident rights orientation of due process advocates; or the pros and cons of indeterminate vs. determinate sentencing schemes. Still, no Progressives would have lamented the expansion of procedures to assure a fair trial, and probably the expansion of right to counsel for adults.

13. See Simon (1993) for an attempt to provide such for the practices of parole supervision.

14. The famous study by Marvin Wolfgang and his colleagues of crime among Philadelphia boys, *Delinquency in a Birth Cohort* (1972), is perhaps the single most influential example of this approach. Contrast that with William Healy's *The Individual Delinquent* (1915).

15. A sign of this is a recent federal district court opinion that upheld the use of a drug courier profile even though it disproportionately targeted African Americans for questioning. The district court reasoned that on its face, the use of a racial classification was justified by the government's compelling interest in controlling drug trafficking and the close relationship between the drug dealing industry and the poverty and unemployment that are endemic in many African-American communities. See United States v. Travis, 62 F.3d 170 (1996).

16. In Milpitas, California, city hall and other municipal services are located in the Mall of America, one of the largest shopping centers under one roof in the United States.

17. As late as the determinate sentence movement in the mid-1970s it unfolded with only moderate levels of public attention.

18. For a long time the division between substantive criminal laws, which focused on the acts sanctioned in court, and the practice of police and corrections on either side of the court sheltered penal strategies from the glare of the most public debates.

19. The debate over the 1994 crime bill serves as a measure of this shift. Liberals have introduced a number of economic development and community investment programs under the guise of crime "prevention." It remains far from clear, however, that the public, which welcomed the massive spending measure, was very conscious of the prevention aspects. The idea of prevention as a mandate for more government is the last thing the Democratic party wants to defend at this point. Indeed the measure is being in part funded through reductions in federal employment.

20. Simon (1994) has analyzed the play of just such deposits of power in the figure of the criminal and human being in one of the most significant public documents of recent times, the Warren Commission Report.

21. Garland (1990:263) suggests usefully that it may traced to the very movement toward privatizing the act of punishment in the eighteenth century.

22. Consider, for example, President Clinton's quest to establish a national health care system. It had been a central component in his campaign as well as those of several key Senators, and polls had revealed that a huge portion of the electorate supported it. Yet, following his election in 1992, when he presented his ideas, they were subjected to ridicule and rejected. He was humiliated in his first major legislative initiative. No doubt there are many reasons for this failure, foremost among them the organized opposition of insurance companies and large corporations. But clearly one reason was that President Clinton presented health care as a technical issue, to be developed by "experts" and financed through a crazy-quilt payments system. Had he presented the idea as a "basic right," much like universal access to public primary and secondary education has been embraced for well over a century, his ideas might have resonated more soundly with the public and he might have been able to avoid the ridicule heaped upon his "experts."

REFERENCES

Anderson, Benedict. 1986. *Imagined Communities: Reflections on the Origin and Spread of Nationalism*, rev. ed. London: Verso.

Austin, James and Barry Krisberg. 1982. "The Unmet Promise of Alternatives to Incarceration." *Crime and Delinquency.* 28:374–409.

Baker, Tom and Jonathan Simon. 2001. *Embracing Risk: The Changing Culture of Insurance and Responsibility.* Chicago: University of Chicago Press.

Barak, Gregg. 1994. *Media, Process, and the Social Construction of Crime: Studies in Newsmaking Criminology.* New York: Garland.

Bayens, Gerald J., Michael W. Manske, and John Ortiz Smykla. 1998. "The Impact of the 'New Penology' on ISP." *Criminal Justice Review* 23:51–62.

Beckett, Katherine. 1997. *Making Crime Pay: Law and Order in Contemporary American Politics.* New York: Oxford University Press.

Blomberg, Thomas G. and Karol Lucken. 1993. "Intermediate Punishments and the Piling Up of Sanctions." in *Criminal Justice: Law and Politics,* Pp. 470–81 edited by George Cole. Belmont, CA: Wadsworth.

Blumstein, Alfred, Jacqueline Cohen, Jerremy A. Roth, and Christy A. Visher (eds.). 1986. *Criminal Careers and "Career Criminals."* Washington, D.C.: National Academy Press.

Braithwaite, John. 1989. *Crime, Shame, and Reintegration.* New York: Cambridge University Press.

———. 1999. "Restorative Justice: Assessing Optimistic and Pessimistic Accounts," Pp. 1–127 in *Crime and Justice Review: A Review of Research,* M. Tonry (ed.). New York: Oxford University Press.

Burchell, Graham, Colin Gordon, and Peter Miller (Eds.). 1991. *The Foucault Effect: Studies in Governmentality.* Chicago: University of Chicago Press.

Bureau of Justice Statistics. 1993. *Sourcebook of Criminal Justice Statistics, 1992.* Washington, DC: GPO.

Calabrese, Guido. 1970. *The Cost of Accidents.* New Haven, CT: Yale University Press.

Cloward, Richard and Lloyd Ohlin. 1960. *Delinquency and Opportunity: A Theory of Delinquent Gangs.* Glencoe, IL: Free Press.

Cohen, Stanley. 1985. *Visions of Social Control.* New York: Polity.

Cohen, Stanley and Jock Young. 1973. *The Manufacture of News: Social Problems, Deviance and the Mass Media.* London: Constable.

Colquhoun, P. 1796. *Treates on the Police of the Metropolis.* London: H. Fry for C. Dilly.

Cotton, Michele. 2000. "Back with a Vengeance: The Resilience of Retribution as an Articulated Purpose of Criminal Punishment." *American Criminal Law Review* 1313–63.

Currie, Elliot. 1987. *Confronting Crime.* New York: Pantheon.

Dionne, E. J., Jr. 1991. *Why Americans Hate Politics.* New York: Touchstone.

Douglas, Mary. 1966. *Purity and Danger: An Analysis of the Concepts of Pollution and Taboo.* London: RKP.

Douglas, Mary and Aaron Wildavsky. 1982. *Risk and Culture.* Berkeley: University of California Press.

Dumm, Thomas. 1987. *Democracy and Punishment: Disciplinary Origins of the United States.* Madison, WI: University of Wisconsin Press.

Durkheim, Emile. [1893] 1947. *The Division of Labor in Society.* Glencoe, IL: Free Press.

Edelman, Murray. 1967. *The Symbolic Uses of Politics.* Champaign-Urbana: University of Illinois Press.

———. 1977. *Words That Succeed and Policies That Fail.* New York: Academic Press.

Elias, Norbert. 1982. *The Civilizing Process,* Edmund Jephcott, trans. New York: Pantheon.

Erickson, Kai. 1966. *Wayward Pilgrims: A Study in the Sociology of Deviance.* New York: John Wiley & Sons.

Ericson, Richard V., Patricia M. Baranek, and Janet B. L. Chan. 1987. *Visualizing Deviance: A Study of News Organizations.* Toronto: University of Toronto Press.

Ericson, Richard V. and Kevin D. Haggerty. 1997. *Policing Risk.* Toronto, ON: University of Toronto Press.

Ericson, Richard V., et al. 1991. *Representing Order: Crime, Law, and Justice in the News Media.* Toronto: University of Toronto Press.

Ewald, Francois. 1986. *L'Etat Provice.* Paris: Grasset.

Feeley, Malcolm M. 1999. "Actuarial Justice, Risk Management, and the Modern State." Pp. 513–28 in *Harmonization in Forensic Expertise.* J. F. Nijboer and W. J. M. Sprangers (eds.). Criminal Sciences. Amsterdam: THELA THESIS, 2000.

Feeley, Malcolm M. and Samuel Kamin. 1996. "'Three Strikes' in the Courts." Pp. 135–54 in *Three Strikes and You're Out: Vengeance as Public Policy,* edited by David Schichor and Dale Sechrest. Thousand Oaks, CA: Sage.

Feeley, Malcolm M. and Edward L. Rubin. 1998. *Judicial Policy Making and the Modern State: How the Courts Reformed America's Prisons.* New York: Cambridge University Press.

Feeley, Malcolm M. and Austin Sarat. 1980. *The Policy Dilemma.* Minneapolis, MN: University of Minnesota Press.

Feeley, Malcolm M. and Jonathan Simon. 1992. "The New Penology: Notes on the Emerging Strategy of Corrections and Its Implications." *Criminology* 30:449–74.

———. 1994. "Actuarial Justice: Power/Knowledge in Contemporary Criminal Justice. "Pp. 173–201 in *The Futures of Criminology,* edited by David Nelken. London: Sage.

Foucault, Michel (ed.). 1975. *I, Pierre Riviere, having slaughtered my mother, my sister, and my brother: A Case of Parricide in the 19th Century.* Frank Jellinek (trans.). New York: Random House.

Foucault, Michel (ed.). 1977. *Discipline & Punish: The Birth of the Prison,* Alan Sheridan, trans. New York: Random House.

Garland, David. 1985. *Punishment and Welfare: A History of Penal Strategies.* Brookfield, VT: Gower.

———. 1990. *Punishment and Modern Society: A Study in Social Theory.* Chicago: University of Chicago Press.

———. 1995. "Penal Modernism and Postmodernism" in *Punishment and Social Control,* T. Blomberg and S. Cohen (eds.). Hawthorne, NY: Aldine de Gruyter.

———. 2001. *The Culture of Control: Crime and Social Order in Contemporary Society.* New York: Oxford University Press.

Gest, Ted. 2001. *Crime and Politics: Big Government's Erratic Campaign for Law and Order.* New York: Oxford University Press.

Giddens, Anthony. 1999. "Risk and Responsibility." *Modern Law Review* 62:1–10.

Gordon, Diana R. 1990. *The Justice Juggernaut: Fighting Street Crime, Controlling Citizens.* New Brunswick, NJ: Rutgers University Press.

———. 1993. *The Return of the Dangerous Classes: Drug Prohibition and Policy Politics.* New York: W. W. Norton.

Greenwood, Peter. 1982. *Selective Incapacitation,* with Alan Abrahmse. Santa Monica: Rand.

Gusfield, Joseph. 1963. *The Symbolic Crusade: Status Politics and the American Temperance Movement.* Urbana: University of Illinois Press.

Hacking, Ian. 1990. *Taming Chance.* Cambridge: Cambridge University Press.

Hall, Stuart, Chas Critcher, Tony Jefferson, John Clarke, and Brian Roberts. 1979. *Policing the Crisis: Mugging, the State, and Law and Order.* London: MacMillan.

Harcourt, Bernard. 2001. *The Illusion of Order: The Failure of Broken Windows Policing.* Cambridge, MA: Harvard University Press.

Healy, William. 1915. *The Individual Delinquent: A Text-Book of Diagnosis and Prognosis for All Concerned in Understanding Offenders.*Boston: Little Brown.

Heath, L. 1984. "The Impact of Newspaper Crime Reports on Fear of Crime." *Journal of Personality & Social Psychology* 47:236–76.

Hofstadter, Richard. 1955. *The Age of Reform.* New York: Vintage.

Humphries, D. 1981. "Serious Crime, News Coverage and Ideology: A Content Analysis of Crime Coverage in a Metropolitan Paper." *Crime and Delinquency* 27:191–205.

Ignatieff, Michael. 1978. *A Just Measure of Pain: The Penitentiary in the Industrial Revolution.* London: Penguin.

Irwin, John. 1970. *The Felon.* Berkeley: University of California Press.

Jackson, Pamela Irving. 1989. *Minority Group Threat, Crime, and Policing: Social Context and Social Control.* New York: Praeger.

Jacobs, James. 1978. *Stateville: The Penitentiary in Mass Society.* Chicago: University of Chicago Press.

Katyal, Neal Kumar. 2002. "Architecture as Crime Control." *Yale Law Journal* 111:1039–1141.

Katz, Michael (ed.). 1992. *The Underclass Debate: Views From History.* Princeton, NJ: Princeton University Press.

Kelling, George and Catherine Coles. 1996. *Fixing Broken Windows.* New York: Free Press.

Kennedy, David W. 1995. "Residential Associations as State Actors: Regulating the Impact of Gated Communities on Nonmembers." *Yale Law Journal* 105:761–93.

Lehman, Nicholas. 1991. *The Promised Land.* New York: Basic Books.

Leps, Marie-Christine. 1992. *Apprehending the Criminal: The Production of Deviance in 19th Century Discourse.* Durham, NC: Duke University Press.

Lowi, Theodore. 1990. "Risk and Rights in the History of American Governments." Pp. 17–40 in *Risk,* edited by E. J. Burger. Ann Arbor: University of Michigan Press.

Lynch, Mona. 1998. "Waste Managers? The New Penology, Crime Fighting, and Parole Agent Identity." *Law & Society Review* 32:839–70.

Melossi, Dario and Massimo Pavarini. 1981. *The Prison and the Factory: Origins of the Penitentiary System.* Totowa, NJ: MacMillan.

Messinger, Sheldon. 1969. *Strategies of Control.* Ph.D. thesis, University of California, Los Angeles.

Messinger, Sheldon and Richard Berk. 1987. "Dangerous People." *Criminology* 25:767–81.

Messinger, Sheldon, et al. 1972. *C-Unit: A Search for Community in Prison.* Aldine: Chicago.

Miller, Lisa. 2001. "Looking for Postmodernism in All the Wrong Places: Implementing the New Penology." *British Journal of Criminology* 41:168–84.

Moore, Mark H., Susan Estrich, Daniel McGillis, and William Spelman. 1984. *Dangerous Offenders: The Elusive Target of Justice.* Cambridge, MA: Harvard University Press.

Newman, Oscar. 1972. *Defensible Space.* New York: Free Press.

Nonet, Philippe and Philip Selznick. 1978. *Law and Society in Transition: Towards Responsive Law.* New York: Harper & Row.

O'Malley, Pat. 1996. "Risk and Responsibility." Pp. 134–15 in *Foucault and Political Reasons,* edited by A. Barry, T. Osborne, and N. Rose. London: UCL.

O'Malley, Pat (Ed.). 1998. *Crime and the Risk Society.* Aldershot, UK: Ashgate.

O'Malley, Pat. 2000. "Volatile Punishments: Contemporary Penality and the Neoliberal Government." *Theoretical Criminology* 3:175.

Ostrom, Brian, Frank Cheesman, A. M. Jones. M. Peterson, and N. B. Kauder. 1999. *Truth in Sentencing in Virginia: Evaluating the Process and Impact of Sentencing Reform.* Williamsburg, VA: National Center for State Courts.

Packer, Herbert. 1968. *The Limits of the Criminal Sanction.* Stanford: Stanford University Press.

Painter, Nell Irvin. 1987. *Standing at Armageddon: The United States 1877–1919.* New York: W. W. Norton.

Pavlich, George. 2000. *Critique and Radical Discourses on Crime.* Aldershot, UK: Ashgate.

Petersilia, Joan. 1987. *Expanding Options for Criminal Sentencing.* Santa Monica, CA: Rand.

Radzinowicz, Leon. 1948–72. *A History of the Criminal Law and Its Administration from 1750.* Five volumes. New York: Macmillan.

Rafter, Nicole. 1990. *Partial Justice: Women, Prisons and Social Control.* New Brunswick, NJ: Rutgers University Press.

Reichman, Nancy. 1986. "Managing Crime Risks: Toward an Insurance-Based

Model of Social Control." In *Research in Law, Deviance and Social Control* 8:151–72.

Rose, Nikolas. 1999. *Powers of Freedom.* Cambridge: Cambridge University Press.

Rothman, David J. 1971 (2002). *The Discovery of the Asylum: Social Order and Disorder in the New Republic.* Hawthorne, NY: Aldine de Gruyter.

———. 1980. *Conscience and Convenience: The Asylum and Its Alternatives in Progressive America.* Toronto: Little Brown.

Ruggiero, Vincenzo, Nigel South, and Ian Taylor. 1998. *The New European Criminology.* London: Routledge.

Savelsberg, Joachim, Ryan King and Lara Cleveland. 2002. "Politicized Scholarship: Science on Crime and the State." *Social Problems* 49: 235–51.

Scheingold, Stuart A. 1984. *The Politics of Law and Order.* New York: Longman.

———. 1991. *The Politics of Street Crime: Criminal Process and Cultural Obsession.* Philadelphia: Temple University Press.

Scull, Andrew. 1977. *Decarceration: Community Treatment and the Deviant—A Radical View.* Englewood Cliffs, NJ: Prentice Hall.

Shaw, Clifford. 1929. *Delinquency Areas: A Study of the Geographical Distribution of School Truants, Juvenile Delinquents, and Adult Offenders in Chicago.* Chicago: University of Chicago Press.

Shichor, David and Dale Sechrest (eds.). 1996. *Three Strikes and You're Out: Vengeance as Public Policy.* Thousand Oaks, CA: Sage.

Simon, Jonathan. 1987. "The Rise of Risk: Insurance, Law & the State." *Socialist Review* 95:61–89.

———. 1993. *Poor Discipline: Parole and the Social Control of the Underclass, 1890–1990.* Chicago: University of Chicago Press.

———. 1994. "Ghosts of the Disciplinary Machine: Lee Harvey Oswald, Life-History, and the Truth of Crime." *Yale Journal of Law and the Humanities* 10:75–113.

———. 1997. "Governing through Crime." Pp. 171–90 in *The Crime Conundrum: Essays on Criminal Justice,* edited by George Fisher and Lawrence Friedman. Boulder, CO: Westview.

———. 1998a. "Managing the Monsters: Sex Offenders and the New Penology." *Psychology, Public Policy and the Law* 3:452–67.

———. 1998b. "Refugees in a Carceral Age: The Rebirth of Immigration Prisons in the United States." *Public Culture* 10:577–606.

———. 2000. "The 'Society of Captives' in the Era of Hyper-Incarceration." *Theoretical Criminology* 4:285–307.

Skogan, Wesley G. 1990. *Disorder and Decline: Crime and the Spiral of Decay in American Neighborhoods.* New York: Free Press.

Skolnick, Jerome and David A. Bayley. 1986. *The New Blue Line.* New York: Free Press.

Spierenberg, Pieter. 1984. *The Spectacle of Suffering: Executions and the Evolution of Repression: From a Preindustrial Metropolis to the European Experience.* Cambridge: Cambridge University Press.

Steiner, Henry. 1987. *Moral Vision and Social Vision in the Court: A Study of Tort Accident Law.* Madison, WI: University of Wisconsin Press.

Sutherland, Edwin H. 1937. *The Professional Thief.* Chicago: University of Chicago Press.

Tyler, Tom and Robert Boeckman. 1997. "Three Strikes and You're Out, But Why?

The Psychology of Public Support for Punishment Rule Breakers." *Law and Society Review* 33:331.

Von Hirsch, Andrew, David Garland, and Alison Wakefield (eds.). 2000. *Ethical and Social Perspectives on Situational Crime Prevention*. Oxford: Hart.

Wakefield, Alison. 2000. "Situational Crime Prevention in Mass Private Property." Pp. 125–46 in *Ethical and Social Perspectives on Situational Crime Prevention*, edited by Andrew Von Hirsch, et al. Oxford: Hart.

Walker, Samuel. 1993. *Taming the System: The Control of Discretion in Criminal Justice: 1950–1990*. New York: Oxford University Press.

Walters, Thomas Franklin. 1994. "Is There Really a New Penology? Evidence to the Contrary." Paper presented at the Annual Meeting of the American Society of Criminology, Miami, Florida.

Weibe, Robert. 1967. *The Search for Order, 1877–1920*. New York: Hill & Wang.

White, Susan O. and Samuel Krislov. 1977. *Understanding Crime: An Evaluation of the National Institute of Law Enforcement and Criminal Justice*. Washington, DC: National Academy of Science.

Wilson, James Q. and George Kelling. 1982. "Broken Windows." *Atlantic Monthly* March, pp. 29–38.

Wilson, William J. 1987. *The Truly Disadvantaged: The Inner City, the Underclass, and Public Policy*. Chicago: University of Chicago Press.

Windlesham, Lord. 1993. *Responses to Crime*, Vol. 2, *Penal Policy in the Making*. Oxford: Clarendon.

Windlesham, Lord. 1996. *Responses to Crime*, Vol. 3, *Legislating with the Tide*. Oxford: Clarendon.

Windlesham, Lord. 1998. *Politics, Punishment, and Populism*. New York: Oxford University Press.

Winter, Stephen. 1989. "Transcendental Nonsense, Metaphoric Reasoning, and the Cognitive Stakes for Law." *University of Pennsylvania Law Review* 137:1105.

Wolfgang, Marvin E., Robert Figlio, and Thorsten Sellin. 1972. *Delinquency in a Birth Cohort*. Chicago: University of Chicago Press.

Young, Jock. 1999. *From Inclusive to Exclusive Society: Nightmares in the European Dream*. London: Sage.

4

Virginia, Criminology, and the Antisocial Control of Women

Pat Carlen

I thought how unpleasant it is to be locked out; and I thought how it is worse perhaps to be locked in.
—Virginia Woolf, *A Room of One's Own*

INTRODUCTION

In 1938, nine years after the publication of her much acclaimed *A Room of One's Own*, Virginia Woolf published *Three Guineas*. It was a book that discomforted some of her family and friends, and it predictably provoked the wrath and derision of her enemies (Bell 1984; Nicolson 1980). For unlike the playful and elegant *Room of One's Own*, which brings an incisive humor to the exposition and analysis of women's inequitable educational opportunities, *Three Guineas* is a passionate and scathing polemic making sustained and condemnatory comparisons between masculism and militarism; between patriarchy and fascism. I had just finished reading it for the first time when I was asked to write this chapter on women and social control. And it seemed to me, as I thought about the meanings of "social control," and the political conundrum posed in *Three Guineas*, that distinguishing between "social control" and "antisocial control" might be a useful way of thinking about both Virginia's conundrum and the puzzle confronting campaigners intent on remedying the wrongs done to women within the criminal justice system. I refer to the dilemma faced by all excluded and oppressed peoples—the question of how they can best penetrate an exclusionary and oppressive structure without their revolutionary objectives being nullified through incorporation into the (thereby strengthened) oppressive structure in question.

The rest of this essay is divided into four parts. The first outlines Virginia's "inclusion/exclusion" conundrum and discusses its relevance to "justice for women" campaigns. (See Carlen [2002a], Hannah-Moffat [2001], Hannah-Moffat and Shaw [2000], for analyses of some of the struggles engaged in at the beginning of this century.) The second examines the concepts of social and antisocial control before going on to discuss their theoretical capacity to inform analysis of the exclusionary and inclusionary modes of social and antisocial control experienced by women. The third part argues that the informal and antisocial control of women is constituted within exclusionary and inclusionary practices, which both preempt and buttress women's (relatively infrequent) criminalization and imprisonment. Then, by way of conclusion, the fourth part returns to Virginia's conundrum and asks, What is to be done?

VIRGINIA'S CONUNDRUM
AND ITS RELEVANCE TO CRIMINOLOGY

Three Guineas was conceived as a sequel to *A Room of One's Own* but it was written in very different circumstances. In 1937 the threat of fascist aggression haunted Europe and in July of that year, when Virginia Woolf was in the middle of writing *Three Guineas*, her nephew Julian Bell was killed in Spain, driving an ambulance for the noncombatant organization Spanish Medical Aid. In *Three Guineas* the author rages at the futility and waste of war; at men's love of uniforms and the seeming continuum between patriarchal mores, militarism, and fascism; and at a societal hypocrisy that, while publicly idolizing women as daughters, wives, and mothers, ruthlessly excluded them from all the public institutions wherein they might be better equipped to contest the aggression and bellicosity of men. The savagery of the ridicule heaped on men and their exclusive and exclusionary institutions may even today startle any reader expecting to find in *Three Guineas* the urbanity of style that characterizes *A Room*. Yet the two books have themes in common: both lay emphasis on the extraordinary feat of (anti-)social control whereby women are both included in and excluded from societies that accord them heavy responsibilities without similarly according them powers and privileges; and both develop this theme to a greater degree (in *Room*) or lesser degree (in *Three Guineas*) by detailing women's exclusion from the level of educational opportunity allowed to men. In *Three Guineas*, however, two other concerns are given equal space: questions about the similarities between patriarchy and fascism; and questions about the possibilities of women entering, and being empowered by, male-dominated institutions, without acquiescing in (and thereby strengthening) the antisocial practices of supremacy and domination fashioned by men to preserve patriarchal social relations.

But what has all this to do with present-day analyses of the social control of women, of contemporary campaigns for justice for women within the criminal justice system? A great deal. For Virginia Woolf's concerns of the 1930s can be translated into the following distinctly criminological questions of the early twenty-first century:

1. What are the relationships between social justice for women and criminal justice for women?

2. How does the informal antisocial control of women (physical, institutional, and ideological) preempt and buttress women's relatively infrequent criminalization and imprisonment?

3. How can analyses of the informal antisocial control of women inform criminal justice campaigns without initiating nonprogressive changes that merely result in (a) more women being dealt with by the criminal courts without any diminution of the antisocial controls brought to bear on them both within and without the criminal justice system; and (b) a concomitant strengthening of the sexist, racist, and class-biased nature of the formal justice systems?

SOCIAL CONTROL AND ANTISOCIAL CONTROL

For analytic purposes, social control is a vacuous term. Unless closely defined it can imply anything from "conspiracy theories," which hold that in any society—"capitalist," "patriarchal" "communist," "fascist," and so on—every social practice is "really" part of a "social control" process (regardless of other ends it may appear to serve), to a very narrow definition that refers only to the state's official apparatuses for controlling crime and other prohibited behaviors. For my purpose here—that of analyzing the different types of "controls" experienced by women—I shall use the following definitions:

Social control: a generic term for a variety of benign institutionalized practices designed to set limits to individual action in the interests of the collectivity's proclaimed ideals of social and criminal justice as instanced in law and dominant ideologies.

Antisocial control: a generic term for a variety of malign institutionalized practices that may *either* set limits to individual action by favoring one set of citizens at the expense of another so as to subvert equal-opportunities ideologies in relation to gender, race, and class (or other social groupings), or (in societies without equal-opportunities ideologies) set limits to individual action in ways that are antisocial because they atrophy an individual's social contribution the grounds of either biological attributes or exploitative social relations.

The advantage of these formal definitions when analyzing the main modes of controlling women both within and without social and criminal justice systems is at least threefold. First, they help avoid libertarian implications that all "social control" is "a bad thing." Second, they help avoid the circularity of conspiracy-type theories, which imply that as a majority of legal and other state bureaucracies have traditionally been dominated by men, *all* their laws, rules, and practices must necessarily be always and already in the interests of men and against those of women (see Cousins 1978, 1980). And third, they allow the same substantive practices to be theorized differently according to the differing combinations of economic, ideological, and political conditions in which they are realized. Thus, for instance (and to illustrate all three foregoing points) the contemporary ideology of child-centeredness encapsulated in the phrase "good parenting" might be seen as a positively benign form of social control when actualized in a society where all have equal opportunities and responsibilities to be "good parents." But it may equally be seen as being a very antisocial form of control in societies where some parents are always-already prevented from being "good parents" by their adverse economic circumstances; or in societies where responsibility for "good parenting" falls systematically upon mothers rather than fathers (or vice versa). In the former example, "good parenting" ideology may be seen as a form of antisocial control because it includes under its "ideal" rule those who are in fact excluded from it by their social circumstances; in the latter example, it may be construed as being an antisocial control because it subverts a society's equal-opportunities rhetoric. In conventional criminological terms, of course, the "anomie" experienced by those concomitantly included under a rule and excluded from the conditions necessary to its fulfillment is a frequent precursor (if not cause) of crime; and the poverty-stricken women who have perennially justified their stealing or soliciting by claiming that "it was only done to feed my kids" are usually seen to have a point (though not one strong enough to absolve them from guilt and its subsequent punishment).

The definitions of social and antisocial control discussed above will now inform this essay's analytic overview of the main ways in which the informal anti- (and ante-)social control of women has both preempted and buttressed their more formal (but relatively infrequent) control by the police, courts, and prisons, as well as by other regulatory agencies such as mental hospitals and welfare bureaucracies.

WOMEN: IN AND OUT OF CONTROL

During the last three decades there has been a much more sustained focus upon the control of women by formal and informal means than there had been prior to the mid-1970s. (For a comparative perspective on the search for a feminist jurisprudence, see Boyle et al. [1985] for Canada; Dahl [1987] for Norway; MacKinnon [1987], Fineman and Thomadsen [1991] for the United States; Redcar [1990], Grbich [1991], Howe [1994] for Australia; and Smart [1989], Bibbings and Nicolson [2000] for England; Hahn Rafter and Heidensohn [1995] for a wide-ranging international collection.) Dominant constructs informing analyses of the control of women have been those relating to control via the politicoeconomic institutions of family, marriage, and welfare; control via the economic systems and ideological structures of patriarchy; control via the ideologies of femininity and the menace and effects of masculist discourses; and, more formally, the sexist, racist, and class-biased control of women in the criminal justice and penal systems. In overviewing the different dimensions of the antisocial control of women, I shall be arguing that they all emanate from the power of one fundamental ideological mechanism for keeping women "in their place": the fracturing of women's subjectivities within complex and contradictory discourses that insist on women's essential "power for good" (femininity) at the same time as engendering social relationships wherein discourses of femininity are incorporated into "Other" discourses ("masculism"—Brittan 1989:4) justifying a close ideological and physical control of women's biological, emotional, and intellectual powers.[1] Anne Worrall has described the anguish of being always and already Other.

> Women . . . are always-already *not men*. Femininity is constructed on the site vacated by masculinity, and this absence of maleness is manifested in two opposing sets of expectations (Eichenbaum and Orbach 1983). On the one hand, femininity is characterised by self-control and independence. Being a normal woman means coping, caring. . . . On the other hand, femininity is characterised by lack of control and dependence. Being a normal woman means needing protection (Hutter and Williams 1981). It means being child-like, incapable, fragile and capricious. . . . The centrality to the construction of femininity of the dilemma of having to be both "in control" and "out of control" poses a routine problem. (Worrall 1990:3,8; cf. Chesler 1974; Allen 1987)

For women, then, the Kafkaesque anterooms of the criminal courts are to be found in the simultaneity of the inclusionary and exclusionary devices of the antisocial family, the antisocial state, and the antisocial practices and discourses of men's violence, men's rea, men's rule, and male menace. Given the strength and elasticity of these informal controls, it is not surprising that the formal system of control has seldom to be invoked against women; nor that, when women are on trial, the courts are doubly punitive toward those who are seen already to have eluded or violated informal gender controls. Theorists have focused on informal controls when analyzing the (anti)social control of women, and it is to three dimensions of these antecedent controls that we will now turn before examining the formal control of women by the courts, prisons, and other regulatory agencies.[2]

Women: In and Out of the Antisocial Family

The strength of the best studies analyzing the social control of white, Western women within the politicoeconomic institution of the family lies first in their historical specificity even though, alas, their *cultural* specificity is too often glossed over. Second, it inheres in a thoroughgoing materialism that, in prioritizing analyses of the social conditions in which women's physical and economic control is accomplished, at the same time is also able to facilitate explanation of the modes of control wherein their *subjective* coercion is achieved. A good example of this type of study is that of Ehrenreich and English, which was published in 1979 and entitled *For Her Own Good*. Subtitled "150 Years of the Experts' Advice to Women," the book shows how nineteenth- and early twentieth-century experts controlled women (and taught middle-class "ladies" how to control working class "housewives") via an attractive mix of rationalist and romanticist discourses that both objectified women's sexuality in the service of men, and denied them their independence for the "good of the family." (See Smart 1992 for a collection of feminist historical essays on the regulation of marriage, motherhood, and sexuality.) As Zedner, also writing on women in Victorian England, has stressed,

> although women gained considerable power within the limited sphere of their influence, in order to protect their own purity they were admonished to leave the house as little as possible. (1991:14)

The woman "simply by being a model of chastity, altruism and morality was supposed to induce men to raise themselves to her level of virtue" (ibid.:17–18). While discriminatory laws relating to public life, education, and the professions combined to keep middle-class women in their place (see Sachs and Wilson 1978), the interrelated institutions of marriage, wage-labor and prostitution kept working-class wives and daughters in theirs. For, though poverty-stricken women might have reason enough to be oft-tempted to rebel against man or master, they had equal reason to fear that no destiny other than prostitution would be the fate of anyone foolhardy enough to risk being cast out "characterless" by either husband or employer. Thus, historically, women have been expected to subject themselves first and perennially to the family—in obedience to the rhetoric that "good mothers make good families make good societies." Then, contradictorily but simultaneously, they have been expected to accept, and be regulated by, an alternative but equally powerful ideology—that the family itself must forever be at the service of the military, the markets, and the man.

Women: In and Out of the Antisocial State

But did women ever have *so* much power within the home? If one examines closely the public/private distinction ("public" referring to the worlds of work, war, and state; "private" to those of family, intimate relationships, etc.) it is easy to establish that the "privacy of the home" ideology has functioned primarily to allow all kinds of physical and sexual abuses to proceed unchecked on the patriarchal assumption that a "man's home is his castle." Moreover, even when domestic violence has not been lacerating families from within, war and poverty have been routinely destroying them from without. Throughout the twentieth century British women were routinely called upon to encourage their men to go to war, *and* twice were called upon to leave their children in order that they themselves might go out to work for the war machine. The wars over, women were then required to give up their jobs to the men, being reminded that their first priority is *of course* with their children once more—until the next time (Woolf [1929] 1989, [1938] 1986:161–63)! However, by the end of the 1940s, it was already being realized that regular war and poverty cycles might no longer be depended upon to discipline families sufficiently to meet the needs of markets. So, the agents of state welfare control made their debuts. Physically, they policed the homes of the poor via their social workers. Ideologically, they interpellated mothers of all classes via the "psy" and "expert" pedagogies of "good parenting" and "child centred familiness" (Donzelot 1979; Rose 1989). Nowadays, women who either cannot or will not pay obeisance to *all* of these opposed ideologies (women who, as one might put it more figuratively, refuse to keep so many balls in the air at once) are likely to be made examples of—by the media, by welfare regulation, or by the courts. Two striking examples from the 1980s were the Greenham Common (antiwar) Women and, most recently, unmarried mothers on welfare.

The founding of the women's anti–cruise missile camp at Greenham Common in 1981 started a women's movement for peace that achieved worldwide acclaim. Its members braved hard weather conditions, separation from families and friends, media derision, arrest, and in some cases, imprisonment. And for over a decade "they were vilified by some of the British tabloids—as dirty lesbians, soviet stooges, [and] irresponsible wives and mothers" (Coote and Campbell 1987:50). In the long tradition of punitive obloquy directed at women who attempt to link feminism and pacifism:

> The women of Greenham Common came in for a particularly nasty brand of misogynist reporting, which characterised them as dirty violent scroungers who were probably in the pay of Moscow. Worse still, the homophobic press invariably described them as lesbians in such a way as to denigrate all lesbians, and by association all Greenham women. (ibid.: 280)

The media's pillorying of unmarried mothers on welfare was, in the 1990s, sparked both by the work of conservative American "underclass" theorist Charles Murray (1984, 1990) and by a British media-inspired scare about persistent young criminals. According to Murray, underclass poor were to be found in neighborhoods containing high numbers of fatherless families reared by unmarried mothers. Having been reared by "permissive" mothers, and a "supportive" welfare state, underclass young men were portrayed as refusing to work and, in lieu of labor, engaging in violent crime. This interlinking of "welfare dependency," single parenthood, undisciplined children, and crime in an unbroken causal chain also coincided with two 1990s concerns: real doubts about the actual success and future redistributionist potential of Western welfare systems, and (in Britain at least) a conservative backlash against feminist struggles for increased female dependence from male-related domesticity. The imagery used by Murray and other underclass theorists was one of disease and infection, a continuation of a long tradition in which misogyny has combined with exploitative class relationships to ensure that "undeserving" poor women have been represented both in life and literature as being especially invidious bearers of social and moral contagion. On the war fronts they have been stigmatized as venereally diseased prostitutes weakening the physical strength of the British army. In the property stakes, they have (like Dumas's *Lady of the Camellias* [1986]) been represented as sexual adventurers threatening class structures by bringing the contagion of the gutter right into the heart of bourgeois society. Murray's solution to "his" problem would have involved a "ghettoization" of underclass families into separate neighborhoods. In the 1980s, governmental responses to increases in single parenthood included increased regulation of women on welfare (see Cook 1988) and occasional threats to develop new policies to "deter" women from choosing to rear children apart from men.

Greenham women took seriously the social values of protecting and nurturing children by rejecting militarism. Single mothers on welfare take seriously their duties to their children—but without embracing male-related domesticity and thereby testing the limits to welfarism in an increasingly illiberal welfare state. For their pains (and for opposing militarism and bucking market morality) they are repeatedly subject to exclusionary and antisocial control measures, antecedent to their regulation (or not) by more formal measures.

Women: In and Out of Men's Violence, Men's Rea, Men's Rule, Male Menace—and an Antisocial Masculism

The antisocial regulation of women has always been as much physical as ideological. Physical exclusion from public space, public institutions, and workplaces has primarily been managed via law, economy, and tradition. Sexual and physical regulation within the home and on the streets has been via either threatened or actual male violence and the peculiar mix of gender ideologies that engender such violence and facilitate its persistence

(Adler 1989; Carrington 1999; Dworkin 1981; Radford and Russell 1992; Stanko 2001). Additionally, from the mid-twentieth century onwards, a further subjection of women has been achieved: by harnessing media and markets in a double targeting of women's bodies as new sites of anxiety and guilt—about body weight, personal appearance, and sexuality (Coward 1984; McRobbie 1991). For women unable to cope, there have been the (overprescribed) tranquillizers and the (oversubscribed) mental hospitals (Chesler 1974; Sim 1990). When men and women have been locked in courtroom battles, again and again the judicial concept of *men's rea* has operated only to reflect an empiricist rationality based on men's worldly experiences, not women's (see Carlen 1993). As Brittan (1989:4) has succinctly put it, "the ideology that justifies and naturalizes male domination" is "masculism." And masculism is already antisocial because

> masculism as an ideology universalizes "man" as the "maker" of history. . . . Man is the "subject" of history. . . . But what this history has glossed and ignored is the systematic objectification of women by men. (ibid.:174)

Drawing the same parallels between masculism and fascism that Virginia Woolf insisted upon, Brittan quotes Theweleit, who noted:

> What fascism promised men was the reintegration of their hostile components under tolerable conditions, dominance of the hostile "female" element within themselves. This explains why the word "boundaries" in fascist parlance, refers primarily to the boundaries of the body. (Theweleit 1987, quoted in Brittan 1989:frontispiece)

In the next section it will be argued that the British criminal justice system is inseminated by a masculism that in denoting crime a male preserve objectifies women who have dared to be other than Other. Such objectification of women within the criminal justice and penal systems is antisocial in that it is one of the two main causes of the liberal state's failure to take seriously the crimes of both men and women. At the boundaries of law— and always calling it into question—today's marketeering and militia men are much more violent and ruthless than they ever were in the 1930s.

Women: In and Out of the Courts, Prisons, and Other Regulatory Agencies

During the 1990s the numbers of women given custodial sentences in Western societies steeply increased (see Cook and Davies 1999). Yet, the moment of sentence is only the endpoint of a series of class-, race-, and gender-biased negotiations, the outcomes of which make criminal women either more or less vulnerable to acquiring the gender-deviant bad characters that result in their receiving harsher sentences than either men or their more conventional sisters. To understand gender biases in criminal justice it is advisable to look not only at sentencing patterns but also to detail the ways in which unconventional, troublesome, or criminal women are discriminated against from the time when they first come to the attention of the state's regulatory agencies.

Since the 1940s when the welfare state ideal was premised on the right to the relief of need, the practice of social work in England and elsewhere has focused on the policing of families in general (Donzelot 1979; Meyer 1977; Carrington, 1993) and the pedagogic regulation of women in particular (Wilson 1977). In exchange for material assistance, twentieth- and twenty-first-century women, especially working-class mothers, have been subjected to an increase of that tutelary supervision (Donzelot 1979) that their predecessors suffered at the hands of late-nineteenth- and early-twentieth-century middle-class charity organizations (Ehrenreich and English 1979). Most women who end up in penal custody, however, have been under state supervision at an earlier age and usually for a nonpenal reason—for example, because their parents are unable to look after them.

In court, girls not living with their families are viewed by sentencers as already being out of their proper place (that is, the family) and are therefore likely to be dealt with more harshly. Older women who have been brought up in state care are often so vehemently against further contact with social workers that they choose to go to prison rather than agree to a renewal of supervision under a noncustodial order (Carlen 1988).

Although there is statistical evidence to support claims that at least some female offenders in England are treated more leniently than men by both the police and the courts (Hedderman and Hough 1994; Hedderman and Gelsthorpe 1997), official figures still indicate that convicted women are guilty of less serious crimes than men and, when given a custodial sentence, are more likely to be imprisoned for a minor crime of theft than for any more serious offence. Even when women have been *victims* of crime, police (and other criminal justice personnel) have often treated them as offenders (see Carrington [1999] for a most significant Australian case study). This has been especially so in cases of rape (Adler 1989); the sexual abuse of adolescent girls (Morgan and Zedner, 1992); and domestic violence (Dobash and Dobash, 1979). Conversely, women found guilty of serious crimes have frequently received more noncustodial sentences than males convicted of similar offenses (Allen, 1987). However, that pattern of more lenient sentencing may now have changed, and the steep rise in female imprisonment in England in the 1990s may have occurred because, as Worrall has recently argued, women who would not previously have received custodial sentences are now being "rendered punishable" in the name of "equality" of sentencing between men and women (Worrall 2002). Whether that be so or not, there are still a number of other social factors that make certain women more prone to a custodial than a noncustodial sentence. They include:

• The inability of many criminal justice personnel to make sense of their female clients whom they often perceive as being less rational and more devious than their male clients (see Worrall, 1990).
• The courtroom domination by the metaphor of the "reasonable man," which can bias the logic of the proceedings against women. For example, the questioning of rape victims or women on charges of carrying offensive weapons or assaulting males is frequently based on moralistic assumptions about what *moral* women *should* do when threatened with rape or attack that are quite opposed to what *reasonable* women with prior experience of male violence actually do (Carlen and Worrall, 1987).
• The relative scarcity of suitable noncustodial programs and hostels for women (as compared with those for men), which result in either probation officers being reluctant to recommend mixed programs and hostels for women who have already suffered male violence or other abuse (see Carlen 1996:67), or women in mixed schemes failing to complete their orders and thus being made more vulnerable to harsher sentences if they should reoffend.
• The general paucity of child-care provision, which makes attendance at noncustodial schemes difficult for mothers with young children.
• The tendency of some officials to recommend custody for pregnant women on the grounds that their material circumstances are so poor that their babies will be better off in prison (Carlen 1998).

Sentencing practices and criminological and popular theories that have repeatedly implied that women criminals and prisoners are either mad, masculine, menopausal, or maladjusted (to conventional female roles) have resulted not only in a denial that they are "real" women, "real" criminals, and "real" prisoners but also in claims that women's prisons are not "real" prisons (Carlen, 1983). Nothing could be further from the truth.

Education, work, and leisure opportunities in many of the women's prisons in Britain, Canada, Australia, and the United States are limited, disciplinary regimes are rigid. The disproportionate numbers of discipline charges leveled against female as compared with male prisoners in Britain result both from regimes that aggravate and multiply the problems that many women already have when they go to prison, and from discriminatory social ideologies that demand higher standards of behavior from women than from men. Moreover, many women feel that prison doctors are unsympathetic about gynecological issues, drug problems, and the many nervous ailments related to their present domestic circumstances and/or their previous sociobiographies as (often abused) daughters, wives, and/or mothers (Ramsbotham 1997; Owen 1998; Malloch 2000).

A number of ideologies constantly undermine attempts to diminish the deprivations suffered by female prisoners.

• The numbers game: The most frequently expressed explanation of inadequacies in custodial provision for women is that as there are relatively few female prisoners it would be uneconomical to provide the range of penal facilities available to males. (The relatively *small* number of women prisoners has also always been used to justify the imprisonment of women far from their homes.)

• Women's prisons must be "real" prisons: Although women's prison regimes have constantly been adapted to the so-called special disciplinary needs of women—that is, their "need" (as deviating women) to be feminized, medicalized, domesticized, and infantilized—the overriding ideological notion that women prisoners should not be better off than their male counterparts has in England resulted in a concomitant demand that pregnancy, motherhood, and other physical and emotional states related to female biology should not result in women prisoners having special privileges. As a consequence, especially high behaviorial standards are expected of pregnant prisoners and inmates in mother and baby units. Allowing imprisoned mothers to have their babies with them or even to receive visits from their children is seen as a privilege, not a right; and the question of continued access to their children is routinely used as another disciplinary weapon in the armory of controls available to the administrators of the women's prisons. More recently both Hannah-Moffat (2001) and Carlen (2002b) have described how even feminist reforming discourses have been incorporated into the program rationales of women's prisons, with the result that prison legitimacy has been strengthened and women resisting penal programming have been consequently defined as authors of their own misfortunes and therefore even more deserving of punishment.

• The main concerns of women prisoners relate to personal relationships: The ideology that women are essentially creatures living primarily according to their emotions and dependent upon personal relationships to give meaning to their lives has not only been responsible for the dependency-inducing domesticity inherent in penal regimes for women, it has also recently resulted in the inception of a variety of in-prison psychologistic "programs" that, in conflating and replacing social need with "criminogenic" risk, have also arguably played a part in legitimating the imprisonment of more and more young women (Kendall 2002)

WHAT IS TO BE DONE?

So back to Virginia's conundrum—and as translated into a gender problem about criminal justice, the question is: How can the criminal justice system be made more user-friendly for women? The short answer is that it cannot be—not without a massive change in present mores in relation to male violence and masculinist principles of (anti-)social (dis-)organization. The reasons are twofold. First, whatever liberal changes are made in the courts (and in recent years some important changes in British judicial attitudes toward women *have* occurred [Kennedy 1992]) the contemporary daily diet of media violence routinely and effectively elevates the rule of male violence above the rule of state law. And if this seems an extreme statement, try to conjure up a picture of *women* engaged in military maneuvers or dramatization involving gun law/lore. It is difficult. Rather, you will find that

> another picture has imposed itself upon the foreground. It is the figure of a man; some say, others deny, that he is Man himself, the quintessence of virility, the perfect type of which all the others are imperfect adumbrations. He is a man certainly. His eyes are glazed; his eyes glare. His body, which is braced in an unnatural position, is tightly cased in a uniform. Upon the breast of that uniform are sewn several medals and other mystic symbols. He is called in German or Italian Führer or Duce; in our own language Tyrant or Dictator. And behind him lie ruined houses and dead bodies—men, women and children. (Woolf [1938] 1986:162)

Arguably, more so in the early twenty-first century than in the 1990s. However, unlike the 1930s, nowadays this celebration of worldwide male violence can be relayed to our homes nightly. For not only are TV audiences around the world injected with a round-the-clock imagery of uniformed males killing each other on the world's battlefields, such "news" is routinely supplemented by cosier (and "sexier") "entertainment" comprising "domestic" dramas in which *men* star as adepts at gun (and other types of) violence.

But second, and much more important, criminal justice reforms are only of indirect importance to women because the greater (and most effective part) of the antisocial control that inseminates their lives is not accomplished by the criminal justice system at all. It is effected informally and antisocially: by the threat and reality of male violence and the continuing exclusion of women from the corridors of power.

Let us, therefore, translate Virginia's conundrum into a broader question of what is to be done about the informal and antisocial control of women. The analyses of this chapter suggest some radical answers. Generally, it seems that women should refuse and resist all antisocial controls in the form of social constraints imposed by masculism. In specific and substantive terms this would at the least involve supporting a variety of household forms other than those of the conventional family type; refusing to countenance all forms of militarism, nationalism, racism, and class exploitation; and resisting all attacks on women's bodies, whether they be by men of violence, media sexual objectification, or marketeering cosmetic or diet "laws." The argument is that, by destroying the informal antisocial controls on women, we may simultaneously refashion the formal controls, re-forming them to be nondiscriminatory and thereby fully social. Then, and not till then, may we have a chance of meeting Virginia's challenge (see Woolf [1938] 1986:78) to cease to be victims of patriarchy, without becoming champions of capitalism.

NOTES

1. Several campaigning authors and feminists have recently criticized structural analyses of the discriminatory effects of institutionalized gender ideologies on the grounds that they always represent women as victims, thereby denying women the agency to resist. As I have argued elsewhere (Carlen 1994) structural analyses are merely a conceptual device for analyzing a specific object of inquiry—here the antisocial control of women. They can no more deny to women the capacity to resist oppression than more voluntaristic analyses can endow them with that same capacity. However, analyses such as Bosworth (1999) and Denton (2001) do indeed provide a corrective to the implication of some social control perspectives that women are always and already passive victims in face of institutionalized oppression.

2. As I have argued elsewhere (Carlen 1993) I am not committed to always privileging gender in explanations of women's oppression; in many specific instances it would be more appropriate to privilege racism or class exploitation. In this essay, however, I do privilege gender. Similarly, the criminal justice system is not the major locus of social control for men. However, men's informal control *qua* men is accomplished via inclusionary *social* control devices such as work and public associations (though, of course, some men also experience an antisocial control via the exclusionary structures of racism , class oppression, and uncongenial gender role demands).

REFERENCES

Adler, Z. 1989. *Rape on Trial.* London: Routledge and Kegan Paul.
Allen, H. 1987. *Justice Unbalanced.* Buckingham: Open University Press.
Bell, A. O. (Ed.). 1984. *The Diary of Virginia Woolf,* Vol. V: 1936–1941. London: Hogarth.
Bibbings, L. and D. Nicolson. 2000. *Feminist Perspectives on Criminal Law.* Oxford: Clarendon.
Bosworth, M. 1999. *Engendering Resistance; Agency and Power in Women's Prisons.* Aldershot: Ashgate.
Brittan, A. 1989. *Masculinity and Power.* Oxford: Blackwell.
Carlen, P. 1983. *Women's Imprisonment.* London: Routledge and Kegan Paul.

———. 1988. *Women, Crime and Poverty.* Buckingham: Open University Press.

———. 1993. "Women, Structural Inequalities and Criminal Justice." Pp. 134–36 in *Inequality, Crime and Social Control,* edited by G. Bridges and M. Myers. Toronto: Westview.

———. 1994. "Why study women's imprisonment? Or anyone else's?" *British Journal of Criminology.* Special Issue.

———. 1996. *Jigsaw: A Political Criminology of Youth Homelessness.* Buckingham: Open University Press.

———. 1998. *Sledgehammer: Women's Imprisonment at the Millennium.* London: Macmillan.

———. 2002a. "Controlling Measures: The Repackaging of Commonsense Opposition to Women's Imprisonment in England and Canada." *Criminal Justice* 2:22:155–72.

———. 2002b. *Women and Punishment: The Struggle for Justice.* Cullumpton: Willan.

Carlen, P. and A. Worrall (Eds.). 1987. *Gender, Crime and Justice.* Buckingham: Open University Press.

Carrington, K. 1993. *Offending Girls: Sex, Youth and Justice.* Sydney: Allen and Unwin.

———. 1999. *Who Killed Leigh Leigh? A Story of Shame and Mateship in an Australian Town.* Sydney: Random House.

Chesler, P. 1974. *Women and Madness.* London: Allen Lane.

Cook, D. 1988. *Rich Law, Poor Law.* Buckingham: Open University Press.

Cook, S. and S. Davies 1999. *Harsh Punishment: International Experiences of Women's Imprisonment.* Boston: Northeastern University Press.

Coote, A. and B. Campbell. 1987. *Sweet Freedom,* 2nd ed. Oxford: Basil Blackwell.

Cousins, M. 1978. "Material Arguments and Feminism." *m/f* 2.

———. 1980. "Men's rea." Pp. 109–02 in *Radical Issues in Criminology,* edited by P. Carlen and M. Collison. Oxford: Martin Robertson.

Coward, R. 1984. *Female Desire.* London: Paladin.

Dahl, T. S. 1987. *Women's Law: An Introduction to Feminist Jurisprudence.* Oslo: Norwegian University Press.

Denton, B. 2001. *Dealing: Women in the Drug Economy.* Sydney, University of New South Wales Press.

Donzelot, J. 1979. *The Policing of Families.* New York: Pantheon.

Dumas, A. 1986. *La Dame Aux Camélias.* Oxford: Penguin.

Dworkin, A. 1981. *Pornography: Men Possessing Women.* London: Women's Press.

Ehrenreich, B. and D. English. 1979. *For Her Own Good.* London: Pluto.

Eichenbaum, L. and S. Orbach. 1983. *What Do Women Want?* London: Michael Joseph.

Fineman, M. and N. Thomadsen (eds.). 1991. *At the Boundaries of Law.* New York: Routledge.

Grbich, J. 1991. "The Body in Legal Theory." Pp. 61–76 in *At the Boundaries of Law,* edited by M. Fineman and N. Thomadsen. New York: Routledge.

Hahn Rafter, N. and F. Heidensohn 1994. *International Feminist Perspectives in Criminology.* Buckingham: Open University Press.

Hannah-Moffat, K. 2001. *Punishment in Disguise.* Toronto: University of Toronto Press.

Hannah-Moffat, K. and M. Shaw 2000. *An Ideal Prison?* Halifax, Nova Scotia: Fernwood.

Hedderman, C. and L. Gelsthorpe. 1997. *Understanding the Sentencing of Women.* London: HMSO.

Hedderman, C. and M. Hough. 1994. "Does the Criminal Justice System Treat Men and Women Differently?" *Research Findings* 10:4. London: Home Office Research and Statistics Department.

Howe, A. 1994. *Punish and Critique.* London: Routledge.

Hutter, B. and G. Williams. 1981. *Controlling Women.* London: Croom Helm.

Kendall, K. 2002. "Time to Think Again About Cognitive Behavioural Programmes." Pp. 182–98 in *Women and Punishment: The Struggle for Justice,* edited by P. Carlen. Collumpton: Willan.

Kennedy, H. 1992. *Eve Was Framed.* London: Chatto and Windus.

MacKinnon, C. 1987. "Feminism, Marxism, Method and the State: Toward Feminist Jurisprudence." in *Feminism and Methodology,* edited by S. Harding. Buckingham: Open University Press.

Malloch, M. 2000. *Women, Drugs and Dealing.* Winchester: Waterside.

McRobbie, A. 1991. *Feminism and Youth Culture.* London: Macmillan.

Meyer, P. 1977. *The Child and the State.* Cambridge: Cambridge University Press.

Morgan, J. and L. Zedner. 1992. *Child Victims of Crime.* Oxford: Clarendon.

Murray, C. 1984. *Losing Ground: American Social Policy. 1950 –1980.* New York: Basic Books.

———. 1990. *The Emerging British Underclass.* London: Institute of Economic Affairs.

Nicolson, N. 1980. *Leave The Letters Till We're Dead: The Letters of Virginia Woolf. 1936–1941.* London: Hogarth.

Owen, B. 1998. *In the Mix: Struggle and Survival in a Women's Prison.* Albany: SUNY Press.

Radford, J. and D. Russell (Eds.). 1992. *Femicide.* Buckingham: Open University Press.

Ramsbotham, D. 1997. *Women in Prison: A Thematic Review by Her HM Chief Inspector of Prisons.* London: Home Office.

Redcar, R. (Ed.). 1990. *Dissenting Opinions.* Sydney: Allen and Unwin.

Rose, N. 1989. *Governing The Soul.* London: Routledge.

Sachs, A. and J. Wilson. 1978. *Sexism and The Law.* Oxford: Martin Robertson.

Smart, C. 1989. *Feminism and The Power of Law.* London: Routledge.

———. (ed.). 1992. *Regulating Womanhood.* London: Routledge.

Stanko, E. 2001. "The Day to Count: Reflections on a Methodology to Raise Awareness about the Impact of Domestic Violence in the UK." *Criminal Justice* I(2):215–26.

Theweleit, K. 1987. *Male Fantasies.* Cambridge: Polity.

Wilson, E. 1977. *Women and The Welfare State.* London: Tavistock.

Woolf, V. [1938] 1986. *Three Guineas.* London: Hogarth.

———. [1929] 1989. *A Room of One's Own.* London: Grafton.

Worrall, A. 1990. *Offending Women.* London: Routledge.

———. 2002. "Rendering Them Punishable." Pp. 47–56 in *Women and Punishment: The Struggle for Justice,* edited by P. Carlen. Collumpton: Willan.

Zedner, L. 1991. *Women, Crime and Custody in Victorian England.* Oxford: Clarendon.

5

Controlling Drug Use
The Great Prohibition

DAVID MATZA AND PATRICIA MORGAN

INTRODUCTION

Next to the now-defunct Russian Revolution, Prohibition was the twentieth century's greatest social engineering project, suffering some of the same defects, but still alive despite a widely shared sense of basic failure. The Great Prohibition has shifted from alcohol to psychoactive drugs as the main substance controlled by penal sanction; users of both alcohol and drugs have been subjected to prohibition this century. After eighty years of governmental effort to enforce the Great Prohibition, prevention of drug use remains an unachieved and elusive goal. The main effect of Prohibition was to magnify the private problems of individual persons using alcohol or drugs. Prohibition created a large public domain devoted to restriction and punishment. If Paul Johnson's *Modern Times* (1983) delivered a definitive call for freedom from the clutches of socialist and welfare state experiments at social engineering, Michael Woodiwiss delivers a similar critique to prohibitions in the United States, 1900–1987:

> U.S. prohibition laws have not succeeded. Instead of solving the problems of excessive drinking, gambling and drug-taking, the laws themselves caused the devastation and termination of countless lives, exacerbated street crime, fostered successful organized crime, nullified or corrupted the law enforcement and criminal justice systems and reduced civil liberties. America's moral crusade has two faces. The rhetoric was righteous, but the reality only highlighted an unlimited capacity for lies, hypocrisy and illegal enrichment. The American people have been the victim of a successful double-cross. (1988:229)

The Great Prohibition did not succeed in controlling alcohol or drug use just as Communism did not succeed in controlling exploitation or economic failure. The difficulties in controlling use have been attributed to greed, to the corruption of authority, to the nature of addiction or dependency, to the role of alcohol or drugs in forming the basis for a way of life or "subculture" in modern society, or to the individual or collective quest for alteration of consciousness (Fingarette 1988; Weil 1972; Reinarman 1983). Whether because of the particular hold of especially demanding substances, or as simply a sign of popular products, effective demand for illegal drugs persists. The mark of the social engineering mentality is to imagine that the reason for failure has been an insufficient effort at law enforcement. Thus the failure in prohibition is thought by its proponents to require an ever greater and greater enforcement.

To understand the history of prohibition, we must separate the intentions from the consequences of meaningful actions, as well as grasp the difference between prohibiting and actually controlling drug use. Moreover, we must include in the social history the changing identities and labels attached to various drugs and users throughout the period. Such an approach leads to the interpretation that public policy toward drugs and alcohol in the United States has gone through cycles utilizing various combinations of public, social, and individual control, depending less perhaps on the inherent danger of any particular substance than on changing social, economic, and political factors. Simply put, social science has provided mounting evidence revealing that these cycles of control and prohibition have not been framed by uniform normative or problem criteria (Helmer 1975; Reinarman 1983; Duster 1970; Cohen 1985). Rather than any inherent standard of danger or harm, different rationales have been employed concerning the use of tobacco, alcohol, heroin, marijuana, and other psychoactive substances. This is most clear when examining separately "intentions" for control and the "consequences" of control for these various substances over time.

In other words, it is not clear—given the known facts of the relative deadliness and the relative danger of tobacco, alcohol, and the psychoactives—why tobacco has been allowed from colonial times to today, why alcohol is ranked second in the scale of danger presumed by law as indicated by a rescinded twenty-five year prohibition, and why psychoactives have been more or less prohibited since between the last quarter of the nineteenth century and the first third of the twentieth century. The inherency thesis that the judgments reflect the inherent dangers of the substances is difficult to take seriously because of the great deadliness associated with tobacco and the high levels of deadliness and danger associated with alcohol. It would be difficult to show that the psychoactives come anywhere near the levels of the two main comparable substances. Thus, the conferral thesis seems preferable to the inherency thesis, which would suggest that the revealed scale of American law is either irrational or haphazard. The scale of American law is to rate tobacco lowest and psychoactives highest in dangerousness. The inferences of such a revealed or presumed scale are not to prohibit tobacco from colonial to contemporary times, to subject alcohol to a twenty-five-year period of prohibition, and to prohibit psychoactives for a much longer though variable period: opiates and cocaine the longest, marijuana since the thirties, and others for shorter periods. The legal treatment of these related matters of tobacco, alcohol, and psychoactives seems better explained in terms of political, social, and economic factors, including ignorance, than by the principle of rationality usually expected in modern law, according to Weber.

The discussion of whether tobacco or marijuana and whether psychoactives or alcohol are more inherently dangerous has yielded no definitive result. To repeat, uniform normative or problem criteria have not been used in framing the discussion.

In this chapter the cycles of prohibition and control are discussed within two broad historical frameworks. The first outlines the process marking the shift from individual to social control taking place in the last half of the nineteenth and the first half of the twentieth century. The second examines how multiple labels of drug and alcohol problems identified as addiction, abuse, and dependency in the late twentieth century promoted a shift back toward selectively applied individual control.

FROM INDIVIDUAL TO SOCIAL CONTROL

The road to contemporary drug prohibition stemmed from the discovery of linking concepts of addiction and loss of control with the use of alcohol in the early part of the nineteenth century. Levine describes how alcohol was transformed from the "good creature of God" in colonial America to "demon rum" by the mid-nineteenth century. Levine notes the positive definition of alcohol before the onset of the Victorian nineteenth century:

> All liquor was regarded as good and healthy; alcohol was tonic, medicine, stimulant and relaxant. It was drunk at all hours of the day and night, by men and women of all social classes, and it was routinely given to children. . . . Puritan ministers praised alcohol but denounced drunkenness as a sinful and willful misuse of the "Good Creature." Most colonials, however, regarded drunkenness as unproblematic and unsurprising; drunkenness was seen as the natural, normal and harmless result of drinking. (Levine 1984:110)

Beginning in the late eighteenth century, Dr. Benjamin Rush led physicians to turn away from colonial notions that drinking was good and Puritan reservations that drunkenness was a willful and sinful choice, a

choice distinguishable from mere drinking. Rush argued that regular drinkers became addicted, experiencing "uncontrollable, overwhelming and ir-
resistible desires for drink . . . what today is referred to as loss of control"
(Levine 1984:110; see also Levine 1980; Wilkerson 1966; Rorabaugh 1979).
The concern with individual drunkenness grew during the first third of the
nineteenth century into a middle-class-elite movement promoting "temperance," then defined as abstinence from distilled liquor and moderation
in the use of beer and wine. Industrialization, urbanization, and the influx
of immigrant workers transformed the meaning and activities of temperance into a broad social movement, which defined alcohol in general as the
basic cause of various social problems. In this emerging ideology—what
was to become prohibitionism—alcohol took the place of urbanization, industrialization, and immigration as the basic cause of the social problems;
the movement to control drinking changed from temperance to prohibition. The conception of the problem became generalized: if individual
drunkenness caused the loss of self-control, societal drinking led to the loss
of social control.

By the end of the nineteenth century, alcohol became a major scapegoat
for the perceived breakdown in social order. Increasing crime, prostitution,
poverty, and the supposed degeneracy of "the undeserving poor" were
caused by alcohol, according to the growing number of adherents to Prohibitionism. Alcohol became the symbol for the Protestant middle classes
of the breakdown in the older, agrarian society (Gusfield 1963). The enemy
of social order became the greed of the liquor industrialists and the local
saloon, as well as the working-class people who frequented saloons. The
evaluation of alcohol was transformed from an earlier focus upon the problems of individual drunkenness to the belief that social control was undermined by drinking in general.

Subsequently, drugs, typically used by immigrant groups, were drawn
into the pattern defined by the prohibition of alcohol. Opiates had first
been available in many forms and were used medicinally and as tonics and
stimulants, following the earlier pattern of alcohol use. Some of the most
common medicinal substances used by middle-class Americans, such as
laudanum, came under attack (Duster 1970). Prohibitions began against
the mainly Chinese immigrants' practice of smoking opium. Influenced by
the newly formed American Medical Association, which wished to gain
control over the dispensing of drugs, federal policy proceeded by 1915, under the Harrison Act, to drive users underground. By 1926, users of pro-
scribed narcotics had become defined as "criminal addicts" (Helmer 1975).

An intolerance to substances has seemed highly correlated with an intolerance toward ethnic groups or social classes using the substances.
Many studies have revealed that drug and alcohol control in the United
States has been aimed specifically at disadvantaged populations for reasons of political expediency, cultural advantage, or economic and social

control (Becker 1963; Duster 1970; Helmer 1975; Himmelstein 1983; Morgan, Wallach, and Buchanan 1988; Reinarman 1983; Trebach 1987).

The transition from tolerance and enthusiasm to intolerance for alcohol in the United States was repeated in the response to opium, cocaine, heroin, marijuana, methamphetamines, psychedelics, and other substances. Temperance served as a midpoint in the reaction against the initial celebration, pointing to moderation instead of total restriction. Whether the accumulation of experience among users or the perception of an association of use with negative effects by nonusers played a greater role in the cycle from tolerance to intolerance is a matter of continuing dispute. Probably internal factors played a smaller role than external opinions in moving public opinion from positive to negative evaluations. A better understanding of the cyclic character of the societal response is possible if we consider the second framework, which has occurred only in the case of alcohol, after the end of Prohibition in 1933. An example of Durkheim's organic solidarity developed in the transition from the prohibition of alcohol to a selectively applied individual control.

INDIVIDUALIZING SOCIAL CONTROL

Following the end of Prohibition, no clear policy emerged until the end of the war. Initially, government and the relegalized alcohol industry joined forces in sustaining the legitimacy of alcohol production and consumption, while the remnants of the Prohibition movement pointed to the continuing problems of alcohol use. Certain federal agencies and some prohibitionist opinion began to shift the focus to marijuana as a problematic substance. Alcoholics Anonymous (AA) formed in the middle thirties but made little headway at first, and formulations of the nature of "alcoholism" were not clearly set. By the middle forties, AA had attracted the attention of some members of the medical community who had favored the establishment of a medical definition of alcoholism as a disease.

The emergent synthesis of a medical model and an AA approach received critical support from the alcohol beverage industry, which was still engaged in a holding action against prohibitionist critics of Roosevelt's New Deal liberal alcohol policy. The alcohol industry funded some of the early research on the disease of alcoholism and was represented in organizations espousing the AA viewpoint politically. By the late forties, AA had attained national recognition as manifested by an address by President Truman to a national AA convention.

By the beginning of the postwar era, several tendencies combined to result in the new pattern of societal response to alcohol use. Despite subsequent change and variation, a relatively stable and functional mix emerged. Social control of alcohol use became individualized. On the one hand, a tolerant attitude, supported and pictured in mass advertising, favored the development of what came to be known as social drinking; on the other hand, a concept of the "alcoholic" was fixed upon a small proportion of problematic drinkers and attributed to individual differences in the capacity to manage alcohol (Moore and Gersten 1981).

The medical model of heavy drinking and problem drinking culminated in the "alcoholic." Addicted to alcohol, the alcoholic suffered from loss of control, manifested characteristic traits of belligerence, poor work habits and, at the extreme, suffered loss of memory and other dysfunctional traits. Alcoholics were perceived within the disease category of the medical perspective. AA promulgated the medical concept that the alcoholic was addicted to alcohol, but AA also developed a distinctive approach to treatment that differed somewhat from the strict medical model, but worked easily with it. The medical model and the AA approach, based upon frequent meetings, group support, and individual sponsorship by veteran members, complemented each other.

Medical facilities specializing in the treatment of alcoholics began to utilize AA meetings and personnel within the treatment programs and referred persons to local AA groups at the end of treatment. There has been significant dispute regarding the effectiveness of the AA treatment model, especially with regard to whether control must be total instead of partial once one has been deemed an alcoholic. For our purposes, however, the important matter is not such disputes but the emergence of the joint AA-medical model as part of the prevailing policy "beyond the shadow of prohibition." This functional mix is part of the cycle in the societal reaction to alcohol, and represents the key development of the post-Prohibition period. The question whether this last part of the cycle could be applied to drug users in addition to alcoholics has already been answered affirmatively by AA organizations. Separate Narcotics Anonymous groups exist, but at the same time many drug users attend AA meetings. Little distinction is made with regard to the nature of the problem and the approach to rehabilitation.

While the labeling of someone as addict or alcoholic can harbor a punitive or degrading implication, it is equally important to recognize that the current mix of societal reaction to alcohol moves back partially to the tolerance of the earlier periods. Most drinkers are tolerated as social or normal. Heavy or problem drinkers come at a certain point to be regarded as alcoholic addicts. Such persons are regarded as problematic alcoholics, but they are not usually imprisoned. The current functional mix of public policy toward alcohol is to that extent an individualization of social control.

Aided by government agencies, including law enforcement, the alcohol industry promoted the mixture of tolerance for social drinking and a medical-organizational model for treating anonymous alcoholic addicts. State and federal agencies were lobbied to develop a "public health" approach. Clearly, such programs served the interest of the alcohol industry by providing an alternative to the demands of temperance or prohibitionist organizations pushing for greater social control of drinking. The function of an addiction concept is to imply that only a small minority of people using alcohol—or some other drug—suffer the negative consequences of losing control over the degree or the consequences of use. The great majority are assumed able to drink normally and socially. The deviance of the alcoholic is medicalized (Conrad and Schneider 1980; Morgan 1988). To the extent that social scientists and medical specialists affirm the concept of addiction, the consumption of alcohol may function within the limits of social tolerance. Such is the mix that currently guides public policy beyond the shadow of prohibition (Moore and Gersten 1981). Whether the mix is a good one is a matter of opinion; nevertheless, the current mix has been remarkably stable. The mix has been able to withstand and adapt to the increasing concern with the disastrous effects of drunk driving or the alleged increase in teenage drinking. The distinction between normal and addicted use seems generally established socially as well as professionally with regard to the drug of alcohol.

Many problems remain in applying the functional mix to a technological society where some people drive after drinking, or even drink while driving cars or locomotives or while operating cranes or office computers. A current dispute regarding the tolerable alcohol level in the legal definition of drunk driving illustrates the continuing conflicts of interest and viewpoint between the American Beverage Institute, a trade organization for restaurants and other businesses that sell alcohol, and citizen's groups wishing to make the standard for legal driving more rigorous. Mothers Against Drunk Driving (MADD) opposes the American Beverage Institute's attempt to maintain the 0.10 percent level of blood alcohol as the permissible standard for driving under the influence of alcohol. Many state legislatures are moving to lower the level to 0.08 percent in defining the level of social drinking permissible when driving. The importance of this debate is clear. Aside from the personal slant of whether Candy Lightner has betrayed MADD (which she founded and headed) by becoming a main lobbyist for the American Beverage Institute, the issue speaks to a critical matter in the definition of social drinking, and indicates that matters of social control and penal sanction maintain their relevance long after the abolition of the general prohibition of alcohol (*San Francisco Chronicle*, 15 January 1994).

CONTROL OF PATHOLOGY: ADDICTION, ABUSE, AND DEPENDENCY

Addiction is the basic English language term referring to the illness of use. Other terms stand in opposition to the implications of the addiction concept, soften or revise the meaning, mimic, repeat, or shift the meaning of this much abused term. To figure the meaning of addiction, one must contemplate the background from which addiction stands out. As in the case of alcohol, addiction takes its meaning in contrast with normal, social use. This background meaning is lost or buried in the case of illegal drugs, since the law does not brook a social usage once an activity is deemed illegal. But in the world of customary users and the social circles in which users work and play, a distinction can be made between social or recreational users and users for whom use is problematic. The legal context of prohibition makes the term *addiction* too broad, for there is an inclination to regard any illegal use of drugs as an addiction. It is for this reason that a legalistic approach quickly develops an intolerance to the addiction concept: Drug use is better regarded as an abuse.

Once considered an individual instance of deviation from a customary notion of normal use, the heavy user may thus be defined in a variety of ways (Smart 1974). Whether the objective judgment of experts, or as subjective judgments apparent in the world of users, the evaluations proceed in several directions. The most common definitions are medical and moral. Most words used in recent history to refer to the 10 to 15 percent of problem users have been overweighted and thus subjected to unwarranted criticism. Each concept has implied or insinuated an explanation of the overuse as well as a meaning, or definition of the usual indications or correlations of the higher than normal degree of drug-taking. The first and most persistent term, *addiction,* follows the medical definition begun by Benjamin Rush at the turn of the nineteenth century. The addiction concept refers to a pressing need because the body's appetites are changed by the chronic use of a particular substance. The body likes the feeling associated with the drug and proceeds from wanting some to needing more than was anticipated at the outset. As the body's tolerance to the substance increases, the person needs more and more to obtain the sought-after feeling. In the event of withdrawal, the body becomes ill or feels bad because of being deprived of the substance. Alfred Lindesmith's (1947) rendition of this concept suggested that if persons did not define an association between withdrawal and the ill effects, the chances of escaping a self-concept as addict might be maximized.

Objections to the addiction concept came from many sources. The allegedly unpleasant symptoms or ill effects of withdrawal varied significantly among differing substances and users. The failure to find an effective treatment adversely affected the acceptance of a medical concept of addiction.

Two of the most professionally endorsed drug treatments of drug addiction—heroin and methadone—proved less than successful, managing only to substitute one strong drug for another. Furthermore, addiction was held by some critics to imply a sense of nonresponsibility. As in the case of mental illness, addiction seemed to imply an excuse or a rationalization for harmful actions or illegal behavior. Because addiction had been found wanting as a basic concept for grasping the phenomenon of "overuse," abuse emerged gradually as a rival idea.[1]

Soon after the widespread increase in drug use during the sixties and early seventies, the concept of drug abuse began to take on a distinctive meaning. More moralistic than medical, the increased popularity of the abuse concept mirrored a negative national reaction to the widespread enthusiasm and popularity of the drug culture. The meaning of abuse and the associated explanation of drug-taking followed two roads, one minimalist and short-lived, the other broader and still prominent.

The minimalist concept of drug abuse referred to the misuse of drugs. Drugs were meant to be taken as treatment for illness, not for pleasure or religious experience or sensual gratification or recreational release. This meaning was widespread among medical professionals, but never quite caught on with the general population. Many countercultural exponents and social scientists challenged the premise that drugs in their nature were to be used only as treatment for illness. Moreover, the increasingly large population opposed to the drug culture thought misuse was too limited a meaning for the concept of drug abuse.

Abuse, in the broader conception of drug abuse, implies more: that drug abuse is taking advantage and is immoral, and that it is justifiable to condemn it and make it illegal. Drug abuse—like sexual abuse or physical abuse—is taking advantage of, an exploitation of close family members and other members of society. People who use drugs, regardless of the amount or patterns of use, were deemed immoral, hedonistic, bending the normative order to their own advantage and for their own pleasure. Culturally, the best symbol of the abuse concept was with reference to athletes who used drugs to enhance their performance. Seeking enhanced performance, pleasure, strength, energy, or alteration of consciousness was endowed with a deviant meaning and intention. Achieving social goals by means of drugs was deviant, abusive.

The explanation provided for drug-taking by the abuse concept is that it is rational, willful. The explanation of addiction is involuntary; the user is captured, controlled by the substance. An abuse is an unfair means to obtain conventional ends. Since conventional means are provided, public opinion is offended by the cutting of corners, the unfair edge, presumed to motivate users of illegal substances.

To a certain extent, the disagreement between the concepts of addiction and abuse has been resolved by a division of attribution. Members of some groups are more likely to be thought of as addictive when coming to the notice of authorities, whereas members of other groups may be assumed abusive. Such attributions of illness and deviation may be further confounded by internal group preferences regarding designation. Middle-class youth and adults may prefer being seen as sick or addicted, rather than deviant and abusive, whereas members of underclass subcultures may prefer the deviant role to attributions of illness or addiction. Such a division of attribution would be consistent with Klein's (1983) observation that being ill and against the law make up two sides of the same coin.

The dispute between the ideas of addiction and abuse has also been mediated by a third alternative. Between addiction and abuse, dependency is usually regarded as the meekest of concepts when applied to drug or alcohol use. Yet precisely because the concept implies neither the medical disease of addiction nor the judgmental moralism of abuse, many practitioners and professionals fall back on a notion of dependency when working with or referring to problematic users of chemical substances. Though dependency is often considered a psychological concept, dependency also has social, economic, and political meanings. The individual meaning of dependency of psychology is augmented by the social meaning of persons dependent on welfare, the economic meaning of dependent nations before they became developing nations, and a political meaning, as in Albert Memmi's (1984) definition of dependency as a state of being dominated. Dependency implies a state of neediness that is not based in either an organic reduction to addiction or the moral outrage of abusiveness. Dependency does not imply a specific explanation of overuse, but remains open-ended. Psychological, social, economic, and political sciences have utilized the concept of dependency, and have often developed ideas of overcoming the state through programmatic aid, political action, or self-help organizations. Given the present state of knowledge regarding the nature of the heavy use of drugs and the societal capacity to control overuse, dependency, the weakest of the most popular conceptions, would seem the wisest choice. Being referred to as being dependent on drugs is slightly less insulting than being called addicted or being held guilty of drug abuse; it is also in most cases probably a more accurate appraisal of the extent of neediness.

When seen from the standpoint of abstinence or withdrawal, the several concepts referring to problematic use appear less competitive. Complementary meanings emerge for what academically or externally appear as rival concepts struggling to account for the phenomenon. There is no reason to favor one concept over another when behavior or feelings associated with each appear during the experience of withdrawal. When the concepts are seen alongside each other, instead of as alternatives, we are forced as analysts or as participants to sharpen the meaning of each concept, so as to remove the overlap that passes unnoticed from the external perspective.

CONCLUSION: CONTROLLING DRUG USE

The idea that persons can achieve a greater self- and social control over drug use in prison is perhaps the greatest single harm committed by the social engineering mentality in the United States. The idea that prison can help someone overcome drugs is one of those ideas that deserves being compared to using the concentration camp to help people not be bourgeois deviationists, or mentally ill. As the Great Prohibition nears the end of its century, the imprisonment of users of prohibited substances should be reconsidered. "Sooner or later," said Walter Lippman, "the American people will have to make up their minds either to bring their legislative ideals down to a point where they square with human nature or they will have to establish an administrative despotism strong enough to start enforcing their moral ideals. They cannot much longer defy the devil with a wooden sword" (quoted in Woodiwiss 1988 [from Walter Lippman, "The Underworld as Servant," *Forum,* January–February, 1931]).

The policy of imprisoning drug-takers has had long-term, permanent effects, most of which have ranged from the sad and bad to the vicious and criminal. Rehabilitation has not been aided by enforced confinement. The drug traffic has continued to flow in and out of prison. People who stop using typically return when out of prison. Prisoners who need drugs (which will now include tobacco in some prisons) and are without money are constrained to obtain drugs by nonmonetary means.

When a person is dependent on drugs, the proper goal for the individual or society is freedom from the necessity to use. To be free of this neediness upon drugs ranging from legal coffee, tobacco, and alcohol, to illegal marijuana, cocaine, and heroin, may mean either consuming in the conventional manner of the social drinker or to stop entirely in the manner of the anonymous, recovering ex-alcoholic. This is the functional mix that defines the public policy in the society beyond Prohibition. In either event, the aim is to achieve a freedom from a reliance upon a particular substance. Social drinkers are drinkers who have not been discredited by their incapacity to imbibe in a controlled manner. They are assumed to be not reliant upon drinking. Addicted, abusive, or dependent drug-takers are labeled persons whose use has led to problematic life circumstances, ranging from arrest or unemployment to divorce or social isolation. To use coercion to impose upon such a person the capacity to be free of a dependency seems the cruelest of hoaxes, the most senseless of punishments. To liken the social control of social work intervention, or even mandatory treatment, to the policy of penal sanction seems a bit insensitive to commonly understood differences of degree. The paradox of controlling drug use is the necessity for freedom, but this does not mean that communities may not insist on some measures of intervention when persons become known or labeled as problematic users. Thus, freedom from the use of drugs may prove a more difficult project than the once celebrated freedom to use.

The possibility of penal sanction for using drugs or alcohol does not end with the end of prohibition. Social control is moved from the simple matter of which substances to prohibit to questions of medical or social work intervention for persons labeled addictive, abusive, or dependent. Penal sanctions in the form of imprisonment for drunk or drugged driving remain; corporations, universities, and government bureaus may require drug testing and fire employees discovered to be drinking or using drugs. Such a shift in focus defines the offense more specifically, but still maintains the expectation of sobriety in driving, working, and other major social roles. Such a complicated mix of attitudes and definitions involves many compromises, apparent inconsistencies, and a political deferring to lobbies, interests, and professional expertise. Whether the functional mix that defines the complex state of social control of alcohol is preferable to the prohibition of psychoactive drugs is the major question of current social policy. Perhaps the dispute between those who support the current prohibition and those favoring legalization of drugs will benefit from the reminder that alcohol remains the model of prohibitionist policy. After the Great Prohibition upon alcohol, social control over the use of alcohol was maintained, though in changed form. Penal sanctions were specified to deal with the dangerous or deadly consequences of drinking, rather than drinking itself. Whether currently prohibited drugs can be expected to follow a similar course is a difficult question to answer. A current reading of public opinion would probably indicate a greater likelihood for the prohibition of tobacco than for the legalization of marijuana. In either event, specialists in the field of drugs and alcohol will continue to profit from continuing research and treatment of afflicted persons.

ACKNOWLEDGMENT

Many thanks to Gresham Sykes for a critical response to an earlier draft of this chapter that discussed addiction but neglected the concept of abuse.

REFERENCES

Becker, H. 1963. *Outsiders: Studies in the Sociology of Deviance.* Glencoe, IL: Free Press.
Cohen, S. 1985. *Visions of Social Control: Crime, Punishment and Classification.* Cambridge: Polity.
Conrad, P. and J. Schneider. 1980. *Deviance and Medicalization.* St. Louis: C. V. Mosby.
Duster, T. 1970. *The Legislation of Morality.* New York: Free Press.
Fingarette, H. 1988. *Heavy Drinking: The Myth of Alcoholism as a Disease.* Berkeley: University of California Press.
Gusfield, J. 1963. *Symbolic Crusade: Status Politics and the American Temperance Movement.* Urbana: University of Illinois Press.
Helmer, J. 1975. *Drugs and Minority Oppression.* New York: Seabury.
Himmelstein, J. 1983. *The Strange Career of Marihuana.* Westport, CT: Greenwood.

Johnson, P. 1983. *Modern Times.* New York: Harper and Row.

Klein, D. 1983. "Ill and Against the Law: The Social and Medical Control of Heroin." *Journal of Drug Issues* 13(1):31–56.

Levine, H. G. 1980. "The Discovery of Addiction: Changing Conceptions of Habitual Drunkenness in America." *Journal of Studies on Alcohol* 39:143–74.

———. 1984. "The Alcohol Problem in America: From Temperance to Alcoholism." *British Journal of Addiction* 79:109–19.

Lindesmith, A. R. 1947. *Opiate Addiction.* Evanston, IL: Principia.

Memmi, A. 1984. *Dependence.* Boston: Beacon.

Moore, M. and D. Gersten (eds.). 1981. *Alcohol and Public Policy: Beyond The Shadow of Prohibition.* Washington, DC: National Academy Press.

Morgan, P. 1988. "Power, Politics and Public Health: The Political Power of the Alcohol Beverage Industry." *Journal of Public Health Policy* 9(2).

Morgan, P., L. Wallach, and D. Buchanan. 1988. "Waging Drug Wars: Prevention Strategy or Politics as Usual." *Drugs and Society* 3:99–124.

Reinarman, C. 1983. "Constraint, Autonomy and State Policy: Notes toward a Theory of Controls on Consciousness Alteration." *Journal of Drug Issues* 13(1): 9–30.

Rorabaugh, W. J. 1979. *The Alcoholic Republic.* New York: Oxford University Press.

Smart, R. 1974. "Addiction, Dependency, Abuse or Use: Which Are We Studying with Epidemiology?" In *Drug Use: Epidemiological and Sociological Approaches,* edited by E. Josephson and E. E. Carroll. New York: Wiley.

Trebach, A. 1987. *The Great Drug War.* New York: MacMillan.

Weil, A. 1972. *The Natural Mind.* Boston: Houghton Mifflin.

Wilkerson, A. 1966. *A History of the Concept of Alcoholism as a Disease.* Ph.D. dissertation, University of Pennsylvania.

Woodiwiss, M. Crimes. 1988. *Crusades and Corruption: Prohibitions in the United States, 1900–1987.* Totowa, NJ: Barnes and Noble.

II
Policing and Surveillance

Introduction to Part II

Although prisons are scrutinized by researchers, practitioners, and inmates, they remain invisible to the public eye, except for the dramatic stories of riots or escapes and the routine stories of budgets and building programs. The public face of punishment and criminal justice is represented more vividly by the police and the courts. The mass media and popular culture transmit the mindless clichs of crime control (Three Strikes and You're Out, Zero Tolerance) and stage its iconic dramas (the O. J. Simpson trial, the video of Los Angeles policemen assaulting Rodney King).

Research on public and private policing is now a major social scientific enterprise. Studies range from the ethnographies of police work to large-scale statistical evaluations of the impact of various forms of policing. Egon Bittner, a pioneering contributor to the sociology of the police, looks in Chapter 6 at the appealing, but largely unclear notion of community policing. The following three chapters are not studies of "the police" as such, but rather of trends in "policing" that raise far wider issues: notably the moral and political implications of extending state and privatized controls by *deception,* by *surveillance,* and by *force.* In Chapter 7, Gary Marx locates the techniques of undercover policing in terms of wider changes in social control strategies. He revisits his well-known 1988 book, *Undercover,* a study of the methods and ethics of the new technologies of covert policing. The arguments about "sting" operations cannot rest on evalutions of "what works" without a wider discussion about trust, secrecy, and deceit. The same applies to new forms of surveillance reviewed by William Staples in Chapter 8. The video monitor (or closed-circuit television, CCTV) in a shopping mall is just one of the many mundane procedures that to which we have become accustomed. "Seemingly benign and relatively inconspicuous," they are part of the scene and behind the scene. They are not "ushered in with dramatic displays of state power" nor do they really threaten democratic rights. Yet, as Staples suggests, they belong on the "soft" side of a continuum that has harder aims ("public security") and intentions (not just monitoring but modifying behavior).

There is little need to point out that the subject of Jerry Skolnick's Chapter 9 is very much at the hard end—away from the gadgetry of private security firms to the very core of political control: the state's monopoly on legitimate violence. If ordinary police (not military or security forces) use violent and illegal techniques of interrogation, two allied questions arise: When does the genuinely strong taboo against torture become flexible? Why does the easy condemnation of torture by those wicked regimes out there suddenly become so hard to apply to our own good and democratic societies?

6

Staffing and Training Problem-Oriented Police

Egon Bittner

Over the course of the twentieth century, reform has been a virtually permanent and ubiquitous element in the structure of municipal policing in the United States. Of course, what was taken as constituting reform varied quite considerably over time and from place to place. A good deal of what was referred to as reform involved changes undertaken to satisfy partisan interests; other reforms were merely responses to local and passing urgencies; and some were merely spurious changes in appearance. Disregarding such variations, it is helpful to distinguish three phases in the reform of policing that are radically different in their substantive orientation—that is, in the perception of what was wrong, and what had to be done to correct it—and that are dynamically related, in that each provided the impetus for moving into the next. Thus, for example, the reformers in the third phase were not merely concerned with the state of policing they inherited from the reformers of the second phase, but were also polemically opposed to the reform aspirations of their predecessors. In each of the three phases, the reformers maintained that the changes they sought to bring about were sufficient to move policing to where it ought to be. But in the progression of time, the reformers changed from an unquestioned to a critical sense of certainty about their respective projects. We happen to believe that the changes in police practice and organization proposed in the most recent phase of reform are generally on the right track. But we also think that a problem of critical importance has not been adequately addressed. To be specific, we propose to discuss staffing, that is, the recruitment of appropriate personnel, for problem-oriented policing, a program formulated by Herman Goldstein, first in a paper published in 1979, then elaborated in other publications, and presently tested, refined, adapted, and adopted in several large police departments, in part or in totality. In order to make the argument, in particular, in order to show why merely raising entry standards from the high school diploma to the baccalaureate does not address staffing problems for problem-oriented policing adequately, we must discuss briefly the two earlier phases of reform, with special attention to their staffing arrangements.

During the first half of this century, the first phase of our story, changes in policing were closely tied to changes in municipal government generally. Civil service rules notwithstanding, access to and advancement in public employment were embedded in the political spoils system. Thus, the electoral victory that brought a new administration into city hall frequently led to a redistribution of power and benefits in the police departments. Since the electoral claims of the new administration included plans for changes that would improve government and public service, they provided the justification for the "shakeup" in the police department. And even though such changes were often enough simply rewards for political loyalty, electoral turnovers were as often preceded by scandals, and the changes in the police departments deserve consideration as reforms of sorts. While it is true that such changes left the prevailing structure of policing unchanged, that they occurred periodically played a part in preventing the police from becoming an independent force in the dynamics of local politics, in which the police was far more often a pawn than a player.

There is no evidence that the recruitment of personnel for the police followed carefully considered selection criteria. The chief officer was a political appointee who served at the pleasure of the mayor. His lieutenants (and it was, of course, always a he) were drawn from among "his people." The line personnel were recruited from among the segments of the population they were expected to police, namely, from among lower class "ethnics," which made it appear that in many cities being of Irish origin was a necessary, even if not a sufficient condition for being a police officer. Depending on their political strength, other ethnic groups have also gained entry into the ranks of the police. Being a police officer was viewed as a rather easily accessible alternative to a blue-collar occupation in public service or industry. No one thought that police work was an intellectually demanding way of making a living, that it might require technical training or skill, or that its performance would be coupled with concern for larger purposes or consequences. Instead, it was assumed that officers who relied on the street smarts one normally acquired in the circumstances of lower-class life would know what to do when their intervention was required to control undesirable behavior. It was also assumed that they would accept the control, and uncritically follow the orders of their superiors. Finally, it was expected that officers would avoid getting into trouble, especially of the sort that might embarrass their superiors. Staying out of trouble did not normally include avoiding the violation of the civil rights of troubled and troublesome people. Quite the contrary, one of the job qualifications was the capacity to impose physical restraint and punishment on those who were thought to require it, not, however, by any rule of law, but by commonsense perception of police sensibility. In sum, the recruitment policies of the police in the first half of this century reflected the view that anyone who had the stomach for it could be expected to be a competent police officer. Though one would not consider it a job qualification in the narrow sense, it might be mentioned that officers were expected to be constrained by a modest sense of public decency epitomized by the concept of "clean graft." Given the low wages officers earned, it was thought reasonable and morally acceptable that they should be free to accept and, if need be, extort gratuities from people who benefited from their service. But, as befits persons in low-grade occupations, they should be humble about it.

In the decade following World War II, the practice of newly elected mayors "bringing in their own people" to run their city's police department continued. But the trusted old ways produced new and unexpected results. Some of the newly appointed chiefs—for example, William Parker in Los Angeles, Stanley Schrotell in Cincinnati, Herbert Jenkins in Atlanta—set in motion an effort to terminate the process that brought them into positions of power, and with it the control city hall exercised over the details of police organization and practice. In those reformers' terminology, they sought to "professionalize" the police. They did not, however, have in mind analogizing police work with the practices and outlook of the traditional professions of divinity, law, and medicine. In fact, quite the opposite was their intention. While the traditional professions always stress the practitioners' independent judgment and responsibility, freedom from any form of supervisory control, and the critical use of complex knowledge and skill, the "professionalization" of the police involved the creation of tight organizational structures, the exercise of close bureaucratic control over line personnel, and an obsessive concern with rules and regulations. Beyond that, the ideal of professionalization entailed the recognition that police work executed a specific, and in the eyes of the reformers, nonpolitical mandate, namely, law enforcement. Law enforcement was seen as the defining social function of policing that needed to be attended to with the kind of sustained and methodical seriousness that was absent in the amateurish ways of the first half of the century. Practical considerations required the recognition that police officers had a good deal of discretionary freedom once they left the police station, and were routinely engaged in the unavoidable activities of peacekeeping that involved a large variety of interventions into urban life that had nothing to do with law enforcement, and were generally viewed as not real police work.

Quite clearly, the professionalization of the police gave the institution a definition of its function and the independence that it lacked before. Admittedly, the function was defined too narrowly. Still, the reformers deserve credit for having set into motion efforts to make explicit what policing is all about and develop some proper ways of doing it. Because the professionalization of the police was a significant departure from the earlier sloth and indolence in policing, it is regrettable that recruitment norms retained the implication that police work is a low-grade occupation. In fact, it could be said that this view became more firmly established. While recruitment in the decades before World War II was haphazard and biased, more a function of history and circumstance than of rationally considered choice, the recruitment of professional police officers involved explicitly formulated selection criteria and thus conscious choice. What was in the past tacitly known was now openly acknowledged: police work was not for people with high aspirations. The ambitious among the recruits sought to move away from actual police work by joining the administrative structure of departments, through promotional exams. Many of those who remained in the ranks of line personnel became skilled practitioners dealing with complex and serious problems, but generally neither receiving nor expecting recognition for their work.

As might be expected, recruitment into the professionalized department became a formalized procedure involving explicitly formulated criteria of selection and elaborate testing and background investigations. Initial appointments were provisional to further test the suitability of recruits. Furthermore, recruits were given a course of training in the police academy that, while not standardized in either content or duration, contained everywhere a very heavy dose of instruction concerning the internal rules and regulation of the department. Following graduation from the academy, recruits were entrusted to the guidance of seasoned officers who, more often than not, instructed the recruits to forget all they had been told in the academy.

While the recruitment procedures conveyed the impression of great care in the selection of suitable candidates, the acceptance of a high school diploma as a condition of employment and the low caliber of the instruction in the academies clearly indicated that suitability did not include high levels of intellectual functioning. It was understood—and probably still is in most places—both inside and outside the police establishment, that police work relied primarily on common sense and an intuitive grasp of the distinction between right and wrong. If there was a need for analysis, it was to be done by management.

The professional police officer's understanding of the nature of his (and it was still generally *his* rather than *her*) role in society and the underlying orientation of his occupational commitment was moralistic. In a sense, this expresses a correct understanding of the mission of the police, which is, after all, the social mechanism for holding people to proper conduct and for ensuring that persons who violate the norms of proper conduct receive their just deserts. But the dominant role of the perception of policing as a *moral* enterprise in the occupational outlook of officers tends to overshadow and diminish the concern for technical practicalities of having to cope with all forms of social deviance. The bright line of distinction that identifies evil tends to evoke unqualified condemnation of the sort that is ordinarily impatient with analysis. Thus, the moralistic attitude of the professional police officer is more compatible with efforts to overpower criminals than with trying to outwit them. That, in turn, favors officers who are impulsively courageous rather than resolutely prudent, and who feel justified in resorting to means that might otherwise be judged unacceptable legally or morally. All this projects a version of police work that can be performed adequately by persons with modest intellectual powers, provided they are of good moral character and are willing to accept a tightly regulated occupational environment. Indeed, given the reformers' preoccupation with organizational coherence and vertical control, not only was it unnecessary to recruit intellectually bright and inquisitive persons, but there would seem to be a positive advantage, from a management point of interest, to staff departments with persons who are not given to raising too many questions and who are content to do what they are told. Chiefs who took seriously the mandate to police a city professionally would not want to have to do it by directing a bunch of geniuses with independent ideas.

It came to be accepted, both inside and outside the police establishment that police work was a lower-level civil service occupation, more or less on the same level of occupational prestige as industrial blue-collar work. While this view is still widely shared, together with all other ideas of professional policing, the lessons of the 1960s and 1970s have convinced many police executives that the original program of professionalization needed to be enriched, on the one hand by programs like "community relations," and on the other by the addition of some psychological consciousness-raising in the training of officers. In many instances this conviction was adopted in response to outside influences, especially from the Law Enforcement Assistance Administration, which as often as not came accompanied by financial incentives in the form of special project support. Interestingly, however, while management was willing to accept programs enriching police services, line personnel did not welcome them and often treated them as unwarranted impositions and unjustified changes in the terms of their employment. That is, the "cops" were quite willing to do what they were told, but they resisted changes that complicated their responsibilities, especially when they involved having to adopt attitudes and procedures that seemed to have the flavor of social work.

The latest phase of reform, problem-oriented policing, emerged in large measure as a reaction to the shortcomings of professional policing, just as the latter emerged in reaction to the shortcomings of its predecessor. While many things could be said to be wrong with professional policing as it emerged in the years following World War II, the shortcomings that were identified most often were (1) its excessive preoccupation with the management of internal departmental affairs, (2) the fragmented and largely reactive nature of police work, combined with an almost total lack of interest in the overall effects of the interventions, and (3) the isolation of the police in the communities they served. It must be emphasized that these features of policing are shortcomings only from a particular perspective. One could, after all, argue (leaving obligatory rhetorical pieties aside) that policing is essentially an emergency service whose function is to arrest untoward tendencies of all sorts, and leaving long-range care of the momentarily immobilized development to others. The police officer's responsibility, and interest, ends with the arrest of criminals; what to do with them is the function of the other parts of the criminal justice system. Similarly, the officer will prevent a family dispute from becoming violent, for the time being, but someone else will have to deal with the underlying problem. This sort of service is best rendered by maintaining a state of response readiness guaranteed by strong managerial control. Moreover, the necessary freedom of officers to act forcefully in the handling of emergencies might be impaired by relations of familiarity and trust with the very people they are supposed to restrain. Hence, the maintenance of distance between the police and the community is functionally efficient. But, of course—and this is the main point of the problem-oriented policing critique—this is an enormously ineffective way of doing police work, all the external appearances of snappy efficiency to the contrary notwithstanding. What is missing in professional policing is the effort to identify, analyze, and understand the problem complexes that create the need for police intervention in the first place; or, to put it differently, there is no interest in the analysis of the substantive problems with which officers are required to cope and, along with it, no interest in the general outcome of police work.

This is not the place to offer a detailed account of the practices and aims of problem-oriented policing. While a good deal has been written about it and some of it has been attempted in practice, much more of it is still being formulated and tried provisionally. It is probably much more than the most ambitious reform ever attempted in policing; it truly redefines the nature and purpose of police work in a fundamental way. In the past, and in many places still today, the police received citizen complaints about vandalism, purse snatching, unruly youth, loud noise, assaults, shoplifting, and the like, and responded to them on a case-by-case basis. The problem is taken as defined in the complaint, and the solution—if the problem could be solved—is the arrest of the miscreant or the abatement of the nuisance while the officers are on the scene. The occasional aggregation of certain complaints may give rise to the consideration of preventive strategies, e.g., by increasing the density of patrols. But this would be a managerial responsibility and the decision would be conveyed to the line personnel whose occupational horizon would remain limited to dealing with isolated incidents.

Contrary to this, to problem-oriented police officers, dealing with an incident is merely the beginning of their involvement with the problem. It leads to a program of inquiries and analyses that place the incident in context, may suggest possibilities of remedies that transcend the specific incident, may involve the engagement of resources outside the police, all undertaken—as needed—in consultation with associated officers. Of course, as in any other professional activity, this all becomes routinized in time and the process works in less ponderous ways than the description might imply. Two points must be stressed: (1) the initiative to engage in the inquiries and analyses of encountered problems is the occupational responsibility of the "street cops," and (2) the "street cops" are also authorized and expected to formulate remedial programs that may include the mobilization of resources outside the police.

Students of police work are aware of the existence of strong resistance among line personnel to any enlargement of responsibilities beyond what is sometimes called the "slam-bang" style of police work. But they have also noted the presence of officers who would be willing and could be trusted to undertake the enlarged responsibilities competently. Indeed, some of these officers practice problem-oriented policing informally and without acknowledgment. Now, it is not unreasonable to expect that starting with this cadre of imaginative and prudent officers one could slowly change from professional to problem-oriented policing. But it would seem more appropriate to try to institutionalize a redefinition of the meaning of police work to bring about a common understanding that the possession and exercise of analytical skills is a basic feature of the occupation. This will not be accomplished by merely liberating the inclinations and talents of some well-meaning officers who are now randomly distributed in police departments from stultifying administrative restrictions, nor by raising educational requirements of recruits in the hope of increasing the numbers of such officers in the future. Instead, it will be more appropriate to have the police follow the example of the other professions. That is, the police will need to institutionalize its training and recruitment in academic institutions in ways more or less analogous to how it is done in schools of education or social work. No doubt there will be voices urging that police work cannot be learned in the classroom. But this is also true of teaching and social work, and both professions require hefty doses of internship training for full acknowledgment of presumptive competence, as should be the case for the police. In fact, it would be necessary to retain a course of in-house training to acquaint recruits with local conditions of police practice.

The purpose of professional education is to provide students with the intellectual background and with habits of critical thought relevant to a field of practice, rather than with the ins and outs of local and timely problem solving. Of course, there is a price to be paid by routing the recruitment and training of teachers and social workers through academic programs. It no doubt discourages some potentially fine teachers and social workers from joining the professions simply because they cannot face the stress of academic work, and there probably are other drawbacks. But on the whole this method has proven indispensable for the professions. While it is not always an unalloyed good, it does serve to ascertain that people who are entrusted with serious, important, and complex responsibilities are adequately prepared for them. They gain the understanding of their function in society that will enable them to act with confidence on their own initiative. Finally, even though it is not guaranteed, academic exercises are the method our society relies on for equipping persons with the mental endurance and the analytic inclination and aptitude for complex problem-solving demands.

There is another reason for creating professional schools of policing after the model of schools of education and schools of social work. Such institutions become centers of research and development in their respective areas. Thus progress in policing would no longer depend on desultory special projects—financed by grants from outside sources and under outside direction—but would acquire an intrinsic continuity and a natural affinity with practice.

We should mention in conclusion that while we argued strongly in favor of the establishment of credentialing schools of policing as preparation for entry into the occupation, our main point is to assert that the success of problem-oriented policing requires a different kind of police officer than was envisioned by the earlier proponents of professional policing. The academic institution is the means for the production of officers who, fully conscious of the nature, the seriousness, and importance of their role in society, will be able to identify, analyze, and address social problems—including crime—entrusted to their care.

7

Developments in Undercover Policing

Gary T. Marx

She [jury member] was extremely liberal. She was a sociologist, and I don't
like sociologists. They try to reason things out too much.
—Florida prosecutor (after losing case involving the
undercover purchase of a 2 Live Crew album)

I have no sympathy for those who are crybabies about the fact that police officers are selling to those who want to buy drugs. We use every legal means
that we can. We want everybody to know that the next drug buy may be from
a police officer.
—Mayor Marion Barry, news conference 1988

In recent decades social control has become more specialized and technical and, in many ways, more penetrating and intrusive.[1] The new surveillance can be contrasted with traditional forms by at least twenty-eight
dimensions (Marx, 2002). Among the most important of these are:

1. It transcends distance, darkness, and physical barriers.
2. It transcends time; its records can be easily stored, retrieved, combined, analyzed, and communicated.
3. It has low visibility or is invisible.
4. It is involuntary.
5. It is preventive.
6. It is capital- rather than labor-intensive.
7. It is decentralized and often involves self-policing.
8. It triggers a shift from targeting a specific suspect to categorical
   suspicion.

9. It is more intensive—probing beneath surfaces, discovering previously inaccessible information.
10. It is more extensive—covering an ever-enlarging number of spatial, temporal, and functional areas.

An important strand of the new surveillance is covert policing. In a previous work (*Undercover*, Marx 1988) I reported the results of an empirical inquiry into covert police practices. That study considered the changing nature of undercover practices; their history; factors responsible for their expansion and changing form; basic types and dimensions; ethical criteria by which the state's use of deception could be judged; intended and unintended consequences for targets, third parties, informers, and police; public policy questions and the social issues raised by the general expansion of the new surveillance. In this chapter, I discuss some developments and research since the publication of *Undercover* and some more general professional questions involved in a project such as this.

The undercover tactic has continued to be used in imaginative if sometimes questionable ways. Recent elaborations include game wardens using a lifelike target device—"robo-deer"—as a means of ensnaring poachers;[2] anticrime decoys used to combat attacks on homosexuals or tourists in rented cars; police as decoy pedestrians in crosswalks seeking drivers who fail to stop for them; stings in which postal authorities mail offers of illegal pornography and then arrest those who respond to their offers (and the use of the Internet in a related fashion); testing cabdrivers to see if they will pick up minority customers; the purchase and sale of endangered species such as Mexican red-kneed tarantulas, or parts of species, such as the genitals of bears and walruses for which there is an Asian aphrodisiac market; the purchase of fish taken from polluted waters; and entering false information into computers to catch those illegally accessing systems. Reverse stings in which police sell rather than buy drugs have also increased in prominence.

A number of first-person accounts have appeared since the publication of *Undercover* (LaBrecque 1987; Goddard and Levine 1988; Pistone and Brasco 1988; Murano and Hoffer 1990; Wansley and Stowers 1989; Wozencraft 1990; Rothmiller and Goldman 1992; Chase and Grimaldi 1993; Rosenthal 2000). Guidebooks for practitioners have also appeared or been updated (e.g., Cheek and Lesce 1988; Carter 1990; VanCook 1996; Fuller 1998; Alvarez 1999; Motto and June 1999), along with journalistic accounts and those of informants (e.g., Kipps 1996; Jakes, Jakes, and Richmond 1998; Eichenwald 2000; Lehr and O'Neil 2000).

There is now enough fictional, biographical, and training material to warrant analysis of this body of work on its own. While offering rich narratives and examples, the more recent work does not suggest the need for major revisions or extensions of *Undercover.* In this sense I think they provide some external validation.[3] Certainly specifics change, but the fundamental social structures, processes, and ethical and policy issues that keep the social analyst in business are more enduring.

Were I to revise the book today I would treat a number of additional topics beyond updating an ever-changing historical record (e.g., issues of culture, international comparisons, and specific topics such as internal affairs uses, jailhouse informing, private stings, and the use of sex in covert investigations).[4] But here I wish to merely update the book by reference to some recent developments and research.

In writing about any contemporary topic, one risks being out of date the minute the writing stops.[5] I recall the case of two political scientists whose book explaining how Lebanon was able to sustain a multiethnic democracy was published just as the Lebanese civil war started. While not in that league, *Undercover* was wrong in suggesting that the political misuses of covert means at the federal level appeared to be behind us. The study documented the increased significance of undercover operations for criminal investigations, but it also reflected a belief that surveillance merely because of a person's legal political beliefs and actions was not likely to be a major problem. The FBI had responded to the abuses revealed during Watergate and the COINTEL programs by severely curtailing political surveillance and by developing restrictive guidelines. A new generation of agents seemed too principled, busy, and regulated to engage in the kinds of often illegal and immoral domestic political surveillance that characterized the 1960s and earlier periods. The undercover activity that had once been directed at persons who held unpopular beliefs came to be directed at those engaged in white-collar and organized crime. Yet soon after the book was published, documents released under the Freedom of Information Act and congressional hearings revealed a massive spying campaign against critics of the administration's Central American policies (Gelbspan 1991).[6] Some of the CISPES (Committee in Solidarity with the People of El Salvador) investigation was illegal and much of it violated the bureau's own policies.

In considering covert means, there is an important distinction between criminal and political investigations. Because the latter rarely result in criminal prosecution and are governed by executive guidelines that can be (and have been) changed at will, they raise very different policy and oversight issues. Of course the line is not always clear. Intensely held political beliefs can lead to crimes and some violators of criminal law see themselves as political prisoners.

But even with criminal investigations additional issues are raised when borders are crossed. Globalization has meant an increase in crime and social control across international borders, including more sophisticated undercover activities focusing on drugs and terrorism. For example, Operation Casablanca, a very large sting operation against drug profit laundering by Mexican and Colombian cartels was partly carried out in Mexico, without the knowledge of the Mexican government (presumably in order to protect the security of the operation). The sting, which lured Mexican bankers, was considered illegal entrapment under Mexican law. Mexico, believing its sovereignty and laws had been broken, asked for the arrest and extradition of the U.S. agents involved in the operation. In 1998 there were at least forty-five DEA agents operating in Mexico (*Seattle Times*, June 6 and 12, 1998). This raises a variety of issues regarding jurisdiction and procedure (Marx 1997a; Passas and Groskin 1995).

This and many cases in Latin America (and elsewhere) also represent a trend toward border-blurring and overlap—not only in geographical and jurisdictional terms but in terms of crime and national security, public and private police, and domestic and military policing.

The Internet offers a new field for criminal and social control innovations. The assumption (although doubtful) of truly anonymous Internet communication creates new opportunity structures. For example, there have been large stings involving the sale of child pornography over the Internet. In 1999, Texas postal inspectors along with other authorities seized control of the Landslide Company, a distributor of child pornography. They then worked with thirty federally financed task forces across the United States in an effort to identify would-be buyers. They pretended that the company was still active and sent e-mails to determine who might buy the illegal materials. One hundred persons were arrested as a result. A similar investigation, Operation Candyman, resulted in ninety arrests (*New York Times* August 8, 2001 and March 19, 2002).

In response to sex crimes involving minors located through the Internet (beyond the provision of prohibited materials), agents visit Internet chat rooms and pretend to be underage females. Over a seven-month period using the name "hotseattle," a technology entrepreneur conversed over the Internet with a "girl" who repeatedly said she was thirteen years old. When the suspect invited "her" to meet him at a Los Angeles beach and promised to take her to his hotel room and show her computer images of copulation, he was arrested and charged with the intent of having sex with a minor and his laptop computer was seized as evidence[6] (*Seattle Times*, September 21, 1999).

Crimes involving intent rather than actual behavior are more difficult to prove. A jury reached a not guilty verdict, concluding that no crime had occurred since there was no thirteen-year-old girl (ibid.).

The tactic continues to be used as an internal means of social control. New York City does about seven hundred stings a year on police officers. For example, in one case information from an anonymous police hotline and from citizens suggested that a patrolman was shaking down bodegas running illegal numbers operations. Internal Affairs Bureau officers identified themselves to the suspect on the beat as undercover officers from the Organized Crime Bureau. They showed him a picture of an individual said to be a major numbers banker. They asked the officer to keep an eye out for the individual (who actually was another IAB officer). They then faked an arrest. As the "suspect" was approaching a bodega, the officers emerged from it, pulling with them the handcuffed, screaming, and resisting "banker." The suspected officer ran up to help and was asked to drive the "banker's" car to the station while they took the banker in. The officer drove to a back street, and was caught on a videotape hidden in the car searching the car and pocketing the marked money planted there.[7]

In 1999, the London Metropolitan police announced plans to use black detectives in undercover roles targeted at officers suspected of racial discrimination. The police union criticized this as a Big Brother tactic and said it would create distrust (*Sunday Times*, February 21, 1999).

"Charlie's Barbershop" in New York, with smoked-glass windows and a locked door, was the setting for a postliminary undercover intelligence investigation that discovered information about the unsolved murder of an off-duty New York police officer. The barbershop was presented to a suspect in a murder case as a social club for gangsters run by the mob. In fact, it was run by the FBI and the "gangsters" were agents. After several visits the suspect "made a swaggering admission" to the club's owner— he had killed a police officer whose murder had never been solved. He offered the information in the hope of gaining what he believed were murder-for-hire contracts. Since he was not under arrest the information was admissible (*New York Times*, May 17, 2001).

In a related "Mr. Big Scenario," which according to one source has been used in Canada, a suspect is targeted by an undercover operative posing as a major crime figure. The suspect is lured into some remunerative petty crime with the promise of still greater profits once his credibility is established and "Mr. Big" knows he can be trusted. If all goes according to plan the suspect then confesses his more serious crimes and is arrested. There is a risk with such confessions, offered under nonjudicially supervised conditions, that defendants will brag about things they have not done in an effort to impress their "criminal" associates. Even if that is not the case, it offers a likely defense if they are charged.

In a deceptive interview, the FBI sought incriminating information from security guard Richard Jewell, initially a suspect in the 1996 bombing at Atlanta's Centennial Olympic Park. Jewell was interviewed on the pretext of helping the FBI produce a "training video" for law enforcement agents about responding to bombing scenes. Jewell was read his Miranda rights and then asked if he'd like to waive those rights for the sake of the training video. He agreed to waive the rights. Is this simply the misguided effort of a clever agent seeking to follow specific orders that a Miranda warning be delivered, or is it "outrageous government misconduct," which would merit the court to overturn a conviction? In this case the interview was terminated and Jewell was cleared as a suspect.

In an example from the United Kingdom, a suspect in a murder placed a lonely hearts advertisement. "Liz," an undercover police officer, responded and pretended to fall in love with the suspect. During one of their meetings the suspect confessed to having killed his wife. He was charged with murder but was acquitted. The trial judge held that the confession was not admissible, because the Police and Criminal Evidence Act of 1984 requires the exclusion of evidence of a confession obtained in "circumstances conducive to unreliability." However, in an unusual step, the judge released the full transcript of the confession (Choo and Mellors 1995).

UNDERCOVER UNDER THE COVERS:
THE MAYOR BARRY CASE

The lure of sex as bait can also be seen in the case of Washington DC Mayor Marion Barry. His arrest and trial after he purchased drugs from an ex-girlfriend raised a variety of ethical and policy issues involving police deception: Is it wise to focus scarce resources on occasional users rather than dealers? If a case for indictment cannot be made before a grand jury or before a judge for permission to search, wiretap, or bug, is it appropriate to move to an undercover temptation for which there is no legal minimum threshold? Was the grand jury used in a manipulative way to obtain a felony indictment (Barry's allegedly lying to it about cocaine use is a felony, while his possession of cocaine was only a misdemeanor)? Was the effort to get Barry on a drug charge undertaken after earlier efforts to obtain direct evidence of corruption against him failed? Is it sound social policy to use criminal law not for prosecution, but as a resource to negotiate (e.g., the prosecutor's hint that he would exchange leniency in return for the mayor's resignation)? Should special criteria be applied before a political figure becomes the target of an undercover investigation? What of the speculation that the highly visible prosecutor in the case had his own political aspirations? Is there a racial patterning to the selection of targets in recent sting operations, or does the apparent pattern simply reflect greater black prominence in political life? Shouldn't the government try to block the flow of drugs rather than provide them? Should it have intervened after he purchased the drugs rather than letting him proceed to use them? What if he had suffered a heart attack or other serious health damage from the cocaine? Should the government be offering its citizens potentially toxic substances?

A particularly interesting question involves friendship and undercover investigations. When, if ever, is it appropriate to use friendship and the lure of sex as part of an investigation? This depends on the context (Marx 1992b). A typology can be created by combining dimensions of whether or not emotional intimacy and sexual intimacy are present. The most problematic law enforcement use of the tactic is seduction (faked emotional intimacy mixed with sexual intimacy). Five situations in which seduction most commonly occurs are (1) blackmail, (2) stigmatization and/or disruption, (3) general intelligence collection, (4) evidence or information collection for a prior offense, and (5) evidence collection for an anticipated offense.

NEW SUPPORTS

Undercover considered a number of material and legal resources that encouraged the use of covert tactics. Judicial rulings and legislation continue to encourage undercover investigations. In an Illinois case, the Supreme Court voted eight to one that the Miranda ruling was not required in prison settings. In this case, an undercover agent posing as a prisoner obtained a confession from a jailed suspect (although it was for a different crime than the one for which he was imprisoned; *Illinois v. Perkins,* 110 S. Ct. 2394, 1990). In another case the Court held that it is legal to rummage around in people's garbage.

But there were new legal restrictions as well. Thus a federal district judge in Phoenix issued a decision that limited the government's authority to send undercover personnel to secretly watch and record church gatherings. The Constitution bars the government from unbridled and inappropriate covert activity that is intended to abridge the First Amendment right of freedom of religion. However, a religious gathering can be infiltrated without a warrant if an agent is invited to participate in criminal activities. The ruling grew out of a case against Arizona churches that had offered sanctuary to illegal aliens from Central America. In the 1986 trial, ministers and priests, among others, were convicted of conspiracy and harboring aliens. The churches claimed they were offering refuge from political persecution. As part of the investigation, informers working for the Immigration and Naturalization Service attended church and recorded sermons (*New York Times,* December 12, 1990).

The issues raised in an Oregon case have the potential to greatly curtail undercover activities, or if not, to have them be carried out without judicial supervision. The latent value conflict between truthfulness and effectiveness against crime became manifest in Oregon as a result of a state Supreme Court mandate requiring all lawyers, including prosecutors overseeing organized crime and narcotics cases, to be truthful. A lawyer seeking information for a civil law insurance suit carried out a private sting and misrepresented himself as a doctor. The lawyer was found by the Oregon Supreme Court to have engaged in dishonest conduct that violated state bar rules. In addition the court found that federal prosecutors were not exempt from state bar ethics rules (based on the 1999 federal McDade law). The Oregon state bar has regulations against dishonesty, fraud, deceit and misrepresentation by lawyers. Encouraging an undercover agent or informant to lie could cause prosecutors to lose their license to practice law. This touches federal prosecutors most clearly since they often play an oversight role in major investigations. After this ruling, "the state attorney general's office, the FBI and the DEA halted virtually all big undercover operations, and local police agencies have cancelled most covert operations in drug cases that could end up in federal court" (*Los Angeles Times,* July 29, 2001).

The state bar sought an amendment that would exclude lawyers involved in "legal covert activity" from this restriction, if they didn't directly participate. However, that was rejected by the state Supreme Court as too broad. This raises an interesting issue for adversarial systems: if prosecutors can legally engage in misrepresentation, why can't defense lawyers use similar tactics? This is logically equivalent to the imbalance in the rewards and other benefits (immunity, lessened sentences, dropped charges, etc.) that the government can offer to informants, relative to what defense attorneys can offer.

A potential boost to covert means in the early 1990s may have come from the largest reallocation of FBI manpower in the bureau's history up to that time. This involved shifting of three hundred agents from cold war counter-intelligence work to the investigation of gang violence and related crimes. Domestic criminal investigation involves a different ethos and methods than political counter-intelligence, but the clandestine cloak and dagger mentality and experience of these agents may have encouraged covert means, whether directly or indirectly.

Congress increased the forfeiture authority of the Justice Department and Customs Service in 1988 and 1992, extending it to pornography, money laundering, and espionage, and permitting the sharing of seized property with local law enforcement agencies. This was revised in 2000. Between 1984 and 1994, there were a large number of federal forfeitures worth $3.6 billion (*Boulder Daily Camera,* December 11, 1994). In 2000 $201 million was received from forfeitures and the sale of recovered property (Department of the Treasury 2001).

With forfeiture may come the risk of going after targets because of what the government stands to gain, rather than because of the seriousness of the offense or offender. In what hopefully will not become a national precedent, the small town of Helper, Utah, is offering to help its police officers by giving them cash bonuses of 12 percent of any seized drug-related assets (*Law Enforcement News*, April 15, 1995). The feeding frenzy potential of such an incentive system is obvious, and personal use of such funds is prohibited at the federal level. Revenue raising and maximizing profit for the government can displace traditional criminal justice goals. There are also issues of justice and equity; since a civil court is involved, the standard is the preponderance of evidence rather than the more stringent beyond a reasonable doubt. One need neither be charged with nor found guilty of a crime to have property seized by the government.

New financial incentives, along with the creation of mandatory life imprisonment or twenty-year minimum sentences and the elimination of parole for certain drug offenses, has made it easier to attract informants.[8] A new (or expanded) class of super-informants has appeared.

The funds available for informing have continued to increase. According to data provided by federal enforcement agencies, funds for informants went from $43 million in 1987 to $63 million in 1989 (*Atlanta Journal-Constitution*, March 31, 1991). By 1995, this was approximately $100 million. DEA's informant budget for 2000 was $20 million (*Los Angeles Times*, March 5, 2000).

The 1988 asset forfeiture law permits prosecutors to share up to 25 percent of seized assets with informants. One informant earned more than one million dollars (including five hundred thousand dollars from a single case in Kansas involving a marijuana ring he infiltrated). He reports he would like to be an undercover officer, "but cops just aren't paid enough" (*Atlanta Journal Constitution*, March 31, 1991). The implications of such incentives for informer abuses, as well as for the morale of the less handsomely rewarded police with whom they work, are worthy of study. Would the adversarial playing field be more level if defendants could also pay witnesses for testimony that results in their being found not guilty? In an adversarial setting where, under penalty of perjury laws, individuals swear to tell the truth, why is payment restricted only to the prosecution? Is justice better served by paying to find one guilty than to find one innocent?

Andrew Chambers spent sixteen years working as an informer for the DEA and other agencies in thirty-one cities. His work on over three hundred cases resulted in 445 arrests, the seizure of "tons" of drugs and $6 million in assets. He reportedly earned $4 million ($2.2 from the DEA), based at least indirectly on his arrests and seizures. However, many of these cases were jeopardized when it was revealed that Chambers had repeatedly lied under oath and that authorities had failed to reveal information about his criminal background to defense attorneys (*Los Angeles Times*, March 5, 2000; *Law Enforcement News*, June 31, 2001). As a freelance agent Chambers moved from city to city (there was no centralized system for keeping track of such informants). The DEA eventually "deactivated" him after an investigation. His continued use, after he had lied about his criminal background and while under oath, was due to mistakes, incomplete files, and communication breakdowns. Given his effectiveness, information on his criminal background is something many agencies would prefer not to know about. Yet this comes with grave risks when the egg cracks. In response DEA has created a central file system with information on an informant's criminal record and a rule that forbids an informant who has lied on the stand from being used again absent "special exemption." It would be interesting to study how often and under what conditions such an exemption is granted.

In 1987, strict federal sentencing guidelines were adopted that mandated harsh penalties for weapons offenses. For example, a convicted felon found guilty of possessing a weapon faces up to ten years in prison. This offered authorities another new resource to persuade those facing such charges to become informants. The definition of violent felon is rather broad, and it permits holding a federal hammer over persons who in the past would have remained in state courts. It also increases the incentive authorities have to manage the environment so that felons are arrested in possession of weapons—in some cases as a result of being sold the weapon by an undercover agent (e.g., through the joint federal-local Achilles Task Force).

Efforts to boost security for U.S. embassies and diplomats abroad have seen the extension of the "concierge principle" in which those in social roles involving contact with the public offer additional eyes to police (e.g., hotel, apartment, restaurant and entertainment workers, taxi drivers, street vendors) (*Seattle Times*, April 27, 2000).

The "hotline" and the offer of rewards have become a more routinized aspect of social control, aided by the ease of communicating through cell phones and the Internet. After September 11 a government TIPS (Terrorism Information and Prevention System) plan to encourage meter readers, transportation workers and others whose jobs regularly take them through public spaces to report what they see was met with considerable public and congressional opposition (*New York Times*, July 21, 2002). The plan, more focused than most hotlines, was offered as a kind of national neighborhood watch. It builds upon a prior program by the American Trucking Association to train drivers to report "something wrong that has security implications" (*Seattle Times*, May 14, 2002).

Florida has a "turkey hotline" and pays informants for providing information on fowl poachers (*St. Petersburg Times*, February 21, 1998). Since Columbine and other high school shootings, there have been increased efforts to encourage students to report suspicious activity, and a number of attacks appear to have been prevented (e.g., the School Safety and Enhancement and Hotline Acts of 1999).

A report by the National School Boards Association's (1995) Council of School Attorneys offers advice to school officials on creating drug-free environments. With no empirical evidence or broad weighing of the factors involved, the report notes that undercover operations in schools can "produce bold and valuable results" and "be quite an effective weapon in the war on drugs."

The report offers guidance for undercover operations in schools. It notes that, "who initiates the operation may be significant to eventual legal challenges." Law enforcement generally needs probable cause, while school officials may carry out searches and seizures based on reasonable suspicion. Goals may involve "simply to gather information" or "alternatively, the goal of an operation could be to identify and prosecute drug dealers, or, in some instances, to target specific individuals." School boards are advised to make it clear that school lockers are the "property of the school system . . . [and] are subject to search and inspection at any time." Students should be required to sign an acknowledgement that the school system retains authority to patrol student parking lots and inspect student automobiles therein. A student's refusal to give access to the interior of a vehicle would lead to disciplinary action. Agents must be carefully trained with respect to the law and given guidance on interaction and involvement with minor students: "(e.g., dating, driving, partying etc.), simulating the use and ingestion of drugs, etc." Care must be taken not to confound school administrative and disciplinary proceedings with the formal protections required of a custodial interview once an arrest has occurred.

With respect to arrests police are said to ". . . prefer to arrest the subjects during school hours, thereby ensuring easier access to students and a high level of visibility" because of its "strong deterrent effect." School officials may not favor this in order to avoid ". . . a perception of 'storm trooper' tactics." If an investigation leads to the arrest of a large number of students the school faces the dilemma of whether to simply "put them on the streets" or provide some alternative form of education.

A Los Angeles police leader, responsible for undercover operations in city schools, expressed the hope that an operation in which 184 students were arrested for drug dealing would send ". . . a strong message to students in every high school that the person seated next to you, in front of you, or behind you in class may be a Los Angeles police officer" (*Los Angeles Times*, June 3, 1999).

Given the publicity covert means and other forms of surveillance receive in the news, entertainment, and marketing media, and the cultural pervasiveness of the idea of the sting, there are many more stings carried out by private individuals and organizations, beyond just private investigators. In India journalists who exposed corruption in military procurement caused the resignation of the Defense Minister. During the seven-month investigation, the journalists posed as arms dealers. Among other things, they documented their provision of prostitutes to three army officers. They said that this was a standard part of winning defense contracts and if they had failed to offer this, their specious role would not have seemed authentic. They claimed that "extraordinary methods" served the public interest. The ". . . story was not about sex, but corruption in governance." The Indian government launched its own investigation of the investigation, claiming "these are not journalists. They are a bunch of criminals, blackmailers and pimps" (*New York Times*, August 24, 2001).

Police may also act as a journalists, a move the latter generally view unfavorably. For example, a man holding children hostage in a daycare center in Luxembourg was lured into the open by a promise of a television interview and then shot by police posing as a TV crew. He was shot with a gun concealed in a television camera (*Seattle Times*, June 2, 2000).

In a rare example of offering positive reinforcement from an undercover investigation, police used underage police cadets who sought to buy liquor in a "compliance check" near Seattle. They found 14 of 64 establishments selling alcohol to minors. The 14 were cited and identified in a news story. Later the stores that were found in compliance with the law also had their names listed as "the good guys" in a news story because they ". . . deserve recognition for their efforts to train clerks and monitor customers" (*Seattle Times*, November 11, 1998).

A number of private information sharing, training, equipment-focused, and contract service provision organizations have appeared in recent decades, as the demand and resources for training and specialized skills has increased. Essentially private, usually profit-making organizations can be contrasted with public agency cross-jurisdictional (whether functional or geographical) networks such as joint task forces.

Consider for example The International Association of Undercover Officers, a private organization founded in 1993 by a former Treasury agent. It is "dedicated to the safety and professionalism of undercover officers." According to its web page (Undercover.org) it offers "a vast international network of intelligence gathering means for today's undercover officers." While noting that "the world of undercover has expanded into all areas of criminal enterprise," much of its focus appears to be on drug enforcement. The organization offers a "confidential database," international intelligence networking, undercover product information and testing, training, conferences and a quarterly magazine, *The Brotherhood*. Apparently in keeping with a need-to-know orientation, my requests for more information received no response.

This and related forms of public, private, and cross-jurisdictional social control organizations raise important issues with respect to accountability, and can offer functional alternatives to localized government forms of control (Marx 1992a; Deflem 2000). Through training conferences and the creation of networks, innovations in social control are brought to peripheral agencies and a national and international police culture is strengthened.

COMPLEXITIES AND VAGARIES OF UNDERCOVER WORK

The conflict of goals between preventing crime and encouraging it in or-der to apprehend is nicely illustrated by a San Francisco officer. He is one of seventeen who patrol the streets in plain clothes, looking for parking vi-olators and meter jammers. He reports that his unit is effective because if a uniformed officer is present, no one is going to wipe off the marked tires (*San Francisco Chronicle*, April 13, 1989). To which the skeptic might re-spond, "Isn't that what we want uniformed officers for—to prevent viola-tions?" Do we really want to encourage people to break the rules because we want them to think no one is there? Underlying the officer's remark is the need to write citations in order to meet productivity goals. The un-stated assumption here is, "We want to create a situation in which, because they never know whether or not a police officer is watching, persons won't wipe off their tires." This myth of surveillance comes with other costs, but it is believed to be more efficient than obtaining that result only when a uniformed officer is actually present. From a standpoint of empirical im-pact, we don't know if it is a myth.

Another goal that appears to have a win/win quality to it can be seen in some special stakeout units whose job it is to watch suspects. In a Los Angeles case the unit watched a man suspected of dozens of thefts. Their mission was "to eliminate him as a suspect by monitoring him while the real criminal struck elsewhere or follow him to the scene of the next theft and clinch the case against him" (*Los Angeles Times*, December 26, 2001).

In response to a high auto-theft rate, police in Seattle leave unlocked sports cars or SUVs, with the engine running, in high-crime areas and watch from a surveillance vehicle. The cars are equipped with hidden in-terior video cameras and remote shutoff devices that permit locking the doors and cutting the engine as patrol cars converge. The cars are donated by insurance companies (*Seattle Times*, July 16, 1991). A key issue here in avoiding what can be called "artifactual crime generation," or deviance amplification, is whether particular individuals in areas where there is a known problem are provided an opportunity to break the law, or whether there is equal opportunity for this by providing opportunities randomly. A second factor is whether ensnarled individuals are approached by a covert agent or whether individuals self-select, as in the case of simply leaving a car running.

The issue of the sometimes conflicting goals of preventing crimes and making arrests can also be seen in the case of Malcolm X's daughter, Qubi-lah Shabazz, who was accused of hiring a pretend hit man to avenge her father's death. When the informant was asked why he didn't try to dis-courage the plot, he said, "I'm supposed to sound like a murderer, re-member? A hit man wouldn't agree to kill someone and then say it's wrong" (*Newsweek,* May 15, 1995). When a suspect is hesitant (e.g., Shabazz indicated that she was leery and wanted to put it on hold, and missed a planned meeting), should the informant respect this apparent withdrawal or ambivalent intent, or persist? In this case, thirty-eight of forty phone calls had been initiated by the informant, and he appears to have done most of the talking on the tapes.

The question of when undercover police should intervene to prevent a crime versus letting it go on too long has continued to raise moral and practical questions. Thus in Dallas an undercover officer watched a woman being raped by a group he had infiltrated. He pretended to be sick to avoid participating. He stated, "You don't want to ruin your credibility" (*New York Times,* August 11, 1989). Would he feel the same way if his wife, sister, or mother had been the victim?

In New York, police had prior information that a drug dealer planned to rob an undercover agent. They did not intervene to stop this and the agent was shot. Some critics within the department claimed that it should have been aborted. Dangers such as this are reflected in agent folktales. Question: What does an undercover agent do? Answer: He's like the kid they use down in Louisiana for alligator bait. They tie him to the end of a rope and he walks out into the swamp. All the kid can do is hope they jerk the rope back in time (Goddard and Levine 1988).

Police in a Long Island sting were criticized for permitting the illegal dumping of toxic waste to continue for what critics saw as an inordinate amount of time. Pollution was created in order to fight it. In a nonenforcement example in Boston, a drug informant was permitted to run an after-hours club in exchange for his cooperation. This led to neighborhood complaints about noise, disorder, and increased crime, and to beliefs about the police corruption that permitted the place to flourish.

An inquiry in Los Angeles found that a nineteen-member special surveillance unit had often failed to prevent those it was watching from attacking people in armed robberies and burglaries. While in many cases they could have been arrested beforehand for lesser offenses or on existing arrest warrants, detectives waited for a violent felony to occur because that would make for a stronger case and a longer sentence. The department subsequently implemented a policy instructing officers to protect potential crime victims even if this jeopardizes an undercover investigation. It reads, "reverence for human life must always be the first priority when considering the extent to which a criminal incident is allowed to progress or deteriorate . . . during a stakeout or the surveillance of known criminals."

The unit has also been accused of dispensing punishment before trial. In a successful civil trial, a federal jury found the Los Angeles chief of police and nine officers in the surveillance unit liable for the death of three robbers and the wounding of a fourth. The suit accused the unit of being a death squad prone to shooting suspects instead of arresting them. In this case police had tracked the robbers for weeks. As the robbers entered their getaway car after holding up a restaurant, the officers opened fire, later claiming the suspects had pointed guns at them. The weapons turned out to be unloaded pellet guns.

In a step that executives did not take "lightly," McDonald's went ahead with a promotional Monopoly giveaway after authorities determined that a contractor had rigged the games. Restaurant customers played "millions of game cards" but did not know they had no chance of winning the biggest prizes. This was justified, according to an executive, because ". . . our No. 1 goal was to get the bad guys, which meant fully cooperating with the FBI . . . and working together with them to put the trap in place." Once the investigation was closed the company offered an alternative "instant giveaway" (*Seattle Times*, August 22, 2001).

The issue of intervention, as well as an example of unintended consequences from covert surveillance, can be seen in a St. Louis case. The FBI, hoping to record evidence of terrorist activities, planted listening devices in the apartment of a Palestinian-American. But instead it recorded the suspect's murder of his teenage daughter. An incriminating statement—"Do you know that you are going to die tonight?"—and the girl's screams as she begged her parents not to kill her, were captured by an automated listening device. Since the FBI surveillance unit was not staffed that night, it is not clear whether authorities could have intervened in time to prevent the murder at that time if they had been listening. However, there were earlier recordings of phone conversations in which the accused discussed various methods of getting rid of the daughter (*New York Times*, October 28, 1991).

Undercover mentions parking tickets given to unmarked vehicles as among the least of the unintended consequences that may occur, but gives no idea of its magnitude. In Boston in 1989, twenty thousand parking violations were dismissed as part of an agreement with agencies engaged in undercover law enforcement or investigative actions. One thousand of these were for the more serious public safety violations such as double-parking and parking by fire hydrants (*Boston Globe*, February 14, 1990).

An example of agency growth as a result of manipulating the numbers game can be seen in the San Juan DEA office. After the arrival of a new department head the pressures for arrests greatly increased. Agents began reporting arrests for small quantities of marijuana or cocaine, rather than for the large-scale quantities that DEA cases usually involve. The first year after the new head's arrival 1,136 arrests were reported, nearly double the previous year's figure. The next year the figure rose to 2,042. The inflated figures meant more resources and almost doubling the size of the staff (from 153 to 304 persons). As much as 70 percent of the agency's "arrests" during this time were for small amounts and made by local police. Agents

who complained about the numbers inflation were reportedly repri-
manded and demoted (*Law Enforcement News*, June 31, 2001).

Rather than arrests generating new resources, the situation may also be
reversed: the available resources may generate an incentive for arrests.
Law enforcement dances rather delicately around the "rewards" issue,
knowing how central, yet also corrupting, it can be.

The resources expended in an undercover operation can also generate
pressures to produce cases to justify the outlay. But when a sting goes awry
the pressures may be even greater. In the largest misconduct award in New
Hampshire's history, a physicist received a one million dollar court settlement. Police received a tip that thieves wanted for working a diamond
swap at a chain store were to try again. A sting was set up; store personnel
went along with the sting and handed over the jewels. Unfortunately the
thieves got away. Under enormous pressure police arrested an innocent
man in spite of having almost nothing to link him to the crime. In their determination to solve the case, police ignored evidence that would have
cleared him and charges were not dropped until fourteen months later
(*Boston Globe*, December 8, 1991).

Panamanian general Manuel Ortega appears to represent the ultimate
in the intermeshing of cops and robbers. His defense claims that his drug-
and gun-smuggling activities were undertaken with the tacit support of
the United States, as part of its anticommunist activities. He worked with
both the DEA and the Medellin drug cartel: he earned praise from the DEA
for his cocaine seizures, which he then appears to have sold back to the cartel. He also sold guns to the cartel and provided photographs and addresses of DEA agents in Panama (*New York Times*, November 24, 1991).

In 1993 there were allegations that top officials of a CIA-funded Vene-
zuelan antidrug unit smuggled several thousand pounds of cocaine into
the United States. The CIA reportedly asked the DEA for permission to let
the dope walk to facilitate intelligence gathering. The permission was denied but the shipment was still made. The chief of the antidrug unit acknowledged that he had run loads to the United States independently, but
claimed that this was done as a law enforcement technique (*Washington
Post*, November 19, 1993).

An example of unintended harm caused to innocent third parties occurred when DEA officers put ninety pounds of cocaine on a flight from
Belize to Miami. When the plane stopped in Honduras, drug-sniffing dogs
discovered it. The three crew members and three passengers, who knew
nothing about the drugs, were beaten and held in prison for twelve days.
One would hope that the risks from loss of control over unaccompanied
evidence in transit could have been anticipated in deciding whether or not
to carry out the plan, and if carried out, that a contingency plan for failures
would have been developed.

The fabrication of evidence and exploitative informers received renewed attention in a Los Angeles scandal involving jailhouse informers. An inmate demonstrated how he could fabricate the confessions of other inmates without ever having talked to them. Using the telephone and given only the name of a murder suspect, the inmate identified himself as a bail bondsman and was able to obtain information from official sources about the crime. He then called the bailiff at the jail where he was a prisoner, identified himself as a district attorney, and ordered himself and the suspect transferred to a court for an interview. He could then say that he was with the suspect on the bus when the latter confessed. This would be admissible in court since authorities had not arranged the confession. The president of the Los Angeles Criminal Courts Bar Association, in commenting publicly on the revelations in the case, said, "All we've done is crack the egg here. The yolk will spill out all over the country."

A nice example of the symbolic and communicative aspects (and the potential for deflating official images) appeared in a speech given by President George Bush from the Oval Office on drug strategy. The president dramatically held up a bag of crack purchased near the White House and said, "I think it's great because it sent a message to the United States that even across from the White House they can sell drugs." Later it also sent a message about manipulation and image creation. It turned out that the seller had been lured to the site by a DEA agent. He did not know where the White House was until the undercover agent who arranged the buy told him how to get there. There are also messages that boomerang with embarrassment. For example, a group of coast guardsmen photographed with the president congratulating them for a job well done against drug smugglers were later themselves indicted for smuggling, and the picture was run a second time in the media.

Barker and Carter (1989) suggest the lovely phrase "fluffing up the evidence" in describing a form of police lying. Undercover means nicely lend themselves to such activity. A police inspector in the Netherlands, in considering deception via omission, states, "We do try to keep things secret, but without lying about it. Sometimes it may seem like we put the judge on the wrong track, lay a mist over it" (Klerks 1995).

HUMOR

As part of a study of cultural images and surveillance I have analyzed visual jokes and cartoons (Marx 1996). The names, props, and sets used in undercover investigations lend themselves to humor that is both intended and unintended, as a result of surprises beyond control. Some humor is in the use of words that have double meanings. As with a play, the audience knows what many of the actors do not. Other humor takes the form of situational comedy, at least for the agents and broader audience. Here I will offer some recent examples.

A drug education and investigation web page has the motto "We make house calls" (The OkieNarc's Home Page). This web page also lists, along with pro and antidrug sites, several sites dealing with drug humor. It reports the 1998 case of a man who threw away the recording device worn by an individual he correctly suspected of being an informant. He was sentenced to ten months in jail and made to pay $3,111.11 to the FBI to replace the property he destroyed.

A case in Bangladesh gives literal meaning to the view held by some of drug dealers being animals. Police reported rescuing two monkeys trained to sell drugs. Those visiting the dealer's house were greeted by the monkeys. If money was offered to the female named Munni, the drugs would be retrieved by a male monkey named Hamid. Three male (human) occupants of the house were arrested and would face the death penalty if convicted. The monkeys remained behind bars of a different sort at the National Zoo.

There are also what can be called last-laugh situations. A seventeen-month sting directed at importers and sellers of illegal eavesdropping equipment in forty spy shops seized pens, calculators, electronic power strips, and telephone jacks with hidden bugs. In another lovely irony that must have given a smile to those in the know, agents used sophisticated listening devices to document their transactions. To the undercover agents' dismay, shop owners refrained from using the antibugging devices they also sell. While many such devices have been illegal since at least 1968, this rare investigation was apparently triggered not by a desire to protect citizens' privacy, but to keep the devices out of the hands of drug dealers after a bug was found in a drug shipment, which alerted smugglers to the police discovery (*New York Times*, April 4, 1995).

While more tragic than funny in the usual sense, given a happy ending, there is an unbelievable quality in the astounding and stupid lengths of the capers of some of those caught in undercover operations. Consider the girlfriend of a New York City police officer who, in an apparent attempt to strengthen their romance, contracted with a specious hit man to have the boyfriend's fourteen-month-old daughter killed. The woman was a psychology student at a Long Island college (*New York Times*, February 5, 1996).

A British case involving a married couple named Dixon ended happily and unhappily for the partners. Intense marital disharmony led both to independently seek to have their respective partner killed. In both cases the hit men they approached informed police. The Dixons survived, but the marriage did not.

The hoisting of morality figures on their own petard has a tragi-comic quality. Among those arrested in an Internet child pornography sting were several priests and a police officer (*New York Times*, March 19, 2002). Such surprises are a part of the drama of secret investigations. The chief state prosecutor for the city of St. Louis, who had spent his fifteen years in office crusading against obscenity, pornography, and prostitution, was arrested on charges of soliciting sex from an undercover police officer. Among other things, he supported changes in the city's laws against prostitution to require mandatory jail sentences for second-time offenders (whether customers, prostitutes, or pimps). Note also the case of a Florida police leader caught on a hidden video surveillance system while videotaping under a woman's skirt in a department store (*Tallahassee Democrat,* August 29, 1998).

EFFECTS ON AGENTS

Undercover noted the unintended social and psychological costs that undercover work can have for its practitioners. Girodo (1991a) offers some systematic data on this in seeking to discover how personality traits interact with work situations to affect mental health and drug problems. He studied 271 federal undercover agents who volunteered (of 350 who were randomly asked). Self-reports of drug and alcohol abuse and disciplinary infractions were positively correlated with the extent of undercover experience. This is related to a prior research finding that accumulated experience in undercover assignments is associated with a variety of social and psychological problems. For example, in a related study Girodo (1991b) found undercover experience to be correlated with job dissatisfaction. But the effect of the undercover experience is mediated by the personality traits of the agent. Agents enter the corrupting undercover environment with varying patterns of character flaws and assets. Problem outcomes were most likely in those agents shown by personality tests to have either poor impulse control, neuroticism, or a desire for new experience. Agents assessed as having a disciplined self-image were at lesser risk.

A study by Farkas (1986) of undercover officers in Honolulu found that more than one-third reported negative changes in their social relations, stress over being with family and friends in public, and anxiety over being unable to discuss their work with those close to them. A study by Pogrebin and Poole (1993) of forty officers with undercover experience from diverse agencies illustrates these and related themes.

Among the implications of the above research is the need for greater vigilance the longer an operation goes on and the greater the accumulated undercover experience of an individual, and the importance of selecting in as well as selecting out.

The contingent and potentially destabilizing aspects of the undercover role are nicely captured in the following quote:

Spinning plates, I thought, *I'm spinning plates again.* Undercover work had always reminded me of the circus act where a guy spins a whole bunch of plates on the end of long flexible sticks, running frantically up and down the row as each one totters, giving another spin so that it doesn't fall. If one falls, it can knock the whole row down. *Phony ID, language, act, cover business, backup documentation and records, phony reputation, secret codes, contacts and agreements, money-money-money, government bureaucrats, Internal Security, murderous gangsters, family, bills, mental and physical health, watch your back, money-money-money—plates to keep spinning, spinning, spinning. How long could it last?* (Levine and Kavanau, 1997)

Among the most tragic of unintended consequences involves the friendly fire shooting or assaults on undercover officers by other police unaware of who they are. In one such incident, a black officer, holding a suspect at gunpoint in a New York subway station, was shot by white officers who thought they had come upon a robbery. Following this, a black officers' association urged its members to refuse plainclothes assignments (*New York Times*, November 19, 1992). An undercover officer in Oakland on a drug stakeout chased a car thief and was holding him at gunpoint when two uniformed officers arrived and shot and killed him (*Los Angeles Times*, January 13, 2001).

A related area also in need of study is of police officers killed by those working undercover, who are unaware or do not believe that they are dealing with police officers. For example, Patrick Dorismond was the third unarmed black man killed by undercover officers in New York City within thirteen months (*Seattle Times*, March 26, 2000). One of the ironies here is that undercover agents, unlike their uniformed counterparts, have traditionally carried lethal weapons, not a baton or mace. Faced with a life-threatening situation they rely on lethal force.

Irony could be the subtitle for any study of the intermeshing of social control with deviance (Marx 1981). To the many ironies and tradeoffs discussed in *Undercover,* one can add the fact that a suspect's not knowing the true identity of an agent puts the agent at greater risk, although it is also a necessary condition for an effective investigation. In discussing the celebrated Florida Mi-Porn case (in which two agents posed as pornographers for several years) LaBrecque notes, "[T]hey pushed out of their consciousness their major fear: that if they made a mistake, their targets might kill them before they found out who they really were. . . . [T]here was safety in being discovered to be an FBI agent" (Marx 1987). In this case there is also irony in the fact that the devious appearance and nervousness that made Pat Livingston (alias Pat Salamone) such a good undercover agent worked against his credibility when he took the witness stand. To enhance their credibility as drug users, agents may bring a variety of props such as a spoon and syringe to their encounters with drug sellers. Yet ironically this effort to appear real can lead the dealer to request that the agent then use the drugs on the spot as a condition for the sale (Jacobs 1992).

DECEPTION

As the work of Erving Goffman and others suggests, there is a generic structure to deceptive and manipulative interaction, regardless of the context. Consider, for example, the similarities between con men and undercover agents. There are parallels between agents and con men in the presentation of false selves and environments and in developmental stages, as one moves from the initial contact, to gaining confidence, to the action, to disclosure.

The mark's motivation to behave illegally is central to both con men and police (when undercover work does not involve entrapment or provocation). Con men say they do not steal: instead the mark literally thrusts a fat bankroll into their hands in hope of illicit gain in which con men willingly oblige. Compare the con man's belief, "You can't cheat an honest man," to the observation by Mel Weinberg (the central figure in the Abscam case) that "a guy's either a crook, or he isn't. If he ain't a crook, he ain't gonna do anything illegal no matter what I offer him or tell him to do." In both cases such beliefs serve to neutralize cultural prohibitions against deception.

Some similar personality characteristics, or at least skills, may be shared by both—especially the ability to read human nature, to persuade and inspire confidence, and to think on one's feet. Maurer's (1974) appreciation of the grand thinking, the unlimited gall, the sure touch, the high intelligence of the best con artists such as Yellow Kid Weil also might characterize some legendary undercover agents, as well as police interrogators (Leo 1996).

The ironic and dramatic possibilities are indeed wonderful should a con man pretending to be a police official cross paths with an agent pretending to be a con man.

The deceptive ploy of using the media to create concern in suspects about a planned arrest in order to get them to talk without benefit of an attorney was illustrated by an FBI investigation of commodities dealers in Chicago. In what appears to be a careful strategy, information about the investigation was leaked in an apparently successful effort to scare potential defendants into cooperating. Authorities have much greater leeway to bluff during questioning before an arrest is made than after it. Apart from due process questions, this also appears to have damaged the reputation of persons who were never arrested (Protess 1989).

Jacobs (1992) has identified four modes of deception used by narcotics agents in one city: prior rehearsal, appearance manipulation, and verbal and physical diversion. He has also studied the counter to agents' efforts at dissimulation—the process by which targets try to discover whether someone is an agent (Jacobs 1993). His interviews with thirty-two heroin user-dealers suggest two major deception clues: trend discontinuity, in which purchasers change their routine behavior (e.g., by bringing in a stranger or by significantly increasing the amount they seek to purchase), and illegitimate appearance and demeanor.

Mike Collison (1995), in an insightful ethnographic study of police and drug enforcement in the United Kingdom, identifies six related motives for drug informers: money, plea-bargaining, fair play, competition, career advancement, and intrigue. An additional motive is fear for one's life from criminal associates. Roger Billingsley (2001) notes that motives may also change over time.

Collison's (1995) notes that "at the core of drug squad activity lies an exchange" and that this exchange ". . . is largely beyond close public, judicial and, sometimes, senior officer, scrutiny." The same proved to be the case with FBI agent John J. Connolly, an irony-drenched, potential screenplay of mythic proportions waiting to happen. Connolly was accused of protecting the criminal activities of two organized crime leaders in Boston (Lehr and O'Neil 2000). In an indictment he was charged with racketeering and the obstruction of justice through regularly falsifying reports and illegally leaking confidential information about grand jury inquiries and wiretaps. This included information on an indictment that permitted a central figure, James Bulger, to become a fugitive. Connolly reportedly told one of them, "You can do whatever you want, just don't clip anybody." The advice was not honored. Connolly claimed that the rules had been changed retroactively, denied any wrongdoing, and said that he was just doing his duty. He drew upon a cost benefit / lesser of evils justification, "we were going to use a gang of 2 to get rid of a gang of 42" (*New York Times*, Dec. 23, 1999).

The case is paradigmatic in raising many of the central issues in undercover work. These include the ubiquity of reciprocity in contexts of democratic policing (and beyond) where the formal means are not maximally effective; the challenge of becoming close to what one is combating without becoming it; the conflicting loyalties of professional role as against family, ethnicity, and neighborhood (the latter often being necessary to carry out the role); the often thin and foggy moral lines in complex contexts; ambivalence as a central human experience; and temptation and the corrosive effects of secrecy on accountability.

PRIVATE EYES

As part of the more general growth of the private security industry (related to public budget constraints) and continuing concerns over drugs and information leaks, private undercover operations have continued to gain in prominence. These vary from full-scale corporate espionage cases to the personals—background investigations requested by individuals. The pool of former government covert agents available for private sector work has continued to grow (including the central figure in the FBI's expanded use of undercover means).

Private investigators, standing between a legal system that is not always good and clients who are not always bad, have a unique vision and freedom. Neither cops nor crooks, their position can be powerful, even if fraught with moral ambiguity and temptation.

The Wackenhut Corporation's division for covert corporate investigations, created in 1990, got off to a rocky start. It was hired by managers of the Trans Alaska Pipeline to investigate the loss of confidential company documents. But according to 1991 hearings held by the House Interior Committee, this escalated into a more questionable investigation of its critics. After six months and $290,000 the investigation was canceled (Committee on Interior and Insular Affairs 1991).

Highly trained investigators, sophisticated eavesdropping equipment, and a sting operation were used against a critic who passed on documents regarding environmental and safety problems to regulators and the news media. In an effort to discover his sources, agents set up a phony environmental organization to gain the target's confidence. He invited the agents to his home, where they stole documents from his desk, went through his garbage, and obtained his personal telephone records. In the logical although not moral equivalent of government targeting the private sector, the agents also considered targeting Congressman George Miller (the new chair of the House Interior Committee) in order to have him indicted for theft of corporate documents and to embarrass him politically.

One expanding specialty niche within the broader field are small firms that monitor activists concerned with social issues such as the environment, nuclear power, and animal rights. Their activities vary from simply using public materials to track persons and issues to undercover operations and infiltration.

Keeping track of protest movements is seen to be a wise thing to do for businesses involved in sensitive work. This is a strand of the broad move toward strategic and anticipatory business planning. There is a perceived need for intelligence not only on markets and suppliers, but also on rivals and critics. The president of Perceptions International in Connecticut states, "We look at the animal-rights movement in general." This includes certain "philosophical and tactical trends" of interest to clients (*Boston Globe*, July 9, 1989). One such client was U.S. Surgical Corporation, a group that was criticized for using anesthetized dogs to demonstrate its surgical staples. But the intelligence firm also gets target specific. One of its employees infiltrated an animal-rights group and befriended a woman who was later arrested for planting a bomb in the parking lot of U.S. Surgical.

Social movements may also use similar tactic in seeking to generate negative publicity and legal difficulties for their opponents, for example, anti-abortion activists who call clinics pretending to be thirteen-year-old girls impregnated by adult boyfriends. According to a leader of the group, a large majority of the time, in tape-recorded calls the clinic indicated that the information would be concealed, which this is may violate state laws that require reporting the sexual abuse of a minor (*The Seattle Times*, May 31, 2002).

No-fault divorce laws have greatly reduced the use of private detectives for domestic investigations. But that is changing. Concern over sexually transmitted diseases and fraud have encouraged increased use of private detectives to investigate possible suitors. Some investigators actively seek out clients by placing ads directed toward singles, such as "Do you know who you're dating? Now more than ever it's important to know." One investigator notes, "[T]wenty years ago this was unheard of, but now we're getting as many single people as married." Women are much more likely to hire such investigators than are men. One investigator reports, "[T]here's nothing we can't get. It may not always be public record, but it can be obtained." Some ways of doing this—by watching targets, going through their garbage, subterfuge, or rewarding or coercing those entrusted with information. For $250, an Ohio company called Test-A-Mate even offers attractive female decoys who will test the loyalty of a partner. They find out where the target is likely to be and then sit near him, but won't speak unless spoken to first.

Individuals are also covertly watched not because of their uniqueness (as with the above), but because they are seen as representatives of more general social types. A development in market research is to make greater use of discreet "people-watchers." As one expert said, "[T]he best way to get an in-depth understanding of consumer values is to watch people buying and using products." Cultural anthropologists now observe and often videotape consumers in stores, shopping malls, and even in their own homes.

Such techniques permit researchers to get underneath the surface. The director of research for one large company states, "We look in the refrigerators, the kitchen cabinets and the closets. We ask people to show us their favorite things. We learn a lot more by looking around than we'd ever find out just asking people about their homes. Nothing is hidden from us." Families that permit researchers to come into their homes presumably give consent and are paid, but in large stores and shopping malls individuals are unlikely to be warned that they are being watched.[9]

SECOND THOUGHTS AND ENDURING TENSIONS

Scholars such as those represented in this volume, who choose to work on criminal justice issues from a broad, interdisciplinary, qualitative, skeptical, and often critical perspective, generally have a more difficult time than their colleagues whose feet are squarely planted in a single discipline and who quantitatively pursue microlevel questions defined by funding agencies and criminal justice establishments.

Here I address some more general professional issues raised by the undercover study.[10] There are empirical or practical answers to some of the questions. Given variation in contexts and value conflicts, others have no fixed resolution. However, heightened awareness of the tension between polarities can be positive.

1. Is it appropriate for social scientists, whose legitimacy and traditions involve ordering micro-empirical measurements with systematic theory, to study broad amorphous topics—such as privacy, deception, authenticity, liberty, autonomy, and justice—in an interpretive fashion? Wouldn't it be better to start with just one question, replicate prior research, or test a few propositions using rigorous methods and quantitative data? Perhaps, but when the topic has rarely been studied there is also a case for beginning by casting a broad net, in the hope of stimulating more delineated studies. Is it better to know things of lesser importance with greater certainty or things of great importance with less certainty? There is no correct answer to the recurring issues of forests, trees, and grasses. They are all there and are all-important.

For social scientists trained in the positivist-happy times of the 1950s and 1960s, one risks (or at least imagines risking) peer rejection, a negative self-image, and guilt in not following the standard linear model of moving from questions to answers, and theories to systematic numerical tests. Yet the specificity and rigidity of this model may not feel right for some projects. For example, I started with an interest in the phenomenon of deception by the state and a feeling that it was wrong, or at least risky, as public policy. I began with an answer—or better, a feeling—and looked for the questions. Some of the most important questions (how to balance the rights of the individual with the needs of the community) cannot be adequately answered by empirical research. I also struggled with finding the right balance between description, classification, measurement, explanation, and prescription/proscription.

2. Even if one opts to focus on a broad topic, should it be approached from a multi- and interdisciplinary perspective, or from a narrower disciplinary base? In an exploratory study there are advantages in using whatever tools are available. But then as a nonspecialist one must confront the issues of poaching. Can/should we trespass with impunity/immunity in other professional vineyards if we like the look of their grapes? In trying to be all things to all people, does one risk being nothing to anyone? Does a book need a disciplinary identity? Does breadth have to come at the cost of depth?

3. What does it mean to understand undercover police practices? What were the goals of my sociological inquiry? What does it mean to be inter-

ested in reasons as well as causes, in subjective experiences understood empathetically, as well as in more easily quantifiable objective factors? How can surveys and experiments be supplemented in the search for broad understanding? How can we make use of the truths of novelists and philosophers?[11] What role does wisdom play in the results of sociological research? How does prediction relate to understanding? How does understanding relate to judgment? What is the difference between a social scientist, a journalist, an essayist, and a novelist? What needs to be added to Robert Park's observation that sociology is slow journalism?

4. Is it possible to balance social science and social criticism so that they are mutually supportive rather than corrosive? We need precision and passion. I don't want my concerns with civil liberties, inequality, and reform to distort my scientific observations—for both intellectual and practical reasons. Scientific understanding should not be sacrificed on the altar of commitment. Yet in this socially important area, I am more than the neutral scientist who just wants the facts (Marx 1972).

5. Can the same work make contributions to both social science and public policy? Must one choose between being an uncontaminated basic scientist seeking fundamental knowledge with little notion of how, when, where, or if it will be used; a hired gun seeking normatively based solutions to an applied problem someone else has defined; or a zealous, self-appointed social engineer-moral entrepreneur, peddling your own brand of expert truth and action? How does and should knowledge relate to action? Do you have to know why in order to know how? Can academics, with their cross-case knowledge and tenure, who act as Monday morning quarterbacks with no responsibility for the consequences of the actions that practitioners must take, really have much to say that is useful?

Is it possible to write so that one's work is well received by both colleagues and the educated public? In trying to reach for (or at least not exclude) a general audience, one runs the risk of dilution and being labeled a popularizer or even a journalist. Books that are accessible are often suspect in the halls of academe. Yet the trappings of academic respectability—literature reviews, sophisticated techniques, jargon, the assumption of a learned audience, and detached and spiritless writing—are hardly endearing to the average reader.

Between starting and finishing the book, my beliefs about the desirability of undercover tactics changed. Rather than seeing them as an unnecessary evil, I came to view their use in the United States, under limited and controlled circumstances, as a necessary evil. I gained excellent access to the FBI (something I would not have predicted from my days of Berkeley student activism). Does the change in my attitude say something about my openness and intellectual honesty in the face of a very complex situation, or was I co-opted? Had I come to that situation the madam warned the prostitute about: when one starts enjoying sex with the customers it's time to quit? At some level did I want to please and be liked by those sometimes heroic figures in almost white hats? Is the change partly a strategic ploy, since I want to affect the policy debate and know that a hostile polemic would likely preclude this? How can one balance and maintain a degree of respect/appreciation for our subjects and the sincerity of their beliefs, reciprocity (at least in so far as one doesn't harm them, since they are giving something to us with little in return), with the need to be objective, to be faithful to our moral concerns, and not to be captured by our subjects?

How do you know when you are done? When do you let go? I stopped largely because of the sponsor's expectations, but could easily have spent several more years working on comparative international materials and on literary and film treatments. I was not quite ready to let go. But I know if I had worked on the book for several more years new topics would have appeared, justifying further work, in an endless spiral. With any book on a contemporary topic, one risks being out of date as soon as the work is published (that of course does not detract from a book's worth as history). As Einstein, in noting the difference between much social inquiry and physical science observed, "politics is for the moment and an equation is for eternity." Web pages that can be continuously updated may be one answer, assuming one does not get bored with the topic. On the other hand, we are in business partly because there *are* regularities as one becomes more abstract, and the analytic ability to draw out generic forms and ideal types and to use them in comparative and explanatory fashion is a vital skill. What obligations do we have once work is done to be sure that the findings come to the attention of appropriate audiences? When this involves reaching wider audiences, how can one deal with the media to be heard without being diluted? In trying to fit into many media formats, one must either appear glib and inauthentic or indecisive and academic. The latter is a surefire method for being edited out or not being asked back.

Yet criminological topics are fascinating partly because there often are no easy solutions in the usual sense, in spite of media and political demands.

In spite of these tensions there is a strong need for qualitative, interdisciplinary, and integrative approaches to broad topics of social importance. The softer social sciences residing between the humanities and the sciences are uniquely qualified for such inquiries. The building blocks of our highly specialized research endeavors must occasionally be brought together in an effort to see the broader landscape.

Comprehensive work on controversial topics takes time and scholarly independence. I spent a decade working on the undercover project and would not want to have been judged for tenure (or anything else) after only five years. The pressure to produce work quickly and to bring in research grants only on topics that established agencies want to fund can be highly dysfunctional. There is no necessary opposition between policy and basic research, nor between writing for colleagues and the educated public. We need to search for wisdom, as well as knowledge. The former is impossible without the latter and the latter is pedantic and lifeless when divorced from the concrete details of everyday life and questions of value.

ACKNOWLEDGMENTS

This chapter extends and revises and the original chapter as it appeared in the first edition of this volume. Some materials (e.g., on quotes and humor) have been cut and new material added. A longer version is available at garymarx.net.

NOTES

1. See for example Bogard (1996), Staples (1997), Ericson and Haggerty (1997), Brin (1998), Froomkin (2000), Smith (2000), Rosen (2000), Garfinkel (2000), and Gutwirth (2002). One manifestation is the expansion of undercover police.

2. The deterrent value of this is another matter. Note a poacher with poor eyesight or memory caught for a second time firing at the decoy in upstate New York. *Seattle Times*, December 20, 1998. New York State has about fifty such deer. One decoy was recently retired after sixty "wounds."

3. Of course, this is not to suggest that just because they are first-person accounts and seem believable they are necessarily correct. Proust's observation that his remembrances were a theory and not a record of the past may apply.

4. Some of these themes are treated in a special September 1992 issue of *Crime, Law and Social Change* devoted to covert policing. Marx (1987, 1992a, 1992b) treats internal affairs units, private police, and sex as they involve undercover means. Fijnaut and Marx (1995) consider undercover means in Europe and across borders. Gensous (1998) offers a comparison of the tactic in France, Canada, and the United States.

5. For example, units that were disbanded came back. Thus the San Diego Police Department's controversial undercover border patrol unit described by Joseph Wambaugh in *Lines and Shadows* was eliminated in 1978 after a scandal. It was reconstituted only to be abandoned again under similar circumstances. In 1989 it was re-created, although in a less aggressive mode.

6. Our understanding of the political uses more generally has been expanded by the good material in Powers (1987), Theoharis (1988), O'Reilly (1989), Keller (1990), and Churchill and Vander Wall (1990).

7. I am grateful to Jim Fyfe for this account.

8. On the other hand, long mandatory sentences may have unintentionally made undercover work more dangerous. Some agents have suggested that suspects, feeling they have nothing to lose, will become more violent in an effort to avoid arrest.

9. Although one couple filed a suit against Nissan, claiming that a researcher

whom they let live in their home was spying on them to gain insight into how American families live. Nissan denied the charge, but did acknowledge that the researcher was engaged in a project to determine how Americans feel about cars (*New York Times,* December 12, 1989).

10. These are treated in more depth in Marx 1990, 1997b, 2002a.

11. For a sensitive and insightful treatment of qualitative understanding see Eisner (1991). In Marx 2002b I use a fictional narrative as an ideal type to convey the sense of watching and being watched.

REFERENCES

Alvarez, T. 1993. *Undercover Operations Survival in Narcotics Investigations.* Springfield, IL: Charles C. Thomas.

Barker, T. and D. Carter. 1989. "Fluffing Up the Evidence and Covering Your Ass: Two Facets of Police Lying." Paper presented at the annual meeting of the American Society of Criminology, Reno, Nevada.

Billingsley, R. 2001. "Informer Careers: Motivation and Change." In *Informers: Policing, Policy, Practice,* edited by R. X. Billingsley et al. Cullompton, U.K.: Willan Publishing.

Bogard, B. 1996. *The Simulation of Surveillance: Hyper Control in Telematic Societies.* New York: Cambridge University Press.

Brin, D. 1998. *The Transparent Society.* Reading, MA: Perseus.

Carter, D. 1990. *Law Enforcement Intelligence Operations.* East Lansing, MI: School of Criminal Justice.

Chase, B. and L. Grimaldi. 1993. *Chased: Alone, Black and Undercover.* Far Hills, NJ: New Horizon.

Cheek, J. and T. Lesce 1988. *Plainclothes and Off-Duty Officer Survival.* Springfield, IL: Charles C. Thomas.

Choo, A. and Mellors, M. 1995. "Undercover Police Operations and What the Suspects Said (or Didn't Say)." *Web Journal of Current Legal Issues.* London: Blackstone.

Churchill, W. and J. Vander Wall. 1990. *Cointelpro Papers: Documents from the FBI's Secret Wars against Domestic Dissent.* Boston: South End.

Collison, M. 1995. *Police, Drugs and Community.* London: Free Association.

Committee on Interior and Insular Affairs. 1991. *Alaska Pipeline Service Company Covert Operation.* Washington DC: U.S. Government Printing Office.

Deflem, M. 2000. "Bureaucratization and Social Control: Historical Foundations of International Police Cooperation." *Law and Society Review* 34(3):601–40.

Department of the Treasury. 2001. *Treasury Forfeiture Fund Accountability Report Fiscal Year 2000.* Washington, DC: Author.

Eichenwald, K. 2000. *The Informant.* New York: Broadway.

Eisner, E. 1991. The Enlightened Eye. New York: Macmillan.

Ericson, R. and K. Haggerty. 1997. *Policing the Risk Society.* Toronto: University of Toronto Press.

Farkas, G. 1986. "Stress in Undercover Policing." Pp. 433–40 in *Psychological Ser-*

vices for Law Enforcement, edited by J. T. Reese and H. A. Goldstein. Washington, DC: U.S. Government Printing Office.

Fijnaut, C. and G. T. Marx. 1995. *Undercover: Police Surveillance in Comparative Perspective.* Rotterdam: Kluwer.

Froomkin, M. 2000. "The Death of Privacy?" *Stanford Law Review* 52(5).

Fuller, C. 1998. *The Art of Undercover.* Youngsville, NC: Law Enforcement Associates, Inc.

Garfinkel, S. 2000. *Database Nation.* Sebastopol, CA: O'Reilly.

Gelbspan, R. 1991. *Break-Ins, Death Threats and the FBI.* Boston: South End.

Gensous, P. 1998. Les Pratiques sous-couverture dans la procedure penale contemporaine Analyse des sytemes Americain, Canadien et francais. Ph.D. thesis, University of Montesquieu Bordeaux.

Girodo, M. 1991a. "Drug Corruption in Undercover Agents: Measuring the Risk." *Behavioral Sciences and the Law* 9:361–70.

———. 1991b. "Personality, Job Stress, and Mental Health in Undercover Agents: A Structural Equation Analysis." *Journal of Social Behavior and Personality* 6:375–90.

Goddard, D. 1988. *Undercover: the Secret Lives of an Undercover Agent.* New York: Random House.

Gutwirth, S. 2002. *Privacy and the Information Age.* Lanham, Maryland: Rowman and Littlefield.

Jacobs, B. 1992. "Undercover Deception Reconsidering Presentations of Self." *Journal of Contemporary Ethnography* 21(2).

———. 1993. "Undercover Deception Clues: A Case of Restrictive Deterrence." *Criminology* 31(2):281–99.

Jakes, D., C. Jakes, and C. Richmond. 1998. *False Prophets: The Firsthand Account of a Husband-Wife Team Working for the FBI and Living in Deepest Cover With the Montana Freemen.* Los Angeles: Newstar Media/Dove Audio.

Keller, W. 1990. *The Liberals and J. Edgar Hoover.* Princeton, NJ: Princeton University Press.

Kipps, C. 1996. *Cop Without a Badge.* New York: Carrol and Graf.

Klerks, P. 1995. "Covert Policing in the Netherlands." In *Undercover: Police Surveillance in Comparative Perspective,* edited by C. Fijnaut and G. T. Marx. Rotterdam: Kluwer.

LaBrecque, R. 1987. *Lost Undercover: An FBI Agent's True Story.* New York: Dell.

Lehr, D. and G. O'Neil. 2000. *Black Mass: The Irish Mob, the FBI, and a Devil's Deal.* New York: BBS.

Leo, R. 1996. "Miranda's Revenge: Police Interrogations as a Confidence Game." *Law and Society Review* 30(2):259–80.

Levine, M. and L. Kavanau. 1997. *Triangle of Death.* New York: Dell.

Marx, G. 1972. *Muckraking Sociology.* New Brunswick, NJ: Transaction.

———. 1981. "Ironies of Social Control." *Social Problems* 23(3):221–46.

———. 1987. "The Interweaving of Public and Private Police in Undercover Work." In *Private Policing,* edited by C. D. Shearing and P. C. Stenning. Newbury Park, CA: Sage.

———. 1988. *Undercover: Police Surveillance in America.* Berkeley: University of California Press.

———. 1990. "Reflections on Academic Success and Failure: Making It, Forsaking

It Reshaping It." In *Authors of Their Own Lives,* edited by B. Berger. Berkeley: University of California Press.

———. 1992a. "When the Guards Guard Themselves: Undercover Tactics Turned Inward." *Policing and Society* 2(3):151–72.

———. 1992b. "Under-the-Covers Undercover Investigations: Some Reflections on the State's Use of Sex and Deception in Law Enforcement." *Criminal Justice Ethics* 11(1):13–24.

———. 1996. "Electric Eye in the Sky: Some Reflections on the New Surveillance in Popular Culture." in *New Technology, Surveillance and Social Control,* edited by D. Lyon and E. Zurick. Minneapolis: University of Minnesota Press.

———. 1997a. "Social Control Across Borders." In *Crime and Law Enforcement Across Borders,* edited by W. McDonald. Cinncinati, OH: Anderson.

———. 1997b. "Of Methods and Manners for Aspiring Sociologists: 37 Moral Imperatives." *American Sociologist* (Spring).

———. 2002a. "Looking for Meaning in All the Right Places: The Search for Academic Satisfaction." In *Lessons of Criminology,* edited by G. Geis and M. Dodge. Cinncinati, OH: Anderson.

———. 2002b. "Tom I. Voire: The Case of Technology and Gender." *Sociological Quarterly.* V. 43, i3, 409–26.

———. 2002c. "What's New About the New Surveillance? Classifying for Continuity and Change." *Surveillance and Society,* Vol. 1, no. 1.

Maurer, D. 1974. *American Confidence Man.* Springfield, IL: C. Thomas.

Motto, C. and D. June. 1999. *Undercover,* 2nd ed. Springfield, IL: Charles C. Thomas

Murano V., with W. Hoffer. 1990. *Cop Hunter.* New York: Pocket Books.

National School Boards Association. 1995. *Legal Guidelines for Curbing School Violence.* Washington, DC, published by National School Boards Association. http://www.keepschoolssafe.org/under.htm

O'Reilly, K. 1989. *Racial Manners: The FBI's Secret Files on Black America. 1960–1972.* New York: Free Press.

Passas, N. and R. Groskin. 1995. "International Undercover Investigations." In *Undercover: Police Surveillance in Comparative Perspective,* edited by C. Fijnaut and G. T. Marx. Rotterdam: Kluwer.

Pistone, J. and Donnie Brasco. 1988. *My Undercover Life in the Mob.* New York: Dutton.

Pogrebin, M. and E. Poole. 1993. "Vice Isn't Nice: A Look at the Ethics of Working Undercover." *Journal of Criminal Justice* 21:383–94.

Powers, R. 1987. *Secrecy and Power. The Life of J. Edgar Hoover.* New York: Free Press.

Protess, D. 1989. "Did the Press Play Prosecutor in Covering an FBI Sting?" *Columbia Journalism Review* 28(2):37–42.

Rosen, J. 2000. *The Unwanted Gaze.* New York: Random House.

Rosenthal, R. 2000. *Rookie Cop: Deep Undercover in the Jewish Defense League.* St. Paul, MI: Leapfrog.

Rothmiller, M. and I. Goldman. 1992. *L.A. Secret Police.* New York: Simon and Schuster.

Smith, R. E. 2002. *Ben Franklin's Website.* Providence: Privacy Journal Press.

Staples. W. 1997. *The Culture of Surveillance.* New York: St. Martin's.

Theoharis, A. 1988. *The Boss: J. Edgar Hoover and the Great American Inquisition.* Philadelphia: Temple University Press.

Van Cook, J. 1996. *Going Undercover: Secrets and Sound Advice for the Undercover Officer.* Boulder, CO: Paladin.

Wansley, L. and C. Stowers. 1989. *FBI Undercover: The True Story of Special Agent "Mandrake."* New York: Pocket Books.

Wozencraft, K. 1990. *Rush.* New York: Ballantine.

8

Surveillance and Social Control in Postmodern Life

WILLIAM G. STAPLES

- Throughout the United States, thousands of criminals are placed under house arrest, their movements monitored electronically by a computer.
- In many states, criminal defendants and judges carry out proceedings over video monitors.
- In Arizona, a welfare mother has a court-ordered contraceptive device surgically implanted in her arm.
- In New York, a high-tech courtroom collects a myriad of information about each defendant that is kept in an electronic file folder.
- Most "clients" in community corrections programs are subjected to random drug and alcohol testing.

At the same time:

- Sixty-seven percent of major U.S. employers engage in some form of electronic monitoring of workers.
- In New York City, more than two thousand private surveillance cameras are taping citizens on public streets.
- In California, all citizens wishing to be issued a driver's license must have their thumb print computer scanned.
- In Massachusetts, a company tracks the Web surfing habits of more than thirty million Internet users.
- Nearly 90 percent of U.S. manufacturers are testing workers for drugs.[1]

The preceding examples illustrate a blurring between the practices of the justice system and the everyday lives of ordinary people. My focus is on relatively small, mundane procedures and practices. These techniques exist in the shadow of large institutions like prisons; they are not ushered in with dramatic displays of state power, nor do they appear as significant

191

challenges to constitutional democracy. These are the more commonplace strategies used by both governmental, but even more likely, private organizations to "keep us in line," monitor our performance, and gather evidence.

The techniques I have in mind range along a continuum. They begin with the "soft," seemingly benign, and relatively inconspicuous forms of monitoring such as those used in, say, a large, corporate bookstore. In such a business, as in thousands across the United States, a security system monitors shoppers' interactions with video cameras, while the store's spatial arrangement has been designed for optimal surveillance of customers and employees alike. Computerized checkout stations keep track of inventory, calculate store performance figures, assess the credit worthiness of patrons through remote data banks, collect personal information about customers so they can be targeted for marketing campaigns, monitor the log-on and log-off times of employees, and calculate the average number of customers those employees process per hour. All this is accomplished behind the scenes, as it were, without disruption to the manufactured ambiance of soft leather chairs, melodic Muzak, and the sound and smell of cappuccino making.

At the "hard" end of the spectrum are the more obtrusive and confrontational practices that often begin with the assumption of guilt and are designed to uncover the "truth," to test an individual's character, and, more generally, to make people consciously aware that they are indeed being watched and monitored. These are what I call "surveillance ceremonies." They include random drug and alcohol testing, the use of lie detectors, preemployment integrity tests, and "sobriety checkpoints" in the streets. They also include the practices of electronically monitored "house arrest," adolescent curfews, and the use of metal detectors. Between these soft and hard types of social control lies a vast array of techniques and technologies designed to watch our bodies, to regulate and monitor our activities, habits, and movements, and, ultimately, to shape or change our behavior. These procedures are often undertaken in the name of law and order, public safety, the protection of private property, or simply "sound business practice"; other procedures are initiated for an individual's "own good" or benefit. But the intent of social control is to mold, shape, and modify actions and behaviors.

My subject, then, is the cultural practices that I will call "meticulous rituals of power." Most generally, I include those microtechniques of social monitoring and control that are enhanced by the use of new information, communications, and medical technologies. I call them meticulous because they are "small" procedures and techniques that are precisely and thoroughly exercised. I see them as ritualistic because they are faithfully repeated and are often quickly accepted and routinely practiced with little question. And they are about power because they are intended to discipline people into acting in ways that others have deemed to be lawful or have defined as appropriate or simply "normal." In this way, meticulous rituals are the specific, concrete mechanisms that operate to maintain unbalanced and unequal authority relationships. These relationships exist between specific clusters of individuals (e.g., between managers and workers, police officers and suspects, probation officials and offenders, teachers and students, parents and children) and, in a larger sense, between individuals and the public and private organizations where these rituals take place. Surveillance and social control of this type, then, are not orchestrated by a few individuals; they are not part of a master plan that is simply imposed on us.

I concentrate on the small, seemingly benign rituals at the intersection of power, knowledge, and the body. Foucault (1977, 1980) challenges us to look at power as being local, continuous, productive, capillary and exhaustive and, potentially, automatic and even anonymous in operation. This kind of "disciplinary power" as he called it, is not a commodity that is held but a technique that is exercised.

Bentham's "Panopticon" (Bentham 1995) was a simple, even elegant, solution to the problem of disciplining people in an enclosed space. But, as Foucault noted: "While on the one hand, the disciplinary establishments increase, their mechanisms have a certain tendency to become 'de-institutionalized,' to emerge from the closed fortresses in which they once functioned and to circulate in the 'free' state; the massive, compact disciplines are broken down into flexible methods of control, which may be transferred and adapted" (Foucault 1977:211). I have attempted to extend this idea into the postmodern era (Staples 1994, 2000).

POSTMODERN SOCIAL CONTROL: A DESCRIPTIVE TYPE

The postmodern social world is characterized by fragmentation and uncertainty. Time as well as social and geographical space are highly compressed by rapidly changing computer and advanced technologies, information storage and retrieval, and scientific and medical knowledge. Ours is a culture deeply penetrated by commodities and consumer "lifestyles." Highly bureaucratic (although increasingly "decentralized") state agencies attempt to order and regulate social life. The media offer nonstop barrage of "crisis-level" social problems, leaving us wondering "what the world is coming to." In turn, we are left cynically mistrusting each other and furthering the disintegration of public life and discourse. This cultural hysteria creates a fertile ground for those selling "science" and the seemingly innocent and "advanced" technological fixes that they claim will ease our fears.

The first characteristic of postmodern social control then is that it tends to be systematic, methodical, and automatic in operation. It is likely to be impersonal in that the observer is rarely seen and is anonymous; further, the "observer" is likely to be a computer system, a videocam, a drug testing kit, or an electronic scanner of some kind. The data that these devices collect may become part of a permanent record in the form of a videotape, a computer file, or some other digital format.

Second, these new meticulous rituals of power often involve our bodies in new and important ways using two tactics: (1) There are types of monitoring and surveillance that enhance our visibility to others and allow us to be watched continuously, anonymously, and automatically. (2) New developments in science, technology, and medicine are making the human body infinitely more accessible to official scrutiny and assessment. This means that the ability of organizations to monitor, judge, or even regulate our actions and behaviors through our bodies is significantly enhanced. It also means that it becomes less important to trust suspects to "speak the truth" or convicted offenders to "mend their ways." Rather, it is the individual's body that will "tell us what we need to know," as in indicating that someone is using drugs or was at the scene of a crime or even has "deviant desires." In this way, the body is treated as an "object" that contains the evidence of any possible deviance.

The third defining characteristic of postmodern social control is a shift in the location of social control and surveillance. There is an attempt to impose a framework of accountability on an individual in everyday life. This framework goes beyond ordinary crime to "lifestyles" of substance (ab)use, alcohol and tobacco consumption, "eating disorders," forms of sexual expression and sexual "promiscuity" and "deviance," teenage pregnancy, out-of-marriage births, domestic violence, child abuse, "dysfunctional" families, various psychological or psychiatric disorders and other "medical" conditions such as "attention deficit disorder," and such diseases as AIDS. How can we possibly institutionalize and control everyone who falls into these rapidly expanding categories of "troublesome" individuals? The incentive now is to develop new ways to control and "keep an eye on" what appears to be an increasing number of "deviants" through an expanding network of formal "community corrections" programs; regulatory welfare, health, and social service agencies; and even schools, workplaces, and other community institutions. New developments in the forensic, medical, and computer and information sciences generated by corporate research and development departments and the post-Cold War military-industrial complex are creating more remote, more flexible, and more efficient ways of making this happen.

When combined with the rampant fear and mistrust generated by the media, the consequence is that we are more willing to condone, even insist, that we adopt more and more disciplinary practices and surveillance ceremonies that soon become routine and commonplace. For example, drug screening had been well-established in the community corrections system before the Supreme Court ruled that, even without probable cause, any student participating in public school athletics could be randomly tested. While prisons have armed guards, metal detectors, and video surveillance cameras, so does the Sunrise Multiplex movie theater in Valley Stream, New York, and so does Mount View High School in West Virginia. These parallels are too significant to ignore. Even prisons themselves "blend in" to everyday life as they are made indistinguishable from other community institutions. In Lockhart, Texas, a small factory no different from the others on Industrial Boulevard makes computer circuit boards and air conditioners. Its 138 "employees" are actually inmates doing time in the medium-security prison run by Wackenhut Corrections Corporation. Other facilities are designed to simulate suburban, high-tech industrial parks and often are referred to as "campuses." In Los Angeles, neighborhood-based, privately run "microprisons" holding illegal immigrants look no different from the surrounding apartment complexes: both have locked gates and bars on the windows. Meanwhile, in downtown Los Angeles, the Metropolitan Detention Center appears to be just another skyscraper or luxury hotel to those who drive by it every day.

In this chapter I move back and forth between the official justice system and the everyday life. I juxtapose the worlds of "community corrections" and the contemporary workplace where we find similar social control and assessment techniques such as video surveillance, "electronic monitoring" and other forms of "intensive supervision," drug and alcohol testing, integrity and personality testing, and the like.

THE HYPERREALITY OF "HOUSE ARREST"

"Clarissa" is a thirty-two-year-old waitress with two children and a drug habit, one of the more than two dozen people I have interviewed who is living under house arrest in the Kansas City area.[2] On the day I spoke with her, Clarissa had slept through a 7:56 A.M. telephone call from the Department of Corrections computer. It had been her fourth random call since midnight. The calls demand that she complete a drill of blowing into an alcohol tester built into a small computerized unit installed in her home while it takes her picture and compares it to a reference photograph stored on a central computer. Missing the call meant that Clarissa had to then drive fifteen miles to present herself at the House Arrest Center to be body searched, have an alcohol breath test, provide urine for a drug test, and offer an explanation of why she had not answered her phone.

Doing time at home, I argue, is a pastiche of old and new, a blending of the institutional confinement of the past and the more futuristic possibility of being monitored in everyday life. It is a virtual world where the values of order, authority, justice, discipline, freedom, consumption, work, and self-help are celebrated, simulated, and presented. For example, when I asked Jill, a working-class women in her early thirties with five children who was arrested for drunk driving, what it is like to live under house arrest, she said:

"Ahm [long pause] . . . of course nobody likes to be monitored, like, twenty-four hours a day, you know, but it's better than sitting in jail. And at least under house arrest you can provide for your family and if you're not out there doing what you're not supposed to be doing then it's not a problem anyway. . . . As long as you're following your schedule and you're honest with the house arrest officer on where you are going to be and what you are going to be doing, then you shouldn't have any problems. And . . . sometimes people that have had problems in the past with maybe drugs or alcohol or situations like that, if they know what's more important then [pause] . . . house arrest can actually be a beneficial thing to a person. You know, for one, you're proving to the community that you can survive, be a part of the community."

The proponents of house arrest claim that it simulates the confinement experience of being in jail. In practice, however, this popular new disciplinary technique bears little relation to any reality. We are told that offenders are "free" to participate in everyday life, yet their movements are highly regulated, the random gaze creating anxiety, obedience, and docility. Is this real freedom or a simulation? Clarissa, and the others I interviewed, are permitted to live at home, but is it "home," or is it "prison"? Is she a "convict" or a "client"? Is her home "private" space or a simulation of the private that can come under the scrutiny of public authorities? These dichotomies no longer make any sense and have been blurred to the point of nondistinction. If it is and at the same time is not "home," "prison," "private," or "freedom," then what is it?

Most of the folks I spoke to had their own versions of what house arrest is all about. "Johnny," an articulate college student, calls it a "cake walk" compared to the county jail where he spent several weeks following an "alcohol-related" car wreck. "Frank" tells me flat-out, "Well, it's just home and jail more or less. You know it's just strict accountability," says the forty-eight-year-old mechanic. He adds, "I don't know any other way to put it." "You might as well say you're locked-down at home too," declares "Jolene," a convicted check forger and recent single mother of one, "You're locked-down, you can't even go nowhere. Might as well say you got to be right there by the phone, cause you don't know when it's gonna ring." "Peter" declares, "It is a lot like jail because, it's all, I *have* to be home. "Jill" tells me that her ten-year-old son was upset when she told him she would be on house arrest because the boy thought his mother would have to wear a ball and chain around her ankle like he had seen on television cartoons.

This jumble of ideas is evident when officials discuss just what "house arrest" means. One advocate calls the concept a "winner" because it enables a person to maintain "the semblance of a normal life, even hold a job" (in other words, a simulated "normal" life). Another is critical, since agencies often fail to provide clients with "the kind of counseling they need to reenter society." But aren't they already in society? Apparently not, according to the Superior Court of Arizona. The court ruled that a person under house arrest may be prosecuted for "escape" for unauthorized leaves, just as a prisoner may be prosecuted for breaking out of prison.[3] So then, "house arrest," once an odd-sounding contradiction in terms, has become part of the discourse and practice of justice officials who have normalized this simulation as accepted public policy. A client's home is characterized in this discourse as simply another "correctional setting." It becomes, then, a "virtual" prison.

Within the "hyperreality" (Baudrillard 1983) of house arrest, clients are rendered docile not through isolation and transformation of their "souls" during their segregation from society but rather through the surveillance of their bodies during integration into everyday postmodern life. Today, "useful" bodies are primarily consuming ones, and everyday life is marked by our dependency on the commodities that signal our desired lifestyles. As "Peter," a salesman in his early thirties with a pregnant fiance and two kids, says about house arrest,

> I guess the biggest thing to why I need it or like it, is because it's either making money for my family or not. If I go to jail, there's a whole lotta stuff, I mean, she's not, can't, make enough money to, I have to be able to go to work to pay the mortgage payments, car payments and all this stuff.

Therefore, if formal, coercive social control is increasingly tied to social integration rather than to segregation, then "freedom" becomes simply that which can create the simulation of freedom.

The original and commonly used house arrest technology deploys a small radio transmitter that is attached to the ankle of the offender. A monitoring box is placed in his or her home or apartment and the client cannot stray more than 150 feet or so from the box without triggering a violation that is recorded by a central computer. The brainchild of a New Mexico judge (who, it is said, was inspired by the use of a similar device in a 1979 *Spiderman* comic book), house arrest programs today tether more than ten thousand individuals in dozens of states to central monitoring systems installed by community corrections officials (Department of Justice 1999). "It's just a given that business is going to grow," says one stock analyst speaking of the corporations that produce the devices. "These are the companies working to solve a social problem. . . . They are going to help develop the industry and . . . the state-of-the-art equipment that is going to be necessary."[4]

In the new disciplinary technology, like the Panopticon, random checks, day or night, bring the discretionary and one-dimensional gaze of authorities onto the clients; they never know when they may be called. One news article about these devices states that "while confinement by monitor does not include bars, correction officials say the psychological loss of freedom should not be discounted." In order to "sharpen a convict's sense of confinement," officials often visit homes or workplaces unannounced, "even reciting the prisoner's every move the previous day" to make it clear to the client that he or she is being monitored. A probation officer stated, "We want them to know we're watching even when they don't know we're watching." Another house arrest system relies on a video camera, instead of the pager-size anklet device. The Visitel camera is described by its manufacturer's agent this way: "The system is unique because there is a human connection that will talk with the offender. That person will ask the offender to smile, or turn his head, wave at the camera, or something like that to make sure it is the offender."[5] But the ultimate application of this panoptic mechanism requires no agent at all. Verifications are completed by the computer itself, programmed to dial at random times. "Hello," says the voice simulator, "this is a Community Control officer calling to verify that the person under our custody is at home. I will pause ten seconds for the person to come to the phone." Whether triggering a spatial violation or offering one's voice, picture, or even breath to the machine, such decentralized control encourages "participatory monitoring" whereby those being watched become active "partners" in their own surveillance (Corbett and Marx 1991:399).

The cybernetic life-world and video technology of contemporary society permit a new partitioning a new "grid" of power that extends into the everyday, in and through the gaze of community corrections. This new grid comes about because the house arrest technology no longer requires the boundaries or the division of space through the architecture of a building. Indeed, this exercise of power can operate more freely, down to the trivial extremities and the remotest corners of everyday life, rather than be confined, like the offenders themselves, within walls of the modern asylum. Disciplinary power, then, has been deinstitutionalized and decentralized. Unlike the somewhat primitive panoptic tower that could practically view only a limited number of cells, the cybernetic machine is capable of creating an infinite number of confinements, as Foucault put it, "like so many cages, so many small theaters, in which each actor is alone, perfectly individualized and constantly visible" (Foucault 1977:200). This technological marvel alters the cost equation. Compared with the cost of building prison beds and the expense of confinement more than $25,000–

$30,000 per inmate per year, house arrest systems require a relatively small initial investment, fewer personnel to administer, and cost only about $4,000 per client per year to operate and, in many programs like the ones I observed, the clients are ordered to pay for their own monitoring.

First used on so-called nonviolent felony offenders who were on parole from prison, house arrest began to proliferate in the mid-1990s to include other populations. For example, in my county, the devices were initially used on juvenile offenders, some as young as twelve, and on others who have been charged but had never been convicted of a crime. Now they are used on a whole range of offenders. Interestingly, the central monitoring office of the computer company that contracted for the service is located somewhere in Texas, about a thousand miles away. These systems cannot track a client who strays outside the range on the monitor. Yet I am told by justice officials that the next generation of devices will be able to report the whereabouts of clients at all times, permitting police to quickly apprehend violators.

With the extended reach of such community-based programs, the authority to judge individuals goes far beyond the walls of the prison that may have formally held them. Now the gaze and surveillance of authorities can go straight into an individual's home, school, or workplace and can evaluate, assess, and enforce, if necessary, the person's "progress" on the road to becoming a model citizen. This kind of power is, indeed, capillary, circulating freely, far below the central administration of the state to the tiniest corners of society, and exercised by low-level criminal justice bureaucrats and technicians armed with a new discourse of accountability and what are referred to by practitioners as "case management devices."

Anyone who thinks that doing time at home is "easy time" knows little about these new programs. One official told me that being sentenced to community corrections programs was, in many ways, much "harder time" than sitting in a jail cell. For example, consider the intensive supervision programs (ISPs) now operating in many communities throughout the country. These are designed for adult, nonviolent felons so that they may, according to one report, "remain in the community while becoming responsible, accountable, and self-supporting." One ISP requires a minimum of four contacts per week between a client and an intensive supervision officer (ISO) during the first year in the program. During this time, the ISO is charged with directing daily job searches, verifying employment through the provision of pay stubs, initiating at least one monthly meeting with employers or training/education providers (not including unannounced visits), coordinating community service work (forty hours per week for those unemployed; five hours for those employed), collecting court-ordered restitution, initiating client curfews (enforced by means of electronic monitoring if deemed necessary), running weekly computerized record checks, and performing random drug and alcohol tests on all participants. After successfully completing the first eight months in the program with no "major violations," an offender may progress to less intensive surveillance "at the discretion of the ISO."

With the advent of community policing and corrections, neighborhood detention centers, offenders under arrest in their own homes, and the proliferation of in-home social welfare models, we see then the process whereby disciplinary power enters into everyday life (Cohen 1979).

The next logical step in "decentralizing" the penal/health/welfare complex is to bring courts to the local level as well. A prototype court of the future was opened in New York City's Times Square district. Supported and financed by private developers who have spent billions rehabilitating the seedy district into a tourist Mecca, this specialized "boutique" court deals only with street hustlers, graffiti artists, prostitutes, and shoplifters, who traditionally had been kicked out by uptown courts too busy with felony cases. The court processes more than fifteen thousand of these so-called quality of life offenders a year. It is characterized as a "computer-driven laboratory," a "fishbowl" that puts a "judge under the same roof as city health workers, drug counselors, schoolteachers and nontraditional community service outlets." A Digital Equipment Corporation computer is at the center of the management information system. It acts, according to one writer who observed the court, as the receptor for an elaborate system of remote feeds that, when combined, create the equivalent of a three-inch court file that can be accessed from a single screen:

> The process usually begins with a beat cop issuing a complaint to an offender, complete with a date for him or her to appear in court. Copies of the complaints are sent to the Manhattan DA's office, which in turn faxes them to the court.
>
> When the defendant arrives in the new courthouse, his presence is noted on large screens that hang in the entrance way like airport flight monitors, displaying the names of all those scheduled to appear that day. . . . In addition, a dozen monitors jam the interior well of the courtroom. . . . If all has worked, the faxed complaint from the DA's office has been scanned into the computer and can be pulled up from any of those monitors. Ditto the defendant's rap sheet, which gets fed into the database by an online hookup with the state's Division of Criminal Justice.
>
> Before long, an interviewer approaches the defendant with a laundry list of queries: Does he or she have a drug habit, a home, a job? Each answer is typed into a laptop computer and downloaded into the DEC machine. . . . By now thousands of bits of information about a single defendant are swimming around the electronic file folder.[6]

As the man who designed the court says, "We know very little about the 100,000 people who come through this system. In three years, we're going to know a whole lot more."[7]

IN THE WORKPLACE

With the "deindustrialization" of the nation, the rise of the service industry and the "information age," the "downsizing" and decentralizing of corporations, and the move toward more "flexible" use of labor, a new class
of white collar and service workers presented a fresh challenge for management. The result has been dramatic changes in the quality and quantity
of watching and monitoring in the workplace and of those workers not tied
to offices and desks. Workers who are increasingly using computers and
other data processing and communication technologies find that these devices become the very tools that management uses to monitor and control
their movements, behavior (what they can say, write, and do in the workplace), and productivity.

For example, in today's workplace, the once friendly-sounding "personal" computer is no longer personal at all; it has been transformed into
a "workstation" connected to a local area network. Those spending their
days at one of these terminals are increasingly vulnerable to managers who
can use the network's operating software to peek at an employee's screen
in real time, scan data files and e-mail at will, tabulate keystroke speed and
accuracy, overwrite passwords, and even seize control of a remote workstation. In a study done by the computer magazine *MacWorld,* 22 percent
of business executives surveyed said that they had rifled through employees' electronic and voice mail and files. Based on this and other findings,
the magazine estimates that as many as twenty million Americans may be
subject to electronic monitoring through their computers on the job. With
a few well-publicized harassment lawsuits against companies based on
computer e-mail, many are arming themselves with sophisticated surveillance tools and monitoring employee e-mail, raising questions about the
proper balance between employee privacy and an employer's need to
know. While some believe that employers have a right, if not an obligation,
to investigate specific complaints of computer-borne harassment, others
think that firms are overreacting. In 1999, the share of major U.S. firms that
checks employee e-mail messages jumped to 27 from 15 percent in 1997,
and overall electronic monitoring of communications and performance increased to 45 from 35 percent, according to an annual survey by the American Management Association (AMA). (Additional forms of watching and
listening, including video cameras, brought the total engaged electronic
monitoring and surveillance to 67 percent in 1999, up from 63 percent in
1997.)[8]

With billions of electronic mail messages flying through cyberspace
every day, few people, it seems, give much thought to how public they really are. This kind of correspondence is openly available to network administrators and others along the line, while so-called deleted mail is

often stored on system backup tapes for quite some time. Even those in corporate boardrooms can have their correspondence scrutinized. It was, after all, the e-mail of Chairman Bill Gates that flatly contradicted his sworn deposition testimony with regard to the federal government's antitrust suit against Microsoft. Like Nixon being thwarted by his own tapes, e-mail is, as Foucault said, a "machine in which everyone [is] caught, those who exercise power, just as much as those over whom it is exercised" (1980:156). And e-mail is increasingly being treated as the "real truth" of the hearts and minds of executives and CEOs alike. For example, employees at Amazon.com, the Internet bookseller, were issued a directive from senior management instructing employees to purge e-mail messages that were no longer required for business or not subject to legal records requirements. This Amazon "document retention" policy is referred to as "sweep and keep." "In the past, message retention policies have been primarily designed for disk space management," says Jim Browning, a senior research analyst at the Gartner Group, a consulting firm. "The new question is how quickly should e-mail be deleted to prevent it from becoming a danger to the organization?" The consulting firm suggests policies that help employees understand what is now "appropriate business language."[9]

To date, the U.S. Supreme Court has yet to hear an e-mail privacy case. Yet lower courts have generally upheld the rights of employers to use surveillance. Federal law prohibits employers from listening in on employees' private telephone conversations, but "there's absolutely no protection when it comes to electronic communications on computers," says Jeremy Gruber, an attorney with the American Civil Liberties Union's Workplace Rights Project. Employers at private sector companies, Gruber contends, "can rifle through your e-mail, computer files and Web-browsing history at will and in most cases don't even have to let you know they're doing it." Fully one-fifth of the companies surveyed in the AMA study cited above did not tell employees they were being watched. Gruber says, "Under current law, if I were an employee I would be extremely hesitant to do any kind of personal business at work."[10]

The World Wide Web comes into play in the workplace, revealing a certain paradox. On the one hand, we have hundreds of companies trying to get us online, visiting their Web pages, buying their products, reading their news, and trading their stocks. On the other hand, the very technology that permits us to do this is installed in our own workplaces, but managers of those businesses insist that computers must be reserved for appropriate productivity uses. The Web, then, is seen as both a source of and a threat to workplace productivity. This issue, as well as the cost of network resource consumption, and the threat of legal liability for the Internet content entering their network, have encouraged companies to look to "Internet access management systems" for help. These software systems, according to one vendor, Websense Enterprise, enable "corporations, schools and other organizations to monitor, report, and manage traffic traveling from their internal network to the Internet." Their systems include the following components:

Monitoring Module: Observes your network-to-Internet traffic and logs the information based on the parameters set in the Management Module. This log data includes network user information, type of sites visited, bandwidth consumed, and attempted violations of your Internet Access Policy.

Management Module: Allows you to set and enforce Internet access privileges for the users on your network. Settings may be configured by type of permitted sites, by user, by time of day, or by day of the week. This module also works in conjunction with the Monitoring Module to block access to undesirable sites and issue warnings of Internet Access Policy violations.

Reporting Module: Generates tabular and graphical reports on your network-to-Internet traffic. This module pulls the information from the logs created by the Monitoring Module and builds visual charts in a variety of formats for easy distribution among departmental managers, supervisors, and others in your organization. The module can generate more than twenty different reports that provide information on observed traffic, type of sites visited (by user), network bandwidth consumed, etc. This module is also a "distributed module," meaning that departmental managers can use it from their desktop to create reports on their personnel and network consumption.

This vendor's "master database" includes the following categories that have been deemed "unacceptable, inappropriate, or undesirable" to access:

- Abortion advocacy
- Personals/dating
- Activist groups
- Politics (advocacy of any type)
- Adult entertainment
- Racism/hate
- Alcohol/tobacco
- Religion
- Alternative journals
- Sex
- Cult/New Age
- Shopping
- Drugs
- Sports
- Entertainment
- Tasteless
- Gambling
- Travel
- Games
- User defined
- Gay/lesbian lifestyles
- Vehicles
- Hacking
- Violence
- Illegal
- Weapons
- Job search
- Web chat
- Militancy[11]

This screening list of "unacceptable" behavior is an extraordinary example of the enforcement of "normalcy." But just how many "Internet abusers" are there in any given workplace? These monitoring systems do not discriminate, but place everyone under suspicion and watch their activities whether or not they have any history of "abuse."

Take the case of American Express travel agent Kathy J., who works out of her home in suburban New Jersey, more than an hour's drive from the central office in Trenton. Customers' calls are routed directly to the computer in the corner of her dining room. "It's skilled work," her supervisor told one journalist. "It can take years to do it well." But just to make sure that the "skilled" worker is doing it well, Kathy's boss can, with a touch of a key on her own computer, look at what her agents are typing on their computers. By hitting a button on her telephone, she can listen in on any of those agents' conversations as well. But rather than calling this technology a surveillance device, management contends that it's a "learning tool."

> [I]t's not used to say, "Hey, you know, we watch what you do." It's basically used for training purposes to say, you know, "Looks like you have some trouble in that area. Let me get you into a class, or get you, you know, something you need to assist you with that."

Kathy J. seems to agree about the productive benefits of being watched and doesn't seem to mind the monitoring: "If they see you doing something on the screen that they think you can do a quicker way, they can tell you, they can advise you of it. They can even tell you ways to talk to people, or they can tell you ways to do things quicker to end your call quicker, so it's pretty helpful." [12]

Recording workers' conversations is increasingly a part of the daily life of telephone operators, the "customer assistant" representatives of financial organizations, and the "sales associates" of catalog merchandisers. Many such organizations have decided that their employees despite their "team spirit" and job titles that proclaim "we're a big happy family" cannot be trusted to conduct business properly and need to have their calls monitored. "This call is being monitored," announces the recording, "to ensure your prompt and courteous service."

Jobs are being influenced throughout the entire occupational structure. Restaurant workers are wearing vibrating beepers that literally prod them through their shift. Bookstore clerks are donning wireless headsets so they can stock shelves and answer phones and queries at the same time. Delivery people, auto rental check-in clerks, parking meter readers, and a host of others are carrying data entry computers that not only make them work "more efficiently" but also keep tabs on their movements and/or keep track of their productivity. If overt monitoring of employees through computers, videocameras, data entry tablets, beepers, and the like were not enough, it is likely that your employer began building a "case file" on you before you were even offered the job. In the face of what employers claim is a rising tide of lawsuits, stringent hiring and firing regulations, drug use, and alleged criminal activity in the workplace, corporations are increasingly turning to preemployment background checks to screen applicants. These investigations can include a criminal records search; access to driver's license, credit, and workers' compensation histories; and verification of educational and professional credentials, along with personal interviews with references. Of course, these kinds of extensive background checks are becoming easy to complete as more and more computerized databases come online and as those who control them are in the business of selling the information.

Assuming you survive this kind of scrutiny, you may find yourself confronted with a preemployment "integrity test" (a favorite substitute for the lie detector, which was outlawed for most preemployment situations back in 1988). Written integrity tests are used, supposedly, to measure a person's level of "honesty or dishonesty." Typically, testers will pose a set of questions that may come right out and ask whether you have committed various offenses (Have you ever stolen products from your place of employment?), or see what you would do under certain circumstances (If you saw a coworker taking money from the cash register would you report it to your supervisor?), or more subtly assess a person's values and attitudes (Do you agree with the idea of once a thief always a thief?). Estimates are that nearly three million of these tests are administered each year in thousands of workplaces across the country. An estimated two million employees every year are required to take written "personality tests" that probe into aspects of their lives such as hygiene habits, sexuality, and family relationships. The 1990 Americans with Disabilities Act put some limits on the use of tests designed to reveal a physical or mental impairment. Yet, in 1998, the AMA reported a "definite upward movement, especially in personality measurements (28 percent this year compared with 19 percent in 1997)" in its annual survey of member organizations.

Estimates are that more than fifteen million Americans were tested for drugs in 1998, up more than 50 percent from five years before at a cost of $600 million. The most common location for testing appears to be the workplace, where the vast majority of the tests are used in preemployment screening rather than on current employees. However, in certain occupational categories, drug and alcohol tests can take place under conditions of "reasonable cause" (or suspicion), after an accident, before treatment, and randomly, as during preemployment. In 1994, the AMA reported that drug testing in the private sector had increased 305 percent since 1987, the year the association first began conducting the survey. Much of this testing was spurred on by President Ronald Reagan's 1986 Executive Order 12564, stating that all federal employees may be tested for drugs; subsequent testing was mandated for specific occupations by the Department of Transportation and the Department of Defense. According to the latest AMA survey of major U.S. corporations, 89.8 percent of manufacturing companies tested their employees in 1993; and 30.6 percent tested periodically or at random. In the transportation sector, 87.5 percent of workers were tested for drugs, and these companies reported the highest rate of periodic or random testing, at 75 percent.[13]

A COMMUNITY OF CORRECTIONS?

Local, meticulous rituals of power are the knowledge gathering activities that involve surveillance, information, and evidence collection and analysis that increasingly compose our daily lives as workers, consumers, and community members. I have argued that these new disciplinary techniques must be understood as a product both of important, long-term processes set in motion with the onset of modernity, and of the emerging cultural context of postmodernity.

I have drawn my examples from and moved back and forth between the justice system and everyday world of the workplace. Much like the reformers of the nineteenth century, contemporary advocates of "community-based" punishment and social control seek to make justice more effective and more efficient. Yet, as they have gone about decentralizing the justice system, we have seen how some the discourses, techniques, and procedures used in the justice system have been adapted for use in schools, workplaces, and other community institutions. One of my goals has been to show how we appear to be building a community of corrections, a tendency to normalize and accept the presence of formal social control in our daily lives. "But perhaps the most important effect of the carceral system and its extension well beyond legal imprisonment is," according to Foucault, "that it succeeds in making the power to punish natural and legitimate, in lowering at least the threshold of tolerance to penalty" (1977:301).

But how did all this happen? "There was no revolution," one journalist declares, "no totalitarian takeover, no war bringing the collapse of worldwide democracy. But by an invention here and a new computer application there, American culture is nearing the point forwarded by those who feared technology could breed a new kind of oppression."[14] Yet, while many of us are subjected to this new despotism, few, it would seem, see or appreciate the implications of this "quiet" revolution. One reason is that some of these surveillance and disciplinary practices often work in the background; we may not even know they exist, and even if we do, they rarely, in and of themselves, give cause for serious concern. Even the more confrontive disciplinary rituals such as random drug screens are quickly routinized into common, everyday practices that soon lose their sense of transgression. "Who cares if someone tapes my conversation at the local donut shop?" someone will declare; "What difference does it make if some big company knows all about me?" another asks. "People should be tested for drugs," most seem to say; "They can test me, I have nothing to hide." Fragmented and piecemeal, quiet and habitual and often convincingly productive meticulous rituals elicit only minor resistance.

Yet these new habits, no matter how small or seemingly trivial, have their own significance, for they define a certain mode of political investment in the body. That is, meticulous rituals of power are the concrete ways in which our bodily lives are shaped, manipulated, and controlled by public and private organizations and by the people who have authority over us. These are the politics of social control in the workplace, the school, the home, and the community. They are also the politics of our "virtual" database(d) identities and who controls them. But since these kinds of practices often appear as a "nudge" here and a "twist" there, few of us experience them as anything like "oppression." Yet, taken together, these "small acts of cunning" constitute the building blocks of what I would argue is a rapidly emerging disciplinary society; a society increasingly lacking in personal privacy, individual trust, or viable public life that supports and maintains democratic values and practices.

Like the invention of the penitentiary itself, the new techniques are said to embody all the ideal virtues of justice preventing crime or deviance, protecting property, or insulating us from harm while being more effective, less expensive, and more "civilized" than what came before. The prison, for example, was more "humane" than the scaffold; now that the reality of the penitentiary can no longer be concealed, house arrest is heralded as "kinder and gentler" and more practical than the institution. Each failure, it seems, only serves to justify and bring about a new generation of disciplinary devices.

Rather than appear simply "from the top down" or originate from a small group of identifiable individuals or even a particular organization, the new surveillance and social control practices, I argue, are advanced, directly or indirectly, by all of us. They are not orchestrated by only a few or as part of some master plan that is simply imposed on us; rather, disciplinary power expands "bidirectionally," flowing from top to bottom and vice versa. So while President Ronald Reagan can issue an executive order that demands that all federal workers be tested for drugs, an ex–auto mechanic can start marketing and selling video cameras to school districts for their buses. While the FBI can help push a wiretap bill through Congress, an employer in your hometown may initiate "integrity" testing of all job applicants.

This is not to suggest that everyday surveillance emerges "by accident." Some people have a vested interest in creating and selling new surveillance technologies, while others may be in a position to exercise this kind of control and benefit from it. Yet even they are, ultimately, not exempt from the gaze of that "long hierarchized network" Foucault refers to. We are all involved and enmeshed within a grid of power relations that are highly intentional and purposeful, arrangements that can be more or less hierarchical and unequal but are never simply one-directional. So while a police officer can surveil suspects with a new high tech scanner, the department can "keep an eye" on that very officer by installing a videocam in the patrol car. Similarly, a teacher can make "normalizing judgments" about students using a computer program, only to find that school administrators can use the same program to assess the teacher's "performance" in the classroom.

How do we maintain anything deserving to be called a democratic society in the face of all this? I am not referring simply to the act of voting (although that is at issue also) as much as I am to the notion of democracy as an ongoing, daily accomplishment that is practiced and maintained both in human relationships and by mediating institutions. Democracy in this sense means not only ensuring our constitutionally given rights but also fostering what we might call the characteristics of a "good society"; a society where citizens are able to maintain a degree of trust in the individuals and organizations that they encounter; a society that is "civil" in every sense of the word; a society that ensures human rights and respects individual privacy and dignity, while at the same time balancing a concern for the "common good." For years, social and political scholars have asserted that a fundamental characteristic of such a society is a viable public life one that includes both public space (e.g., streets, parks, community markets, meeting places, schools) and a civic discourse (i.e., something such as "public opinion"). If Enlightenment reason and democratic ideals offer us any hope, it is in the notion that people can come together and rationally decide what is in their best interest and for the common good.[15]

But in today's culture, how is this possible? As more and more of this "public" space is brought under the gaze of surveillance, and as meticulous rituals permeate our daily lives, "there is nowhere to hide," as Gary Marx puts it. "A citizen's ability to evade this surveillance is diminishing. To venture into a shopping mall, bank, subway, sometimes even a bathroom is to perform before an unknown audience" (Marx quoted in Berko 1992:68). Even if this kind of surveillance is relatively "seamless," as I have argued, it may function to undermine our willingness to participate in civic life and "to speak our minds as clearly, openly, and imaginatively as we can" (Goldfarb 1991:182). Like those subjected to the gaze of the Panopticon, we are increasingly "awed to silence," systematically manipulated and progressively unable to question private authority, challenge public officials, or engage in political dissent. We become, in essence, a "docile" citizenry, "disciplinary" subjects rather than democratic ones.

Driven out of the public sphere, we retreat to the "private life" of home only to find that, increasingly, it is not private at all. Here, public opinion has been replaced by the mass-mediated "storytelling" of high profile media stars who "inform" us about how to vote and what is and what is not a "social problem." Our homes will be increasingly "hardwired" with new telecommunication links that offer corporations unprecedented access to our habits, buying preferences, and financial status. Meanwhile, some of the same technologies can be used to convert some people's homes into "virtual" prisons as they are remotely monitored under the watchful eye of authorities or, in other instances, similar devices enable suspicious parents to listen in on their teenagers' phone calls, to videotape the babysitter, or to rifle through each other's e-mail. With the contemporary blurring of boundaries between notions of "public" and "private," between "real" freedom and its simulation, it is easy to see how "democracy" could become little more than a media illusion on the postmodern landscape.

NOTES

1. Some parts of this chapter are adapted from my book, *Everyday Surveillance: Vigilance and Visibility in Postmodern Life* (copyright August 2000, William G. Staples) and are reproduced with kind permission of Rowman & Littlefield Publishers.

2. Between August and October of 2001 I interviewed twenty-five clients in two house arrest programs in the metropolitan Kansas City area. Clients were asked by corrections officials if they were interested in participating. If they agreed, the interviews took place in an empty office at the facility and took approximately thirty minutes to conduct. The interviews were taped and later transcribed by myself. The names used here are fictitious. The research protocol was conducted within the ethical and procedural guidelines set out by the Human Subjects Committee of the University of Kansas, the American Correctional Association, and the American Sociological Association.

3. "New Growth in a Captive Market," *New York Times*, 31 December 1989, p. 12(E); and *Arizona Republic*, 13 May 1992, p. 5(B).

4. *New York Times*, 31 December 1989, p. 12(E).

5. Ibid., and "Jail Has Alternatives," *University Daily Kansan*, University of Kansas, Lawrence, 18 September 1990, p. 1.

6. A former student, who is an ISO officer, supplied this information. I must ensure confidentiality of this individual and of the agency.

7. Shaun Assael, "Robocourt," *Wired*, March 1994, pp. 106.

8. AMA (1999). The greater share of this oversight is focused on selected job categories and is most often performed as spot checks rather than ongoing surveillance, the survey found, and an average 84 percent of companies with such practices inform their employees of their policies. The financial services sector, including the banking, brokerage, insurance, and real estate industries, lead in elec-

tronic monitoring (68 percent), followed by business and professional service providers (51 percent) and wholesalers and retailers (47 percent). As defined by the AMA, electronic monitoring includes storage and review of e-mail (27 percent, up from 15 percent in 1997); recording and review of telephone conversations (11 vs. 10 percent in 1997); storage and review of voice mail messages (6 vs. 5 percent); storage and review of computer files (21 vs. 14 percent); and video recording of employee job performance (16 percent, as in 1997). Additional surveillance practices include tracking telephone numbers called and time spent on calls (39 vs. 34 percent in 1997); computer time and keystrokes entered (15 vs. 16 percent); and video surveillance to counter theft, violence, or sabotage (33 vs. 34 percent in 1997). The annual survey included 1,054 AMA member organizations, and was conducted in January–March 1999. The survey's margin of error is ±3.5 percent.

9. "Corporate Delete Keys Busy As E–Mail Turns Up in Court," *New York Times*, 11 November 1998, p. 1(A).

10. "Privacy Clashes with Employer Need to Monitor E-Mail," *Dallas Morning News*, 22 July 1998.

11. "Internet Access Management Solutions," WebSENSE Enterprise, Inc. <http://www.netpartners.com> [accessed 23 November 1999].

12. "High-Tech Spy Equipment in the Workplace," National Public Radio, "All Things Considered," 1 April 1996.

13. "Labor Pains," Kansas City, *Pitch Weekly*, 7 October 1999, p. 12.

14. "Surveillance Extends Everywhere," *Lincoln Star*, 19 May 1994, 7

15. See Bellah et al. (1991). The communitarian sociologist Amitai Etzioni argues that excessive protection of individual privacy, in certain situations, may threaten the common good. See Etzioni (1999). Deciding what is best for the "common good," however, is a political process.

REFERENCES

AMA. 1994. *Survey on Workplace Drug Testing and Drug Abuse Policies.* New York: American Management Association.

AMA. 1999. *Survey on Workplace Monitoring and Surveillance.* New York: American Management Association.

Baudrillard, Jean. 1983. *Simulations.* New York: Semiotext(e).

Bellah, Robert N., Richard Madsen, William M. Sullivan, Ann Swindler, and Steven M. Tipton. 1991. *The Good Society.* New York: Knopf.

Bentham, Jeremy. 1995. *The Panopticon Writings.* Edited by Miran Bozovic. London: Verso.

Berko, Lili. 1992. "Surveying the Surveilled: Video, Space, and Subjectivity." *Quarterly Review of Film and Video* 14(1–2):61–91.

Cohen, Stanley. 1979. "The Punitive City: Notes on the Dispersal of Social Control." *Contemporary Crisis* 3(4):339–63.

Corbett, Ronald and Gary T. Marx. 1991. "Critique: No Soul in the New Machine: Technofallacies in the Electronic Monitoring Movement." *Justice Quarterly* 8(3, September):399–414.

Department of Justice. 1999. *Prisons and Jail Inmates at Mid-Year. 1998.* Bureau of Justice Statistics Bulletin. Washington, DC: Author, March.

Etzioni, Amitai. 1999. *The Limits of Privacy.* New York: Basic Books.

Foucault, Michel. 1977. *Discipline and Punish: The Birth of the Prison.* Translated by A. M. Sheridan. New York: Pantheon.

———. 1980. *Power/Knowledge: Selected Interviews and Other Writings, 1972–1977.* Edited by Colin Gordon. New York: Pantheon.

Goldfarb, Jeffrey C. 1991. *The Cynical Society.* Chicago: University of Chicago Press.

Staples, William G. 1994. "Small Acts of Cunning: Disciplinary Practices in Contemporary Life." *Sociological Quarterly* 35(3, Summer):645–64.

———. 2000. *Everyday Surveillance: Vigilance and Visibility in Postmodern Life.* Lanham, MD: Rowman & Littlefield.

9

On Controlling Torture

Jerome H. Skolnick

Torture is a powerful and brutal form of social control, explicitly forbidden by international law. Article 5 of the Universal Declaration of Human Rights holds that "no one shall be subjected to torture or to cruel, inhuman or degrading treatment or punishment." The 1987 United Nations Convention Against Torture allows for no justifications:

> No exceptional circumstances whatsoever, whether a state of war or a threat of war, internal political instability or any other public emergency, may be invoked as a justification of torture. An order from a superior officer or a public authority may not be invoked as a justification of torture.

The international community's prohibition of torture seeks to impose a Kantian aspiration, a common conscience, with no allowable excuses. But a sense of world history or contemporary reality cautions that the aspiration has scarcely been achieved, or likely will be. In 2002 the issue has resurfaced as Western democracies consider how to respond to homicidal bombings and other forms of terror.

There is, nevertheless, a positive story to be told about the elimination of torture, but only in the context of criminal justice. In this chapter, I briefly tell some of the story of torture's evolution and control in civil law jurisprudence. I follow with a narrative of torture in the United States. The history of U.S. torture fits within the international community's definition, but has been called such terms as "lynching" and "the third degree." Finally, I reach the pessimistic conclusion that it will be difficult, if not impossible, to exclude torture when its purpose is to elicit information to prevent an attack by a terrorist organization, rather than to produce evidence leading to a criminal conviction.

THE NATURE OF TORTURE

The 1987 United Nations Convention defined torture as:

> any act by which severe pain or suffering, whether physical or mental, is intentionally inflicted on a person for such purposes as obtaining from him or a third person information or a confession, punishing him for an act he or a third person has committed or is suspected of having committed, or intimidating or coercing him or a third person, or for any reason based on discrimination of any kind, when such pain or suffering is inflicted by or at the instigation of or with the consent or acquiescence of a public official or other person acting in an official capacity. It does not include pain or suffering arising only from, inherent in or incidental to lawful sanctions.

The practice of torture within and outside criminal justice has a long and loathsome history. The archetypal vision is of the "chamber" or "room" where implements of pain were available to burn, beat, shock, drown, and terrify the torture victim (Kerrigan 2001). In the Inquisition, where the goal was a confession, torture was a last resort and a powerful threat. Rules were developed by Nicolas Eymeric, Aragon's papal inquisitor during the second half of the fourteenth century. Eymeric well understood the effectiveness of torture's threat, writing in his *Directorium Inquisitorum:*

> One must not resort to the question until other means of discovering the truth have been exhausted. Good manners, subtlety, the exhortations of well intentioned persons, even frequent meditation, and the discomforts of prison, are often sufficient to induce the guilty to confess. (quoted in Innes 1998:41)

Torture's inevitable link with interrogation may make it appear that it is legally sanctioned. But since evidence gained by torture is inadmissible in civil and common law systems, contemporary torture will more likely be used to gain information. Or torture may be used to intimidate or punish those considered to be enemies. An interrogator may ask questions, but may not care about the truth of the answer. "That something is asked *as if* the content of the answer matters," writes Elaine Scarry "does not mean that it matters" (Scarry 1985:29). Since torture is forbidden by law it has been interpreted as "conduct that seeks to trump law" (Nagan and Atkins 2001:88).

Scarry's vivid portrait of "the structure of torture" mentions a number of regimes where specially equipped torture sites have been used to terrorize political enemies (Scarry 1985:38–45). Such torture, Scarry writes, is usually employed when power is "highly contestable" and the regime "unstable" (ibid.:1). Paul Chevigny, who extended his studies of police violence in New York to Latin America and the Caribbean, describes torture methods of Latin American police in democracies as well as dictatorships. The preferred method of the Sao Paulo police in the 1980s (because it did not leave marks) was the *pau de arrara*, the parrot's perch:

> On the parrot's perch, the victim is hung over a horizontal pole inserted behind his knees, head down, with his hands tied to his ankles; there he may be subjected to other tortures, or just left to contemplate his sins until he has had enough. (Chevigny 1995:149)

Alternative forms of pressure were used by British authorities in Northern Ireland. After beating prisoners with batons and fists, they employed practices of detention and interrogation that included forcing detainees or prisoners to stand for long hours; placing black hoods over their heads; detention in rooms with hissing sounds prior to interrogation; and deprivation of sleep and food and drink (Conroy 2000). The European Court of Human Rights ruled that these practices were "cruel, inhuman and degrading" but refused to characterize them as "torture" (Nagan and Atkins 2001:115).

Even those who deplore torture may be convinced of its necessity, a good end justifying bad means. David Rothman and Aryeh Neier, for example, report torture by police interrogators in India, the world's largest democracy. They say that police brutality during interrogation flourishes because it is widely accepted among the middle classes as a necessary form of social control (Rothman and Neier 1991).

More commonly, torture in contemporary democracies is justified as a response to terror. Israel's General Security Services (GSS) have used "physical means" such as shaking suspects violently, sleep deprivation, and forcing suspects to wait in painful positions, when interrogating Palestinians who are thought to be terrorists or potential terrorists. The GSS practices were challenged by a number of Israeli civil rights groups. The GSS argued that these tactics were a necessary defense against terrorism.

That defense was rejected by the Israeli Supreme Court in a widely heralded case in 1999. The court recognized "the difficult reality in which Israel finds herself," and that "this decision does not ease dealing with that reality." But it concluded that "this is the destiny of democracy, as not all means are acceptable to it, and not all practices employed by its enemies are open before it" (Supreme Court of Israel, H.C. 5100/94, September 6, 1999). However, Israel civil rights groups, notably *B'tselem,* have charged that such interrogation practices continued as terrorist attacks against Israel escalated.

Torture has, of course, also been used by terrorists, perhaps most frighteningly by terrorists who recognize no regime. The Pakistani tormentors and murderers of Daniel Pearl, a journalist employed by the *Wall Street Journal*, tortured and mutilated him as a spectacle, demonstrating their ruthlessness and hatred of Western democracy, and particularly of Jews.

The fruits of torture have been and will likely continue to be used by democratic nations as well as by terrorists, either directly or indirectly, when the primary purpose of the "pressure" is to produce intelligence. For example, the *New York Times* reported that an Al-Qaeda terrorist, Jamal Beghal, was arrested in the Dubai airport, an arrest that thwarted a planned bombing of the U.S. embassy in Paris and nearly prevented the bombing of the World Trade Center in New York. After some weeks in captivity, he talked to his interrogators and "out poured a wealth of information." His lawyer charged that he had been "tossed into a darkened cell, handcuffed to a chair, blindfolded and beaten and that his family was threatened" (Erlanger and Hedges 2001).

Torture and Jurisprudence

That torture in the legal process is deplorable, but necessary, is an idea found in Roman canon law, where torture was permitted as a supplement to strong circumstantial evidence. Standing alone, circumstantial evidence was not considered convincing enough to convict. Even someone caught running away from a corpse, in possession of the murder weapon and the stolen goods, could not be convicted solely on that evidence.

Roman canon law justified torture in the belief that, under torture, a guilty person would reveal detailed knowledge of the crime that an innocent person would not know. But torture was not permitted to be routinely used against criminal suspects. "Half proof" (the testimony of one eyewitness, or strong circumstantial evidence) was required to protect the innocent from pain infliction and false confession (Langbein 1977:4,5).

Foucault argues that this "penal arithmetic" was not nearly so precise at the margins. French criminal procedures were carried out in secret by magistrates who needed to weigh the persuasiveness of circumstantial evidence and the credibility of witnesses. Consequently, the confession took on added significance. It relieved the prosecutor of the obligation of providing further evidence. Moreover, it vindicated the "unequivocal authority" of the criminal law enforcement procedures, including torture, that were being applied. To achieve a "real victory" over the accused demanded confession and contrition. Those accused must if possible "judge and condemn themselves" (Foucault 1977:37–38).

Nevertheless, torture was permitted and its results were persuasive, Foucault argues, because it was regulated. "It was certainly cruel, but it was not savage" (ibid.:40). The rules for torture were codified, but under different local customs and practices. And the magistrate took risks. Under torture, the suspect might die or he might embarrass the magistrate by holding out and forcing the magistrate to drop the charges. That innocent suspects experienced pain was not considered an issue since, if the suspect was innocent, the pain he had endured proved his innocence. If he was guilty, the pain was deserved (ibid.:41).

Nor was the innocent subject of the torture considered a victim. Since he was a suspect, with a reasonable belief based on "half proof" that he was guilty, he could not be completely innocent. As Foucault concludes, "In the eighteenth century, judicial torture functioned in that strange economy in which the ritual that produced the truth went side by side with the ritual that imposed the punishment" (ibid.:42).

Langbein argues that the criticisms of torture by such Enlightenment thinkers as Beccaria and Voltaire were not the main reason for the abolition of torture in civil jurisprudence. He explains the dissolution in terms of a jurisprudential culture lag, arguing that changes in the law of proof had been building through centuries of dissatisfaction. When judges were eventually permitted to evaluate evidence freely, much like English juries who could convict on the basis of strong circumstantial evidence, judicial torture became outmoded.

But if torture for the purpose of obtaining evidence was no longer countenanced in civil law after 1780, torture as *punishment* for those already convicted was retained until 1788 and was even defended by Voltaire (Langbein 1977:17). The rationale for postconviction torture was that convicted felons became the property of the state and therefore, Langbein wryly observes, "the state might put him to some better use first" (ibid.:16). An instance of "better use" was made famous by Foucault's riveting description of the public torture of Damiens the regicide. Public tortures, including hangings in seventeenth-century England, were lessons of deterrence, of just deserts, and of the state's power to impose punishments.

Torture in the United States

Citizens of the United States do not usually register torture as an aspect of the nation's history. Yet, much like the torment of Damien, lynchings were public spectacles employed mostly against southern blacks to maintain a caste social order. In this extrajudicial arena of vigilante justice, victims were whipped and otherwise mutilated. The tortured body was hanged for all to see and remember, the "strange fruit" of Lillian Smith's celebrated novel (Smith 1944).

Although lynchings were intentional homicides, perpetrators were rarely, if ever, prosecuted. Lynchings were accepted by the post-civil war white power structure as individual and general deterrence against those who violated the laws, customs, and institutions that had arisen to keep blacks in a subordinate place (Skolnick and Fyfe 1993:23–42).

The Ku Klux Klan, the secret organization responsible for much of the lynching, was illegal, but its members had infiltrated the institutions of southern justice. Those who carried out the lynching were rarely subject to arrest. Police usually ignored and occasionally participated in the brutal homicides. "Nothing has more nourished dreams of racial revenge," Randall Kennedy writes, "than the knowledge that buried in American history are scores of black victims of lynching whose murderers, though known, escaped punishment" (Kennedy 1997:49).

By the mid-1930s, southern law enforcement officials tried to direct into the criminal justice system incidents that might earlier have provoked a lynching. Charges of murdering a white man were more likely to find their way into court than charges of raping a white woman, an offense more likely to elicit a lynching (Beck, Massey, and Tolney 1989:329).

This was true in the sociologically revealing—and legally groundbreaking—United States Supreme Court case, *Brown v. Mississippi* 297 U.S. 278 (1936), decided in 1936 (Cortner 1986). No evidence, except for their confessions, was produced against three black tenant farmers accused of murdering a white planter. It took only ten days from the time of their arrest to convict them of capital murder. "A speedy trial for the suspected blacks would go a long way," a local newspaper editorialized, "toward removing any apprehension of attempted violence on the part of allegedly enraged citizens of Kemper." And a speedy capital trial with its outcome understood would prevent a lynching (ibid.:8).

To prevent a lawless and uncontrollable public lynching, Mississippi law enforcement officials, who were becoming sensitive to accusations that Mississippi was a lawless state, arrested the suspects, kept the lynch mob at bay, and tortured the men themselves. How the confessions were induced is described by the United States Supreme Court's Chief Justice, Charles Evans Hughes:

> Dial, a deputy sheriff, accompanied by others, came to the home of Ellington, one of the defendants, and requested him to accompany them to the house of the deceased, and there a number of white men were gathered, who began to accuse the defendant of the crime. Upon his denial, they seized him, and with the participation of the deputy they hanged him by a rope to the limb of a tree, and having let him down, they hung him again, and when he was let down the second time, and he still protested his innocence, he was tied to a tree and whipped, and still declining to accede to the demands that he confess, he was finally released and he returned with some difficulty to his home, suffering intense pain and agony. The record of the testimony shows that the signs of the rope on his neck were plainly visible during the so-called trial. A day or two thereafter the said deputy, accompanied by an-

other, returned to the home of the said defendant and arrested him, and departed with the prisoner towards the jail in an adjoining county, but went by
a route which led into the State of Alabama; and while on the way, in that
State, the deputy stopped and again severely whipped the defendant, de-
claring that he would continue the whipping until he confessed, and the defendant then agreed to confess to such a statement as the deputy would
dictate, and he did so, after which he was delivered to jail. (*Brown v. Mississippi* 281–82)

The two other men were similarly whipped and brutalized until they
confessed. The sheriff's deputy who had presided over the beatings did
not deny that one of the defendants had been whipped. The whipping, he
testified, was "not too much for a Negro, not as much as I would have done
if it were left to me" (*Brown v. Mississippi* 284). Despite this acknowledgment, the "confessions" were admitted as evidence by the Mississippi trial
court. Even more shocking, on appeal, the Supreme Court of Mississippi
upheld the trial court's ruling. Nevertheless, a powerful and influential
dissent by Judge Virgil A. Griffith joined by Judge William D. Anderson,
was to influence the Supreme Court of the United States.

Mississippi justice was not uniformly racist or in league with the KKK.
The lawyers who defended the accused blacks were, in their own way,
heroic. John Clark lost law business, friends, and health defending the men
and bringing their appeal to the Mississippi Supreme Court. Against powerful odds, former governor Earl Brewer brought the case to the U.S.
Supreme Court, and reluctantly agreed to a plea of guilty to a lesser degree
of murder, with time served to count against the sentence.

When the case was appealed to the United States Supreme Court, the
justices, a collection of conservatives known as "the nine old men" were
shocked not only by the conduct of the Mississippi police, but that the
highest court of Mississippi could accept confessions that had been elicited
by extraordinary, acknowledged torture by police. The U.S. Supreme Court
opinion virtually adopts Judge Griffith's dissent and concludes:

"It would be difficult to conceive of methods more revolting to the sense of
justice than those taken to procure the confessions of these petitioners," Chief
Justice Charles Evans Hughes wrote, "and the use of the confessions thus obtained as the bases for conviction and sentence was a clear denial of due
process." (*Brown v. Mississippi* 286)

As it turned out, however, victory in the U.S. Supreme Court was not
the end of troubles for the defendants. The case was remanded to the Mississippi District Court and retried by District Attorney John Stennis (later
an influential United States Senator). Stennis negotiated a plea bargain
with attorney Earl Brewer, which was accepted by the defendants, who
had already served years in jail and were given time off their sentences for

their jail service. They believed that no matter how tainted the evidence against them, a retrial would result in a conviction and another death sentence (Cortner 1986:153).

The Jurisprudence of Interrogation

Although coerced confessions had been inadmissible in federal courts since the nineteenth century, *Brown v. Mississippi* set a new judicial standard for state courts. Henceforth, to be admitted as evidence, all confessions in the United States needed to conform to "due process" and be "voluntary" (Cortner 1986).

THE THIRD DEGREE

Whatever the law on the books, however, controlling police during interrogation proved to be elusive largely because, as the Wickersham Commission found, the "third degree" was practiced in most of the United States (Wickersham 1931). Language is interesting here. Under contemporary human rights law, the treatment of the suspects in *Brown v. Mississippi* would surely qualify as torture. Nevertheless, what the court termed "revolting methods" to force the confessions is never referred to by that name. Nor is it in a recent decision upholding *Miranda* by Chief Justice William Rehnquist, who references the Mississippi beatings in *Brown* as "physical coercion" (*Dickerson v. U.S.* 433).

Why not? It may be that the word "torture" connotes a room or chamber designated for that purpose by constituted authorities. In the inquisitorial system, described above by Langbein and Foucault, torture was an established practice, somewhat regulated by legal rules, and performed by magistrates or their agents. Torture had never been sanctioned under the common law as it was in the civil law system. There were no official torturers trained to administer carefully measured doses of pain to test pleas of innocence. Moreover, coerced confessions were regarded as inherently untrustworthy. English judges excluded confessions obtained by promises, threats, and force. "A free and voluntary confession is deserving of the highest credit, because it is presumed to flow from the strongest sense of guilt . . . but a confession forced from the mind by the flattery of hope or the torture of fear, comes in so questionable a shape . . . that no credit ought to be given to it, and therefore it is rejected" (*Dickerson v. U.S.* 1045).

American police north of the Mason-Dixon line (the line that separated slave from free states) understood that the law did not accept confessions that had been elicited by coercion. So did southern police, but they applied different, unwritten rules, to the treatment of blacks. Nevertheless, police in the nineteenth century, and the first third of the twentieth century, developed a set of coercive interrogation practices that today would qualify as torture under international law. They called it "the third degree" and used it against suspects regardless of race.

The origin of the term "third degree" is one of those obscure legal mysteries (like why criminal trial juries in the United States are composed of twelve persons). Richard Sylvester, President of the International Association of Chiefs of Police in 1910–1915, found its origins in the criminal justice system. The first degree is presumably the arrest, the second degree the transport to a place of confinement, and the third degree the interrogation. Whatever its origin, the "third degree" was a euphemism for what we would today call torture.

Sylvester describes the "sweat box," which was introduced after the Civil War to combat the "marauder, the bank robber and the highwayman, thieves and criminals of every kind, [who] took advantage of the exciting times to engage in their nefarious undertakings." The "sweat box" he describes as:

> a cell adjoining which in close proximity was a high iron stove of drum formation. The subject indisposed to disclose information which might be securely locked within his bosom, without ceremony or formality . . . would be confined within the cell. A scorching fire would be encouraged in the monster stove adjoining, into which vegetable matter, old bones, pieces of rubber shoes and kindred trophies would be thrown, all to make a terrible heat, offensive as it was hot, to at last become so tortuous and terrible as to cause the sickened and perspiring object of punishment to reveal the innermost secrets he possessed as the compensation for release from the "sweat box." (Sylvester 1976:71–72)

Captain Cornelius Willemse of the New York City police department, in a book titled *Behind the Green Lights* (of the stationhouse), contrasted the public and the police idea of the third degree, which is resonant of the carefully calibrated, "cruel but not savage" practice of torture in medieval Europe. "To the public," wrote Captain Willemse, ". . . the 'third degree' suggests only one thing—a terrifying picture of secret merciless beating of helpless men in dark cells of the stations." Detectives, said Willemse, saw it as strategic, *purposeful* pressure, not the imposition of punishment for the sake of retribution (Hopkins [1931] 1972:191–92).

Although Willemse acknowledged a repertoire of coercive and deceptive police tactics, he took care to point out that these were not necessarily violent, and were calibrated. Detectives might roll up their sleeves and carry a rubber hose but would not actually beat the suspect. But Willemse acknowledges that there were no limits on how far police might go to break down a suspect: "I never hesitated," he boasted. "I've forced confessions—with fist, blackjack and hose" (ibid.:192).

Unlike the Mississippi sheriff who admitted that the suspect had been whipped, police in cities like New York and Chicago who used fists or blackjacks routinely compounded their offense by giving false testimony. Prosecutors and judges must surely have understood that the police were often lying about how a confession was obtained, but nevertheless accepted the perjured testimony.

But if whippings in the southern United States, and fist, blackjacks, and hose in the northern, were no longer permitted to elicit confessions, what degree and kind of coercion would henceforth be acceptable under the Constitution? For thirty years after the decision in *Brown*, the U.S. Supreme Court faced and struggled with a succession of cases to ascertain the contours of the "due process-voluntariness" standard. Clearly, police could not lawfully whip suspects or beat them with a rubber hose to elicit a confession. Nor could an incriminating admission that led to physical evidence of the crime, such as the murder weapon, be used at trial under the "fruit of the poisonous tree" doctrine. But could police threaten a suspect with a beating? For how many hours could they grill a suspect? How long could they hold him incommunicado? How long could they deny food, or sleep? Could a detective pretend to be a priest? Did it matter whether the suspect was a college graduate or slightly retarded? Could the police lie about the evidence they held against the suspect?

MIRANDA

These were the sorts of questions that made their way to the U.S. Supreme Court following the decision in *Brown*. Of all the U.S. Supreme Court decisions addressing police interrogation, *Miranda v. Arizona* 384 U.S. 436 (1966), narrowly decided by the Warren Court only thirty years after *Brown*, is the lynchpin. It is the case most widely discussed among legal scholars, and surely the best known among television and movie viewers for the famous warnings that have come to be known as "Miranda rights." A suspect must be told that he "has the right to remain silent, that anything he says can be used against him in a court of law, that he has the right to the presence of an attorney, and that if he cannot afford an attorney one will be appointed prior to any questioning if he so desires" (*Miranda v. Arizona* 479). To the surprise of many legal scholars, the legal authority of the decision was recently reaffirmed 5–4, by the U.S. Supreme Court, in a decision written by Chief Justice William Rehnquist (*Dickerson v. U.S.* 530 U.S. 428, 2000).

Nevertheless, *Miranda* remains controversial for three principal reasons: Critics from the right, notably Paul G. Casell, charge that *Miranda* has permitted small but significant numbers of guilty persons to go free (Casell 1996). This allegation has been effectively challenged, particularly by Stephen Schulhofer (1998).

Critics from the left invoke what might be called the "waiver paradox." *Miranda* requires that if a suspect waives his or her right to remain silent, the waiver must have been given "knowingly and intelligently." But, critics ask, is it possible for most suspects to make a "knowing and intelligent" waiver, without the advice of counsel, in what may be the most important legal decision of the suspect's life? But if a lawyer were to be routinely consulted before the decision, few suspects, if any, would waive their right to silence. Moreover, once the waiver is given, many of the coercive pressure tactics that the *Miranda* court decried are then available under the "due process-voluntariness" standard (Skolnick 1982).

A middling position is evident in Justice Rehnquist's unexpected majority decision in *Dickerson*, affirming the necessity for *Miranda* warnings. He notes that the warnings have become embedded in our national culture, and are required as a matter of legal precedent. Moreover, subsequent decisions have reduced *Miranda's* impact on law enforcement. Rarely can a defendant make a "colorable argument" that a self-incriminating statement was unconstitutionally compelled. Critics of the court would agree that the police have adapted to *Miranda*, undermining its original intent. Yet critics from the left have difficulty resolving the waiver paradox. A suspect who has the advice of an attorney on the question of whether to waive his or her right to remain silent would routinely be advised not to waive, to keep silent, virtually eliminating custodial police interrogation (Rosenberg and Rosenberg 1989).

The waiver paradox has been largely resolved by the police and by the courts in two ways. The police have learned to substitute "interviewing" for custodial interrogation. Suppose, for example, a divorced woman has been found murdered in a public park. The police may want to "interview" her former husband, a current friend or recent lover, a business partner, or a neighbor. They can make an appointment and meet each "interviewee" at his or her home or a restaurant. Since the interviewee is not yet a suspect in custody, and is presumptively free to leave, the detectives may question without giving *Miranda* warnings. Based on the answers, each interviewee may appear to be innocent. But if any interviewee's answers seem to be incriminating, and the police make an arrest, they must give *Miranda* warnings before further questioning the suspect in a police interrogation room. Yet police have sometimes failed to give *Miranda* warnings even when the suspect is in a police interrogation room. Ofshe and Leo report cases where the suspects are told that they are free to leave, that this is simply a conversation, and give no *Miranda* warnings (1997:1001).

Suspects who are placed under arrest, handcuffed, given *Miranda* warnings, and taken into custody know that they are in trouble, that the police believe they are guilty of a serious crime. Lacking an attorney with whom to consult about whether to waive their right to silence, they often "cooperate" with the police, and try to tell a story of innocence or exculpation. They believe that asserting their right to silence and representation will signify guilt to the police. They believe that they will help their legal position by trying to justify what they did to the police.

But the police well understand how to manipulate such suspects. Typically, they will suggest incriminating justifications for the suspect's role in the crime. There are many such ploys, usually involving leading questions. In a case of rape, the police may point to the complicity of the victim. "She has a real sexy walk, right, so you knew she wanted it?" or "You were just driving the car, right, you didn't know Joe was going to shoot the liquor store manager? If you had, you never would have driven the getaway car, right?"

Although police are not permitted to use physical coercion, they are permitted to lie to suspects who agree to talk while in custody, even deceiving them about the evidence the police have in their possession. "We found your DNA at the crime scene" or "Your partner has confessed, so why not tell the truth—things will go better for you that way" (Skolnick and Leo 1993). In some cases, police have made up stories so convincing that suspects begin to mistrust their own memories, believe the stories, and falsely confess even to capital crimes (Leo 1998).

CONCLUSION

The whippings of the Jim Crow era, and the fists and blackjacks of the early twentieth century period of the third degree, have virtually disappeared in U.S. interrogation rooms. However much we may think we deplore deception by American police, the post-*Miranda* era of deceptive questioning has ushered in an era of psychological pressure during custodial interrogation, as an alternative to physical brutality. This is not to claim that police brutality has disappeared on the streets and the stationhouses. But physical force rarely, if ever, occurs when the police are seeking *evidence* that can be introduced in a trial (Skolnick and Fyfe 1993:43–66).

Contemporary cases of American police brutality are usually retributive. The most famous brutality cases of the past decade are the street beating of Rodney King in Los Angeles and the beating and sodomizing of Abner Louima in a stationhouse bathroom in New York City. Other known cases follow this retributive pattern of violence against a victim who, the police believe, has assaulted or insulted them. The police may justify the assault (know in the New York City police culture as a "tune up") by filing charges of resisting arrest, as was done in both the King and Louima cases (Skolnick 2000). Such charges are so common that police executives use "resisting arrest" filings as an indicator of a "problem" officer who is likely to employ excessive force.

As terror invades—as it has New York City and Washington DC—will U.S. interrogations resemble the torture rooms of Latin American and other dictatorships? Will they resemble the sometimes physically forceful interrogations in other democracies, such as Great Britain and Israel, which have been the victims of urban terrorist attacks? The tactics used by U.S. interrogators, and the rights of the detainees from the war in Afghanistan held at the U.S. naval base in Guantanamo Bay, Cuba, have come under considerable scrutiny in the American press. "Military officials say torture is not an option," writes Eric Schmitt of *The New York Times.* "But, they said, under the Geneva Conventions, anything short of torture is permissible to get a hardened Qaeda operative to spill a few scraps of information that could prevent terrorist attacks" (Schmitt 2002).

I need here to restate my argument, to distinguish again, as I have throughout this essay, between (a) American police detectives who are seeking evidence to convict a criminal suspect in a courtroom and (b) police or military security officers who are seeking intelligence about terrorist organizations and plans for attack.

If the former, the historical evidence suggests that norms of procedural jurisprudence have limited torture, even in the pre-Enlightenment civil law systems. At the turn of the twentieth century, American detectives tortured suspects whom they considered particularly hardened and uncooperative criminals. They knew it was against the law to do so, but they considered it necessary for the public good. The tortures could be obfuscated by the euphemism "the third degree" to make them appear acceptable.

Judicial oversight provided antidotes to station house brutality during interrogation by developing explicit normative standards (due process, voluntariness, Miranda warnings) for police to consider when contemplating custodial interrogation to produce evidence that would be acceptable in a court of law. Norms governing police interrogation can work well in democracies (and better in some than in others) when the issue is guilt or innocence of traditional victim crimes such as murder, rape, and robbery; and where there is a rule excluding evidence when the incriminating admissions have been physically coerced.

By contrast, when we leave the territory of ordinary crime and enter the perplexing terrain of crimes of terror, with multiple homicides and serious injuries, we encounter a different and more unsettled normative world. Punishment for ordinary crime is traditionally justified as appropriate retribution and incapacitation. We also consider the prevention function of punishment through the general and specific deterrence that the punishment offers.

Aside from general and laudatory human rights declarations by the international community, and the remote possibility of conviction in a so far nonexistent international criminal court, there is comparably little to deter torture by an official from a nation attacked by terrorists. Assuming, as we must, that there are few explicit sanctions to deter torture to prevent terror attacks, do not the antitorture admonitions of the United Nations exert a powerful normative force?

They do. But in the context of terror, competing normative forces—the pressure to save innocent lives, to prevent attacks—are also powerful. Our jurisprudence of police interrogation has evolved in the context of enforcing ordinary crimes enumerated in a penal code. Terror is different and more frightening. Its consequences are death, injury, and the destruction of property. Its costs are unfathomable. Michael Walzer explains terrorism's purpose as the destruction of "the morale of a nation or class, to undercut its solidarity; its method is the random murder of innocent people" (Walzer [1977] 2000:197). Those who would violate—or more likely, test the limits of—the torture conventions may place a higher value on the safety of such innocent people as against the pain experienced by the terrorist.

Consequently when we leave the familiar environment of judicial evidence regarding crime and enter the region of war and terror, we find ourselves on confusing and slippery normative terrain. Consider that before World War II, wars were fought between states and armies of men. Combatants needed rules to protect prisoners, and there was an expectation of reciprocity between the antagonists as to how prisoners of war would be treated. This was true during World War II as well.

But World War II was the first where *states* also used terror on a major scale as part of their strategy (Walzer [1977] 2000). This was done by both sides. German planes and rocket launchers dropped bombs on English cities. In retaliation, the bombing of Germany was not limited to industrial sites and included such major cities as Berlin and Dresden. The most noteworthy, some would say infamous, terrorist bombings were of Hiroshima and Nagasaki, the nuclear bombing of two Japanese cities by the air force of the United States. The attacks were supposedly based on a utilitarian calculus valuing the lives of American soldiers over the lives of Japanese civilians. The bombings were intended to terrorize the Japanese government and its civilian population into surrender. The strategy worked to end World War II and the victors were vindicated.

Suppose bombings could be prevented by interrogatory torture producing information leading to the destruction of the planes delivering nuclear bombs. How forceful would be a "human rights" position allowing for "no exceptional circumstances . . . as a justification of torture"? Yet it requires little imagination to think of such situations, for example, preventing a nuclear attack.

Alan Dershowitz has proposed that we introduce a "torture warrant" so as to exercise judicial control over the torture that, he argues, will inevitably occur in the "ticking bomb" scenario (Dershowitz 2002). In response, Amnesty International's William Schulz acknowledges that although the hypothetical works well enough as a classroom thought experiment, "its defenders are unable to cite even one case that mirrors its conditions" (Schulz 2002). Schulz points out that the authorities must have knowledge of a ticking bomb that is about to explode, must have a suspect in custody who knows where it is and how to disable it. If tortured, the suspect will, in a few minutes, yield the precise information needed to disable the bomb. Moreover, the "torture warrant" assumes that there is time to communicate the facts and circumstances to the judge who would issue the warrant.

Michael Ignatieff has also criticized the "ticking bomb" hypothetical on grounds that it is unrealistic, based on the French experience in Algeria (Ignatieff 2002). He argues that while even those who detest torture might be willing to torture once to prevent a disaster, that is unrealistic. Torture, Ignatieff argues, is a political strategy, as it was in Algeria, and will occur again and again. Moreover, it is a face-to-face activity that exposes our own agents to "unnecessary moral harm."

A torture warrant implies boundaries separating permissible from impermissible torture. Should we institutionalize torture chambers, selecting certain instruments and practices and rejecting others? Should we develop courses on the application of such torture to interrogators? If not torture chambers, what will a judge be agreeing to permit if he or she signs such a warrant? The idea of a torture warrant implies that interrogators who lie about the evidence leading to the warrant, or who exceed the terms of the permitted torture, will be sanctioned. But given the assumption of "necessity" for torture to be imposed, what sanctions should or would we apply if its terms of permissible torture were exceeded?

Judicial oversight of torture raises many problems. It implies case law and precedent and, ultimately, some degree of legitimacy for anything just short of what a court will call "torture." (Recall that the European Court of Human Rights ruled that the beatings and torments carried out by British authorities in Northern Ireland were "cruel, inhuman and degrading," but not "torture.")

As a free and democratic nation, the United States has largely succeeded in eliminating "third degree" interrogation by police. With the reaffirmation of the *Miranda* warnings and the "due process-voluntariness" test for confessions by Supreme Court of the United States, we seem to have reached something like a consensus concerning the limits of police interrogatory pressure for ordinary crimes. Even those who continue to oppose the *Miranda* warnings affirm the limits placed by these standards, which clearly outlaw the pressure tactics of the "third degree."

Crime, however deplorable, is a familiar part of the world that police, citizens and courts inhabit. But war and terror do and will challenge the normative stability of everyday life. However commendable and seemingly firm the "no exceptional circumstances" clause of the United Nations proscription against torture, it is unlikely to persuade American (or European) interrogators in the context of terrorist plans to attack innocent civilians. But if we try to control them through judicial oversight, we probably will not succeed. And we may, as an unintended consequence, legitimize "cruel, inhuman and degrading" police practices—so long as we do not designate these practices by the universally condemned label "torture."

REFERENCES

Beck, E. M., James L. Massey, and Stewart E. Tolney 1989. "The Gallows, the Mob and the Vote: Lethal Sanctioning of Blacks in North Carolina and Georgia, 1882–1930." *Law and Society Review* 23:317.

Brown v. Mississippi 297 U.S. 278 (1936).

Casell, Paul G. 1996. "Miranda's Social Costs: An Empirical Reassessment," Pp. 175–90 in *The Miranda Debate: Law, Justice and Policing,* edited by R. A. Leo and G. C. Thomas. Boston: Northeastern University Press.

Chevigny, Paul. 1995. *Edge of the Knife: Police Violence in the Americas.* New York: New Press.

Conroy, John. 2000. *Unspeakable Acts, Ordinary People: The Dynamics of Torture.* Berkeley: University of California Press.

Cortner, Richard C. 1986. *A "Scottsboro" Case in Mississippi: The Supreme Court and Brown v. Mississippi.* Jackson: University Press of Mississippi.

Dershowitz, Alan. 2002. *Shouting Fire: Civil Liberties in a Turbulent Age.* Boston: Little, Brown.

Dickerson v. U.S. 530 U.S. 428 (2000).

Erlanger, Stephen and Chris Hedges. 2001. "A Nation Challenged: The Trail: Terror Cells Slip Through Europe's Grasp." *New York Times,* December 28, p. A1.

Foucault, M. 1977. *Discipline and Punish: The Birth of the Prison.* London: Allen Unwin.

Hopkins, Ernest Jerome. [1931] 1972. *Our Lawless Police: A Study of the Unlawful Enforcement of the Law.* New York: De Capo.

Ignatieff, Michael. 2002. "The Torture Wars." *New Republic,* April 22, pp. 40–43.

Innes, Brian. 1998. *The History of Torture.* New York: Saint Martins.

Kennedy, Randall. 1997. *Race, Crime and the Law.* New York: Pantheon.

Kerrigan, Michael. 2001. *The Instruments of Torture.* London: Amber.

Langbein, John H. 1977. *Torture and the Law of Proof: Europe and England in the Ancient Regime.* Chicago: University of Chicago Press.

Leo, Richard A. 1998. "*Miranda* and the Problem of False Confessions." Pp. 271–82 in *The Miranda Debate: Law, Justice and Policing,* edited by R. A. Leo and G. C. Thomas. Boston: Northeastern University Press.

Nagan, Winston P. and Lucie Atkins. 2001. "The International Law of Torture: From Universal Proscription to Effective Application And Enforcement." *Harvard Human Rights Journal* 14:87–121.

Ofshe, Richard J. and Richard Leo. 1997. "The Decision to Confess Falsely: Rational Choice and Irrational Action." *Denver University Law Review* 74(4):979–1122.

Rosenberg, Irene M. and Yale L. Rosenberg. 1989. "A Modest Proposal for the Abolition of Custodial Confessions." Pp. 142–52 in *The Miranda Debate: Law, Justice and Policing,* edited by R. A. Leo and G. C. Thomas. Boston: Northeastern University Press.

Rothman, David and Aryeh Neier. 1991. "India's Awful Prisons." *New York Review of Books* (May 16):53–56.

Scarry, Elaine. 1985. *The Body in Pain.* New York: Oxford University Press.

Schmitt, Eric. 2002. "There Are Ways To Make Them Talk." *New York Times: Week in Review,* June 16, p. 1.

Schulhofer, Stephen. 1998. "Miranda's Practical Effect: Substantial Benefits and Vanishingly Small Social Costs." Pp. 191–207 in *The Miranda Debate: Law, Justice and Policing,* edited by R. A. Leo and G. C. Thomas. Boston: Northeastern University Press.

Schulz, W. 2002. "The Torturer's Apprentice." *The Nation.* May 13, 2002.

Skolnick, Jerome H. 1982. "Deception by Police." *Criminal Justice Ethics* (Summer/Fall):40–54.

Skolnick, Jerome H. 2000. "Code Blue: Prosecuting Police Brutality Requires Penetrating the Blue Code of Silence." *American Prospect* (March 27–April 10):49–53.

Skolnick, Jerome H. and James J Fyfe. 1993. *Above The Law: Police and the Excessive Use of Force.* New York: Free Press.

Skolnick, Jerome H. and Richard A. Leo. 1993. "The Ethics of Deceptive Interrogation." Pp. 75–91 in *Issues in Policing: New Perspectives,* edited by J. Bizzack. Lexington: Autumn House.

Smith, Lillian. [1944] 1992. *Strange Fruit.* New York: Harcourt Brace Jovanovich.

Sylvester, Richard. 1976. "A History of the 'Sweat Box' and the 'Third Degree.'" in *The Blue and the Brass: American Policing 1890–1910.* Gaithersburg, MD: IACP.

Walzer, Michael. [1977] 2000. *Just and Unjust Wars.* New York: Basic Books.

Wickersham, George W. 1931. "Report on Lawlessness in Law Enforcement." *National Commission on Law Observance and Enforcement.* Washington, DC: U.S. Government Printing Office.

III

Punishment: Measuring and Justifying

Introduction to Part III

Mainstream work on the sociology of punishment and control (see Part I) takes the form of historical narratives: tales of changes and continuities, trends and interruptions, rare successes and frequent failures. The chapters in this section deal with two frequent interruptions of these tales:

(1) There is the question of *evidence:* what data, measurements, or indicators do we use to establish that rates of incarceration (or whatever) are actually increasing and moreover, increasing "significantly"? Extravagant theories about grand "trends" need grounding in the detailed statistical record of what the system actually does. "Social control" is not an abstract process; it leaves behind measurable traces of its operations. At the descriptive level, we need raw information about what is done to what number of people over what time. At the more complicated evaluative level, we need reliable data to assess the impact of all these operations.

In Chapter 10, Richard Berk and David Freedman consider some of the methodological problems in measuring the impact of penal policy. Can the natural science model of experimental group/control group be adapted to evaluating particular programs? Moreover, as the authors conclude, statistical maneuverings and analyses of the results of prior studies that characterize the meta-analysis approach will not yield better empirical generalizations than those resulting from simply reading prior studies, thinking about their results, and summarizing them into meaningful categories. In Chapter 11, Alfred Blumstein, who has pioneered the use of systems theory to study the criminal justice process, uses the measurable variable of imprisonment rates to examine the "stability of punishment" hypothesis. Whether or not some internal adjustment mechanism ever operated to stabilize amounts of punishment, Blumstein's characterization of the correctional system as being "out of control" clearly points to the breakdown of such internal regulation.

(2) Crime control systems do not operate like conveyor belts. Each component part "stops" the machine: to make decisions, use discretion, review "alternatives." At each stage—whether before, during, or after the decision—there are appeals to a set of justifications and rationalizations, a language drawn from the jurisprudential catalog of "aims of punishment." Debates about the aims of the criminal law in general and judicial sentencing in particular often revolve around the contrast between utilitarian

and nonutilitarian rationales. The legal scholar Andrew von Hirsch has been a major figure in this debate and is identified with the "back to justice" or "just deserts" model. In Chapter 12, he reflects on the attractions and criticisms of the principle of proportionality in sentencing. What is the influence of this model in the movement toward the fixed, determinate, or mandatory sentencing guidelines that are associated (causally or not) with increased rates of imprisonment?

Gary Kleck (Chapter 13) enters the debate from two directions quite different from von Hirsch's. First, he takes a utilitarian rationale for granted and concentrates on its strongest appeal: the doctrine of general deterrence. Second, he looks less for philosophical justifications than for criminological evidence about criminal behavior. In particular: the nature of the link "required" by the legal doctrine (general deterrence) between (1) rational decision-making and (2) some (if not perfect) correspondence between contingencies and the perception of these contingencies.

In the thoughts and on the bodies of punished criminals, it might not matter too much whether they are sitting in a prison cell as a result of either utilitarian or of nonutilitarian jurisprudence. What does matter, irrespective of the original justification, is whether the process of judicial allocation (sentencing) was efficient and fair. Waldo and Paternoster (Chapter 14) could hardly find a better case to illustrate this principle than the ugly story of failed reforms in the administration of the death penalty in the United States. Their title comes from Justice Blackmun's commitment to tinker no longer with the machinery of death, but to concede that the death penalty "experiment" has failed. Sadly, there are stronger and familiar forces that will rewrite this moral lesson into a quite different historical imperative: Rothman's motto for the perpetuation of the prison: "legitimation despite failure."

10

Statistical Assumptions as Empirical Commitments

RICHARD A. BERK AND DAVID A. FREEDMAN

INTRODUCTION

Researchers who study punishment and social control, like those who study other social phenomena, typically seek to generalize their findings from the data they have to some larger context: in statistical jargon, they generalize from a sample to a population. Generalizations are one important product of empirical inquiry. Of course, the process by which the data are selected introduces uncertainty. Indeed, any given dataset is but one of many that could have been studied. If the dataset had been different, the statistical summaries would have been different, and so would the conclusions, at least by a little.

How do we calibrate the uncertainty introduced by data collection? Nowadays, this question has become quite salient, and it is routinely answered using well-known methods of statistical inference, with standard errors, t-tests, and p-values, culminating in the "tabular asterisks" of Meehl (1978). These conventional answers, however, turn out to depend critically on certain rather restrictive assumptions, for instance, random sampling.[1]

When the data are generated by random sampling from a clearly defined population, and when the goal is to estimate population parameters from sample statistics, statistical inference can be relatively straightforward. The usual textbook formulas apply; tests of statistical significance and confidence intervals follow.

If the random-sampling assumptions do not apply, or the parameters are not clearly defined, or the inferences are to a population that is only vaguely defined, the calibration of uncertainty offered by contemporary statistical technique is in turn rather questionable.[2] Thus, investigators who use conventional statistical technique turn out to be making, explicitly or implicitly, quite restrictive behavioral assumptions about their

235

data collection process. By using apparently familiar arithmetic, they have made substantial empirical commitments; the research enterprise may be distorted by statistical technique, not helped. At least that is our thesis, which we will develop in the pages that follow.

Random sampling is hardly universal in contemporary studies of punishment and social control. More typically, perhaps, the data in hand are simply the data most readily available (e.g., Gross and Mauro 1989; MacKenzie 1991; Nagin and Paternoster 1993; Berk and Campbell 1993; Phillips and Grattet 2000; White 2000). For instance, information on the use of prison "good time" may come from one prison in a certain state. Records on police use of force may be available only for encounters in which a suspect requires medical attention. Prosecutors' charging decisions may be documented only after the resolution of a lawsuit.

"Convenience samples" of this sort are not random samples. Still, researchers may quite properly be worried about replicability. The generic concern is the same as for random sampling: if the study were repeated, the results would be different. What, then, can be said about the results obtained? For example, if the study of police use of force were repeated, it is almost certain that the sample statistics would change. What can be concluded, therefore, from the statistics?

These questions are natural, but may be answerable only in certain contexts. The moment that conventional statistical inferences are made from convenience samples, substantive assumptions are made about how the social world operates. Conventional statistical inferences (e.g., formulas for the standard error of the mean, t-tests) depend on the assumption of random sampling. This is not a matter of debate or opinion; it is a matter of mathematical necessity.[3] When applied to convenience samples, the random sampling assumption is not a mere technicality or a minor revision on the periphery; the assumption becomes an integral part of the theory.

In the pages ahead, we will try to show how statistical and empirical concerns interact. The basic question will be this: what kinds of social processes are assumed by the application of conventional statistical techniques to convenience samples? Our answer will be that the assumptions are quite unrealistic. If so, probability calculations that depend on the assumptions must be viewed as unrealistic too.[4]

TREATING THE DATA AS A POPULATION

Suppose that one has data from spouse abuse victims currently residing in a particular shelter. A summary statistic of interest is the proportion of women who want to obtain restraining orders. How should potential uncertainty be considered?

One strategy is to treat the women currently residing in the shelter as a population; the issue of what would happen if the study were repeated does not arise. All the investigator cares about are the data now in hand. The summary statistics describe the women in the dataset. No statistical inference is needed because there is no sampling uncertainty to worry about.

Treating the data as a population and discarding statistical inference might well make sense if the summary statistics are used to plan for current shelter residents. A conclusion that "most" want to obtain restraining orders is one thing; a conclusion that a "few" want to obtain such orders has different implications. But there are no inferences about women who might use the shelter in the future, or women residing in other shelters. In short, the ability to generalize has been severely restricted.

ASSUMING A REAL POPULATION AND IMAGINARY SAMPLING MECHANISM

Another way to treat uncertainty is to define a real population and assume that the data can be treated as a random sample from that population. Thus, current shelter residents could perhaps be treated as a random sample drawn from the population of residents in all shelters in the area during the previous twelve months. This "as-if" strategy would seem to set the stage for statistical business as usual.

An explicit goal of the "as-if" strategy is generalizing to a specific population. And one issue is this: are the data representative? For example, did each member of the specified population have the same probability of coming into the sample? If not, and the investigator fails to weight the data, inferences from the sample to the population will likely be wrong.[5]

More subtle are the implications for estimates of standard errors.[6] The usual formulas require the investigator to believe that the women are sampled independently of one another. Even small departures from independence may have serious consequences, as we demonstrate later. Furthermore, the investigator is required to assume constant probabilities across occasions. This assumption of constant probabilities is almost certainly false. Family violence has seasonal patterns. (Christmas is a particularly bad time.) The probabilities of admission therefore vary over the course of the year. In addition, shelters vary in catchment areas, referral patterns, interpersonal networks, and admissions policies. Thus, women with children may have a low probability of admission to one shelter, but a high probability of admission to other shelters. Selection probabilities depend on a host of personal characteristics; such probabilities must vary across geography and over time.

The independence assumption seems even more unrealistic. Admissions policies evolve in response to daily life in the shelter. For example, some shelter residents may insist on keeping contact with their abusers. Experience may make the staff reluctant to admit similar women in the future. Likewise, shelter staff may eventually decide to exclude victims with drug or alcohol problems.

To summarize, the random sampling assumption is required for statistical inference. But this assumption has substantive implications that are unrealistic. The consequences of failures in the assumptions will be discussed below.

AN IMAGINARY POPULATION AND IMAGINARY SAMPLING MECHANISM

Another way to treat uncertainty is to create an imaginary population from which the data are assumed to be a random sample. Consider the shelter story. The population might be taken as the set of all shelter residents that could have been produced by the social processes creating victims who seek shelter. These processes might include family violence, as well as more particular factors affecting possible victims, and external forces shaping the availability of shelter space.

With this approach, the investigator does not explicitly define a population that could in principle be studied, with unlimited resources of time and money. The investigator merely assumes that such a population exists in some ill-defined sense. And there is a further assumption, that the dataset being analyzed can be treated as if it were based on a random sample from the assumed population. These are convenient fictions. The source of the fiction is twofold: (1) the population does not have any empirical existence of its own, and (2) the sample was not in fact drawn at random.

In order to use the imaginary-population approach, it would seem necessary for investigators to demonstrate that the data can be treated as a random sample. It would be necessary to specify the social processes that are involved, how they work, and why they would produce the statistical equivalent of a random sample. Hand-waving is inadequate. We doubt the case could be made for the shelter example or any similar illustration. Nevertheless, reliance on imaginary populations is widespread. Indeed, regression models are commonly used to analyze convenience samples: as we show later, such analyses are often predicated on random sampling from imaginary populations. The rhetoric of imaginary populations is seductive precisely because it seems to free the investigator from the necessity of understanding how data were generated.

WHEN THE STATISTICAL ISSUES ARE SUBSTANTIVE

Statistical calculations are often a technical sideshow; the primary interest is in some substantive question. Even so, the methodological issues need careful attention, as we have argued. However, in many cases the substantive issues are very close to the statistical ones. For example, in litigation involving claims of racial discrimination, the substantive research question is usually operationalized as a statistical hypothesis: certain data are like a random sample from a specified population.

Suppose, for example, that in a certain jurisdiction there are 1084 probationers under federal supervision: 369 are black. Over a six-month period, 119 probationers are cited for technical violations: 54 are black. This is disparate impact, as one sees by computing the percentages: in the total pool of probationers, 34% are black; however, among those cited, 45% are black.

A *t*-test for "statistical significance" would probably follow. The standard error on the 45% is $\sqrt{0.45 \times 0.55/119} = 0.046$, or 4.6%. So, $t = (0.45 - 0.34)/0.046 = 2.41$, and the one-sided p is .01. (A more sophisticated analyst might use the hypergeometric distribution, but that would not change the outlines of the problem.) The null hypothesis is rejected, and there are at least two competing explanations: either blacks are more prone to violate probation, or supervisors are racist. It is up to the probation office to demonstrate the former; the *t*-test shifts the burden of argument.

However, there is a crucial (and widely ignored) step in applying the *t*-test: translating the idea of a race-neutral citation process into a statistical null hypothesis. In a race-neutral world, the argument must go, the citation process would be like citing 119 people drawn at random from a pool consisting of 34% blacks. This random-sampling assumption is the critical one for computing the standard error.

In more detail, the *t*-statistic may be large for two reasons: (1) too many blacks are cited, so the numerator in the *t*-statistic is too big, or (2) the standard error in the denominator is too small. The first explanation may be the salient one, but we think the second explanation needs to be considered as well. In a race-neutral world, it is plausible that blacks and whites should have the same overall citation probabilities. However, in any world, these probabilities seem likely to vary from person to person and time to time. Furthermore, dependence from occasion to occasion would seem to be the rule rather than the exception. As will be seen below, even fairly modest amounts of dependence can create substantial bias in estimated standard errors.

In the real world of the 1990s, the proportion of federal probationers convicted for drug offenses increased dramatically. Such probationers were often subjected to drug testing and required to participate in drug treatment programs. The mix of offenders and supervision policies changed dramatically. The assumption of probabilities constant over time is, therefore, highly suspect. Likewise, an assumption that all probationers faced the same risks of citation is almost certainly false. Even in a race-neutral world, the intensity of supervision must be in part determined by the nature of the offender's crime and background; the intensity of supervision obviously affects the likelihood of detecting probation violations.

The assumption of independence is even more problematic. Probation officers are likely to change their supervision policies, depending on past performance of the probationers. For example, violations of probation seem likely to lead to closer and more demanding supervision, with higher probabilities of detecting future violations. Similarly, behavior of the probationers is likely to depend on the supervision policies.

In short, the translation of race neutrality into a statistical hypothesis of random sampling is not innocuous. The statistical formulation seems inconsistent with the social processes on which it has been imposed. If so, the results of the statistical manipulations—the p-values—are of questionable utility.

This example is not special. For most convenience samples, the social processes responsible for the data likely will be inconsistent with what needs to be assumed to justify conventional formulas for standard errors. If so, translating research questions into statistical hypotheses may be quite problematic: much can be lost in translation.

DOES THE RANDOM SAMPLING ASSUMPTION MAKE ANY DIFFERENCE?

For criminal justice research, we have tried to indicate the problems with making statistical inferences based on convenience samples. The assumption of independence is critical, and we believe this assumption will always be difficult to justify (Kruskal 1988). The next question is whether failures of the independence assumption matter. There is no definitive answer to this question; much depends on context. However, we will show that relatively modest violations of independence can lead to substantial bias in estimated standard errors. In turn, the confidence levels and significance probabilities will be biased too.

Violations of Independence

Suppose the citation process violates the independence assumption in the following manner. Probation officers make contact with probationers on a regular basis. If contact leads to a citation, the probability of a subsequent citation goes up, because the law enforcement perspective is reinforced. If contact does not lead to a citation, the probability of a subsequent citation goes down (the law enforcement perspective is not reinforced). This does not seem to be an unreasonable model; indeed, it may be far more reasonable than independence.

More specifically, suppose the citation process is a "stationary Markov chain." If contact leads to a citation, the chance that the next case will be cited is 0.50. On the other hand, if contact does not lead to a citation, the chance of a citation on the next contact is only 0.10. To get started, we assume the chance of a citation on the first contact is 0.30; the starting probability makes little difference for this demonstration.

Suppose an investigator has a sample of 100 cases, and observes 17 citations. The probability of citation would be estimated as $17/100 = 0.17$, with a standard error of $\sqrt{0.17 \times 0.83 / 100} = 0.038$. Implicitly, this calculation assumes independence. However, Markov chains do not obey the independence assumption. The right standard error, computed by simulation, turns out to be 0.058. This is about 50% larger than the standard error computed by the usual formula. As a result, the conventional t-statistic is about 50% too large. For example, a researcher who might ordinarily use a critical value of 2.0 for statistical significance at the .05 level should really be using a critical value of about 3.0.

Alert investigators might notice the breakdown of the independence assumption: the first-order serial correlation for our Markov process is about 0.40. This is not large, but it is detectable with the right test. However, the dependencies could easily be more complicated and harder to find, as the next example shows.

Consider a "four-step Markov chain." The probation officer judges an offender in the light of recent experience with similar offenders. The officer thinks back over the past four cases and finds the case most like the current case. If this "reference" case was cited, the probability that the current case will be cited is 0.50. If the reference case was not cited, the probability that the current case will be cited is 0.10. In our example, the reference case is chosen at random from the four prior cases. Again, suppose an investigator has a sample of 100 cases, and observes 17 citations. The probability of citation would still be estimated as $17/100 = 0.17$, with a standard error of $\sqrt{0.17 \times 0.83 / 100} = 0.038$. Now, the right standard error, computed by simulation, turns out to be 0.062. This is about 60% larger than the standard error computed by the usual formula.

Conclusions are much the same as for the first simulation. However, the four-step Markov chain spreads out the dependence so that it is hard to detect: the first-order serial correlation is only about 0.12.[7] Without a priori knowledge that the data were generated by a four-step Markov chain, a researcher is unlikely to identify the dependence.

Similar problems come about if the Markov chain produces negative serial correlations rather than positive ones. Negative dependence can be just as hard to detect, and the estimated standard errors will still be biased. Now the bias is upward so the null hypothesis is not rejected when it should be: significant findings will be missed.

Of course, small correlations are easier to detect with large samples. Yet probation officers may use more than four previous cases to find a reference case; they may draw on their whole current caseload, and on salient cases from past caseloads. Furthermore, transition probabilities (here, 0.50 and 0.10) are likely to vary over time in response to changing penal codes, administrative procedures, and mix of offenders. As a result of such complications, even very large samples may not save the day.

The independence assumption is fragile. It is fragile as an empirical matter because real world criminal justice processes are unlikely to produce data for which independence can be reasonably assumed. (Indeed, if independence were the rule, criminal justice researchers would have little to study.) The assumption is fragile as a statistical matter, because modest violations of independence may have major consequences while being nearly impossible to detect. The Markov chain examples are not worst-case scenarios, and they show what can happen when independence breaks down. The main point: even modest violations of independence can introduce substantial biases into conventional procedures.

DEPENDENCE IN OTHER SETTINGS

Spatial Dependence

In the probation example, dependence was generated by social processes that unfolded over time. Dependence can also result from spatial relationships rather than temporal ones. Spatial dependence may be even more difficult to handle than temporal dependence.

For example, if a researcher is studying crime rates across census tracts in a particular city, it may seem natural to assume that the correlation between tracts depends on the distance between them. However, the right measure of distance is by no means obvious. Barriers such as freeways, parks, and industrial concentrations may break up dependence irrespective of physical distance. "Closeness" might be better defined by travel time. Perhaps tracts connected by major thoroughfares are more likely to violate the assumption of independence than tracts between which travel is inconvenient. Ethnic mix and demographic profiles matter too, because crimes tend to be committed within ethnic and income groups. Social distance rather than geographical distance may be the key. Our point is that spatial dependence matters. Its measurement will be difficult, and may depend on how distance itself is measured. Whatever measures are used, spatial dependence produces the same kinds of problems for statistical inference as temporal dependence.

Regression Models

In research on punishment and social control, investigators often use complex models. In particular, regression and its elaborations (e.g., structural equation modeling) are now standard tools of the trade. Although rarely discussed, statistical assumptions have major impacts on analytic results obtained by such methods.

Consider the usual textbook exposition of least squares regression. We have n observational units, indexed by $i = 1, \ldots, n$. There is a response variable y_i, conceptualized as $\mu_i + \epsilon_i$ where μ_i is the theoretical mean of y_i while the disturbances or errors ϵ_i represent the impact of random variation (sometimes of omitted variables). The errors are assumed to be drawn independently from a common (Gaussian) distribution with mean 0 and finite variance. Generally, the error distribution is not empirically identifiable outside the model; so it cannot be studied directly—even in principle—without the model. The error distribution is an imaginary population and the errors are treated as if they were a random sample from this imaginary population—a research strategy whose frailty was discussed earlier.

Usually, explanatory variables are introduced, and μ_i is hypothesized to be a linear combination of such variables. The assumptions about the μ_i and ϵ_i are seldom justified or even made explicit—although minor correlations in the ϵ_i can create major bias in estimated standard errors for coefficients. For one representative textbook exposition, see Weisberg (1985). Conventional econometric expositions are for all practical purposes identical (e.g., Johnston 1984).

Structural equation models introduce further complications (Freedman 1987, 1991, 1995, 1997, 1999; Berk 1988, 1991). Although the models seem sophisticated, the same old problems have been swept under the carpet, because random variation is represented in the same old way. Why do μ_i and ϵ_i behave as assumed? To answer this question, investigators would have to consider, much more closely than is commonly done, the connection between social processes and statistical assumptions.

Time Series Models

Similar issues arise in time series work. Typically, the data are highly aggregated; each observation characterizes a time period rather than a case; rates and averages are frequently used. There may be T time periods indexed by $t = 1, 2, \ldots, T$. The response variable y_t is taken to be $\mu_t + \epsilon_t$, where the ϵ_t are assumed to have been drawn independently from a common distribution with mean 0 and finite variance. Then, μ_t will be assumed to depend linearly on values of the response variable for preceding time periods and on values of the explanatory variables. Why such assumptions should hold is a question that is seldom asked, let alone answered.

Serial correlation in residuals may be too obvious to ignore. The common fix is to assume a specific form of dependence between the ϵ_t. For example, a researcher might assume that $\epsilon_t = \alpha \epsilon_{t-1} + \delta_t$, where now δ_t satisfy the familiar assumptions: the are drawn independently from a common distribution with mean 0 and finite variance. Clearly, the game has not changed except for additional layers of technical complexity.

Meta-Analysis

Literature reviews are a staple of scientific work. Over the past twenty-five years, a new kind of review has emerged, claiming to be more systematic, more quantitative, more scientific: this is "meta-analysis." The initial step is to extract "the statistical results of numerous studies, perhaps hundreds, and assemble them in a database along with coded information about the important features of the studies producing these results. Analysis of this database can then yield generalizations about the body of research represented and relationships within it" (Lipsey 1997:15). Attention is commonly focused on the key outcomes of each study, with the hope that by combining the results, one can learn what works. For example, Lipsey (1992) assesses the efficacy of a large number of juvenile delinquency treatment programs, while Sherman and his colleagues (1997) consider in a similar fashion a wide variety of other criminal justice interventions. Meta-analysis is discussed in any number of accessible texts (e.g., Lipsey and Wilson 2001). Statistical inference is usually a central feature of the exposition.

A meta-analysis identifies a set of studies, each of which provides one or more estimates of the effect of some intervention. For example, one might be interested in the impact of job training programs on prisoner behavior after release. For some studies, the outcome of interest might be earnings; do inmates who participate in job training programs have higher earnings after release than those who do not? For other studies, the outcome might be the number of weeks employed during the first year after release. For a third set of studies, the outcome might be the time between release and getting a job. For each outcome, there would likely be several research reports with varying estimates of the treatment effect. The meta-analysis seeks to provide a summary estimate over all of the studies.

We turn to a brief description of how summary estimates are computed. We follow Hedges and Olkin (1985:Sections 4E, A), but relax some of their assumptions slightly. Outcomes for treated subjects ("experimentals") are denoted Y_{ij}^E, while the outcomes for the controls are denoted Y_{ij}^C. Here, i indexes the study and j indexes subject within study. Thus, Y_{ij}^E is the response of the jth experimental subject in the ith study. There are k studies in all, with n_i^E experimentals and n_i^C controls in the ith study. Although we use the "treatment-control" language, it should be clear that meta-analysis is commonly applied to observational studies in which the "treatments" can be virtually any variable that differs across subjects. In Archer's (2000) meta-analysis of sex differences in domestic violence, for example, the "treatment" is the sex of the perpetrator.

One key assumption is that for each $i = 1,\ldots,k$,

(A) Y_{ij}^E are independent and identically distributed for $j = 1,\ldots,n_i^E$; these variables have common expectation μ_i^E and variance σ_i^2.

Similarly,

(B) Y_{ij}^C are independent and identically distributed for $j = 1,\ldots,n_i^C$; these variables have common expectation μ_i^C and variance σ_i^2.

Notice that μ_i^E, μ_i^C, and σ_i^2 are parameters—population-level quantities that are unobservable. Notice too that the variances in (A) and (B) are assumed to be equal. Next, it is assumed that

(C) The responses of the experimentals and controls are independent.

Assumptions (A) and (B) specified within-group independence; (C) adds the assumption of between-group independence. Finally, it is assumed that

(D) studies are independent of one another.

Let $\overline{Y}_i^E$ be the average response for the experimentals in study i, and let $\overline{Y}_i^C$ be the average response for the controls. These averages are statistics, computable from study data. It follows from (A) and (B) that, to a reasonable approximation

$$\overline{Y}_i^E \sim N(\mu_i^E, \sigma_i^2/n_i^E), \qquad i = 1,\ldots,k \tag{1}$$

and

$$\overline{Y}_i^C \sim N(\mu_i^C, \sigma_i^2/n_i^C), \qquad i = 1,\ldots,k. \tag{2}$$

For the ith study, the "effect size" is

$$\eta_i = \frac{\mu_i^E - \mu_i^C}{\sigma_i}. \tag{3}$$

It is assumed that

$$\eta_1 = \eta_2 = \ldots = \eta_k = \eta. \tag{4}$$

The goal is to estimate the value of η. For instance, if $\eta = 0.20$, the interpretation would be this: treatment shifts the distribution of responses to the right by 20% of a standard deviation.[8]

There are a number of moves here. Assumptions (A), (B), and (C) mean that treatment and control subjects for each study are drawn as independent random samples from two different populations with a common standard deviation. The standardization in (3) eliminates differences in scale across studies.[9] After that, (4) requires that there is but a single parameter value for the effect size over all of the studies: there is only one true treatment effect, which all of the studies are attempting to measure.

Now the common effect can be estimated by taking a weighted average:

$$\hat{\eta} = w_1\hat{\eta}_1 + \ldots + w_k\hat{\eta}_k, \tag{5}$$

where

$$\hat{\eta}_i = \left(\overline{Y}_i^E - \overline{Y}_i^C\right)/\hat{\sigma}_i. \tag{6}$$

In (6), the statistic $\hat{\sigma}_i$ estimates the common standard deviation from the sample; the weights w_i adjust for differences in sample size across studies. (To minimize variance, w_i should be inversely proportional to $1/n_i^E + 1/n_i^C$; other weights are sometimes used.) Moreover, we can compute standard errors for $\hat{\eta}$, because this estimator is the product of a convenient and well-defined chance process. For details, see Hedges and Olkin (1985:Chapter 6).

The outcome is both pleasing and illusory. The subjects in the treatment and control groups (even in a randomized controlled experiment, as discussed below) are not drawn at random from populations with a common variance; with an observational study, there is no randomization at all. It is gratuitous to assume that *standardized* effects are constant across studies: it could be, for instance, that the average effects themselves are approximately constant but standard deviations vary widely. If we seek to combine studies with different kinds of outcome measures (earnings, weeks worked, time to first job), standardization seems helpful. And yet, why are standardized effects constant across these different measures? Is there really one underlying construct being measured, constant across studies, except for scale? We find no satisfactory answers to these critical questions.

The assumed independence of studies is worth a little more attention. Investigators are trained in similar ways, read the same papers, talk to one another, write proposals for funding to the same agencies, and publish the findings after peer review. Earlier studies beget later studies, just as each generation of Ph.D. students trains the next. After the first few million dollars are committed, granting agencies develop agendas of their own, which investigators learn to accommodate. Meta-analytic summaries of past work further channel the effort. There is, in short, a web of social dependence inherent in all scientific research. Does social dependence compromise statistical independence? Only if you think that investigators' expectations, attitudes, preferences, and motivations affect the written word—and never forget those peer reviewers.[10]

The basic model represented in Equations (1–4) can be—and often is—extended in one way or another, although not in any way that makes the model substantially more believable. Perhaps the most common change is to allow for the possibility of different effect sizes. That is, Equation (4) no longer applies; there is no longer an η characterizing all of the studies. Under a "random-effects model," the η_i's are assumed to be drawn as a random sample from some population of η_i's. Now the goal is to estimate the grand mean μ of this population of η_i's. However, insofar as meta-analysis rests on a convenience sample of studies, if not a whole population, the random-effects model is at a considerable distance from the facts.[11]

But wait. Perhaps the random-effects model can be reformulated: the ith study measures η_i, with an intrinsic error whose size is governed by Equations (1), (2), and (3). Then, in turn η_i, differs from the sought-for grand mean μ by some random error; this error (i) has a mean value of 0 across all potential studies, and (ii) a variance that is constant across studies. This second formulation (a "components of variance" model) is equally phantasmagorical. Why would these new assumptions be true? Which potential studies are we talking about,[12] and what parameter are we estimating? Even if we could agree on answers to those questions, it seems likely—particularly with nonexperimental data—that each study deviates from truth by some intrinsic bias, whose size varies from one study to another. If so, the meta-analytic machine grinds to a halt.

There are further variations on the meta-analytic model, with biases related to study characteristics through some form of regression analysis. The unit of analysis is the study, and the response variable is the estimated effect size. Statistical inference is driven by the sort of random sampling assumptions discussed earlier, when regression analysis was initially considered. However, with research studies as the unit of analysis, the random sampling assumption becomes especially puzzling. The interesting question is why the technique is so widely used. One possible answer is this. Meta-analysis would be a wonderful method if the assumptions held. However, the assumptions are so esoteric as to be unfathomable and hence immune from rational consideration: the rest is history. For other commentaries, see Oakes (1990) or Petitti (1999).

Observational Studies and Experiments

We return to the basic assumptions (A)–(C) above. How are these to be understood? Meta-analysis is on its most secure footing with experiments, so we begin there. By way of example, consider an experiment with 1,000 subjects. Each subject has two possible responses. One response will be manifest if the subject is put into the treatment condition; the other, in the control condition. For any particular subject, of course, one and only one of the two responses can be measured: the subject can be put into treatment or control, but not both.

Suppose 500 out of our 1,000 subjects are chosen at random, and put into treatment; the other 500 are put in the control condition; the treatment and control averages will be compared. This is the cleanest of study designs. Do assumptions (A)–(C) hold? No, they do not—as a moment's reflection will show. There are two samples of size 500 each, but these are dependent, precisely because a subject assigned to treatment cannot be assigned to control, and vice versa. Thus, (C) fails. Similarly, the treatment group is drawn at random without replacement, so there is dependence between observations within each group: the first subject drawn cannot appear also as the second subject, and so forth. So the independence assumption in (A) fails, as does the corresponding assumption in (B).

To secure assumptions (A)–(C) in an experimental setting, we need an extremely large pool of subjects, most of whom will not be used. Suppose, for instance, we have 10,000 subjects: 500 will be chosen at random and put into treatment; another 500 will be chosen at random for the controls; the remaining 9,000 will be ignored. In this unusual design, we have the independence required by (A)–(C), at least to a first approximation. But we are not there yet. Assumptions (A) and (B) require that the variance be the same in treatment and control conditions. In effect, treatment is only allowed to add one number—the same for all subjects—to the control response. If different subjects show different responses to treatment, then the constant-variance assumption is likely to be wrong.

To sum up, (A)–(C) hold—to a good approximation—for an experiment with a large pool of subjects, where a relatively small number are chosen at random for treatment, another small number are chosen at random for controls, and the only effect of treatment is to add a constant to all responses. Few experiments satisfy these conditions.[13]

Typically, of course, a meta-analysis starts not from a set of experiments, but from a set of observational studies. Then what? The basic conceit is that each observational study can be treated as if it were an experiment; not only that, but a very special kind of experiment, with the sampling structure described above. This is exactly the sort of unwarranted assumption whose consequences we have explored earlier in this essay. In brief, standard errors and p-values are liable to be quite misleading.

There is one situation where the assumptions underlying meta-analysis can be shown to give reasonable results, namely, combining a series of properly designed randomized controlled experiments, run with a common protocol, to test the global null hypothesis (treatment has no effect in any of the experiments).[14] Of course, even if the global null hypothesis is rejected, so the treatment has some effects on some subjects in some studies, the model underlying meta-analysis is far from demonstrated: the treatment may have different effects on different people, depending on context and circumstance. Indeed, that seems more plausible a priori than the hypothesis of a constant additive effect.[15]

RECOMMENDATIONS FOR PRACTICE

Convenience samples are a fact of scientific life in criminal justice research; so is uncertainty. However, the conventional techniques designed to measure uncertainty assume that the data are generated by the equivalent of random sampling, or probability sampling more generally.[16]

Real probability samples have two great benefits: (1) they allow unbiased extrapolation from the sample; (2) with data internal to the sample, it is possible to estimate how much results are likely to change if another sample is taken. These benefits, of course, have a price: drawing probability samples is hard work. An investigator who assumes that a convenience sample is like a random sample seeks to obtain the benefits without the costs—just on the basis of assumptions.

If scrutinized, few convenience samples would pass muster as the equivalent of probability samples. Indeed, probability sampling is a technique whose use is justified because it is so unlikely that social processes will generate representative samples. Decades of survey research have demonstrated that when a probability sample is desired, probability sampling must be done. Assumptions do not suffice. Hence, our first recommendation for research practice: whenever possible, use probability sampling.

If the data-generation mechanism is unexamined, statistical inference with convenience samples risks substantial error. Bias is to be expected and independence is problematic. When independence is lacking, the p-values produced by conventional formulas can be grossly misleading. In general, we think that reported p-values will be too small; in the social world, proximity seems to breed similarity. Thus, many research results are held to be statistically significant when they are the mere product of chance variation.

We are skeptical about conventional statistical adjustments for dependent data. These adjustments will be successful only under restrictive assumptions whose relevance to the social world is dubious. Moreover, adjustments require new layers of technical complexity, which tend to distance the researcher from the data. Very soon, the model rather than the data will be driving the research. Hence another recommendation: do not rely on post hoc statistical adjustments to remove dependence.

No doubt, many researchers working with convenience samples will continue to attach standard errors to sample statistics. In such cases, sensitivity analyses may be helpful. Partial knowledge of how the data were generated might be used to construct simulations. It may be possible to determine which findings are robust against violations of independence. However, sensitivity analysis will be instructive only if it captures important features of the data-generation mechanism. Fictional sensitivity analysis will produce fictional results.

We recommend better focus on the questions that statistical inference is supposed to answer. If the object is to evaluate what would happen were the study repeated, real replication is an excellent strategy (Freedman 1991; Berk 1991; Ehrenberg and Bound 1993). Empirical results from one study can be used to forecast what should be found in another study. Forecasts about particular summary statistics, such as means or regression coefficients, can be instructive. For example, an average rate of offending estimated for teenagers in one neighborhood could be used as a forecast for teenagers in another, similar neighborhood. Using data from one prison, a researcher might predict which inmates in another prison will be cited for rule infractions. Correct forecasts would be strong evidence for the model.

Cross validation is an easier alternative. Investigators can divide a large sample into two parts. One part of the data can be used to construct forecasting models, which are then evaluated against the rest of the data. This offers some degree of protection against bias due to overfitting or chance capitalization. But cross validation does not really address the issue of replicability. It cannot, because the data come from only one study.

Finally, with respect to meta-analysis, our recommendation is simple: just say no. The suggested alternative is equally simple: read the papers, think about them, and summarize them.[17] Try our alternative. Trust us: you will like it. And if you can't sort the papers into meaningful categories, neither can the meta-analysts. In the present state of our science, invoking a formal relationship between random samples and populations is more likely to obscure than to clarify.

CONCLUSIONS

We have tried to demonstrate that statistical inference with convenience samples is a risky business. While there are better and worse ways to proceed with the data at hand, real progress depends on deeper understanding of the data-generation mechanism. In practice, statistical issues and substantive issues overlap. No amount of statistical maneuvering will get very far without some understanding of how the data were produced.

More generally, we are highly suspicious of efforts to develop empirical generalizations from any single dataset. Rather than ask what would happen in principle if the study were repeated, it makes sense to actually repeat the study. Indeed, it is probably impossible to predict the changes attendant on replication without doing replications. Similarly, it may be impossible to predict changes resulting from interventions without actually intervening.

NOTES

1. "Random sampling" has a precise, technical meaning: sample units are drawn independently, and each unit in the population has an equal chance to be drawn at each stage. Drawing a random sample of the U.S. population, in this

technical sense, would cost several billion dollars (since it requires a census as a preliminary matter) and would probably require the suspension of major constitutional guarantees. Random sampling is not an idea to be lightly invoked.

2. As we shall explain below, researchers may find themselves assuming that their sample is a random sample from an imaginary population. Such a population has no empirical existence, but is defined in an essentially circular way—as that population from which the sample may be assumed to be randomly drawn. At the risk of the obvious, inferences to imaginary populations are also imaginary.

3. Of course, somewhat weaker assumptions may be sufficient for some purposes. However, as we discuss below, the outlines of the problem stay the same.

4. We use the term "parameter" for a characteristic of the population. A "sample statistic" or "estimate" is computed from the sample to estimate the value of a parameter. As indicated above, we use "random sampling" to mean sampling with replacement from a finite population: each unit in the population is selected independently (with replacement) and with the same probability of selection. Sampling without replacement (i.e., simple random sampling) may be more familiar. In many practical situations, sampling without replacement is very close to sampling with replacement. Stratified cluster samples are often more cost-effective than purely random samples, but estimates and standard errors then need to be computed taking the sample design into account. Convenience samples are often treated as if they were random samples, and sometimes as if they were stratified random samples—that is, random samples drawn within subgroups of some poorly defined superpopulation. Our analysis is framed in terms of the first model, but applies equally well to the second.

5. Weighting requires that the investigator know the probability of selection for each member of the population. It is hard to imagine that such precise knowledge will be available for convenience samples. With the wrong weights, estimates will be biased, perhaps severely.

6. The standard error measures sampling variability; it does not take bias into account. Our basic model is random sampling. In the time-honored way, suppose we draw women into the sample one after another (with replacement). The conventional formula for the standard error assumes that the selection probabilities stay the same from draw to draw; on any given draw, the selection probabilities do not have to be identical across women.

7. The standard error is affected not only by first-order correlations, but also by higher-order correlations.

8. We are not quite following the notation in Hedges and Olkin (1985): our standardized effect size is η rather than δ, corresponding to d in Cohen (1988).

9. Temperature can be measured in degrees Celsius or degrees Fahrenheit. The two temperature scales are different, but they are linearly related: $F° = (\frac{5}{9})C° + 32°$. The Hedges-Olkin model for meta-analysis described above does not account for transformations more complicated than the linear one. In short, units do not matter; but anything more substantive than a difference in units between studies is beyond the scope of the model.

10. Meta-analysts deal with publication bias by making the "file-drawer" calculation: How many studies would have to be withheld from publication to change the outcome of the meta-analysis from significant to insignificant? Typically, the number is astronomical. This is because of a crucial assumption in the procedure—

that the missing estimates are centered on zero. The calculation ignores the possibility that studies with contrarian findings—significant or insignificant—are the ones been withheld. There is still another possibility, which is ignored by the calculation: study designs may get changed in midstream, if results are going the wrong way. See Rosenthal (1979), Oakes (1990:158), or Petitti (1999:134).

11. The model now requires two kinds of random sampling: a random sample of studies and then a random sample of study subjects.

12. If the answer is "all possible studies," then the next question might be, with what assumptions about government spending in fiscal 2025? or for that matter, in 1975? What about the respective penal codes and inmate populations? The point is that hypothetical superpopulations don't generate real statistics.

13. With a binary response variable—"success" or "failure"—there does seem to be a logical contradiction in the model: changing the probability p of success automatically changes the variance $p(1 - p)$. Naturally, other models can then be used, with different definitions for η. But then, combining binary and continuous responses in the same meta-analysis almost seems to be a logical contradiction, because the two kinds of studies are measuring incommensurable parameters. For example, in Lipsey (1992), half the studies use a binary response variable (item 87, p. 111). Following Cohen (1988), Lipsey (p. 91) handles these binary responses by making the "arcsine transformation" $f(x) = 2 \arcsin \sqrt{x}$. In more detail, suppose we have n independent trials, each leading to success with probability p and failure with the remaining probability $1 - p$. We would estimate p by $\hat{p}$, the proportion of successes in the sample. The sampling variance of $\hat{p}$ is $p(1 - p)/n$, which depends on the parameter p and the sample size n. The charm of the arcsine transformation—which is considerable—is that the asymptotic variance of $\hat{p}$ is $1/n$, and does not depend on the unknown p.

If now $\hat{p}^E$ is the proportion of successes in the treatment group, while $\hat{p}^C$ is the proportion of successes in the control group, $f(\hat{p}^E) - f(\hat{p}^C) = f(p^E) - f(p^C)$, up to an additive random error that is asymptotically normal with mean 0 and variance $1/n^E + 1/n^C$. Lipsey—like many others who follow Cohen—would define the effect size as $f(\hat{p}^E) - f(\hat{p}^C)$. But why is a reduction of 0.20 SDs in time to rearrest—for instance—comparable to a reduction of 0.20 in twice the arcsine of the square root of the recidivism rate, i.e., a reduction of 0.10 in the arcsine itself? We see no rationale for combining studies this way, and Lipsey does not address such questions, although he does provide a numerical example on pp. 97–98 to illustrate the claimed equivalence.

14. Although (A)–(C) are false, as shown above, the statistic $\hat{\eta}_i$ in (6) should be essentially normal. Under the global null hypothesis that all the η_i are zero, the expected value of $\hat{\eta}_i$ is approximately zero, and the variance of $\hat{\eta}_i / \sqrt{1/N_i^E + 1/N_i^C}$ is approximately 1, by a combinatorial argument. Other tests are available too. For example, the χ^2-test is a more standard, and more powerful, test of the global null. Similar calculations can be made if the treatment effect is any additive constant—the same for all subjects in the study. If the treatment effect varies from subject to subject, the situation is more complicated; still, conventional procedures often provide useful approximations to the (correct) permutation distributions—just as the χ^2 is a good approximation to Fisher's exact test.

15. Some readers will, no doubt, reach for Occam's razor. But this is a two-edged sword: (i) Isn't it simpler to have one number than 100? (ii) Isn't it simpler to drop

the assumption that all the numbers are the same? Finally, if the numbers are different, Occam's razor can even cut away the next assumption—that the studies are a random sample from a hypothetical superpopulation of studies. Occam's razor is to be unsheathed only with great caution.

16. A probability sample starts from a well-defined population; units are drawn into the sample by some objective chance mechanism, so the probability that any particular set of units falls into the sample is computable. Each sample unit can be weighted by the inverse of the selection probability to get unbiased estimates.

17. Descriptive statistics can be very helpful in the last-mentioned activity. For one lovely example out of many, see Grace, Muench, and Chalmers (1966).

REFERENCES

Archer, J. 2000. "Sex Differences in Aggression Between Heterosexual Partners: A Meta-Analytic Review." *Psychological Bulletin* 126(5):651–80.

Berk, R. A. 1988. "Causal Inference for Statistical Data." Pp. 155–74 in *Handbook of Sociology,* edited by N. J. Smelser. Newbury Park, CA: Sage.

Berk, R. A. 1991. "Toward a Methodology for Mere Mortals." Pp. 315–24 in *Sociological Methodology,* Volume 21, edited by P. V. Marsden. Washington, DC: American Sociological Association.

Berk, R. A. and A. Campbell. 1993. "Preliminary Data on Race and Crack Charging Practices in Los Angeles." *Federal Sentencing Reporter* 6(1):36–38.

Cohen, J. 1998. *Statistical Power Analysis for the Behavioral Sciences.* Second edition. Hillsdale, NJ: Lawrence Erhham.

Ehrenberg, A.S. C. and J. A. Bound. 1993. "Predictability and Prediction." *Journal of the Royal Statistical Society,* Series A,156, Part 2:167–206 (with discussion).

Freedman, D. A. 1987. "As Others See Us: A Case Study in Path Analysis" (with discussion). *Journal of Educational Statistics* 12:101–223.

Freedman, D. A. 1991. "Statistical Models and Shoe Leather." Pp. 291–313 in *Sociological Methodology,* Volume 21, edited by P. V. Marsden. Washington, DC: American Sociological Association.

Freedman, D. A. 1995. "Some Issues in the Foundation of Statistics" (with discussion). *Foundations of Science* 1:19–83. Reprinted in *Some Issues in the Foundation of Statistics* edited by B. van Fraasen. Dordrecht: Kluwer.

Freedman, D. A. 1997. "From Association to Causation via Regression" (with discussion). Pp. 113–82 in *Causality in Crisis?* edited by V. McKim and S. Turner. Notre Dame, IN: University of Notre Dame Press.

Freedman, D. A. 1999. "From Association to Causation: Some Remarks on the History of Statistics." *Statistical Science* 14:243–58.

Grace, N. D. H. Muench, and T. C. Chalmers. 1966. "The Present Status of Shunts for Portal Hypertension in Cirrhosis." *Gastroenterology* 50:684–91.

Gross, S. R. and R. Mauro. 1989. *Death and Discrimination.* Boston: Northeastern University Press.

Hedges, L. V. and I. Olkin. 1985. *Statistical Methods for Meta-Analysis.* New York: Academic Press.

Johnston, J. 1984. *Econometric Methods.* New York: McMillan.

Kruskal, W. 1998. "Miracles and Statistics: The Casual Assumption of Independence." *Journal of the American Statistical Association* 83(404): 929–40.

Lipsey, M. W. 1992. "Juvenile Delinquency Treatment: A Meta-Analysis Inquiry into the Variability of Effects." Pp. 83–127 in *Meta-Analysis for Explanation.* T. C. Cook, D. S. Cooper, H. Hartmannn, L. V. Hedges, R. I. Light, T. A. Loomis, and F. M. Mosteller (eds.). New York: Russell Sage.

———. 1997. "What Can You Build with Thousands of Bricks? Musings on the Cumulation of Knowledge in Program Evaluation." *New Directions for Evaluation* 76(Winter):7–24.

Lipsey, M. W. 2001. *Practical Meta-Analysis.* Newbury Park, CA: Sage Publications.

MacKenzie, D. L. 1991. "The Parole Performance of Offenders Released from Shock Incarceration (Boot Camp Prisons): A Survival Time Analysis." *Journal of Quantitative Criminology* 7(3):213–36.

Meehl, P. E. 1978. "Theoretical Risks and Tabular Asterisks: Sir Karl, Sir Ronald, and the Slow Progress of Soft Psychology." *Journal of Consulting and Clincal Psychology* 46:806–834

Nagin, D. S. and R. Paternoster. 1993. "Enduring Individual Differences and Rational Choice Theories of Crime." *Law & Society Review* 27(3):467–96.

Oakes, Michael W. 1990. *Statistical Inference.* Chestnut Hill, MA: Epidemiology Resources Inc.

Petitti, Diana B. 1999. *Meta-Analysis, Decision Analysis and Cost-Effectiveness Analysis,* 2nd ed. New York: Oxford University Press.

Phillips, S. and R. Grattet. 2000. "Judicial Rhetoric, Meaning-Making and the Institutionalization of Hate Crime Law." *Law & Society Review* 34(3):567–606.

Rosenthal, R. 1979. "The 'File Drawer' and Tolerance for Null Results." *Psychological Bulletin* 86:638–41.

Sherman, L. W., D. Gottfredson, D. MacKenzie, J. Eck, P. Reuter, and S. Bushway. 1997. *Preventing Crime: What Works, What Doesn't, What's Promising?* Washington, DC: U.S. Department of Justice.

Weisberg, S. 1985. *Applied Linear Regression.* New York: John Wiley.

White, M. D. 2000. "Assessing the Impact of Administrative Policy on the Use of Deadly Force by On- and Off-Duty Police." *Evaluation Review* 24(3):295–318.

11

Stability of Punishment

What Happened and What Next?

ALFRED BLUMSTEIN

INTRODUCTION

The continuing debate about what is known as the "stability-of-punish-ment" hypothesis is relevant not only for the study of social control, but also for its policy implications. The hypothesis was generated in a paper I wrote with Jacqueline Cohen in 1973 (Blumstein and Cohen 1973) propos-ing a theory of the stability of punishment. That was challenged by Berk, Rauma, Messinger, and Cooley (1981) in a paper that analyzed California data on prison admissions, and argued that these data did not confirm the stability-of-punishment hypothesis. Their challenge was based mostly on the technical aspects of the definition of "stability" in a time series and was based on data from California.[1] My colleagues and I raised some objections to the challenges raised (Blumstein, Cohen, Moitra, and Nagin 1981) and we thought they were appropriate, but I have no desire here to reopen that discussion.

The stability-of-punishment hypothesis was stimulated on a theoretical level by some ideas of Durkheim and on an empirical level by examining the time series of incarceration rates in the United States from the 1920s through the early 1970s, which displayed an impressive stability over that period. The U.S. incarceration rate averaged 110 per 100,000, with a coeffi-cient of variation[2] over that 50-year period of only 8 percent. When the same pattern was repeated in some foreign countries over even longer pe-riods, that gave rise to some attempts to figure out what processes could account for that very stable pattern.

Even though subsequent events have certainly made it clear that we are no longer in a stable-punishment regime, I continue to believe that the ar-guments advanced in that original paper and in a number of succeeding papers refining aspects of the theory were a reasonably valid assessment of the processes at work at the time. It is clear, however, that whatever stability prevailed in the fifty years leading to 1973, they certainly do not prevail today.[3] The U.S. incarceration rate at the end of 2000 reached a level of 470 per 100,000 in state and federal prisons[4] (with an additional 50 percent or so in local jails). This rate is more than four times the rate that had prevailed for the 50 years prior to 1973, and reflects an exponential growth rate averaging about 6.5 percent per year since 1973.

In this chapter, I would like to revisit that initial hypothesis, explore some of the earlier debate, and examine what happened to take us from the originally stable regime (stable in at least some reasonable definitions) to one that now seems to be out of control. I would then like to examine where our current policies might be taking us, and what possible restoring forces might yet appear to tame this exponential growth, at least to some degree.

THE STABILITY-OF-PUNISHMENT DEBATE

The Original Hypothesis

In examining a time series of incarceration rates in the United States, I was struck by how little variation they displayed. Figure 11.1 presents that information from 1925 to 1975. Looking at those data, it is striking how closely they adhered to the mean of 108.5 per 100,000 and how well the great majority of the points stayed within even *one* standard deviation of 11.0.[5] The most significant deviation (after the early years of the series, which started in 1925 with a rate of 79 per 100,000) was in the late 1930s, when the Great Depression gave rise to a maximum deviation at 137 per 100,000 in 1939. This was followed by a rapid decline during World War II, when the nation had much better uses for its young men of prison age, and the incarceration rate dipped to a local minimum of 100 (still well within one standard deviation of the mean rate) in 1945.

The only other deviation was in the late 1960s, when the move to community-based treatment and "prison reform" led to a dip to a rate of 94 in 1968. This low rate could also be partly artifactual because of the small cohort sizes in the prime imprisonment years at that time as a result of the low number of births in the later depression years and the wartime years.[6]

We were struck by the flatness of this curve, by its trendlessness, and by the presumed existence of "homeostatic" forces that kept this process in reasonable balance. The fact that a similar pattern was displayed in Norway over even a longer period (1880 to 1964) albeit at a lower rate (52.5 per 100,000 with a standard deviation of 8.2) and in other Scandinavian coun-

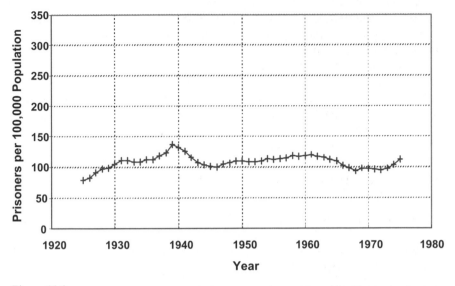

Figure 11.1

tries as well strengthened the conviction that there must be some kind of stabilizing process at work, and led to a search for explanation and interpretation.

The hypothesis, in short, recognizes the possibility that crime rates would be climbing and falling depending on a wide variety of social conditions that were far less amenable to control than would be the case with prison populations. The proposed mechanism was one of shifting thresholds. As crime rates went up, the threshold of the seriousness of the offense or of the offender's prior criminal history (or other attributes that might enter into sentencing decisions) would be raised in order to avoid imposing an excessive burden on the prison system. This recognized a degree of common interest that was shared by judges and prosecutors (who were generally far more subservient to judges in those days). With indeterminate sentences (one year to life was not uncommon in states like California), parole boards had a broad range of discretion. They, too, could shift thresholds on their readiness to tolerate risk in the released offenders as necessary to accelerate departures when admissions increase in order to avoid overcrowding of the state's prisons.

The process could also work similarly when crime rates were decreasing. If crime rates were to decline appreciably, then behaviors that were tolerated but complained about became candidates for passing new laws or more aggressively enforcing old laws (e.g., laws prohibiting prostitution or drunk driving).

This is a modification of the Durkheim (1964) argument that *crime* (rather than punishment) is a natural—and even in some sense desirable— aspect of society, and that societies without crime will seek to redefine certain behaviors as crimes partly to reinforce the norms in that society. This is an argument that was developed in rich detail by Kai Erikson in *The Wayward Puritans* (1966).

With a variety of other collaborators I pursued the issue to provide more elaborate structure of the dynamics of the process maintaining a homeostatic relationship (Blumstein, Cohen, and Nagin 1977). Some of that work explored the stability phenomenon within individual states and the similarity across neighboring states of the nature of their individual incarceration rate time series (Blumstein and Moitra 1979).

The Challenge by Berk et al.

The principal issues in the challenge by Berk, Rauma, Messinger, and Cooley (1981) and in a separate paper by David Rauma (1981) derive from an analysis of a long time series, more than twice as long as our fifty-year series for the United States as a whole, and hinges on an elaborate analysis of the autoregressive integrated moving average (ARIMA) time series model outlined by Box and Jenkins (1976) and a finding that the longer time series for California was not "stationary" in the terms of that model. Our response (Blumstein, Cohen, Moitra, and Nagin 1981) was to argue that this technical definition of "stationary" was not the principal relevant criterion, but rather that our emphasis was on trendlessness and small variation around that flat trend. We argued that the time series we were studying both in many of the states as well as in the nation as a whole displayed those aspects of "stability." Of course, this is not the time to reopen that old debate. Rather, I wanted to use this as a departure point for examining what has happened since.

Figure 11.2 extends the graph of Figure 11.1 to 2000. It is difficult to pinpoint the precise year in which the dramatic growth of the right-hand portion of the graph began, but it does appear to be in the period 1973 to 1975, and so we can identify 1974 as an important turning point, but with significant acceleration beginning in 1981.

Even the simplest examination of that figure would challenge any presumption of stability after 1980. The period between 1974 and 1980 might be argued as within the reasonable range of the prior stable rate. But that would be reasonable only if the rate had turned down after 1980 instead of accelerating upward.

Many who have looked at Figure 11.2 question whether that dramatic change does more harm than it does good: the trend over the last twenty-five years must raise many more questions than those of "stability." There

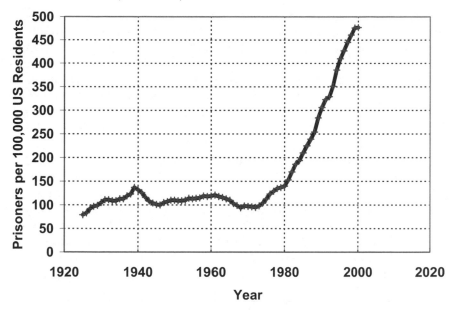

Figure 11.2

must be considerable concern about the political forces that have given rise to this dramatic growth in incarceration that had over 1.3 million people in state or federal prisons by the end of 2000, with another 620,000 in local jails, a total approaching 2 million prisoners in the United States (Beck and Harrison 2001).

SUBSEQUENT DEVELOPMENTS
IN THE INCARCERATION RATE

It is clear that, whatever forces did maintain the homeostatic process from the 1920s through the mid-1970s, they had been fractured by 1975 and totally abandoned by 1980. Several factors have contributed to that shift.

Ironically, most of the initial attacks on the stable process appear to have come from the liberal Left, which is generally hostile to any increase in punishment. But the Left provided the opening that was exploited by the conservative Right, which seems to continually demand more punishment.

Some of the initial assault on the previous regime of control by parole boards was stimulated by a succession of findings through the 1960s that reported on various kinds of experimental and quasi-experimental evaluations of correctional treatment alternatives. Most of these found a null effect, or no difference between the innovation being tested and any other approach.[7] The accumulation of these null-effect results led to a clamor that "nothing works." The initial response by the Left to these findings argued that, since the correctional system could not claim to rehabilitate (then the reigning ideology of corrections), then one ought to intervene less in the lives of those convicted. An exemplar of this stance was Robison and Smith (1971), who made this reduced-intervention argument particularly vigorously.

Such an argument was clearly in conflict with the view of the Right, whose perspectives were certainly enthusiastically endorsed by the public more broadly. At that time, in the early 1970s, crime rates were soaring significantly from the low rates characteristic of the early 1960s to the values that prevailed from the mid-1970s through the mid-1990s. That growth was attributable to a mixture of the arrival of the baby-boom cohorts (starting with the 1947 cohort, which reached age fifteen in 1962 and nineteen in 1966) the peak crime ages. That demographic shift gave impetus to the "crime in the streets" theme of Barry Goldwater's 1964 presidential election campaign. That growth continued with the increasing cohort sizes until the largest cohorts (those born around 1960) began to recede from the high-crime ages after 1980.

Those demographic shifts were exacerbated by the disruptions and challenges to forces of authority that characterized the 1960s. The most salient challenges were associated with the civil rights struggles in the early 1960s and the protests against the Vietnam War in the late 1960s and early 1970s. The effects of the changing demographic composition (more people in the high-crime ages) were augmented also by the contextual effect of larger cohort sizes, which increased the age-specific crime rates within the high-crime ages. Both the composition and the contextual effects contributed to higher aggregate crime rates.

With crime an increasing concern to the general public and with the traditional crime-control methods and prison populations maintained in a stable mode by the now discredited "corrections" functionaries, the policy issues were fully ripe for major reconsideration. There was little doubt that the arguments for punitiveness would prevail. An article entitled "Lock 'Em Up" by James Q. Wilson (1975) articulated the basic incapacitation argument that appealed to the general public—an offender in prison cannot be committing in the community the crimes that he might have committed if he were free.

The deterrence argument also has a natural appeal to legislatures and to the middle-class perception generally. With the growth of the public's concern about crime, there followed an intense battle among political figures to show who was acting more "tough" on offenders, and a corresponding scramble for political opportunities to label their opponents "soft on crime."

This battle emerged along with the growing use of the thirty-second TV sound-bite as a central feature of political campaigns. It was much easier to incorporate a slamming prison cell door into one of those sound-bites than to discuss the complex tradeoffs surrounding incarceration, its incapacitative effects, its opportunity costs, and its potentially criminogenic effects on the offender.

Aside from its symbolic nature, this battle to be the toughest candidate seems to be based largely on a presumption of the deterrent effectiveness of toughness. The underlying presumption is that increasing the threat of criminal sanctions (usually articulated in terms of sentence severity) is a very powerful influence in inhibiting criminal activity. While there is little doubt that deterrence works to some degree, there must be important differences between its effectiveness in conventional middle-class populations—who have so much to lose from the condemnation and relative deprivation associated with a prison sentence—compared to the lower-class populations that comprise the great majority of the offenders who engage in the crimes that lead to imprisonment. The political effectiveness of the toughness stance must derive from the projection of the response of the bulk of the middle-class voters to the deterrent threat, and their difficulty in appreciating the diminished responsiveness of the principal targets of the threat. They recognize that the threat of imprisonment keeps *them* from committing crimes, and so it should work comparably with others who do commit crimes. They then seem to believe that, if current sanctions are not working, then they should be increased in order to cross a response threshold. That threshold for people who do crime would probably be somewhat higher, but not necessarily out of reach.

It does not seem to enter the public debate that the rational weighing of costs and benefits—a salient characteristic of middle-class behavior—is not necessarily characteristic of everyone's decision to engage in a criminal offense. Or that actions that could lead to gaining "respect"[8] would have great saliency to some people, enough to warrant risking their lives, let alone risking imprisonment. Or that the loss in personal well-being (or "utility" in terms of the cost-benefit calculation) associated with imprisonment is considerably greater for a person who is employed and lives with his family than it is for an unemployed person with no such stable attachments. Indeed, for some, the opportunity for reasonable room and board in prison may not be much worse than life on the streets, especially if one has some protective affiliates in prison who will serve as a shield against the predators that make prison life so threatening to many.

The attempts to curry favor with the electorate also give rise to efforts to point to individual cases where an offender who committed a serious crime was let out on probation, parole, or with a surprisingly small sentence. Given the diversity of judges, their values, and the variety of variables that they take into account, it is not surprising that such cases can readily be found in any jurisdiction. Pointing to such errors of commission[9] usually leads to a further call for toughness in limiting the opportunity to release a prisoner. It also gives rise to a cry for "mandatory-minimum" legislation, which requires judges to sentence all offenders convicted of a particular offense specified by the statute to at least the specified minimum sentence, regardless of whatever mitigating circumstances might be present in the case.

Along with this came a general scapegoating of judges as being too "lenient," a cry that was often encouraged by prosecutors, many of whom harbor ambition for higher office.[10] These mandatory minimum sentences started as low as one year in the 1970s (or even thirty days for drunk-driving convictions) and have escalated since then to values as high as ten years or more for individual convictions, most notoriously for drug offenses. Drug offenses, which have been the focus of many of the mandatory-minimum sentencing laws, are offenses for which incarceration is so largely an inappropriate and ineffective sanction because the offenders deterred by the threat of the sanction or incapacitated by its imposition are readily replaced from a willing labor market (see Blumstein 1993).

Another means by which the conservative perspective has come to hold greater sway in the development of punishment policy also derives from the generally liberal concern about "disparity." Disparity occurs when two offenders equally placed (the idealized case where the two crimes are identical and the offenders' prior record and other relevant attributes are identical) receive different punishment, perhaps because they came from different jurisdictions (urban areas tend to be more lenient than rural areas for the same offense) or because they face judges who use different criteria. The pressure for reducing disparity gave rise in some places (most notably California) to determinate sentencing laws, which tried to specify by statute a sentence to be associated with each of the major offense categories. Of course, given the diversity of burglaries and the diversity of prior records and other relevant offender characteristics, this introduced its own form of disparity by bringing cases that were unlike into the same box. It also provided an opportunity for the political pressure toward greater severity to ratchet up the prescribed sentence for any particular offense. This could happen, for example, when a particularly heinous version of the offense was reported in the newspaper headlines—or, with much greater impact, on the evening television news. There would then follow a rush by legislators to get a bill into the hopper calling for an increase in the prescribed sentence for that generic offense class.

This introduction of determinate sentences was also usually associated with elimination of the parole function, and the parole release decision in particular. Parole boards, charged with making the release decision within the bounds of the indeterminate sentences prescribed by the judges, were branded as evildoers fully as much as judges were. The public could always be reminded that they made a decision that in retrospect was wrong when a released prisoner recidivated by committing a serious felony.[11]

The next stage in the escalation of sanctions, and its assault on judicial "leniency" was the mandatory-minimum sentencing law. If it could be shown that an offender put on probation (for a first offense with mitigating circumstances, say) committed a serious crime while on probation, then that was taken as proof of judges' leniency, and so the legislature would require that all such offenders would have to go to prison for at least the prescribed minimum sentence. This would apply to all offenders convicted of the specified crime, regardless of the mitigating circumstances; only the prosecutor, with discretion over the charges filed, could make any accommodation. There may be good reason to suspect that people sentenced under mandatory-minimum sentencing laws do not have appreciably more serious prior records compared to others sent to prison.

The large majority of people sentenced to prison under mandatory minimum laws are those sentenced for drug offenses. These are demonstrably the offenses for which prison is least appropriate in terms of incapacitation (as noted above) as well as from the viewpoint of deterrence (since those driven out of the business by the threat of extremely high sanctions will also be replaced by others whose disutility for prison may be lower or whose view of other forms of gainful economic activity is less attractive). If the intention is less utilitarian and more retributive, even then the hostility to the drug seller seems largely to have abated in the general public. The evil represented by the leading character in *The Man with the Golden Arm* no longer seems to represent the general public view of a drug seller, especially at the retail level on the street. Rather, the public has come to view the seller as one more individual willing to take the risks in order to pursue that line of economic activity, either for inevitably small economic gain, merely for sustenance, or—most likely—because his drug abuse prevents him from earning income in the legitimate economy. It was undoubtedly this last consideration that caused California voters to endorse Proposition 36[12] in 2000 by a 61 percent majority. A similar initiative was passed in Arizona and a number of other states are considering similar policies. Despite all of the shortcomings of incarceration for drug offenses, by the end of 1999, 57 percent of federal prisoners and 21 percent of state prisoners were there on a drug charge.[13] Many of them are first offenders serving time under a mandatory-minimum sentence.

The latest weapon in the armamentarium of those intent on greater use of incarceration is the "Three Strikes and You're Out" laws that were passed by public referendum in Washington in 1993, subsequently in California and a large number of other states. A three-strikes provision was also included in the Federal Violent Crime Control and Law Enforcement Act of 1994. Variants of this principle (mandatory life imprisonment without parole for conviction of a third "strike"—a third conviction of one of a set of specified serious offenses) somehow built on the presumption that this baseball metaphor was particularly appropriate for sentencing policy.

It is not clear to what extent the three-strike laws are intended to achieve retribution or crime control. If the latter, it would be through deterrence and incapacitation. For either, this is a relatively inefficient means for achieving those effects. If focused on the most serious violent felonies, the twice-convicted offender should already be facing a long sentence, and it is not clear how much more deterrent threat will be added by posing this extension to life. In terms of incapacitation, the laws keep people in prison well after their active criminal careers have ended—very likely by age 50, almost certainly by age 60. If the choice arises about whom to release—a currently violent offender not under such a mandatory law and an aging one imprisoned under a three-strikes law—the system will have to release the currently serious offender. Once such laws are passed, even when restricted to the most serious offenses, they then provide a platform for expanding the scope of offenses that can be counted as "strikes." Indeed, the federal law initially was confined to serious violent felonies, but ended up permitting drug convictions to be counted as one of the strikes. One can reasonably anticipate seeing other kinds of offenses added in the future as they capture the attention of the moment.

Much of the growth in the prison populations since 1980 is attributable to the growth in drug offenders, who comprised only about 6 percent of prison populations in 1979. The adult incarceration rate for drugs increased by a factor of ten from 1980 to 1996. Thus, the obsession with the drug war has been a major contributor to the growth in prison populations. Aside from drug offenses, there has been a general upward trend in the general sanction level since 1980 for the five other crime types that are important for prison (murder, robbery, burglary, aggravated assault, and sexual assault), which, together with drugs, account for about 80 percent of state prisoners. This is reflected in Figure 11.3, which shows the incarceration rate for these offenses. Analysis of the factors contributing to the growth from 1980 through 1996 shows that none was attributable to more crime nor to more arrests per crime, but was entirely attributable about equally to growth in prison commitments per arrest (an indication of tougher prosecution or judicial sentencing) and to longer time served (an indication of longer sentences, elimination of parole or later parole release, or greater readiness to recommit parolees to prison for either technical violations or new crimes).[14]

It turns out that one of the most important recent sources of growth in prison population is the level of recommitment of parolees. Parole boards have received the same political message that they too ought to become tougher to keep up with the political tenor of the times, and indeed have been more aggressive in performing urinalysis on parolees, in delaying release decisions, and in making recommitments for technical violations.

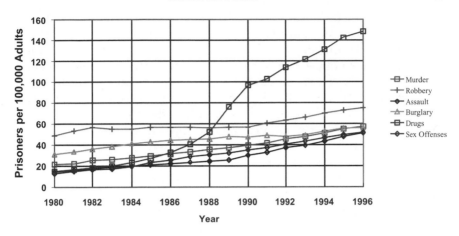

Figure 11.3

Another factor that was a significant contributor to the growth in prison populations through the 1980s was the same demographic shift that contributed to the growth of crimes in the 1960s and 1970s—the baby boomers. Since the peak age for crime occurs in the late teens, and the peak age for imprisonment is in the early 30s, the population bulge associated with that generation was expected to impact the prison population about a decade later than it impacted the crime rates.[15] The impact of that demographic shift on prison populations was relatively small, however, compared to the shift associated with the drug war, and in the same order of magnitude as the shifts in the punishment of the more common street crimes. In any event, those effects should have saturated by the early 1990s as the baby boomers passed out of the high imprisonment ages, and should already have begun working the other way, waiting for the arrival of the echo boom following the demographic trough associated with the 1976 cohort, the smallest cohort in the U.S. population under age fifty.

TOWARD THE FUTURE

This process of escalating incarceration must certainly pain an individual like Sheldon Messinger with his deep concerns about social justice. He would certainly want to seek ways to reverse this trend toward open-ended growth in punitiveness. The number of options, however, is limited.

One approach that might be pursued is finding means of enhancing public education, to counter the naive reaction to the argument that more punishment will lead to less crime, regardless of the social dynamics of the particular crime (the substitution in drug markets, for example) or the offenders on whom the punishment is targeted (offenders with relatively low disutility for prison, for example). Somehow, the subtleties of those differences have not been able to get through the emotion and the rhetoric of sanction policy. It does appear that too much of the policy debate is from the perspectives of the ideological poles—arguing broadly for more incarceration at one extreme (with no concern for where it can be most effectively applied) or, at the other extreme, against incarceration as a broad generality rather than with a sharp focus on where it is least effective and most wasteful or even harmful.

In economic policy, in contrast, there still remain sharp ideological differences between the Left and the Right, but there has emerged a level of theoretical agreement and strong empirical observations that has brought the poles much closer together than has been the case in criminal justice policy. In part, this is attributable to the much more backward state of empirically grounded theory in criminology, which could force resolution on at least some aspects of the debate. A major rise in the level of support for research in the whole area of crime and crime control through the National Institute of Justice (whose annual discretionary budget has been about $25 million for a large number of years, in marked contrast to the $20 billion for the National Institutes of Health) could help move that process forward.[16]

In policy terms, one could argue for more widespread use of sentencing commissions as an instrument for generating at least some degree of coherence in sentencing structures. It represents an antidote to the passionate response to a particularly heinous crime or the mood of the moment and could sometimes serve as an inhibitor of the frequent legislative response of mandatory minimum sentences. That approach is limited, however, because even sentencing commissions have to respond politically (in most cases, their guidelines must be approved by the legislature). Sentencing commissions that operate under capacity constraints make even more sense because the capacity constraint imposes a discipline that even the most conscientious sentencing commissions are sometimes forced to ignore. It is rare that a sentencing commission hears a demand for reduction of any sentences. Almost all the communications call for increased sentences, and so the capacity constraint provides a basis for asking for which offenses the sentence should be reduced in order to provide the capacity for the sentence to be increased. Alternatively, when appropriate, the capacity should be increased through the expenditure of public funds.

One might also require the development of prison-impact statements to be provided to the legislature before any change in sentencing policy is enacted. This is done as a matter of course for other programs that have budgetary implications (and the Congressional Budget Office was established by the Congress for this purpose), but changes in sentencing policy are usually enacted first by a Judiciary Committee and then the legislative body without consideration of their costs and prison-population impacts. Changes in the legislative process here might force more responsible consideration of sentencing policy.

Probably the most likely prospect for change in consideration of sentencing will be through the emergence of a coalition between fiscal conservatives (as they become appalled at the costs of incarceration, and the inefficiency associated with much of that) and liberals (who want to reduce sentences and use the funds for other social programs that might promise to reduce crime in the longer run). There are some glimmerings of the emergence of those coalitions, and one might hope to seem them coalesce over the next decade.

In the early years of the twenty-first century, those effects may be starting to show themselves as the growth in prison population seems to be flattening out. This is undoubtedly a reflection of the crime decline of the 1990s (Blumstein and Wallman 2000), when crime rates declined to levels not seen since the mid-1960s. Thus, one might speculate about the future directions of national incarceration rates in the United States.[17] It is possible that these rates might decline as the crime rate declines, as the public anxiety about crime declines as a result, and as the political benefit of being "tough on crime" diminishes. Fiscal stress on state governments may also contribute to that decline. Certainly the moves reflected in California's Proposition 36 to use treatment rather than incarceration for drug offenders can move significantly in that direction.

On the other hand, there has developed a significant political interest group with a stake in avoiding too rapid a reduction in prison populations. The California Correctional Peace Officers Association, representing prison guards, for example, has been reported to be a major political contributor to gubernatorial campaigns in California. They obviously have a strong economic interest in keeping prison levels high. Thus, it is entirely possible that prison populations may have reached a new homeostatic level four times above the previous level.

Maybe one day we might even revert to a new stable regime of incarceration rate, although I have my doubts that that will happen as long as sentencing policy remains a salient aspect of the political process. And that is likely to continue as long as crime rates—even as low as they have become—are a troubling part of life in America.

NOTES

1. One could readily concede that California could be an exception to almost any social theory without seriously threatening the validity of the theory.

2. The "coefficient of variation" of the series is the ratio of the standard deviation of the observations to their mean.

3. Since our initial paper was written in 1973, this may be just one more example of nature's perversity, which rebels whenever social science tries to pin down its behavior.

4. Available from the Bureau of Justice Statistics website, http://www.ojp.usdoj.gov/bjs/glance/tables/corr2tab.htm.

5. The numbers used here are more recent ones, and are slightly different from those used in the original paper. They are based on Table 3-7 in Cahalan (1986). Information for more recent years was obtained from annual Bureau of Justice Statistics updates (Beck and Harrison [2001]).

6. The denominator of the incarceration rate is the total national population. A more appropriate denominator would be a population weighted by some measure of the age-specific incarceration rate, which tends to peak in the early 30s. To some limited extent, this would boost the rate during the 1960s and reduce it during the 1980s, when the peak of the "baby boom" generation moved into the peak imprisonment ages.

7. A paper by Robert Martinson (1974) attracted considerable attention to the null-effect findings. His paper was based on a more comprehensive survey in Lipton, Martinson, and Wilks (1975).

8. See Elijah Anderson's (1994) discussion of the importance of "respect" to the people he characterizes as "street people." See also Anderson (1999).

9. The errors of omission—failure to release an offender who is a good risk and would not recidivate—are never seen.

10. Can one require prosecutors to take an oath of further political celibacy?

11. Willie Horton, who was made infamous by the George Bush presidential campaign of 1988, was a notorious example of such a release that led to a heinous recidivist offense. That occurrence was eventually used to reach up to condemn the governor at the time, Michael Dukakis, who was running for president.

12. Known officially as the Substance Abuse and Crime Prevention Act.

13. Based on data in Beck and Harrison (2001).

14. Based on Blumstein and Beck 1999).

15. These impacts of the demographic shifts on crime and on prison populations are examined in some detail in Blumstein, Cohen, and Miller (1981).

16. Joan Petersilia and I have argued for an annual doubling of the NIJ budget to a level of $1 billion per year. See Blumstein and Petersilia (1995).

17. It is interesting in this context to compare incarceration rates internationally. The highest rate (including local jails) in the world is that of the United States (700 per 100,000 population), followed by Russia (665). Two-thirds of the nations have rates under 150, and most of Western Europe has rates under 100. Data from Wolmsley (2002).

REFERENCES

Anderson, Elijah. 1994. "The Code of the Streets." *Atlantic Monthly* 273(May):80–94.
Anderson, Elijah. 1999. *Code of the Street: Decency, Violence, and the Moral Life of the Inner City.* W.W. Norton & Company.

Beck, Allen J. and Paige M. Harrison. 2001. "Prisoners in 2000." BJS Bulletin No. NCJ-188207, August.

Berk, Richard, David Rauma, Sheldon Messinger, and Thomas Cooley. 1981. "A Test of the Stability of Punishment Hypothesis: The Case of California, 1851–1970." *American Sociological Review* 46(December):805–29.

Blumstein, Alfred. 1993. "Making Rationality Relevant—The American Society of Criminology Presidential Address. *Criminology* 31(1):1–16.

Blumstein, Alfred and Allen J. Beck. 1999. "Population Growth in U.S. Prisons, 1980–1996. Pp. 17–61 in *Crime and Justice,* Vol. 26, *Prisons,* edited by Michael Tonry and Joan Petersilia. Chicago: University of Chicago Press.

Blumstein, Alfred and Jacqueline Cohen. 1973. "A Theory of the Stability of Punishment." *Journal of Criminal Law and Criminology* 64(Summer):198–207.

Blumstein, Alfred, Jacqueline Cohen, and Harold Miller. 1981. "Demographically Disaggregated Projections of Prison Populations." *Journal of Criminal Justice* 8(1):1–26.

Blumstein, Alfred, Jacqueline Cohen, Soumyo Moitra, and Daniel Nagin. 1981. "Testing the Stability of Punishment Hypothesis: A Reply." *Journal of Criminal Law and Criminology* 72(4):1799–1808.

Blumstein, Alfred, Jacqueline Cohen, and Daniel Nagin. 1977. "The Dynamics of a Homeostatic Punishment Process." *Journal of Criminal Law and Criminology* 67(3):317–34.

Blumstein, Alfred, and Soumyo Moitra. 1979. "An Analysis of the Time Series of the Imprisonment Rate in the States of the United States: A Further Test of the Stability of Punishment Hypothesis." *Journal of Criminal Law and Criminology* 70(3):376–90.

Blumstein, Alfred, and Joan Petersilia. 1995. "Investing in Criminal Justice Research." Chapter 20 in *Crime,* edited by Joan Petersilia and James Q. Wilson. San Francisco: ICS.

Blumstein, Alfred and Joel Wallman (Eds.). 2000., *The Crime Drop in America.* Cambridge: Cambridge University Press.

Box, George E. P. and Gwilym M. Jenkins. 1976. *Time Series Analysis; Forecasting and Control.* San Francisco: Holden-Day.

Cahalan, Margaret. 1986. "Historical Corrections Statistics in the United States, 1850–1984." Bureau of Justice Statistics Report No. NCJ-102529, December.

Durkheim, E. Emil. 1964. *The Rules of Sociological Method.* Trans. by S. Solovay and J. J. Mueller.

Erikson, Kai. 1966. *The Wayward Puritans.* New York: Wiley.

Lipton, Douglas, Robert. Martinson, and Judith Wilks. 1975. *The Effectiveness of Correctional Treatment: A Survey of Treatment Evaluation Studies.* New York: Praeger.

Martinson, Robert. 1974. "What Works? Questions and Answers about Prison Reform." *Public Interest* 35(2):22–54.

Rauma, David. 1981. "Crime and Punishment Reconsidered: Some Comments on Blumstein's Stability of Punishment Hypothesis." *Journal of Criminal Law and Criminology* 72:1772.

Robison, James O., and Gerald Smith. 1971. "The Effectiveness of Correctional Programs." *Crime and Delinquency* 17(1):67–80.

Wilson, James Q. 1975. "Lock 'Em Up." *New York Times Magazine,* 9 March, p. 11.

Wolmsley, Ray. 2002. "World Prison Population List," 3rd ed. *Findings* No. 166, Home Office.

12

The Future of the Proportionate Sentence

ANDREW VON HIRSCH

The idea of the proportionate or "deserved" sentence has had considerable influence during the last two decades. In actual sentencing policy, that influence is not so widespread as sometimes has been supposed. In the United States, only a few jurisdictions—Oregon and Minnesota, for example[1]—have relied on it in systematic fashion. In Europe, three jurisdictions —Finland in 1976, Sweden in 1988, and England and Wales in 1991[2]—have adopted sentencing framework legislation that stresses explicitly the idea of proportionality. Canada is expected shortly to adopt a juvenile justice law that gives proportionality a central role.[3] But even where laws and policies have not changed so much, proportionalism has considerably altered thinking about punishment (see, e.g., Canadian Sentencing Commission 1986).

In previous writings,[4] I have tried to develop a substantive case for proportionate sentencing. Here, my interest will shift to political/ideological questions. What has made proportionalism an attractive idea? What concerns or worries does it generate that limit its potential attractiveness? What are the prospects of survival of the idea? My focus will be less on the "rightness" of the idea on its merits, as on the possible reasons of its influence and on the extent to which that influence is likely to abide. (I shall also consider, in this connection, the bearing of some developments in sentencing policy occurring during the years since publication of the earlier version of this essay in the book's first 1995 edition.[5])

THE ATTRACTIONS OF PROPORTIONALISM

The Appeal to Fairness

Traditional preventively-oriented penal theories, even if they purported to be humane, focused on instrumental concerns: how a sentencing strategy can better protect *us* from the depredations of *them,* the criminals. Such an instrumental perspective threatens unjust results: if the aim is prevention, why not do whatever works for that purpose? During the heyday of rehabilitation, that threat seemed muted—for the rehabilitative sentence was supposed to further the offender's interests as well as ours. But as faith declined in the identity of the offender's interests with those of the larger society, the potential oppressiveness of purely crime-preventive sentencing strategies has become more apparent.

Proportionalism gives notions of fairness a central role in sentencing theory. It rests on the idea that the penal sanction should fairly reflect the degree of reprehensibleness (that is, the degree of harmfulness and culpability) of the actor's conduct (see, more fully, von Hirsch 1993:Ch. 2; Duff 2001). This viewpoint helps deal with the tension over whether penal policy should favor societal interests or the interests of offenders. In a "just deserts" theory, societal interest is expressed in the recognition that typical crimes (e.g. those of force and fraud) are *wrongs,* for which public condemnation through the criminal sanction is due. The individual's interest is protected through his entitlement to no severer a sanction than the degree of blameworthiness of the conduct would warrant, even if a harsher sentence might possibly have better preventive effects.

It was fashionable for a time to dismiss such fairness claims as a mere facade, behind which social theories or practices are espoused for wholly ulterior, self-interested motivations. I think this is a mistake. Granted, a theory or practice is unlikely to gain widespread adherence *merely* because of its claims to justice. But, as David Garland (1990:Ch. 10) notes, sensibilities about humane or fair treatment of criminals have influenced attitudes about punishment, at least among some influential groups.

Proportionalism in punishment sometimes has been characterized as a reversion to pre-Enlightenment notions: as returning to Old Testament conceptions of an eye for an eye, or "going back" to Kant. However, the desert rationale rests on the idea of *proportion* rather than harm-for-harm equivalence: penalties need not visit as much suffering as the harm done by offenses. A substantial deflation in overall penalty levels is permissible (indeed, desirable), so long as penalties are graded in the order of crimes' seriousness.[6] Kant, it should also be remembered, was not an Old Testament prophet but a major Enlightenment thinker. There always were two strands of Enlightenment thinking: one a consequentialist version, concerned with calibrating state responses to achieve certain desired social effects; the other, a version that sought to regulate state responses on the basis of certain justice imperatives or equity requirements. Modern proportionalist theory does not rely on Kant's brief (and unsatisfactory) comments about punishment,[7] but on his larger ethical assumptions that a person's claim to just treatment should take precedence over the pursuit of collective societal aims.

Practical Guidance

Proportionalism has the additional attraction of providing a degree of practical guidance: it suggests a way of scaling penalties. Traditional crime-preventive penal conceptions have in large part failed to offer such guidance.

Consider deterrence and rehabilitation. If one asks how sentences might be arrayed according to their supposed deterrent impact, the answer is indeterminate, because not enough is known about the comparative marginal deterrent effects of different degrees of sentence severity (see von Hirsch et al. 1999). With rehabilitation, matters are scarcely better. To the extent treatment programs work at all, they succeed only for carefully selected subgroups of offenders; no "cure" is known for routine cases of car theft, burglary, or robbery. There also is considerable difficulty translating rehabilitative concerns—which address modalities of treatment—into the kind of decisions sentencers must make, about the type and duration of the sanction.[8]

What about incapacitation? It has been possible, for many years already, to make rough-and-ready forecasts about which offenders are the more likely to return to crime.[9] That would seem to offer a practical alternative to desert-based scaling: namely, calibrating sentences according to offenders' degree of risk. Proposals of this kind have been advocated, most notably in the "selective incapacitation" schemes promoted by some American penologists in the early 1980s (see, e.g., Greenwood 1982; Wilson 1983: Ch. 8). But there are ethical objections—for example, those concerning misclassification. Because predictions of dangerousness yield high false-positive rates, it is known that a substantial number of those classified as bad risks (and hence given longer sentences) would not offend were they to remain at liberty. A further drawback is the link to social class: many of the statistical indicia of risk are matters such as drug use, employment and school background, residential stability, and early offending. When these factors are relied upon in sentencing, lower-class offenders will tend to get the tougher sentences precisely in virtue of their class status.

There are also practical impediments. One is selective incapacitation's limited apparent effectiveness, when judged by its prospective impact on overall crime rates. Enthusiasm for selective incapacitation began to wane with the publication of a 1986 U.S. National Academy of Sciences report suggesting how small that net preventive impact might be (National Research Council 1986; see also von Hirsch 1988). The strategy also has potential for political embarrassment, because it presents itself as able to foretell who will and will not reoffend. This involves not only designating some offenders as dangerous, but designating others (convicted of similar crimes) as "better" risks—and giving the latter (comparatively) lower sentences. Because any prediction system yields "false negatives" as well as false positives, a significant number of those deemed better risks will commit serious new offenses anyway, and the sentencing authorities will be held responsible. It is thus not surprising that most American sentencing guidelines systems have avoided explicit reliance on selective incapacitation.[10] An actuarial, risk-oriented "new penology" is not about to take over sentencing policy,[11] whatever its possible influence elsewhere.

A proportionalist sentencing theory provides fuller guidance on scaling matters: sentences are to be ranked in severity to reflect the comparative seriousness of crimes. Granted, there are problems. The theory gives less specific guidance (albeit still some) on how a penalty scale should be anchored. A theory for assessing crimes' comparative seriousness is only beginning to develop. There also are knotty conceptual questions about how much weight, if any, should be accorded to prior convictions.[12] Nevertheless, grading is not an unmanageable task. The Minnesota and Oregon sentencing commissions, for example, anchored the penalty scale by reference to existing prison capacities—a practical choice based in part on the need to limit expenditures for building new prisons. Given this target, they were able to grade crimes in seriousness without great dissent, to assign a weight to the criminal record (a smaller weight in Oregon than Minnesota[13]), and to construct presumptive sentence ranges on that basis.

Guidance for sentencers does not necessarily require numerical guidelines; it can be provided instead through statutory guiding principles, as Finland and Sweden have done. Formerly, the courts in those countries tried to develop a sentencing tariff on the basis of a not-very-well-delineated rationale in which deterrence and rehabilitation was supposed to carry considerable weight. The adoption of statutory principles, in 1976 and 1988, respectively, furnished a rationale—through a stated criterion that the gravity of the criminal act should primarily be determinative (see Jareborg 1995). It became easier for courts to judge whether one crime is typically more serious than another than to decide the penalties for those crimes on the basis of their supposed preventive effects.

Proportionalism can also be useful as an aid to implementing other practical sentencing aims. Consider a matter that has drawn much interest in the last two decades: intermediate, noncustodial penalties. Such sanctions can successfully function as a substitute for imprisonment only if they are targeted to crimes of intermediate rather than lesser seriousness, and if incarceration may be used only sparingly as the penalty for those who breach the terms of their community sentences. A proportionalist sentencing rationale calls for observance of these policies: noncustodial sanctions of middle-level severity would be appropriate only for offenses of middling (not lesser) gravity; and mere breaches of program conditions would not be serious enough to deserve substantial stints of confinement (see more fully, von Hirsch 1993:Ch. 7). Crime prevention aims, by contrast, have greater difficulty supplying a workable basis for grading such penalties, and make it more difficult to limit the onerousness of breach penalties (ibid.:64–68).

So far, my point is a modest one: that proportionality theory has a certain moral appeal, and helps scale penalties. The theory has not, however, generated the kind of broad consensus that supported rehabilitationism in earlier decades: substantial resistance to the idea continues. Some of the doubts have been raised by penal theorists and reformers who share proportionalists' ultimate aims of the fair and humane treatment of offenders, but worry about whether a desert theory can promote those aims. What, then, are the sources of disquiet?

MULTIPLE AIMS?

Proportionalism sets priorities among sentencing aims. A desert model assumes that it is more important to have proportionately ordered sanctions than to seek other objectives—say, incapacitating those deemed higher risks. This understandably evokes discomfort: why cannot one seek proportionality *and* pursue other desired ends, whether they be treatment, incapacitation, or something else?

While proportionalism involves priorities, it is not exclusive. In the 1970s in the United States, notions of proportionality came into prominence together with growing skepticism about the feasibility of effective treatment. However, the exclusion of treatment considerations is not presupposed. Treatments may be offered to imprisoned offenders within the duration of their deserved sentence; and where two noncustodial sanctions of approximately equivalent severity are available (say, a unit-fine of so many days' earnings and intensive probation of a specified duration), desert constraints are not offended when one is chosen over the other on rehabilitative grounds (von Hirsch 1993:Ch. 7).

However, a desert model remains a somewhat constraining one: ulterior factors may be relied upon only where those do not significantly alter the comparative severity of penalties. Giving extra prison time to persons deemed higher risks would breach the model's limits, for example. Why not, then, relax the model's constraints to allow greater scope to other, seemingly reasonable aspirations?

A possibility—sometimes referred to as a "modified" desert model—is to relax the constraints to a limited extent. Proportionality would ordinarily determine comparative punishment levels, but upward deviations would be permitted in case of extraordinarily harmful conduct or extraordinarily dangerous individuals. Or else deviations from the deserved sanction might ordinarily be permitted, but these would be restricted ones: say, a deviation of no more than 10 or 15 percent. These approaches still make desert the primary determinant of the ordering of penalties, but give some extra scope for ulterior aims.[14] Such schemes, however, also remain constraining. Especially dangerous offenders may be given extra prison time, but not the ordinary recidivist. Some extra leeway may be granted in choosing a noncustodial penalty suited to an offender's apparent treatment needs, but not much.

Could more scope be given to nondesert considerations? In a mixed rationale, either desert will predominate or something else will. If—in the ordinary case—the seriousness of the current crime remains the primary determinant of the severity of the penalty, the system still is desert dominated. This has the attractions of which I have spoken: it seems fairer, and gives some useful guidance to decision-makers. Our limited knowledge of how to achieve preventive effects will also be no great obstacle: we do know something about treatment or risk in *some* situations, and when we do that may (to the requisite limited degree) affect the disposition. If ulterior aims are given still greater scope, however, that creates a system dominated by those aims. Desert then can serve only as a (much less important) outer limit. This reintroduces the difficulties of which I spoke earlier: those of apparent injustice, and insufficient practical guidance.

The writings of some of the proponents of "mixed" models reflect these tensions. Norval Morris (1982:Ch. 5) has advocated what he calls "limiting retributivism." According to this view, desert would set only outer bounds on the severity of punishment, within which the sentence would be fixed on incapacitative or deterrence grounds. The difficulty has been that of delineating the breadth of these bounds. If the limits are fairly narrow, then the scheme is akin to the modified-desert scheme just mentioned. If the limits are broad, then incapacitation and deterrence will chiefly determine penalties, with problems of which I already have spoken. As long as the breadth of the limits is unspecified, Morris's scheme remains indeterminate (more fully, see von Hirsch 1985:Ch. 12).

Another possible variant is treating desert as only an *upper* constraint on punishment, below which sentences could be fixed on other grounds. That, however, leaves unresolved what those other grounds should be— and poses the problem of what other conception sustains *any* level of punishment above zero. If crime prevention is invoked as the sustaining rationale, there reappears the problem of the poor guidance such rationales provide. There is also the additional hazard of a skewed ordering of penalties: what is to prevent those convicted of a lesser crime category from receiving a penalty near that crime's applicable upper limit (say, because its perpetrators are expected often to reoffend) whereas a more serious offense might be penalized much more leniently (say, because it occurs more infrequently)? To avoid such bizarre results, lower bounds based on the gravity of the crime need to be supplied. Perhaps these lower bounds might be "softer" than the upper limits, allowing departures below them to be made more readily (see von Hirsch 1994:45–48). But this still would constitute some kind of modification of a desert theory—perhaps not so dissimilar to desert-based hybrids just discussed.[15]

JUSTIFYING PUNITIVENESS

Proportionality and Punitiveness

Does proportionalism justify or lead to harsher sanctions? The idea of proportionality does not itself prescribe harsher punishments; indeed, it permits (indeed, supports) considerable reduction in sanction levels (see discussion below and von Hirsch 1993:Chs. 5, 10). Several of the jurisdictions that have relied on proportionality as guiding rationale have succeeded either in reducing penalty levels (as Finland has since 1976), or in limiting penalty increases (Sweden and, albeit somewhat less successfully in recent years, Minnesota).[16] The systems calling for large penalty increases—for example, the U.S. Sentencing Commission's guideline scheme for federal crimes—tend explicitly or implicitly to reject the idea of proportionality (see, more fully, von Hirsch 1993:91–94; Roberts 1994; Doob 1995).

But is this a sufficient answer? Even if proportionalism has no direct causal links to tougher sanctions, the theory does focus on penal deprivations. (Indeed, it is largely concerned with *how much* deprivation can be visited for various crimes.) Once we admit that punishment should be about "pain delivery," in Nils Christie's (1980) phrase, are we not legitimating the infliction of suffering? And once suffering is legitimated, what is to stop more from being inflicted?

It should be borne in mind, however, that a proportionalist sentencing theory is not about pain delivery as an end in itself. It is only traditional retributivism that insists that deprivation is the only justifiable response to wrongdoing. Current desert theories—including R. A. Duff's (2001) and my own (von Hirsch 1993:Ch. 2)—place much more emphasis on punishment's function of expressing *censure* for criminal acts. The shift to censure is important, because it permits significant reductions in punishment levels, so long as these adequately express blame for the conduct involved. Indeed, escalated sanction levels interfere with penal censure's moral functions: the higher overall penalty levels rise, the less the normative reasons for desistence supplied through penal censure will matter, and the more penal sanction becomes merely a system of threats (see more fully, von Hirsch 1993:13, 41–45).

Proportionalism does call attention to the deprivations of punishment, by insisting that comparative severities reflect the gravity of the conduct involved. Insisting on this scrutiny might help induce greater awareness of the hurt one is visiting on the offender. Consider the sanction of probation. This was once considered not really punishment at all, but as help to the offender. Benign as that "help" was supposed to be, it could be quite burdensome (involving, for example, residential custody in drug treat-ment facilities). Insisting on proportionality can make one aware of the pains involved in such a sentence.

Is this not too optimistic? Perhaps a greater awareness of the penal con-tent of punishments will make the tender-hearted more careful about in-flicting pain. But what of the uncompassionate—the proponents of law and order? Will they not utilize the greater awareness of punishments' severity precisely in order to advocate harsher sanctions?

Interestingly, however, today's law-and-order advocates have not flown retributivist colors. To the extent any conception is invoked, it is crime pre-ventive and instrumentalist: what should count is not what criminals pur-portedly deserve, but how "decent, law-abiding citizens" can best be protected from victimization. Given this instrumentalist emphasis, it is not surprising that academic defenders of law-and-order approaches, such as Dan Kahan, have little use for proportionality constraints (Kahan 1996).

Indeed, desert theory has features that the penological right finds posi-tively objectionable. Proportionalism, with its emphasis on the degree of gravity of the current offense, restricts the ability to impose markedly higher penalties on recidivists who are deemed greater risks. Moreover, the theory's emphasis on equity toward offenders is suspect: it is said that the penal system should pay more attention to protection of the law-abiding, and less attention to the rights of lawbreakers. Ernest van den Haag, one of the most committedly right-wing modern penologists, exemplifies this way of thinking. In an early volume (van den Haag, 1975), he flirted with the idea of retribution: his book attempted to combine deterrence with desert to produce a policy of scaled, tough sentences. Soon thereafter, how-ever, he became skeptical of desert as an undue limitation of the state's punitive power. Indeed, he took that skepticism to its logical conclusion, holding that an offender has *no* legitimate equity claims regarding the severity or character of his punishment, once he has voluntarily submitted himself to the risk of being punished through his decision to offend (van den Haag 1987).

Punitiveness and the Politics of Resentment

Law-and-order approaches involve not only sharp increases in penal-ties, but also escalated rhetoric concerning crime and criminals. Convicted criminals are to be subjected to drastic sanctions, in view of their supposed depravity and their status as moral outlaws. "Populist punitiveness," as Anthony Bottoms (1995) terms it, has come to shape sentencing policy in many jurisdictions.

The law-and-order[17] approach tends to utilize what Arie Freiberg (2001) characterizes as "forfeiture": convicted offenders are deemed to have ex-cluded themselves from the body politic, and have forfeited any claims to be treated as citizens entitled to even a minimum of equity. In one version of law-and-order, offenders are to be subjected to degrading penalties as an expression of community indignation at their crimes (Kahan 1996). Because the offender is deemed to have no moral standing, such penal responses may disregard the degree of blameworthiness of the offender's conduct, as well as any claims he might have to dignified treatment; what counts, instead, is giving vent to respectable citizens' animus at criminals and their behavior.

The emphasis on substantive penal goals is also rejected. Proportionality of sentence is jettisoned, and the recommended sanctions tend to be quite disproportionate to the gravity of the offense or with the penalties for other offenses. A notorious example is California's "three strikes" law, according to which two convictions for burglary and a third conviction for a lesser offense suffices for near-lifetime imprisonment. In a substantial number of cases under this statute, the third "strike" was a conviction for marijuana possession (Dickey and Hollenhorst 1998).

Notwithstanding rhetorical claims about "prison works" and such, there is also little serious interest in crime-prevention effects; symptomatic is the fact that the measures are almost never accompanied by any serious efforts to estimate the likely crime-preventive effects. Thus the former British home secretary, Michael Howard, when introducing his version of three strikes in the mid-1990s (providing for substantial mandatory sentences for third-time burglars and drug dealers[18]), asserted in his accompanying White Paper that these measures would reduce the rates of burglary and drug dealing by 20 percent (U.K. Government White Paper 1996:54–55). The figure was pulled out of the air, however, with no supporting evidence offered whatever.

If law-and-order approaches are not well suited for reducing crime, what other functions might they serve? Their primary function, it appears, is to mobilize and exploit popular resentment at crime or criminals—a strategy that can, in certain political environments, be a way of garnering political support. In England, for example, Home Secretary Michael Howard's campaign of the early 1990s, that "prison works," became a useful unifying theme for an otherwise divided Conservative party. Once introduced into political discourse, law and order also has a tendency to spread. In the late 1990s, for example, several European parties of the moderate left endorsed some repressive penal policies.[19] At least in part, the strategy seems to be one of seeking protection from vulnerability to attacks for being "soft" on crime.

Where law-and-order dominates the debate on crime, sentencing reform of the kind I am speaking of in this chapter becomes very difficult to accomplish. A notable example is the U.S. federal sentencing guidelines. Congress passed legislation in the mid-1980s creating a U.S. Sentencing Commission to write guidelines for sentences in federal cases. By the time the Reagan-appointed members of the commission were drafting its standards, law and order had become a much-emphasized theme for the administration and Congress. A study by Anthony Doob (1995) shows the results. The federal sentencing guidelines adopt no particular penal philosophy and do not show any consistent substantive approach. There is, however, one clear (and clearly intended) effect of the guidelines: that of large increases in penalty levels.

In Chapter 18 in this volume, David Rothman argues that the liberal reform efforts of the 1970s—particularly the liberals' espousal of explicit guidance for sentencing decisions—were in part responsible for the subsequent rises in punishment levels in the United States. He argues, essentially, that it was such reform efforts that legitimated restraints on sentencing discretion; that such restraints have since been used to increase penalties; and that in the absence of the reforms, sentencing would still be discretionary today, and hence not so easily escalated.

In actual fact, the chief vehicle for raising sentence levels throughout the United States has been the mandatory minimum sentence, which is no sense a byproduct of liberal reforms (see Tonry 1992). The mandatory minimum was effectively initiated by the Rockefeller drug laws adopted in New York at the outset of the 1970s, well before guidelines and comparable sentence-reform measures became influential. Rothman's examples of the impact of sentencing guidelines are also highly selective. He disregards state guideline systems (such as Minnesota's) that have made a serious effort to limit rises in imprisonment levels, and focuses on the federal system, which did significantly raise penalty levels—and indeed, seems to have been designed to do so.

Rothman's thesis appears to rest on the assumption that the penological right can achieve its aims chiefly by taking advantage of liberal reforms and turning them to its own purposes. If something goes amiss, it must be because liberals unwisely have espoused one particular kind of reform rather than another. This perspective, however, overestimates the extent to which progressive reformers control the criminal justice agenda. The politics of resentment have not needed liberal reforms to legitimate the quest for harsher punishment. The appeal is to the public's loathing of criminals, and the policy mechanisms can be quite varied—ranging from a policy of denouncing "lenient" judges to enactment of mandatory-minimum and habitual-offender laws. "Three-strikes-and-you're-out" legislation is not a co-optation of some benevolently minded penal measure; it draws its force, instead, from popular images of habitually violent criminals.

"NEGATIVISM" AND RESTORATIVE JUSTICE

Another kind of worry about proportionalist sentencing theory has concerned its seeming negativism. It can, at most, provide a fairer distribution of the penalties. Major positive benefits are not offered.

Rehabilitation purported to satisfy all interests: the citizenry would benefit through reduced recidivism, and the offender would gain through programs aimed at his needs. Whether rehabilitative programs in fact were so designed is doubtful: traditionally, their criterion for success has been whether recidivism is reduced; such a reduction helps *us* but does not necessarily aid the offender himself. Nevertheless, much of the rehabilitative ideal's attractiveness lay in its apparent commitment to "doing good."

With the decline of rehabilitationism as the dominant penal rationale, the desire for a happy ending has not disappeared. Another conception has been emerging: restorative justice. Crime is perceived as conflict. The response to the crime should seek to resolve that conflict: to "restore" the victim, give the perpetrator insight into the injuriousness of his conduct, and reassure other citizens.

I shall not attempt here to assess the merits of restorative-justice conceptions in any detail—a considerable literature already exists on this subject (for a variety of perspectives, see the selections in von Hirsch and Ashworth [1998:Ch. 7] and in von Hirsch, Roberts, et al. [2003]). I am somewhat skeptical, however. Most crimes do not seem to me to be "conflicts" in any ordinary sense. I wonder whether "reassurance" of the citizenry can be made to amount to much more than crime control under a new name. Above all, I perceive in the literature of restorativism that unhappy combination, once apparent in traditional rehabilitationism, of excessive ambitiousness about ends and insufficient specification of means and limits. The aims of restorativism are said to be to restore the victim *and* reintegrate the offender *and* repair bonds of community ruptured by the offense. However, the means (how, exactly, this felicitous concatenation of results is to be achieved) are left sketchy, at best. And the limits on permissible intervention—to what degree the offender's rights may be intruded upon—are not delineated in comprehensible, principled fashion. And with this lack of specificity about means, amounts, and limits comes the familiar problem of insufficient guidance: it is difficult to know what kind of responses, for what kind of offenses and offenders, would and would not be appropriate under restorativism.

These characteristics could be viewed by a critic as suggesting that restorativism is primarily aspirational in character: to express aspirations rather than to adopt substantive goals that guide the choice of dispositions. True, the stated aspirations are somewhat different than those of the traditional pre-1980s discretionary sentencing model—having more to do with "healing," "conflict-resolution," and the like. There is also a shift on who officiates: it is no longer the judge, but rather the offender, victim, and community representatives. (This shift might be compared with substituting the congregation for the priest in a religious ritual.) But the actual mission, on this interpretation, would be to express a variety of aspirations: that the victim should be restored, that the offender should be made to recognize his wrong; that the "conflict" be healed; that the breach in the community's sense of trust be repaired; that the community should be reassured against further offending; that fear of crime be diminished, and so forth. There would be no need to choose among these ambitious and varying goals, because these are all things to which we may wish to aspire, and the restorative disposition serves to express these aspirations.

What would be wrong with such a purely aspirational approach? Someone might wish to defend it along the following lines: we feel that *something* needs to be done to the criminal offender, but what exactly is done is difficult to decide and will not make much difference in its consequences for the community. So why not have a discretionary response that expresses chiefly what we *wish* would occur? Restorative dispositions, however, involve *impositions:* the offender stands to suffer deprivations of his rights or interests. Such impositions stand in need of substantive justification: either in terms of harm prevention, or of the appropriate application of ethical norms, or both. People should not lose their rights just as a means of conveying hopes or aspirations.

A critical task confronting restorative justice, therefore, is that of defining aims and limits more carefully. There would need to be clearer specification of what, among the numerous desiderata restorativists mention, should be the principal guiding rationale; and the criteria for success or failure should be defined accordingly. And there needs to be a much more definite specification of limits. Some (although not all) restorativists assert that dispositions should be constrained by certain outer limits of proportionality—although what those limits might be and how they might be rationalized remains uncertain.[20]

Such skepticism, however, does not diminish the force of the desire for a seemingly more "positive" response to crime. If restorative justice fades because of its intrinsic problems and limitations of practical application, we can expect some other idea that purports to combine offender interests and societal interests. And, from those who find such ideas attractive, we can expect a continuing sense of discomfort with the "negativism" of the desert model.

PROSPECTS FOR PROPORTIONALIST SENTENCING POLICIES

What are the prospects for the proportionate sentence? Will the features of proportionalist sentencing spoken of in this chapter—the appeal to fairness, and the practical guidance offered to sentencers—continue to attract those who fashion sentencing policy? Or will the approach gradually recede, as a once-fashionable but no longer influential idea? Proportionalism's attraction, in my judgment, depends on the degree of influence of certain normative assumptions that are worth spelling out.

The proportionalist approach to sentencing is one version of what might be called the "liberal reform project" (or, as I have termed it elsewhere, the "project of sentencing reform" [von Hirsch 2001]). Such an approach, which has been influential since the mid 1970s, involves the following postulates:

First, a principled approach to sentencing: sentencing reform, it is assumed, should be guided by a coherent set of aims or principles.[21] A principled approach does not require that there be a single, exclusive penal purpose. Several aims may properly be pursued, so long as there are explicit norms concerning their interrelationship. A desert rationale gives primacy to notions of penal censure, and to proportionality of punishment to crime seriousness. Within a desert framework, however, other penal purposes may properly be taken into account, to the extent this is consistent with proportionality requirements.[22] "Limiting retributivism" operates with two rather than one penal goal: desert and crime prevention. Desert sets the limits for the possible sentence, within which crime prevention goals (including rehabilitation) may be pursued (Morris 1982:Ch. 5). Having the sentence depend on two main aims may be permissible, however, provided that the theory can help account for the relationship between those aims.

This principled approach rules out primarily intuitive approaches to sentencing, or the ad hoc adoption of differing sentencing goals for various different kinds of cases: that the drug offender should get a deterrent sentence, the repeat burglar an incapacitative one, and the shoplifter a rehabilitative one, and so forth.[23] It also precludes what I have described above as the aspirational approach—according to which sentencing aims set forth aspirations or desiderata that the sentence might symbolize, rather than actual goals in terms of which the sentence is to be fashioned and evaluated.

Second, an emphasis on "parsimony" in punishment: the preference should be for less rather than more intervention. Parsimony, properly understood, does not involve the adoption of a particular sentencing rationale, be it one of desert or of crime-prevention (see von Hirsch 1984:1105–07). It is, instead, a principle of self-restraint: of preferring moderate criminal sanctions, in the interest of reducing the extent to which convicted offenders' lives are disrupted. Either a desert-oriented or a more preventively oriented theory can be implemented with greater or less parsimony. Parsimony does, however, call for norms that explicitly set limits on permissible sanctions.

Parsimony is based on certain normative grounds. Convicted defendants are assumed to have continued human status, and continuing membership in the legal and moral community, and as such, are entitled to concern for their welfare and dignity. Punishment—involving as it does the censure of the offender and the purposeful infliction of deprivations on him or her—is viewed as something painful and humiliating; and imprisonment particularly so. Such impositions, if they must be inflicted at all, need to be imposed with restraint.

Third, an emphasis on notions of fairness: the sentence, it is assumed, should visit an equitable sanction on the offender. Debate exists about the criteria of fairness—and particularly, on how great a restraining role proportionality should have. Notwithstanding these divergences of view, however, fairness is to be treated as an important, not just a marginal, constraint. This concern with the justice of sentences depends also on the assumption of convicted offenders' having continued membership in the moral and legal community.

The attractiveness of a proportionalist approach to sentencing will depend, in important part, on whether these general assumptions are accepted. To the extent these assumptions are influential, an approach to sentencing emphasizing proportionality will continue to be attractive—because, as noted earlier, of its appeal to fairness and because of the degree of guidance that it offers. To the extent the assumptions do not prevail, however, the rationale's influence will diminish. Where the law-and-order ethos is strong, for example, the rationale is likely to have reduced influence—because that ethos simply rejects notions of parsimony and equity in sentencing. When the focus becomes that of using sentencing to express popular resentment of crime and criminals, it is not surprising that liberal sentencing approaches have diminished impact.

This point, about the importance of the underlying assumptions, is illustrated when one compares developments during the past decade regarding the sentencing reforms adopted in the late 1980s and early 1990s in Sweden and England. The English 1991 Criminal Justice Act made proportionality the primary criterion for deciding the use of imprisonment and of noncustodial punishments (Ashworth 2000:84–89). Sweden adopted comparable legislation in 1988, although its statutory sentencing principles are more fully and carefully delineated (Jareborg 1995). In both countries at the time of these schemes' adoption, proportionality occupied center stage in academic discussions.

In Sweden, the reform has survived. The sentencing statute has remained fundamentally intact, and continues to make the seriousness of the offense the primary criterion for deciding the severity of sentence. This proportionalist approach continues, by and large, to draw substantial support from justice ministry officials, senior judges, and academics (see the collection of essays in Jareborg 1999). In England, the comparable reform is under serious threat. Senior government officials, beginning in 1993, have increasingly voiced a "get tough" posture on sentencing; have diluted important provisions of the 1991 Act (for example, on the role of prior convictions—see Wasik and von Hirsch 1994); and have adopted mandatory minimum sentences without regard to proportionality concerns

(Ashworth 2000:177–80). Now, the government proposes to scrap the proportionalist framework of the 1991 Criminal Justice Act entirely, and replace it with a sentencing scheme that provide a menu of possible aims for the courts to consider, and call for toughened penalties for repeat offenders (Home Office 2001; 2001b; von Hirsch 2002; Roberts 2002; Home Office 2002).

Why these differing outcomes? They relate, in my judgment, to development of differing background assumptions. Swedish policymakers continue to subscribe to the liberal reform project, stressing identifiable sentencing aims, parsimony, and notions of equity—and, given these assumptions, continue to find a proportionalist perspective attractive. In England, the judiciary never really accepted the idea of explicit guidance for sentencing decisions—preferring wide sentencing discretion, treatment of sentencing aims as largely aspirational, and only limited guidance by the Court of Appeal; as a result, the judiciary has tried to water down the 1991 act's proportionality requirements from the outset.[24] Government officials, who in the late 1980s had supported goals of providing clearer guidance for sentencing and limiting prison populations, have been moving increasingly toward a law-and-order stance. How far this trend will go is still uncertain—it will be of interest to see what kind of sentencing scheme actually does emerge as the replacement of the 1991 Act. But to the extent the aim has become that of demonstrating ferocity toward criminals (particularly the more tiresome kinds of criminals such as repeat offenders) concerns about parsimony and equity attract less interest; and with it, proportionality loses much of its attractions to policymakers.

How will a proportionality-oriented approach to sentencing fare, then? It depends on what policymakers' more fundamental priorities are. In settings where there still is interest in developing sentencing principles that actually help guide sentencing decisions and that can provide a modicum of equity, a desert rationale will continue to seem attractive for the reasons that I have endeavored to describe in this chapter. In places where priorities have shifted to demonstrating fierceness on crime to the public, such a rationale will no longer seem appealing—but then, neither will alternative sentencing rationales making comparable assumptions about the need for meaningful guidance, parsimony, and fairness.

NOTES

1. For a description and analysis of the Minnesota and Oregon sentencing schemes, see von Hirsch (1995).

2. For a description of these three systems, see for Finland, Lappi-Seppälä (1992); for Sweden, Jareborg (1995); and for England and Wales, Ashworth (2000).

3. See Canada's Youth Criminal Justice Act, now a bill (C-7) under parliamen-

tary review (at present before the Senate). The bill is likely to become law late in 2002. The relevant paragraph of the bill provides that "the sentence must be proportionate to the seriousness of the offense and the degree of responsibility of the young person for that offence."

4. See von Hirsch (1976, 1985, 1993).

5. The fourth and fifth section of this chapter are thus substantially revised.

6. For arguments favoring a deflation of sanction levels in fixing the penalty scale's anchoring points, see von Hirsch (1993:Ch. 5).

7. For the difficulties of ascertaining Kant's penal views, see, e.g., Murphy (1987).

8. For issues relating to rehabilitation as the basis for sentence, see von Hirsch and Ashworth (1998:Ch. 1).

9. For issues concerning incapacitation, see von Hirsch and Ashworth (1998:Ch. 3).

10. The major state guideline systems—those of Minnesota, Oregon, Washington State, and North Carolina—do not rely on prediction methods, for example. For a survey of state guideline systems, see Tonry and Hatlestad (1997).

11. The term "new penology" is taken from Feeley and Simon (1992), who assert that an actuarial, risk-oriented penal practice has been developing—and cite selective incapacitation as an example. However, actuarial forecasting schemes have had a surprisingly small influence on sentencing policy, as just noted.

12. These issues have been discussed in the following previous writings: for anchoring points, von Hirsch (1993:Ch. 5); for crime-seriousness, von Hirsch (1993:Ch. 6), von Hirsch and Jareborg (1991); for the role of prior convictions, von Hirsch (1981, 1985:Ch. 7, 1998).

13. For a comparison of the role of the criminal record in the Minnesota and Oregon guidelines, see von Hirsch (1995).

14. For a fuller discussion of the structure and rationale of such "modified desert" schemes, see von Hirsch (1993:Ch. 6).

15. For the extent to which modified-desert and the more recent versions of "limiting retributivism" may tend to converge, see von Hirsch (2001:408–10).

16. For the Swedish experience, see Jareborg (1995); for the Finnish, Lappi-Seppälä (1998); for Minnesota's and Oregon's see von Hirsch (1994, 1995), Frase (1995).

17. For fuller discussion of law-and-order approaches to sentencing, see von Hirsch and Ashworth (1998:Ch. 9); see also Garland (2001:182–86) on the "criminology of the other."

18. Howard's "three strikes" provisions were embodied in the 1997 Crime (Sentences) Act, legislation that passed immediately before the dissolution of the Conservative government in the spring of 1997. He did not have time before dissolution to put the statute's provisions into effect, but his Labour successor, Jack Straw, took that step. Straw implemented the Act's seven-year minimum sentence for a third drug-dealing offense shortly after he took office, and implemented the three-year minimum for third burglary convictions in January 1999.

19. In Germany, the social democratic government's interior minister, Otto Schilly, has put forward some strongly prosecution-oriented changes in criminal procedure. The German government has not, however, proposed extensive changes in sentencing policy for ordinary offenders.

20. Some writers on restorative justice, however, suggest a more modest role for

restoration: as a procedure reserved for a certain range of cases, within limits specified by the criminal justice system (see von Hirsch, Ashworth, and Shearing 2003). On this view, it might be easier to accommodate restorative dispositions within bounds of proportionality (on these issues, see more fully the various essays in von Hirsch, Roberts et al. 2003).

21. For discussion of the importance of specified, prioritized aims, see Council of Europe (1993).

22. Since the principle of proportionality addresses only the deserved *severity* of punishment, crime-preventive goals (say, rehabilitation) may be considered when choosing among penalties of approximately comparable severity (see, von Hirsch 1993:Ch. 7).

23. True, Morris and Tonry (1990:at 104) speak of "purposes at sentence," whereby the court may adopt different aims for different kinds of cases; this choice, however, is constrained within their basic principles of limiting retributivism. The repeat burglar's incapacitative sentence, for example, may not exceed the upper desert limits for offenses of this degree of seriousness.

24. See, more fully, Ashworth (2000:86).

REFERENCES

Ashworth, Andrew. 2000. *Sentencing and Criminal Justice*. 3rd ed. London: Butterworths.

Bottoms, Anthony. 1995. "The Philosophy and Politics of Punishment and Sentencing." In *The Politics of Sentencing Reform*, edited by R. Morgan and C. Clarkson. Oxford: Oxford University Press.

Canadian Sentencing Commission. 1987. *Sentencing Reform: A Canadian Approach*. Ottawa: Canadian Government Publishing Centre.

Christie, Nils. 1980. *Limits to Pain*. Oslo: Universitetsforlaget.

Council of Europe. 1993. "Consistency in Sentencing: Recommendations to Member States and Explanatory Memorandum." *Criminal Law Forum* 4:355–92.

Dickey, Walter and Pam Steibs Hollenhorst. 1998. "Three Strikes Law: Massive Impact in California and Georgia, Little Elsewhere." *Overcrowded Times* 9(6):2–8.

Doob, Anthony. 1995. "The United States Sentencing Commission Guidelines." In *The Politics of Sentencing Reform*, edited by R. Morgan and C. Clarkson. Oxford: Oxford University Press.

Duff, Antony. 2001. *Punishment, Communication and Community*. Oxford: Oxford University Press.

Feeley, Malcolm and Jonathan Simon. 1992. "The New Penology: Notes on the Emerging Strategy of Corrections and Its Implications." *Criminology* 30:449–74.

Frase, Richard. 1995. "Sentencing Guidelines in Minnesota and Other American States: A Progress Report." In *The Politics of Sentencing Reform*, edited by R. Morgan and C. Clarkson. Oxford: Oxford University Press.

Freiberg, Arie. 2001. "Three Strikes and You're Out—It's Not Cricket: Colonization and Resistance in Australian Sentencing." In *Sentencing and Sanctions in Western Countries*, edited by M. Tonry and R. Frase. New York: Oxford University Press.

The Future of the Proportionate Sentence

Garland, David. 1990. *Punishment and Modern Society.* Oxford: Oxford University Press.

———. 2001. *The Culture of Control: Crime and Social Order in Contemporary Society.* Oxford: Oxford University Press.

Greenwood, Peter. 1982. *Selective Incapacitation.* Santa Monica, CA: RAND Corporation.

Home Office. 2001a. *Criminal Justice: The Way Ahead.* London: Home Office.

———. 2001b. *Making Punishments Work: Report of a Review of the Sentencing Framework for England and Wales.* London: Author.

Home Office. 2002. *Justice For All.* London: HMSO.

Jareborg, Nils. 1995. "The Swedish Sentencing Reform." In *The Politics of Sentencing Reform,* edited by R. Morgan and C. Clarkson. Oxford: Oxford University Press.

——— (Ed.). 1999. Påfoljdsbestämning. In *Svensk Juristtidning* 84(2).

Kahan, Dan. 1996. "What Do Alternative Sanctions Mean?" *University of Chicago Law Review* 63:591–653.

Lappi-Seppälä, Tapio. 1992. "Penal Policy and Sentencing in Finland." *Canadian Journal of Law and Jurisprudence* 5:95–120.

———. 1998. *Regulating the Prison Population: Experiences from a Long-Term Policy in Finland.* Helsinki: National Research Institute of Legal Policy, Research Communication No. 38.

Morris, Norval. 1982. *Madness and the Criminal Law.* Chicago: University of Chicago Press.

Morris, Norval and Michael Tonry. 1990. *Between Prison and Probation: Intermediate Punishments in a Rational Sentencing System.* New York: Oxford University Press.

Murphy, Jeffrie G. 1987. "Does Kant Have a Theory of Punishment?" *Columbia Law Review* 87:509–32.

National Research Council, Panel on Research and Criminal Careers. 1986. *Report.* In *Criminal Careers and "Career Criminals,"* vol. 1, edited by A. Blumstein, J. Cohen, J. Roth, and C. Visher. Washington DC: National Academy Press.

Roberts, Julian. 1994. "The Role of the Criminal Record in the Federal Sentencing Guidelines." *Criminal Justice Ethics* 13(1):21–30.

———. 2002. "Alchemy in Sentencing: An Analysis of Reform Proposals in England and Wales." *Punishment and Society* 4:425–442.

Tonry, Michael. 1992. "Mandatory Penalties." *Crime and Justice: A Review of Research* 16:243–73.

Tonry, Michael and Kathleen Hatlestad (Eds.). 1997. *Sentencing Guidelines in Overcrowded Times: A Comparative Perspective.* New York: Oxford University Press.

U.K. Government White Paper. 1996. *Protecting the Public.* London: H.M. Stationery Office.

van den Haag, Ernest. 1975. *Punishing Criminals: Concerning a Very Old and Painful Question.* New York: Basic Books.

———. 1987. "Punishment, Desert and Control." *Michigan Law Review* 85:1250–60.

von Hirsch, Andrew. 1976. *Doing Justice: The Choice of Punishments.* New York: Hill & Wang.

———. 1981. "Desert and Previous Convictions in Sentencing." *Minnesota Law Review* 65:591.

————. 1984. "Equality, 'Anisonomy,' and Justice." *Michigan Law Review* 82:1093–1112.

————. 1985. *Past or Future Crimes: Dangerousness and Deservedness in the Sentencing of Criminals.* New Brunswick, NJ: Rutgers University Press.

————. 1988. "Selective Incapacitation Reexamined: The National Academy of Sciences' Report on Criminal Careers and 'Career Criminals.'" *Criminal Justice Ethics* 7(1):19–35.

————. 1993. *Censure and Sanctions.* Oxford: Oxford University Press.

————. 1994. "Sentencing Guidelines and Penal Aims in Minnesota." *Criminal Justice Ethics* 13(1):39–49.

————. 1995. "Proportionality and Parsimony in the U.S. Sentencing Guidelines: The Minnesota and Oregon Standards." In *The Politics of Sentencing Reform,* edited by R. Morgan and C. Clarkson. Oxford: Oxford University Press.

————. 1998. "Desert and Previous Convictions." In *Principled Sentencing,* 2d ed., edited by A. von Hirsch and A. Ashworth. Oxford: Hart Publishing.

————. 2001. "The Project of Sentencing Reform." In *Sentencing and Sanction in Western Countries,* edited by M. Tonry and R. Frase. New York: Oxford University Press.

————. 2002. "Record-Enhanced Sentencing in England and Wales: Reflections on the Halliday Report's Proposed Treatment of Prior Convictions." *Punishment and Society* 4:443–457.

von Hirsch, Andrew and Andrew Ashworth (Eds.) 1998. *Principled Sentencing,* 2nd ed. Oxford: Hart.

von Hirsch, Andrew, A. Ashworth, and C. Shearing. 2003. "Specifying the Aims and Limits of Restorative Justice: A 'Making Amends' Model?" In *Restorative Justice and Criminal Justice: Competing or Reconcilable Paradigms?* edited by A. von Hirsch, J. Roberts, A. E. Bottoms, K. Roach, and M. Schiff. Oxford: Hart.

von Hirsch, Andrew, A. E. Bottoms, E. Burney, and P-O Wikström. 1999. *Criminal Deterrence and Sentence Severity: Analysis of Recent Research.* Oxford: Hart.

von Hirsch, Andrew and Nils Jareborg. 1991. "Gauging Criminal Harm: A Living Standard Analysis." *Oxford Journal of Legal Studies* 11:1–38.

von Hirsch, Andrew, J. Roberts, A. E. Bottoms, K. Roach, and M. Schiff (Eds.) 2003. *Restorative Justice and Criminal Justice: Competing or Reconcilable Paradigms?* Oxford: Hart Publishing.

Wasik, Martin and Andrew von Hirsch. 1994. "Section 29 Revised: Previous Convictions in Sentencing." *Criminal Law Review* 409:18.

Wilson, James Q. 1983. *Thinking About Crime,* rev. ed. New York: Basic Books.

13

Constricted Rationality and the Limits of General Deterrence

Gary Kleck

THE DETERRENCE RATIONALE FOR PUNISHMENT

Punishment can be justified solely on moralistic grounds as retribution, inflicting suffering on the wicked because it is right to do so. And for many people, this and similar justifications may indeed be their only important reason for favoring the punishment of criminals. For others, however, other justifications are crucial.

In culturally diverse societies where consensus on moral issues is often far from complete, many advocates prefer to justify punishment as a rational means to the end of crime reduction. As one scholar of deterrence recently argued, deterrence-based arguments for crime control policies allow advocates to avoid passionate and "illiberal" confrontations over unresolvable cultural conflicts, by providing rationales grounded in the promised consequences of the policies. Further, this style of justification may actually be a socially beneficial mode of debate over contentious public issues. "By muting expressive controversy, deterrence arguments make it easier for citizens of diverse moral and cultural commitments to agree on policy outcomes. . . . Deterrence theory secures the goals of liberal public reason, which enjoins us to disclaim privileged moral insight when we engage in public deliberations" (Kahan 1999:498–99).

One simple utilitarian justification for imprisoning convicted criminals is the assertion that incarceration produces incapacitative effects, i.e., crime-reducing effects that are due to the obvious fact that criminals cannot victimize members of the general public while physically isolated and restrained in prisons and jails. While incapacitative effects of incarceration undoubtedly operate, their magnitude is unclear and heavily dependent on how successful the criminal justice system is in identifying high-frequency offenders and selectively sentencing them to prison or jail terms (Spelman 1994).

The considerable crime control potential of selective incapacitation sentencing policies has not been realized, due in part to a severely limited ability of court actors to distinguish high-frequency offenders from other defendants using information that is both available in court records and that reflects legally permissible sentencing factors, and to do so early enough in offenders' careers to have significant crime preventive impact. The best available predictors of future criminal behavior, among those that can legally be used to determine criminal sentences, are measures of past involvement with the criminal justice system, but unfortunately by the time criminals have accumulated enough arrests and convictions to be identifiable as chronic offenders they are usually past their peak crime-committing years. As a result, sentencing them to prison prevents fewer crimes than if they could somehow have been identified as high-frequency offenders, and sentenced to prison, before their peak years (Spelman 1994).

Another utilitarian rationale for punishment, however, is its potential to reduce crime through deterrent effects. Punishment can make some people, who otherwise would have been willing to commit crimes, fearful enough of punishment to avoid it by refraining from committing crimes. When punishment of a particular person causes that person to subsequently refrain from crime, it is called "special deterrence," and when punishment of criminals in general causes people in general, punished or unpunished, to refrain from crime, it is called "general deterrence" (Zimring and Hawkins:72–73). While incapacitation, like special deterrence, can restrain the behavior only of the relatively small share of criminals who have been caught and convicted, general deterrence can potentially influence anyone, including both noncriminals and heretofore uncaught criminals, as well as caught criminals. (From this point on, we use "deterrence" to refer to general deterrence.) For this reason, deterrent effects are potentially far more potent sources of social control than incapacitative effects.

But unlike incapacitative effects, which occur regardless of how criminals perceive their punishment, deterrence can occur only to the extent that the risk of punishment is perceived by prospective offenders. Without perception of the risk of punishment, there can be no deterrent effect (Zimring and Hawkins 1973; Spelman 1994:294). The dimensions of punishment that affect its deterrent impact on criminal behavior are summarized in the proposition that "the greater the certainty, severity, and swiftness (celerity) of punishment, the lower the crime rate will be" (e.g., Gibbs 1975:5). However, a more precise restatement of this proposition, which stresses the essential role of perceptions, would be: The greater the *perceived* certainty, severity, and swiftness of punishment, the lower the crime rate will be.

Of course, the abstract possibility of punishment for crime is perceived by virtually everyone. There are few people who do not know that at least some criminals suffer legal punishments for at least some crimes. Some people may believe that these risks are low, or that they are themselves unlikely to be caught and punished for any crimes they might commit, but almost everyone recognizes at least the theoretical possibility that they might suffer legal punishment if they broke the law.

Nevertheless, this does not necessarily imply that increases in punishment levels (i.e., increases in actual certainty, severity, or swiftness of legal punishment) will increase deterrent effects and thereby reduce crime, since variations in actual punishment levels may or may not cause variations in the average perceived level of punishment among prospective offenders. Indeed, critics of deterrence as crime control, such as Leslie Wilkins, have long pointed to this reality-perception gap as a key weakness in deterrence-based crime control policies (cited in Zimring and Hawkins 1973:45). More recently, in a review of the deterrence literature, Nagin (1998) has placed research on the policy-perception link as one of the three top priorities for future deterrence research.

Because punishment for crime is to a great degree justified on moralistic grounds, some level of punishment will persist regardless of its utility for controlling crime. The answer to the simple yes/no question, Can punishment deter crime? is almost certainly yes, since some people almost certainly refrain from some crimes due to a fear of legal punishment. But this is obviously an irrelevant question from a policy standpoint since no policymakers are asking the simple yes/no policy question, Shall we have punishment?

But in response to the very real policy question, Shall we have, as a means to crime reduction, *more* punishment than we have now? it is by no means obvious that more punishment would yield more deterrent effect. Even if one were willing to assume that there are no deviance-amplifying effects of punishment to counterbalance deviance-suppressing effects, it would still be unclear whether more punishment would reduce crime via deterrence because it would be uncertain whether increases in actual punishment levels would cause an increase in the level of perceived risk of punishment. And even if one could assume that there is some prevailing "baseline" deterrent effect from the mere existence of legal punishment and widespread awareness of it, this would still not resolve the policy question of whether higher punishment levels would increase the deterrent effect of punishment beyond its currently prevailing level.

This way of framing the issue is pertinent because much of contemporary debate over crime control in policymaking circles is confined to variations on the theme of legal punishment, and a great deal is even more narrowly confined to strategies for increasing the severity and certainty of punishment. Thus, legislators debate bills that would mandate minimum sentences for certain crimes, "three-strike" penalties for some repeat offenders, enhanced penalties for crimes committed with guns or in connection with drug trafficking, and many other strategies for increasing the severity of punishment. Likewise, law enforcement officials lobby for increased budgets and enforcement authority so that they can arrest more criminals, thereby increase the certainty of arrest for crime, and thus enhance the likelihood of legal punishment. Prosecutors make similar appeals to enable them to increase the certainty of conviction, and thus the certainty of punishment. And many advocates argue for building more prisons so that both the probability and severity (length) of prison sentences can be increased. In sum, advocates push for increased punishment levels above existing levels.

These policies proposals are frequently, and perhaps even usually, justified at least partly on the grounds that they will reduce crime through increased deterrence, by "sending a message," "getting the word out" that crime will not tolerated, that criminals will be "taught a lesson," that crime will not be "coddled," and that punishment will surely follow crime. In sum, it is asserted that policy changes producing increases in punishment levels will reduce crime by means of deterrence, that is, by means of an increased perception of legal risk among prospective offenders.

And the question of whether punishment increases can reduce crime via deterrence, or whether punishment decreases will increase crime due to a decline in deterrent effects, turns on the question of whether perceptions of punishment levels bear at least a rough correspondence with actual punishment levels.

PERCEPTION-REALITY CORRESPONDENCE
AND THEORIES OF CRIMINAL BEHAVIOR

Leaving public policy aside, many scientific explanations of criminal behavior, and indeed human behavior in general, rely heavily on assumptions of a reality-perception correspondence. Legal punishments are, of course, but one class of contingencies that can affect criminal behavior. Many explanations of criminal behavior stress the role of a wide array of costs and benefits, punishments and reinforcements, undesirable and desirable consequences of potential courses of action. Thus, criminological theories ranging from Beccaria's "classical criminology" to social learning theory, economic theories of crime, the routine activities perspective, and rational choice theory all rely on an assumption, explicit or implicit, of a correspondence between contingencies and perceptions of those contingencies among prospective offenders (Beccaria [1764] 1963; Akers 1973; Becker 1968; Hindelang, Gottfredson, and Garofalo 1978; Cornish and Clarke 1986).

The validity of rational decision-making theories does not, however, require a perfect correspondence between contingencies and perceptions of contingencies, but does require some correspondence if the theories are to have any explanatory or predictive power. The stronger this correspondence, the stronger the theories' explanatory and predictive power.

No matter how inclined and able people may be to rationally process and weigh information and to consider potential costs and benefits of various courses of action, they cannot actually decide and act rationally unless there is at least some accuracy to their perceptions of those costs and benefits and thus some correspondence between reality and their perceptions of reality.

In some realms of human activity, it is perfectly reasonable to assume a fairly close correspondence between perceptions and the realities of costs and benefits. Certainly, in the sphere of economic behavior, narrowly construed, the assumption is plausible, mainly because there is such a large volume of relevant information, and a relatively high degree of accuracy to that information, available to actors. Consumers generally know exactly the price of different brands of goods, while investors know not only the price of a share of stock in any given business firm, but also a great deal about the assets, liabilities, and past profit performance of that company. Relevant information in the sphere of market behavior is voluminous, fairly accurate, and easily obtained. Rational behavior, and predictable responses to changes in costs and benefits, is to be expected in such information-rich environments. Shaped by research experiences in this context, it is not surprising that economists appear to consider it self-evident that there be at minimum a significant positive, albeit imperfect, correlation between actual risks and perceived risks (Becker 1968; Ehrlich 1973).

Criminal behavior, on the other hand, may be quite different, especially with regard to one of the main risks associated with it, punishment. If information about legal risks were limited, often inaccurate, and hard to obtain, the correlation of actual risks and perceptions of those risks would be considerably weaker than in the realm of market behavior. And if prospective offenders' perceptions of punishment risk bore no systematic relationship to punishment reality, variations in that reality would have no effect on deterrence of criminal behavior. People might well be deterred by the possibility of punishment, but they would be no more likely to be deterred in settings where punishment risks were actually higher than in settings where they were lower.

Under such circumstances, investment in policies increasing punishment levels would be wasted, at least from a deterrence standpoint. Putting it even more broadly, though a bit too strongly, one scholar has stated that "absent some linkage between policy and perceptions, behavior is immune to policy manipulation" (Nagin 1998).

One recent illustration of the extent of offender ignorance of legal risks is worth noting, since it suggests that huge numbers of criminals are not even aware of the most highly publicized changes in the legal status of some behaviors, never mind details such as the degree to which the behaviors are punished. Perhaps the most widely publicized criminal law enacted in the past decade was the Brady Act, a federal law that mandated a criminal background check on all persons seeking to buy a gun from a licensed dealer. Becoming effective in February of 1994, the law made it impossible for convicted felons to legally buy a gun from a licensed gun dealer.

A search of the Lexis-Nexis database on January 30, 2002, indicated that in the twenty-eight major U.S. newspapers covered by the database, there were 1,166 stories on the "Brady bill" in 1992–1997, i.e., about 194 per year, or seven per newspaper per year. If criminals were aware of any change in the legal status of a behavior, the Brady Act's provisions concerning criminal background checks should surely have been such a change. Even the most minimally aware convicted criminals should have known that if they tried to buy a gun from a licensed dealer, they would have to go through a background check, which they would certainly fail.

Yet, in the first three years and nine months following the law's effective date, 207,000 people, 63 percent of them convicted felons, attempted to buy guns from dealers and were turned down after a background check (U.S. Department of Justice, Bureau of Justice Statistics 1999a:1). That is, 207,000 criminals and other persons forbidden from buying guns, almost all of whom surely knew of their own criminal convictions or other disqualifying characteristics, were not aware of the most highly publicized new law of the decade, a law whose main provision made it impossible for them to legally buy a gun from a licensed dealer.

PRIOR RESEARCH ON CRIME AND DETERRENCE

Prior deterrence studies can be divided into two broad categories: (1) macrolevel studies of the relationship between the actual punishment levels and measured crime rates of aggregates such as cities, counties, states, and nations, (e.g., Ehrlich 1973) and (2) individual-level survey studies of the relationship between perceived punishment levels and self-reported criminal or delinquent behavior, or hypothetical willingness to commit crimes (e.g., Paternoster, Saltzman, Waldo and Chiricos 1982). The main concepts addressed by these studies are illustrated in Figure 13.1. Concepts in brackets were not measured.

The perceptual deterrence studies using survey data on individuals address the *scientific* issue of whether perception of legal risks affects criminal behavior, but do not address the *policy* issue of whether policies that change actual punishment levels, such as increasing the share of convicted persons who are sentenced to prison, affect crime rates via deterrence. It is perfectly possible that perceptions of legal risk *do* affect criminal behavior,

Macro-level: Punishment --> [Perception of --> Crime
                 Levels   Punishment]   Rates

Individual-level: [Punishment --> Perception of --> Criminal
                   Levels]   Punishment   Behavior

Figure 13.1.   Body of research.

yet variations in policy and punishment activities of the criminal justice system do *not* influence prospective offenders' perceptions of risk. It is the first causal link in each of the Figure 13.1 diagrams that is the focus of the present research, i.e., the link between actual punishment levels (levels of certainty, severity, or swiftness of punishment) and perceptions of those levels.

While it might seem self-evident to some that there is bound to be some positive correlation between actual and perceived levels of punishment, there is good reason to question the linkage, and a fair amount of research on related topics that casts doubt on the assumption that the link is strong.

Few people, whether criminals or noncriminals, are consumers of criminal justice statistics (CJS), and even among criminals, most have only limited personal experience with crime and punishment. Further, depending on hearsay and gossip among their criminal associates may be an unreliable basis for forming even approximately accurate notions of levels or trends in CJS punishment activities.

On the other hand, the news media provide neither criminals nor noncriminals with much reliable information on levels of either crime or punishment. At the macrolevel, the amount of news coverage of legal *punishment* is unlikely to bear a very strong relation to the general level of actual punishment, given that studies of the relationship between the volume of news coverage of *crime* and actual rates of crime find the relationship to be close to nonexistent (Garofalo 1981; Marsh 1989). If common punishment events such as court sentencings or admissions to prison get no more publicity than the crimes that gave rise to them, it would be optimistic to suppose that people could formulate even minimally accurate perceptions of punishment risks from news media coverage.

Indeed, various documented news media biases in coverage of crime and punishment could cause, in an irregular fashion, either overstated or understated perceptions of punishment risk. For example, some scholars have found that newspapers exaggerate the certainty of arrest by overreporting solved crimes (Roshier 1973:37; Parker and Grasmick 1979:371). On the other hand, studies reviewed by Roberts (1992) indicate that news stories about suspects who "got off on a technicality" or who got a "slap on the wrist" sentence from a judge leads to the public perceiving the severity of sentences to be lower than they really are. Further, since estimates of the certainty of punishment necessarily reflect perceptions of the volume of criminal acts relative to punishments, the lack of correspondence between the volume of news media coverage of crime and actual crime rates would contribute to weaker reality-perception correlations regarding the certainty of punishment.

On the other hand, already active criminals might draw on their own experiences and those of close associates to formulate their perceptions of punishment risk. To the extent that they accurately observed, remembered, and assessed these past experiences, it could improve both perceptions of past legal risks and forecasts of future risks, should they attempt further crimes. The research on personality traits common among known offenders, however, does not encourage a view of criminals as disciplined and careful processors of information, likely to bother recalling and assessing such past experiences. Indeed, within a population of persons who already evince tendencies toward risk-taking, past experience of punishment could even lead to a variant of the gambler's fallacy: "My string of past bad luck in getting caught is due to end; my chances of avoiding arrest are bound to improve because I've exhausted my share of bad luck."

It is unnecessary for present purposes to review in detail the findings of deterrence research. Nagin summarizes the individual-level survey research as follows: "I believe that a consensus has emerged among perceptual deterrence researchers that the negative association between sanction risk perceptions and offending behavior or intentions is measuring deterrence" (1998:15). Concerning the macrolevel research, findings are both mixed and, due to uncertainty about how to deal with simultaneity of the punishment-crime relationship, inconclusive (Nagin 1998).

The salient implication of Figure 13.1 is that neither macrolevel nor individual research has addressed the main issue considered here—the effect of actual punishment levels on perceived punishment levels. Thus, prior research has provided only weak indirect tests of deterrence theory. The individual-level studies address whether perceptions of punishment, however arrived at, influence criminal behavior, but say nothing about whether actual punishment levels, and crime control policies, influence the formation of those perceptions in the first place. On the other hand, macrolevel studies address whether actual punishment levels somehow affect crime rates, but do not address intervening causal mechanisms and thus can say little of a persuasive nature about whether any alleged effects actually involved deterrence. For example, most studies purporting to find a negative effect of clearance, conviction, and imprisonment rates on crime rates may be detecting nothing more than incapacitative effects, since all those measures of punishment levels could contribute to a higher share of the active criminal population being incarcerated and thus incapacitated.

While some self-report studies have treated perceptions of punishment as a dependent variable (e.g., Cohen 1978; Parker and Grasmick 1979; Richards and Tittle 1981, 1982; Paternoster, Saltzman, Waldo, and Chiricos 1985; Horney and Marshall 1992), none have assessed the impact on those perception of actual punishment levels prevailing in the person's area. Coming closest to our concerns, a single study conducted over twenty years ago did examine, in a limited way, the association between actual and perceived punishment levels. Erickson and Gibbs surveyed a random sample of Phoenix residents, asking them to estimate the probability of arrest for ten different offenses. Comparing their collective estimates with police statistics on arrest probabilities, they found a 0.55 Pearson correlation (rho=.39) between objective and perceived certainty of arrest, across ten offenses (1978:259).

This study addressed only variation in arrest certainty across offenses, rather than across areas or time periods. The authors stated that a study examining variation across areas would be desirable, but claimed that it would be prohibitively expensive (ibid.:255, fn. 6). Using offense types as the unit of analysis was problematic because perceived certainty of punishment, while it varied considerably across individuals, showed very little variation, for the Phoenix population in the aggregate, across offenses (ibid.:260). This unit of analysis also meant that the study was limited to a sample of just ten "cases" (offense types), favoring unstable findings. Further, the study was limited to a single jurisdiction, addressed only certainty of punishment, and only the police contribution to certainty.

THE PRESENT STUDY

Our study, in contrast, is designed to address perceived and objective levels of severity and swiftness of punishment as well as its certainty, and to consider the contributions of courts and correctional institutions to perceptions of those aspects of punishment levels. The general strategy was to survey urban residents and measure their perceptions of punishment risks prevailing in their area, and then relate these perceptions to actual punishment risks as measured in official criminal justice system data.

METHODOLOGY

To properly address this topic, it was necessary to identify aspects of punishment for which we can measure both actual and perceived levels. Since we would like to be able to generalize our findings to the entire United States, this means we would prefer to select objective measures of actual punishment-related CJS activities that are available across the nation, for which we can also measure corresponding perceptions. Unfortunately, there are no systematic national data on the swiftness of punishment, while data on severity of punishment, such as mean lengths of prison sentences imposed or served, are available only for varying subsets of the states or for selected local areas.

A much richer set of measures of actual punishment risk, however, is available for a smaller set of local, primarily urban, jurisdictions. Approximately three hundred counties participate in the Bureau of Justice Statistics' National Judicial Reporting Program (NJRP). The counties are selected to be representative of the entire United States but disproportionately cover larger urban counties (U.S. Department of Justice, Bureau of Justice Statistics 1999b). Within each sampled county, NJRP staff select a representative sample of criminal convictions from court records. They then gather data on the number of convictions (allowing the computation of conviction rates—adults convicted or plead guilty per hundred charged or arrested), the number of convicted adults who received prison sentences (allowing computation of adults sentenced to prison per hundred adults convicted), the average maximum sentence imposed, and the average number of days between arrest and sentencing.

The number of felony convictions is too low in the smaller of the counties participating in the NJRP to yield stable estimates of sentencing-related parameters for specific crime types in individual counties, even when aggregated across multiple years. Therefore, we used data only from the fifty-four largest NJRP counties. Because these counties were selected to be representative of the seventy-five largest (by population) counties in the United States, results based on our urban sample are generalizable to the nation's seventy-five biggest urban counties. In 1998, these seventy-five counties accounted for 50.2 percent of the nation's murders, 61.9 percent of robberies, and 51.4 percent of all violent crimes known to the police (analysis of U.S. Department of Justice, Federal Bureau of Investigation 2000). In sum, our results can be generalized to the areas that account for most of the nation's serious crime problem.

Combining county-level Uniform Crime Reports (UCR) data on crimes and arrests and NJRP data on convictions and sentences allowed us to measure the following kinds of punishment levels, for each of four offense types. The actual punishment variables pertain to the county in which the respondent resides.

Certainty of punishment:

- Total arrests per hundred offenses known to the police
- Adults convicted per hundred adults arrested

Severity of punishment:

- Adults sentenced to prison per hundred adults convicted
- Average maximum sentence imposed

Swiftness of punishment:

- Average number of days from arrest to sentencing

MEASUREMENT

To measure perceptions of punishment levels, we surveyed representative samples of adults (age eighteen and over) in each of the fifty-four urban counties. For each county-level measure of actual punishment levels (whether a measure of certainty, severity, or swiftness of punishment), we devised closely matching questions for the survey, which measured respondents' perceptions of the levels of these risks.

These perceptions were measured by asking questions of the following form: "In your county, out of every 100 *robberies* known to the police, about how many do you think resulted in the arrest of the robber?" In each case, to put all respondents (Rs) on an equal footing, interviewers provided a simple nontechnical definition of the offense type being asked about. Rs were asked about the preceding ten year period, 1988–1998. This was done to ensure a reasonably close correspondence between the period to which perceptions pertained and the period for which reliable data on actual punishment levels could be obtained. It was necessary to go back as far as 1988 to insure enough sample convictions to have reliable estimates of actual punishment levels in individual counties for each offense type. The NJRP data are gathered only for even-numbered years, and the most recent NJRP data available at the time of data analysis were for 1996. Thus, we used NJRP data on representative samples of convictions obtained in 1988, 1990, 1992, 1994, and 1996.

We obtained data on actual punishment levels for as much of the 1988–1998 period as were available. Data on crimes and arrests for counties were available for all five years from 1994 to 1998; pre-1994 county UCR data are unusable because they have not been adjusted for nonreporting agencies (U.S. Department of Justice, Federal Bureau of Investigation 2000, and preceding years). Data on conviction rates were available for 1994 and 1996, and data for all other punishment measures for even-numbered years from 1988 through 1996 (U.S. Department of Justice, Bureau of Justice Statistics 1999b).

We asked about punishment of four types of crime: criminal homicide, robbery, aggravated assault, and burglary. These four offenses are all serious crimes, and include both violent and property crimes. They encompass most of the offenses that are likely to be publicized, and respondents are likewise probably more likely to hear about punishment of these offenses than almost any other crime types. We were confined to using the seven traditional FBI/UCR Crime Index offenses because these were the only offenses for which data were available on crimes known to the police. The only two serious Index crimes we could not study were rape and motor vehicle theft. We could not include rape because sexual assault statutes are so different from one state to another that NJRP data on actual punishment levels for rape were not likely to be comparable across states. And we could not cover motor vehicle theft because some states do not have a separate statutory category for this crime, which is lumped in with other grand larcenies. Thus, there are no separate data on punishment of this crime from the NJRP for some states.

Sampling

The survey sample consisted of 1,500 adult respondents (Rs) selected using conventional random-digit dialing procedures. This sampling method allows access to the 95 percent of the U.S. households that have a telephone, including those with unlisted numbers. The sample was drawn exclusively from the fifty-four largest NJRP counties, with samples for each county proportionate to the population size of the county. Within each household contacted, an adult respondent was randomly selected by the interviewer asking to speak to the resident age eighteen or older who had most recently celebrated a birthday.

Telephone interviews were conducted by Research Network, Inc., of Tallahassee, Florida, a professional polling firm that has conducted hundreds of telephone surveys, including many concerning crime. The interviews were conducted in April and May of 1998. Our focus was on the simple bivariate association between perceived and actual punishment levels, so Pearson correlation coefficients were computed, along with their significance levels.

SENSITIVITY TO PUNISHMENT LEVELS AMONG CRIMINALS AND NONCRIMINALS

It might be argued that deterrence is not relevant to the bulk of the general population, because most people would remain largely noncriminal regardless of perceived or actual punishment levels. According to this view, a more relevant subset of the population for present purposes would be criminals because they are the people who most need to be deterred to reduce crime. This argument is dubious, since deterrence doctrine supporters assert that the prospect of punishment is precisely why many *non-criminal* persons remain noncriminal. Thus, it would be high perceptions of punishment risk among noncriminals that would provide the most important support for the deterrence doctrine.

Alternatively, it might be argued that perceptions of punishment should correspond more closely to reality among criminals, because they are the ones most likely to be knowledgeable about actual punishment levels. Already-active criminals have both the strongest incentives to acquire information on punishment risks, and a larger store of information from their own crime-punishment experiences and those of associates than non-criminals.

On the other hand, research on the personality of known offenders portrays them as impulsive, impatient, easily distracted, narrowly focused on the short-term consequences of their actions, and biased toward behaviors that are immediately gratifying, regardless of long-term risks (summarized in Vold, Bernard, and Snipes 2002:77–81). Since the risks of punishment for crime are fairly low in the short term, and substantial only in the long term, such persons should be especially unlikely to be responsive to legal risks, because they would give them relatively little thought and consideration. Further, despite strong incentives to acquire and retain accurate information about legal risks, people with such personality traits would be especially unlikely to exercise the patience and forethought to actually do so.

If this view of criminals is accurate, to focus solely on already-active criminals would bias results against finding a reality-perception correlation, by examining only those least inclined and able to acquire reasonably accurate information about punishment levels. Nevertheless, it was possible to address this issue by asking Rs whether they had ever been arrested for a nontraffic offense (using a question asked in seven national General Social Surveys between 1973 and 1984). This allowed us to estimate the correlation between actual and perceived punishment levels separately for self-reported arrestees and for nonarrestees. Our sample of the general urban population included 182 admitted arrestees, and thus included many significantly criminal individuals as well as noncriminals.

HYPOTHESES

The validity of the deterrence doctrine does not depend on an assumption that people are able to accurately estimate the absolute levels of actual punishment levels. Rather, the doctrine depends only on there being a positive correlation between perceived and actual punishment levels, such that higher actual levels generally lead to higher perceived levels. For example, Rs might perceive the average prison sentence for robbery to be double what it really is, but the deterrence doctrine would still be supported if people in areas with longer actual sentences generally provided larger estimates of sentence length (however inaccurate in absolute terms they might be) than people in areas with shorter actual sentences.

Thus the null hypothesis was that there is no statistically significant correlation between actual and perceived punishment levels. This basic hypothesis was tested with respect to each of four specific types of crime for which punishment data are gathered, for each of the five measures of certainty, severity, and swiftness previously described. We further hypothesized that criminals' perceptions of punishment would not correspond any closer to reality than those of noncriminals.

FINDINGS

Table 13.1 shows the correlations between perceived and actual punishment levels. They are all extremely weak to nonexistent. None of them reached 0.13 in the full sample, and they averaged a negligible 0.02. Many were even negative. Only four of twenty correlations were even statistically significant, despite the fairly large sample sizes, which ranged from 1,142 to 1,330, depending on missing data. Even the largest correlation of 0.122, pertaining to swiftness of punishment for robbery, implies that variation in actual punishment levels accounts for less than 1.7 percent of the variation in perception of punishment levels. Further, there was no clear pattern regarding either crime type or dimension of punishment, among the few correlations that were statistically significant.

Supporters of the deterrence doctrine might argue that while criminals might not directly perceive overall punishment levels prevailing in their local areas, they should be indirectly influenced by those levels via their own personal experiences with crime and punishment and the experiences of their close associates. Criminals are familiar with their own rate of past criminal behavior and their own experiences with legal punishment, and have at least some knowledge of such experiences among associates. Thus, if the personal experiences of any one criminal tend to reflect, on average, the aggregate experiences of all criminals in an area, perceptions of punishment risk might correlate well with actual punishment risk. This presupposes, of course, that criminals reasonably accurately recall their own criminal behavior and punishment experiences, have reasonably accurate perceptions of the experiences of associates, and bother to take account of these experiences when deciding whether to commit crimes.

In any case, the hypothesis that criminals are more closely attuned to actual punishment risks than noncriminals is clearly not supported by the evidence. Examining Table 13.1 again, it is clear that correlations between perceived and actual punishment levels were even weaker among self-reported arrestees (middle two columns) than among nonarrestees (last two columns). Indeed the average perception-reality correlation among arrestees is slightly negative, though not significantly different from zero. Evidently, urban criminals' perceptions of punishment risks prevailing in their areas have virtually no systematic correspondence with reality. Only one of the twenty correlations estimated was statistically significant at the .05 level, one-tailed. Thus, the notion that perceptions correspond to reality more strongly among criminals, and that deterrence therefore works

Table 13.1. Correlations of Perceived and Actual Punishment Levels; Pearson's r, 1-tailed significance*

	Total Sample ($n = 1142–1330$)		Arrestees ($n = 150–182$)		Nonarrestees ($n = 910–1251$)	
Certainty	r	p	r	p	r	p
Arrest rates[a]						
Murder	**0.048**	0.04	−0.030	0.35	**0.071**	0.01
Robbery	0.011	0.34	−0.043	0.29	0.004	0.45
Aggravated assault	0.006	0.42	−0.120	0.06	0.028	0.18
Burglary	0.015	0.29	−0.145	0.03	0.047	0.06
Conviction rates[b]						
Murder	−0.030	0.14	0.072	0.18	−0.042	0.08
Robbery	0.020	0.24	0.107	0.08	0.019	0.26
Aggravated assault	0.040	0.07	**0.130**	0.05	0.019	0.27
Burglary	**0.053**	0.03	0.084	0.14	0.046	0.06
Severity						
Prison rates (%)[c]						
Murder	−0.027	0.15	−0.074	0.16	−0.017	0.27
Robbery	0.026	0.16	−0.014	0.43	0.041	0.07
Aggravated assault	0.026	0.16	0.028	0.35	0.028	0.16
Burglary	**0.058**	0.01	−0.068	0.18	**0.079**	0.00
Average maximum sentence						
Murder	−0.000	0.50	−0.023	0.38	0.008	0.40
Robbery	0.009	0.37	−0.008	0.46	0.020	0.26
Aggravated assault	−0.011	0.35	−0.027	0.37	−0.006	0.42
Burglary	0.006	0.41	0.095	0.12	−0.002	0.48
Swiftness: Average time, arrest to sentencing						
Murder	0.026	0.21	−0.013	0.44	0.039	0.14
Robbery	**0.122**	0.00	0.016	0.44	**0.144**	0.00
Aggravated assault	0.025	0.23	−0.045	0.32	0.037	0.16
Burglary	−0.013	0.35	0.001	0.50	−0.015	0.35
Average correlation:	0.020		−0.004		0.027	

*Correlations in bold are significant at .05 level, 1-tailed.
[a]Number of persons arrested per 100 offenses known to police.
[b]Number of adults convicted per 100 adults arrested.
[c]Number of adults who received a jail or prison sentence per 100 adults convicted.

best in shaping the perceptions of those who most need to be influenced, is contradicted by the evidence.

It should be noted that, in at least three important ways, these are generous estimates of the reality-perception association. First, in all of our analyses we had to exclude the 15–20 percent of respondents who were not willing to even guess at punishment levels in their area. Thus, by excluding what were presumably the least knowledgeable respondents, we biased results in favor of finding a higher correspondence between reality and perception, yet still found virtually no association. Second, we asked Rs for these perceptions in a context favoring accuracy. Rs were in the relative comfort and security of their homes, and could calmly reflect on punishment risks. In contrast, prospective offenders, at the moment when they consider committing a criminal act, especially a violent act, are often under considerable emotional stress and thus less likely to make reasonable assessments of legal risks. Third, because samples of the general household population exclude incarcerated criminals, our sample excluded people who were undeterred by, and thus least responsive to, threats of legal punishment. Thus, one could view the sample as excluding those whose perceptions of punishment risks were the most weakly correlated with actual risks (again, compare the arrestee correlations with nonarrestee correlations in Table 13.1).

On the other hand, no measurements are perfect, and to the extent that our measurements of actual and perceived punishments are affected by random error, the correlations will be attenuated toward zero, favoring the null hypothesis. Perhaps perfect measurement of the variables would have resulted in strong correlations, but the attenuation due to measurement error would have to be substantial indeed to suppose that the near-zero correlations actually observed are concealing strong ones.

It should also be acknowledged that it is impossible to prove a negative and thus to prove the null hypothesis. Thus, the most precise way to summarize these findings is to say that they fail to support the hypothesis that higher actual punishment levels routinely lead to higher perceived punishment levels.

CONCLUSIONS AND POLICY IMPLICATIONS

The policy implications of these findings are important. There is generally no significant correlation between perceptions of punishment levels and the actual levels of punishment that CJS agencies work hard to achieve, implying that increases in punishment levels do not routinely reduce crime through general deterrence mechanisms. Increases in punishment might reduce crime through incapacitative effects, through the effects of treatment programs linked with punishment, or through other mechanisms, but they are not likely to do so in any way that depends on producing changes in perceptions of risk in the population.

The results do *not*, on the other hand, imply that punishment does not exert any deterrent effect. Rather, they support the view that any deterrent effect, however large or small it may be, does not covary with actual punishment levels to any substantial degree, since the perceptions of risk on which deterrent effects depend generally do not covary with punishment levels. There may be, as earlier suggested, some baseline level of deterrent effect generated by punishment-generating activities of the criminal justice system, but this level apparently is one that will not consistently increase with increased punishment levels or diminish with decreased punishment levels. Thus, increased punishment levels are not likely to increase deterrent effects, while decreased levels are not likely to decrease them.

For those seeking ways to improve existing levels of ability to control crime, these findings suggest a need for either (1) a shift in crime control resources toward strategies whose success does not depend on general deterrence effects, or (2) different, nonroutine methods for generating effective deterrence messages. One approach in the latter category is to more narrowly target very specific deterrence messages at audiences who are at especially high risk of committing crimes in the near future. This was the main idea behind a program implemented in Boston and aimed at reducing youth gang violence. Rather than using apprehension, prosecution, and punishment to send very broad "wholesale" deterrence messages aimed at the general population, the Ceasefire program delivered direct and explicit "retail deterrence" messages to a relatively small target audience of gang members and potential members. Unfortunately, there has been no rigorous evaluation of this program or any similar one, so it is impossible to say whether more narrowly targeted delivery of deterrence messages works better than traditional deterrence (Kennedy 1997).

It is also possible that unusually highly publicized punishment events may generate deterrent effects that the routine, largely unpublicized punitive activities of the criminal justice system ordinarily do not. It has, for example, been claimed that highly publicized executions exert an effect, albeit a possibly temporary one, on homicidal behavior (Phillips 1980; Stack 1987), and the same might be true of events linked with less extreme punishments such as incarceration. There is, however, no persuasive evidence bearing on publicized punishment events other than executions or death sentencings. When criminals are sentenced to prison in court, or start serving those sentences, such events are much less likely to receive publicity than the rarer and more dramatic executions.

Criminals' awareness of legal risks may be largely confined to the most conspicuous features of their immediate environments at the time a crime is contemplated. They are aware of the presence of a police officer, patrol car, or potential witness who might intervene or summon the police, but are not sensitive to, directly or indirectly, the overall likelihood of arrest in their areas. Likewise, they can recall punishments they themselves have experienced in the past, yet are not sensitive to the average severity of prison sentences or swiftness of punishment prevailing in their areas.

In light of the present study's evidence of even worse reality-perception correlations among arrestees than among nonarrestees, the data support the conclusion that neither news media information, nor personal experiences of the actor and his associates, nor any other sources of information in practice provide an even minimally adequate foundation for forming accurate perceptions of punishment levels.

Thus, it may be useful to view prospective offenders' responses to punishment levels as characterized by a severely constricted rationality. While many people are capable of weighing perceived risks and rewards when deciding whether to do crime, they typically possess so little accurate information about key risks and rewards that this capacity for rational decision-making remains to a great extent inoperative.

These findings suggest that conventional efforts to increase general deterrent effects beyond their current level may be so ineffective that policymakers should consider more productive alternatives to deterrence. Punishment-generating activities will, of course, be continued regardless of the evidence bearing on general deterrence, either for the sake of justice and retribution, or for the sake of crime control via incapacitation, the treatment associated with apprehension and conviction, and whatever continuing, though perhaps hard to increase, general deterrent effects that punishment produces.

Other alternatives to deterrence-based crime control, however, could be more seriously explored, such as generating a larger supply of stable, well-paying jobs in high-crime areas, and delivering job training, daycare, and health services to enable more young people to enter the job market, hold on to jobs, and form and maintain stable families, so as to reduce crime among members of the next generation.

ACKNOWLEDGMENTS

This research was supported by a grant from the Charles E. Culpepper Foundation. The author wishes to gratefully acknowledge Professors Brion Sever and Marc Gertz for their valued contributions to this research.

REFERENCES

Akers, Ronald L. 1973. *Deviant Behavior: A Social Learning Approach.* Belmont, CA: Wadsworth.

Beccaria, Cesare. [1764] 1963. *On Crimes and Punishments*. Translated by Henry Paolucci. Indianapolis: Bobbs-Merrill.

Becker, Gary S. 1968. "Crime and Punishment: An Economic Approach." *Journal of Political Economy* 76:169–217.

Cohen, Larry. 1978. "Sanction Threats and Violation Behavior: An Inquiry into Perceptual Variation." Pp. 84–99 in *Quantitative Studies in Criminology*, edited by Charles Wellford. Beverly Hills, CA: Sage.

Cornish, Derek B. and Ronald V. Clarke (Eds.). 1986. *The Reasoning Criminal*. New York: Springer-Verlag.

Ehrlich, Isaac. 1973. "Participation in Illegitimate Activities." *Journal of Political Economy* 81:521–65.

Erickson, Maynard L. and Jack P. Gibbs. 1978. "Objective and Perceptual Properties of Legal Punishment and the Deterrence Doctrine." *Social Problems* 25:253–64.

Garofalo, James. 1981. "Crime and the Mass Media." *Journal of Research in Crime and Delinquency* 18:319–50.

Gibbs, Jack. 1975. *Crime, Punishment, and Deterrence*. New York: Elsevier.

Hindelang, Michael J., Michael R. Gottfredson, and James Garofalo. 1978. *Victims of Personal Crime*. Cambridge, MA: Ballinger.

Horney, Julie and Ineke Haen Marshall. 1992. "Risk Perceptions among Serious Offenders: The Role of Crime and Punishment." *Criminology* 30:575–92.

Jacob, Herbert. 1979. "Rationality and Criminality." *Social Science Quarterly* 59:584–85.

Jensen, Gary F. 1969. "Crime Doesn't Pay: Correlates of a Shared Misunderstanding." *Social Problems* 17:189–201.

Kahan, Dan M. 1999. "The Secret Ambition of Deterrence." *Harvard Law Review* 113:413–500.

Kennedy, David. 1997. "Pulling Levers: Getting Deterrence Right." *National Institute of Justice Journal* 236:2–8.

Marsh, H. L. 1989. "Newspaper Crime Coverage in the U.S., 1983–1988." *Criminal Justice Abstracts* 21:506–14.

Nagin, Daniel S. 1998. "Criminal Deterrence Research at the Outset of the Twenty-First Century." Pp. 1–42 in *Crime and Justice: A Review of Research*, Volume 23, edited by Michael Tonry. Chicago: University of Chicago Press.

Parker, Jerry and Harold G. Grasmick. 1979. "Linking Actual and Perceived Certainty of Punishment." *Criminology* 17:366–79.

Paternoster, Raymond. 1987. "The Deterrent Effect of the Perceived Certainty and Severity of Punishment: A Review of the Evidence and Issues." *Justice Quarterly* 4:173–217.

Paternoster, Raymond, Linda E. Saltzman, Gordon P. Waldo, and Theodore G. Chiricos. 1982. "Perceived Risk and Deterrence." *Journal of Criminal Law and Criminology* 73:1238–58.

———. 1985. "Assessments of Risk and Behavioral Experience: An Exploratory Study of Change." *Criminology* 23:417–36.

Phillips, David P. 1980. "The Deterrent Effect of Capital Punishment: New Evidence on an Old Controversy." *American Journal of Sociology* 86:139–48.

Richards, Pamela and Charles R. Tittle. 1981. "Gender and Perceived Chances of Arrest." *Social Forces* 59:1182–99.

Richards, Pamela and Charles R. Tittle. 1982. "Socioeconomic Status and Perceptions of Personal Arrest probabilities." *Criminology* 20:329–46.

Roberts, Julian V. 1992. "Public Opinion, Crime, and Criminal Justice." Pp. 99–180 in *Crime and Justice: A Review of Research,* Volume 16, edited by Michael Tonry. Chicago: University of Chicago Press.

Roshier, Bob. 1973. "The Selection of Crime News by the Press." Pp. 28–39 in *The Manufacture of News,* edited by Stanley Cohen and Jock Young. London: Constable.

Saltzman, Linda E., Raymond Paternoster, Gordon P. Waldo, and Theodore G. Chiricos. 1982. "Deterrent and Experiential Effects: The Problem of Causal Order in Perceptual Deterrence Research." *Journal of Research in Crime and Delinquency* 19:172–89.

Spelman, William. 1994. *Criminal Incapacitation.* New York: Plenum.

Stack, Steven. 1987. "Publicized Executions and Homicide, 1950–1980." *American Sociological Review* 52:532–40.

Tittle, Charles R. 1980. *Sanctions and Social Deviance: The Question of Deterrence.* New York: Praeger.

U.S. Department of Justice, Bureau of Justice Statistics. 1999a. *Presale Handgun Checks: The Brady Interim Period, 1994–98.* Washington, DC: U.S. Government Printing Office.

———. 1999b. National Judicial Reporting Program, 1996: *[United States]* [Computer file]. Compiled by U.S. Department of Commerce, Bureau of the Census. ICPSR ed. Ann Arbor, MI: Interuniversity Consortium for Political and Social Research [producer and distributor].

U.S. Department of Justice, Federal Bureau of Investigation. 2000. *Uniform Crime Reporting Data [United States]: County-level Detailed Arrest and Offense Data, 1998* [Computer file]. 2nd ICPSR ed. Ann Arbor, MI: Interuniversity Consortium for Political and Social Research [producer and distributor].

Vold, George B., Thomas J. Bernard, and Jeffrey B. Snipes. 2002. *Theoretical Criminology,* 5th ed. New York: Oxford.

Zimring, Franklin E., and Hawkins, Gordon J. 1973. *Deterrence: The Legal Threat in Crime Control.* Chicago: University of Chicago Press.

14

Tinkering with the Machinery of Death

The Failure of a Social Experiment

GORDON P. WALDO AND RAYMOND PATERNOSTER

From this day forward, I no longer shall tinker with the machinery of death. . . . I feel morally and intellectually obligated to concede that the death penalty experiment has failed.

—Justice Harry Blackmun (*Callins v. Collins* 1994)

INTRODUCTION

It seems apparent that the machinery of death is broken, as well as the promises of those who said they were "fixing it."[1] Despite well-intentioned tinkering in an attempt to patch some cracks, it appears the cracks are larger and more numerous than previously believed, and the capital punishment system may be broken beyond any hope of repair. Good intentions do not always produce positive consequences,[2] and this clearly applies to efforts at criminal justice reform, and the death penalty in particular. The evidence suggests that the time may have come to accept Justice Blackmun's conclusion that the death penalty experiment has failed, and follow his lead by tinkering no more with the machinery of death (ibid.).

Evidence of a broken system comes from many sources. In recent years, for example, higher state and federal courts of appeal have reversed the majority of death penalty cases sentenced by trial courts (Liebman, Fagan, and West 2001). This, by itself, has suggested that something is seriously wrong with the system, and is one factor that lead George Ryan, Republican governor of Illinois, a death penalty supporter, to place a moratorium on the use of the death penalty in Illinois until a commission appointed to examine the evidence could arrive at conclusions about the nature and scope of the problem and make recommendations for fixing the system once again.[3] When the moratorium and special commission were announced Governor Ryan said, "I cannot support a system which, in its administration, has proven so fraught with error, and has come so close to the ultimate nightmare, the state's taking of an innocent life" (Taylor 2000). Parris Glendening, Democratic Governor of Maryland, who had earlier commissioned a study on the use of the death penalty in Maryland, has also recently declared a moratorium on the death penalty while awaiting the results of the study. In announcing the moratorium, Governor Glendening, who has supported the death penalty, stated, "It is imperative that I, as well as our citizens, have complete confidence that the legal process involved in capital cases is fair and impartial" (Sandon 2002).

Additionally, all of the cases involving people on death row who have been exonerated recently by incontrovertible DNA evidence have raised doubts even in the minds of many death penalty supporters.[4] While rightly concerned about the cases that have been cleared by DNA evidence, it has also become apparent that these cases only represent the tip of the iceberg. DNA evidence is available for testing in only a small portion of death row cases, and in some states it is still difficult to have this testing done. Other than being able to test for DNA, there are no other characteristics that would suggest that the DNA-exonerated cases are any more likely to be innocent than all of the other cases on death row, with the possible exception of simply "blind luck."

If it is assumed that the same proportion of people on death row are innocent when DNA evidence is not available as was found in cases where it is, this would suggest that there are a lot of innocent people still on death row, and probably many others who already have been executed. Unfortunately, for those cases where DNA evidence is not available it is not known which of these people are innocent, and it is not yet known how to prove or disprove their innocence with the same level of confidence provided by DNA testing. It can be assumed, however, at a high level of probability, that an alarming proportion of these death row inmates is very likely to be innocent. Some have estimated it to be as low as 1 percent (69 out of 6,000),[5] others have said 14 percent (1 out of 7) ("Death Penalty" 1998), and still others have suggested it may be as high as 33 percent, or even more, based on the findings from several different types of DNA tests.[6] The exact number of innocent people executed, or the percentage they make up of the total, can never be known with any degree of certainty, but it is clearly a significant number, and likely to be much higher than proponents of the death penalty have yet to acknowledge.

It is also becoming more readily apparent that many sources of evidence that were previously accepted as incontrovertible have more potential sources of error than might have been considered conceivable in the past.

A suspect's signed confession, once considered sacrosanct, is now known to be "suspect" in numerous instances even when given in a completely voluntary and noncoerced manner. Eyewitness testimony, once considered irrefutable by some, has lost credibility and is now considered one of the weaker forms of evidence.[7] "Jailhouse witnesses" who trade favors for testimony with prosecutors is being viewed with more and more suspicion. In a similar vein, information provided by law enforcement "snitches" on the street, or by accomplices in the crime being investigated, is being viewed as more and more problematic, yet witnesses such as these continue to be used quite frequently by prosecutors in capital cases.[8]

Most problematic, however, at least for purposes of this chapter, are actions or inactions by members of the criminal justice system who are involved in a case. This chapter is specifically concerned with the behavior of defense attorneys who are representing defendants in capital cases, and the quality of that representation. It is also concerned with the behavior of law enforcement officers and prosecutors who are representing the state, and the behavior of judges who are supposed to assure that justice is being done. Because the behavior of police, prosecutors, and judges overlaps and intermingles at times, their roles will be discussed in the same general context. Stuart Taylor captures the major concern of this chapter very well in a recent article:

> In case after case, death row prisoners . . . have been cleared by DNA or other new evidence amid revelations of gross prosecutorial misconduct, shockingly incompetent defense-lawyering, egregious judicial errors, and even use of torture by police to force confessions. (Taylor 2000)

TINKERING WITH THE MACHINERY OF DEATH— *FURMAN v. GEORGIA*

In its 1972 decision *Furman v. Georgia,* the United States Supreme Court vacated the death sentences of two Georgia inmates and one from Texas. The impact of *Furman,* however, extended beyond these two states in that it implicitly called into question the administration of the death penalty in all other states. The Georgia and Texas statutes were not declared unconstitutional because capital punishment itself was thought to be cruel and unusual punishment. Rather, with a very divided voice, the Court held that while capital punishment was not *per se* cruel and unusual, the manner in which the death penalty was administered resulted in a product that was unconstitutional.[9] More specifically, these state statutes gave judges and juries too little guidance or direction in making the decision as to which convicted defendants should live and which should be put to death. This created an unacceptable risk that the death penalty was "wantonly and freakishly imposed" (*Furman v. Georgia* 1972:310). The constitutionally impermissible product was sentences of death wherein "there is no meaningful basis for distinguishing the few cases in which it is imposed from the many cases in which it is not" (ibid.:313).

Of course, the *Furman* decision did not foretell the abolition of capital punishment in the United States. On the contrary, it simply provided the motivation for states to "tinker" with their capital statutes to bring them in line with the requirements suggested by the Court's decision. *Furman* did make it clear that if they wanted their statutes to pass constitutional muster, state legislatures would have to squarely address the issue of unguided sentencing discretion in capital cases, even if at the same time it suggested no specific remedy.[10] State legislatures immediately went to work to draft new death penalty statutes that they thought would comply with the requirements of *Furman*. Attempts to tinker with or reform state capital statutes took one of two general forms. Guided discretion capital statutes sought to remedy the defect of jury discretion by identifying factors that the sentencing body should explicitly consider before imposing sentence in capital cases. The path to statutory reform these statutes took, then, was to channel or direct the discretion of the judge or jury in a capital case.[11] Mandatory statutes sought to eliminate judge or jury sentencing discretion by narrowly defining new forms of capital murder and making a sentence of death mandatory upon conviction of these crimes.[12]

In a series of decisions that were handed down in July 1976,[13] the U.S. Supreme Court struck down mandatory statutes as unconstitutional, but upheld the constitutionality of guided discretion capital statutes. Mandatory statutes were constitutionally infirm because they failed to allow the sentencing body to consider information about the unique culpability of capital defendants. In essence, mandatory statutes did not allow the individualization of death sentences and instead treated "all persons convicted of a designated offense not as uniquely individual human beings, but as members of a faceless, undifferentiated mass to be subjected to the blind infliction of the penalty of death" (*Woodson v. North Carolina* 1976:304). Guided discretion statutes, however, were accepted by a majority of the Court because they possessed three features that made it unlikely that the arbitrary and capricious death sentences that were condemned by *Furman* would be repeated: (1) bifurcated trials, (2) statutorily enumerated aggravating and/or mitigating factors that focused and guided the attention of the sentencing body, and (3) appellate review of death sentences for consistency and fairness. Writing for the Court that approved Georgia's guided discretion statute, Justice Stewart observed that the lesson of *Furman* was that "where discretion is afforded a sentencing body on a matter so grave as the determination of whether a human life should be taken or spared, that discretion must be suitably directed and limited so as to minimize the risk of wholly arbitrary and capricious action." The new Georgia statute proposed legal reforms that meaningfully narrowed those subject to the penalty of death such that "no longer can a jury wantonly and freakishly impose the death sentence" (*Gregg v. Georgia* 1976:206–7).

The capital punishment decisions of the U.S. Supreme Court in July 1976 did a number of things, three of which are important for our current concerns. First, it affirmed *Furman*'s "death is different" doctrine,[14] which stated that because the penalty of death is qualitatively different than any other penalty "there is a corresponding difference in the need for reliability in the determination that death is the appropriate punishment in a specific case" (*Woodson v. North Carolina* 1976:305). In other words, because death is the ultimate sanction in the quiver of the state (because mistakes cannot be rectified, because death is a complete repudiation of the person as a member of the human community), we must ensure that it is *reliably* imposed. Reliably in this case means that the process of administering capital punishment must effectively cull out the most deserving and morally blameworthy offenders while sparing less culpable others. This in turn means that there must be legal mechanisms or legal machinery in place that will ensure that there is a "meaningful" difference between those who live and those sentenced to die.[15]

A second important thing achieved by the 1976 death cases was that they essentially announced that, at least for the time being, the U.S. Supreme Court would get into the death penalty business. Normally criminal procedure in state trials is a matter for states to decide. However, the Court in this instance was to take a proactive stance in imposing on the states what they thought states needed to do in order to have a capital statute that was constitutional at the federal level. In other words, it was the U.S. Supreme Court that would both develop and impose upon the states the *legal machinery* it thought would most likely enhance the reliability of death sentences.

The Court in its 1976 cases first laid down the content of this legal machinery in capital cases. In *Gregg* and its progeny, the Court began the creation of this "machinery of death" in its holding that bifurcated trials, focusing and guiding the discretion of the sentencing body to appropriate aggravating and mitigating factors, and the opportunity to examine the effectiveness of these legal reforms via direct and automatic appellate review held promise of remedying the defects identified by *Furman*. While the *Gregg* Court was clear that the three procedural reforms put in place by its decision (bifurcated trials, aggravating and mitigating factors, and appellate review) were not the only safeguards that would be acceptable under *Furman*, it was equally clear that some new legal machinery needed to be in place to enhance the reliability of state death penalty systems.

Third, while the Court had no direct evidence that the reforms of state death penalty procedures that it began to implement starting with *Gregg* would drastically reduce or eliminate arbitrary and capricious death sentences, it did make the pronouncement that such procedural reforms *promise* to remedy such defects. The Court, in other words, held out the hope that this legal machinery would make for more reliable capital sentencing. Writing for the plurality, Justice Stewart in *Gregg* wrote that:

> Georgia's new sentencing procedures require as a prerequisite to the imposition of the death penalty, specific jury findings concerning the circumstances of the crime or the character of the defendant. Moreover, to guard further against a situation comparable to that presented in *Furman*, the Supreme Court of Georgia compares each death sentence with the sentences imposed on similarly situated defendants to ensure that the sentence of death in a particular case is not disproportionate. *On their face*, these procedures seem to satisfy the concerns of *Furman*. No longer should there be "no meaningful basis for distinguishing the few cases in which [the death penalty] is imposed from the many cases in which it is not." (*Gregg v. Georgia* 1976:198; emphasis added)

In this passage, Justice Stewart is referring to the fact that in submitting its capital statute to constitutional review, the state of Georgia provided no information that the new statute was performing better than the old one condemned by *Furman*.[16]

Everyone (except, of course, the defendant in *Gregg*)[17] agreed that the machinery of death that was initiated by the *Gregg* Court simply held out the promise that "no longer can a jury wantonly and freakishly impose the death sentence" (ibid.:206–7).

Beginning in 1976, the Supreme Court of the United States began to actively impose legal machinery on state and federal trial courts with the expectation and promise that such machinery would result in more reliable death sentences. The *Gregg* decision, however, simply marked the beginning of its effort to construct and impose a legal machinery for death sentences. In subsequent cases it was to install other components of this machinery, such as what kind of evidence the sentencing body could and should hear in a capital case,[18] the precise function of aggravating circumstances,[19] and the parameters of effective legal representation in capital cases (*Strickland v. Washington* 1984; *Murray v. Giarratano* 1989). Although the Court was also to make its mark in the more substantive area of trying to define for which class of crimes the penalty of death was appropriate,[20] the lion's share of its work was in the area of procedural reform of the death penalty—creating a legal machinery of death. With each new cog in this machinery in place, the Court maintained the belief and held out the hope that their efforts would produce reliable death sentences. This expectation is captured (though with wistful hindsight) by Justice Blackmun in his dissent on a denial for a writ of certiorari to the Court after this legal machinery had been in place for nearly two decades:

We hope, of course, that the defendant whose life is at risk will be represented by competent counsel—someone who is inspired by the awareness that a less than vigorous defense truly could have fatal consequences for the defendant. We hope that the attorney will investigate all aspects of the case, follow all evidentiary and procedural rules, and appear before a judge who is still committed to the protection of the defendant's rights—even now, as the prospect of meaningful judicial oversight has diminished. In the same vein, we hope that the prosecution, in urging the penalty of death, will have exercised its discretion wisely, free from bias, prejudice, or political motive, and will be humbled, rather than emboldened, by the awesome authority conferred by the State. (*Callins v. Collins* 1994:1141)

The point being made in this chapter, and the conclusion ultimately made by Justice Blackmun, is that the substantial machinery of death that was erected by the Court has failed to ensure that death sentences are fair and consistent.[21] In other words, the machinery of death has broken down; the death penalty experiment has failed. Moreover, the breakdown has been precipitated by failures in the very areas that Justice Blackmun wrote so hopefully about in the passage above in his dissent in *Callins v. Collins*. All too often, attorneys are not competent, energized, or inspired, and prosecutors and police frequently do not exercise their power and discretion with wisdom and impartiality. In the remainder of this chapter we intend to document the breakdown in this legal machinery by illustrating a few of the many instances where the primary actor for the defendant (defense counsel), and the primary actors for the state (police and prosecution) have fallen far short of the standard anticipated by Justice Blackmun.

THE FAILURE OF DEFENSE COUNSEL

Ever since *Powell v. Alabama* was decided in 1932, capital defendants in state trials have had the constitutional right to the assistance of counsel (*Powell v. Alabama* 1932).[22] The right to counsel may be the most important right any criminal suspect may have because counsel is the tool that secures other legal rights suspects enjoy. It is also critical because without competent counsel to raise and preserve contested issues of law at trial, they may not be reviewed by appellate or postconviction proceedings. The right of counsel is particularly critical for capital defendants for several additional reasons: (1) bifurcated capital trials are more complex than noncapital criminal trials, (2) defendants are at risk of losing their life should they lose, and (3) because of restrictions and limitations placed on the postconviction process, the state trial in a capital case has become the "main event" (*Wainwright v. Sykes* 1977).[23]

More than just the assistance of counsel, the U.S. Constitution requires that capital defendants are entitled to the *effective assistance* of counsel.[24] That is, the mere appointment or appearance of counsel in a capital case is not sufficient; counsel must provide adequate or effective legal assistance. Effective counsel is necessary in order to ensure the fundamental fairness of the criminal trial. What effective counsel does for the criminal defendant is to provide a strong counterweight to the case made by the prosecution. The defining characteristic of our adversarial system is that truth is best discovered when both sides have powerful champions, and that "partisan advocacy on both sides of a case will best promote the ultimate objective that the guilty be convicted and the innocent go free" (*Herring v. New York* 1975:862). The right to the effective assistance of counsel, then, is the right that defendants have counsel acting as their advocate, because only counsel as advocate can both present favorable evidence on behalf of the defendant and also seek to cast doubt on the prosecution's case. Ultimately, the principle of effective counsel "is the right of the accused to require the prosecution's case to survive the crucible of meaningful adversarial testing" (*United States v. Cronic* 1984). When this breaks down, the trial for the defendant with ineffective assistance of counsel becomes "a sacrifice of unarmed prisoners to gladiators" (*United States ex rel. Williams v. Twomey* 1975:640).

The provision of effective assistance of counsel is, then, a critical part of the legal machinery of capital punishment. In 1984, the U.S. Supreme Court in the case of *Strickland v. Washington* (1984:688) acknowledged this and set up a two-pronged test for the effective assistance of counsel. The first prong of the test is that a defendant must demonstrate that the performance of counsel was deficient under "prevailing professional norms" and that the attorney's conduct "fell below an objective standard of reasonableness" (ibid.:687). Moreover, the Court argued that it is *counsel* that must be given a strong presumption of reasonable performance, and that the burden of proof of ineffective counsel falls squarely on the shoulders of the defendant. The second prong of the *Strickland* test stated that even if the defendant could demonstrate that counsel's conduct fell below prevailing professional standards of competence, it must further be shown that the attorney's performance was so deficient that it prejudiced the outcome of the trial. In other words, the defendant is forced to demonstrate that the outcome of the trial would have been different had it not been for counsel's ineffective defense.

Critics of the *Strickland* decision have argued that its two-pronged test places a crippling burden on the defendant, and ensures that ineffective assistance of counsel claims are not provided adequate remedy.[25] Whatever the merits of that argument, there is ample evidence indicating that counsel in capital cases all too frequently does not provide the kind of vigorous "meaningful adversarial testing" of the evidence envisioned by the rulings of an earlier U.S. Supreme Court.[26] There is also ample evidence indicating that even in the face of an appalling lack of effort on the part of defense counsel the courts are reluctant to conclude that the performance was ineffective.

Although *Powell v. Alabama* promised defendants the effective assistance of counsel, they clearly are not entitled to their own legal "dream team." In the vast majority of capital cases in the United States, defendants are indigents, unable to hire their own lawyers, and must make do with counsel appointed by the state. In far too many instances, appointed counsels' performance has been abysmal. The evidence to substantiate this claim consists both of broad-based examinations of the role of counsel in capital cases, and case-specific anecdotal evidence that perhaps more vividly demonstrates the role played by incompetent defense counsel in the breakdown of the machinery of death. The examples that follow are by no means exhaustive, merely illustrative of the problem.

In 1985, Jesus Romero was convicted of raping and murdering a teenage girl in San Benito, Texas (*Romero v. Lynaugh* 1989:871, 875). Following his conviction for capital murder, Romero's trial entered the critical penalty phase during which the defendant's attorney, at least theoretically, mounts a vigorous argument to the jury in support of a sentence less than death. The penalty phase of a capital trial has been described as a kind of morality play in which the defense counsel brings as much evidence in mitigation of the offense as possible, by humanizing the defendant in such a way that the offense appears explicable, if not excusable.[27] In this effort, counsel attempts to strike a chord of compassion with the jury by arguing that the defendant's dysfunctional and destructive past has deformed a normal human being. The "humanization" of the just-convicted capital murderer requires considerable time and effort on the part of defense counsel. Typically the defense must investigate the defendant's immediate family, friends, employers, children, ministers, and any relevant expert witnesses (psychiatrists, psychologists, social workers) who would assist in the construction of the defendant as a redeemable human being, in spite of an obviously malignant act.

Jesus Romero's attorney appeared to put little time and effort into his penalty phase testimony. He offered only the following observation to the jury in pleading for his client's life:

Defense Counsel: Ladies and Gentlemen, I appreciate the time you took deliberating and the thought you put into this. I'm going to be extremely brief. I have a reputation for not being brief. Jesse, stand up. Jesse?
Defendant: Sir?
Defense Counsel: Stand up.
[defendant Jesus Romero rises]

Defense Counsel:	You are an extremely intelligent jury. You've got that man's life in your hands. You can take it or not. That's all I have to say.

Jesus Romero's court-appointed defense counsel employed fewer than one hundred words in his meager attempt to try to convince the jury to save his client's life. He called no witnesses, he provided no evidence in mitigation of the penalty of death other than the few words he spoke, and he offered no resistance to the prosecution's argument that Romero should be sentenced to death for his grisly deed. It should not be too surprising to learn that the jury sentenced Jesus Romero to death. It might, however, be surprising to learn that counsel's performance in the Romero case was deemed "effective" according to the standard established in *Strickland.* In determining that the attorney's performance satisfied *Strickland,* the U.S. Court of Appeals for the Fifth Circuit characterized it as a "dramatic ploy," and offered their own observation that had the jury returned a life sentence, the lawyer's acts might have been perceived as "a brilliant move." Jesus Romero was executed by the state of Texas on May 20, 1992, and his lawyer was later suspended from his law practice for other reasons.

Paradoxically, Jesus Romero was lucky in at least one respect. Although arguably incompetent, unprepared, and ineffective, at least his lawyer was awake! The same could not be said for the lawyer for Carl Johnson, another Texas convicted murderer. During his state trial in 1979 for armed robbery and murder, Johnson had two court-appointed lawyers to represent him. One of these lawyers had been out of law school for less than a year and had no experience in capital cases, the other, Joe Frank Cannon, had tried many capital cases—almost all of them unsuccessful. In Johnson's case, Cannon was sound asleep during portions of the jury selection process and the trial itself (Dow 1996). Johnson was executed in 1995 after appeal's courts rejected his claim of ineffective assistance of counsel. Disturbingly, this was not the first time Cannon had fallen asleep during a capital trial. While representing another Texas capital offender, Calvin Burdine, Cannon was caught dozing "in particular during the guilt-innocence phase when the State's solo prosecutor was questioning witnesses and presenting evidence" (*Ex parte Burdine* 1995:456–57). The clerk of the court testified at a later hearing that Cannon "fell asleep and was asleep for long periods of time during the questioning of witnesses" (ibid.*:457).*[28] Burdine's trial lasted only thirteen hours, after which he was sentenced to death. Cannon's entire presentation to the jury at the penalty phase of the case consisted of the following (ibid.).

Attorney Cannon:	Calvin, do want to take the stand and plead for your life?
Calvin Burdine:	No, sir, they didn't listen to me the first time, I don't see . . .

The Court: What says the Defense, gentlemen?
Attorney Cannon: We close, your honor.

The Texas Court of Criminal Appeals affirmed Burdine's death sentence.[29]

A third Texas capital defendant, George McFarland, also was the recipient of a sleeping lawyer. John Benn spent only four hours preparing for the trial, did not examine the crime scene, failed to interview a single witness, issued no subpoenas, filed no motions, and visited his client only twice. According to the *Houston Chronicle,* Benn spent most of the trial in deep sleep, with his mouth falling open, occasionally snapping his head and sitting upright (Makeig 1992:A35). When the trial court judge asked Benn if he truly had been sleeping during the capital murder trial, the seventy-two-year old lawyer answered, "It's boring." Judge Doug Shaver dismissed the relevance of the sleeping lawyer, noting that "the Constitution says everyone's entitled to the attorney of their choice. The Constitution doesn't say the lawyer has to be awake." The Texas Court of Criminal Appeals determined that Benn's performance satisfied the demands of *Strickland.* In fact the court argued that Benn's sleeping might have been a strategic decision, to get sympathy from the jury (*McFarland v. State* 1996: 500–5).

In a Georgia murder case, a court-appointed defense lawyer presented virtually no mitigating evidence during the penalty phase of the trial. The attorney's sole reference to his client for the jury's behalf was as follows:

> You have got a little ole nigger man over there that doesn't weigh over 135 pounds. He is poor and he is broke. He's got an appointed lawyer. . . . He is ignorant. I will venture to say that he has an IQ of not over 80. (*State v. Dungee* 1986:39)

Actually, had defense counsel bothered to investigate the case it would have discovered that the defendant was not merely "ignorant," but mentally retarded, with an estimated IQ of 68. As a result of his subnormal intelligence he was rejected from the military and unable to perform either in school or the most menial of jobs. This is precisely the kind of mitigating evidence that should be presented to a jury during the penalty phase of a capital trial. The jury sentenced the defendant to death in the absence of this critical evidence. Of course, this is not to say that the defendant would have been sentenced to life had the jury had such information; however, the adversarial system would seem to require that the jury be given the opportunity to hear all evidence that would argue in the defendant's favor before rendering its decision.

Clearly, Georgia murder defendant James Messer's attorney did not perform in such a manner as "to require the prosecution's case to survive the crucible of meaningful adversarial testing." Messer's court appointed attorney, John Sawhill, gave no opening statement at the guilt phase of the trial, made no objections, and cross-examined the prosecution's witnesses with obvious reluctance. In fact, he seemed to openly join the prosecution's own side when he acknowledged his opinion to the jury that Messer was guilty of committing an egregious act that likely deserved the death penalty! During his closing argument at the guilt/innocence phase of the Messer's trial for the kidnapping and murder of a child, Sawhill told jury:

> As to what the evidence has been I don't contend what the evidence is, I haven't said anything about it. I would be no less honest with each and every one of you if I tried to tell you the evidence said something other than what [the prosecutor] indicates occurred on that day so I am not going to. . . .I'm a parent too and I can't explain or give you some easy explanation for why so I won't try. . . . I dare say you've got five hundred years of common sense and experience and there is not one bit . . . not one bit that's seen anything like this before and I pray to God that none of you or myself . . . will ever see anything like this again. (*Messer v. Kemp* 1985:1089)

In "arguing" to the jury during the penalty phase, Sawhill said:

> I dare say, and it has been suggested to me . . . , that I ought to argue to this jury to leave him alive is a more cruel punishment because he's got to live with it, so I don't know what to say to you. I really don't. . . . [The decision you have to make] is an awesome responsibility and I dare say I would rather be over here than in y'all's seats, because as a parent under these circumstances. (ibid.:1097)

It is readily apparent from this "defense" mounted by counsel that the adversarial process fundamentally broke down with defense counsel virtually joining the prosecution against the defendant. The jury apparently agreed with defense counsel's assessment of his defendant's character and sentenced him to death. After reviewing the record, the Georgia Court of Appeals found no deficiency in counsel's performance. Messer was later executed by the state of Georgia.

Harris County (Houston), Texas, attorney Ronald Mock is an old hand in trying capital cases. He has frequently been the court-appointed counsel in cases involving poor defendants. He has represented clients in nineteen capital cases, in sixteen of those the defendant was sentenced to death, four of which have already have been executed while the others await their turn on Texas's death row. Attorney Mock has been disciplined five times by the state bar, and he has served jail time after being held in contempt of court for his mishandling of previous criminal cases under his charge. One of Mock's clients was Gary Graham, executed by Texas on June 22, 2000. The Graham case is an excellent example of defense counsel not acting as a powerful champion or partisan advocate for their client. Graham was convicted primarily on the testimony of one eyewitness, who claimed to be able to accurately identify him even though she saw the assailant's face for only a few seconds, at night, through her car windshield, from a distance of thirty to forty feet. No physical evidence linked Graham to the crime, the pistol found on him was found by ballistics tests not to be the one that killed the victim, and two other eyewitnesses claimed that they say saw the actual killer and it was not Gary Graham. They were never called by the defense to testify, and Ronald Mock acknowledged that he did virtually no investigation of the case (Rimer and Bonner 2000).[30] In fact, Mock's own investigator who assisted in the case testified that he and Mock spent little time on the case because they believed that Graham was guilty (*Graham v. Johnson* 1999:762, 767).

The difference between having and not having a dedicated defense attorney can be vividly seen in the case of Gary Nelson (Bright 1994). A court-appointed lawyer who had never before tried a capital case represented Nelson. The prosecution's case relied entirely on circumstantial evidence and included questionable scientific evidence from the state's expert witness who testified that a hair found on the victim's body could have come from Nelson. Nelson's lawyer was not provided funds for his own investigator and did not seek any funds for his own expert witnesses to independently verify the state's claim. The lawyer provided virtually little in the way of a defense, and his closing argument to the jury was only 255 words long. He was later disbarred for reasons unrelated to his defense of Nelson. Through fortuitous circumstances, or just dumb luck, Nelson was represented in his postconviction proceedings by *pro bono* lawyers willing and able to spend their own money. Through their own investigation of the case, they were able to determine that the hair on the victim's body, which was linked to Nelson by the prosecution's expert witness, lacked sufficient characteristics to be compared to Nelson, a fact confirmed by the FBI lab. Because of this extensive work, which threw considerable doubt on the state's case, Nelson was released from prison, but not before he had served eleven years on Georgia's death row (ibid.).

These cases provide individual examples of the ineffectiveness of many lawyers for capital offenders. It may be argued, however, that these cases, though horrific, are exceptions to the rule. The rule being, that lawyers for defendants on trial for their life, court-appointed or not, are generally quite effective, competent, and professional. What may put the lie to this assumption, however, is evidence of a more general sort that indicates that lawyers in death cases are not the "cream" of their profession. The *National Law Journal* (1990) reported on a six-month investigation of the lawyers in capital cases in six southern states. These states were selected because they were responsible for the execution of nearly 80 percent of the death row prisoners put to death since 1977.

This study found that lawyers in these states who represented defendants charged with capital crimes were substantially more likely to have

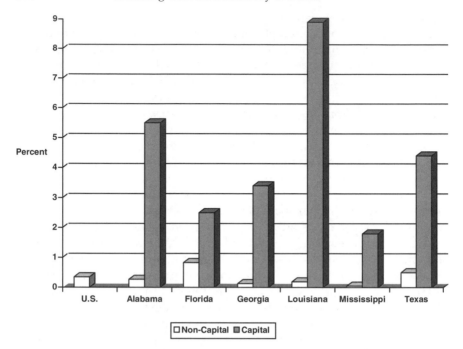

Figure 14.1.   Sanctioning rates for capital and noncapital lawyers. *Source:* National
Law Journal (1990:44).

been disbarred, suspended, or otherwise professionally disciplined (public reprimand, resignation, probation, fine, restitution, and costs) than
lawyers in their state who had not handled a capital case. Figure 14.1 represents these data. It shows that for the nation as a whole the rate at which
lawyers are disciplined is 0.35 percent, or less than one-half of one percent.
In other words, out of every 1,000 practicing attorneys in the United States,
about 3.5 have experienced some type of professional disciplinary sanction, such as a suspension, disbarment, or other disciplinary action. Figure
14.1 reports that for the six southern states with a majority of the executions in the United States, the disbarment rate for lawyers in the state who
have not handled a capital case is 0.27 percent in Alabama, 0.83 percent in
Florida, 0.13 percent in Georgia, 0.19 percent in Louisiana, 0.05 percent in
Mississippi, and 0.50 percent in Texas. These state-level sanctioning rates
for noncapital lawyers are not substantially different from the sanctioning
rate for U.S. lawyers in general.
     When one compares these figures to the sanctioning rate for lawyers
who handle capital cases in the state, however, a different picture emerges.
Lawyers in Florida who handle death penalty cases are three times more
likely to have been disciplined (2.5 vs. 0.83 percent) than lawyers who do

not handle death penalty cases. In Texas, death penalty lawyers are almost nine times more likely to have been professionally sanctioned than lawyers who do not try death cases (4.4 vs. 0.50 percent). In Georgia they are twenty-six times more likely (3.4 vs. 0.13 percent), and in Alabama, lawyers who handle death penalty cases are approximately twenty-seven times more likely to have received some professional sanction than non-death penalty lawyers (5.5 vs. 0.27 percent). In Mississippi death penalty lawyers are thirty-six times more likely to have been disciplined than non-death penalty lawyers (1.8 vs. 0.05 percent), and in Louisiana they are almost 47 times more likely (8.9 vs. 0.19 percent) to have been sanctioned. While it is true that the sanctions imposed on these lawyers were in many cases unrelated to their defense of a capital defendant, the fact that lawyers who are more likely to act as attorneys in death penalty cases are disciplined at a rate substantially higher than other lawyers in their state is some clear indication of the generally poor representation that most defendants who are on trial for their life are likely to receive (*National Law Journal* 1990).

Reporters for the *Chicago Tribune* recently conducted an investigation of the quality of representation in death penalty cases in Texas, the state that has executed more people than any other (Mills, Armstrong, and Holt 2000). They examined all 131 executions that occurred while George W. Bush was governor of Texas. They reported that in forty cases (30 percent) defense counsel presented either no evidence at all in mitigation, or only one witness during the trial's crucial penalty phase. As suggested earlier, this is particularly critical because it is at the penalty phase where the defense has the opportunity to present virtually any evidence to the court that would argue for a life rather than a death sentence. In one-third of the cases the defendant was represented by an attorney who had been or was later disbarred, suspended from practice, or professionally disciplined in another way. This was recently corroborated by Liebman and his colleagues (2001, 2002:414) who found that about 40 percent of the reversals in state postconviction hearings and between 25 ands 35 percent of those reversed in federal habeas proceedings are due to the incompetent lawyers of capital defendants.

POLICE, PROSECUTOR, AND JUDICIAL MISCONDUCT

Law enforcement officers, prosecutors, and judges are given the simultaneous responsibilities of protecting society from dangerous criminal offenders while also protecting the rights of individuals accused of committing a crime. An elaborate set of procedural laws is in place that has evolved in order to accomplish these two conflicting goals.[31] When these procedures are followed to the letter by the most conscientious and honest public servants, mistakes will still be made and innocent defendants will be found guilty and sent to death row. However, the concern here is not with unavoidable errors that even the most conscientious public servant or citizen might commit, but rather with egregious avoidable errors and overt misconduct and law violations that dramatically increase the probability of an innocent person being executed. Moreover, this situation exists because the procedural laws to protect the rights of the accused were violated by the very people charged with upholding them. To illustrate this point in very concrete terms, the case of Frank Lee Smith is presented here in considerable detail, not because it is the most blatant example of misconduct, but because it is recent, his innocence was clearly established, and to one degree or another all of the components of the system must share the blame for failing to protect his rights and seeing that justice was done, even after his death.

The Case of Frank Lee Smith

The state of Florida cheated Frank Lee Smith, and Frank Lee Smith in turn cheated the state of Florida. Eight-year-old Shandra Whitehead was brutally raped, sodomized, and strangled with her pajama bottoms as she was sleeping at home in her bed on April 14, 1985. Although there was no physical evidence linking him to the crime, no eyewitness who saw him at the scene, and he never made a confession, Frank Lee Smith received the death penalty.[32]

During fourteen years on death row Smith consistently proclaimed his innocence, at least as well as an incoherent, mentally ill, impoverished, brain-damaged person could do. His attorneys initiated numerous appeals, the governor signed his death warrant, new evidence concerning another suspect was discovered, and the state's star witness recanted her testimony. Nevertheless, the police, prosecutors, and judges involved in the case remained adamant that the process followed by the criminal justice system leading to Smith's conviction, as well as in the subsequent hearings, and the original sentence received were appropriate, justified by the evidence, and did not require modification.

Nonetheless, Frank Lee Smith became one of the lucky few death row inmates who were eventually cleared of the crime for which they were on death row. Based on DNA evidence reluctantly tested by the state, Frank Lee Smith was exonerated of the crime on December 14, 2000, fifteen years and eight months after the crime was committed and two years after his defense attorney made the original request for DNA testing to be conducted. Unfortunately, it was also eleven months after Frank Lee Smith had died on death row from pancreatic cancer. He was unlucky in the timing, but nevertheless Frank Lee Smith was lucky still in that most inmates who die on death row do not have the exoneration process continue after their death.[33]

How could this miscarriage of justice have happened? Some defense attorneys say, "It happens all the time" (Grimm 2001a), while an assistant state attorney said "It's a nightmare. . . . I was sure of his guilt" (De Vise 2001), and the person most responsible for the conviction, Detective Richard Scheff, could only say "It's like an epiphany" (ibid.).

In the end, Frank Lee Smith was sent to death row primarily because of two factors: an incriminating statement he supposedly made during the initial interrogation and a mistaken eyewitness identification (later recanted) made by a teenage neighbor who saw someone in the neighborhood at the approximate time of the crime.[34] Most importantly, however, the lead detective in the case took these two pieces of information and converted them into evidence that led to a death sentence for an innocent man.

Conducting an apparently routine but fruitless interrogation, Detective Scheff told the defendant a lie in an attempt to get him to incriminate himself, a questionable interrogation tactic to say the least. Scheff told Smith that Shandra's brother had seen the crime and could identify the killer although in fact the brother slept through the entire crime and had not been able to provide the police with any useful information. Although there was no video or audio recording of the interrogation, Scheff's handwritten notes say that Smith said, "No way that kid could've seen me, it was too dark" (ibid.). Although everyone else who had talked with Frank Lee Smith said he seldom made a coherent statement and it was difficult to understand and interpret what he was saying because of his brain damage and mental illness, this handwritten note by Detective Scheff containing the "quote" from Smith was treated like a confession of guilt and used by the prosecutor accordingly, despite the fact that Smith denied he ever made the statement (Bikel 2002).

Moreover, the eyewitness identifications were questionable from the start. Dorothy McGriff, Shandra's mother, came home from work around midnight and found a man lurking around her home and chased him away with a sling blade. She identified Smith from a photo and later in the courtroom, but upon cross-examination said she had not seen the intruder's face, only the back of his shoulders as he ran from the scene in the dark (De Vise 2001). Gerald Davis, a nineteen-year-old who lived in the neighborhood said "A scruffy man had propositioned him on the street nearby" (De Vise 2001). But the "star" witness was nineteen-year-old Chiquita Lowe, "who said a 'delirious' man had stopped her car near the crime scene and asked for 50 cents" (ibid.). Lowe and Davis provided a description that led to a composite drawing of a scraggly-haired, delirious black man with a droopy eye, a pockmarked face, and no eyeglasses (Bikel 2002; De Vise 2001). The only physical resemblance between Frank Lee Smith and the witnesses' descriptions and the composite drawing by the police artist was that he was black! Moreover, Smith had 20-400 vision and was dependent on his "coke-bottle-thick glasses" for normal daily functioning and was never seen without them (De Vise 2001).

Chiquita Lowe acknowledges now that when she appeared in court she had many doubts. "When I went into the courtroom and seen [Smith], he was too skinny, too tall, and he did not have the droopy eye" (Bikel 2002). Nevertheless, she identified Frank Lee Smith as the man who had approached her car.[35] She later said she was "pressured by my family, people that's in my neighborhood, and the police officer, they kept telling me that I'm the only one that seen that man that night" (ibid.).

Interestingly, however, there was someone else in the neighborhood, Eddie Lee Mosely, who fit the description and the composite photo perfectly. Eddie Lee Mosely was well-known to law enforcement in south Florida, had been in and out of prison, was a suspect in many rape and murder cases, and was living in the neighborhood at the time of the crime. Most importantly, and unfortunately for Frank Lee Smith, Mosley was the cousin of Dorothy McGriff (mother of Shandra Whitehead), who denied that he was the man she had chased from her yard on the night of the murder, although she only saw this intruder from the rear and in the dark.

After a death warrant was signed for Frank Lee Smith in 1989, an investigator for his defense team went through old files on the case and found the photo of Mosely and realized immediately that it matched the composite photo. Chiquita Lowe was apparently shocked and relieved to see the photo and she stated in an affidavit, "When I looked at the picture, everything came back to me. . . . I swear on my mother's grave that the man in the photo is the man I saw on the street the night when the little girl was raped and killed" (De Vise 2001). On national television she told Frontline reporters, "I seen the man like I seen him yesterday, I seen the droopy eye, I see the look on his face and it just shook me up" (Bikel 2002).

Given Lowe's recantation, the Florida Supreme Court stopped the pending execution and immediately ordered a new hearing to examine Lowe's claims (De Vise 2001). At the hearing in 1991, Detective Scheff threw a curve at the defense saying that he had shown Mosley's photo to all three eyewitnesses before the trial and none of them had identified Mosley (ibid.). However, an important inconsistency in his testimony suggested he was not telling the truth.

Scheff's new testimony contradicted his words at the trial, when he said he had not shown Mosley's picture to anyone. His handwritten notes did not mention a Mosley picture. Even Dimitrouleas, currently a Federal judge, but the prosecutor at Smith's trial, disputes Scheff's account by his statement, "I have no recollection of my ever seeing a photo lineup containing Eddie Lee Mosley" (ibid.).

Unfortunately for Frank Lee Smith, and the United States legal system, Broward Circuit Judge Robert Tyson accepted Scheff's testimony and rejected Lowe's recantation as "not to be credible." Tyson went on to say in his court order following the hearing, "Additionally, this court finds absolutely no credible evidence to support the defendant's claim that it was Eddie Lee Mosley who committed the murder of Shandra Whitehead" (ibid.). On December 14, 2000, the same DNA testing process that exonerated Frank Lee Smith indicated that the person who had brutally raped, sodomized, and murdered Shandra Whitehead was none other than Eddie Lee Mosely!

But even after the DNA evidence had exonerated him, the prosecution still did not rest its case against Frank Lee Smith. Lawrence Mirman, an assistant state attorney from an adjacent county was appointed to investigate Scheff's inconsistent testimony in the case to determine if there was sufficient evidence to prosecute Scheff. After determining that there was insufficient evidence to prosecute Scheff, Mirman then proceeded to create a "theory" to explain how an innocent man could die on death row, without the system having erred. It was true that Frank Lee Smith was not the person who raped and murdered Shandra Whitehead; the DNA testing had shown this was Eddie Lee Mosley. But according to the story presented by Mirman, Smith had burglarized the Whitehead home the same night that Shandra Whitehead had been murdered. According to the prosecutor's explanation, it was just a coincidence that both Smith and Mosley, without any connection between them being demonstrated, committed their respective crimes in the same house, on the same night, at approximately the same time! While theoretically possible, the likelihood of the occurrence of a bizarre happening such as this was not lost on the news media. "The odds of two separate, unrelated breakins at the same house on the same night—without the murderer and the burglar stumbling across one another—would daunt the boldest gambler" (Grimm 2001b). This would clearly exceed, by some exponential power, the standard of "reasonable doubt" required for conviction in any felony case, particularly when there was no evidence presented that Frank Lee Smith had burglarized anything, much less Shandra Whitehead's home! In the end, however, the prosecutor's explanation was simply an ad hoc concoction made to fit the known facts, as well as the inconsistencies, so a series of deadly mistakes made by the system could be explained in a "logical" manner and made to disappear:

> This wasn't, he [Mirman] found, rogue cops gone berserk. Instead, the policemen acted responsibly, the judges acted responsibly, even when they rejected Chiquita Lowe's recantations, the prosecutors acted responsibly. Everyone acted responsibly. But at the end of the day, at the end of a murder trial and two hearings, Frank Lee Smith was on Death Row for a murder he didn't commit. . . . Mirman seems to have found that the policemen, prosecutors and judges, all operating in good faith, could send an innocent fellow to his death without a bit of physical evidence and with a witness who, when she tried to recant, they described as without credibility. The innocent

explanation [of how everyone in the system acted responsibly] is more chilling than a frame-up by rogue cops. (ibid.)

At one level it is easy to understand how mistakes can occur and an innocent person can become a prime suspect in a murder—this is a common occurrence. Knowing the limitations of the criminal justice system it is also possible to envision how a verbally incoherent, brain-damaged, mentally ill suspect with a prior record and no financial resources can be convicted of murder, and even wind up on death row. This is particularly true when the police are eager to close the case, the investigating officer is convinced of the suspect's guilt and twists the limited evidence to fit the case he is building against him, ignores all other logical suspects and inconsistencies, and the prosecutor is so convincing in his presentation to the jury that a couple of pieces of flimsy evidence become a solid and convincing case, especially when he was able to inform the jury of the defendant's prior record without a mistrial being called by the presiding judge.

But what is difficult to fathom, in a system that is functioning at even the lowest minimal level of credibility and efficiency, is how a person can remain on death row for fifteen years and even have a death warrant signed, when the primary witness has recanted her testimony, a secondary witness has acknowledged that another potential suspect she failed to implicate was her cousin, and from the outset the case was lacking any physical evidence, an eyewitness, or a confession connecting the suspect to the crime! Finally, after Smith was posthumously cleared of the crime using DNA testing grudgingly permitted by the state, to have the prosecutor's office concoct the "two burglar theory" rather than concede they had made a mistake was unconscionable.

Other Atrocities in the Name of Justice

Unfortunately, the Frank Lee Smith case is only one small story in the ongoing saga of the treatment of criminal defendants, and as extreme and bizarre as this case appears, it is not the most horrific. There are many others that can compete for that honor.

A team of independent experts determined that a forensic scientist for the West Virginia State Police "lied about, made up, or manipulated evidence" in at least thirty-six cases over a ten-year period, in an attempt to prove that he was a "team player" by bolstering the cases that investigators were trying to make ("Police Chemist Surrenders" 1994:14). In a similar scenario, state troopers in New York admitted fabricating fingerprint evidence in over twenty-five cases in order to increase their chances of getting a conviction ("Ex-Trooper Gets Prison" 1993:26). The Kerry Max Cook capital murder case in Tyler, Texas, shares some similar characteristics to the situation in New York. In order to prove that the defendant was at the scene when the murder was committed, the district attorney forced a fingerprint specialist to falsely testify that the fingerprints found at the scene were between ten and twelve hours old, which coincided with the time the crime occurred. It is well-known, however, that it is virtually impossible to put a time and date on fingerprints taken from the scene of a crime (McClosky 1995:5).

This is not to suggest that all law enforcement officers use illegal tactics in order to secure a conviction. In fact, it is frequently the diligent work of dedicated law enforcement personnel that exposes the mistakes and wrongdoings of other officers. For example, Special Agent Michael Breece of the Florida Department of Law Enforcement found new evidence that indicated that the Broward Sheriff's Office (BSO) had incarcerated the wrong three men for a homicide. "When I told them they had the wrong guys, they laughed at me, I was dumbfounded" (DeMarzo, De Vise, and Lebowitz 2002). But this only made him more determined. The real murderers were eventually caught and the three innocent men were freed. Breece stated, "They [BSO] never, ever admitted they had the wrong guys" (ibid.), even after they were released. One indication of the weakness of the BSO case came when one of the three original suspects produced seventeen eyewitnesses to testify that he was in Rhode Island at the time of the murder. With many similarities to the Frank Lee Smith case, the BSO investigators offered other explanations when their case started to unravel. According to Breece, "If they didn't have an answer, they made one up" (ibid.).

When President George W. Bush was governor of Texas he presided over more executions than any other governor. He stated that he was "absolutely confident" that none of these people were innocent, saying "I haven't been wrong in any of these incidences" (Saletan 2000), but the case of David Spence may yet prove him wrong. Originally, in order to protect themselves from the death penalty, two key witnesses said Spence had helped them commit the murders, but they now say he was not involved. Moreover, the prosecutor withheld evidence concerning the false alibi of another suspect, and a lead detective who had worked on the case said he no longer believed Spence was guilty. But Governor Bush failed to intercede and David Spence was executed on April 3, 1997, still proclaiming his innocence (ibid.).

Illinois has had a number of problems with the death penalty, resulting in the current moratorium called by the governor. "Charges of police misconduct—from manufacturing evidence to concealing information that could help clear suspects—are central to at least half of the 13 Illinois cases where a man sentenced to death was exonerated" (Mills and Armstrong 1999a, 1999b). For example, Rolando Cruz and Alejandro Hernandez spent eleven years on death row in Illinois for the rape and murder of a ten-year-old. They were convicted even though a repeat sex offender and murderer had already confessed to the murder. Some of the evidence used to convict them included testimony by several law enforcement officers that Cruz and Hernandez made incriminating statements, and testimony from sheriff's officers that Cruz admitted to having "visions" that revealed detailed features of the crime that only the murderer would know. These alleged conversations about the visions were never tape recorded by the police. Cruz's second trial was reversed by the Illinois Supreme Court in large part because Brian Dugan, a convicted rapist-murderer, admitted that he had committed the crimes. In fall of 1995, DNA evidence not available at the time of the original trial indicated that neither Cruz nor Hernandez was the likely assailant, and that Dugan could not be eliminated as the offender. In response to this event the state merely changed its theory of the crime arguing that although Dugan may have committed the rape, Cruz and Hernandez were still at the crime scene as active participants. At Cruz's last trial one of the police officers substantially modified his story about the vision statements, creating considerable doubt about the guilt of Cruz. This reversal in testimony, together with Dugan's confession and the DNA evidence, led to all charges being dropped against Cruz and Hernandez.[36]

The Illinois Supreme Court has ordered a new trial or sentencing hearing in almost half of the death penalty cases it has reviewed because of judicial error, inadequate defense counsel, or prosecutorial misconduct, so it is clear that it has not acted simply as a "rubber stamp" for lower court death penalty decisions. This makes the case of Anthony Porter all the more frightening and disturbing because the same Illinois Supreme Court that had granted new trials or sentencing hearings to 49 percent of the cases it had heard denied all of the appeals of Anthony Porter, and he came within forty-eight hours of being executed (Armstrong and Mills 1999).

Porter was charged with the shooting deaths of Jerry Hillard and Marilyn Green on the south side of Chicago on August 15, 1982. Porter, whose IQ had been measured at different times between 51 and 75, was convicted based largely on the testimony of William Taylor, who claimed that he had witnessed the killings. Porter's death warrant had been signed and he was scheduled for execution in September 1998. He came within two days of being executed when his lawyer convinced the Illinois Supreme Court to stay the execution until Porter's mental fitness could be determined. During this period, Taylor recanted his testimony to a private investigator and a Northwestern University student taking a journalism class with Professor David Protess. Subsequent to this, Professor Protess and several of his other students interviewed a woman named Inez Jackson, who admitted that her husband, Alstory Simon, had killed Hillard and Green. In February of 1999, Simon confessed to the killings and after sixteen years on death row Anthony Porter was finally released (ibid.).

Unfortunately, credit for correcting a mistake and righting a wrong in the case of Anthony Porter cannot be attributed to the U.S. Supreme Court, or the Illinois Supreme Court, or to defense attorneys who discovered another grounds for an appeal, or to prosecutors who found the real perpetrator in the process of interviewing witnesses for another case, or a dishonest cop with a guilty conscience who confessed to tampering with the evidence. No, Anthony Porter came within two days of being executed and no one from the criminal justice system familiar with his case came forth to prevent it from happening. Luckily, he was saved from execution by a group of journalism students working on a class project (ibid.)!

Illinois, and Chicago in particular, has another claim to fame in regard to the death penalty. One team of detectives led by Chicago Police Commander Jon Burge have been responsible for putting at least ten people on death row. Unfortunately, it appears that they accomplished this by obtaining confessions using physical torture, psychological threats, and other extreme measures that have been illegal in the United States for many years (Mills and Armstrong 1999a, 1999b; Justice Project 2002a).

"Among the accusations leveled at the Burge regime: that detectives, from the late 1970s to the late 1980s, beat suspects, shocked them with electric wires and put guns to their heads or in their mouths in an effort to get confessions" probably represent only a small portion of the illegal acts conducted (Mills and Armstrong 1999a, 1999b). In responding to a death row inmate's appeal, U.S. District Judge Milton Shadur included in his response, "It is now common knowledge that in the early- to mid-1980s, Chicago Police Cmdr. Jon Burge and many of the officers working under him regularly engaged in the physical abuse and torture of prisoners to extract confessions. [This appeared to be an] established practice, not just on an isolated basis" (Armstrong and Mills 1999).

An examination of the literature reveals that Jon Burge was neither the originator of these illicit techniques nor the only one using them. Indeed, they appear to be well known, widely dispersed, and frequently used. When confessions obtained through the use of physical torture and psychological abuse are combined with the creation or modification of physical evidence, the failure to report evidence to the defense that would help the defendant's case, the bullying, badgering, and threatening of witnesses, the use of unreliable "jailhouse witnesses" (some who actually make a career out of these activities in order to gain more lenient sentences for themselves[37]), and the unwillingness to follow leads that do not support the crime scenario they have concocted, it is readily apparent that police and prosecutors literally hold the lives of both innocent and guilty suspects in their hands, and the outcome may well hinge on factors completely unrelated to the specific crime, or the criminal behavior or nonbehavior of the defendant.

"DOUBLE JEOPARDY" OR "NEGATIVE SYNERGISM"

While this chapter has separated for discussion the problems of bad defense attorneys from the problems associated with judicial, prosecutorial,
or police misconduct, frequently bad lawyering and unethical behavior by
criminal justice personnel occur in the same case. In these cases the deck is
stacked even more and could be thought of as "double jeopardy" or "negative synergism" in that the defendants are extremely likely to find themselves on death row because virtually every element in the system is
working against them.

Ernest Willis was a disabled Texas oil worker who was prosecuted for
murder by District Attorney J. W. Johnson. Johnson had Willis drugged
with psychotropic medication without his knowledge during his trial, and
suppressed exculpatory evidence. There was no physical evidence linking
Willis to the murder, and another person, on death row for other murders,
confessed to the crime. At his trial Willis's court-appointed lawyer spent a
total of three hours with his client, and until two months before his appointment as Willis's attorney he had worked for the district attorney's office that was prosecuting Willis. The attorney had been disciplined by the
state bar association, and subsequently lost his license after being convicted for cocaine possession. Given these factors it is no surprise that
Ernest Willis found himself on death row (Texas Civil Rights Project 2000).

William Bracy received a death sentence for the murder of three drug
dealers in Chicago, but the trial had a bizarre set of circumstances surrounding it. First, the key witness confessed to being an accessory to the
crimes, but placed the blame for the murders on Bracy in order to receive
leniency. This is not unusual, but as discussed earlier it is frequently problematic in that the real murderer may get off with a minimum sentence
while an innocent person is convicted. Second, the presiding judge was
convicted a few years later for fixing murder cases and received a sixteen-
year prison sentence. Third, the court-appointed attorney that the judge selected was a convicted felon who was emotionally unstable and had an
alcohol problem. He had just been reinstated to the bar shortly prior to representing Bracy. This attorney went on to become the only Illinois attorney
to be disbarred twice; unfortunately it was not the Bracy case that led to
his second disbarment. Fourth, the prosecutors were notorious for misconduct in previous cases, with court records showing they had committed thirty-five inappropriate or illegal acts in one case alone. There was no
reason to assume that their approach to the Bracy case would be any different. Fifth, the jury was all white (Bracy was black). Sixth, the jury included the wife of a judge who had sentenced Bracy to prison on an earlier
unrelated charge. The outcome was predictable and William Bracy has
been on the Illinois death row since 1981. Higher courts have shown

concerns over numerous issues in the case, but none have found it necessary to overthrow the lower court's decision. But then again, these are the same state courts that rejected all of the appeals of Anthony Porter (Armstrong and Mills 1999).

Earl Washington, Jr. was arrested in 1983 and during his interrogation for the crime was asked about the murder of Rebecca Lynn Williams, which had take place in Culpeper, Virginia, one year earlier. Washington, who is a mentally retarded special education dropout, was asked by a police investigator:

"Did you stab a woman in Culpeper?" Washington nodded.

"Was this woman white or black?" the detective asked.

"Black," replied Washington, thus creating a problem for the detective since the victim was white.

After a few additional questions, the detective returned to the question, "Was she white or black?"

This time, Washington replied, "White," and the police interrogation continued, after which Washington was arrested for the murder of Rebecca Williams. In addition to Washington's inability to determine the race of his alleged victim, there were a number of other inconsistencies. He told police investigators, for example, that he had stabbed Rebecca Williams "once or twice," when in fact she had thirty-eight stab wounds. He said he and the victim were alone in the room when the murder took place, when in fact there was a baby in the playpen and a toddler walking around the victim's apartment. There were no eyewitnesses or physical evidence that place Washington at the crime scene, and his blood type did not match semen at the scene. How did Washington get convicted with all of these inconsistencies? Easy, his inexperienced lawyer who had a copy of the blood report indicating that Washington's blood type did not match the semen at the scene never informed the jury of this important fact.[38] The only "evidence" linking Earl Washington, Jr., to the crime was the "confession" of a retarded man (Washington) taken during an interrogation over one year after the crime, who was never an original suspect in the crime, and who was being interrogated in reference to an entirely different case (*Washington v. Commonwealth* 1984).

POLICY IMPLICATIONS

In 1994 Justice Harry A. Blackmun wrote that the legal machinery surrounding the death penalty that he had helped to establish was in ruins, that as a result he would no longer "tinker" with the system, and that ultimately the social experiment with capital punishment was a failure. This chapter has provided evidence to support Justice Blackmun's claims.

More Tinkering or Abolition?

There is a growing consensus that there is something terribly wrong with the death penalty, but less consensus about what should be done. In the face of evidence that the legal machinery of death is breaking down there have been calls for abolition as well as for additional tinkering. After their comprehensive study of legal errors in capital cases, Liebman and his colleagues made several recommendations, one being the abolition of the death penalty. Should states desire to retain capital punishment, however, they also suggested several reforms, such as requiring that a conviction of a capital offense be based on the more demanding requirement of proof beyond any doubt, requiring that aggravating circumstances substantially outweigh mitigating factors before a sentence of death is imposed, requiring that states include life without parole as a sentencing option in capital cases, and appointing and adequately compensating qualified defense counsel in capital cases (Liebman *et al.* 2002:v–vi).

The Governor's Commission on Capital Punishment appointed by Illinois Governor George H. Ryan made eighty-five recommendations to modify the handling of capital cases. These recommendations included requiring police to keep a schedule of all evidence (including exculpatory evidence), videotaping police interrogations, reducing the number of aggravating factors that subject people to the death penalty, review of death eligibility by a statewide committee, and specialized training and experience for legal counsel in death cases (Governor's Commission on Capital Punishment 2002).

Finally, the Innocence Protection Act is an attempt by the U.S. Congress to reform the system of capital punishment by instituting new safeguards in capital cases. Among these safeguards is the requirement that states include life without parole as a sentencing option in capital cases, ensuring that defendants can request DNA testing on evidence, providing experienced and adequately compensated defense lawyers in death cases, and providing adequate compensation for those who are falsely convicted and imprisoned.[39]

Many critics of the way the death penalty is currently administered in the United States are, like Justice Blackmun, skeptical of the utility of any additional tinkering. Justice Blackmun has recently been joined in his skepticism by two other justices, Powell[40] and Ginsburg. Blackmun, Powell, and Ginsburg all had a hand in creating some of the legal machinery of capital punishment and they now have expressed grave reservations about the operation of the death penalty and suggest that it should be abolished. Some others who have made public statements about changes in their positions on the death penalty are Sandra Day O'Connor, justice of the United States Supreme Court,[41] Gerald Kogan, former chief justice of the Florida Supreme Court,[42] Moses Harrison II, justice of the Illinois Supreme Court,[43] and Jesse Ventura, governor of Minnesota.[44] Still other recently converted opponents are conservative commentators Oliver North, George Will, and Gerald Seib (*Wall Street Journal*), and religious figures such as the Reverend Pat Robinson (Green 2000).

Some of these, like Blackmun, have concluded that the social experiment with capital punishment in the United States is a proven failure, and after years of building a complex web of procedural and substantive reforms, are ready to end the experiment. Others recognize that the system is badly broken and want to "tinker" some more with the machinery. What the "tinkerers" may not recognize, however, is that the best possible system will be imperfect and innocent people will continue to be executed under any process that can be devised by mere mortals. It is a mathematical and statistical certainty that cannot be challenged, regardless of the safeguards that are established—in sum, human beings are fallible, and mistakes will be made![45] Tinkering with a broken system and drastically reducing the number of executions might proportionately reduce the number of mistakes, but the only way to eliminate the execution of innocent people is to abolish the system entirely. Furthermore, it is clear that recent efforts to provide finality by expediting executions through the truncation of the appeals process will exacerbate rather than ameliorate the problems noted in this chapter. It is also clear that the highest court in the land will provide little comfort to those concerned about the execution of innocent persons. In *Herrera v. Collins* the petitioner, Leonel Herrera, sought relief from his Texas death sentence on the grounds that newly discovered evidence corroborated his claim of innocence. The problem for Herrera, however, was that this evidence came some ten years after his original conviction and death sentence for the murder of two police officers. In rejecting Herrera's plea for either a new trial or new sentence, Chief Justice Rehnquist writing for the Court argued that a claim of actual innocence even by one facing execution must surmount a high hurdle "because of the very disruptive effect that entertaining claims of actual innocence would have on the need for finality in capital cases."[46]

Life without the Possibility of Parole (LWOP)

If additional tinkering with the administration of capital punishment is not the answer, then what should be done to those who commit the most egregious crimes? One obvious alternative to the death penalty, currently used in many jurisdictions, is a sentence of life without the possibility of parole (LWOP). Under an LWOP sentence, those convicted of the most serious murders would be sent to prison for the rest of their life, without the possibility of being released. Life without parole can provide most, if not all, of the benefits of capital punishment without the risk of mistakenly executing an innocent person.

Arguments against LWOP by Death Penalty Advocates

Those who support the death penalty make several arguments concerning why the death penalty is more appropriate than an LWOP sentence. The main arguments are:

• The public demands the death penalty for serious offenders, particularly murderers (social support).
• The death penalty deters others from committing murder because of the fear of execution (general deterrence).
• Executing a convicted murderer makes it impossible for that person to murder again (incapacitation).
• The death penalty is far less costly than an LWOP sentence (cost savings).
• Capital punishment is the only morally appropriate punishment for those who have committed the most serious crimes (moral necessity).

Each of these points will be examined briefly, and an argument will be made that LWOP can achieve all of the policy objectives of the death penalty, without the unnecessary risk of executing an innocent person.

Those who use the social support argument for the death penalty have pointed to public opinion polls indicating that Americans want to have capital punishment imposed on those who commit murder. These polls have shown that when asked if they "approve" of the death penalty for convicted murderers, a majority of Americans, nearly two-thirds, respond in the affirmative. Realistically, however, what is to be made of these poll results? Americans state that they approve of the death penalty for murderers, but they do not seem to be saying that they either demand the death penalty for the most serious crimes or that they even prefer the death penalty over an alternative form of punishment.

Research by William Bowers (1993) has shown that expressed "support" for the death penalty weakens considerably when people are asked if they prefer a death sentence or an LWOP sentence for convicted murderers. For example, in California 67 percent of those asked expressed a preference for LWOP over capital punishment while only 26 percent said that they preferred the death penalty. Similar results were obtained from polls taken in Nebraska, Florida, and New York—less than one-third of those asked said that they preferred the death penalty over LWOP. When given a choice between executing those convicted for the most serious crimes and putting them in prison for a "real" life sentence, people show a strong preference for the latter. Consequently, the social support argument collapses under the weight of responses to more clearly worded public opinion surveys.

The deterrence argument states that capital punishment is the preferred sanction because it will deter potential murderers more effectively than an LWOP sentence. The deterrence argument has been challenged, however, by a large number of studies. For example, if the argument is true that executions deter would-be murderers more than do LWOP sentences, then (1) states with capital punishment should have lower homicide rates than those without it, and (2) states that have capital punishment during some period of their history but not during another period should have lower homicide rates during the periods when capital punishment was in use. Numerous studies have been devoted to both of these issues, some using very sophisticated statistical techniques, and there is simply no convincing evidence that capital punishment is a more effective deterrent than an LWOP sentence, and in many cases the murder rate may actually be higher in capital punishment states (brutalization effect).[47] What this evidence seems to show is that murder rates are responsive to numerous factors, such as the proportion of young males in the population, the level of unemployment and poverty, and the accessibility of handguns, but it does not make much difference whether the sentencing policy requires capital punishment or an LWOP sentence.

The incapacitation argument is a little different. It is difficult to argue with the fact that capital punishment is effective in incapacitating murderers. An executed murderer cannot kill (or do anything else) again. But this oversimplifies the argument because there are other sanctions short of death that can effectively keep murderers from killing again. An LWOP sentence, for example, could keep murderers behind bars where they would be denied the opportunity to take another life. Proponents of the death penalty might argue, however, that murderers serving LWOP could kill other inmates or correctional staff, or could escape and kill a citizen. The evidence would indicate, however, that even though the probability that a murderer sentenced to a life term will kill again is not zero, it is very, very low. Marquart and Sorensen (1988, 1989) studied the behavior of a sample of defendants who were sentenced to die, but had their death sentences modified to life imprisonment due to a court decision. They found that these former death row offenders did not constitute a threat to their fellow inmates or correctional staff. In fact, they were less likely to commit a murder or a serious violation of prison rules than were prisoners serving terms for much less serious crimes. They concluded that putting convicted murderers behind bars is an effective way of keeping them from either killing again or committing another serious crime.

Upon initial perusal, the cost savings argument would appear to have some obvious merit. Proponents of the death penalty argue that it is clearly more costly to incarcerate for life than to execute murderers and suggest that the cost savings can be used to meet other needs of the criminal justice system. This position is assuming the cost savings, however, based on "common sense" rather than empirical data. The question that must be asked, however, is "What is the true and complete cost of administering capital punishment in comparison to an LWOP sentence?" There is ample evidence to suggest that the administration of capital punishment is much more costly than might be assumed based on casual observation. First, since defendants are on trial for their lives, many more motions are filed than in noncapital cases. Combined with the fact that capital law is more complex, it means there are more motions to file, more motions to be decided by the courts, and a greater chance of reversible error. It has been estimated that the number of pretrial motions in capital cases is twice that in noncapital cases (Spangenberg and Walsh 1989; Cook and Slawson 1993). The costs of investigating a case are higher when defendants are on trial for their life because investigators and counsel must prepare both for the guilt phase and penalty phase hearings. The process of jury selection or *voir dire* is more detailed and longer in capital cases—jurors are often *voir dired* separately and sequestered during the jury selection process as well as the trial itself. Finally, the appeals process is longer and more detailed in a capital case and courts give capital cases a great deal of scrutiny. Liebman and his colleagues (2001) have estimated that more than two-thirds of the capital trials that took place between 1973 and 1995 have been reversed on appeal. This means thousands of new guilty and penalty phase hearings, new juries, new investigations, and added costs. When all of these costs are compiled, the best estimates suggest that a death sentence costs much more than an LWOP sentence (Bohm 1998; Dieter 1997).

There is a final argument that proponents of the death penalty sometimes use. They argue that someone who has taken a life has forfeited his right to live in the human community and must be expelled—through death (moral necessity). This position is a kind of "payback" retributivism of the *lex talionis*—"an eye for an eye"—the murderer has taken a life and the only morally equivalent punishment is to take the life of the murderer. In trying to understand this seemingly compelling moral view, we must recognize that as a society this kind of retribution is almost never used for other types of crime. There is virtually never a situation where the punishment exactly matches the injury or suffering of the victim. For example, all those who kill another are not executed. Those cases lacking premeditation and/or malice or those murders where there is no statutory aggravating circumstance do not receive the death penalty.[48] Society does not try to duplicate the grotesque brutality of other murders because it is recognized that such behavior on the part of the state would be demeaning and uncivilized. Rather, society tries to cull out the most egregious blameworthy murderers and then impose a penalty that is harsh enough to symbolize the moral condemnation of the act and one not so lenient that it trivializes the crime.

Unlike "payback" or exact retribution, proportional retribution (Nathanson 1987) would not require that the punishment imposed by the state on an offender strictly duplicate the harm done to the victim, or that the severity of the punishment be identical to the severity of the crime. The only requirements of proportional retribution are that those who commit more serious crimes must be punished more severely than those who commit less serious crimes, and that no punishment should be so lenient that it trivializes the moral gravity of the offense. Proportional retribution, then, would not morally require the death penalty for those who commit murder. Given the two requirements of proportional retribution it can be argued that the death penalty is not the only punishment that murderers may morally receive. Those who commit murder could be punished by life without the possibility of parole, it could be restricted to the most serious murders who currently receive the death penalty, and it certainly is a severe penalty that does not minimize the moral magnitude of murder.

CONCLUSIONS

This chapter has discussed some of the factors that result in the wrongful conviction and execution of innocent people under the current system of justice. It has shown that defense attorneys in death penalty cases are all too often inexperienced, understaffed, and poorly compensated. Although a human being is on trial for his or her life, capital defendants, at least poor ones, often get the worst that the legal profession has to offer. Moreover, the Supreme Court through its *Strickland* decision has created a high hurdle for any defendant wishing to make a claim that their counsel was ineffective (*Strickland v. Washington* 1984). Evidence has also been provided indicating police and prosecutors frequently act in highly unethical ways, suppressing evidence that may be exculpatory for defendants, manufacturing evidence, giving and knowingly using false testimony, and using jailhouse informants whose credibility is highly questionable.

Moreover, there is an inexorable link between the breakdown of the legal machinery of death and the mistaken conviction and possible execution of innocent persons. The Innocence Project has reported that of the first seventy DNA exonerations there was evidence of false confessions in fifteen cases, the use of jailhouse informants in sixteen, evidence of incompetent lawyers in twenty-three, prosecutorial misconduct in thirty-four, and evidence of police misconduct in thirty-eight cases (Innocence Project 2000).[49] Further, in their examination of error in capital cases, Liebman et al. found that during the period 1973–1995 approximately 68 percent of all death sentences imposed and reviewed by an appellate court in the United States were reversed due to serious errors at trial (Liebman *et al.* 2001). Two major sources of these errors were the misconduct of prosecutors and police and the incompetence of defense lawyers. In 82 percent of the cases that were sent back for retrial or resentencing, the defendant ultimately received a sentence other than death, and was acquitted in an additional 9 percent of the cases (ibid.).

In sum, if the death penalty continues to be used, all of the best-intended tinkering to improve the system will not eliminate the inevitable consequence that innocent people will be executed. The only way to avoid the execution of the innocent is to do what virtually every other industrialized nation has done: abolish the death penalty (Amnesty International 2001)! None of the arguments in favor of capital punishment hold up under careful scrutiny, and a sentence of life in prison without any possibility of parole provides the same benefits as a sentence of death, without the risk of executing the innocent. This would be a win-win situation, and provide a sound and sane policy alternative.

NOTES

1. In the numerous court cases and laws that have been passed by legislative bodies since the landmark case of *Furman v. Georgia* (1972), the courts and legislatures continuously promised that the latest tinkering would "fix" the system. Subsequent sections of this chapter show that the problems with the death penalty are as big today as they have ever been, suggesting that the tinkering has failed, the system is indeed irreparably broken, and the promises of politicians and the judiciary are either empty or broken, but certainly not fulfilled.

2. The problems encountered in this area are reminiscent of the old expression, the road to Hell is paved with good intentions.

3. The fact that Illinois had executed twelve offenders since 1977 while exonerating thirteen innocent people on death row provided ample evidence that Governor Ryan's concerns were not misguided.

4. On April 8th, 2002, Arizona convicted murderer Ray Krone became the one hundredth person to be exonerated by DNA evidence. Krone spent ten years on death row before being released as an innocent man (Justice Project 2002b).

5. "During the past 25 years, 69 people who had been sentenced to death in the United States were eventually found to be innocent and released from their death-row prison cells. . . . [During this same period] about 6,000 people have been sentenced to death in this country. At that rate, more than one of every 100 death-row inmates awaiting execution is innocent" (Smart 1997).

6. "One third of the 2,500 rape suspects the FBI is asked by local police agencies to do DNA testing on are exonerated. These men are suspects based primarily on eyewitness testimony. To be wrong thirty-three percent of the time is scary" (McClosky 1996).

7. "Eyewitness evidence is notoriously unreliable in any kind of case or situa-

tion, yet it is constantly used in capital cases. . . .Five years ago, concern about eye-witness reliability prompted England to ban trials where the only evidence against a suspect is an eyewitness" (McClosky 1996).

8. "Prosecutorial use of nefarious criminals as star witnesses is also rather commonplace and leads to false convictions. These can take the form of career criminals looking to get out of their own serious troubles or real perpetrators and accomplices who will falsely incriminate an innocent person in exchange for generous sentencing leniency such as noncustodial sentences. I see this so often it sickens me, especially where the real killer is the one who dispatches the innocent to death row as the chief witness for the prosecution" (McClosky 1996).

9. *Furman* was a 5-4 decision, with each of the nine Justices writing their own opinion. Only two of the justices, Justice Brennan and Justice Marshall, adopted the *per se* position that capital punishment itself violates the 8th Amendment's prohibition against cruel and unusual punishment. The other three justices who made up the plurality in *Furman,* Justices Stewart, White, and Douglas, took the view that the manner in which the death penalty was being administered in the states was unconstitutional.

10. In his dissenting opinion, however, Chief Justice Burger made reference both to the Court's fractured ruling, and two possible statutory remedies that legislatures (both state and federal) might want to pursue: "While I would not undertake to make a definitive statement as to the parameters of the Court's ruling, it is clear that if state legislatures and the Congress wish to maintain the availability of capital punishment, significant statutory changes will have to be made. . . .Legislative bodies may seek to bring their laws into compliance with the Court's ruling by providing standards for juries and judges to follow in determining the sentence in capital cases or by more narrowly defining the crimes for which the penalty is to be imposed. If such standards can be devised or the crimes more meticulously defined, the result cannot be detrimental" (*Furman v. Georgia* 1972:400).

11. An example of a guided discretion statute was that of Florida. Florida's capital sentencing statute called for a bifurcated trial, with a distinct guilt/innocence phase and a penalty phase. During the penalty phase, the jury was to focus its attention on a list of statutorily enumerated aggravating and mitigating circumstances. The jury could not recommend a sentence of death (under the new Florida statute, the judge sentenced in a capital case with the presumptive sentence being that which was recommended by the jury) unless it found beyond a reasonable doubt at least one statutory aggravating mitigating circumstance. Even in the presence of one or more aggravating circumstances, however, the jury was not required to recommend a death sentence. It had to balance the aggravating circumstances it found with statutorily enumerated mitigating factors and determine if the mitigating circumstances outweighed the aggravating circumstances.

12. The North Carolina legislature opted for a mandatory capital statute in response to *Furman.* Its new statute enacted in 1974 defined murder in the first degree as a "murder which shall be perpetrated by means of poison, lying in wait, imprisonment, starving, torture, or by any other kind of willful, deliberate and premeditated killing, or which shall be committed in the perpetration of attempt to perpetrate any arson, rape, robbery, kidnapping, burglary or other felony." Conviction for this newly created crime of first degree murder resulted in the automatic imposition of the death penalty (N.C. Gen. Statute 1975).

13. *Gregg v. Georgia* 1976; *Proffitt v. Florida* 1976; *Jurek v. Texas* 1976; *Woodson v. North Carolina* 1976; *Roberts v. Louisiana* 1976.

14. In *Furman v. Georgia,* Justice Stewart wrote that "the penalty of death differs from all other forms of criminal punishment, not in degree but in kind. It is unique in its total irrevocability. It is unique in its rejection of rehabilitation of the convict as a basic purpose of criminal justice. And it is unique, finally, in its absolute renunciation of all that is embodied in our concept of humanity "(*Furman v. Georgia* 1972:306). In *Gregg v. Georgia,* Justice Stewart again observed that *Furman* "recognized that the penalty of death is different in kind from any other punishment imposed under our system of criminal justice. Because of the uniqueness of the death penalty, *Furman* held that it could not be imposed under sentencing procedures that created a substantial risk that it would be inflicted in an arbitrary and capricious manner" (*Gregg v. Georgia* 1976:188). In *Woodson v. North Carolina,* Justice Brennan in concurring with the judgment that mandatory death statutes are unconstitutional, noted that "this conclusion rests squarely on the predicate that the penalty of death is qualitatively different from a sentence of imprisonment, however long. Death, in its finality, differs more from life imprisonment than a 100 year prison term differs from one of only a year or two" (*Woodson v. North Carolina* 1976:305).

15. This is often stated as since "death is different," there must be *super due process* afforded potentially capital defendants to ensure that only those truly deserving are sentenced to death (see Radin 1980). More recently, however, it has been observed that "the Rehnquist court's perverse interpretation of the 'death is different' formulation has led to some strange outcomes. . . . The court has even abandoned the commitment to insuring review for innocent men and women facing imminent execution. In *Herrera v. Collins* (1993), the Court held that the constitution does not protect condemned state prisoners from execution even if there is new evidence of innocence. Chief Justice Rehnquist wrote the opinion, which rejected federal protections for such prisoners because of 'the very disruptive effect that entertaining claims of actual innocence would have on the need for finality in capital cases'" (Stevenson 1996:16).

16. In its decision, the Court did have information about the Georgia Supreme Court and the role that it was playing (at least initially). Under the new Georgia statute, the state Supreme Court was charged with reviewing each death sentence to determine the factual validity of the aggravating circumstance(s), whether the sentences were imposed under the influence of passion, prejudice, or some other illicit factor, and if the death sentence was proportionate to the sentence imposed in comparable cases. In *Gregg,* the U.S. Supreme Court had before it instances where the Georgia Supreme Court conducted its review under these provisions and concluded that "it is apparent that the Supreme Court of Georgia has taken its review responsibilities seriously" (*Gregg v. Georgia* 1976: 205).

17. Petitioner Gregg argued that the proposed procedural reforms of the Georgia capital statute were merely cosmetic, designed to gloss over the real defects that continued to exist, and that the new statute would result in the same kind of arbitrary and capricious death sentences that the Court condemned in *Furman.*

18. *Eddings v. Oklahoma* 1982; *Lockett v. Ohio* 1978; *California v. Ramos* 1983; *Caldwell v. Mississippi* 1985; *Skipper v. South Carolina* 1986; *Booth v. Maryland* 1987; *Payne v. Tennessee* 1991.

19. *Zant v. Stephens* 1983; *Barclay v. Florida* 1983; *Barefoot v. Estelle* 1983.

20. In the area of substantive matters, the Court ruled on such issues as the constitutionality of a mandatory death penalty for certain narrow categories of murder (*H. Roberts v. Louisiana* 1977; *Sumner v. Shuman* 1987); the execution of the mentally ill and mentally retarded (*Ford v. Wainwright* 1986; *Penry v. Lynaugh* 1989); the execution of juveniles (*Thompson v. Oklahoma* 1988; *Stanford v. Kentucky* and *Wilkins v. Missouri* 1989); and the execution of nonmurderers (*Coker v. Georgia* 1977; *Enmund v. Florida* 1977; *Tison v. Arizona* 1987).

21. In *Eddings v. Oklahoma* (1982:112), the Court declared that the penalty of death must be imposed "fairly, and with reasonable consistency, or not at all."

22. In *Powell v. Alabama* (1932), seven black youths (historically known as the "Scottsboro boys" because the offense occurred near and the trial took place in Scottsboro, Alabama) were accused of sexually assaulting two white girls on a freight train passing through Alabama. The youths were all residents of other states, illiterate, and their arrest for what at the time was an incendiary offense required that they be kept under the protection of the state militia. At their arraignment, the presiding Alabama trial judge appointed the entire local bar to represent the defendants, though assigned individual responsibility to no one. No attorney from the local bar stepped forward to take the case, although an attorney from Tennessee who was not a member of the Alabama bar indicated that he would be willing to appear with any counsel that the court might appoint. On the day of the trial a member of the local bar did ambiguously indicate that he would help with the case, but had not prepared anything. The defendants were immediately rushed to trial, all were convicted that day and sentenced to death.

23. In *Wainwright v. Sykes* (1977) the U.S. Supreme Court observed that the state trial in a capital case should be the "main event," and not a "tryout on the road" before postconviction review.

24. "It has long been recognized that the right to counsel is the right to the effective assistance of counsel" (*McMann v. Richardson* 1970).

25. See, for example, Goodpaster (1986), Klein (1986), Bright (1994, 1999), and Geimer (1995).

26. See *United States exrel. Williams v. Twomey* (1975).

27. Goodpaster has noted that in adequately preparing for the penalty phase of a capital trial, the defense counsel should strive to achieve four basic objectives: (1) convey to the jury that the defendant is a member of the human community who possess redeeming attributes, (2) to demonstrate that while the defendant's act may not be forgivable, it is at least understandable given the defendant's life experiences (child or sexual abuse, history of alcoholism or drug addiction, etc.), (3) to attempt to put the death penalty on trial by arguing that it is an inappropriate punishment for a civilized society either generally or in the immediate case, and (4) rebut the prosecution's evidence in aggravation. See Goodpaster (1983) and Mello (1988).

28. *Ex parte Burdine* 1995 at 457. See also, Texas Defender Service (2002).

29. Burdine appealed to the federal district court, which ruled in his favor, concluding that "sleeping counsel is equivalent to no counsel at all" (*Burdine v. Johnson* 1999). Subsequent to that, a three-judge panel of the U.S. Court of Appeals for the Fifth Circuit concluded in a 2-1 opinion that a sleeping counsel did not violate the defendant's right to effective assistance of counsel. The court reasoned that in the case at hand the record did not demonstrate that the attorney slept through an important part of the trial (*Burdine v. Johnson* 2000), reversing *Burdine v. Johnson* (1999).

In August of 2001, an *en bac* Fifth Circuit Court of Appeals agreed with the district court's ruling that Burdine failed to receive the effective assistance of counsel.

30. See also Texas Civil Rights Project (2000).

31. In 1935 the United States Supreme Court said "The prosecutor's interest in a criminal prosecution is not that it shall win a case, but that justice shall be done. . . . While he may strike hard blows, he is not at liberty to strike foul ones. It is as much his duty to refrain from improper methods calculated to produce a wrongful conviction as it is to use every legitimate means to bring about a just one" (*Berger v. United States* 1935).

32. Not wanting to make him bigger than life, it should be noted that Frank Lee Smith was neither a "choir boy" nor a "model citizen." At age thirteen and suffering from brain damage, he was placed in a juvenile facility for a manslaughter that occurred in a fight following a football game, and at age eighteen he served fifteen years on a felony murder that occurred during the course of a robbery committed with his older brother. He was, unfortunately, like too many others in similar situations, a child of the streets, who had, according to someone who got to know him well, "suffered a lifetime of poverty, abandonment, neglect, abuse, alcoholism, mental illness, and, ultimately, incarceration" (Walsh 2002).

33. Frank Lee Smith is thus far the only death row inmate to be exonerated by DNA evidence after dying in prison.

34. It should be noted that there was no physical evidence linking Frank Lee Smith to the crime, no eyewitnesses to the crime or anyone who saw Smith at the crime scene, and no confession signed by Smith.

35. The fact that Dorothy McGriff and Chiquita Lowe were both able to identify Frank Lee Smith at the defense table was likely aided by the fact that Smith was the only adult black male in the court room (De Vise 2001).

36. See also Justice Project (2002a).

37. Some jailhouse informants are well known as pathological liars and mistrusted even by prosecutors, but used by them anyway. Tommy Dye has served at least four prison sentences, is wanted in four states, has more than a dozen aliases, and lies even when under oath, sometimes about mundane and trivial things, as well as things that can place a defendant on death row. He was called a "menace to society" by a parole officer and a federal prosecutor called him "a pathological liar . . . not worthy of this court's trust." But it was his testimony, and very little else, that put Steve Manning, a former Chicago police officer, on death row. Although a six-hour jailhouse tape recording did not contain it, Dye supposedly got a confession from Manning. Dye said the brief confessions were lost in two different two-second gaps in the tape, one caused by a malfunction, one when the waistband of his underwear covered the microphone (ah, Watergate remembered), but Dye was apparently so believable that Manning was convicted anyway! In another scenario, this one in Los Angeles, Leslie White "demonstrated how simple it was to concoct a confession and convince prosecutors it was genuine. Using a jail telephone, White . . . posed as a police officer, prosecutor and bail bondsman to obtain information about a murder suspect he had never met, then falsified jail records to show he had shared a cell with the suspect" (Mills and Armstrong 1999a, 1999b).

38. At an evidentiary hearing in district court in Virginia, a claim that Washington's counsel was ineffective was rejected. Applying the *Strickland* standard, the court argued that counsel's conduct did not fall below acceptable professional

conduct and that even if it did the failure to provide the jury with the exculpatory blood evidence was not prejudicial.

39. The Innocence Protection Act is a bipartisan bill designed to prevent the mistaken execution of innocent persons. This bill was introduced into the U.S. House of Representatives (H.R. 912) by Representatives Roy LaHood (Republican-Illinois) and William Delahunt (Democrat-Massachusetts). The Senate version of the bill was cosponsored by Senators Patrick Leahy (Democrat-Vermont), Gordon Smith (Republican-Oregon), and Susan Collins (Republican-Maine) (Innocence Project 2002: Legislation).

40. In his biography, Justice Powell said that the one vote that he would like to change was in *McClesky v. Kemp*. He was the deciding vote in a 5-4 decision that prevented capital punishment from being abolished, at least temporarily, in 1987, based on evidence of racial bias in the administration of the death penalty. Four years later he had changed his mind and wished that he had voted differently. In his biography he is quoted as saying, "I have come to think that capital punishment should be abolished . . . it serves no useful purpose" (Jefferies 1994:451–2).

41. In a speech in Minneapolis, Supreme Court Justice Sandra Day O'Connor said that "there were 'serious questions' about whether the death penalty was being fairly administered in the United States, telling lawyers that 'if statistics are any indication, the system may well be allowing some innocent defendants to be executed'" (MSNBC 2001).

42. "'There are several cases where I had grave doubts as to the guilt of a particular person' who was executed, former Florida Chief Justice Gerald Kogan has said" (Taylor 2000). More recently, an article in the *Miami Herald* suggests that the next judge appointed to Florida's Supreme Court might have some concerns as well. "As some of Florida's leading lawyers and jurists compete for a seat on Florida's Supreme Court, nearly all agree on this: The state's death penalty system is deeply flawed and in dire need of an overhaul. That consensus emerged from two days of presentations by 18 men and three women from across the ideological spectrum" (Wallsten 2002).

43. Justice Harrison stated, "The system is not working. Innocent people are being sentenced to death. If these men dodged the executioner, it was only because of luck and the dedication of the attorneys, reporters, family members and volunteers who labored to win their release. They survived despite the criminal justice system, not because of it. . . . One must wonder how many others have not been so fortunate" (Armstrong and Mills 1999).

44. Although residing in an abolitionist state, Governor Jesse Ventura had been a supporter of the death penalty, but recently changed his mind. "I do not support the death penalty anymore. Imagine what you'd feel like if someone were put to death, and a year or two later, [you] found out that the person didn't do it" (Saletan 2000).

45. Perhaps this is why Justice Sandra Day O'Connor recently "told Minnesota lawyers they 'must breathe a big sigh of relief every day' that their state does not allow the death penalty" (MSNBC 2001).

46. *Herrera v. Collins, United States Law Week.* Supreme Court Opinions. At 4115.

47. See Thorsten Sellin (1967, 1980), Peterson and Bailey (1988), Klein, Forst, and Filatov (1978), Lempert (1983), Bailey (1983, 1990), Phillips (1980), Stack (1987), McFarland (1983), Bailey and Peterson (1989; 1997).

48. It would never be suggested that the proper punishment for rape would be to rape the rapist, or to sexually molest the child molester, or to burn down the house of the arsonist.

49. There are other recent and very visible manifestations that the death penalty experiment has failed. On April 8, 2002, Ray Krone was released from the Arizona State Prison after DNA evidence conclusively proved that he was not responsible for the murder for which he had been convicted and sentenced to death. Krone spent ten years on Arizona's death row before he became the one-hundredth person exonerated by DNA evidence since 1973 (Justice Project 2002b). As of December 18, 2002, the number of innocent people released from death row based on DNA evidence had increased to one hundred two (Death Penalty Information Center 2002).

REFERENCES

Amnesty International. 2001. Abolitionist and Retentionist Countries. http://www.amnestyusa.org/abolish/abret.html.

Armstrong, Ken and Steve Mills. 1999. "Death Row Justice Derailed." *Chicago Tribune,* November 14.

Bailey, William C. 1983. "Disaggregation in Deterrence and Death Penalty Research: The Case of Murder in Chicago." *Journal of Criminal Law and Criminology* 74:827–59.

———. 1990. "Murder, Capital Punishment, and Television: Execution Publicity and Homicide Rates." *American Sociological Review* 55:631–33.

Bailey, William C. and Ruth D. Peterson. 1989. "Murder and Capital Punishment: A Monthly Time-Series Analysis of Execution Publicity." *American Sociological Review* 54:722–43.

———. 1997. Murder, Capital Punishment and Deterrence: A Review of the Literature (in Bedau, Hugo Adam, *The Death Penalty in America: Current Controversies*). New York: Oxford University Press.

Barclay v. Florida, 103 S. Ct. 3418 (1983).

Barefoot v. Estelle, 103 S. Ct. 3383 (1983).

Berger v. United States, 55 S. Ct. 629 (1935).

Bikel, Ofra (Producer). 2002. "Requiem for Frank Lee Smith." *Frontline,* April 11. Boston: Public Broadcasting Service.

Bohm, Robert M. 1998. The Economic Costs of Capital Punishment: Past, Present and Future. (In Acker, James R., Robert M. Bohm, and Charles S. Lanier, 1998. America's Experiment with Capital Punishment: Reflections on the Past, Present and Future of the Ultimate Penal Sanction. Durham, Carolina Academic Press.)

Booth v. Maryland, 482 U.S. 496 (1987).

Bowers, William J. 1993. "Capital Punishment and Contemporary Values: People's Misgivings and the Court's Misperceptions." *Law and Society Review* 27:157–75.

Bright, Stephen B. 1994. "Counsel for the Poor: The Death Penalty Not for the Worst Crime, but for the Worst Lawyer." *Yale Law Journal* 103:1835–83.

Bright, Stephen B. 1999. "Neither Equal Nor Just: The Rationing and Denial of Legal Services to the Poor When Life and Liberty are at Stake." *New York University School of Law Annual Survey of American Law* 1997:783–836.

Burdine v. Johnson, 234 F. 3d 1339 (5th Ct. 2000), reversing *Burdine v. Johnson*, 66 F. Supp. 2d 854, 866 (Southern District of Texas, 1999).

Burdine v. Johnson, 66 F. Supp. 2d 854, 866 (Southern District of Texas, 1999).

Caldwell v. Mississippi, 105 S. Ct. 2633 (1985).

California v. Ramos, 103 S. Ct. 3446 (1983).

Callins v. Collins, 510 U.S. 1141, 1145 (1994).

Coker v. Georgia, 433 U.S. 584 (1977).

Cook, Phillip J. and Donna B. Slawson. 1993. *The Costs of Processing Murder Cases in North Carolina*. Durham, North Carolina: Terry Sanford Institute of Public Policy, Duke University.

Death Penalty Information Center. 2002. The Death Penalty in 2002: Year End Report. *http://www.deathpenaltyinfo.org*. (Retrieved December 19, 2002).

"The Death Penalty: One in Seven Wasn't Guilty." 1998. *Economist (U.S.)*, November 28, 29(1).

De Vise, Daniel. 2001. "For 14 Years, Justice Failed a Man Condemned to Die." *Miami Herald*, June 25.

DeMarzo, Wanda, Daniel de Vise, and Larry Lebowitz. 2002. "Handling of Behan Case Part of a Pattern." *Miami Herald*, March 4.

Dieter, Richard C. 1997. "Millions Misspent: What Politicians Don't Say About the High Costs of the Death Penalty." (In Bedau, Hugo Adam, 1997. *The Death Penalty in America: Current Controversies*.) New York: Oxford University Press.

Dow, David R. 1996. "The State, The Death Penalty, and Carl Johnson." *Boston University Law Review* 37:691–711.

Eddings v. Oklahoma, 455 U.S. 104 (1982).

Enmund v. Florida, 458 U.S. 917 (1977).

Ex parte Burdine, 901 S.W. 2d 456, 457 (Texas Criminal Appeals, 1995) (Maloney, J., dissenting).

"Ex-Trooper Gets Prison for Faking Evidence." 1993. *New York Times*, June 6, 26.

Ford v. Wainwright, 477 U.S. 399 (1986).

Furman v. Georgia, 408 U.S. 238 (1972).

Geimer, William S. 1995. "A Decade of Strickland's Tin Horn: Doctrinal and Practical Undermining of the Right to Counsel." *William and Mary Bill of Rights Journal* 4:91–178.

Goodpaster, Gary. 1983. "The Trial for Life: Effective Assistance of Counsel in Death Penalty Cases." *New York University Law Review* 58:299–362.

———. 1986. "The Adversary System, Advocacy and the Effective Assistance of Counsel in Criminal Cases." *New York University Review of Law and Social Change* 14:59–92.

Governor's Commission on Capital Punishment. 2002. *Report of the Governor's Commission on Capital Punishment, George H. Ryan Governor of Illinois*. April 15.

Graham v. Johnson, 168 F. 3d 762, 767 (5th Ct. Court of Appeals, 1999).

Green, Frank. 2000. "Death Penalty Foes Gaining? Virginia Executed Eight Inmates in 2000. *Richmond Times-Dispatch*, December 27.

Gregg v. Georgia, 428 U.S. 153 (1976).

Grimm, Fred. 2001a. "One Detective's Behavior Reveals Larger Truths." *Miami Herald,* March 4.

Grimm, Fred. 2001b. "Scenario Can't Justify Condemning Wrong Man." *Miami Herald,* July 8.

H. Roberts v. Louisiana, 431 U.S. 633 (1977).

Herrera v. Collins, 506 U.S. 190, 113 S.Ct. 853 (1993).

Herring v. New York, 422 U.S. 853 (1975).

Innocence Project. 2002. "Causes and Remedies." http://www.innocenceproject. org. (Retrieved June 14, 2002.)

Jefferies, J. C., Jr. 1994. *Justice Lewis F. Powell, Jr.: A Biography.* New York: Charles Scribner & Sons.

Jurek v. Texas, 428 U.S. 262 (1976).

Justice Project. 2002a. "Profiles of Injustice." http://justice.policy.net/cjreform. (Retrieved June 14, 2002.)

Justice Project. 2002b. "100th Prisoner Exonerated by DNA Evidence." http://justice. policy.net/cjreform. (Retrieved June 14, 2002.)

Klein, Lawrence R., Brian E. Forst, and Victor Filatov. 1978. "The Deterrent Effect of Capital Punishment: An Assessment of the Estimates." In *Deterrence and Incapacitation: Estimating the Effects of Criminal Sanctions on Crime Rates,* edited by A. Blumstein, J. Cohen, and D. Nagin. Washington, DC: National Academy of Sciences Press.

Klein, Richard. 1986. "The Emperor Gideon Has No Clothes: The Empty Promise of the Constitutional Right to Effective Assistance of Counsel." *Hastings Constitutional Law Quarterly.* 13:625–693.

Lempert, Richard O. 1983. "The Effect of Executions on Homicides: A New Look in an Old Light." *Crime and Delinquency* 29:88–115.

Liebman, James, Jeffrey Fagan, and Valerie West. 2001. *A Broken System, Part I: Error Rates in Capital Cases, 1973–1995.* http://www.law.columbia.edu/ instructionalservices/liebman/; Columbia Law School.

Liebman, James, Jeffrey Fagan, Andrew Gelman, Valerie West, Garth Davies, and Alexander Kiss. 2002. *A Broken System, Part II: Why There Is So Much Error in Capital Cases and What Can Be Done About It.* http://www.law.columbia.edu/ brokensystem; Columbia Law School.

Lockett v. Ohio, 438 U.S. 586 (1978).

Makeig, John. 1992. "Asleep on the Job: Slay Trial Boring, Lawyer Said." *Houston Chronicle,* August 14, p. A35.

Marquart, James and John R. Sorensen. 1988. "Institutional and Post-Release Behavior of *Furman*-Commuted Inmates in Texas." *Criminology* 26:677–93.

———. 1989. "A National Study of the *Furman*-Commuted Inmates: Assessing the Threat to Society from Capital Offenders." *Loyola of Los Angeles Law Review* 23:5–28.

McClosky, James. 1996. "The Death Penalty: A Personal View." *Criminal Justice Ethics* 15(Summer-Fall).

McFarland, Sam. 1983. "Is Capital Punishment a Short-Term Deterrent to Homicide? A Study of the Effect of Four Recent American Executions." *Journal of Criminal Law and Criminology* 74:1014–31.

McFarland v. State, 928 S.W. 2d 482, 500–5 (Texas Criminal Appeals, 1996).

McMann v. Richardson, 397 U.S. 759 (1970).

Mello, Michael. 1988. "Facing Death Alone: The Post-Conviction Attorney Crisis On Death Row." *American University Law Review* 7:513–607.

Messer v. Kemp, 760 F. 2d 1080 (11th Ct., 1985).

Mills, Steve and Ken Armstrong. 1999a. "The Jailhouse Informant." *Chicago Tribune*, November 16.

———. 1999b. "A Tortured Path to Death Row." *Chicago Tribune*, November 17.

Mills, Steve, Ken Armstrong, and Douglas Holt. 2000. "GW Bush Has Executed 131 Inmates—Many With Seriously Flawed Trials." *Chicago Tribune*, June 11.

MSNBC. 2001. "O'Connor Questions Death Penalty." Staff and Wire Reports. *http://www.msnbc.com/news/595670.asp*, July 2.

Murray v. Giarratano, 109 S. Ct. 2765 (1989).

N.C. Gen. Statute, Sec. 14–17 (Cum. Supp., 1975).

Nathanson, Stephen. 1987. *An Eye for an Eye? The Morality of Punishing by Death.* Totowa, NJ: Rowman and Littlefield.

National Law Journal. 1990. *Fatal Defense, Death Row Defense: Lawyers in Trouble.* June 11 (Monday).

Payne v. Tennessee, 501 U.S. 808 (1991).

Penry v. Lynaugh, 109 S. Ct. 2934 (1989).

Peterson, Ruth D. and William C. Bailey. 1988. "Murder and Capital Punishment in the Evolving Context of the Post-*Furman* Era." *Social Forces* 66:774–807.

Phillips, David. 1980. "The Deterrent Effect of Capital Punishment: New Evidence on an Old Controversy." *American Journal of Sociology* 86:139–47.

"Police Chemist Surrenders in Perjury Case." 1994. *New York Times*, August 5, p. 14.

Powell v. Alabama, 287 U.S. 45 (1932).

Proffitt v. Florida, 428 U.S. 242 (1976).

Radin, Margaret Jane. 1980. "Cruel Punishment and Respect for Persons: Super Due Process for Death." *Southern California Law Review* 53:1143–85.

Rimer, Sara and Raymond Bonner. 2000. "Texas Lawyer's Death Row Record a Concern." *New York Times*, June 11.

Roberts v. Louisiana, 428 U.S. 325 (1976).

Romero v. Lynaugh, 884 F. 2nd 871, 875 (5th Ct., 1989).

Saletan, William. 2000. "Calculating the Risk—Does the Death Penalty Protect Innocent Life, or Endanger It?" *Mother Jones* 25:4.

Sandon, Leo. 2002. "Unease With Capital Punishment Mounts." *Tallahassee Democrat*, May 18, p. D1.

Sellin, Thorsten 1967. *Capital Punishment.* New York: Harper and Row.

——— 1980. *The Penalty of Death.* Beverly Hills, CA: Sage.

Skipper v. South Carolina, 106 S. Ct. 1669 (1986).

Smart, Christopher. 1997. "Innocence Found on Death Row." *Salt Lake City Weekly*, August 4.

Spangenberg, Robert L. and Elizabeth R. Walsh. 1989. "The Cost of Taking a Life: Dollars and Sense of the Death Penalty." *University of California Law Review* 8:1221–70.

Stack, Steven 1987. "Publicized Executions and Homicide, 1950–1980." *American Sociological Review* 52:532–40.

Stanford v. Kentucky and *Wilkins v. Missouri* 109 S. Ct. 2969 (1989).

State v. Dungee, Record Excerpts at 102, (11th Ct.) (No. 85-8202), *decided sub nom.*

Stevenson, Bryan. 1996. "The Hanging Judges: Once the Court Said 'Death Is Different.' Now It Says, Let's Get On with It. (The Supremes: Which Way Will the Court Swing?)" *The Nation,* October 14, v. 263(11).

Strickland v. Washington, 466 U.S. 688 (1984).

Sumner v. Shuman, 483 U.S. 66 (1987).

Taylor, Stuart, Jr. 2000. "The Death Penalty: To Err Is Human." *National Journal,* February 12, v. 32, p. 7.

Texas Civil Rights Project. 2000. *The Death Penalty in Texas: Due Process and Equal Justice or Rush to Execution? The Seventh Annual Report on the State of Human Rights in Texas.* Author.

Texas Defender Service. 2002. *A State of Denial: Texas Justice and the Death Penalty.* Houston: Texas Defender Service, *http://www.texasdefender.org* (Retrieved June 14, 2002).

Thompson v. Oklahoma, 108 S. Ct. 2687 (1988).

Tison v. Arizona, 107 S. Ct. 1676 (1987).

United States ex rel. Williams v. Twomey, 510 F. 2d 634 (1975).

United States v. Cronic, 466 U.S. 648 (1984).

Wainwright v. Sykes, 433 U.S. 72, 90 (1977).

Wallsten, Peter. 2002. "State High-Court Hopefuls Urge Death Penalty Change." *Miami Herald,* June 7.

Walsh, Jeff. 2002. "Frank Lee Smith's Long Hard Life." http://www.pbs.org/frontline/shows/smith/etc/longhard. (Retrieved April 12.)

Washington v. Commonwealth, 323 S.E. 2nd 577 (Va., 1984).

Woodson v. North Carolina, 428 U.S. 280 (1976).

Zant v. Stephens, 103 S. Ct. 2733 (1983).

IV

The Expanding Prison:
Life Inside, Policy, and Reform

Introduction to Part IV

We referred in our Introduction to the continued presence of the prison. It would be hard to imagine another institution with such apparently specialized functions that has been so intensively scrutinized. Historians have debated its origins; sociologists have studied its internal structure and culture; policy analysts have tried to evaluate its effectiveness; social critics, reformers, and prisoners themselves have exposed its inhumanity. The prison invariably emerges from this scrutiny as little more than a crude instrument for punishment and disposal—of dubious utility and near-certain harm. Yet prison systems throughout the world not only remain intact but keep expanding. They are seemingly impervious to criticism and resistant to attempts to replace them by alternatives that are more humane, efficient, and cheaper.

The first chapter in our subsection "Inside" comes from an unfortunately declining interest in the sociological study of prison life. In 1958, Gresham Sykes published *The Society of Captives,* the pioneering sociological study of imprisonment. The themes he raised in this study—what imprisonment does to prisoners, the social relationship between inmates and staff, the prison as a miniature society—remain just as relevant and interesting today. In Chapter 15, Sykes reflects on how this line of enquiry began.

Ethnographic studies of microcontrol within the prison gave way to macro- and historical enquiries. In typical academic fashion, this move went too far: how, we might ask, does something like "late-modern penality" look to its (unwilling) recipients? Gartner and Kruttschnitt (Chapter 16) give us a model for answering such questions. Their case study of women in two Californian prisons is explicitly designed to see how macroshifts in the penal landscape are reflected in the women's experience of imprisonment. The rare feature of this research is not so much the inside/outside comparison, but access to data that allow for comparisons over time: the California Institution of Women from the early sixties to the mid-nineties.

Our *Policy and Reform* subsection starts with a different interface between "life inside" and "policy and reform outside." In Chapter 17, James Jacobs examines one particular strand of prison reform: the use of the legal system to improve prison conditions and protect prisoners' rights. However important the quest for alternative forms of social control, democratic societies cannot allow internal prison regimes to be insulated from conventional mechanisms of legal accountability. But how far have the courts succeeded in penetrating the closed walls of the prison?

In Chapter 18, the historian David Rothman, whose 1971 book *The Discovery of the Asylum*, was a breakthrough in understanding the origins of the penitentiary in early 19th century America, now reflects on the current dramatic rise in rates of imprisonment. His emphasis on the determinate sentencing model raises important issues about the causal relationship between ideas and penal policy. In Chapter 19, Blomberg looks outside the prison walls, actually following up the immediate effects and long-term fate of alternatives to imprisonment. Metaphors like "net-widening" expressed the first wave of disappointment of many reformers (and cynicism of many criminologists) at the failure to stop correctional expansion. Blomberg's series of local-level studies show the more ambiguous results to be expected of programs that are classified as forms of "intermediate punishment" and located somewhere on a "continuum of care." Some results were indeed positive, but close empirical observation shows how cumulative effects (intended or not) run clearly toward "accelerated social control" and "piling up sanctions."

We end with three rather grim chapters on the expansion of the US prison system. They represent very different styles of academic enquiry. Austin, Irwin, and Kubrin (Chapter 20), as if trying to justify the sarcastic term "binge," are relentlessly empirical. They well know that the methodological complexities behind straightforward attributions such as "system expansion," "population growth," or "higher rates" require many different indicators: state and federal prisons; jails; "correctional supervision" through probation and parole; incarceration rates (number of prisoners per 100,000 of the population on a given day). Wacquant (Chapter 21) has the identical data in mind. But instead of scrutinizing their internal patterns, he launches outward from the one statistical cluster that is too shameful to ignore: the massive overrepresentation of black males in the prisons. Not everyone will be comfortable with his master image of the ghetto, but more conventional criminological "models" hardly do better.

Elliott Currie, a consistent voice of liberal criminology for nearly four decades, seems in Chapter 22 to be addressing a rather restricted issue: how mass imprisonment distorts our measurements of the rates/distribution of *criminality*, hence making such statistics even less suitable for generating causal theory and social policy. However, we placed this contribution as the last chapter because its modest thesis points to a major subject ahead: not punishment and social control as *dependent* but as *independent* variables, that is, *causes* of something else. If this "something else" turns out to be criminality itself, then this self-perpetuating cycle can only be broken from the outside—or by a new constellation of knowledge and power from inside.

15

The Structural-Functional Perspective on Imprisonment

Gresham M. Sykes

I

The emergence of a structural-functional perspective on the prison, in the decades immediately following the end of World War II, can be explained in part by the particular interests, personal experiences, and intellectual training of those involved in penology in those years. I believe, however, that the temper of the time—the dominant intellectual fashions, the events in the headlines, the social and political trends of those years—also played a role, providing a spur for a particular kind of theorizing as well as a receptive audience. And pure chance, I think, had an influence as well, in the sense that quite fortuitous events led a number of people—many at the beginning of their academic careers—to immerse themselves in the study of punishment of criminal offenders, bringing a variety of new approaches to the issues. These notes, then, are a form of intellectual history, admittedly impressionistic, anecdotal, personal, and incomplete.

In my own case, for example, I was assigned the criminology course in my first year of teaching as an instructor at Princeton University, although I knew almost nothing about the field, a kind of assignment of little concern apparently to sociology departments then and now. But I began learning what I could, one step ahead (often a misstep) of my students. I was appalled to find that textbooks in the field made almost no effort to examine what I would have thought to be basic issues such as varying conceptions of crime, how and why society defined some behavior criminal, and the meaning of crime from the viewpoint of the offender. The vast body of writing in the law (which I was dimly aware existed) was largely ignored, including the analysis of criminal intent that evidently played a large part in legal thought. And punishment was almost uniformly viewed as a barbarism, and ineffective to boot. A number of liberal sentiments, which I largely shared, seemed to have hardened into a set of clichs that closed off inquiry. But my experience in the army had persuaded me that, for better or for worse, people often became whatever they were assigned regardless of personal proclivities or skills, and I set about becoming a criminologist.

At Princeton in those days many classes were split between lectures and "precepts," or small groups meeting to discuss the lecture material. What was unusual was that the precepts were led not by graduate students but by faculty members, from junior instructors to senior professors. Enrollments in my criminology course began to go up sharply, with the result that the number of necessary precepts increased greatly, requiring more preceptors; and the sociology department persuaded Lloyd McKorkle, the warden of the New Jersey State Maximum Security Prison in the nearby city of Trenton, to meet with one of the discussion groups twice a week.

Lloyd and I became good friends, although I am sure he was more than a little bemused by my naivete and ignorance, and he urged me to make a closer study of the prison. The friendship had two important consequences. For one thing, Lloyd provided me with free and easy access to all parts of the prison, to both guards and inmates, and to the records of the institution. And in frequent, long conversations spread over a number of years, Lloyd and other prison officials provided intimate and detailed accounts of institutional life which proved invaluable.

Donald Cressey tells of a similar chance encounter with another Lloyd—Lloyd Ohlin, in his case—involving a missed connection after a meeting of the American Sociological Association in Urbana, and a shared ride to Chicago, leading to an invitation to study prisons in Wisconsin. Others seem to have had like experiences, in the sense that often seemingly whimsical, random, or accidental events led them into criminology and penology and the establishment of close and prolonged relationships with penal institutions. So much for the idea of an orderly, logical development of an intellectual career. But the important point is that these links with penal institutions produced detailed, intimate knowledge of prison life over a period of years, a knowledge that transcended what could be obtained through questionnaires or interviews, although these too played a part. And the knowledge was different, I think, from that obtained by being an official with an administrative role or being an inmate, although both have made important contributions to the literature of penology.

II

In the first half of this century, interest in the prison had taken six major forms. First, humanitarian concerns centered attention on the brutal and degrading conditions of confinement, and offered various programs of reform. Second, the prison was examined with an eye to the possibilities of rehabilitating the offender, with the deterrent effect of imprisonment largely discounted, as I have noted. Third, a good deal of anecdotal material was offered for public consumption, since tales of life behind bars seemed to feed an endless curiosity about the confinement of dangerous felons. Fourth, linked to this anecdotal material, prisons were periodically subject to expose detailing mismanagement, graft, and other forms of wrongdoing on the part of officials, with prison scandals serving as a convenient weapon for the party out of power. Fifth, penal institutions served as a topic for historical investigations, although this interest remained limited until the shape of historical inquiries changed and "history from below" became more popular. And finally there was a sociological concern with penal institutions—a concern often marked by a humanitarian impulse and utilitarian considerations of finding more effective means of rehabilitation, but laying claim to scientific objectivity and sociological relevance, and examining such things as patterns of socialization and status.

This sociological work provided an indispensable base for later studies, but with some notable exceptions it was mainly descriptive, an ethnography of the confined. Much of the theorizing centered on the question of "prisonization," or the process by which the individual acquired the values, norms, and attitudes of the inmate subculture, with less attention paid to the question of why the subculture existed in the first place. The diversity of inmate roles was made clear, but their relationship to one another and to the regime of the custodians remained relatively neglected.

After the end of World War II, however, American sociology began to change. Many of the changes were actually a flowering or a development of ideas produced in the 1930s and 1940s, ideas that had simply lain dormant or received little attention in a country preoccupied with war. In any event, research design became much more elaborate and sophisticated, as did the statistical techniques for sample selection and the analysis of data. This push toward quantification was closely linked to the growth of federal funding for scientific research, with skills in quantification becoming an important qualification for securing funds while at the same time large federal grants provided the resources that made more elaborate quantification possible. "Big time" research was becoming a notable feature of modern sociology. While some substantive areas fell out of fashion, others such as stratification gained increasing attention. And in the area of theory, the ideas of Parsons and Merton, along with those of their disciples, rose into prominence.

Criminology and penology were inevitably influenced to some extent by these developments. As far as the study of the prison was concerned, however, quantitative research with large numbers of respondents and the precise measurement of variables remained relatively rare. The suspicion bordering on paranoia in the prison posed a major problem, since it was extremely difficult and time-consuming to establish the trust necessary for the collection of reliable data by means of questionnaires and interviews, with both guards and inmates. Generally, empirical research on the prison continued to take the form of community studies or participant observation. But a way of looking at the prison, influenced by the ideas of Parsons and Merton, did become much more evident. First, the prison as a whole was taken as the object of study, a small-scale society or social system, with questions about the problems of continuity and order assuming major theoretical significance. Second, the parts of the system—the objectives of the custodial institution, the social and physical environment, the perceptions and social roles of guards and inmates, and so on—were seen as interrelated elements to be analyzed for their impact on one another and the system as a whole. Emphasis was placed not simply on the intended consequences of rules and behavior but on the unintended or latent outcomes as well. Third, the prison was seen as providing an opportunity for "middle-range" theorizing, with the special conditions of custodial institutions setting definite limits on generalization but offering the possibility of greater insights on the nature of totalitarian control. And fourth—and perhaps most important—the norms of both guards and inmates were seen as being significantly shaped by the system of power in which they played out their social roles. The existence of norms was not to be taken as a given, with commitment to those norms seen as a matter of socialization, enculturation, the transmission of culture, learning theory, differential association, and so on. Instead, the existence of norms was a problem to be solved, and the task was to analyze norms as a function of the social structure or social system in which individuals found themselves.

These themes were not original nor were they unique to the study of the prison. Albert Cohen, for example, in his book *Delinquent Boys* (1955), had set forth a clear and powerful argument for the need to explore the origins of subcultures rather than merely to study the process of their acquisition, and had traced his ideas to Pitirim Sorokin's concern with the rise and fall of total systems. But the combination of these themes, the emphasis given to them, and the primary interest in the prison itself rather than the effectiveness of the prison for rehabilitation, deterrence, or retribution all brought something different to penology.

Two other things were important, I think, in the development of a changed perspective on imprisonment. First, there were some forty riots in eighteen months in American prisons, beginning in the early part of 1952. Prisons, obviously, were not working very well, and public concern with the issue encouraged an academic interest. Thus, for example, funds were provided by the Social Science Research Council for a series of meetings, in 1956 and 1957, for a group of social scientists working in this area, leading to the publication of *Theoretical Studies in the Social Organization of the Prison* (1960). Second, the 1950s saw an increased interest in systems of total power as more and more information about Nazi concentration camps became available. This factor acted in a very indirect fashion, I believe, and the analysis of concentration camps never became a part of American criminology in any full or systematic way. Nevertheless, reports on concentration camps became an important part of the intellectual climate, particularly through Bruno Bettelheim's "Individual and Mass Behavior in Extreme Situations" (1943) in the early 1940s, and books such Eugen Kogan's *The Theory and Practice of Hell* (1950) in the 1950s, and Hannah Arendt's *Eichmann in Jerusalem* (1963) in the 1960s.

III

The structural-functional approach to the prison rarely concerned itself with precise definitions, conceptual elaboration, or the logical analysis of causal chains—or, indeed, the accumulation of a large mass of empirical data. Instead, I think its claim to attention rested on a set of basic insights that found a sympathetic audience:

1. It was recognized that prison, like any other complex social system persisting through time, could not be run by the use of force alone, that some degree of voluntary cooperation on the part of those who were ruled was necessary. The problem then was how this cooperation could be obtained.

2. The rewards and punishments legally available to the prison authorities were generally inadequate, as far as securing cooperation was concerned. Furthermore, the task of running the prison and securing cooperation was severely hampered by the fact the prison was assigned objectives that were often contradictory or in conflict with one another. Thus, for example, efforts to rehabilitate inmates were frequently undone by the requirements of maintaining security and preventing disorder.

3. Some degree of cooperation could be obtained—and usually was— by a system of illegal or forbidden rewards, such as guards ignoring the infraction of prison rules by inmates. Prisoners were allowed to engage in various forms of deviant behavior—ostensibly of a minor sort—in exchange for a quiet institution. This pattern of the custodians breaking the rules for the sake of peace and quiet was part of an extensive pattern of "corruption" based on friendship and the innocuous encroachment on the guards' duties on the part of inmates.

4. Imprisonment involved a set of deprivations that went far beyond the loss of liberty or material comfort. Prisoners were faced with a number of psychological threats to their self-conception or sense of worth, such as be-

ing reduced to childhood's dependence or being forced into homosexual liaisons.

5. Much of the behavior of inmates could be interpreted or understood as attempts, conscious or unconscious, to meet and counter the problems posed by the deprivations of prison life, including the potent threats to the ego. In later years, critics such as John Irwin (1970) would claim that the behavior patterns of inmates were rooted in a thieves' subculture, and much was made of an indigenous versus an imported model of the inmate social system. From the structural-functional perspective, however, the important issue was how the behavior of inmates was related to their present predicament rather than the possible influence of life before confinement. And although inmates' behavior was probably conditioned by prior criminal patterns, the crucial issue was how these general tendencies—such as the vaunted loyalty among thieves or the instrumental use of violence—might be reinforced or called into play by the realities of prison life. (I think there was a common feeling that the inmate social system seen in prisons at the time would very likely come into existence almost without regard to inmates' criminal histories. I suppose this idea was based at least in part on assumptions about the power of totalitarian systems to shape behavior and the limited possibilities of dealing with the threats posed by imprisonment.)

6. It was claimed that the behavior patterns of inmates sprang from a set of values, attitudes, and beliefs that found expression in the so-called inmate code couched in prison argot. This code held forth a pattern of approved conduct, but as Shelly Messinger and I tried to make clear, it was an ideal rather than a description of how inmates behaved. It was argued that an important theoretical and empirical variable was to be found in the extent to which inmates actually did or did not conform to the inmate code with its demands for inmate solidarity, and this variation was likely to be a vital factor in determining the extent to which rehabilitation was possible in a prison setting.

These ideas came to be labeled "the structural-functional perspective on the prison," and I suppose that designation was appropriate, in the sense that interest in the prison centered on (1) the social structure of the prison as a whole; and (2) the ways in which beliefs, norms, and behavior of both inmates and guards functioned to maintain the prison as an ongoing system. The astonishing thing about prisons, from this viewpoint, was the fact that they did not degenerate into perpetual chaos on the one hand or, on the other, into the frozen order of masses of men locked in solitary confinement. Somehow, a social system, involving complex interaction, was kept going. It was precisely this fact, I think, that Shelly and I concentrated on in our discussion of the inmate beliefs and norms that we saw, not as an extension of the outlaw's code—a somewhat romantic notion, perhaps—

but as an understandable response to the rigors of confinement, specifi-cally addressed to the problems of prison life.

IV

As I look back on the development of these ideas, some forty years after the fact, I still think they were a worthwhile innovation despite their limi-tations. Obviously, the nature of imprisonment has changed in a number of ways, such as the greatly increased balkanization of the inmate popula-tion along racial and ethnic lines described by James Jacobs (1983), court intervention in the legal powers of the custodians, and shifts in the com-position of the inmate population, and these changes must modify our view of the social system of the custodial institution. The neglect of race re-lations in the prisons in the 1950s is rather striking, and I think this was probably due to two things, First, the sociologists writing about the prison were almost exclusively white, and I suspect this helped to shape not only the range of their concerns but also their ability to establish relationships of trust with black inmates. And second, there was an assumption that the social systems of black and white inmates—and their relationships with the power structure of the prison—were essentially the same. Along with this it was assumed that blacks and whites in prison frequently achieved a kind of modus vivendi and, indeed, that the solidarity of inmates would, to some extent, override the antagonisms of race.

All this changed, of course, in the ensuing decades, and group conflict rather than inmate solidarity became a paramount feature of many custo-dial institutions. Not only did blacks and whites often move to violent con-frontations, but bikers, different factions of Hispanics, political radicals, and others formed contesting alliances. Nonetheless, I believe the struc-tural-functional perspective continues to provide a valid picture of the broad outlines of the nature of imprisonment in America today, with the recognition that inmate solidarity has fractured, in many institutions, along a variety of fault lines.

However, I must admit I am also struck by the fact that academic stud-ies of the prison seem to have had little impact on public policy. A good deal of the research on prisons has been linked to the hope that society can build a more humane and more effective system of criminal justice, with a decreased reliance on punishment; what has happened in fact, in the last twenty-five years or so, is that the philosophy of "lock 'em up and throw away the key" has gained ground in the United States rather than being diminished. Rates of imprisonment have increased sharply. For a compre-hensive review of what is commonly referred to as mass imprisonment in the United States, see Garland (2001). Public support for parole has gone down, and programs of treatment within prisons have been eliminated or reduced. Harsher sentences have become more popular, as in the case of the so-called war on drugs, but with little apparent effect on crime rates.

It is possible of course, that the problems of the prison are beyond the reach of the social engineering often envisioned by social sciences—and it must be admitted that the social sciences have unquestionably suffered from an amazing hubris as far as their power to change social reality is concerned. It is also possible that more punitive public policies of recent years might be seen as a misguided but sincere effort to come to grips with changing circumstances, such as high crime rates, or as an acceptance of empirical research claiming nothing much works when it comes to treatment without prison walls. I suspect, however, that the increased strength of the punitive viewpoint is only marginally related to increases in crime rates or an objective analysis of the outcome of efforts at reformation. In my opinion, when all is said and done about rehabilitation, incapacitation, and deterrence, the prison continues to be seen primarily as a flawed but essential instrument of retribution, as far as the great majority of the public is concerned. Stories of crime and punishment have an ancient lineage and exercise a perennial appeal, and it is undoubtedly true that our ideas about how to handle the criminal are likely to be shaped by the entertainments of the mass media and the emotional rhetoric of political speeches. But it is also probably true that our ideas about punishment are shaped as well by deep-seated cultural dictates and persistent personal inclinations. Sociology has been inclined to dismiss the demand for punishment largely as an irrelevant barbarism or as the expression of fluctuations in the political climate. If we are to achieve a better, more complex understanding of the forces that shape punishment in general or imprisonment in particular, I think we will need to work out a more profound analysis of the public's view of punishment, and to examine it as a moral choice filled with the ambiguities, uncertainties, prejudices, and efforts to be rational that shape so much of human behavior.

REFERENCES

Arendt, Hanna. 1963. *Eichmann in Jerusalem: A Report of the Banality of Evil.* New York: Viking.

Bettelheim, Bruno. 1943. "Individual and Mass Behavior in Extreme Situations." *Journal of Abnormal and Social Psychology* 38:447–51.

Cloward, Richard (ed.). 1960. *Theoretical Studies in the Social Organization of the Prison.* New York: Social Science Research Council.

Cohen, Albert K. 1955. *Delinquent Boys.* New York: Free Press.

Garland, David (ed.). 2001. "Special Issue on Mass Imprisonment in the USA." *Punishment & Society* 3(1):5–199.

Irwin, John. 1970. *The Felon.* Englewood Cliffs, NJ: Prentice-Hall.

Jacobs, James B. 1983. *New Perspective on Prisons and Improvement.* Ithaca, NY: Cornell University Press.

Kogan, Eugene. 1966. *The Theory and Practice of Hell.* New York: Berkeley.

16

Women and Imprisonment

A Case Study of Two California Prisons

ROSEMARY GARTNER AND CANDACE KRUTTSCHNITT

In 1970, when the number of women incarcerated in U.S. state and federal prisons (5,635) was at its lowest point since 1938, scholarly interest in women in prison was limited and largely concerned with how women's ways of coping with imprisonment compared to men's. In 2000 the United States imprisoned over 85,000 women[1] and, perhaps not surprisingly, the literature on women in prison had expanded accordingly to include overviews of the demographic characteristics and life histories of female inmates, detailed needs assessments and reviews of gender-specific programs, and qualitative research on the culture of women's prisons and women's adaptations to prison life.[2] This literature suggests that even as the female prison population in the United States increased fifteenfold, there was a dreary monotony both in the types of women going to prison—the poor, racial minorities, and single mothers continued to be overrepresented; and in the problems they faced inside—access to adequate medical care, to education and vocational training, to drug treatment, and to programs addressed to their histories of physical and sexual abuse.

Studying women in prison in order to understand their backgrounds, adaptations, and needs is undoubtedly important, but research with this as its primary goal may miss an opportunity to raise broader questions about the purposes and practices of imprisonment, and the ways in which these are gendered. The scholarly literature on penality has characterized the last third of the twentieth century as a time of unusual change in the discourses, objectives, and techniques of punishment, but has done so largely without reference to the experiences of those in prison. For women prisoners and women's prisons, what Garland (1995:203) has called "the closing of a long period of naive enthusiasm and optimism" and the emergence of "a deep moral ambiguity" with regard to penality may have had particularly profound consequences. The punishment of criminal women has historically been based on assumptions and expectations different in important ways from the punishment of men. Among these was the view that women were generally more reformable, or at least more tractable and hence controllable, than men; and the belief that a disciplinary regime grounded in an ideology of domesticity could best effect women's rehabilitation. But shifts in the penal landscape have eroded these assumptions and altered the ways in which punishment is practiced on women in the United States.

In this chapter, we turn to women in three different prison contexts in California—a "bellwether state" (Clear 1994:54) in trends and practices of imprisonment—to provide insights into whether and how the discursive and technical shifts of the last forty years are reflected in their experiences of imprisonment. Our interest is in what women in prison can tell us about the practices of punishment and how these operate within different penal regimes. To provide a broader context for these women's experiences, we first outline some of the important changes in California's female prison population and in the ways imprisonment was practiced on women in California during the last third of the twentieth century.

CHANGES IN CALIFORNIA'S FEMALE PRISON POPULATION

One of the most obvious indicators of recent changes in penality in the United States is the enormous growth in the size of the prison population that began in the mid- to late 1970s (Blumstein 1995). California was among the states leading this growth, just as it was a leader in repudiating the rehabilitative model it had so warmly embraced in the 1950s (Simon 1993). Until 1987, California had only one prison for women. Within the next eight years three more prisons for women opened, each of which filled to capacity almost immediately. This building boom did little to ease overcrowding: Throughout the 1990s, the occupancy rate of women's prisons in California ranged from 150 to 178 percent. By 2000, California imprisoned over 10,000 female felons, close to 15 percent of all female felons in the nation and 18 times the number of women in prison in 1970 (California Department of Corrections 2000).

Another indicator of changes in penality during this period is who was sent to prison, for how long, and why. Throughout the 1970s between 40 and 50 percent of the women in California's prisons were serving time for violent crimes and about 25 percent were imprisoned for drug crimes. By the late 1990s, these percentages had reversed so that the typical female prisoner was serving time for the possession, sale or manufacture of narcotics.[3] As a consequence, the average time women served before being paroled dropped from 27 months in 1975 to 14 months in 1995, reflecting the shorter sentences for drug crimes compared to violent crimes. For female felons, parole became a major avenue back into prison. In the 1970s an average of about 100 women were returned to prison for parole violations each year, compared to over 5,000 by the mid-1990s.[4]

These changes—massive growth in prison populations fed to a greater and greater extent by parole returnees and nonviolent offenders—have been seen as important indicators of not only a new penal regime, but also an emerging "social management instrument" aimed at governing "the underclass" (Feeley and Simon 1992). The repercussions of this new regime were particularly pronounced for women, who relative to men commit a larger share of nonviolent offenses—especially drug offenses—than they do of violent offenses. Consequently, in California in the 1990s imprisonment was no longer the exceptionally rare event for women that it had been a generation earlier: California's female imprisonment rate grew from 8 per 100,000 female population in 1970 to almost 90 per 100,000 by 2000.

California's female prison population changed in other ways between the 1960s and the 1990s.[5] Women in prison became more ethnically diverse over time, as did women in the general population; even so, African-American women were overrepresented in the state's prisons throughout this period. By the 1990s women in prison were also distinctly older than they had been in the 1960s, with over half aged 36 or older compared to only about one-third over 35 in the 1960s. Despite being older, women in California's prisons in the 1990s were much less likely to be married (approximately 16 percent) than either their counterparts in the 1960s (approximately 35 percent) or women in the general population in the 90s (approximately 50 percent). However, in the 1990s over 80 percent of imprisoned women had children compared to 68 percent of women in prison in the 1960s and 58 percent of women in the general population in the 1990s. In other words, single mothers were increasingly the targets of California's unfurling carceral net.

As we compare women's experiences in the three prison contexts, we need to keep in mind these changes over time in their background characteristics. But, as we will see, the differences across the three contexts in women's views of other inmates, staff, and the prison in general are unlikely to be a simple function of changes over time in who was sent to prison.

THE THREE PRISON CONTEXTS

Our research began as a comparative study of women's experiences at the California Institution for Women (CIW) in the early 1960s and mid-1990s. Opened in 1952 when California led the nation in the implementation of new rehabilitative methods, CIW was designed to embody the assumptions about women's needs for a domestically oriented correctional regime. Located in an agricultural area forty miles east of Los Angeles, CIW's rural isolation was expected to encourage women to identify with the prison as a home. Its "residents" wore their own clothing and lived in single rooms in "cottages" staffed by nonuniformed "matrons;" only a cyclone fence surrounded the "campus," which was planted with flower gardens; and state law mandated that CIW's "superintendent" must be a woman. In the early 1960s, when David Ward and Gene Kassebaum conducted their now-classic study of women in prison at CIW (Ward and Kassebaum 1965), the 850 or so women imprisoned there received vocational training in cosmetology, laundry, sewing, and quantity cooking; were required, if they were under fifty-five years old, to take a homemaking class; and participated in voluntary and mandatory individual and group therapy.

What were assumed to be women's distinctive needs dictated that their imprisonment be conducted according to rules and procedures that differed in some respects from those governing men in prison, and so CIW was run according to its own "local institution rules" (California Department of Corrections 1960). The training manual issued to new employees in the early 1960s was developed specifically for CIW and emphasized that CIW "does not separate its custody and treatment functions" (California Department of Corrections 1957:5). Nevertheless, the language used in the manual, particularly in its conclusion, suggests that the treatment function and CIW's "dynamic rehabilitative program" were expected to be primary concerns of staff:

> The atmosphere that we create in our relationship with the women under our care is more important than the beauty of our buildings, the richness of our equipment, the perfection of our program structure, the words that we speak. Unless our relationship is one of genuine professional interest, seasoned with warmth and friendliness, it has no value. Only if we create a treatment atmosphere can there be treatment. (ibid.:21)

Treatment required something more concrete than professional interest or an appropriate atmosphere, however; it also required information. Each woman at CIW had a detailed case file that included the results of her psychological testing upon admission to prison and notes from correctional counselors who conducted therapy groups and from the psychiatrist or psychologist who met with her individually. This was to be the basis for a treatment program designed to meet the woman's particular "psychological, psychosexual, and symbiotic needs," as well as addressing problems with her family and social adjustment, and with her "self-limitation variables" (Cassel and van Vorst 1961). Knowing the individual was the first step toward normalizing her, a task CIW took very seriously.

Through the 1960s and 1970s, CIW remained the only prison for women in California and operated with relative autonomy from the California Department of Corrections (CDC). By the early 1980s, however, dramatic changes in penality were under way in California. Rehabilitation was officially renounced as a goal of imprisonment in 1977 when indeterminate sentencing was replaced by determinate sentencing, and the war on drugs was about to be launched. Between 1977, the year the Uniform Determinate Sentencing Law was passed, and 1983 the state's prison population more than doubled, to over 39,000 prisoners. CIW's population followed a similar trend, rising from approximately 600 women in the early 1970s to almost 2,500—or just over 10 percent of all female inmates in the United States—by the late 1980s. With the opening of the Central California Women's Facility (CCWF) in 1990—the third prison for women in California and then the largest women's prison in the world—CIW's overcrowding eased somewhat, but it faced new challenges as the CDC moved to bring women's prisons into conformity with the policies and procedures applied to men's prisons. This move was welcomed by CIW's administrators, who claimed that female felons were becoming more like men in the crimes they committed[6] and therefore required a less gender-typed prison regime.

By the time we began our research at CIW in 1995, the 1,600 or so women imprisoned there lived two to a room, wore state-issued clothing, and were guarded by uniformed male and female correctional officers. Towers with armed guards and a perimeter fence reinforced with razor wire had been added, but otherwise the physical layout of the prison had changed little since the early 1960s. In the 1990s, vocational training had expanded to include electronics, plumbing, computer programming, and fire fighting, but counseling and treatment programs had been greatly scaled back and many of these were conducted by community volunteers or by prisoners themselves. Although subject to an obligation to work, over one-third of CIW's prisoners were "involuntarily unassigned" to jobs, which meant they could not earn credits toward sentence reduction. Many of the staff had worked at CIW for years, learning their jobs "when there was a reformatory philosophy," as one administrator put it; but newer staff, according to this same administrator, tended to have a much different "us versus them," "inmates don't deserve anything" attitude. Another senior staff member voiced the same opinion and attributed younger staff's inability to "communicate with inmates in human terms" to their having been "born and raised in more punitive times."

What prisoners called the "robocop" mentality of some staff at CIW reflected a very different penal climate from that of the early 1960s when Ward and Kassebaum conducted their research, and was a source of concern for CIW's warden and her immediate deputies. The warden, like her predecessors, stressed the importance of open communication between staff and prisoners. One long-time staff member praised this and other efforts by the warden to reinvigorate aspects of CIW's therapeutic community of the 1960s and 1970s. This included encouraging prisoners to form self-help groups to address their histories of substance abuse and domestic violence, which, according to the warden, were major barriers to their rehabilitation. Offering herself as a role model, the warden told us she urged women to "use that adversity in their lives to try and turn themselves around" and to get involved in community service work while in prison as a way to boost their self-esteem.

Rehabilitation, then, was still on CIW's agenda in the 1990s but it was no longer viewed as CIW's responsibility. As the warden told us: "We're not rehabilitating anyone. We're creating an atmosphere in which women can change themselves, where they can start thinking about themselves as being able to change." As O'Malley (1992) has argued and Lynch (2001) has demonstrated in her study of parole agents in California, this represents the emergence of a strategy of responsibilization or prudentialism whereby the criminal justice system offloads the responsibility for rehabilitation onto the criminal subject. Like CIW in the 1960s, then, CIW in the 1990s still assumed women could be reformed by imprisonment. Unlike the 1960s, however, this reformation would not be guided by expert knowledge of a woman's particular needs nor made possible through training her in her proper domestic role. In the 1990s rehabilitation would occur at CIW only when women made the choice to change. "Prison," said one senior administrator, "can only provide the means and the time for women to make that choice."

The question our research was designed to address was whether the experiences of women serving time at CIW in the 1960s and the 1990s would differ in distinctive ways, given these differences in philosophy and practice. We had access to interview and survey data Ward and Kassebaum collected at CIW in 1963. Using a similar methodology, we intended to conduct in-depth interviews with about forty women and gather survey data from the general inmate population at CIW. Our research design changed, however, after our initial interviews at CIW in the summer of 1995. A number of the women we talked with expressed concern that they might be transferred to Valley State Prison for Women (VSPW), which had just opened across the road from CCWF. VSPW was rumored by prisoners to be "the female Pelican Bay,"[7] but welcomed by administrators at CIW who saw it as a way to relieve overcrowding and cull out inmates whom they felt were not well-suited to CIW's distinctive culture.

From our first visit to VSPW it was clear that it embodied an ideology of imprisonment and a view of female prisoners very different from CIW's, even though it, like CIW, housed women of all security levels. VSPW's physical plant and staff practices conveyed a preoccupation with security, danger, and control. Prisoners' movements were restricted by walled yards, electrified fences, and requirements to line up when walking to and from meals or between different parts of the prison. Unlike at CIW, guards carried batons along with pepper spray and handcuffs. The warden at VSPW told us that his overriding concern was with the safety of inmates and staff, a concern he acknowledged was somewhat different from that of the wardens of the other prisons for women in California. As a consequence, he had instituted policies—such as restricting the value of personal property to discourage extortion—that some prisoners considered to be harsh, but that he felt made the prison safer.[8] The warden's emphasis on safety was accompanied by his lack of faith that imprisonment—at least the way it was currently practiced—could do much of anything else for women; rehabilitation was not mentioned in our interview with him.

The warden's pessimism about imprisonment exemplifies the diminished expectations many claim characterized penality in the late-twentieth century. If the prison cannot reform its charges, it can at least strive to house them safely and efficiently, and this appears to have been VSPW's raison d'être. "At design," its mission statement opens, "Valley State Prison for Women provides 1,980 women's beds for California's overcrowded prison system." The implication is that VSPW serves and services the prison system rather than performing any larger function. This is the "managerialism" identified by Bottoms (1983), Feeley and Simon (1992), and others —"a new and pronounced concern with system management, resource allocation, cost-benefit considerations, and organizational efficiency" (Garland 1995:190).

Notwithstanding the pastel institutional furniture in the public areas of the prison, then, almost nothing about VSPW reminded us of the domestic disciplinary regime and faith in rehabilitation that had dominated women's imprisonment for so many decades and continued to shape CIW's culture. How, we wondered, would women's experiences in this new prison—built so that it could be converted to a men's prison should the need arise, headed by a male warden, and housing eight women per cell[9]—compare with those of women at CIW in the early 1960s and in the mid-1990s?

WOMEN'S EXPERIENCES OF DOING TIME IN DIFFERENT PRISON CONTEXTS

What can women at CIW and VSPW tell us about the practice of imprisonment under different penal regimes? Did women's views of other prisoners, staff, and the prison differ depending on when and where they served their time? We address these questions drawing first on Ward and Kassebaum's and our interviews with women at CIW, and our interviews with women at VSPW. We then present responses to a series of survey questions we asked of the general population at each prison.

Interviews with Women at CIW and VSPW

Because little was known about how women "did time" in the early 1960s, Ward and Kassebaum began their study by conducting interviews with forty-five inmates. The women they chose to interview included "inmate politicians," women in prison for the first time, and women who had served time at CIW more than a decade earlier. The interviews asked the women to reflect upon "the major problems of confinement" they experienced and "the general inmate behavior patterns" they saw at CIW (Ward and Kassebaum 1963:5). More specific questions included: (1) What are the most difficult aspects of doing time? (2) What are the specific problems of prison life for you? (3) What is the nature of inmate-staff relations? (4) What are the various types of inmates and how would you characterize relations among inmates?

In our interviews with women at CIW and VSPW in the mid-1990s, we asked the same set of questions because we wanted information as comparable as possible to that obtained by Ward and Kassebaum. We planned to use these interviews to design a survey for the general population at each prison, and so we attempted to interview women at different stages in their prison careers, women committed for different offenses, and women of different racial and ethnic backgrounds and ages. We were reasonably successful in this effort[10] and were able to interview thirty-two women at CIW and thirty-eight women at VSPW.

In many respects, the major problems of imprisonment for women did not differ over time or across prisons. Separation from their families, particularly their children, was the predominant concern of the women interviewed in the 1960s and the 1990s. Ward and Kassebaum (1964:162) saw this "psychological pain of prison" as "particularly severe for a woman who is a mother" and found that it "does not appreciably lessen over time." Virtually all of the women we interviewed also reported that separation from their children and families was the most difficult aspect of doing time. Some cited it as the reason for the relative absence of serious violence, racial tension, and collective action in women's prisons compared to men's prisons. As one woman at VSPW told us: "We're talking about 3,000, or nearly 3,000 mothers, you know? So whether they have their kids when they're out or not, when they're in here, they think about wanting to get out to their kids."[11] What Carlen (1998:99) calls "the material consciousness of their family responsibilities; as well as all the ideological baggage about appropriate and legitimated femininities and women's proper place" means that separation from children is cited in study after study as the most uniformly distressing aspect of imprisonment for women, and one which Carlen argues was "sharpened and amplified" in the 1990s. While our data do not allow us to determine whether the latter claim was true for women at CIW and VSPW in the 1990s, it is the case that more women experienced this separation: Recall that over 80 percent of the women at CIW and VSPW in the 1990s had children compared to about two-thirds of the women at CIW in the 1960s.

One of the specific problems of imprisonment that was identified by women in all three prison contexts was a tension between their desire for consistency in the application of rules and their desire that staff take account of their individual differences. Ward and Kassebaum (1965:21–22) described this as "an inherent conflict in the system. . . . The problem here for staff is in reconciling the need to treat each inmate as a distinctive case with the demands of individual inmates and some staff members for standard practices which would make expectations more consistent and predictable." Despite the deemphasis on individualized treatment in the 1990s, the women we interviewed continued to hold out hope that they might be treated as individuals, even as they expressed the apparently contradictory complaint that, in the words of one woman at CIW, "the only thing that's consistent around here is the inconsistency." Women at VSPW in particular felt they had the worst of both worlds. Many claimed that "the rules change when the shift changes" but what did not change was how guards viewed them: "They figure that we're all criminals and we're all animals, and all we want to do is hurt, steal, and kill people. And that's not true. I know they can't get on a personal level. I understand that. But they shouldn't classify us." Others (e.g., Liebling, Price, and Elliot 1999; Bosworth 1996) have identified the tension between uniform and individualized treatment as an important and intractable paradox of staff-prisoner relationships, which staff often struggle with as well. As such, this tension needs to be seen as a fundamental feature of imprisonment, rather than an example of the "contrariness" of female prisoners, as some staff characterized it to us.

Women's relationships with staff and with other prisoners have greater influence on their daily lives in prison than do official discourses about penality or abstract logics of power, and these relationships were extensively commented upon in the interviews. Every woman interviewed complained about staff and in ways that, for the most part, varied little across the three contexts. The women resented being treated like children by staff, felt they could not trust staff with personal information, and railed over staff's pettiness and "superior attitude." But there were also important differences over time and between prisons in women's views of staff. Appreciation for the efforts and professionalism of at least some staff was more commonly expressed in the 1960s than in the 1990s. Of the women interviewed by Ward and Kassebaum, only two had nothing positive to say

about staff; of the women we interviewed, many of those at CIW and almost all of those at VSPW spoke about staff only in negative terms.

Some of the criticisms of staff were also context-specific. For example,
only at CIW in the early 1960s did women reprove staff who tried to be too
friendly toward them. A woman interviewed for Ward and Kassebaum's
study "complained of new staff who try to be like one of the inmates" and
said that staff should "know their place—they're not inmates." This type
of concern was never expressed to us. Rather, the women we interviewed
frequently complained that staff, especially new correctional officers
treated prisoners as "a different category from them." The view expressed
by a woman at CIW was common: "Now we got this new breed of staff
that has no respect. You're a criminal and that's it, and you're never gonna
be nothin' else and they talk to you so bad." The women we interviewed
at VSPW were the most critical of staff and related encounters that were
unparalleled in the other prisons.[12] One woman at VSPW described how
staff "make you feel like you're a failure and you're not gonna' make it out
there. They'll say 'Oh, you'll be back.' I've heard them say that when somebody's paroled. 'Oh, I'll see you next week.'" Another said "There are officers that don't care whether you learn or not. This is their job, and if
you're gone, they lose their money. 'We need your money. If you don't
come back, could you send somebody in your place, because it's a job.'" A
lifer at CIW explained this type of attitude in a very similar fashion to that
of the CIW administrator quoted earlier:

> They're taking the reflection that society has for inmates. . . . I think that
> whatever's happening out there is happening in here, whether it's in the gov-
> ernment or just in society in general. . . . The pendulum swung so far in one
> direction, you know, toward rehabilitation . . . that it's back in the other di-
> rection. It hasn't quite reached as far as it's going to go.

Interactions and relationships with other prisoners are at least as central
to how women experience imprisonment as are those with staff, and in
many ways are more complex because they are not as predetermined by
power differentials. Women's intimate sexual relationships became the focus of Ward and Kassebaum's analysis, and were characterized by them as
"the major adaptation employed by women in a prison setting" (1965:102).
The women we talked with also saw what they called "homosecting" as
very common, but they did not ascribe it major significance for how they
did their time. The apparent difference in how important these relationships were for defining women's prison experience in the 1960s and the
1990s could be due to a number of factors, including the possibility that the
then-novelness of Ward and Kassebaum's finding encouraged them to assume its significance.

Another factor in the declining significance of women's sexual relationships in prison is undoubtedly the change over time in official reactions to them. As we have seen, in the 1960s CIW was attempting to prepare its charges to assume traditional domestic roles upon release from prison; and same-sex relationships, whether in prison or not, were defined as highly deviant (if pruriently fascinating). One of the ways of defying prison authority, then, was to become sexually involved with other women while in prison, and some of the women interviewed by Ward and Kassebaum indicated that they thought of their relationships that way (Gartner and Kruttschnitt 2001). In the 1990s, in contrast, sex between prisoners remained illegal but was not the preoccupation for authorities that it had been in the 1960s. A woman we interviewed at CIW echoed the view of many other prisoners; she said that staff "just shine it on. They know it's happening, and it's like 'If it's private, as long as you're not throwing it in my face, I don't care.' So if you keep a low profile everything's OK."[13]

In part because of the prevalence of women's consensual sexual relationships, women's prisons have traditionally been seen as characterized by cooperative and caring relations among prisoners (Giallombardo 1966). However, our and Ward and Kassebaum's interviews suggest this is true only relative to men's prisons. Women in the 1960s and the 1990s expressed considerable distrust of other prisoners and most said that they kept a distance from them, choosing to have at most one or two confidantes. The reasons for this distrust were not entirely the same across the three contexts, however. For example, at CIW in the 1960s, a number of women pointed to the "kiss-asses," "brownnosers," and women who identified more with staff than with prisoners as a major problem. They believed that these were the women who might very well snitch in an effort to "get in good" with the administration. In the 1990s, concern was more often expressed about women who simply did not care about anyone or anything, and who would create trouble for others not to gain the good graces of the administration but because they were basically "treacherous" and "no-good."

Still, women at CIW in the 1960s and 1990s also described positive relationships with other prisoners. A woman interviewed for Ward and Kassebaum's study, explaining why adjusting to prison was not as difficult as she expected, said: "The girls as a whole are not rough or tough, they've got more heart than the people I associated with outside. We can talk to each other." A first-timer at CIW in the 1990s was also pleasantly surprised by other prisoners: "You kind of wonder, 'Wow, what did they do to get here?' you know? They look like real caring people . . . there's people here who are really, really nice." However, as we have described in greater detail elsewhere (Kruttschnitt, Gartner, and Miller 2000), other prisoners were viewed much more unidimensionally by women at VSPW, where "everybody's on edge, attitudes flyin' left and right. . . . There's a lot of animosity and a lot of stress. . . . You learn in here that you have no friends and nobody likes you." As a consequence, avoidance and isolation were more common adaptations to imprisonment at VSPW, at least among the women we interviewed.

We had two predominant impressions after completing our interviews at CIW and VSPW, and after reading the transcribed interviews conducted for Ward and Kassebaum's research. First, we were struck by the many similarities in women's experiences of imprisonment despite differences in penal regime and prison context. Distress over separation from their families, frustration at being infantilized and dehumanized by prison authorities, and distrust of other prisoners were common not only over time and between prisons, but also across prisoners of different ages, races, institutional histories, and criminal experiences. Our second impression was that some of these experiences were also profoundly shaped by where and when women served their time. In particular, the intensity and uniformity with which women described their negative experiences in prison seemed to us to be greatest at VSPW, the prison that most clearly exemplified the "new penology" of the late twentieth century. To test these impressions with information from more representative samples of prisoners, we turn to a comparison of responses to general population surveys carried out in each of the three prison contexts.

Survey Data from Women at CIW and VSPW

After close consultation with their inmate respondent group, Ward and Kassebaum designed and administered a survey to a 50 percent random sample of the women imprisoned at CIW in the early 1960s. Of the 387 women randomly selected, 314 (81 percent) reported to fill out the questionnaire, and 293 (42 percent of the total prison population) completed usable surveys. Following a similar procedure, we designed a survey based on the interviews and focus groups we conducted with women at CIW and VSPW and drawing from Ward and Kassebaum's questionnaire. We pretested the survey on women at CIW and discussed its wording and content with them. In the summer of 1998 we administered the survey to the general population of women at CIW and VSPW. At CIW, we were allowed to personally distribute 1,224 surveys to six housing units; 887 of these were returned in a completed and usable form. At VSP, we were not allowed to distribute the survey ourselves. Instead we left 2,500 surveys at VSPW for distribution by staff; 1,214 of these were returned, 934 of which were completed and usable. We believe the response rates—72 percent at CIW and 37 percent at VSPW—were quite different because of differences in the method of distribution and in the culture and organization of the two prisons.

Characteristics of the women who responded to the surveys are shown in Table 16.1. Women at CIW and VSPW who participated in our survey

Table 16.1.   Characteristics of Survey Respondents at CIW in 1963 and 1998, and at VSPW in 1998 (%)

	CIW 1963 (N = 832)	CIW 1998 (N = 887)	VSPW 1998 (N = 934)
Ethnicity			
White	54	42	39
Black	28	29	27
Hispanic	11	15	17
Other	6	14	17
Age			
21 and younger	10	2	3
22–25	17	5	9
26–35	41	42	41
36 and older	32	51	47
Age at first arrest			
16 or younger	23	17	21
17–18	13	17	14
19–20	13	10	9
21–23	18	11	15
24 and older	33	45	41
Age at first conviction			
16 or younger	9	14	17
17–18	4	14	14
19–20	5	9	9
21–23	11	11	14
24 and older	68	51	46
Prior prison commitments			
0	76	46	48
1	18	26	26
2 or more	6	28	26
Offense of conviction			
Forgery or theft	43	17	21
Narcotics	24	33	35
Burglary	5	8	8
Assault	3	6	7
Robbery	4	8	8
Murder, manslaughter, attempts	14	22	13
Other	5	6	8

are quite similar to each other in their racial backgrounds, ages, and criminal justice histories, and quite similar to the general population of inmates at the two prisons, according to CDC data (California Department of Corrections 1999). One notable difference is that a larger proportion of respondents at CIW compared to VSPW were incarcerated for homicide-related offenses. This parallels a difference in the general populations of the two prisons and reflects the fact that women sentenced to life imprisonment prior to 1987—i.e., when CIW was the only prison for women in California—have, in a crude sense, "stacked up" at CIW. CIW administrators have tended to let long-time lifers remain at CIW rather than transferring them to any of the newer prisons.

As discussed earlier, the types of women sent to prison in California changed over time, and this can be seen by comparing characteristics of survey respondents at CIW in the early 1960s with those at CIW and VSPW in 1998. Women at CIW in the 1960s tended to be less racially and ethnically diverse and younger, and, while arrested at younger ages on average than women in prison in the 1990s, they were institutionalized later in life, and had less extensive institutional careers. The consequences of the war on drugs are apparent from differences in the offenses for which women were convicted in the 1960s and the 1990s: a much smaller percentage of women at CIW in the early 1960s were in prison on drug-related offenses.[14]

In our and in Ward and Kassebaum's survey, women were asked a number of questions about their views of other prisoners, staff, and the prison experience generally (see Table 16.2). For most of these, we have data from women in all three prison contexts, but we also include answers to questions in our survey that were not asked by Ward and Kassebaum because they highlight differences between women's experiences at CIW and VSP in the 1990s.

The first six questions listed in Table 16.2 ask about women's views of other prisoners, and the responses to these questions suggest that women became more distrustful of and distant from other prisoners over time. Moreover, consistent with our analysis of the interview data, women at VSPW were the most disenchanted with other prisoners. At VSPW women were the least likely to want to associate with other prisoners, had the least faith in the loyalty of other prisoners or their willingness to stand up for their rights, and were the most condemnatory of snitching.[15] The views of women at CIW in 1998 fell between those of women at CIW in 1963 and those of women at VSPW on each of the items about other prisoners that were common to the three surveys. But it is important to emphasize that even at CIW in 1963—where women held the most benign attitudes toward each other—most women wanted little contact with and did not expect loyalty from other prisoners. Thus, in the early 1960s, a time when women at CIW were encouraged to share their feelings with other prisoners in group therapy and work together in "community living groups" to solve problems, the survey data suggest that women did not see their peers as generally trustworthy nor did they want much to do with them. These findings support the conclusions we drew from our analysis of the interview data and suggest that even when imprisonment is couched in an optimistic rhetoric of rehabilitation, treatment, and care, those subject to it

Table 16.2.   Survey Data on Prisoners' Attitudes about Other Prisoners, Staff, and Doing Time (%)

	CIW 1963 (N = 293)	CIW 1998 (N = 887)	VSPW 1998 (N = 934)
Agreeing with the following statements:			
Attitudes about other prisoners			
In some situations, it's OK to inform on another inmate	43[b,c]	35[a,c]	23[a,b]
When inmates stick together, it's easier to do time	77[c]	80[c]	84[a,b]
Most inmates aren't loyal when it really matters	72[b,c]	83[a]	84[a]
The best way to do time is to mind your own business and have as little to do with other inmates as possible	72[b,c]	88[a,c]	93[a,b]
I would prefer to have more time alone (rather than time with other inmates)		46[c]	68[b]
Inmates here would protest if the administration took away our privileges		38[c]	25[b]
Attitudes about prison staff			
Correctional officers have to keep their distance in dealing with inmates	32[b,c]	51[a,c]	57[a,b]
If you reveal too much about yourself to staff the information will be used against you	53[b,c]	72[a,c]	78[a,b]
An inmate should stick up for what she feels is right and not let staff set her standards	92	92	93
The best way to do time is grin and bear it, and not let staff know when you're down	61[c]	61[c]	76[a,b]
Most staff don't care about us, they're just doing their jobs		78[c]	86[b]
Attitudes about the prison			
I feel I have no control over my life in here		43[c]	63[c]
Doing time here is not as bad as I expected		66[c]	39[b]
What do you think this place is about?			
It's a place that helps women in trouble		6[c]	2[b]
It's a place for sending women who get in trouble		24	21
It's a place to punish women for doing wrong		70	77

[a]Significantly different ($p < .05$) from respondents at CIW in 1963.
[b]Significantly different from respondents at CIW in 1998.
[c]Significantly different from respondents at VSPW in 1998.

recognize their vulnerability and the necessity of protecting themselves from others, even similarly powerless others.

Women's attitudes toward staff and how to relate to them are tapped by the next five questions in Table 16.2. Regardless of time period or prison, most women felt they should not open up to staff nor allow staff to dictate how they lived their lives. These views were, again, particularly pronounced at VSPW, as we concluded from the interview data. Whereas only a third of the women at CIW in 1963 felt that staff needed to keep their distance from prisoners—perhaps reflecting the emphasis placed on "warmth and friendliness" in staff-inmate relations in this period—most women in 1998 endorsed a detached approach by staff, particularly women at VSPW. In addition, over three-fourths of women in 1998 felt staff cared little about them, a view that was—again—strongest at VSPW. Variations across the three prison contexts in attitudes toward staff, as with attitudes toward prisoners, tend to be differences of degree and not kind. So, for example, even in the early 1960s, when CIW was attempting to implement a therapeutically based rehabilitative program, most women did not trust staff with personal information, preferred to hide their emotions from staff, and did not seek to emulate staff standards.

The last three items in Table 16.2 ask women about the prison experience in general, but because they were not included in Ward and Kassebaum's survey, permit comparisons only between CIW and VSPW in 1998. Responses to these items portray imprisonment at VSPW as a substantially more alienating and punitive experience than imprisonment at CIW. Almost two-thirds of the women at VSPW felt they had no control over their lives in prison, compared to less than half the women at CIW. In contrast, two-thirds of the women at CIW said that serving time there was not as bad as they had expected, whereas less than 40 percent of women at VSPW felt this way. Women at CIW and VSPW did share a similar view of what prison was about: the vast majority saw their prison as a place of punishment, not as a place of help or even just incapacitation.

Overall, women's perceptions of imprisonment show distinct and consistent differences across the three prison contexts, according to both the interview and survey data. Women at CIW in 1963 held the least negative views of other prisoners and staff, women at VSPW in 1998 held the most negative views of prisoners and staff, and the views of women at CIW in 1998 fell somewhere between these two. This pattern of responses suggests, first, that transformations in the discourses and objectives of penality since the 1960s had uneven consequences for prisoners, depending on where they served their time. It appears that CIW retained a culture that blunted some of the more alienating effects of the new punitiveness on prisoners. Second, the responses also suggest that imprisonment—even in the early 1960s at CIW, a prison designed to "create a non-punitive environment in which . . . true rehabilitation could take place" (Bookspan

1991:86)—was typically characterized by relations of distrust and prisoners' wariness toward those around them.

Finally, the interview and survey data suggest that where administrators were preoccupied with reducing the risks of imprisonment—as they were at VSPW in 1998—rather than with increasing its potential benefits, prisoners were particularly disaffected, suspicious, and isolated. VSPW's warden worried that staff might become too complacent and "let their guard down," which likely sent a message to prisoners as well as staff that the environment was unsafe. Whether intended or not, this may have had the consequence of pushing prisoners at VSPW to rely largely or solely on themselves to manage their imprisonment and to see others as threatening, exploitative, or untrustworthy. Their answers to an open-ended question on our survey support this conclusion. When asked to name "the type of inmate I have the most respect for," twenty-one women at VSPW wrote "none" or "no one" and seventeen wrote "myself." In contrast, only one woman at CIW wrote "myself" and no one wrote "none." The views of women at VSPW, then, appear to more homogeneous and more negative than the views of women at CIW in either time period, a finding consistent with other analyses we have conducted (Kruttschnitt et al. 2000).

CONCLUSION

Imprisonment for women in California underwent substantial changes in the last third of the twentieth century. The domestic disciplinary regime and therapeutic community model were dismantled and replaced with a more punitive and apparently degendered approach to imprisonment; the women's "institution" (as in CIW) was superseded by the women's "prison" (as in VSPW). The rate at which women were imprisoned increased so dramatically during this period that by 2000 it was equivalent to the combined male and female imprisonment rate of the late 1970s. And while the public and prison staff may still have viewed women prisoners as less dangerous than men, they had lowered their expectations regarding women prisoners' ability or willingness to be reformed or, given the rise of responsibilization strategies (O'Malley 1992; Garland 1996), to reform themselves.

The ways in which women perceived imprisonment and related to other prisoners and to prison staff to some extent reflected these and other changes in the discourses, goals, and practices of imprisonment. In the 1960s, when the rhetoric (if not always the practice[16]) of individualized treatment reigned, women's attitudes toward other prisoners and staff were more varied than they were in the 1990s, when a managerial strategy addressed toward governing aggregates had emerged. Indeed, at VSPW, the prison where this managerial approach was most fully realized, women's attitudes were the most crystallized—as if their treatment as members of a group had homogenized their subjectivities. Another, potentially complementary way to view the change over time in how women related to imprisonment is to link it to the greater punitiveness of the 1990s. As one of the women we interviewed put it: "It seems like the more they strip from us, the tougher we get." Our interviews and survey data support her portrayal of women's imprisonment in California in the 1990s.

This is not, however, a story of how women in prison became "more like" men in prison as the ways in which imprisonment was practiced on women and men became less dissimilar. Women in prison in the 1990s continued to be preoccupied with how their relationships with their children and their families would be affected by their imprisonment—a preoccupation not generally shared by men in prison according to both staff and prisoners to whom we talked.[17] And unlike in men's prisons, at CIW and VSPW in the 1990s, serious violence, overt conflict over race or gang allegiance, and organized rebellion were rare, as they had been in the 1960s. Because of this, women at VSPW could be housed eight per cell and VSPW's warden had the luxury of worrying that correctional officers might become too complacent around prisoners. For these reasons, serving time in a women's prison, even one built and run along the lines of a men's prison, remained a very gendered experience.

It also was an increasingly alienating and anomic experience, which is not surprising given the greater deprivations that accompanied imprisonment for women in California in the 1990s. Does this mean that we might expect a more woman-centered approach to imprisonment, one emphasizing healing, therapy, and caring relations, to encourage positive, trusting relationships among prisoners and staff and to provide a setting in which empowerment and rehabilitation could occur? The evidence from CIW in the 1960s suggests not, as does evidence from more recent efforts to "create a feminized technology of penal governance" (Hannah-Moffat 2001:189). Such efforts may be doomed to fail because of the fundamentally coercive and involuntary character of imprisonment. As Hannah-Moffat (ibid.:197) concludes in her analysis of correctional reform in Canada:

> When we reform the content of a regime, we tend to obscure the oppressive aspects of prisons and the unequal relations of power that characterize this sanction. Prisons are governed by material structures, cultural sensibilities, and mentalities that limit the extent to which the content of a regime can be changed. Regardless of the form and content of a woman-centered regime, it is still in many respects about punishment, security, and discipline.

While reformers may forget this—or may hope to overcome the repressive tendencies of imprisonment—prisoners cannot, and as a consequence their experiences, even across decades and under different penal regimes, are circumscribed by the denial of their freedom.

NOTES

1. This number excludes women imprisoned in jails, or under correctional supervision in the community.

2. See Kruttschnitt and Gartner (2002) for a review of this literature.

3. The proportion of men in prison for drug crimes also rose during these years. However, men imprisoned for violent offenses continued to outnumber men imprisoned for drug offenses. In California, the ratio of violent offenders to drug offenders in men's prisons was about 2:1 in the late 1990s; in contrast, the ratio of violent offenders to drug offenders in women's prisons was about 1:2.

4. Approximately three-quarters of female parole violators were returned to prison for violating parole conditions in the 1990s; only about one-quarter were returned with a new felony court commitment.

5. The data in this paragraph are taken from Zalba (1964), Ward and Kassebaum (1965), Owen and Bloom (1995), and the California Department of Corrections (1999).

6. In 1989 CIW's warden was quoted in a newspaper article as saying that female prisoners "are just equalizing and rivalling their male counterparts at this point" (Wares 1989:13). Data on serious violent crimes in California provide little support for this claim. For example, women accounted for about 15 percent of all arrests for homicide in the 1960s, but only about 11 percent of all arrests for homicide in the 1990s. In the 1990s, the only major crime for which women accounted for more than one-third of arrests was forgery, where they were responsible for about 36 percent of arrests (California Bureau of Criminal Statistics/California Department of Justice, various years).

7. Pelican Bay State Prison, according to its institutional mission statement, "is designed to house the state's most serious [male] criminal offenders in a secure, safe, and disciplined 'state-of-the-art' institutional setting." Its two Security Housing Units, the largest in the state, are designed "for inmates who are management cases, habitual criminals, prison gang members and violence-oriented maximum custody inmates." During the 1990s it was under investigation for some of the methods used on its inmates.

8. As another example of his efforts at making VSP safe, the warden told us that he had submitted a proposal to the state legislature to have any sex between staff and inmates defined as rape, because, in his view, it is inevitably exploitative and/or coercive. The proposal was not acted upon.

9. If VSPW were converted to a men's prison, administrators acknowledged that its population would drop dramatically because it would not be safe to house eight men per cell.

10. See Kruttschnitt et al. (2000) for a more detailed description of the characteristics of our interview samples.

11. In Bosworth's (1996:9) interviews with women in English prisons, some women offered the same explanation for the higher levels of compliant behavior in women's compared to men's prisons.

12. See Kruttschnitt et al. (2000) for a discussion of how women at VSPW, but not CIW, compared their experiences of abuse outside prison to their interactions with staff in prison.

13. Bosworth (1999:137–38) found a similar attitude on the part of prison authorities in England. She also notes that prisoners were ambivalent about sexual relationships among prisoners for a variety of reasons, including "prejudice" and the infringements on their privacy. Some of the women we spoke with were critical of sexual relationships for the same reasons, but more commonly because they felt many of them were exploitative or abusive.

14. The percentages of survey respondents at CIW and VSPW in the 1990s who were in prison for drug-related offenses underestimates the percentages in for drug-related offenses in the general population of the two prisons. CDC data indicate that just over 40 percent of the women at both VSPW and CIW were incarcerated on drug-related crimes (California Department of Corrections 1999).

15. The question about informing on other inmates was included in Ward and Kassebaum's survey to tap endorsement of the "inmate code." Disagreement with this question is typically interpreted as indicating a stronger identification with the convict social system, which is opposed to cooperation with the authorities. In this sense, responses are an expression of how the women relate to prison authorities as much as they reveal attitudes toward other inmates.

16. See Gartner and Kruttschnitt (2001) for a discussion of how CIW's goal of individualized treatment was compromised in practice.

17. Most of the women at CIW and VSPW in the 1990s had male relatives who had been in prison. For example, about 60 percent of the women who responded to our survey indicated that their brothers had served time and about 28 percent indicated that their husbands had served time. In our interviews, women often commented on how they thought men "did time" differently from women. One of the important differences, in their view, was that men did not think about how their actions in prison might affect their relationships with their families. A woman at VSPW whose husband and brothers had done time gave us her view on why men riot or challenge authorities in prison more than women: "A women always puts her family first. A man will say 'OK, I'm with you all the way,' and they don't think 'I gotta go home to my kids.' That's the last thing a man says and the first thing a woman says 'I gotta go home to my kids.'" To illustrate her point she told us about one of her brothers who, some months ago, had called her from prison: "He said 'I think I got a 115,' and I say 'For what?' And he said 'Because the police told me to get up and I wasn't through eating.' 'You wasn't through eating? Why didn't you get up? I want you to come home on your date.' And he said 'I ain't thinking about that date. I wanted to eat my food. I wasn't going to be hungry.'"

REFERENCES

Blumstein, Alfred. 1995. "Stability of Punishment: What Happened and What Next?" Pp. 259–74 in *Punishment and Social Control*, edited by Thomas Blomberg and Stanley Cohen. Hawthorne, NY: Aldine de Gruyter.

Bookspan, Shelley. 1991. *A Germ of Goodness: The California State Prison System, 1851–1944*. Lincoln: University of Nebraska Press.

Bosworth, Mary. 1996. "Resistance and Compliance in Women's Prisons: Towards a Critique of Legitimacy." *Critical Criminology* 7:5–19.

———. 1999. *Engendering Resistance: Agency and Power in Women's Prisons*. Aldershot, UK: Ashgate.

Bottoms, Anthony E. 1983. "Neglected Features of Contemporary Penal Systems." Pp. 166–202 in *The Power to Punish*, edited by David Garland and P. Young. London: Heinemann.

California Bureau of Criminal Statistics/California Department of Justice. Various years. *Crime and Delinquency in California*. Sacramento: Author.

California Department of Corrections. 1957. *Orientation to Employment in State Correctional Service*. Sacramento: CDC.

———. 1960. *Rules of the Director of Corrections and of the Superintendent of the California Institution for Women*. Sacramento: CDC.

———. 1999. "Characteristics of Population in California State Prisons by Institution, December 31, 1999." Sacramento: Data Analysis Unit, CDC.

———. 2000. "Historical Trends: Institution and Parole Population, 1979–1999." Sacramento: Data Analysis Unit, CDC.

Carlen, Pat. 1998. *Sledgehammer: Women's Imprisonment at the Millennium*. London: Macmillan.

Cassel, Russell and Robert B. Van Vorst. 1961. "Psychological Needs of Women in a Correctional Institution." *American Journal of Corrections* (January–February):22–24.

Clear, Todd. 1994. *Harm in American Penology: Offenders, Victims, and Their Communities*. Albany NY: SUNY Press.

Feeley, Malcolm and Jonathan Simon. 1992. "The New Penology: Notes on the Emerging Strategy of Corrections and Its Implications." *Criminology* 30: 449–74.

Garland, David. 1995. "Penal Modernism and Post-Modernism." Pp. 181–209 in *Punishment and Social Control*, edited by Thomas Blomberg and Stanley Cohen. Hawthorne, NY: Aldine de Gruyter.

———. 1996. "The Limits of the Sovereign State: Strategies of Crime Control in Contemporary Society." *British Journal of Criminology* 36:445–71.

Gartner, Rosemary and Candace Kruttschnitt. 2001. "A Brief History of Doing Time: The California Institution for Women in the 1960s and the 1990s." Unpublished manuscript.

Giallombardo, Rose. 1966. *Society of Women: A Study of a Women's Prison*. New York: Wiley.

Hannah-Moffat, Kelly. 2001. *Punishment in Disguise: Penal Governance and Federal Imprisonment of Women in Canada*. Toronto: University of Toronto Press.

Kruttschnitt, Candace and Rosemary Gartner. 2002. "Women's Imprisonment." Pp. 55–135 in *Crime and Justice: An Annual Review of Research*, Vol. 30. Edited by Michael Tonry. Chicago: University of Chicago Press.

Kruttschnitt, Candace, Rosemary Gartner, and Amy Miller. 2000. "Doing Her Own Time? Women's Responses to Prison in the Context of the Old and the New Penology." *Criminology* 38:681–718.

Liebling, Alison, David Price, and Charles Elliot. 1999. "Appreciative Inquiry and Relationships in Prison." *Punishment and Society* 1:71–98.

Lynch, Mona. 2001. "Rehabilitation as Rhetoric: The Ideal of Reformation in Contemporary Parole Discourse and Practices." *Punishment and Society* 2:40–65.

O'Malley, Pat. 1992. "Risk, Power, and Crime Prevention." *Economy and Society* 21:252–75.

Owen, Barbara and Barbara Bloom. 1995. "Profiling the Needs of California's Female Prisoners: A Needs Assessment." Washington DC: Department of Corrections.

Simon, Jonathan. 1993. *Poor Discipline: Parole and the Social Control of the Underclass, 1890–1990.* Chicago: University of Chicago Press.

Ward, David and Gene Kassebaum. 1963. "Patterns of Homosexual Behavior among Female Prison Inmates." Los Angeles, CA: School of Public Health, University of California.

———. 1964. "Homosexuality: A Mode of Adaptation in a Prison for Women." *Social Problems* 12:159–77.

———. 1965. *Women's Prison: Sex and Social Structure.* Hawthorne, NY: Aldine de Gruyter.

Wares, Donna. 1989. "Hard Time at Frontera: Women's Jail Overcrowded, Treacherous." *Orange County Register,* September 3, p. J11.

Zalba, Serapio R. 1964. *Women Prisoners and Their Families.* Sacramento: State of California Department of Social Welfare and Department of Corrections.

17

Judicial Impact on Prison Reform

JAMES B. JACOBS

Beginning in the 1960s, federal courts started to become deeply immersed in institutional reform litigation involving schools, prisons, mental hospitals, and other institutions. Sweeping decisions in one case after another forced states to spend large sums of money to bring institutional conditions and practices up to minimum constitutional requirements and forced administrators to extend due process, rationalize their decisions, and limit their discretion. While such judicial activism had many champions and supporters, it also generated a great deal of criticism. Some critics objected to judicial efforts to reform institutions on grounds that federal courts lacked constitutional and political authority to play this kind of role, and that federal judges had usurped the authority that properly belongs to state legislators and executive branch officials. Other critics stressed the courts' lack of competence in fixing problems rooted in inadequate resource funding and malfunctioning bureaucracies. They warned that judicial intervention was as likely to make things worse as to improve them.

One of the most powerful critiques of the role that courts have played in reform litigation is Gerald Rosenberg's *The Hollow Hope: Can Courts Bring About Social Change?* (1991). Professor Rosenberg, a legally trained political scientist on the University of Chicago faculty, forcefully challenges the proposition that the federal courts, the Supreme Court in particular, have been successful in their efforts to produce social change. Rosenberg argues that courts have had a much more limited role in producing social change than is commonly thought. He sets out a formal model demonstrating the conditions necessary and sufficient for courts to achieve social change, and attempts to support his thesis with empirical data and studies on social change in a number of contexts, particularly school desegregation and opportunities for abortion, but also including prison reforms. Although Rosenberg deals with prison reform briefly, he raises important questions for American and foreign scholars trying to assess the capacity of courts to reform prisons. If courts have not been the primary impetus for prison reform since the 1960s, as Rosenberg seems to argue, then prison scholars are left to determine what is the force that drives prison reform.

Rosenberg sets out his thesis clearly:

> courts will generally not be effective producers of significant social reform for three [structural] reasons: the limited nature of constitutional rights, the lack of judicial independence and the judiciary's inability to develop appropriate policies and its lack of powers of implementation. (ibid.:10)

Rosenberg further argues that when "political, social and economic conditions have become supportive of change, courts can effectively produce significant social reform" (ibid.:3). He believes, however, that court decisions are neither necessary nor sufficient for producing significant social reform.[1]

While Rosenberg does not rule out the possibility of judicially mandated reform, he is skeptical about the ability of American courts to transform or even lead the way in reforming American institutions. Rosenberg tests his revisionist thesis in the contexts of school desegregation and freedom of choice with respect to completing or terminating pregnancy. He finds that despite widespread belief that the Supreme Court's decision in *Brown v. Board of Education* (347 U.S. 483 [1954]) brought about school desegregation and that *Roe v. Wade* (419 U.S. II 3 [1973]) expanded opportunities to obtain abortions, the Court's decisions actually were small (and by no means necessary) steps along the way to inevitable social changes. In other words, change would have occurred without the Supreme Court's intervention. In the context of school desegregation and abortion, Rosenberg marshals impressive data.

The purpose of this essay is to examine how well Rosenberg's thesis stands up when applied to prison reform. I take no position on the validity of his thesis when applied to other contexts, although I believe that my criticisms of his methodology might be more generally applicable. I conclude that even if Rosenberg is right that the courts played only a limited role in bringing about school desegregation and abortion opportunities, he is wrong when it comes to prison reform.

There are two key problems with the application of Rosenberg's thesis to prisons. The first problem is his failure to consider money variables that can significantly impact prison reform litigation. The second problem is that there is an inadequate database from which to draw generalizations about the amount of prison reform and the extent to which it depends upon litigation and court interventions.

Unfortunately, Rosenberg addresses the issue of prison reform in only fifteen pages of his book, and the data that he presents in behalf of his thesis constitute only a fraction of the evidence that he brings forward in the school desegregation and abortion contexts. Equally unfortunate, in applying his thesis to prisons, he is far less persuasive.

WHAT COUNTS AS SIGNIFICANT SOCIAL REFORM?

Rosenberg's thesis requires him first to consider whether there has been significant social reform in prisons. On that question, he says, "In sum, it appears that change has been uneven. Many of the worst conditions have been improved to at least minimal standards, but problems still abound" (1991:307). This is not enlightening; in fact, it is almost vacuous. One might safely offer the same "assessment" of any institution or social problem.

Many of the key terms in Rosenberg's analysis are vague or indeterminate (see Schuck 1993). Consider "significant social reform." This term has both normative and positive components. First, Rosenberg should determine what counts as court-generated prison reform and how much of it exists. Then, he should tell us how to determine whether court-generated prison reform qualifies as "significant."

Rosenberg fails to define significant social reform. At times, he equates significant social reform with the stated goals of the lawyers who bring institutional change litigation. Even assuming that the stated goals of prisoners' rights lawyers could be reliably ascertained and summed up (or averaged), this is a strange criterion. For instance, at that outset, lawyers may have had unrealistic expectations for their litigation, may have parroted, without believing to be realistic, the goals of their most vocal clients, or may have articulated goals for tactical reasons. Surely it does not follow that if the activist lawyers' goals were only partially achieved, significant social reform has not occurred.

THE PROBLEMS IN ASSESSING THE SCOPE OF PRISON REFORM

The complexity and ambition of Rosenberg's project is mind-boggling. How can one "assess" the status of prison reform in several thousand prisons and jails throughout the United States? Likewise, how can one assess the impacts of twenty-five years of prisoners' rights litigation in all these diverse prisons and jails? There have been thousands of lawsuits, many hundreds of important ones, and hundreds of major decisions and consent decrees imposing wide-ranging reforms on various institutions and whole prison systems. Regrettably, this massive volume of legal activity has not been systematically transformed into a database; indeed, there have been only a few case studies of "judicial impacts" on prison reform and these themselves have been controversial (DiIulio 1990a).

Great epistemological and methodological problems cloud our ability to assess the overall status of prison reform in America. Rosenberg concludes that the extent of positive social change that has been achieved in prisons is debatable: "while some changes have been made, serious problems remain" (1991:306). This "conclusion" does not respond to the question, whether significant social change has occurred. For example, massive social change may have occurred in Eastern Europe and an observer might still rightly conclude that "while some conditions have gotten better, some have gotten worse." One can rightly argue that all major social reform has some negative consequences, direct and indirect.

Furthermore, in assessing the status of prison reform it is difficult to weigh negative impacts against positive achievements. For example, how can the deterioration in quality of food be weighed against enhancements of fundamental rights like freedom of speech and due process? Should the achievements of prison reform be discounted by increased risks of AIDS and tuberculosis?

Rosenberg rightly notes that prison overcrowding has neutralized much prison reform. He argues that while judicial intervention in prisons has flowered, prisons have become more crowded and have suffered all of the strains that flow from crowding. It is inappropriate, however, to conflate the significance of court-sponsored prison reform with negative developments unconnected to prisoners' rights litigation. Prison reform litigation does not produce prison crowding; in many cases it has ameliorated crowding through population caps, square footage requirements for cells, etc. Rather, prison crowding flows from tougher sentencing and law enforcement policies of legislatures, police, prosecutors, state trial courts, and parole boards.

Aside from the issue of crowding, Rosenberg is on the right track when he argues that a proper accounting for court-ordered prison reform must include the negative direct and indirect consequences of litigation, like the weakening of staff control and the breakdown of order (see Jacobs 1983; DiIulio 1990b).

In tracing the negative consequences of prisoners' rights litigation and court-ordered prison reform, we face another incredibly complicated methodological problem and again find ourselves befuddled by the absence of a database or a set of systematic case studies. What should be the "time frame" in assessing the positive and negative consequences of litigation-generated prison reform? At what point(s) in time after a court has mandated change should an observer make an assessment? Is six months after a judicial decree sufficient? Is it better to wait one year? Or five years? In the short-term, a court decision may have undermined administration, but in the long run led to a more competent administrative regime.

Disentangling causes is a problem that goes to the core of Rosenberg's project. How can we be sure that court-ordered prison reform caused short-term, medium-term, or long-term deterioration of control? Rosenberg states that court-ordered prison reform has led to a decrease in safety and security. To support this conclusion, he quotes a Texas inmate and a former member of the court-appointed special master's staff in *Ruiz* (the Texas prison case) who states, "Contemporary wisdom in corrections is that despite more than a decade of close scrutiny and mandated reforms, many prisons are less safe than they were in the pre-reform days" (1991: 307). The person quoted here may not be correct. However, even if he is correct, is the deterioration of prison safety directly (or even indirectly) attributable to prison litigation? Obviously, other independent variables are also at work, including an upsurge in violence in American society generally, deteriorating race relations, and gang activity. Might the inability of prison management to adapt to the new requirements of greater prisoners' rights also be counted as a "cause"?

Rosenberg's belief that prisons are less safe is debatable. Violence was a pervasive characteristic of prison life that existed well before the intervention of the courts. In fact, it was one of the prime reasons for court intervention in the first place. Recall Chief Judge Henley's moving depiction of the violence in the Arkansas prison system that stirred him to hold that prison in violation of the Eighth Amendment:

> In a very real sense trusty guards have the power of life and death over other inmates. Some guards are doubtless men of good judgment; others are not. It is within the power of a trusty guard to murder another inmate with impunity, and the danger that such will be done is always clear and present. Very recently a gate guard killed another inmate "carelessly." One wonders. And there is evidence that recently a guard on night duty fired a shotgun into a crowded barracks because the inmates would not turn off the television set. In any event the rankers [ordinary inmates] live in deadly fear of the guards. (*Holt v. Sarver,* 309 F. Supp. 362 [D.C. Ark 1970])

The opinions in such cases as *Ramos v. Lamm* (485 F. Supp. 881 [1972]) in Colorado, *Gates v. Collier* (349 F. Supp. 881 [1972]) in Mississippi, and *Ruiz v. Estelle* (503 F. Supp. 1265 [1980]) in Texas graphically describe horrendous violence that triggered judicial interventions. Some observers of the Texas prison system argue that the pre-Ruiz days amounted to a reign of terror for inmates (Martin and Eklund-Olson 1987), while others characterize this period as peaceful and orderly (DiIulio 1987). Moreover, while there seems to be a consensus that the Texas prisons experienced a period of destabilization and deterioration of control in the mid-1980s occasioned by inability or unwillingness to implement court-ordered reforms, some scholars soon foresaw the reestablishment of control (Eklund-Olson 1986; Eklund-Olson and Martin 1988).[2]

ATTRIBUTING SOCIAL CHANGE IN PRISON TO LITIGATION AND COURTS

If, for the sake of argument, we accept that significant social change has occurred, we must next examine whether it can be attributed to litigation and court intervention. Rosenberg finds that the judicial effort to protect prisoner's constitutional rights conforms his thesis about the limited efficacy of courts in producing significant social change. He argues that

> for change to occur as a result of litigation, reformers [had to] overcome the three constraints and then have present at least one of four [facilitating] conditions. With prison reform, courts overcome only one of the constraints entirely. In individual cases, other constraints were overcome. When this occurred, and when one of the conditions were present, meaningful change occurred. (1991:308)

Rosenberg argues that the presence or absence of facilitating conditions "explain[s] both why change has been uneven and when it has occurred." He believes that political support was much more influential than litigation in bringing about prison reform:

> There is little evidence that prison reform litigators have put as much time, energy, and resources into political and social change as into litigation. Without that change, litigation will not be effective. Reliance on courts will not bring much change. The political change must be faced directly. Litigation, as the executive director of the ACLU's National Prison Project has come to understand, "is not, of course, the real answer." (ibid.:313–14)

There is a tautological quality to this argument: where litigators and courts have been successful in implementing reform, it is because they have overcome "impediments"; but where they have been unsuccessful, they have not overcome "impediments." Moreover, the tautology is compounded because, according to Rosenberg, the existence of insurmountable impediments is proved by the absence of change.

In attempting to account for the occurrence of significant social change in prison, it is implausible to assign a key causal role to the political branches of government. While here and there, governors and legislators sympathetic to prison reform may have appeared, political reality practically always assigns prison reform the lowest priority. It is hard, if not impossible, to convince the citizenry that money should be invested to upgrade prison conditions rather than to upgrade schools, roads, health care, the state university, police, job training, and practically anything else. Even if politicians and prisoners are *not opposed in principle* to prison reform, and they often are, it is highly unlikely that they would lead a campaign for safer and better conditions and programs.

The only other possible contender for chief causal agent in the occurrence of prison reform is the corrections establishment itself.[3] Prison reformers have worked within the system throughout American history, although ideas about what constitutes reform have varied, rarely corresponding to the view of theorists and activists "outside" the system. It is possible that in the 1960s and 1970s, a new generation of prison officials sympathetic to a broad range of prison reforms appeared throughout the United States, and that they were able to obtain (independent of litigation threats) significant resources to implement their reform vision. I doubt, however, that empirical evidence can support this hypothesis. Nevertheless, Rosenberg is right that in the late 1970s and 1980s some prison officials came to recognize that they could leverage litigation or the threat of litigation to obtain resources (especially more staff) and improvements.[4]

Rosenberg's thesis does not withstand scrutiny in the case of prison reform. Prison reform is different than desegregation or abortion because there are no strong interest groups, supportive public opinion, or legislative or executive branch politics that press for expanding prisoners' rights or improving their living conditions. Prisons occupy a unique place among institutions targeted for reform by litigation precisely because of the lack of popular and political support for their reform. Clearly, courts did not simply and gently nudge along powerful outside forces of change that were destined to make their mark. Courts became embroiled in prison reform despite strenuous claims by legislators that there was not enough money for implementation and claims by prison officials that the courts' orders would set off maelstroms.

TRACING CHANGE TO THE LOWER COURTS

The Supreme Court has been only minimally involved in judicial intervention in prison affairs. Certainly it has not played the pivotal role that it did in school desegregation and decriminalization of abortion. True, the Court did hand down a few liberal decisions in the early 1970s that opened the door to prisoners' suits,[5] but no sooner was the door opened a crack than the Court began to close it. The Burger Court backed away from prisoners' rights suits very quickly, frequently emphasizing the importance of judges deferring to prison officials (*Hudson v. Palmer*, 468 U.S. 517 [1984]; *Block v. Rutherford*, 468 U.S. 589 [1984]). The *Wolf v. McDonald* (194 S. Ct. 2963 [1974]), *Estelle v. Gamble* (429 U.S. 97 [1976]), and *Bounds v. Smith* (430 U.S. CT. 817 [1977]) marked the watershed for prisoners' rights victories in the Supreme Court; since then, most cases that reached the Supreme Court have resulted in victories for prison officials (e.g., example, *Bell v. Wolfish*, 441 U.S. 520 [1979]; *Rhodes v. Chapman*, 452 U.S. 337 [1981]; *Hewitt v. Helms*, 459 U.S. 460 [1983]; *Ponte v. Real*, 471 U.S. 491 [1985]; *Whitley v. Albers*, 475 U.S. 312 [1986]).

In part, it is analytically difficult to apply Rosenberg's thesis to court-ordered prison reform. Unlike school desegregation, where Rosenberg turned to the Supreme Court's decision in *Brown v. Board of Education*, or abortion, where he assessed the impact of the Supreme Court's decision in *Roe v. Wade*, Rosenberg does not and cannot focus on the impact of a particular Supreme Court decision or series of Supreme Court decisions in the area of prison reform. Most court-ordered prison reform has been accomplished by federal district courts after lengthy trials (and negotiated consent judgments) that have turned on specific conditions in one prison or prison system rather than on appellate court decisions announcing new constitutional principles. Thus, the most important (albeit not necessarily representative) prison cases are *Ruiz v. Estelle* (503 F. Supp. 1265 [S.D. Tex 1980]) in Texas, *Guthrie v. Evans* (93 F.R.D. 390 [S.D. Georgia 1981]) in Georgia, the "Tombs" (*Rhem v. Malcolm*, 389 F. Supp. 964 [S.D. N.Y. 1975]) litigation in New York City, and *Morales Feliciano v. Romero Barcelo*, in Puerto Rico (672 F. Supp. 591 [D. Puerto Rico 1986]).

As important, perhaps even more important, than *court-ordered* reforms have been negotiated reforms that have been implemented without a trial.[6] In many instances, the initiation of litigation or even the *threat* of litigation has produced significant prison reform. State officials may choose to settle because they wish to avoid the expense and negative publicity of a trial or the risk of even more expensive court-ordered reforms.

In any event, the key question for Rosenberg is not why the courts stayed the course, but "why the change has been so uneven—why there was some change, but only some" (1991:307). This question is hard to understand. Is Rosenberg asking why some judges were receptive to prisoners' cases, while others were not? Or, why among those judge who were receptive to prisoners' claims, some succeeded in remedying unconstitutional practices and conditions while others did not? Or is the key question, why did judges succeed in remedying with some practices and conditions but not others?

The fact that many district courts remained receptive to and actively involved in "totality of conditions suits," while the Supreme Court withdrew from the field, has never been adequately explained. I believe that the answer lies in the deplorable prison conditions, the superior lawyering skills of a highly specialized prisoners' rights bar, and the poor quality of the state's representation in many of these cases.

WHAT ACCOUNTS FOR JUDICIAL SUCCESS AND FAILURE?

The question why, among courts that found in favor of prison reform, some were more successful at implementing change than others is intriguing and important. A satisfactory answer would require a strong empirical knowledge base, criteria for "success," and a coherent position on what time frame to use. Of course, because all prisons did not suffer from the same operational and physical deficiencies, "success" would have to be defined in terms of each change from each institution's baseline. Furthermore, different lawsuits asked for different relief, so it would be wrong to compare the achievements of a massive "totality of conditions" with the achievements of a more limited suit.

Assuming that we could adequately deal with the dependent variable "success" and with the time frame problem, empirical studies are needed to identify those independent variables that account for judicial success. A full-blown empirical study of cases in which judges wanted to achieve prison reform ought to focus on a number of independent variables, including resources, skills, and commitment of the prisoners' lawyers; the determination of the judge; whether the judge appointed a special master to supervise implementation of the decree; the special master's legal powers, resources, skills, commitment, and intelligence; the kinds of prison problems targeted for reform; the attitude of the prison's and prison department's officials toward reform, the attitude of the department's legal counsel toward reform, the attitude of the rank and file corrections officers toward reform; the attitude of the governor toward reform; the attitude of the legislative leadership and rank and file legislators toward reform; and the resources of the state.

Another phenomenon that needs to be explained is the tremendously complex process by which courts obtain the support of prison officials. The strategies that judges and their special masters have used include the contempt power, publicly reprimanding prison officials, threatening to close down prisons, and persuading prison officials that reform is in their interest.

Rosenberg engages in a cursory reading of some limited descriptions or impressions of two or three prison cases and concludes that "the active support of administrators and staff is required. And without the presence of factors external to the courts, that support will not be available" (1991:311). By "factors external to the courts," he apparently means political support for reform from the executive and legislative branches:

Prison reform issues are essentially political, and prison reform is highly dependent upon the political process. When political leaders are willing to act, this constraint can be overcome. When they do nothing, or oppose court decisions, little change occurs. (ibid.:308)[7]

These observations do not take us very far. Court-ordered prison reform obviously cannot be achieved without cooperation from prison officials. If, in response to a court's prison reform decision, prison officials went on strike (or worse), no reform would occur (unless the court were able to remove the recalcitrant officials from their jobs and substitute compliant replacements).

Rosenberg himself notes that the constraint on a court's ability to achieve social change can be overcome by an alliance with prison officials, who see an opportunity to leverage the court's decision to obtain more resources and other reforms that they themselves want. This point is well taken. Many prison officials have seen the velvet glove around the iron fist; in fact, some prison cases have resulted in something like collusion between prisoners' rights advocates and prison officials to obtain more resources from the legislature. Unfortunately, Rosenberg does not provide a formula for predicting when such collusions will occur and, if they occur, when they will be successful. What he provides is a truism: if prison officials support court-ordered reform, success will be more likely.

Another Rosenberg truism is that broad-scale prison reform cannot be achieved without some support from the executive and legislative branches. But without a full-scale empirical study, it is impossible to know how much variation there is from state to state in the process of obtaining fiscal support for court-ordered prison reform, or the different means courts have used to obtain necessary funding. Whether access to funding ultimately depends upon the skill and commitment of the judge and the parties to the lawsuit or on the predisposition of the governor and legislative leadership is unknown. Research is needed to illuminate how judges have or have not overcome political intransigence and resistance.

CONCLUSION

In the context of prison reform, Rosenberg's thesis is not persuasive. At every point along the way, he fails to define crucial terms. Testing his thesis against empirical reality presents Herculean difficulties. It is unclear what he means by "significant social reform" is unknown. Further, he lacks an adequate methodology to determine where "significant social reform" has occurred and how much can properly be attributed to courts. If courts have been the driving force behind reform, the process by which they have been able to enlist enough support to enforce their decrees remains mystery.

Rosenberg's inquiry is overly ambitious. In a single volume, he seeks to prove with empirical evidence a complex thesis about the role of courts in producing social change in a number of massively complex contexts: school desegregation, abortion, environmental protection, and prisons, among others. He did not collect data or make observations himself, but summarized and synthesized the work of others. Therefore, his work can be no better than the underlying empirical scholarship on which it is based. Unfortunately, at least in the prisons context, the existing scholarship does not begin to address the vast amount of legal activity.

Finally, two-thirds or more of the nation's prison systems have been operating, in whole or in part, under significant court decrees dealing with issues like disciplinary procedures and conditions, transfers, food services, ventilation, sewage, fire safety, recreation opportunities and facilities, lighting, cell size and assignments, guard training, and many more (National Prison Project 1993). To anyone who has been part of or closely watched this legal activity, it seems naive to ask whether litigation has produced significant social change. Every prison has changed its practices and reconstructed parts of its physical plant as a direct consequence of prisoners' rights litigation. Construction, renovation, and rehabilitation of physical plants as required by court orders have led to huge expenditures in a number of states. Both Kentucky and Tennessee estimate court-ordered prison reform costs in excess of $250 million. Puerto Rico is currently engaged in a physical rehabilitation project estimated at $100 million. Since 1985, the Texas legislature has made biennial appropriations in excess of $1 billion for prison construction and renovation, much of which was precipitated by the massive Ruiz litigation. Florida estimates that it has spent $600 million in construction and compliance costs. North Carolina has had direct compliance costs of $200 million and, in 1991, presented plans for $400 million in new prison construction.

Against this tidal wave of apparent court-ordered prison reform, Rosenberg's revisionist view is not persuasive. I do not doubt that judicial intervention in prisons has been the most significant vehicle of prison reform in the latter quarter of the twentieth century. But why this development occurred, especially when the Supreme Court did not encourage it and no other formidable political and social forces were behind it, remains to be adequately explained. By the same token, much more needs to be known about how prison reform was implemented. No doubt the importance of lawyering skills, the personalities and politics of district court judges, and the stance and competency of prison administrators and staff will all turn out to be important.

In *The Hollow Hope,* Rosenberg has kept the issue alive. For those of us interested in writing the contemporary social history of the American prisons, it should serve to stimulate both more research and more theorizing.

ACKNOWLEDGMENTS

The author is very grateful for the extensive and insightful comments of Steve Martin and for the research and editing assistance of Jessica Henry.

NOTES

1. "They are not necessary because much reform takes place outside the judicial system and because courts lack independence. They are not sufficient because courts lack effective tools of implementation and require the existence of [at least one of several] particular conditions[:] a) Positive incentives are offered to induce compliance, b) Costs are imposed to induce compliance, c) Court decisions allow for market implementation or d) Administrators and officials crucial for implementation are willing to act and see court orders as a tool for leveraging additional re-sources or hiding behind. Without the presence of at least one of these conditions, court decisions will not produce significant social reform" (Rosenberg 1991:35–36).

2. See also *Feliciano v. Barcelo* (672 F. Supp. 591 [1986]) for a discussion of violence in Puerto Rican prisons.

3. Actually, riots are another possible causal factor for the occurrence of prison reform that are beyond the scope of this chapter.

4. Prison officials in Texas routinely relied on "Ruiz Requirements" to justify their funding requests to the legislature. A former chairman of the Board of Corrections openly advocated including a certain level of staffing in the final settlement in order to ensure that the legislature would provide the funds necessary to operate the prison properly.

5. See *Wolf v. McDonald* (94 S.Ct. 2963 [1974]), *Johnson v. Avery* (89 S.Ct. 747 [1968]), and *Cruz v. Beto* (92 S.Ct. 1079 [1972]). These decisions were devoted to civil rights. They did not require spending money or reorganizing prison administration. The really important prison reform cases were district court cases that did not flow from Supreme Court doctrine but from the judges' revulsion at squalid prison conditions.

6. For example, the states of Kansas, Nevada, New Mexico, and Texas entered into consent decrees before.

7. Rosenberg goes on to note that political support for court-ordered prison reform has been encouraged by the existence of the larger rights movement and prison violence.

REFERENCES

DiIulio, John J. Jr. 1987. *Governing Prisons: A Comparative Study of Correctional Management*. New York: Free Press.

———. 1990a. "The Old Regime and the Ruiz Revolution: The Impact of judicial

Intervention on Texas Prisons." Pp. 51–72 in *Courts, Corrections and the Constitution,* edited by John J. DiIulio, Jr. New York: Oxford University Press.

———. 1990b. *Courts, Corrections, and the Constitution: The Impact of Judicial Intervention on Prisons and Jails.* New York: Oxford University Press.

Eklund-Olson, Sheldon. 1986. "Crowding, Social Control, and Prison Violence: Evidence from the Post-Ruiz Years in Texas." *Law and Society Review* 20:389.

Eklund-Olson, Sheldon and Martin, Stephen J. 1988. "Organizational Compliance with Court-Ordered Reform." *Law and Society Review* 22:359.

Jacobs, James B. 1983. "The Prisoners' Rights Movement and Its Impacts." Pp. 33–60 in *New Perspectives on Prisons and Imprisonment,* edited by James B. Jacobs. Ithaca, NY: Cornell University Press.

Martin, Steven J. and Eklund-Olson, Sheldon. 1987. *Texas Prisons: The Walls Came Tumbling Down.* Austin: Texas Monthly Press.

National Prison Project. 1993. "Status Report: State Prisons and the Courts—January 1, 1992." *National Prison Project Journal* 8(1, Winter).

Rosenberg, Gerald N. 1991. *The Hollow Hope: Can Courts Bring About Social Change?* Chicago: University of Chicago Press.

Schuck, Peter H. 1993. "Book Review: Public Law Litigation and Social Reform" (reviewing *The Hollow Hope*). *Yale Law Journal* 102:1763–86.

18

The Crime of Punishment

David J. Rothman

INTRODUCTION

Beginning in the 1970s, and continuing to this day, an impressive body of factual findings and theoretical overviews has discredited each component of our inherited criminal justice system. Foreign observers, who once flocked to visit American prisons, are now appalled by current conditions and sentencing practices, astonished to find them so retrogressive. Christie was so repelled by American prisons that after opening his analysis with the apologetic phrase: "Whom one loveth, one chasteneth," he went on to draw an analogy with Nazi Germany: "The extermination camp was a product of industrialization . . . a combination of thought-patterns, social organization and technical tools. My contention is that the prison system in the USA is rapidly moving in the same direction" (Christie 1993).

American critics are no less indignant. Human Rights Watch, having investigated prison conditions throughout the world, turned its eye to the United States and "numerous human rights abuses and frequent violations of the UN Standard Minimum Rules for the Treatment of Prisoners" (Human Rights Watch 1994). The most conspicuous sign of failure, cited by Christie, Human Rights Watch, and many other critics, is the heavy American reliance on keeping people in prison. For example, Tonry reports that in mid-1998, America's imprisonment rate of 668 per 100,000 residents reached a historical high. In relation to other Western countries' use of prisons, between 50 and 135 residents per 100,000 are in prison or jail on an average day. Sweden's rate of 1 resident per 800 is the lowest of these other Western countries. In comparison, America imprisons 1 resident per 150 population, which is 6 to 12 times higher than the imprisonment rate of other Western countries (Tonry 1999:429–37). To be sure, a low rate of incarceration may reflect pervasive police brutality; in India, for example, police prefer to beat up petty criminals rather than imprison them

(Rothman and Neier 1994). But such conduct is irrelevant to comparisons one might make between America's mass imprisonment policy with other Western countries' disproportionately low rate of imprisonment policies.

Moreover, the American prison population is growing at the fastest rate in the world. Between 1980 and 1998, the number of inmates in state and federal prisons rose by 295 percent, from 329,821 to 1,302,019. The increase in the number of offenders sentenced to probation instead of prison, or paroled from prison, is no less dramatic. In 1980 1.1 million adults were serving sentences on probation and 220,000 were on parole. From 1985 to 1995, offenders on probation rose 57 percent and prisoners out on parole rose 133 percent (Austin and Irwin 2001).

Keeping people in prison, as would be anticipated, places a heavy burden on state budgets. In 1997, the United States spent $43.5 billion dollars on its prison system, making it the second fastest growing item, after Medicaid, among state government expenditures. New York, for example, between 1983 and 1990 built twenty-seven new prisons at the short-term cost of 1.6 billion dollars, and eventual cost of 5.4 billion over thirty years if one includes the interest payable on state bonds floated for the construction. It was once commonplace to observe that a year in jail was as expensive as a year at Harvard, but by now jail costs in many cities are much higher. Maintaining one inmate for one year in New York City costs $58,000, at least twice the tuition and living expenses at a private university. Unforeseen contingencies push costs still higher. New York State spends well over $50 million dollars a year for inmates with AIDS, and New York City, to abide by a court order, recently built eighty-four isolation cells at $450,000 each, to house inmates with tuberculosis (Edna McConnell Clark Foundation 1993:2–3).

Despite these expenditures, prisons remain overcrowded. On average, federal prisons are 46 percent and state prisons are 31 percent over capacity. Cells built for one inmate often hold two or even three. Prisoner rights groups have successfully sued to reduce overcrowding. In the mid-1990s, forty states and the District of Columbia were under court orders to correct overcrowding and improve substandard conditions. So were one-third of all the jails in the country. But courtroom victories do not consistently get translated into prison realities.

CYCLES OF REFORM

The justice system is most troubling in its impact on minorities, particularly on African-Americans. As Miller reports, 50 percent of black men in Washington, D.C., between the ages of eighteen and thirty-five are either in prison or on probation or parole, out on bail, or being sought on an arrest warrant. For black men in Baltimore, the comparable figure is 57 percent.[1] Nationwide, blacks make up 48 percent of prison inmates, as against 12 percent of the population. The disparity is even more flagrant if one looks, as did Tonry, at rates of confinement per 100,000. For whites, it is 289, for blacks, 1,860.[2] The likelihood of being in prison or in jail is seven times higher for black Americans than for whites.

Among the many reasons why so many blacks are in prison—including high rates of unemployment and inadequate urban schools—none is more decisive than the changes in the administration of criminal justice, particularly the sentencing practices that have been adopted since the 1980s. During the 1970s, liberal reformers became disillusioned with the Progressive principle that indeterminate sentences would encourage greater justice in punishment. The new view, expressed in many reports and studies,[3] was that open-ended sentences adapted to the personal characteristics of the offender—his education, jobs, marital state, and so on—gave judges and parole boards the discretion to penalize blacks and lower-class offenders more heavily than white, middle-class ones. The reports also argued that rehabilitation programs were a sham. Not only were they ineffectual, but they made imprisonment seem legitimate and desirable. The rehabilitative model, as Gaylin and I wrote in 1975, "has been more cruel and punitive than a frankly punitive model would probably be." Fostering the illusion that inmates were locked up for their own good, rehabilitation made sentences of five, ten, and fifteen years appear benevolent.

From this diagnosis came a proposed cure: encourage legislators to enact fixed sentences, reduce the discretion of the judge to set the penalty, and restrict, or even eliminate, the power of the parole board to determine the moment of release. The aim was to let the crime and the previous criminal record of the offender dictate the punishment, without any reference to the social characteristics of the criminal, including race, gender, occupation, or work history. Sentencing guidelines, drawn up in advance, could set the punishment within narrow ranges. In this way, virtually all first-time burglars would get, for example, a sentence of between twelve and eighteen months, regardless of whether the burglar was white or black, male or female, from the urban or rural part of the state, or standing before a judge with a reputation for leniency or harshness.

The reformers were aware of the possibility that fixed sentences might turn out to be even longer than indeterminate ones. They recognized that longer sentences were the goal of the conservative and right-wing thinkers who also advocated fixed sentences. Such conservatives argued, none more vigorously than Wilson, that indeterminate sentences put offenders back on the streets too quickly. Since the actual time served almost always turned out to be less than the maximum provided in the original sentence, the criminal, they said, was being prematurely released and allowed to return to a life in crime. When "twenty-five years to life" turned out to be eight years, because parole boards often released inmates at one-third the minimum sentence, conservatives warned that the safety of society was being compromised. Thus fixed sentences represented a long overdue return to "truth in sentencing," which would make offenders serve out their time.

The oddness of the alliance did not weaken reformers' enthusiasm. They fully expected that the sentences indicated in guidelines would reduce the severity of penalties, starting with less serious crimes, and they believed that the number of prison cells available would limit the numbers put in prison. Why were they so optimistic? In retrospect, they exaggerated the appeal that a claim to fairness would have. But they were so appalled by the existing system that they were overeager to find an alternative to it. In 1972, Frankel, then a federal judge in New York, published a highly influential book, *Criminal Sentences: Law without Order*, arguing that judges exercised "almost wholly unchecked and sweeping authority." He found it "terrifying and intolerable for a society that professes devotion to the rule of law" to perpetuate these sentencing practices. His passionate language conveys just how anxious he and others were that changes be made.

Moreover, during the early 1970s a fierce attack took place on the legitimacy of "total institutions," to use Goffman's term. Partly as a result, the number of prison inmates, along with mental hospital inmates, was actually declining. Indeed, the sense that prisons were losing their hold on public policy was reinforced by reactions to the Attica riot. The official New York State report on Attica expressed shame at the wretchedness of prison conditions, not hostility to the rebellious inmates. Reformers also expected their legislators to vote in ways that would cost the taxpayers less. Since prisons were expensive and becoming more so because of court-ordered improvements, politicians, they believed, would welcome a reduction in the number of prisoners.

Finally, reformers were attracted by the prospect that appointed commissions, not individual judges or parole boards, would set the scale of penalties. The advocates of commissions, it must be said, did not spend much time discussing who would actually serve on them or how their decisions would be translated into law or practice. Rather, they were convinced that sentencing decisions should be removed from politics and the criminal justice system insulated from popular pressures. Sentencing commissions, like other administrative bodies (most notably, the Securities and Exchange Commission and the Food and Drug Administration), would, it was thought, bring expertise and rational decision-making into bitterly contested disputes over sentences. Once decisions on punishment were removed from arbitrary judges, from overly conservative parole boards, and from legislators trying to please constituents, prison time would be doled out more sparingly and alternatives to prison would be used more frequently.

The reformers proved wrong on all counts. Fixed sentences were introduced in the 1980s, both in the federal system and in roughly one-third of the states. But apart from a few jurisdictions (most notably Minnesota), sentencing guidelines have increased the time served and have had relatively little effect on disparity in sentences. They have promoted prison overcrowding and reduced the importance of judges in sentencing, while giving more discretion to prosecutors. The distaste for rehabilitation has also contributed to making prisons into human warehouses. If educational and training programs are seen as futile, why should the state spend money on them?

Hostility to indeterminate sentences also made it easier for the federal government and the states to enact mandatory minimum statutes, which inevitably increase the time to be served. Once decisions about punishment became more mechanical—a matter of consulting a chart—and less concerned about what would be a just sentence for a particular criminal, mandatory minimum sentences seemed to have their own logic. Over one hundred provisions for mandatory sentences are now to be found in the federal code, with crimes involving guns and drugs accounting for most of them. Thus, between 1984 and 1990, sentences for drug offenders who did not carry firearms increased from thirty-six months, with the possibility of earlier release on parole, to sixty-six months with no parole. Moreover, mandatory minimum sentences have greatly increased the authority of prosecutors. In return for a guilty plea, they will indict on a lesser offense, which does not carry a minimum. And prosecutors continue their discriminatory practices: far more often than blacks, whites get the chance to plead guilty to lesser crimes and thereby receive sentences below the mandatory minimums (Schulhofer 1993).

UNINTENDED CONSEQUENCES

Why did the good intentions of the reformers lead to such unintended results? Part of the answer is the changed political environment of the 1980s. Reagan and Bush were able to make crime and sentencing procedures an issue that middle-class Americans could use to express their frustrations not only with unsafe streets but with affirmative action and the costs of welfare. Reformers also forgot that many bondholders see prisons not as a drain upon public resources but as a sound investment, while some job seekers see them as a source of employment.

More important, reformers were wrong to think that sentencing commissions would be insulated from politics. The history of sentencing practices in Washington State, as explained by Boerner, is an excellent case in point (Boerner 1993). Politicians there wanted to change sentencing standards not so much because of a rising crime rate as because of a widely shared belief that sentencing should be less discretionary and that something had to be done to reduce overcrowding in the state's prisons (which a federal court ruled violated constitutional standards). The legislation approving a sentencing commission and determinate sentences was drawn up by two state representatives, Mary Kay Becker, a Democrat, and Gene Struthers, a Republican, who were otherwise so opposed to each other politically that their collaboration, Becker said, was like "Jane Fonda and John Wayne co-authoring a book on the Vietnam War."

The Washington State sentencing commission was dominated by insiders: it included four judges, two prosecutors, two defense attorneys, three state criminal justice officials, the state director of finance, and three private citizens. The commission set out explicit guidelines for sentencing, which the legislature subsequently adopted, and judges were obliged to follow. Prison sentences were reserved for violent offenders, with time to be served based exclusively on the crime itself and the offender's past criminal history; nonviolent offenders were to be put on probation and sentenced to community service.

These guidelines initially reduced the imprisonment rate so that Washington State soon had a surplus of prison cells (which it then leased to other states). But beginning in 1990, the prison population grew (by 23 percent the first year, 10 percent the second), mostly because the legislature, with the concurrence of the commission, revised the fixed sentences upward. It set tougher penalties for drug sales, responding to pressures from prosecutors who said the system was too soft on dealers. In the new scheme, judges were not allowed to sentence first-time offenders to probation and treatment programs, so 92 percent of first-time drug offenders went to prison. The legislature also increased punishments for all drug offenders so that average sentences became three times as long. (In 1988, the average sentence for possession and delivery of heroin or cocaine was nineteen months; in 1992, it was fifty-six months.) At the same time, after the mutilation of a young boy by a sex offender who had served his maximum sentence and had just been released from prison, the commission, responding to explicit legislative directions, revised the penalties for all sex abuse crimes. The average sentences served then increased from thirty-three months to seventy-six months. Parallel examples occurring now are the growing outcry for stronger law enforcement and tougher punishment for sex offenders in response to the highly publicized series of child abductions during 2002 and America's Missing Broadcast Emergency Response (Amber Alert) system to facilitate the apprehension of child abductors.

As the Washington State experience suggests, transferring authority from judges and parole boards to a commission made sentencing at least as much and probably more of a political issue than it had been before. Outrageous crimes can be used as evidence to support long-term changes in penal codes. In the past, a public outcry often affected judges' behavior, and when there was a rash of robberies or a vicious child abuse case, the next person to commit such a crime often received a harsher sentence in the hope of deterring future crimes. But when sentencing commissioners and legislators feel they must show they are tough, the repercussions go beyond an increased sentence for one highly publicized case and result, for years to come, in harsher penalties for entire categories of crimes. The real problem, as Christie shrewdly observed, is that once sentencing becomes a "tool in the hands of politicians," we get "democratic crime control" (Christie 1993:191). That is, there are no limits to punishment so long as those limits do not adversely affect the majority.

Probably the most serious drawback of the 1970s reform program was the failure to anticipate the prominence that would be given drug control, the issue that now dominates criminal justice procedures. Attempts to correlate crime rates with changing criminal policy are usually futile because one-to-one correlations will not stand up. A notable decline in crime rates occurred over the 1990s, especially in New York City. Murder there, for example, dropped from 2,245 in 1990 to 1,177 in 1995. Rudolph Giuliani, then mayor, took credit for the change, linking it to a combination of aggressive policing, targeted policing to high-crime areas, and mostly, increased imprisonment. But as Mauer persuasively demonstrates, New York crime rates dropped much more dramatically than the national rates (violent crime was down by 34 percent, property crime by 39 percent), but its incarceration rate was actually lower than the national rates (Mauer 1999). New York's state prison population did increase by 25 percent between 1990 and 1995, but in the United States as a whole, the increase was 43 percent. The city's jail population actually declined over the period by 9 percent. If incarceration was the secret to combating crime, why did New York fare better than other states? Clearly some other dynamic was at work.

What is apparent is that arrests, convictions, and imprisonment for drug offenses, as distinguished from other crimes, have risen sharply. Everyone agrees that the increase reflects a change not in street behavior but in patterns of enforcement and punishment. Drug arrests increased during the 1980s by 88 percent and then increased even more in the 1990s. In 1980, for example, there were 581,000 arrests for drug offenses; in 1997, the arrests skyrocketed to 1,584,000, and remained at that level through 1999. Further, between 1981 and 1996, the proportion of prison admissions for drug crimes tripled from 9 to 30 percent (Austin and Irwin 2001). As a result, 21 percent of all inmates in state prisons, and an astonishing 58 percent of all inmates in federal prisons, are serving time for drug offenses. Not only the number of prisoners but the length of the drug sentence has climbed. In the 1980s, drug offenders served on average some 22 months in federal prisons. Offenders sentenced in 1999 were expected to serve some 62 months.

Drug law enforcement and punishment are aimed mostly at minorities, and the "war on drugs" is in large part a war on blacks. The proportion of blacks among all those arrested for drug possession increased from 22 percent in 1981 to 37 percent in 1990. In Baltimore, among adult offenders, blacks are five times more likely than whites to be arrested for drug offenses; among juveniles, blacks are ten times more likely. Of all drug possession offenders who received a prison sentence in New York, 91 percent were black or Hispanic; in California, 71 percent of those sentenced to prison for drug possession were black or Hispanic (Human Rights Watch 1997).

In crimes involving drugs, as with crime more generally, it is almost impossible to sort out whether the disparity in convictions and punishment between whites and blacks reflects actual behavior. Do blacks commit more of the heavily penalized crimes, or do police, prosecutors, and judges come down harder on blacks than whites? Undoubtedly both statements are true, but discrimination is especially apparent in drug enforcement. For example, some state penal codes punish the possession or use of heroin far more severely than cocaine, a tactic so obviously biased against blacks and Hispanics that one federal court held the provision unconstitutional.

Racial discrimination also helps to explain the disparity in punishment between drunk driving and drug use. Mauer and Shine recently calculated that although drunk driving causes as many deaths as drug use, it is punished far less severely. It is true that drug use is often linked with violent crimes. But Mauer and Shine suggest that the difference may also lie in the fact that all but a few of those convicted of drunk driving are white, while those convicted for drug offenses are mostly black or Hispanic (Sentencing Project 1993). Prison overcrowding, the increasing disappearance from city streets of young black urban males, and the fate of the 1970s reformers' hopes for the fixed sentence are largely explained by the system's response to the use of drugs.

The short, unhappy history of the new federal sentencing code starkly demonstrates how the new reform program produced rigid and punitive policies. Stith and Koh (1993) skillfully analyze the fate of the initiative for revising federal sentencing codes in the 1970s, which originated with Senator Ted Kennedy. His aim was to create a commission that would bring greater equity to sentencing by not allowing such factors as schooling, income, and family life to alter the severity of the punishment. In Kennedy's original proposal, the commission was also to insure that time served did not increase, that prisons did not become overcrowded, and that alternatives to prison were incorporated into the system. But Kennedy never could make up his mind. Sometimes he made it seem as though the guidelines were advisory, at other times as though they were binding. But his goal was to restrict judges' discretion so as to reduce discrimination.

The Kennedy bill did not pass during the Carter administration, in part because the House of Representatives was far less attracted to mandatory guidelines, and in part because sentencing became entangled with conservatives' efforts to revise the entire federal criminal code. But rather than abandon his proposal when Reagan became president, Kennedy continued to campaign for it; and he too readily accepted a number of compromises. The bill that was signed into law by President Reagan in 1984 had none of the nuances of the original proposal. The earlier instructions to the commission to decrease the amount of time served and not to overcrowd prisons were weakened. More important, the commissioners were appointed by the president with William Wilkens, a federal appeals court judge from South Carolina and a close associate of the very conservative Senator Strom Thurmond, as chairman. Under Wilkens's leadership the commission adopted Reagan's rhetoric about "law and order" and "getting tough with the criminal." Its interpretations of the statute consistently curtailed judicial discretion and made penalties more severe. The commissioners ruled, for example, that sentences were to be meted out on the basis of "real offense"—that is, what the offender had presumably done, not what he had pleaded guilty to in bargaining with the prosecutor or been convicted for in court (ibid.).

In day-to-day practice, as Tonry has noted, the judge must consult a set schedule to reach his sentence. He starts at the "base offense level," say, burglary, which has a score of 20, and then adds points to it on the basis of how the crime was carried out. If the offender discharged a gun, he adds seven points. If the crime resulted in bodily injury, he adds two. If it was serious bodily injury, another two. If $10,000 or less was stolen in the burglary, he adds nothing, but if the sum was between $10,000 and $50,000, he adds two. If it was more than $250,000 he adds three, and so on. The judge then adds up the points and consults the guideline chart, which has the offense level scores running down the left, and, running across the top, six columns scoring the offender on the basis of his past criminal record. So if the burglar fired a gun, caused serious bodily injury, and made off with $300,000, he gets a score of 34; if this was his first offense, his sentence must fall between 151 and 188 months. If he has a long record, let us say IV on the scale of VI, his sentence must fall between 210 and 262 months (Tonry (1993; Weinstein 1992).

The only two factors a judge may use to reduce the guideline's sentence are the offender's "acceptance of responsibility," i.e., by pleading guilty, which can bring a modest reduction, and his willingness to provide "substantial assistance" to the government, i.e., by turning state's evidence and implicating others, which can bring a major reduction. The judge may not reduce sentence time because of the offender's age, his employment record, his having a stable family life, the fact that he has children at home to support, or any other personal characteristic.

The impact of these guidelines has been to increase the prison population and the average time served from twenty-four months in July 1984 to forty-six months in June 1990. Sentences of probation have declined. The guidelines have clearly elevated the prosecutor over the judge. Because sentences are severe, offenders may be tempted to go to trial rather than to plea bargain; to make certain this does not happen, prosecutors define the "base offense" downward to bring about a reduction in penalty, and hide their action so that the "real offense" on which the guidelines are set cannot be known. Thus in return for a guilty plea, the prosecutor will agree to charge the defendant with robbery without the use of a weapon, although he carried a pistol. Defendants and their lawyers understand that judges no longer control sentencing, bound as they are to the guidelines. All the real bargaining has to be done with the prosecutors.

Are convicted offenders now more likely to receive the same punishment regardless of their race or which judge presides over their case? Research findings are too meager for us to know for certain, and to the degree that prosecutors bury their tracks, the answers will remain hidden. Still, the Government Accounting Office, the research organization for Congress, finds that no decline in disparity can be demonstrated. Most other analysts are less cautious, and are convinced that the disparity has not decreased. What is clear is that judicial authority has weakened and judicial anger and frustration have mounted. Federal Judge Jack Weinstein spoke for many of his colleagues when he said: "Whereas sentencing once called for hours spent reflecting on the offense and the person, we judges are becoming rubber-stamp bureaucrats. When we come to see ourselves as judicial accountants, freed from the awful responsibility of imposing a sentence, we will have abdicated our judicial role entirely" (Weinstein 1992)

LOOKING TO THE FUTURE

Prison analysts tend to agree on the flaws in current policies but they are uncertain about what should be done next. Christie, who is critical of determinate sentences, would like to restore sentencing discretion to the judges, but recognizes that to do so would only revive the dilemmas faced in the 1960s, when judges exercised unchecked and often biased authority. He believes that drawing up sentencing formulas is a hopeless task. But he refuses to suggest alternatives: "As a criminologist I feel more and more that my function is very similar to that of a book-reviewer or art critic" (Christie 1993:202).

Morris and Tonry (1994) are more ambitious, urging the establishment of a range of intermediate alternatives to prison. They want a system that would make use of substantial fines, residential control, electronic monitoring, sentences to community service and treatment, and supervised probation and parole. Judges would continue to sentence many violent criminals to prison but they would not be forced to choose between imprisonment and sending a criminal home.

Morris and Tonry recognize the problems with such a proposal. First, it is entirely possible, even likely, that judges will use the alternatives to prison mainly on behalf of white, middle-class offenders and not for blacks, thereby making the prison system even more of an apartheid institution than it is now. Second, and as we have seen in the Progressive era, alternatives to prison tend to become supplements to prison thereby "widening the net" of punishment. Judges would likely apply the new range of punishments not to those they consider hardened criminals but to those that they have formerly tended to treat more leniently. So a sentence to twelve months of community service is imposed not on people who otherwise would have entered a maximum security prison but on those who would have been released on probation without conditions. The net effect, then, is to increase, not reduce, the severity of sanctions and the number of people under state control. Nevertheless Morris and Tonry believe that these risks are worth taking. At least some offenders who are guilty of nonviolent crimes (including blacks) will be spared the miseries of confinement. Perhaps, too, those who run the criminal justice system will be able to learn from the experience and deal more intelligently with offenders generally (Blomberg and Lucken 2000).

Other would-be reformers of current conditions focus on the need for a new drug policy in criminal justice. They urge greater efforts to treat rather than punish the users, a principle now supported in California and elsewhere. To this end, public defenders should be given the resources to assess the right service plans for their clients. Drug courts should be established so that more defendants would be eligible for rehabilitative services. And of course, they recommend the repeal of mandatory sentencing laws particularly for nonviolent drug offenders so as to allow judges more discretion to fashion a sentence to meet the particular needs of the offender (Human Rights Watch 1997; Sentencing Project 2001).

More broadly still, reformers are advocating for alternatives to incarceration—not the building of enormous regional prisons and boot camps. Increasingly severe punishments are no remedy for the thwarted life circumstances that account for much of the crime being committed today, and they promise to create an even greater prison industry without effectively reducing crime. But to break out of our current fixation on prisons would require the kind of political leadership, that so far has been absent. It seems to be the fate of each generation to try to reform the inherited system of criminal justice and incarceration, and ours is no exception. This is not an uplifting history to trace but it does demonstrate the need for continuing engagement with these ever so difficult issues.

ACKNOWLEDGMENTS

An earlier version of this chapter appeared as the epilogue to the new edition of David J. Rothman, *Conscience and Convenience: The Asylum and its Alternatives in Progressive America*. Hawthorne, NY: Aldine de Gruyter. Copyright 1980 (2002) by David J. Rothman.

NOTES

1. Miller (1992a, 1992b). Both reports are available from the center's offices in Alexandria, Virginia.
2. Tonry (1994). Tonry notes that the United States is no worse in this respect than England (blacks), Canada (native population), and Australia (aboriginal people). His point is not to exculpate but to demonstrate how pervasive the problem is.
3. Among others, American Friends Service Committee (1971), Twentieth Century Fund (1976), and Von Hirsch (1976).

REFERENCES

American Friends Service Committee. 1971. *Struggle for Justice* 1st ed. New York: Hill & Wang.
Austin, James and John Irwin. 2001. *It's About Time: America's Imprisonment Binge*, 3rd ed. Belmont, CA: Wadsworth.
Blomberg, Thomas G. and Karol Lucken. 2000. *American Penology*. Hawthorne, NY: Aldine de Gruyter.
Boerner, David. 1993. "The Role of the Legislature in Guidelines Sentencing in The Other Washington." *Wake Forest Law Review* 28:381–420.
Christie, Nils. 1993. *Crime Control as Industry: Towards GULAGS, Western Style?* New York: Routledge.
Edna McConnell Clark Foundation. 1992. *Americans Behind Bars*. New York: Author.
Human Rights Watch. 1994. "Prison Conditions in the United States." New York: Author.
———. 1997. "Cruel and Usual: Disproportionate Sentences for New York Drug Offenders." March. New York: Author.
Mauer, Marc. The Sentencing Project, 1999. *Race to Incarcerate*. New York: New Press. Distributed by W.W. Norton.
Miller, Jerome G. 1992a. *Hobbling a Generation*. Alexandria, VA: National Center on Institutions and Alternatives.
———. 1992b. *Search and Destroy: The Plight of African-American Males in the Criminal Justice System*. Alexandria, VA: National Center on Institutions and Alternatives.

Morris, Norval and Michael Tonry. 1994. *Between Prison and Probation: Intermediate Punishments in a Rational Sentencing System.* New York: Oxford University Press.

Rothman, David J. and Aryeh Neier. 1994. "India's Awful Prisons." *New York Review of Book.* May 16, 1991. v. 38, n. 9, p. 53–54.

Schulhofer, Stephen J. 1993. "Rethinking Mandatory Minimums." *Wake Forest Law Review* 28(Summer):199–222.

Sentencing Project. 1993. "Does the Punishment Fit the Crime? Drug Users and Drunk Drivers, Questions of Race and Class." Report, March. Washington DC.

Sentencing Project. 2001. "Drug Policy and the Criminal Justice System." Report, May 2. Washington DC.

Stith, Kate and Steve Y. Koh. 1993. "The Politics of Sentencing Reform." *Wake Forest Law Review* 28:223–90.

Tonry, Michael. 1994. "Racial Disproportion in US Prisons." *British Journal of Criminology* 34:97.

———. 1993. "The Failure of the U.S. Sentencing Commission's Guidelines." *Crime and Delinquency* 39:131–49.

———. 1999. "Why Are U.S. Incarceration Rates So High?" *Crime and Delinquency* 45(4):419–38. New York.

Twentieth Century Fund. Task Force on Criminal Sentencing. 1976. *Fair and Certain Punishment: Report of the Twentieth Century Fund Task Force on Criminal Sentencing.* New York: McGraw-Hill.

Von Hirsch, Andrew. 1976. *Doing Justice: The Choice of Punishments: Report of the Committee for the Study of Incarceration.* New York: Hill & Wang.

Weinstein, Jack B. 1992. "A Trial Judge's Second Impression of the Federal Sentencing Guidelines." *Southern California Law Review* 66:357–66.

19

Penal Reform and the Fate of "Alternatives"

Thomas G. Blomberg

INTRODUCTION

During the past three decades a series of studies have appeared that have assessed the intentions and consequences of various nineteenth- and twentieth-century penal reforms. This literature has included considerations of the prison and asylum reform efforts of Jacksonian Americans in the early nineteenth century (Rothman 1991), the subsequent Progressive era reforms of parole, probation, and the juvenile court at the turn of the twentieth century and continuing into the 1950s (Platt 1977; Rothman 1980), the deinstitutional and diversion reforms of the 1960s and 1970s (Blomberg 1977), as well as the more recent intermediate punishment strategies that began in the 1980s and continue today (Blomberg, Bales, and Reed 1993). The recurring theme emerging from these studies has been the pattern of good intentions leading to bad consequences.

In attempting to capture this seemingly enduring contradiction, the metaphors of net-widening, wider and stronger nets, dispersal of discipline, transcarceration, minimum security society, maximum security society, and new penology have been used (i.e., Blomberg 1977; Austin and Krisberg 1981; Lowman, Menzies, and Palys 1987; Feeley and Simon 1992). In trying to account for this contradiction, one of several theoretical models has dominated the penal reform literature. Nonetheless, while these findings, metaphors, and theoretical interpretations have been helpful, we have yet to adequately grasp the full meaning of this seemingly unending cycle of reform and failure. Clearly, until we are able to grasp and understand this cycle of good intentions leading to bad consequences its repetition will continue. In fact, the metaphor of choice that is being employed in attempts to capture penal reform's current continuation of the intentions and consequences cycle of contradiction is "the culture of control" (Staples 2000; Garland 2001).

It has been in response to our fragmented understanding of penal reform that several authors have suggested a different approach to its study. Matthews (1987), for example, argues that an additional issue emerging from the findings of net-widening and the dispersal of discipline is that while there are inherent dangers associated with the expansion of social control, simultaneous attention must be given to the positive outcomes that may result from penal reforms. Matthews elaborates that penal reforms involve complex processes that result in not one outcome or result but several potentially mixed outcomes or results. Consequently, to make sense of these reforms and their processes requires a more comprehensive "approach than is realizable through overgeneralization, directionless statistical manipulation, and the kind of relentless pessimism which characterizes much of the literature" (ibid.:356).

Cohen (1985) specifies further that five theoretical models have dominated the literature attempting to interpret the contradictions between the intentions and consequences of penal reforms: progress, organizational convenience, ideological contradiction, professional interest, and political economy. Cohen argues that while each model can be emphasized for different purposes, ultimately all may be necessary to provide more comprehensive and compelling interpretation of the contradictions in the intentions and consequences of penal reforms. Cohen concludes that any satisfactory interpretation of penal reform must necessarily sift through the various theoretical models and assign them relative explanatory weight in relation to the different but interrelated processes characterizing penal reform (ibid.:112–13).

The need, then, is to move the study of penal reform beyond narrowly conceived empirical depictions and theoretical overgeneralization. In response to this need, Garland (1990) recommends a return to the empirically concrete coupled with an integration and synthesis of different theories in a way that approximates the real world components and interrelated processes of penal reforms. He argues that specific microstudies informed by the more general context would seem capable of providing more meaningful empirical and theoretical understanding of penal reform. These microstudies, as envisioned by Garland, would describe and capture the multiple components and processes that constitute the "wholeness" of penal reforms, namely, the interrelationships between their origins, implementation, operations, and potentially mixed outcomes. Moreover, the results of these microstudies should provide a number of timely and specific policy and practice predictions relevant to the fate of subsequent penal reform efforts.

This chapter identifies and discusses some of the ways to implement Garland's recommendation for a microstudy approach informed by an integrated theoretical framework for the study of penal reform. Included is a review of prior literature addressing the intentions and consequences of a series of penal reforms implemented during the past three decades. The review is intended to identify some of the contributions and shortcomings of this prior literature. From this literature review, an alternative microstudy approach that is informed by an integrated theoretical framework is described, applied, and concluded to be capable of providing more comprehensive description, explanation, and penal reform policy and practice predictions.

PENAL REFORM CONSEQUENCES

Major interest in the intentions and consequences of penal reforms emerged in the 1970s. Many of these early studies were focused upon determining the social control consequences produced by juvenile diversion programs that exploded throughout the United States during the 1960s and 1970s. The fundamental question addressed in these studies was whether diversion was providing an alternative or supplement to preexisting juvenile court practices. Several studies revealed that diversion services were being provided largely to youth and families who in the absence of diversion would not have been subject to any form of juvenile court contact or control (Blomberg 1977; Klein 1979; Lemert 1981; Austin and Krisberg 1981). This finding became communicated through the metaphor of net-widening or one of several other metaphors (wider or stronger nets, accelerated social control, etc.). These metaphors were used to characterize the gap between diversion's formal intentions and actual consequences. While the increased social control or net-widening finding did not go unchallenged in the literature, no contradictory empirical evidence was provided by such net-widening critics as Binder and Geis (1984) or McMahon (1990).

For example, while presenting no empirical evidence to support their argument, Binder and Geis (1984) concluded that concern over net-widening in diversion programs was without merit. They claimed that it was merely fashionable within "sociological criminology" to criticize diversion. According to the authors, those involved in diversion's criticism used "catchy words and phrases (like 'widening the net'), and frequently substituted rhetoric for logic in their argumentation aimed both at gaining cultic recognition and winning over the unwary" (ibid.:624). Additionally, while acknowledging net-widening's occurrence in both juvenile and adult community correctional reforms, McMahon argued that "wider," "stronger," and "different" nets, while useful in focusing attention upon trends in the expansion and extension of penal control, could direct attention away from any possible reduction in penal control that might have taken place as a result of these reform efforts (McMahon 1990:144).

The 1980s rise of various get-tough-on-crime approaches resulted in continued interest in measuring social control outcomes. Several studies found that the various get-tough strategies were, like earlier progressive and more recent diversion and community corrections reforms, being implemented as supplements rather than alternatives, thereby resulting in an expanded proportion of the base population subject to some form of penal control. In these get-tough program instances, mandatory jail sentences for drunk drivers, flat or determinant prison sentencing, and stiffer penalties for drug offenders coupled with preexisting diversion, community, and other traditional probation, parole, and prison strategies were cumulatively resulting in a larger proportion of the base population subject to some form of penal control (NCCD 1989; Blomberg 1987; Hylton 1982).

National Council on Crime and Delinquency (NCCD) (1989), in a consideration of the impact of the war on drugs policy, for example, predicted that by 1994, the 1989 incarceration rate of 250 per 100,000 population would increase to 440 per 100,000 and when combined with the offender populations in various community programs would result in not only more reliance upon incarceration but substantially more penal control over the base population. Similarly, other studies documented unprecedented increases in prison admissions and populations during the 1980s, which when considered in combination with the offender populations in various community correctional programs, documented unprecedented increases in the proportion of the base population subject to some form of penal control (Hylton 1982; Blomberg 1987).

Beginning in the late 1980s, America's preoccupation with getting tough on crime became subject to challenge by a growing public demand for simultaneous protection from crime and higher taxes. The rapidly rising costs of building and operating prisons were being felt throughout the country as state correctional budgets became the fastest growing component of state expenditures. With an average prison cell construction cost of $50,000, it was projected that states would have to raise over $20 billion for prison construction (NCCD 1989). The response to this fiscal dilemma was the nationwide call for various intermediate punishment programs that were promoted as a way to provide less costly but still tough sanctions for offenders requiring more supervision than nominal probation but less than incarceration. As intended, intermediate punishment was to provide a range of punishment and treatment sentence alternatives to prisons and jails that could include intensive supervision, home confinement, electronic surveillance, daily reporting, work release, and numerous other private treatment services (e.g., chemical abuse, impulse control, and marital counseling).

Like earlier penal reform efforts, the net-widening finding resurfaced in several empirical assessments of the intentions and consequences of intermediate punishment. Again, the question being addressed in these assessments was whether intermediate punishment was redistributing control away from prisons and jails or merely expanding penal control to those offender groups previously not subject to imminent jail or prison sentences. For example, we concluded that during the late 1980s, and despite the operation of a statewide Florida intermediate punishment program alternative to prison that involved an average daily caseload of more than 10,000 offenders, Florida's use of prisons experienced major increases disproportionate to the state's population, arrests, and conviction increases (Blomberg et al. 1993).

In another study of a local jurisdiction's intermediate punishment program alternative to jail, we documented not only net-widening but what we termed the "piling up of sanctions" on participating offenders (Blomberg and Lucken 1994). In this case, we found that the jurisdiction's use of its jail did not decline as intended but instead experienced substantial inmate population growth with simultaneous growth in the use of intermediate punishments that together were disproportionate to the jurisdiction's increases in population, arrests, and convictions. Moreover, and beyond the net-widening findings, it was found that the piling up of intermediate sanctions on participating offenders was resulting in numerous violations of sentence conditions and subsequent jail sentences followed by a recycling of the offender back through intermediate punishment. In sum, by piling up sanctions, the program was having the latent effect of literally entangling offenders with multiple sanctions (probation, home confinement, chemical abuse treatment, impulse control treatment, etc.) often coupled with overlapping conditions and requirements resulting in frequent sentence violations, new jail sentences, and resulting increased jail populations (see also Petersilia and Turner 1990).

The characteristic empirical assessments of the consequences of various penal reforms over the past three decades demonstrate increased penal control despite the intention of these reforms to result in alternative control. Further, these increases in penal control have been shown to be disproportionate to increases or changes in population, arrests, or convictions. Additionally, several latent and negative consequences have been documented including the piling up of sanctions, sentence violations, return to court, new jail sentences, and subsequent recycling of offenders back through intermediate punishment.

TOWARD MICRO- AND THEORETICALLY INTEGRATED STUDY OF PENAL REFORM

Contemporary penology is a complex and dynamic system continuously undergoing reform and proliferation. The current penal system subsumes within its structure expanding prison and jail facilities, probation and parole services, ever-enlarging systems of intermediate punishments, and growing numbers of private-provided penal services. Moreover, most states have enacted crime victim bill of rights laws guaranteeing victims of crime the right to be notified, present, and heard at all phases of their assailant's legal and correctional hearings. As a result, penal systems are implementing and operating various crime victim services as well.

These and other developments are resulting in more interagency activities between police, courts, corrections, victim services, and private organizations. Further, each of these agencies is undergoing independent changes related to additional and often-conflicting goals and functions. Also, ever-increasing public fear over crime and higher taxes are leading politicians to lay their respective claims that they are not only "tougher" on crime than their political adversaries but that they can "deliver" more cost effective policy solutions as well. Consequently, contemporary penology is an increasingly politicized, and dynamic system not easily described or interpreted.

Intermediate punishment policies provide useful illustration of the need to employ several theoretical models and more comprehensive and detailed empirical designs in order to adequately describe and interpret penal reform. In our study of a large local jurisdiction's intermediate punishment program, we identified several contextual factors that shaped the idea, and development of the program (Blomberg and Lucken 1994). Specifically, the idea of "punish and treat" turned out to be embraced by not only local key decision-makers ultimately responsible for developing the program but by the general public as well. Further, the official claims underlying intermediate punishment, a cost-effective and responsible approach were well received by both liberals and conservatives in and out of local government. This jurisdiction, like many other local jurisdictions throughout the country, was experiencing lawsuits and other fiscal problems related to jail overcrowding. Approximately one-third of all local jails across the United States were under court orders to reduce overcrowding during the early 1990s (Proband 1993). Moreover, much of this local jurisdiction's jail population was comprised of misdemeanor offenders. Intermediate punishment was promoted as a cost-effective strategy to reduce jail overcrowding and related lawsuits, which the county commissioners were eager to accomplish, and as a means to deal more responsibly with the growing number of misdemeanor offenders in the jurisdiction. Overall, the punish and treat approach to misdemeanors was welcomed by local law enforcement, judicial and penal personnel, policymakers, as well as interested citizens.

Ultimately, a consolidation of jail and correctional services was approved with the guiding philosophy of a punish and treat "continuum of care." This became the jurisdiction's intermediate punishment philosophy and we found that a number of local individuals were central to the development and implementation of this philosophy and program including several county commissioners, judges, the sheriff, and the program's director. However, the motives and efforts of these individuals must be understood within the larger context of local concerns and needs related to overcrowded jail conditions and ongoing lawsuits, increasing fiscal constraints as well as increasing public outcries for protection from crime and higher taxes. Intermediate punishment emerged as a "strategy for the times" that an increasingly dissatisfied public, criminal justice professionals, and fiscally conservative-minded policymakers could collectively embrace. Unfortunately this broadly embraced philosophy of treat and punish through a continuum of care contributed to an inherent capacity for unintended and negative consequences.

The implementation of a penal reform philosophy and program initiates a series of events that determine the practices and consequences resulting from the reform. Specific items of information can be collected to describe the reform's implementation process. Central among these items of information are the perspectives of those individuals implementing the reform. How do these individuals view the reform's goals, practices, and consequences? Does the reform challenge or reinforce their professional ideology and major organizational interests? Certainly the perceptions of program administrators, line staff, judges, and private agency personnel are central to the form and operational features of a penal reform regardless of the reform's official intentions. Further, these perceptions can be identified and assessed. The task involves soliciting the perspectives of those personnel associated with the implementation of the penal reform. When asked with genuine interest, penal system personnel will routinely share not only their daily routines, problems, and practices, but the commonsense constructs that guide their everyday practices and decisions. Additionally, program rules and prescribed practices are recorded in some form, providing additional information about penal system practices and procedures.

In our study of intermediate punishment, we found the program's major operational feature to be what we termed "the piling up of sanctions." In the "piling up of sanctions" process various intermediate punish and treat program components consistent with the intermediate punishment idea and philosophy were intentionally implemented as supplements to each other, whereby offenders received several simultaneous sanctions. Offenders would routinely receive a period of incarceration followed by a term of probation, community service, and/or a fine. When a period of incarceration and probation were imposed and the offender qualified for work release or home confinement, the offender could be supervised simultaneously by a probation officer and work release counselor or home confinement officer. In these instances, offenders were supervised by two officers and were required to comply with the conditions of both programs (Blomberg and Lucken 1994:66).

Through this process of implementation, intermediate punishment was resulting in a number of predictable unintended and negative consequences. However, we determined that various intermediate punishment personnel viewed the "piling up of sanctions" as both responsible and an appropriate implementation of the treat and punish continuum of care philosophy of intermediate punishment rather than program subversion. Different program personnel including jail staff, probation officers, program administrators, judges, and private treatment staff communicated common assumptions about how to deal with offenders. Specifically, they shared a "middle-class measuring rod" with regard to offender expectations. Successful compliance with the piling up of sanctions required offenders to have characteristics of middle-class, law-abiding citizens with higher education, stronger community ties, and greater financial resources. However, the bulk of participating offenders in the program did not possess these middle-class characteristics, which would facilitate their compliance with various simultaneous program requirements. For example, if the offender was employed, he or she may have had the money to enroll in private treatment programs but not the necessary time to attend the required weekly meetings because of work obligations. If unemployed, the offender had the time to attend meetings but not the money required to participate. The piling up of sanctions required offenders to use their limited resources across several often costly programs. The characteristic requirements for satisfactory participation and successful completion of multiple programs and conditions, namely, money, transportation, and a sense of responsibility, were not characteristics held by most participating offenders.

While sanctioning agents expressed awareness of these offender characteristics and obstacles, they did not excuse the offender from the consequences of their lawbreaking. Such offender characteristics and circumstances were not viewed as unusual or deserving of special consideration. Rather, the prevailing perception was that strict enforcement of various program conditions and requirements was essential to the ultimate redirection of the offender's behavior. To accommodate or sympathize with the offender's circumstances was considered inappropriate, lenient, or enabling to the offender's lifestyle. These sanctioning agent perceptions and expectations coupled with offender characteristics and associated limited program participation capabilities set the stage for frequent violations of intermediate punishment's multiple program sentence requirements.

Meaningful interpretation of intermediate punishment's piling up of sanctions practices and consequences clearly involves several theoretical dimensions. For example, aspects of organizational convenience, professional interest, and ideological contradiction are relevant and helpful in understanding how and why the piling up of sanctions practice was implemented and came to characterize the program's operations. With regard to organizational convenience, a number of organizational dynamics contributed to the process. Private treatment agencies, for example, had a vested organizational self-interest in gaining and maintaining clients. This process is fundamental for the survival of these agencies since their funding is determined by the number of offenders served and length of service. Moreover, various professional interests shaped the piling up of sanctions process since various program sanctioning agents and private treatment staff hold what are often common views concerning the value and appropriateness of multiple punish and treat program services for offenders. Additionally, ideological contradictions are exemplified in intermediate punishment's punish and treat philosophy that gain direct expression through the piling up of sanctions process and resulting pattern of frequent offender violation of sentence requirements. Further, aspects of political economy arguments are helpful in explaining intermediate punishment's overriding focus on lower-class, undereducated, and unemployed misdemeanor offenders, and the subsequent attempt to hold these offenders to "middle-class" standards and expectations with multiple program requirements.

Ultimately penal reform philosophy and practices are measured in relation to consequences or outcomes. Typically, and as shown in the earlier review of prior research, only select aggregate statistics have been employed for outcome measures but other items of data can provide more comprehensive outcome measures. For example, to provide more complete measurement of the control outcomes requires consideration of not only changes in the proportion of population subject to control but description of the specific type and character of control being administered. Specifically, the length of time individuals are subject to control, description of the requirements and nature of control, and any follow-up consequences are all important considerations for any meaningful measurement and understanding of penal reform and social control (e.g., twenty-four hours per day home confinement compared to once a day reporting to a community center). Moreover, the perceptions of offenders concerning the character of control they are subject to is integral if the full range of a penal reform's control consequences are to be described, measured, and understood. Further, and beyond social control descriptions and measurements, other outcomes should be sought for offenders, families, communities, and penal agencies. The empirical task is to collect various outcome measures that together provide a more comprehensive and accurate description of a penal reform's overall and potentially mixed outcomes.

In our study of intermediate punishment, we found a number of negative outcomes associated with the piling up of sanctions, but we also found positive program outcomes. With regard to negative outcomes associated with the piling up of sanctions, there was a chain of unintended events and consequences associated with this practice. As mentioned previously, by involving offenders in multiple vocational, education, and substance abuse programs with multiple demands and requirements, offenders were often found to be in noncompliance. This pattern of noncompliance resulted in return to court for new sentencing, often leading to jail followed by a return to the same combination of intermediate punishment programs, in which some offenders were recycled several times because of repeated sentence violations. As a result, intermediate punishment resulted in increased demands for jail space, with the jurisdiction finding it necessary to expand its incarceration capacities initially by 300 beds and later by adding a 768-bed minimum-security facility.

The piling up of sanctions, however, was not detrimental to all offenders on intermediate punishment. For example, the intermediate punishment program included a work release component. The work release component selected each of its program participants from the jail population thereby providing an alternative rather than supplement to jail. While on work release the offenders were housed in a residential facility. One requirement of work release was to either have a General Education Diploma before entering work release or earn the diploma while in the program. All offenders selected for work release were either employed or quickly placed in jobs with assistance from the work release counselors. The maximum term for offenders on work release was one year. Typically, offenders worked during the day and completed various counseling or chemical abuse treatment during the evenings. The offender's financial obligations were automatically deducted from their payroll checks including child-support and restitution. Offenders with satisfactory work release performance could qualify for program release into the daily reporting program. In these instances the offenders would live at home, continue to work and be subject to automatic payroll deductions, and report to the daily reporting centers. Numerous offenders, employers, and program staff viewed work release and its multiple requirements as successful in terms of offender accountability, treatment, and vocational assistance.

The home confinement program component of intermediate punishment operated similarly to work release. Offenders were selected from the jail population and required to work and meet all of their financial obligations and to participate in various other treatment programs deemed necessary. The program provided an alternative to jail with regular offender monitoring. Again, offenders, employers, and program personnel considered home confinement as a responsible alternative to jail that enabled offenders to participate in treatment, to work and to provide for their families, and to meet other financial obligations.

Drawing upon another example, during the late 1990s, the State of Florida embarked upon major reform of its juvenile justice system. Underlying this reform effort were different quality, accountability, research, cost-effective as well as get-tough rationales that ultimately resulted in the broad use of privatization, a move toward larger and more prisonlike juvenile commitment facilities, and a statewide accountability and research-driven approach to juvenile justice education programs operating in these commitment facilities. The subsequent outcomes of this sweeping reform effort have indeed been clearly mixed.

With regard to privatization, approximately 50 percent of the more than 16,000 youth handled annually in Florida's commitment facilities receive private-provided education services. Since 1998, we have evaluated the quality differences between these private- and public-provided education programs in relation to annual quality assurance reviews and scores. Over the years, public-operated education programs have, as a group, received consistently higher-quality assurance scores than have private-operated education programs. We have determined that these quality assurance score differences between public and private education programs have related directly to the qualifications of the teachers and the educational activities taking place in the classrooms. Most of the private-operated juvenile justice education programs do not employ as many professionally certified teachers as do the public-operated programs. For example, in 2001, public-provided education programs throughout the state employed 79 percent full-time professionally-certified teachers, as compared to 33 percent for private not-for-profit, and only 21 percent for private for-profit providers. It is important to acknowledge, however, that several private not-for-profit providers received very high-quality assurance scores for their education programs, so the situation is not completely one-sided. As a result, although it can be concluded that privatization has generally reduced the overall quality of education services, in certain instances privatization can provide the flexibility for innovation that increases quality education (Chester, Tracy, Earp, and Chauhan 2002).

In relation to Florida's tough-love and economy-of-scale driven move toward larger and more prisonlike juvenile commitment facilities, we have evaluated the quality of education programs in relation to facility size. We included analyses of the educational program quality assurance scores of larger facilities compared to smaller facilities. These analyses showed that education programs operating in larger facilities (one hundred or more youths) scored substantially lower than the educational programs operating in smaller facilities (less than one hundred youths). Based on the findings reported in the prior literature and these quality assurance scores, we argued that Florida's employment of tough-love and economy-of-scale rationales for larger juvenile justice institutions was resulting in a number of negative outcomes for the education programs in these facilities (Major et al. 2002).

In contrast, and occurring simultaneously to the move to privatization and larger custodial juvenile facilities has been Florida's implementation of ongoing quality accountability and research-based best practices into its juvenile justice education programs. Our ongoing assessment that began in 1998 and continues today has demonstrated that higher-quality scoring juvenile justice education programs have the highest proportion of promising or best practices, with the middle scoring programs having fewer promising or best practices, and the low scoring programs having the least of such practices. With regard to academic outcomes, there is a positive correlation between high-quality performing programs and various pre- and post-academic outcome gains related to academic pre- and post-assessment test score gains, credits earned, and diplomas and certificates received. Moreover, our longitudinal results related to community reintegration documents that programs with high-quality scores and higher pre- and post-academic gains have less official and self-reported misconduct or recidivism, more students returning to school and staying in school longer than the lower-quality scoring education programs (Blomberg and Waldo 2002). What this suggests is the capacity of quality education and academic gains to serve as a "positive turning point" in life course of delinquent youth.

The preceding penal reform efforts demonstrate both alarming and encouraging implications. Further, it is evident that penal reform should not be oversimplified—it is complex and often involves the blurring of conflicting rationales and operational features. Moreover, these rationales and operational features are themselves products of larger social, political, and economic influences and imperatives that can be identified, interpreted, and applied.

SUMMARY AND DISCUSSION

This chapter has identified elements and strategies for a microstudy approach that views the origins, operations, and consequences of penal reform as interrelated. Specific data sources have been identified as useful in describing the origins, operations, and consequences of penal reform. Further, it has been shown that several theoretical models are necessary to provide compelling interpretation of these penal reform components and interrelationships. Garland (1990) suggests that a level of abstraction is a necessary first step during the initial study of complex areas with competing abstractions and particular explanations resulting from these early studies. This is how much of the prior penal reform literature has developed. But as Garland concludes, "the ultimate objective of research must be to return to the concrete, to integrate and synthesize different abstractions in a way that simulates the over determination of real-world objects and approximates their complex wholeness" (ibid.:15). This is the task now facing penal reform researchers in their continuing effort to provide more comprehensive empirical description, compelling theoretical interpretation, and policy and practice predictions.

It is important to understand that it is possible to develop penal reform program strategies from theory and to implement those strategies with integrity through careful evaluation and accountability measures that ensure encountered impediments to appropriate implementation are overcome. Moreover, the outcomes produced from these reforms can be documented to test the ultimate adequacy of the reform's underlying theory, and program strategy. Clearly, given current U.S. incarceration trends or what is being characterized as a "mass imprisonment society," the need for more effective and humane penal reform alternatives to incarceration has never been more crucial. For example, considering only adult incarceration trends between 1980 and 2000, prison populations have increased by 319 percent, and jail populations by 279 percent. According to the U.S. Department of Justice (2001) during the year 2000, over two million adults were either held in jails or prisons compared to fewer than 500,000 during 1980. The question is why do we continue to rely increasingly upon these crude, inhumane, ineffective, and costly mechanisms? No doubt, many politicians would respond to this question with their own question: What are the proven alternatives to jails and prisons? One would be hard pressed to identify such proven incarceration alternatives from the existing penal reform literature.

While the degree of incarceration growth in state prisons is now experiencing some slowdown, the Federal Bureau of Prisons is currently undergoing the largest prison expansion in its history. The numerous social and economic costs of this mass imprisonment policy have and will continue to be felt for many years to come. An often-cited example of the social costs associated with our mass imprisonment policy is higher education funding, which has experienced major declines during the past decade while prison spending has exploded. Further, and largely overlooked in the literature, are the unknown multitude of other potential social costs associated with the ongoing release of hundreds of thousands of inmates sentenced to prison during the get-tough era. Many of these releasees have been incarcerated for two decades or longer in prisons characterized by overcrowded and violent conditions and without satisfactory vocational, educational, or treatment services. The prospects of these releasees in our vastly changed and ever-increasingly technological and competitive society are dismal at best, which could give rise to still another "lock them up longer" outcry from frightened citizens and politicians alike. In fact, newspapers across the country are reporting from the most recent FBI Uniform Crime Report (U.S. Department of Justice 2002) that murder and other serious crimes have increased overall by 2 percent in

2001 following a sustained nine-year decline. One of the major reasons being cited for this crime increase turnabout is the 600,000 inmate felons being released annually from our prisons.

A timely and crucial penal policy question, therefore, is whether there are penal reform alternatives to incarceration that can offer something beyond the routinely documented intentions and consequences contradiction. Is it possible for penal researchers to provide concrete and politically authoritative statements on what specific prison, prison alternatives, or other penal reforms can and cannot do and for whom? Certainly, such policy recommendations will not be forthcoming until our empirical and theoretical understanding of penal reforms becomes substantially improved. Yet, without grasping the meaning of this seemingly unending cycle of reform and failure, the cycle will continue to repeat itself with ever more ominous implications (see, for example, Blomberg and Lucken 2000:226–32).

REFERENCES

Austin, James and Barry Krisberg. 1981. "Wider, Stronger and Different Nets: The Dialectics of Criminal Justice Reform." *Journal of Research in Crime and Delinquency* 18(1):165–96.

Binder, Arnold and Gilbert Geis. 1984. "Ad Populum Argumentation in Criminology: Juvenile Diversion as Rhetoric." *Crime and Delinquency* 30(4):624–47.

Blomberg, Thomas G. 1977. "Diversion and Accelerated Social Control." *Journal of Criminal Law and Criminology* 68(2):274–82.

———. 1987. "Criminal Justice Reform and Social Control: Are We Becoming a Minimum Security Society?" Pp. 218–26 in *Transcarceration: Essays in the Sociology of Social Control*, edited by J. Lowman, R. J. Menzies, and T. S. Palys. England: Gower.

Blomberg, Thomas G., William Bales, and Karen Reed. 1993. "Intermediate Punishment: Redistributing or Extending Social Control?" *Crime, Law and Social Change* 19:187–201.

Blomberg, Thomas G. and Karol Lucken. 1994. "Stacking the Deck by Piling Up Sanctions: Is Intermediate Punishment Destined to Fail?" *Howard Journal* 33(1):62–80.

———. 2000. *American Penology: A History of Control*. Hawthorne, NY: Aldine de Gruyter.

Blomberg, Thomas G. and Gordon P. Waldo. 2002. "Evaluation Research, Policy, and Politics." *Evaluation Review* 26(3):340–51.

Chester, Deborah R., Jessamyn A. Tracy, Emily Earp, and Reetu Chauhan. 2002. "Correlates of Quality Education Programs." *Evaluation Review* 26(3):272–300.

Cohen, Stanley. 1985. *Visions of Social Control*. Cambridge: Polity.

Feeley, Malcolm M. and Jonathan Simon. 1992. "The New Penology: Notes on the Emerging Strategy of Corrections and Its Implications." *Criminology* 30(4): 449–74.

Garland, David. 1990. *Punishment and Modern Society: A Study in Social Theory.* Oxford: Clarendon.

———. 2001. *The Culture of Crime and Social Order in Contemporary Society.* New York: Oxford University Press.

Hylton, John. 1982. "Rhetoric and Reality: A Critical Appraisal of Community Corrections Programmes." *Crime and Delinquency* 28(3):341–73.

Klein, Malcolm W. 1979. "Deinstitutionalization and Diversion of Juvenile Offenders: A Litany of Impediments." Pp. 145–201 in *Crime and Justice: An Annual Review of Research,* edited by Norval Morris and Michael Tonry. Chicago: University of Chicago Press.

Lemert, Edwin M. 1981. "Diversion in Juvenile Justice: What Hath Been Wrought." *Journal of Research in Crime and Delinquency* 18(1):34–46.

Lowman, John, Robert J. Menzies, and T. S. Palys. 1987 *Transcarceration: Essays in the Sociology of Social Control.* England: Gower.

Major, Aline K., Deborah R. Chester, Ranee McEntire, Gordon P. Waldo, and Thomas G. Blomberg. 2002. "Pre-, Post-, and Longitudinal Evaluation of Juvenile Justice Education." *Evaluation Review* 26(3):302–21.

Matthews, Roger. 1987. "Decarceration and Social Control: Fantasies and Realities." Pp. 338–57 in *Transcarceration: Essays in the Sociology of Social Control,* edited by J. Lowman, R. J. Menzies, and T. S. Palys. England: Gower.

McMahon, Maeve. 1990. "Net-Widening: Vagaries of the Use of a Concept." *British Journal of Criminology* 30(2):121–49.

National Council on Crime and Delinquency. 1989. *The 1989 NCCD Prison Population Forecast: The Impact of the War on Drugs.* San Francisco, CA: National Council on Crime and Delinquency.

Petersilia, Joan and Susan Turner. 1990. "Comparing Intensive and Regular Supervision for High Risk Probationers." *Crime and Delinquency* 36(1):87–111.

Platt, Tony. 1977. *The Child Savers: The Invention of Delinquency.* Chicago: University of Chicago Press.

Proband, Stan C. 1993. "Jail Populations Up—Racial Disproportions Worse." *Overcrowded Times* 4(4):4.

Rothman, David J. 1980. *Conscience and Convenience: The Asylum and its Alternatives in Progressive America.* Boston: Little, Brown.

———. 1991. *The Discovery of the Asylum: Social Order and Disorder in the New Republic,* rev. ed. Boston: Little, Brown.

Staples, William G. 2000. *Everyday Surveillance: Vigilance and Visibility in Postmodern Life.* Maryland: Rowman and Littlefield.

U.S. Department of Justice, Bureau of Justice Statistics. 2001. *Prisoners 2000.* Washington, DC: U.S. Government Printing Office.

———. 2002. *Crime in the United States, 2001.* Washington, DC: U.S. Government Printing Office.

20

It's About Time

America's Imprisonment Binge

JAMES AUSTIN, JOHN IRWIN, AND CHARIS KUBRIN

AMERICA'S GROWING CORRECTIONAL INDUSTRIAL COMPLEX

Over the past two decades, the United States has been engaged in an unprecedented imprisonment binge. Between 1980 and 2000, the prison population ballooned from 329,821 to 1,381,892—a rise of 319 percent.[1] The increase was so great that by 2000 the number of citizens incarcerated in state and federal prisons exceeded or approximated the resident populations of thirteen states and was larger than all of our major cities with the exceptions of Chicago, Houston, Los Angeles, New York, and Philadelphia.[2] The incarceration rate (number of persons in state and federal prison on any given day per 100,000 population) increased during the same time period from 138 to 478, as compared to only 26 in 1850. We now imprison at a higher rate than any nation in the world, having recently surpassed South Africa.

Most Americans are unaware that the adult prison population represents no more than one-fifth of the entire correctional industrial complex. There are another 621,149 people in jail, nearly 3.9 million on probation, and 725,527 on parole. In total, almost 6.5 million adults—about 1 of every 32 adults—were under some form of correctional supervision in 2000. In 1980 the ratio was only 1 of every 91 adults.

The rise in prison populations has been accompanied by equally large increases in these other forms of correctional supervision. Between 1980 and 2000, the probation, parole, and jail populations (facilities that typically house pretrial defendants and offenders sentenced to short jail terms of one year or less) grew almost as rapidly as the prison population, as

Table 20.1.   Adult Correctional Populations, 1980–2000

	1980	2000	Change (%)
Probation	1,118,097	3,839,532	243
Jails	164,994	621,149	279
Prison	329,821	1,381,892	319
Parole	220,438	725,527	229
Totals	1,832,350	6,568,100	258
Population	162,800,000	209,100,000	28
Adults under supervision (%)	1.1	3.1	182
Arrests	6,100,000	9,100,000	49
Reported index crimes	13,400,000	11,600,000	(13)

Sources: U.S. Department of Justice, Federal Bureau of Investigation, *Uniform Crime Reports: Crime in the United States, 1980 and 2000;* U.S. Department of Justice, Bureau of Justice Statistics, *Prisoners in 2000;* U.S. Department of Justice, Bureau of Justice Statistics, *Probation and Parole Populations in the United States, 2000.*

Table 20.1 shows. Probation grew by 243 percent during the same time and remains the dominant form of correctional supervision.

It should also be noted that more Americans experience jail time than any other form of correctional control. In 1994, the U.S. Department of Justice reported 9.8 million admissions to the nation's 3,300-plus jails.[3] Assuming that approximately 75 percent of these admissions represent mutually exclusive adults, this means that nearly 1 of every 25 adults in America goes to jail each year. But even these staggering numbers do not account for all Americans involved in the correctional system. Not counted in the six million daily correctional population figure are nearly 110,000 children incarcerated and nearly 2,500 prisoners held by the military. Although there are no firm government estimates, there are several hundred thousand juveniles on probation or parole plus the same number of adults and juveniles on some form of pretrial supervision. Based on these estimates, one can safely assume that over 7 million Americans are under the control of one of several adult and juvenile correctional systems.

Yet after decades of steady growth, there is some evidence that the accelerating use of imprisonment may be subsiding. Between January 1 and December 31, 2000, thirteen states experienced decreases, led by Massachusetts (down 6 percent), followed by New Jersey (down 5 percent), New York (down 4 percent), and Texas (down 3 percent). Between 1990 and 1999, the prison population grew an average of nearly 6 percent a year, but in 2000, the annual rate of growth declined to 4 percent. Still, many states who have adopted "truth in sentencing" and other mandatory sentencing policies, which serve to increase the number of persons incarcerated and lengthen their sentences, continue to experience growth in their inmate populations. Five states—Idaho (up 14 percent), North Dakota (14 percent), Mississippi (11 percent), Vermont (11 percent), and Iowa (10 percent)—had increases of at least 10 percent in 2000.

RACE, ETHNICITY, AND GENDER AND HIGHER IMPRISONMENT RATES

Those under the control of correctional authority do not represent a cross section of the nation's population. They tend to be young African-American and Hispanic males who are uneducated, without jobs, or, at best, marginally employed in low-paying jobs. African-Americans comprise about 13 percent of the population but according to the most recent data from the U.S. Department of Justice, blacks constitute about 46 percent of the sentenced prisoners under state and federal jurisdiction. Furthermore, more than one-third of probationers and more than two out of five adults on parole in 2000 were black. At the same time, persons of Hispanic origin, who are of any race, comprised 16 percent of the probation population and 21 percent of the parole population. As Table 20.2 illustrates, there are great disparities in incarceration rates by race and ethnicity; black and Hispanic males have incarceration rates that are three to nearly seven times higher than white males.

These disparities by race and ethnicity are even more troubling when age is factored into the analysis. In 2000, nearly 10 percent of black males, age 25–29, were in prison. It is interesting to note, however, that while the incarceration rate for African-American males steadily increased over the last decade, the incarceration rates for white and Hispanic males have be-

Table 20.2. Male Incarceration Rates per 100,000 Male Population by Race and Ethnicity, 1990–2000

Year	All	White	Black	Hispanic
1990	564	338	2,234	1,016
1995	781	449	3,095	1,264
1996	810	468	3,164	1,279
1997	841	491	3,253	1,272
2000	904	449	3,457	1,220
Change (%)	60	33	55	20

Source: U.S. Department of Justice, Bureau of Justice Statistics, *Prisoners in 2000* (Washington, DC: U.S. Government Printing Office, August 2001).

gun to decrease in the last three years. The incarceration rate for white males dropped from 491 to 449 and the rate for Hispanic males from 1,272 to 1,220 from 1997 to 2000; on the other hand, the rate for black males increased from 3,253 to 3,457 over the same time period. Thus, the subsiding increase in the use of incarceration that was mentioned earlier appears to be related primarily to decreases in the incarceration rates of whites and Hispanics, not blacks.

At year end in 2000, 91,612 women were in state or federal prisons—6.6 percent of all prison inmates. While the number of male prison inmates has grown 77 percent since 1990, the number of female prisoners has increased 108 percent. Female incarceration rates, though substantially lower than male rates at every age, reveal similar racial and ethnic disparities, as Table 20.3 shows. For example, black non-Hispanic females (with an incarceration rate of 205 per 100,000) were more than three times as likely as Hispanic females (60 per 100,000) and 6 times more likely than white non-Hispanic females (34 per 100,000) to be in prison. Similar to Hispanic male incarceration rates, Hispanic female rates have begun to decline substantially in the last three years; from 1997 to 2000, the rate dropped from 87 to 60 per 100,000. For white and black females, however, the opposite is true, as both rates have steadily increased over the last decade.

These disparities for both men and women have a real impact on the relative life chances of the different groups. In 1997, the Bureau of Justice Statistics calculated the lifetime likelihood of a person going to prison, assuming that rates of first incarceration and death remained at their 1991 levels. This analysis revealed that if the 1991 rates prevailed throughout the life of a cohort, about 16 percent of the blacks, 9 percent of the Hispanics, and 3 percent of the whites would be sentenced to prison at some time in their lives. These chances were much greater for men (9 percent) than for women (1 percent), and reached their highest level for African-American males. As shown in Table 20.1, nearly one in three black males (29 per-

Table 20.3.   Female Incarceration Rates per 100,000 Female Population by Race and Ethnicity, 1990–2000

Year	All	White	Black	Hispanic
1990	31	19	117	56
1995	47	27	176	64
1996	51	30	185	78
1997	53	32	192	87
2000	59	34	205	60
Change (%)	90	79	75	7

Source: U.S. Department of Justice, Bureau of Justice Statistics, Prisoners in 2000 (Washington, DC: U.S. Government Printing Office, August 2001).

cent) could expect to be incarcerated at some time in their life given the 1991 rates. The comparable rates for Hispanic and white males were 16 and 4 percent, respectively. More importantly, these rates of incarceration have continued to rise since 1991, and especially for African-Americans and Hispanics.

THE POLITICS OF THE FEAR OF CRIME

Several factors have fueled the imprisonment binge. The most powerful has been the public's growing fear of crime. Bill Chambliss has documented the well-orchestrated effort by powerful interest groups since the 1960s to make crime the most important issue on the public's mind. Chambliss points out that prior to the 1960s crime was not cited by the public as a major concern.[4] Yet led by a well-funded cartel of conservatives who were greatly concerned about the civil rights and anti-Vietnam war movements, a "War on Crime" was formally launched by an increasingly defensive President Johnson. Part of the increasing concern regarding crime was fueled by a substantial increase in the major "index" crimes (homicide, assault, rape, burglary, theft, and arson) reported to police in the late 1960s and early 1970s. Despite massive increases in the amount of money being spent on law enforcement and corrections coupled with a tapering off in the crime rate, the public has continued to believe that crime has been on the rise and their fear of crime remains high. The most recent Gallup Poll national poll shows that violent crime tops the list of the most important problems facing the country.

Through the 1980s, the fear of crime and drug abuse was elevated each election year by the attention that politicians (both Democrats and Republicans) and the media gave to crime and drug problems. The most blatant example of these tactics was then Republican presidential candidate George Bush's successful effort to erase his opponent's (Michael Dukakis) early lead in the 1987 presidential campaign by blaming the tragic Willie Horton incident on liberal Democratic party politics. Smarting from this poignant lesson in dirty politics, Democrats have fully embraced "get tough on crime" policies in an effort to outflank and neutralize what has traditionally been a Republican perspective.

It was under a Democrat-controlled Congress that the controversial Federal Sentencing Guidelines, which mandated long prison terms for possession of crack cocaine, were adopted. And it was President Clinton's administration that endorsed the most expensive crime bill in the nation's history to fund 100,000 police officers and boot camps, and to help pay for prison construction for states willing to pass laws that would require long prison terms. Ironically, the public shifted its focus (or more correctly has had its focus shifted by the media) on violent crime even as the crime rate has declined.

Politicians harangue on the street crime problem because it is a safe issue. It is easy to cast in simple terms of good versus evil and no powerful constituency is directly offended by a campaign against street crime. Some politicians also use street crime to divert attention away from other pressing social problems—such as the threat of nuclear war, unemployment, high living costs, and the economy—all of which persistently top the list of public concerns. Measures to solve these problems would require changes that would offend powerful interest groups.[5]

THE WAR ON DRUGS

The public's concern over drug use has also been used as a political football to justify the ever-increasing use of imprisonment for drug users. The public's attention on drugs accelerated dramatically at the end of this decade and then declined but rose again in 1997 and 1998 as Republicans and Democrats began to worry about modest increases in the use of marijuana by high school students. In her analysis of the nation's early rationale for the War on Drugs, Marsha Rosenbaum points out that the drug problem has received similar treatment:

> The Reagan administration initiated a "War on Drugs" in the early 1980s. The Bush administration appointed a "Drug Czar," and recently offered a major plan to remove the "scourge" of drugs from the American landscape. The media have reported on the violence occurring in our inner cities and in cocaine-source nations like Colombia. The public is bombarded with news about drugs, like the drug death of sports figure Len Bias and the confessions of celebrities about personal struggles with substance abuse.[6]

In addition to increased imprisonment rates, the War on Drugs spurred a movement toward more punitive sentencing policies for drug offenders. Moreover, mandatory drug testing and a reduction in affordable publicly funded drug treatment programs have meant that more and more released felons are being returned to prison for use of illegal drugs. Most important, because this war is focused on crack cocaine, which is mainly sold and used in inner-city communities, it is increasing the already disproportionately high number of African-American and Hispanic prisoners. For example, in 1926, the first year that the race of prison admissions was recorded on a national basis, only 21 percent of all prison admissions were African-American. By 1970, that figure had increased to 39 percent; by 2000, it had further grown to 46 percent.[7]

In their steady and unrelenting harangues on the crime and drug problems, politicians have argued that steady and dramatic expansion of prison populations is absolutely necessary to maintain a safe society. They contend that massive increases in imprisonment are positive signs—indications that the nation is increasingly intolerant of criminals and their antisocial and frequently violent behavior. Moreover, they claim that increasing the use of punishment in general and incarceration in particular has reduced crime.

THE ECONOMICS OF THE HAVES AND THE HAVE-NOTS

Many unsettling developments have made Americans more fearful, conservative, and mean-spirited, which is turn has also fueled the perceived need for more prisons. The perception of steady increases in crime is one contributing factor, but more fundamental are nationwide economic difficulties. Soaring inflation, high unemployment, and a decline in real wages of a significant proportion of the middle class have caused uncertainty about the economic future. Also, the proliferation of materialistic, ostentatious parvenus and the expansion of an underclass perceived as menacing have offended the public. These disturbing developments have been aggravated by the perception that, because of global, unmanageable economic processes, our society's economic problems are insolvable.

In terms of lowering our crime rate or in reducing the need for prisons, the following social and economic trends offer little reason for optimism for the future:

• Between 1980 and 1996, the number of persons living in poverty rose from 29 million to 37 million (27 percent increase).
• Fourteen million children, or more than one of every five children, live in poverty.
• For minority children, the figures are even more desperate: 40 percent of African-American children and Hispanic children live in poverty.
• The number of single-parent families, predominantly headed by females, increased from 22 percent in 1980 to 32 percent by 1997.
• Between 1980 and 1995, the number of births to unmarried women increased from 666,000 to 1,254,000. Approximately 13 percent of all births are to unmarried teenagers. The rates of illegitimate birth rates are highest among black and Hispanic women.[8]

Why did these disturbing trends emerge in the past decade? Part of the explanation lies in fundamental shifts in the distribution of wealth, as first documented by Kevin Phillips in his book *The Politics of Rich and Poor*.[9] Phillips, using a wide variety of official data, argued that the government economic policies of the past decade have improved the economic status of the rich at the expense of the lower and middle classes. These trends have continued to the present. Although the middle and upper class recently enjoyed the prosperity of a booming U.S. economy, not all Americans are benefiting from the current economic situation. In economic terms, the United States is becoming a more fragmented and segregated society. These trends not only contribute to crime rates and other social problems but also fuel a growing public demand to fund criminal justice services. In particular, the number of those Americans who are uneducated and raised in impoverished conditions will continue to grow and justify the need to further expand the correctional system. As Phillips stated:

> For women, young people, and minorities the effect of economic polarization during the 1980's was largely negative. The nation as a whole also suffered as unemployable young people drove up the crime rate and expanded the drug trade. Broken families and unwed teenage mothers promised further welfare generations and expense. And none of it augured well for the future skills level and competitiveness of the U.S. work force.[10]

These economic factors created an enormous public policy dilemma. On the one hand, we were expending a greater portion of our public dollars on incarcerating, punishing, treating, and controlling persons who are primarily from the lower economic classes in an effort to reduce crime. On the other hand, we had set in motion economic policies that serve to widen the gap between the rich and the poor, producing yet another generation of impoverished youths who will probably end up under the control of the correctional system. By escalating the size of the correctional system, we were also increasing the tax burden and diverting billions of dollars from those very public services (education, health, transportation, and economic development) that would reduce poverty, unemployment, crime, drug abuse, and mental illness. Although we have become more punitive than at any other time in our history, the public still believes that America is soft on crime and wants legislators and the courts to "get tougher" on crime.

Edward Luttwak, in his analysis of the impact of the economy on the middle class, argues that the growing insecurity of the middle class has translated into an almost "insatiable demand" for even more punitive sentencing practices:[11]

> The insecure majority does not realize that the economy too can be subject to the will of the majority . . . so it vents its anger and resentment by punishing, restricting, and prohibiting everything it can. The most blatant symptom is the insatiable demand for tougher criminal laws, longer prison terms, mandatory life sentences for repeat offenders, more and prompter executions, and harsher forms of detention (including, of late, chain gangs). Politi-

cians have heard the people, and the result is a mass of new federal and state legislation that will greatly add to the staggering number of Americans already behind bars.

In many ways, this situation is similar to that of eighteenth-century England, which was passing through even more unsettling changes than we are today, and was faced with unprecedented crime waves in its new, crowded, filthy, polluted, slum-encircled, rabble-ridden cities.[12] After experimenting with extraordinary punishments, particularly wholesale hanging and the use of prison barges, England turned to banishment as its primary penal measure. An important difference between eighteenth-century England and modern-day America, however, is that the world offered England locations to which it could send its felons: first America and then Australia. Between 1787 and 1868, hundreds of thousands of convicts (over 100,000 in the first fleet) were transported to Australia. It is ironic that Australia's incarceration rate is currently below 100 per 100,000 residents.

America has had to construct its locations of banishment within its borders. This has been done at a feverish pace. As was done in eighteenth-century England, we have even tried using barges in New York City. Although we lack an Australia where we can set up prison colonies, we are increasingly building huge megaprison settlements in isolated rural locations where land is cheap and recession-starved communities are anxious for the economic benefits that a major prison will bring.

THE FINANCIAL COSTS OF IMPRISONMENT

Few advocates of imprisonment have addressed just how expensive the imprisonment binge in the United States has been. As shown in Figure 20.2, there has been a steady rise in the costs of the criminal justice system and prisons in particular. We are spending over $135 billion per year on criminal justice costs and approximately $45 billion on corrections. But even these figures have dramatically underestimated the amounts of money spent on housing prisoners (operating costs) and building new prisons (construction costs). In the final result, it is cheaper to build prisons than to operate them.

Operating Costs

On average, costs to operate our jails and prisons consumed 7 percent of state budgets in 2000.[13] It cost nearly $40 billion to imprison approximately two million state and local inmates in 2000, up from $5 billion in combined prison and jail expenditures in 1978.[14] To determine the costs per inmate per day or year, prison administrators typically calculate operating costs by dividing their annual budget by the average daily prison population. Using this crude method, the daily cost is estimated at $56 or about $20,500 per year. There is wide variation among the states, with some reporting operational costs of over $30,000 and others below $15,000 per year. The most expensive prison systems tend to represent relatively smaller, more affluent states, with low crime rates and low incarceration rates, with organized labor and a predominantly white prisoner population, led by Minnesota ($37,825), Rhode Island ($35,739), Maine ($33,771), Alaska ($32,415), and Utah ($32,361). The least expensive prison systems are located in the south and tend to be in states that are less affluent, have high crime rates and high incarceration rates, and lack organized labor. These prisons house predominantly black inmate prisoner systems and are led by Alabama ($7,987), Oklahoma ($10,601), Mississippi ($11,156), Texas ($12,832), and Louisiana ($12,304).[15]

However, this accounting practice is misleading and produces patently low estimates of the true costs of imprisonment. For example, agency budgets often exclude contracted services for food, medical and mental health care, legal services, and transportation provided by other government agencies. According to two studies conducted in New York, these additional expenses increased the official operating costs by 20–25 percent.[16] An independent audit of the Indiana prison system found that actual expenditures were one-third higher than those reported by the agency.[17] Besides these "hidden" direct expenditures, other costs are rarely included in such calculations. To name only a few, the state loses taxes that could be paid by many of the imprisoned, pays more welfare to their families, and maintains spacious prison grounds that are exempt from state and local real estate taxation.

Construction Costs

The other enormous cost is prison construction. Because prisons vary dramatically in their "mission," construction (and operating) costs will be vary dramatically. Prisons are also enclosed, "total" institutions in which prisoners are not only housed but guarded, fed, clothed, and worked. They also receive some schooling and medical and psychological treatment. These needs require—in addition to cell blocks or dormitories—infirmaries, classrooms, laundries, offices, maintenance shops, boiler rooms, and kitchens. Dividing the total construction costs of one of these institutions by the number of prisoners it houses produces a cost per "bed" of as low as $5,000 for a minimum-security prison in Alabama to $128,000 for a maximum-security prison in Washington State. As of 1998, there were approximately 83,500 new prison beds under construction with another

86,500 being planned, for a total of 170,000 new prison beds. Assuming an average construction cost of $50,000, we will be spending $8.5 billion in direct prison construction costs.

But these costs are just part of the costs associated with building a new prison. First, the prison construction often needs to be financed. Instead of using current tax revenues to pay directly for this construction, however, the state does what most citizens do when they buy a house, that is, borrow the money, which must be paid back over several decades. The borrowing is done by selling bonds or using other financing instruments that may double or triple the original figure depending on the prevailing interest rates.

Second, other costs are associated with the construction costs themselves. These include architectural and legal fees, project management fees, prison equipment and site improvement costs for removing existing structures, hazardous waste materials, and landscaping.

Third, prison construction costs are further increased by errors in original bids by contractors and cost overruns caused by delays in construction, which seem to be the rule rather than the exception. A survey of fifteen states with construction projects revealed that cost overruns averaged 40 percent of the original budget projections.[18] Because of these almost predictable overruns, prison construction projects typically have "contingency fees" set aside to cover such expenses.

The Million Dollar Cell

From the above discussion, its obvious that states will spend a lot more than $25,000 per year to house a prisoner and to build a cell for him or her to live in. But just how much more? In a recent study conducted for the U.S. Department of Justice, estimates were made on the costs of operating and constructing new prison beds for the District of Columbia. Table 20.4 uses the assumptions made in that study for developing the likely costs of a typical prison bed that will cost at least $50,000 to build. The results show that in total, a state will likely spend over $1 million in operating and construction costs over the projected thirty-year life cycle of that prison bed. The vast majority of those costs will be operations.[19]

Prisons versus Education

The states are just beginning to feel these enormous increases in the cost of imprisonment. Budgetary battles in which important state services for children, the elderly, the sick, and the poor are gutted to pay for prisons have already begun. In coming years, great cutbacks in funds for public education, medical services for the poor, highway construction, and other

Table 20.4. The Million Dollar Cell: Typical 30-Year Life Cycle Costs
of a Prison Bed

Cost Item	Costs
I. Construction costs	
A. Direct construction costs	$50,000
B. 20-year debt services costs at 7.15% per year	$45,000
C. Project management at 4% of construction costs	$2,000
D. Legal fees/testing and inspection at 2% of construction costs	$1,000
E. Architectural and engineering fees at 8% of construction costs	$4,000
F. Fixtures and equipment at 6% of construction costs	$3,000
G. Project Contingencies at 5% of construction costs	$2,500
H. Site improvements at 8% of construction costs	$4,000
Total Construction and Debt Service Costs (Items A–H)	$111,500
II. Operating Costs	
A. Direct operating costs	$25,000
B. External indirect government support at 25%	$6,250
Total Operating Costs (Item A and B)	$31,250
III. 30-Year Operating Costs in 1999 Dollars	$937,500
IV. Total Costs for One Prison Bed in 1999 Dollars	$1,049,000

Source: James Austin, Darlene Grant, David Bogard, and Curtiss Pulitzer, *District of Columbia Department of Corrections Long-Term Options Study* (Washington, DC: National Institute of Corrections, U.S. Department of Justice, January 31, 1997).

state services will occur. A recent analysis of the "tradeoff" of prison beds for higher education was conducted by the Justice Policy Institute and the Correctional Association of New York. They found that since 1988, spending for New York's public universities had dropped by 29 percent while funding for prisons had increased by 76 percent. In terms of real dollars, the state's annual prison budget had increased by $761 while funding the New York city and state university systems had declined by $615 million. Currently, the state is spending $275 million more per year on prisons than on state and city colleges. And these costs do not include the $300 million now approved to construct an additional 3,100 new prison beds (at $96,775 per bed).[20]

THE "INCARCERATION REDUCES CRIME" DEBATE

Perhaps the most hotly debated topic today is whether the imprisonment binge has actually reduced crime rates. Those who are largely responsible for this state of affairs—elected officials who have harangued on the street crime issue and passed laws resulting in more punitive sentencing policies, judges who deliver more and longer prison terms, and government crim-

inal justice functionaries who have supported the punitive trend in criminal policies—promised that the great expansion of prison populations
would reduce crime in our society.

Table 20.3 shows historical crime rate and incarceration rate data. As
the chart indicates, prior to the 1970s, there were relatively low crime and
incarceration rates. Thereafter, both measures grew steadily. Only in the
past five years have crime rates began their steady decline while incarceration rates have continued to increase. And, as we have noted throughout
the book, the continuing increase in the prison population is not due to
more people being sentenced to prison but due to prisoners serving longer
sentences.

Does this chart prove or disprove the arguments for and against the "incarceration reduces crime" equation? In this section, we review the scientific basis that has been offered by criminologists in support of the
imprisonment binge. In making this assessment, we maintain that there are
several basic requirements for their argument to hold. First, there must be
a steady and consistent association over time between incarceration rates
and crime rates. Where departures exist from the basic relationship they
must be reported and explained. Second, other changes in other factors
known to be associated with crime rates must also be controlled for, or
at least acknowledged. Failure to meet either of these two requirements
would be sufficient reason to reject the proincarceration position.

The Argument in Favor of Incarceration Reduces Crime

The proincarceration advocates have a very simplistic two-variable
equation: as incarceration goes up, crime rates must go down. To provide
the scientific basis for this argument, the U.S. Department of Justice has
played a key role in both articulating this proposition as a reasonable policy and by funding a number of studies to demonstrate the causal relationship between imprisonment and crime. Beginning in the late 1980s,
several key officials in the Bush administration's Department of Justice
launched a major information campaign to solidify the scientific basis for
supporting incarceration as the best means for reducing crime as follows:

Statisticians and criminal justice researchers have consistently found
that falling crime rates are associated with rising imprisonment rates, and
rising crime rates are associated with falling imprisonment rates.[21]

Former Attorney General William Barr restated this position, arguing
that the country had a "clear choice" of either building more prisons or tolerating higher violent crime rates. This view implied that increasing the
government's capacity to imprison is the single most effective strategy for
reducing crime. Barr listed twenty-four steps the government should take
to reduce violent crime, including "truth in sentencing," which requires in-

mates to serve the full amount of their sentences, increased use of mandatory minimum prison sentences, relaxation of evidentiary rules to increase conviction rates, greater use of the death penalty, and higher numbers of police officers.[22]

Similarly, President Clinton successfully campaigned for 100,000 police officers to be added to the streets to increase arrests. The 1994 Crime Bill, advocated by the then Democrat-controlled Congress and eventually adopted in 1996 by the Republican-controlled Congress, was designed to encourage states to increase the use of imprisonment by adopting "truth in sentencing laws" that would require inmates convicted of violent crimes to serve 85 percent of their sentences. States that adopted such laws were rewarded with federal funds to help pay for the construction of more prison beds. Clearly, both political parties have decided that we need to get even tougher with criminals.

During this period, a number of reports and studies were issued by the U.S. Department of Justice to support the proposition that increases in incarceration reduce crime. A primary tactic was to compare Uniform Crime Reports (UCR) and the National Crime Survey (NCS is now referred to as the National Criminal Victimization Survey, NCVS) for violent crime rates (homicides, robbery, assault, rape, and kidnapping) with imprisonment rates between 1960 and 1990 in ten-year increments.[23] By selectively using these ten-year increments, the Justice Department's bar chart shows that, during the 1960s, imprisonment rates dropped by 19 percent while reported violent crime rates increased by 104 percent. During the 1970s, violent crime rates continued to increase again, but by only 47 percent, whereas imprisonment rates increased by 39 percent. And, in the 1980s, as imprisonment rates increased by 99 percent, violent crimes rates again increased, but by only 11 percent.

In other words, although violent crimes rates steadily increased over the past three decades, the rates of increase were lowest during the 1980s, when imprisonment rates were at their highest levels. These data led a Justice Department spokesperson to claim that violent crime will decline even more if more persons are imprisoned:

> No one knows for sure what the 1990s will bring. But my guess, based on the lessons learned over the past three decades, is this: If imprisonment rates continue to rise, overall violent crime rates will not increase and could actually fall in the 1990s. A big "if," of course, is whether imprisonment rates will continue their steady upward climb.[24]

The Argument against "Incarceration Reduces Crime"

The major flaw in the "incarceration reduces crime" policy is its simplistic nature. For some reason, imprisonment advocates have completely rejected or ignored the long and rich history of criminology that has shown that many other social forces, in addition to the response of the criminal justice system, affect crime rates. It would be hard to find any credible social scientist or reasonable person who would agree that the rate of crime in any society is the sole product of how many of its citizens are incarcerated. Rather, crime is the product of a society's many very complex individual, social, economic, political and even random circumstances. What is being asked of the American people is to exclude all other factors known and to put all of our crime-fighting eggs in the incarceration basket. We believe a more careful examination of all available information demonstrates major inconsistencies in this argument and lends greater support to the conclusion that more imprisonment has little to do with crime rates.

Inconsistencies in the Incarceration Leads to Lower Crime Rate National Trend

Returning to the argument set forth by the U.S. Department of Justice that crime rate increases were lowest in the decade of the 1980s and highest in the 1960s, a more careful year-by-year analysis of the same UCR data cited by the Justice Department shows that the nation's overall crime rates have had relative periods of stabilization in all four decades and usually during the initial part of the decade (1960–1962, 1970–1973, 1975–1978, 1980–1984, and 1990–1994), only to be followed by crime rate increases despite increases in the use of imprisonment. For the imprisonment theory to be valid, these countervailing trends either should not have occurred or should somehow be explained by the imprisonment theory. If there were a direct causal relationship between imprisonment and crime rates, stabilization in crime rates during these time periods should not have taken place.

The imprisonment advocates also claimed at one time that crime has been reduced since 1973 by over 30 percent, with most of the decline occurring since 1980. They have based their case exclusively on the 1973–1992 NCVS household surveys. During this same time period, imprisonment rates more than tripled, from 98 to 329 per 100,000. Like the UCR rates, the NCVS data also show a decline in household reported crime beginning in 1980. Beginning in 1985, however, both the UCR and NCVS violent crime rates began to increase despite the fact that the imprisonment rate continued to escalate. In fact, the overall violent victimization rate in 1995 is virtually the same as it was in 1973 when the number of people in prison was only 200,000.

Inconsistencies among Selected States over Time

If we were to pick three states to test the imprisonment theory, Texas, California, and New York would be the obvious choices. As shown in Table

Table 20.5.   Comparisons between Crime Rates and Incarceration Rates:
California, Texas, and New York, 1990–1998

	California		Texas		New York	
Year	Crime	Prison	Crime	Prison	Crime	Prison
1990	6,604	311	7,827	290	6,364	304
1991	6,773	318	7,819	297	6,245	320
1992	6,680	339	7,058	344	5,858	340
1993	6,457	368	6,439	385	5,510	354
1994	6,174	384	5,872	637	5,071	367
1995	5,831	416	5,684	677	4,560	378
1996	5,208	446	5,709	666	4,132	383
1997	4,865	475	5,481	717	3,911	386
1998	4,343	477	5,112	700	3,589	384
Change (%)	−34	53	−35	141	−44	26

20.5, both California and Texas are the nation's leaders in increasing prison populations. In 1992, then attorney general William Barr believed that California should serve as the model for the rest of the country. In fact, he was urging Texas to follow California's lead: "California quadrupled its prison population during the 1980s and various forms of violent crimes fell by as much as 37 percent. But in Texas, which did not increase prison space, crime increased 29 percent in the decade."

Under Democratic governor Ann Richards's leadership, Texas launched the largest prison construction program in the state's history. As shown in Table 20.5, both California and Texas continued to increase their imprisonment rates in the 1990s. California increased its imprisonment rates by over 50 percent while Texas tripled its rate. Both reported the same decline in crime rates (about 35 percent) as the national rate. Not surprisingly, politicians in favor of imprisonment point to these two states as examples of how imprisonment reduces crime. However, if we add New York to the analysis we see how the "greater imprisonment, lower crime" thesis fails. New York has only slightly increased its prison population and imprisonment rates. Yet it has reported an even larger decrease in its crime rate. Furthermore, despite its lower incarceration rate, the overall crime rate is significantly lower in New York than in California and Texas.

Inconsistencies within States

The proincarceration argument also fails to explain why within a state, jurisdictions that exercise very different sentencing policies report similar declines in crime rates. The most recent example of this situation is in Cal-

Table 20.6. San Francisco Crime and Sentencing Trends, 1990–1998

Year	Population		Serious Crime	Crime Rate	Felony Arrests All	Sentences Prison	Jail	Jail/Prob.
1990	724,100	3,443.0	34,810	4,807	7,335	1,239	1,146	2,973
1991	724,200	3,503.3	35,125	4,850	7,946	1,211	929	3,086
1992	744,500	3,491.5	38,642	5,190	8,740	1,314	1,051	3,690
1993	749,400	3,367.8	36,095	4,817	8,630	1,512	1,063	4,109
1994	753,400	3,147.7	28,389	3,768	7,941	953	656	3,465
1995	751,500	2,929.0	26,548	3,533	8,563	923	580	3,477
1996	768,200	2,558.9	25,737	3,350	8,244	816	775	4,305
1997	777,400	2,381.4	23,314	2,999	7,786	484	869	4,351
1998	789,500	2,072.1	20,990	2,659	7,301	NA	NA	NA
Change (%)	9.0	−39.8	−39.7	−44.7	−0.7	−60.9	−24.2	46.4

Source: Institute on Crime, Justice and Corrections, *San Francisco Jail Crowding Study*

ifornia, where in San Francisco a remarkable experiment in deincarceration occurred. As shown in Table 20.6, the county has reduced the number of offenders it sends to state prison each year by over 60 percent. According to some, this should certainly produce a huge crime wave, but in fact, the crime rate went down by almost 40 percent—virtually the same decline reported for the state and Los Angles (Table 20.7).

Table 20.7. California Crime Rates and Prison Sentences, 1990–1997

Year	Statewide Reported Crime	Prison Sentences	San Francisco Reported Crime	Prison Sentences	Los Angeles Reported Crime	Prison Sentences
1990	3,443	32,265	4,807	1,239	4,596	13,803
1991	3,503	37,288	4,850	1,211	4,710	15,560
1992	3,492	43,199	5,190	1,314	4,661	16,532
1993	3,368	49,730	4,817	1,512	3,845	17,682
1994	3,148	42,388	3,768	953	3,528	12,105
1995	2,929	44,659	3,533	923	3,155	13,830
1996	2,559	47,283	3,350	816	2,762	17,574
1997	2,381	46,850	2,999	484	2,352	16,648
Change (%)	−45	45	−38	−61	−49	27

Source: Crime and Delinquency in California

Bad Math: The Numbers Don't Add Up

A number of criminologists and major studies have greatly contributed to the scientific basis for expanding the use of incarceration. Much of this "science" is grounded in a small number of studies funded by the U.S. Department of Justice in the 1970s, conducted by the Rand Corporation and its leading researchers (Jan and Marcia Chaiken, Joan Petersilia, Peter Greenwood, and Alan Abrahamse).[25] These studies had newly admitted prisoners self-report how many crimes they had committed prior to being incarcerated. Based on these survey results, the Rand researchers concluded that a small number of prisoners had committed a very large number of crimes before they were incarcerated. Assuming they would continue to commit crimes at the same rate for an extended period of time, crime rates could be lowered by "selectively incapacitating" them. Lost in the discussion was the finding that most inmates sentenced to prison have very low or even nonexistent rates of criminal activity, suggesting that many prisoners posed little threat to public safety and need not be incarcerated. Nonetheless, policymakers were urged to adopt selective incapacitation sentencing strategies.[26]

A review by the National Academy of Sciences and by Rand's own followup research later discovered that the selective incapacitation policy was incorrect for two reasons. The National Academy reanalysis of Rand's research found that it had significantly overestimated the incapacitation effects of their original sample of inmates. And Rand itself found that its criteria for identifying high-risk inmates at the time of sentencing was invalid. But these findings did not deter others from arguing that incapacitation was a proven cost-effective approach to fighting crime.

The first major effort to promote incapacitation was a report written by Edwin Zedlweski that was published with great fanfare by the U.S. Department of Justice, National Institute of Justice (NIJ) in 1987. Zedlweski argued that by incarcerating high-rate offenders as defined by the Rand studies, crime would be significantly reduced and society would reap enormous economic benefits. Specifically, he states that although one year of incarceration would cost $25,000, society would avert $430,000 in social costs. Most of these averted costs were be realized by assuming that each incarcerated offender would have committed 187 crimes per year, which would have cost victims and society's response to crime about $2,300 per crime.[27]

A related but later study conducted by Mark Cohen and his colleagues tried to quantify the "true" costs of crime. The study was first published in 1988 with another version released in 1996 by the U.S. Department of Justice's NIJ. It took the cost of crime a major step higher by adding the costs of "pain and suffering" to the cost benefit equation. Remarkably, this piece of research claimed that the true cost of crime was actually $450 billion per year, with $345 billion being linked to so called "quality of life" issues.

These cost figures are well above the government's own estimates of $17.6 billion.[28]

These two studies have formed the basis for many politicians to argue that increased incarceration will significantly reduce crime and yet save money—in fact hundreds of billions of dollars. Policies that served to reduce lengths of stay were criticized as "ineffective." Instead, "truth in sentencing," "three strikes and you're out," and other efforts to lengthen prison terms were advocated by many politicians who now had a scientific basis for their ideology. For example, John DiIulio, using these data claimed that "prisons were a bargain" and California's then-governor Pete Wilson's chief economist promised that by passing the "three strikes and you're out" legislation, the crime rate in California would drop by 20 percent and the state would save $55 billion.[29]

These studies have been roundly criticized largely because the numbers presented do not add up to what is well-known regarding number of crimes and their costs. With respect to the number of crimes associated with incarcerated felons, Zimring and Hawkins have simply noted that assuming the 187 crimes per offenders were true and given the large increase in the prison population, crime would have been eliminated in the United States many years ago.[30] Clearly, something is very wrong with the assumption that the average number of crimes committed per year for sentenced inmates is so high.

With respect to the cost benefit claim by Cohen et al., Austin and Zimring and Hawkins have pointed out the inappropriateness of using rarely-awarded jury awards for "pain and suffering" for all crimes regardless of their relative pettiness:

> These estimates are applied to all crimes despite the fact that virtually none of them result in jury awards. . . . Even if one assumes that the $345 billion estimate of "quality of life" is accurate, what does it mean in real dollars? The answer is very little. The number is only a monetary symbol, it has nothing to do with real dollars, and has no economic significance.[31]

The specific cost estimates are opportunistic, arbitrary, inconsistent, and too high. The schema lacks an articulated theory of either public or private cost. Moreover, Cohen's analysis reveals no relationship between its cost estimates and its conclusions about the cost-effectiveness of the investment in further crime control resources.[32]

Failure to Control for Other Factors Known to Be Associated with Crime Rates

All of the data presented here point to an inescapable conclusion: crime rates are much more the products of other aspects of our society. Here, we return to the themes articulated by others, namely, factors other than incarceration rates, which are known to be linked to crime rates. In order for the "incarceration reduces crime" thesis to be valid, one must shown that these other crime-related factors remained constant or were controlled in the analysis.

Demographics

Since most crimes are committed by males between the ages of fifteen and twenty-four, as that population grows or subsides, one can expect associated fluctuations in the crime rates. Before changes in crime rates can be attributed to changes in imprisonment rates, the influence of demographic changes must be considered.

Beginning in the early 1960s, the size of this age group began to grow and continued to grow through the 1970s—the exact period of the rise in crime rates. By 1980, this growth had peaked and began to decline—just as the crime rate also began to decline. An article by two criminologists found that most of the decline in crime rates observed since 1979–1985 was a direct result of a declining "at-risk" population. Unlike the proincarceration rate analysis, this study controls for changes in incarceration rates. When we take into account the influence of this demographic shift, reductions in the NCVS from 1980 to 1988 are largely attributable (60 percent of the crime reduction explained) to reductions in the fifteen to twenty-four age group, the high crime rate population. The same analysis, when applied to the UCR data, actually shows an increase in UCR during the same period.[33]

Demographics also influence how crime is reported in the NCVS rates. Since they are based on the number, characteristics, and location of U.S. households, changes in the attributes of households over the past two decades will influence reported crime rates. For example, the Justice Department has acknowledged that, since 1973, the size of the American household has (1) declined, (2) shifted from urban areas to suburban locations, and (3) shifted from the Northeast and Midwest to the South and the West.[34]

The first two conditions automatically reduce crime rate estimates because smaller households located in suburban areas are less likely than larger and urban households to experience crime. The third condition, relocation to the West where crime rates are highest, increases the likelihood of households being victimized. These trends in the NCVS must be more carefully analyzed before conclusions can be made that a tripling of the incarceration rate is solely responsible for declines in personal and household theft.

The Economy and Other Social Economic Indicator

The 1990s have also witnessed major improvements in a number of areas know to be related to crime rates (see Table 20.8). We have already

Table 20.8.   Social Demographic Indicators Related to Crime Rates, 1990–1997

Year	Crime Rate	Median Age	Population 15–24 (%)	Unemployment Rate (%)	AFDC Recipients (in 1000s)	Abortions (in 1000s)	Teenage Birthrate (per 1000)
1990	5820	35.2	14.8	6.2	12,159	1,609	83.8
1991	5898	35.3	14.4	7.0	13,489	1,557	83.2
1992	5660	35.4	14.2	7.4	14,035	1,529	80.7
1993	5484	35.6	14.0	6.6	14,115	1,500	80.1
1994	5374	35.7	13.9	5.6	14,276	1,431	78.8
1995	5276	35.8	13.8	5.4	13,931	1,364	77.7
1996	5087	35.9	13.7	4.8	12,877	1,366	70.6
1997	4923	36.1	13.7	4.6	11,423	NA	NA
Change (%)	−15	3	−7	−26	−6	−15	−16

Sources: Poverty and Health Statistics Branch/HHES Division, U.S. Bureau of the Census, U.S. Department of Commerce, *Current Population Survey* Washington, DC: Author, March 1999). Population Division, U.S. Census Bureau, *Population Estimates Program* (Washington, DC: Author, Internet Release, December 23, 1999).

noted the effects of demographics—namely the aging of the U.S. population. Unemployment in general has declined from 6.2 percent of the work-eligible population to 4.1 percent in 1999. There are also indications that the number teenage births and public welfare rolls have declined as well. And there are many more indicators of social well-being that also point in a positive direction. Many of these indicators are reflective of the earlier-cited study by Linsky and Straus. As these indicators continue to improve, we can continue to expect further declines or at least stabilization in the crime rates. Clearly, these factors should also be accounted for in assessing fluctuations in crime rates.

VOODOO/ENRON CRIMINOLOGY

The failure of the massive expansion of prison populations to accomplish its most important objective—the reduction of crime—should come as no surprise, because the idea that increased penalties will reduce crime is based on a simplistic and fallacious theory of criminal behavior. It starts with the idea that every person is an isolated, willful actor who makes completely rational decisions to maximize his or her pleasure and to minimize his or her pain. Consequently, individuals only commit crimes when they believe it will lead to more pleasure, gain, or satisfaction, and with minimal risk for pain or punishment. If penalties for being caught are small or nonexistent, then many persons who are not restrained by other factors (for example, strong conventional morals or the disapproval of close

454 It's About Time

friends or family) will commit crimes—indeed, a lot of crimes. Only by increasing the certainty and severity of punishment, this thinking goes, will people "think twice" and be deterred.

The punishment/incapacitation/deterrence theory assumes that all individuals have access to the same conventional lifestyles for living out a law-abiding life. This is not true for most of the individuals who are caught up in our criminal justice system. For many, particularly young members of the inner-city underclass, the choice is not between conventional and illegal paths to the good life but between illegal and risky paths or no satisfaction at all. They are faced with a limited and depressing choice between a menial, dull, impoverished, undignified life at the bottom of the conventional heap, or a life with some excitement, some monetary return, and a slim chance of larger financial rewards, albeit with great risks of being imprisoned, maimed, or even killed. Consequently, many "choose" crime despite the threat of imprisonment.

For many young males, especially African-Americans and Hispanics, the threat of going to prison or jail is no threat at all but rather an expected or accepted part of life. Most minority males will be punished by the criminal justice system during their lifetime. Deterrence and punishment are effective only when the act of punishment actually worsens a person's lifestyle. For millions of males, imprisonment poses no such threat. As a young black convict put it when Claude Brown told him that his preprison life meant that there was a "60 percent chance he will be killed, permanently maimed, or end up doing a long bit in jail":

> "I see where you comin' from, Mr. Brown," he replied, "but you got things kind of turned around the wrong way. You see, all the things that you say could happen to me is dead on the money and that is why I can't lose. Look at it from my point of view for a minute. Let's say I go and get wiped [killed]. Then I ain't got no more needs, right? All my problems are solved. I don't need no more money, no more nothing, right? Okay, supposin' I get popped, shot in the spine and paralyzed for the rest of my life—that could happen playing football, you know. Then I won't need a whole lot of money because I won't be able to go no place and do nothin', right? So, I'll be on welfare, and the welfare check is all the money I'll need, right? Now if I get busted and end up in the joint [prison] pullin' a dime and a nickel, like I am, then I don't have to worry about no bucks, no clothes. I get free rent and three squares a day. So you see, Mr. Brown, I really can't lose."[35]

Voodoo criminology also espouses a fatalistic perspective that there is little one can do to change humans. This perspective has been argued most strongly by John DiIulio. In making his statements on crime and the criminal justice system DiIulio makes use of the entire range of tactics employed by the academic apologists. He uncritically accepts unverified, frequently outlandish statements of facts and builds his own arguments upon them. He draws conclusions from a single case—an anecdote. He selects facts or relationships, plucks them from their full context, and then twists them to suit his conservative agenda. Sometimes, it appears he just makes things up.[36]

Nonetheless, DiIulio and his fellow supporters (including former drug czar and Department of Education secretary William Bennett) have argued that many wayward youthful offenders should be viewed almost as human garbage and dumped behind bars for as long as possible.

> America is no home to thickening ranks of juvenile "super-predators"—radically impulsive, brutally remorseless youngsters, including ever more pre-teenage boys, who murder, assault, rape, rob, burglarize, deal deadly drugs, join gun-toting gangs and create serious communal disorders. They do not fear the stigma of arrest, the pains of imprisonment or the pangs of conscience."[37]

This dark futuristic view of America has led others to warn of an impending crime wave. James Alan Fox, a criminologist who often appears before congress to give advice on policy predicted that juvenile crime rates—especially crimes of violence—could only go up: "We are facing a potential bloodbath of teenage violence in years ahead that will be so bad, we'll look back at the 1990s and say those were the good old days."[38]

DiIulio himself recommended that the juvenile prison system be increased threefold to handle the new wave of "superpredators." Fortunately, as before, these dire predictions and calculations have been way off the mark, with juvenile crime and especially juvenile violent crime dropping—not increasing as forecasted.

AMERICA'S FARM SYSTEM FOR CRIMINALS

We have a less deterministic view of human nature. Most people who engage in crime do so not as isolated individuals, but—like all of us—as participants in various social organizations, groups, or "social systems," each of which has its own rules and values. Some groups in our society (often because of subjection to reduced circumstances such as poverty, idleness, and incarceration over an extended period of time) develop preferences for deviant lifestyles. For example, young males who were abused as children, dropped out of school, lived in poverty, abused drugs, and served many juvenile jail and prison sentences have become immersed in deviant values and are distanced from any set of conventional values. They are most satisfied when engaging in specialized deviant practices related to their unique culture—wild partying involving drug use and sex along with extremely risky behavior involving displays of machismo.[39]

Since crime is not the sole product of individual motives, efforts, especially by the state, to punish the individual without addressing the social
forces that produced that individual will fail. Individuals do not decide to
sell drugs, purchase drugs, and set up single-proprietor operations on their
own. Most street crime involves groups, organizations, and networks.
Drug dealers are persons who have been involved in groups and networks
of people who use drugs, have connections, and know or are dealers. The
same is true of gang bangers, hustlers, and thieves.

In effect, America has created a lower-class culture designed to produce
new cohorts of street criminals each generation. Similar to organized
sports, most of these criminal operations have major leagues, minor
leagues, and a bench. Children come up through the ranks, learn the game,
and finally move into the starting lineup once they reach their adolescent
years. When they are temporarily or permanently removed (that is, arrested, imprisoned, or killed), they are replaced by others from the bench
to continue the game. When the bench is depleted, someone comes up from
the minors. Much as in professional and college sports, the span of their
career is short, with their most active crime years taking place between the
ages of fifteen and twenty-four. Our impoverished inner-city neighborhoods (or what is left of them as neighborhoods) have almost unlimited re-
serves milling about who are kept out of the starting lineup by managers
and first-string players. As soon as the police arrest the "kingpin" drug
dealer, the leaders of a gang, or some of the top pimps or hustlers, new recruits move in to take over these positions.

This characterization of criminal operations also explains why the War
on Drugs, which has been going on for two decades, has failed. During the
1980s, the government spent billions of tax dollars and arrested millions
for drug possession or drug trafficking. Regularly, the media reported that
a new large-scale drug operation and some kingpin drug dealers had been
caught. Drugs continue to be at least as available as they were before the
new arrests, however, as new kingpins quickly and often violently replace
the recently departed leaders.

Even if a particular type of criminal operation dies out, new crime
games appear. In the late 1980s, the news media and government officials
were blaming crack cocaine dealing for unprecedented numbers of homicides in Los Angeles inner-city neighborhoods. However, sociologist Jack
Katz discovered that, contrary to the media's reports, homicide rates in the
crack neighborhoods had not changed over the last decade.[40] Earlier in the
1980s, rival gangs were killing each other over territory. It seems, using the
sports analogy, that the number of players available for crime games is related to broader social conditions, such as the existence of a large under-
employed population of young males who have the ordinary youthful
desires for respect, excitement, and gratification but are confronted with
extremely limited access to legitimate means of acquiring them. Thus, the

number of potential players remains constant over an extended period. Only the types of games being played change from season to season.

OUR PRISON SYSTEM IN THE TWENTY-FIRST CENTURY

Where Are We Headed?

Unless we find a way to reverse the trends that have been set in motion we will continue to pay a heavy price. Unless we wanted to strip down or abandon many other government enterprises—education, welfare, transportation, medical services—we would have to greatly increase state taxes to pay for this massive experiment in imprisonment. In many ways—the financial costs, the social disruptions, the removal of a very large percentage of young males—this current policy would be like World War II, prolonged for decades.[41]

Of course, other consequences would arise. Since a large percentage of the current prison population is black, it would mean that most of the nation's 5.5 million black males ages eighteen to thirty-nine would be incarcerated or under the criminal justice system, and we would look a lot like South Africa of the 1950s and 1960s.[42]

Its now clear that this increase would have little if any impact on the crime rate The prison population would become increasingly older, filled with hundreds of thousands of aging adults who pose a minimal threat to public safety. It is impossible to anticipate what new forms of social problems, crime, and upheavals this punitive experiment would cause. The massive social disruptions—such as the removal of most young black males—might result in unanticipated new types of violent criminal activities. Each year hundreds of thousands of prisoners are being released to society—many of them with no parole supervision. Many of them will be socially crippled and embittered by their long prison terms.

For the most part, their chances of pursuing a merely viable, much less satisfying, conventional life after prison are small. The contemporary prison experience has converted them into social misfits and cripples, and there is a growing likelihood that they will return to crime, violence, and other forms of disapproved deviance. They will at least be an enormous nuisance and burden.

This ultimate cost of imprisonment—that which society must suffer when prisoners are released—continues to be confirmed by research. The Rand Corporation found that convicted felons sent to prison or granted probation had significantly higher rates of rearrest after release than those on probation.[43] Linsky and Straus found that states with higher rates of incarceration have higher rates of violence and suicide. Sampson and

458 It's About Time

Laub found persons who experienced incarceration had higher rates of criminality:

> One clear possibility is that current [sentencing] policies are producing un-intended criminogenic effects. From our perspective, imprisonment may have powerful negative effects on the prospects of future employment and job employment. In turn, low income, unemployment, and underemploy-ment are themselves linked to heightened risks of family disruption. Through its negative effects on male employment, imprisonment may thus lead indi-rectly through family disruption to increases in future rates of crime and vi-olence. The extremely high rate of young black males renders this scenario very real.[44]

Even if we assume that crime would eventually decline, how long would we have to maintain such a large prison system to continually de-ter and incapacitate each successive generation of potential criminals? Be-cause we do not believe Americans are ready for this costly solution to the crime problem through imprisonment, we are left with its failure.

On another dimension, our national punishment policies and rising in-carceration rates have significantly weakened the capacity of certain com-munities to perform crucial traditional functions: raise children, provide a healthy environment for families, provide jobs for young and old, and sustain a vibrant civic life. According to a number of theories of crime, in-cluding social disorganization theory, removing large numbers of com-munity residents weakens informal social control mechanisms that are necessary to help prevent crime. In fact, some researchers are testing the hypothesis that the level of incarceration is so high that we have weakened the capacity of communities to control crime. These researchers believe that if strong families, financially viable communities, and social cohe-sion—what is now commonly termed "collective efficacy," or the ability of the collective to be efficacious—contribute to lower crime rates, then it is possible that a weakening of community capacity through a policy of mass incarceration might actually result in higher crime rates.

A related consequence of U.S. incarceration policies has to do with the fact that the communities hardest hit by these policies are often the poor-est, and particularly poor communities of color. The cycle of arrest, re-moval, and incarceration is highly concentrated in communities that are already facing the enormous challenges of poverty, crime, disinvestment, and inadequate social services. For example, new federal laws authorize housing authorities and Section 8 providers to evict individuals with cer-tain criminal convictions. What impact does this policy have on access to housing, homelessness, and family life in public housing? Consider the re-search finding that imprisonment has the effect of decreasing the lifetime earnings of former prisoners. As a higher percentage of men have prison experiences, particularly African-American and Latino men living in inner cities, what is the net effect of imprisonment policies on the financial health of those communities? Researchers are just beginning to understand these dynamics of our criminal justice policies.

Our Vindictive Society

Crime has incurred another profound cost: the increase of general vindictiveness in our society. Historically, Americans (as compared to Europeans and Japanese, for example) have been highly individualistic, which means, for one thing, that they are prone to blaming individuals for their actions. In America, according to the dominant ideology, everyone is responsible for his or her acts, and every act is accomplished by a willful actor. Consequently, every undesirable, harmful, "bad" act is the work of a blameful actor. This belief has resulted in our being the most litigious people in the world and has given us the world's largest legal profession. It has also led us to criminalize more and more behavior and to demand more and more legal action against those who break laws. Today many Americans want someone blamed and punished for every transgression and inconvenience they experience.

Social science should have taught us that all human behavior is only partially a matter of free will and that persons are only partially responsible for their deeds. Everyone's actions are always somewhat influenced or dominated by factors not of one's own making and beyond personal control (with economic situation being the most influential and obvious).

Moreover, seeking vengeance is a pursuit that brings more frustration than satisfaction. It has not only been an obstacle in solving many social problems and in developing cooperative, communal attitudes (the lack of which is one of the important causes of the crime problem), but it is in itself a producer of excessive amounts of anxiety and frustration. Ultimately, vindictiveness erects barriers between people, isolates them, and prevents them from constructing the cooperative, communal social organizations that are so necessary for meaningful, satisfying human existence. Ironically, it is just these social structures that contain the true solution to our crime problem.

The Crime Problem as a Diversion

Our tendency toward vindictiveness is greatly nurtured by the media, politicians, and other public figures who have persistently ranted about the crime issue. They do this largely because the crime issue is seductive. It is seductive to politicians because they can divert attention away from larger and more pressing problems, such as the economy and pollution, whose solutions would require unpopular sacrifices, particularly for them and other more affluent segments of the society.[45] Street crime is seductive to the media because it fits their preferred "sound bite" format of small bits of sensational material. Likewise, it is deeply seductive to the public, who, though they fear crime, possess at the same time a deep fascination for it.

IT'S ABOUT TIME

We *must* turn away from the excessive use of prisons. The current incarceration binge will eventually consume large amounts of tax money, which will be diverted from essential public services such as education, child care, mental health, and medical services—the very same services that will have a far greater impact on reducing crime than building more prisons. We will continue to imprison millions of people under intolerably cruel and dangerous conditions. We will accumulate a growing number of ex-convicts who are more or less psychologically and socially crippled and excluded from conventional society, posing a continuing nuisance and threat to others. We will severely damage some of our more cherished humanitarian values, which are corroded by our excessive focus on blame and vengeance. And we will further divide our society into the white affluent classes and a poor nonwhite underclass, many of them convicts and ex-convicts. In effect, we are gradually putting our own apartheid into place.

We believe that these trends can be reversed without jeopardizing public safety. But how should we accomplish a turnaround of this magnitude? First, we must recognize that crime can, at best, be marginally reduced by escalating the use of imprisonment. If we are to truly reduce crime rates, we as a society must embark on a decade-long strategy that reverses the social and economic trends of the previous decade. In particular, we must jettison the overly expensive and ineffective criminal justice approach and redirect our energies toward the next generation of youth, who already are at risk of becoming the generation of criminals.

The "crime reduction" reforms we have in mind have little to do with criminal justice reform. Rather, these reforms would serve to reduce poverty, single-parent families headed by females, teenage pregnancies and abortions, welfare dependency, unemployment, high dropout rates, drug abuse, and inadequate health care. These are the social indicators that have proven to be predictive of high crime rates.

The programs and policies that will work, such as better prenatal health care for pregnant mothers, better health care for children to protect them against life-threatening illnesses, Head Start, Job Corps, and Enterprise Zones, have been well documented and may well be contributing to the current decline in crime.[46] But we will also need a level of commitment from our major corporate leaders to reduce the flight of jobs, especially blue-collar and industrial jobs, from this country to Third World nations where cheap labor can be exploited for profits but at tremendous cost to this country.

So how do we go about cutting our losses? We begin by reducing, or at least reducing the rate of growth in, the prison population and reallocating those "savings" to prevention programs targeted at-risk youth and their families. But is it realistic to assume that prison populations and their associated costs can be lowered without increasing crime? How, exactly, should we proceed?

Reduce Prison Terms

Many methods of reducing prison populations have been advocated. Some argue that certain classes of felony crimes should be reclassified as misdemeanors or decriminalized completely. In the late 1960s, there was a great deal of support to do this for many minor drug offenses. Others claim that a significant number of those convicted of felonies could be diverted from prison to probation and new forms of alternatives to prison, including intensive probation, house arrest, electronic surveillance, and greater use of fines and restitution.

We are persuaded, however, that these "front-end" reforms would not substantially reduce prison crowding. Historically, well-intentioned alternatives have had marginal impact on reducing prison populations. Instead, they have had the unintended consequence of widening the net of criminal justice by imposing more severe sanctions on people who otherwise would not be sentenced to prison.[47] They have little support with public officials, who, like the public, are increasingly disenchanted with probation and other forms of community sanctions. Moreover, the current problem is not increasing prison admissions but increases in the length of stay and the number of parole violators.

For alternatives to work, legislators, prosecutors, police, judges, and correctional agencies would all have to agree on new laws and policies to implement them. Such a consensus is unlikely to occur in the near future, since these measures are replete with controversy and disagreement. Even if the forces that are presently driving the punitive response to crime abated considerably, it would take several years to work through these disagreements and effect changes in the laws and policies that would slowly produce an easing of prison population growth. Such a slow pace of reform would not allow states to avoid the catastrophe that is rapidly developing in our prisons.

Even diversion of a substantial number of offenders from prison would not have a major impact on prison population growth. "Front-end" diversion reforms are targeted for those few offenders who are already serving the shortest prison terms (usually less than a year). The recent flood of tougher sentencing laws has greatly lengthened prison terms for offenders charged with more serious crimes and repeat property or drug offenders. Consequently, it is this segment of the prison population that is piling up in the prisons. The problem is that inmates with long sentences are unlikely to be candidates for diversion from prison.

For these reasons, we believe the single most direct solution that would have an immediate, dramatic impact on prison crowding and would not affect public safety is to shorten prison terms. This reform can be done swiftly and fairly through a number of existing mechanisms, such as greater use of existing good-time credit statutes, accelerating parole eligibility, developing reentry programs for inmates, and altering existing parole revocation policies.

Indeed, many states have launched such programs with no impact on crime rates. Between 1980 and 1983, the Illinois director of corrections released more than 21,000 prisoners an average of ninety days early because of severe prison crowding. The impact on the state's crime rate was insignificant, yet the program saved almost $50 million in tax dollars. A study of the program found that the amount of crime that could be attributed to early release was less than 1 percent of the total crime of the state. In fact, the state's crime rate actually declined while the early release program was in effect. Based on these findings, the state expanded its use of "good time" by another ninety days. A recent study of that expanded program found that the state was now saving over $90 million per year in state funds, even taking into account the costs of early release crimes (which represented less than 1 percent of all crimes committed in Illinois) to crime victims.[48]

An earlier demonstration of how swiftly and easily prison populations can be reduced occurred in California from 1967 to 1970. When Ronald Reagan became governor, he instructed the parole board to reduce the prison population. The board began shortening sentences, which it had the power to do within the indeterminate sentence system, and in two years lowered the prison population from 28,000 to less than 18,000. Many other states are following these examples. At the time of this writing, the Texas prison system has dropped by nearly 10,000 inmates as the result of the parole board adopting parole guidelines. Other large states such as Michigan, Ohio, and New York are also reporting declines.

All of these states have found a way to reduce prison terms including inmates serving lengthy sentences for crimes of violence who, because of their age, no longer pose a threat to public safety. Because the average prison stay in the United States is approximately two to three years, even marginal reductions in the length of stay for large categories of inmates would have substantial effects on population size. Using the 1997 figure of approximately 540,748 prison admissions, and assuming that 80 percent of those inmates (representing those who are nonviolent and have satisfactory prison conduct records) had their prison terms reduced by thirty days, we can see that the nation's prison population would have declined by about 36,000 inmates. A ninety-day reduction would result in nearly 110,000 fewer prisoners. Assuming a conservative average cost of $25,000 per inmate, the nation would avert as much as $2.8 billion a year in operating costs and virtually eliminate the need to construct new prisons except for replacement purposes.

Humanize Our Prisons

Whether or not we make any progress toward rational sentencing policies and succeed in dramatically reducing our prison populations, we must confront another issue. Our prisons are at best warehouses where prisoners stagnate and are rendered less and less capable of coping with outside society or, at worst, cruel and dangerous maxiprisons where prisoners are damaged and suffer severely. As a civilized people, we must not tolerate this.

The consequences to our society of supporting or even tolerating inhumane prisons are varied and profound. There is the obvious consequence of having to receive back into our society released prisoners who have been critically damaged by their imprisonment. Less obvious is that the general society itself is polluted by the mistreatment of its prisoners. In the first place, guards and other staff persons who must work in the inhumane prison environment are contaminated by it, as are their families and the townsfolk near the prison. It is virtually impossible to be part of or witness to the systematic mistreatment of other human beings without experiencing some deleterious effects. More generally, support for an inhumane prison system requires that citizens embrace the simplistic concept that prisoners are less worthy beings who deserve their extreme punishment. This belief, which is advanced by unscrupulous and self-serving politicians for their self-gain, rests on—and then in turn, in a looping process—promotes invidiousness, hate, fear, and other emotions that are inimical to the functioning of a cohesive, orderly, beneficent society.

Prisons where prisoners are systematically treated as less that human and denied dignity, basic human rights, and life necessities and are physically and mentally mistreated are festering sores that poison the entire society. The state does not have to make prisons into country clubs or mollycoddle felons to treat prisoners humanely. Prisons are inherently punitive and can operate efficiently and effectively while treating prisoners in a manner consistent with the minimum standards and rights for prisoners that have been formulated by many private and public bodies.[49] Many of these were proposed in the late 1960s and early 1970s, when considerable concern and effort to reform the prison were manifest. Some have been realized in many prison systems. But many have not, and at present most people who decide or influence prison policy completely ignore prisoners' rights and welfare. The courts, particularly the U.S. Supreme Court, after almost completely ignoring the plight of prisoners (the "hands-off" policy, which prevailed until the early 1960s), began ruling on issues regarding prisoners' rights, cruel and unusual punishment, and due process. However, after the mid-1970s, the court effectively returned to the hands-off policy.[50]

Given the anti-prison reform climate, we believe that presenting an argument in support of a full prisoners' rights agenda would be futile at this time. However, several features of a system of incarceration should be acceptable to anyone interested in accomplishing the prison's dominant goals—punishment and incapacitation—and not engaging in unnecessary and counterproductive punitive practices. These are as follows:

1. No cruel and unusual punishment.   Prison overcrowding, adoption of control practices in reaction to prison violence, the lack of concern on the part of the public has resulted in an increase in extremely punitive policies and practices. These include denial of adequate medical services, excessive use of physical punishment in the management of prisoners, and housing prisoners in extremely punitive arrangements, all of which, when delivered maliciously, have been ruled in violation of the Eighth Amendment of the Constitution.[51]

2. Safety.   Prisoners should be able to avoid being attacked, raped, and murdered and in other ways being preyed on by other prisoners and staff. Effective strategies such as adequate surveillance, voluntary access to safe living areas within prison systems, housing prisoners in small units, and single celling should be introduced.

3. Health.   Prisoners should have access to the resources and services required to maintain their physical and mental health. These include access to medical and psychiatric services, adequate diet, and recreation. It also means that they should not be subjected to incarceration regimens that are physically and mentally deleterious, such as extended periods of isolation and restriction on mobility.[52]

4. Rehabilitation.   As suggested earlier, there has been considerable disagreement on whether rehabilitative programs as they have been practiced have been effective in reducing recidivism. However, it appears obvious to us and certainly consistent with a rational system of punishment that prisoners should have access to programs that, according to their and appropriate experts' judgment, improve their chances to adjust to life after prison. This approach would include education, vocational training, and a wide variety of treatment programs that have been experimented with in the past or will be created in the future.

5. Reentry Assistance.   Given the large number of inmates being released and the high rate of parole violations, it will be increasingly important to start building supportive reentry programs for these inmates. Most inmates receive little if any preparation for their release or assistance in the three areas where they require the most help: employment, residence, and family support. Certainly it makes little sense to simply dump inmates out of prison with no more than $20 to $50 and expect them to make it on the outside as an ex-convict with few if any marketable or social skills. Community-based programs operated in particular by nonprofit organizations are needed to help facilitate the reentry process.

This is a minimum list of features that would serve as a foundation for a humane and rational system of incarceration. Many other characteristics should be introduced to achieve a truly effective and humane system.[53] But these features are crucial. Without them we will continue to deliver excessive and irrational punishment to our prisoners and dump them back out into the "streets," damaged and handicapped, ready to descend into the growing urban pit called the "underclass" or to be recycled once again through prison.

ACKNOWLEDGMENTS

This chapter is largely based on the book of the same title (James Austin and John Irwin, *It's About Time: America's Imprisonment Binge*, 3rd ed. Belmont, CA: Wadsworth, 2001).

NOTES

1. U.S. Department of Justice, Bureau of Justice Statistics, *Prisoners in 2000* (Washington, DC: U.S. Government Printing Office, August 2001).

2. U.S. Department of Commerce, Bureau of the Census, *Statistical Abstract of the United States 1998* (Washington, DC: U.S. Government Printing Office, October 1998).

3. U.S. Department of Justice, Bureau of Justice Statistics, *Jails and Jail Inmates 1993–1994* (Washington, DC: U.S. Government Printing Office, 1994).

4. William J. Chambliss, *Power, Politics , and Crime* (Boulder, CO: Westview, 1999).

5. John Irwin and James Austin, *It's About Time* (San Francisco: National Council on Crime and Delinquency, 1987).

6. Marsha Rosenbaum, *Just Say What?* (San Francisco: National Council on Crime and Delinquency, 1989), p. 1.

7. U.S. Department ofjustice, Bureau of Justice Statistics, *Race of Prisoners Admitted to State and Federal Institutions, 1926–86; Sourcebook of Criminal Justice Statistics, 1989* (Washington, DC: U.S. Government Printing Office, 1991); and *National Corrections Reporting Program, 2000* (Washington, DC: U.S. Government Printing Office, 2001).

8. U.S. Department of Commerce, Bureau of the Census, *Statistical Abstract of the United States, 1998* (Washington, DC: U.S. Government Printing Office, September–October, 1998).

9. Kevin Phillips, *The Politics of the Rich and Poor* (New York: Random House, 1991).

10. Ibid., p. 208.

11. Edward Luttwak, "The Middle-Class Backlash," *Harper's* 292 (January 1996):15–16.

12. See Robert Hughes, *The Fatal Shore* (New York: Random House, 1988), Chapter 2, for an excellent discussion of threats from crime, the "urban mobs," or the "dangerous classes" in England, which led to an expansion of transportation as a remedy for the crime problem.

13. National Association of State Budget Officers, *The Fiscal Survey of States* (Washington, DC: Author, 2001).

14. Camille Graham Camp and George M. Camp, *The Corrections Yearbook* (South Salem, NY: Criminal Justice Institute, 1997).

15. In addition to the data provided by the Criminal Justice Institute on daily operating costs, the U.S. Department of Justice reported that in 1996, the operating costs were $20,100. The state-by-state comparisons are located in the DOJ report. See *State Prison Expenditures, 1996* (Washington, DC: U.S. Department of Justice, Office of Justice Programs, Bureau of Justice Statistics, August 1999).

16. See D. McDonald, The *Price of Punishment* (Boulder, CO: Westview, 1989), and Carl Loeb, "The Cost of Jailing in New York City," *Crime and Delinquency* (October 1978): 446–52.

17. See Bruce Cory and Stephen Gettinger, *Time to Build? The Realities of Prison Construction* (New York: Edna McConnell Clark Foundation, 1984).

18. See Cory and Gettinger, *Time to Build?*

19. Austin, James, Darlene Grant, David Bogard, and Curtiss Pulitzer. *District of Columbia Department of Corrections Long-Term Options Study* (Washington, DC: National Institute of Corrections, U.S. Department of Justice, January 31, 1997).

20. Robert Gangi, Vincent Schiraldi, and Jason Ziedenberg. *New York State of Mind? Higher Education vs. Prison Funding in the Empire State, 1988–1998* (New York: Justice Policy Institute and the Correctional Association of New York, 1999).

21. See Steven D. Dillingham, Bureau of Justice Statistics, *Remarks: The Attorney General's Summit on Law Enforcement Responses to Violent Crime: Public Safety in the Nineties,* March 4–5, 1991, Washington, D.C.

22. William Barr, *Combating Violent Crime: 24 Recommendations to Strengthen Criminal Justice* (Washington, DC: U.S. Department of Justice, Office of the Attorney General, July 22, 1992).

23. Crime in the United States is measured by two different methods. The first is the Uniform Crime Reports (UCR), which includes all crimes reported to the police and tabulated by the FBI. The UCR only captures a limited number of crimes (homicide, rape, aggravated assault, robbery, burglary, larceny theft, and motor vehicle theft). A second method involves annual surveys of households conducted by the Census Bureau to determine how many have been victimized by one of seven crimes (rape, robbery, assault, personal theft, household theft, burglary, and motor vehicle theft) each year. This crime reporting system, known as the National Crime Victim Survey, or NCVS, began in 1973. The NCVS does not include crimes against

businesses (shoplifting, commercial burglaries), drug crimes, homicides, or crimes against children under the age of twelve. Furthermore, the NCVS tends to record a large number of trivial crimes that are ordinarily not reported to the police.

The UCR, unlike the NCVS, does include homicides, crimes committed against businesses or commercial properties, and crimes committed against children under the age of twelve and those not living in households. For these reasons, most criminologists believe that the UCR is a more reliable measure of crime.

For a review of the methodological merits of the UCR and NCVS, see Darrell Steffensmeier and Miles Harer, "Did Crime Rise or Fall During the Reagan Presidency?" *Journal of Research in Crime and Delinquency* 283(3, 1991):330–59.

24. See Dillingham, *Remarks*.

25. For a review of the Rand research, see Zimring and Hawkins, *Incapacitation: Penal Confinement and the Restraint of Crime*.

26. Richard B. Abell, "Beyond Willie Horton: The Battle of the Prison Bulge." *Policy Review* (Winter, 1989):32–35. William P. Barr, Speech to California District Attorney's Association. *Federal Sentencing Reporter* 4(6, 1992):345–46. John J. DiIulio and Anne Morrison Piehl, "Does Prison Pay? The Stormy National Debate over the Cost-Effectiveness of Imprisonment." *Brookings Review* (Fall, 1991):28–35.

27. Edwin W. Zedlweski, *Making Confinement Decisions* (Washington, DC: National Institute of Justice, 1987).

28. Mark A. Cohen, "Pain, Suffering, and Jury Awards: A Study of the Cost of Crime to Victims." *Law and Society Review* 22(3, 1988):537–55. Ted. R. Miller, Mark A. Cohen, and Brian Wiersema, *Victim Costs and Consequences. Research Report* (Washington, DC: U.S. Department of Justice, National Institute of Justice, 1996). U.S. Department of Justice, Bureau of Justice Statistics, *Criminal Victimization in the United States; 1992* (Washington, DC: Author, 1994, Table 91).

29. Phillip J. Romero, *How Incarcerating More Felons Will Benefit California's Economy.* (Sacramento, CA: California Governor's Office of Planning and Research, March 31, 1994).

30. Franklin E. Zimring and Gordon Hawkins, "The New Mathematics of Imprisonment," *Crime and Delinquency* 34(1988):425–36.

31. James Austin, "Are Prisons Really a Bargain?" *Spectrum* (1996):10.

32. Zimring and Hawkins, note 30, p. 138.

33. U.S. Department of Justice, *Crime and the Nation's Households, 1991* (Washington, DC: Office of Justice Programs, Bureau of Justice Statistics, July 1992, pp. 5–6).

34. See note 33.

35. Claude Brown, "Manchild 1984," *This World,* September 23, 1984, pp. 7–8.

36. The most blatant display of DiIulio's use of these tactics appeared in a *Readers Digest* article titled "Crime in America, It's Going to Get Worse" (1995). He begins his piece with a story about a guy, a "career criminal," who shot a man strolling on the street in a robbery attempt. According to DiIulio, the shooter had thirteen previous convictions for robberies, burglaries, theft and drug possession, but had slipped past "forgiving" judges for years.

This case is out of line with what is happening in Florida and misplaces the "blame" for this situation on liberal judges. Florida has had a habitual offender law for many years that allows for life sentences on the third conviction of a serious felony (including property or drug violations). It is up to the prosecutor to apply this extremely tough sanction to defendants. Judges have little control once the prosecutor decides to file charges a certain way. DiIulio knows very well that making points from a single case, an anecdote, is fudging. This case, if it did happen anything like DiIulio contends, is a weird anomaly and no conclusions about criminal justice policy can be drawn from it.

37. See Peter Elikann, *SuperPredators*, p. 4.

38. Elikann, *SuperPredators*, p. 25.

39. Jack Katz, in a study of street criminals, found that the excitement of criminal behavior was one of the strong attractions it holds for many offenders. See *Seductions in Crime* (New York: Basic Books, 1990). In a much earlier study, Joan Moore documented the culture of urban Chicanos in Los Angeles and how their involvement in gangs inevitably leads to drugs, arrests, and prison. See *Homeboys: Gangs, Drugs and Prison in the Barrios of Los Angeles* (Philadelphia: Temple University Press, 1978).

40. "If Police Call It Gang Crime, That Doesn't Make It True," *Los Angeles Times*, September 28, 1989, part 11, p. 7.

41. Todd R. Clear has presented evidence that this is in fact occurring already with great increases in incarceration of some categories of the population, particularly African-Americans. See "The Unintended Consequences of Incarceration," paper presented to the National Institute of Justice Workshop on Corrections Research, February 14–15, 1996.

42. Bureau of Prisons, *1990 Census, Race and Hispanic Origin by Age and Sex for the United States, Regions, and States* (Washington, DC: Bureau of the Census, Racial Statistics Branch, 1992), and Bureau of Justice Statistics, *Sourcebook of Criminal Statistics* (Washington, DC: Author, 1991, Table 6.82).

43. Joan Petersilia and Susan Turner, *Prison Versus Probation in California: Implications for Crime and Offender Recidivism* (Santa Monica, CA: Rand, 1986).

44. Sampson and Laub, 1993: 255.

45. When he was U.S. attorney general under Ronald Reagan, Edwin Meese was one of the best examples of a powerful politician who made great use of the crime issue to divert attention. Throughout his public career, he barely avoided prosecution on various charges involving his and his friends' receiving money illegally. All the while he persistently ranted about the crime problem, defined it as a problem of career criminals, and called for more punitive action, even suspension of constitutional procedures to keep career criminals in prison. In April 1988, the press reported on his possible involvement in the Wedtech scandal, which led to the conviction of several persons, one a very close personal friend of Meese. In the midst of all this, he delivered a speech to the nation's mayors in which he again fulminated against the new dangerous criminals, drug users.

46. See Lisbeth Schorr and Daniel Schorr, *Within Our Reach* (New York: Anchor Books, 1990), for an exhaustive list of such programs and policies.

47. See James Austin and Barry Krisberg, "The Unmet Promise of Alternatives to Incarceration," *Crime and Delinquency* 28(3, 1983):374–409.

48. James Austin and Melissa Bolyard, *The Effectiveness of Shorter Prison Terms* (San Francisco: National Council on Crime and Delinquency, March 1993). See James Austin, "Using Early Release to Relieve Prison Crowding." *Crime and Delinquency* 32:404–502.

49. As early as 1955 at Geneva, the United Nations Congress on the Prevention

of Crime and the Treatment of Prisoners adopted a set of Standard Minimum Rules for the Treatment of Prisoners. See *Human Rights: A Compilation of International Instruments* (United Nations publication, Sales No. E.88.XIV 1), section G.

50. See Jack E. Call, "The Supreme Court and Prisoners' Rights," *Federal Probation* (March 1995):36–46, for a discussion of the Court's shift in prisoners' rights matters.

51. The Federal District Court of Northern California ruled that treatment of prisoners at Pelican Bay SHU (segregated housing unit) was cruel and unusual in these regards. See *Madrid v. Gomez*, 889 F.Supp. 1149 (N.D. Cal. 1995).

52. In the opinion delivered by the Federal District Court regarding the conditions of confinement at Pelican Bay SHU, the Court found that "many, if not most, inmates in the SHU experience some degree of psychological trauma in reaction to their extreme social isolation and the severely restricted environmental stimulation in the SHU." See *Madrid v. Gomez*.

53. In *The Struggle for Justice* (New York: Hill & Wang, 1971), the Working Party for the American Friends Service Committee, which consisted of persons with a variety of experiences with prison systems, produced one of the best thought out lists of these. See pp. 168–69.

21

America's New "Peculiar Institution"

On the Prison as Surrogate Ghetto

Loïc Wacquant

Not one but several "peculiar institutions" have operated to define, confine, and control African-Americans in the history of the United States. The first is *chattel slavery* as the pivot of the plantation economy and original matrix of racial division from the colonial era to the Civil War. The second is the *Jim Crow system* of legally enforced discrimination and segregation from cradle to grave that anchored the predominantly agrarian society of the South from the close of Reconstruction to the civil rights revolution, which toppled it a full century after abolition. The third device for containing the descendants of slaves in the Northern industrial metropolis is the *ghetto*—which corresponded to the conjoint urbanization and proletarianization of African-Americans from the Great Migration of 1914–1930 to the 1960s, when it was rendered partially obsolete by economic transformation and the mounting protest of blacks against continued caste exclusion, climaxing with the explosive urban riots chronicled in the Kerner Commission Report.[1] The fourth, I contend here is the novel institutional complex formed by the *remnants of the dark ghetto and the carceral apparatus* with which it has become joined by a linked relationship of structural symbiosis and functional surrogacy.

Viewed against the backdrop of the full historical trajectory of racial domination in the United States, the glaring and growing "disproportionality" in incarceration that has afflicted African-Americans over the past three decades[2] can be understood as the result of the " extrapenological" functions that the prison system came to take on in the wake of the crisis of the ghetto after the mid-seventies. The main impetus behind the stupendous expansion of America's penal state is not crime, but the need to shore up an eroding caste cleavage and the emergent regime of desocialized wage labor to which most blacks are fated by virtue of their lack of marketable cultural capital—and which the most deprived among them resist by escaping into the illegal street economy.

PREFACE: RACIAL DISPROPORTIONALITY IN U.S. IMPRISONMENT

Three brute facts stand out and give a measure of the grotesquely disproportionate impact of mass incarceration on African Americans:

(1)The ethnic composition of the inmate population of the United States has been virtually *inverted* in the last half-century, going from about 70 percent (Anglo) white at the mid-century point to less than 30 percent today. Contrary to common perception, the predominance of blacks behind bars is not a long-standing pattern but a novel and recent phenomenon, with 1988 as the turning point: the year when then vice president George Bush ran his infamous "Willie Horton" advertisement during the presidential campaign, featuring sinister images of the black rapist of a white woman as emblematic of the contemporary "crime problem," as well as the year after which African-American men began to supply a majority of prison admissions for the country as a whole.[3]

(2) Whereas the difference between arrest rates for whites and blacks has been stable (the percentage black oscillating between 29 and 33 percent of all arrestees for property crimes and between 44 and 47 percent for violent offenses between 1976 and 1992,),[4] the white-black *incarceration* gap has grown rapidly in the past quarter-century, jumping from 1 for 5 in 1985 to about *1 for 8 today*. This trend is all the more striking for occurring during a period when significant numbers of African-Americans have entered into and risen through the ranks of the police, the courts, and the corrections administration: institutions in which the more overt forms of racial discrimination commonplace into the seventies have been greatly reduced, if not stamped out.[5]

(3)The lifelong cumulative probability of "doing time" in a state or federal penitentiary based on the imprisonment rates of the early 1990s is 4 percent for whites, 16 percent for Latinos, and a staggering 29 percent for blacks.[6] Given the class gradient of incarceration, this figure suggests that a majority of African-American males of (sub-)proletarian status are facing a prison term of one or several years (and in many cases several terms) at some point in their adult life, with all the family, occupational, and legal disruptions this entails, including the curtailment of social entitlements and civil rights and the temporary or permanent loss of the right to vote. As of 1997, nearly one black man in six nationwide was excluded from the ballot box due to a felony conviction, and more than one-fifth of them were prohibited from casting a vote in Alabama, Connecticut, Florida, Iowa,

Mississippi, New Mexico, Texas, Washington, and Wyoming.[7] A short thirty-five years after the civil rights movement finally gained African-Americans effective access to the voting booth, and a full century after Abolition, this right is being taken back by the penal system via legal dispositions that are of dubious constitutional validity and in many cases (notably lifetime disenfranchisement) violate international conventions on human rights ratified by the United States.

Beyond the specifics of this recent U.S. incarceration policy, there is much to be learned from an historical-cum-analytic comparison between ghetto and prison. For both belong to the same class of organizations, namely, *institutions of forced confinement:* the ghetto is a manner of "social prison" while the prison functions as a "judicial ghetto." Both are entrusted with enclosing a stigmatized population so as to neutralize the material and/or symbolic threat that it poses for the broader society from which it has been extruded. And, for that reason, ghetto and prison tend to evolve patterns and cultural forms that display striking similarities and intriguing parallels, calling for comparative study in other national and historical settings.

VEHICLES FOR LABOR EXTRACTION AND CASTE DIVISION

America's first three "peculiar institutions" (slavery, Jim Crow, and the ghetto) were all instruments for the conjoint extraction of labor and social ostracization of an outcast group deemed inassimilable by virtue of the indelible threefold stigma it carried. African-Americans arrived in bondage in the land of freedom. They were accordingly deprived of the right to vote in the self-appointed cradle of democracy (until 1965 for residents of the southern states). And, for lack of a recognizable national affiliation, they were shorn of ethnic honor, which implies that, rather than simply standing at the bottom of the rank ordering of group prestige in American society, they were barred from it ab initio.[8]

Slavery is a highly malleable and versatile institution that can be harnessed to a variety of purposes but in the Americas property-in-person was geared primarily to the provision and control of labor.[9] Its introduction in the Chesapeake, Middle Atlantic, and Low Country regions of the United States in the seventeenth century served to recruit and regulate the unfree workforce forcibly imported from Africa and the West Indies to cater to the tobacco, rice, and mixed-farming economy. By the end of the eighteenth century, slavery had become self-reproducing and expanded to the fertile crescent of the southern interior. It supplied a highly profitable organization of labor and was the basis for a plantation society, distinctive for its feudal-like culture, politics and psychology.

An unforeseen byproduct of the systematic enslavement and dehumanization of Africans and their descendants on North American soil was the creation of a racial caste line separating what would later become labeled "blacks" and "whites." Racial division was a consequence, not a precondition, of U.S. slavery, but once it was instituted it became detached from its initial function and acquired a social potency of its own. Emancipation created a double dilemma for southern white society: how to secure anew the labor of former slaves, without whom the region's economy would collapse, and how to sustain the cardinal status distinction between whites and "persons of color," i.e., the social and symbolic distance needed to prevent the odium of "amalgamation" with a group considered inferior, rootless, and vile. The solution came in the form of the so-called Jim Crow regime, an ensemble of social and legal codes that prescribed the complete separation of the "races" and sharply circumscribed the life chances of African-Americans,[10] while binding them to whites in a relation of submission backed by legal coercion and violence.

Imported from the North where it had been experimented with in cities, this regime stipulated that blacks travel in separate trains and streetcars and use separate waiting rooms; that they reside in the "darktown" slums and be educated in separate schools (if at all); that they patronize separate service establishments and use their own bathrooms and water fountains; that they pray in separate churches, entertain themselves in separate clubs, and sit in separate "nigger galleries" in theaters; that they receive medical care in separate hospitals and exclusively from "colored" staff; and that they be incarcerated in separate cells and buried in separate cemeteries. Most crucial of all, laws joined mores in condemning the "unspeakable crime" of interracial marriage, cohabitation, or mere sexual congress so as to uphold the "supreme law of self-preservation" of the races and the myth of innate white superiority. Through continued white ownership of the land and the generalization of sharecropping and debt peonage, the plantation system remained virtually untouched as former slaves became a "dependent, propertyless peasantry, nominally free, but ensnared by poverty, ignorance, and the new servitude of tenantry."[11] While sharecropping tied African-American labor to the farm, a rigid etiquette ensured that whites and blacks never interacted on a plane of equality, not even on the track field or in a boxing ring. Whenever the "color line" was breached or even brushed, a torrent of violence was unleashed: Ku Klux Klan and vigilante raids; public floggings, mob killings and lynching—ritual caste murder designed to keep "uppity niggers" in their appointed place. All this was made possible by the swift and near-complete disenfranchisement of blacks, as well as by the enforcement of "Negro law" by courts that granted the latter *fewer* effective legal safeguards than slaves had enjoyed earlier by dint of being both property and persons.

The sheer brutality of caste oppression in the South, the decline of cotton agriculture due to floods and the boll weevil, and the pressing short-age of labor in northern factories caused by the outbreak of World War I created the impetus for African-Americans to emigrate en masse to the booming industrial centers of the Midwest and Northeast (over 1.5 million left in 1910–1930, followed by another 3 million in 1940–1960). But as migrants from Mississippi to the Carolinas flocked to the northern me-tropolis, they discovered not the "promised land" of equality and full cit-izenship but another system of racial enclosure, the ghetto, which, though it was less rigid and fearsome than the one they had fled, was no less en-compassing and constricting. To be sure, greater freedom to come and go in public places and to consume in regular commercial establishments, the disappearance of the humiliating signs pointing to "Colored" here and "White" there, renewed access to the ballot box and protection from the courts, the possibility of limited economic advancement, release from per-sonal subservience and from the dread of omnipresent white violence, all made life in the urban north incomparably preferable to continued peon-age in the rural south: it was "better to be a lamppost in Chicago than Pres-ident of Dixie," as migrants famously put it to Richard Wright.[12] But restrictive covenants forced African-Americans to congregate in a "black belt," which quickly became overcrowded, underserved, and blighted by crime, disease, and dilapidation, while the "job ceiling" restricted them to the most hazardous, menial, and underpaid occupations in both in-dustry and personal services. "Social equality," understood as the possi-bility of "becoming members of white cliques, churches, and voluntary associations, or marrying into their families," was firmly and definitively denied.[13]

Blacks had entered the Fordist industrial economy, to which they con-tributed a vital source of abundant and cheap labor, willing to ride along its cycles of boom and bust. Yet they remained locked in a precarious po-sition of structural economic marginality and consigned to a secluded and dependent microcosm, complete with its own internal division of labor, social stratification, and agencies of collective voice and symbolic repre-sentation: a "city within the city" moored in a complex of black churches and presses, businesses, and professional practices. Continued caste hos-tility from without and renewed ethnic affinity from within converged to create the ghetto as the third vehicle to extract black labor while keeping black bodies at a safe distance, to the material and symbolic benefit of white society.

The era of the ghetto as paramount mechanism of ethnoracial domina-tion had opened with the urban riots of 1917–1919. It closed with a wave of clashes, looting, and burning that rocked hundreds of American cities from coast to coast, from the Watts uprising of 1965 to the riots of rage and grief triggered by the assassination of Martin Luther King in the summer of 1968.[14] By the end of the sixties, the ghetto was well on its way to becoming functionally obsolete or, to be more precise, increasingly *un-suited* to accomplishing the twofold task historically entrusted to America's "peculiar institutions." On the side of *labor extraction*, the shift from an urban industrial economy to a suburban service economy and the accompanying dualization of the occupational structure (along with the upsurge of working-class immigration from Mexico, the Caribbean, and Asia), meant that large segments of the work force contained in the "black belts" of the northern metropolis were simply no longer needed. On the side of *ethno-racial closure*, the decades-long mobilization of African-Americans against caste rule finally succeeded—in the propitious political conjuncture of crisis stemming from the Vietnam war and assorted social unrest—in forcing the federal state to dismantle the legal machinery of caste exclusion. Having secured voting and civil rights, blacks were at long last full citizens who would no longer brook being shunted off into the separate and inferior world of the ghetto.[15]

But while whites begrudgingly accepted "integration" in principle, in practice they strove to maintain an unbridgeable social and symbolic gulf with their compatriots of African descent. They abandoned public schools, shunned public space, and fled to the suburbs in the millions to avoid mixing and to ward off the specter of "social equality" in the city. They attacked the welfare state and those social programs upon which the collective advancement of blacks was most dependent, and gave enthusiastic support to "law-and-order" policies that vowed to firmly repress urban disorders connately perceived as racial threats.[16] Such policies pointed to yet another special institution capable of confining and controlling, if not the entire African-American community, at least its most disruptive, disreputable, and dangerous members: the prison.

THE GHETTO AS ETHNORACIAL PRISON, THE PRISON AS JUDICIAL GHETTO

To grasp the deep kinship between ghetto and prison, which helps explain how the structural decline and functional redundancy of the one led to the unexpected ascent and astonishing growth of the other during the last quarter-century,[17] it is necessary first to characterize accurately the ghetto. The social sciences have failed to develop a robust analytic concept of the ghetto; instead they have been content to borrow the folk concept current in political and popular discourse at each epoch. This has caused a good deal of confusion, as the ghetto has been successively conflated with—and mistaken for—a segregated district, an ethnic neighborhood, a territory of intense poverty or housing blight, and even, with the rise of the policy myth of the "underclass" in the more recent period, a mere accumulation of urban pathologies and antisocial behaviors.[18]

A comparative and historical sociology of the reserved Jewish quarters in the cities of Renaissance Europe, as well as America's "Bronzeville" in the Fordist metropolis of the twentieth century, reveals that a ghetto is essentially a socio-spatial device that enables a dominant status group in an urban setting to ostracize and simultaneously exploit a subordinate group endowed with negative symbolic capital: an incarnate property perceived to make mere contact with it degrading by virtue of what Max Weber calls "negative social estimation of honor." The relation between ethnoracial control and closure is built out of four elements:(1) stigma, (2) constraint, (3) territorial confinement, and (4) institutional encasement. The resulting formation is a distinct *space*, containing an ethnically homogeneous *population*, which finds itself forced to develop within it a set of interlinked *institutions* that duplicates the organizational framework of the broader society from which that group is banished and that supplies the scaffoldings for the construction of its specific "style of life" and social strategies. This parallel institutional nexus affords the subordinate group a measure of protection, autonomy, and dignity, but at the cost of locking it in a relationship of structural subordination and dependency.

The ghetto operates as an *ethnoracial prison:* it confines a dishonored category and severely curtails the life chances of its members in support of the "monopolization of ideal and material goods or opportunities" by the dominant status group[19] dwelling on its outskirts. Recall that the ghettos of early modern Europe were typically delimited by high walls with one or more gates that were locked at night, and within which Jews had to return before sunset on pain of severe punishment,[20] and that their perimeter was subjected to continuous monitoring by external authorities. Note next the structural and functional homologies with the prison conceptualized as a *judicial ghetto:* a jail or penitentiary is in effect a reserved *space* that serves to forcibly confine a legally denigrated *population* and wherein this latter evolves its distinctive *institutions*, culture, and sullied identity. It is thus formed of the same four fundamental constituents—stigma, coercion, physical enclosure, and organizational parallelism and insulation—that make up a ghetto, and for similar purposes.

Much as the ghetto protects the city's residents from the pollution of intercourse with the tainted but necessary bodies of an outcast group, the prison cleanses the social body from the temporary blemish of those of its members who have committed crimes. In Durkheim's terms, these individuals have violated the sociomoral integrity of the collectivity by infringing on "definite and strong states of the collective conscience."[21] Students of the "inmate society" have noted time and again how the incarcerated develop their own argot roles, exchange systems, and normative standards, whether as an adaptive response to the "pains of imprisonment" or through selective importation of criminal and lower-class values from the outside, much like residents of the ghetto have elaborated or intensified a "separate subculture" to counter their sociosymbolic immurement.[22] As for the secondary aim of the ghetto, to facilitate exploitation of the inmates, this was central to the "house of correction," the direct historical predecessor of the modern prison, and it has periodically played a major role in the evolution and operation of the latter.[23] Finally, both prison and ghetto are authority structures with inherently dubious or problematic legitimacy whose maintenance is ensured by intermittent recourse to external force.

By the end of the seventies, as a backlash against the democratic advances won by the social movements of the preceding decade were in full swing, the prison abruptly returned to the forefront of American society and offered itself as the universal and simple solution to all manners of social problems. Chief among these problems was the "breakdown" of social order in the "inner city," which is scholarly and policy euphemism for the patent incapacity of the dark ghetto to contain a dishonored and supernumerary population henceforth viewed not only as deviant and devious, but as downright dangerous in light of the violent urban upheavals of mid-sixties. As the walls of the ghetto shook and threatened to crumble, the walls of the prison were correspondingly extended, enlarged, and fortified. "Confinement of differentiation," aimed at keeping a group apart, gained primacy over "confinement of safety" and "confinement of authority"— to use the distinction proposed by Claude Faugeron.[24] Soon the black ghetto, converted into an instrument of naked exclusion by the concurrent retrenchment of wage labor and social protection, and further destabilized by the increasing penetration of the penal arm of the state, became bound to the jail and prison system by a triple relationship of functional equivalency, structural homology, and cultural syncretism. The ghetto and prison constitute a single *carceral continuum* that entraps a redundant population of younger black men (and increasingly women) who circulate in closed circuit between these two poles in a self-perpetuating cycle of social and legal marginality with devastating personal and social consequences.[25]

The carceral system had already functioned as an *ancillary* institution for caste preservation and labor control in America during one previous transition between regimes of racial domination, that between slavery and Jim Crow in the South. On the morrow of Emancipation, southern prisons turned black overnight as "thousands of ex-slaves were being arrested, tried, and convicted for acts that in the past had been dealt with by the master alone"[26] and for refusing to behave as menials and follow the demeaning rules of racial etiquette. Soon thereafter, the former confederate states devised "convict leasing" as a response to the moral panic of "Negro crime," which presented the double advantage of generating prodigious funds for the state coffers and furnishing abundant bound labor to till the fields, build the levees, lay down the railroads, clean the swamps, and dig the mines of the region under murderous conditions.[27] Indeed, penal labor, in the form of the convict-lease and its heir, the chain gang, played a major role in the economic advancement of the New South during the Progressive era, as it "reconciled modernization with the continuation of racial domination."[28]

What makes the racial intercession of today's carceral system different is that unlike slavery, Jim Crow, and the ghetto of mid-century, it does not carry out a positive economic mission of recruitment and disciplining of an active workforce. It serves only to warehouse the precarious and de-proletarianized fractions of the black working class, whether because they cannot find employment owing to a combination of skills deficit, employer discrimination, and competition from immigrants, or because they refuse to submit to the indignity of substandard work in the peripheral sectors of the service economy—what ghetto residents commonly label "slave jobs." But there is mounting financial and ideological pressure, as well as renewed political interest, to relax restrictions on penal labor so as to (re-)introduce mass unskilled work in private enterprises inside American prisons. Putting most inmates to work would help lower the country's "carceral bill" as well as effectively extend to the inmate poor the workfare requirements now imposed upon the free poor as a requirement of citizenship.[29] The next decade will tell whether the prison remains an appendage to the dark ghetto or supersedes it to go it alone and become America's fourth "peculiar institution."

ACKNOWLEDGMENTS

This is adapted from an article that first appeared in *Theoretical Criminology* 4(3, 2000):377–89, special issue on "New Social Studies of the Prison" (edited by Mary Bosworth and Richard Sparks).

NOTES

1. See, respectively, on slavery, Kenneth M. Stampp, *The Peculiar Institution: Slavery in the Ante-Bellum South* (New York: Vintage, 1956, reprinted 1989), and Ira Berlin, *Many Thousands Gone: The First Two Centuries of Slavery in North America* (Cambridge, MA: Harvard University Press, 1998); on the Jim Crow regime, C. Vann Woodward, *The Strange Career of Jim Crow* (New York: Oxford University Press, 3rd rev. ed. 1989, orig. 1957); Leon F. Litwack, *Trouble in Mind: Black Southerners in the Age of Jim Crow* (New York: Knopf, 1998); and William Chaffe et al. (Eds.), *Remembering Jim Crow* (New York: New Press, 2001); on the rise and crisis of the ghetto as instrument of ethnoracial control and containment, Allan H. Spear, *Black Chicago: The Making of a Negro Ghetto, 1890–1920* (Chicago: University of Chicago Press, 1968), and Kerner Commission, *The Kerner Report: The 1968 Report*

of the National Advisory Commission on Civil Disorders (New York: Pantheon, 1988, orig. ed. 1968).

2. Michael Tonry provides a systematic analysis of the increasing enmeshment of African-Americans in the criminal justice system over the past two decades: *Malign Neglect: Race, Class, and Punishment in America* (New York: Oxford University Press, 1995).

3. David C. Anderson, *Crime and the Politics of Hysteria: How the Willie Horton Story Changed American Justice* (New York: Times Books, 1995).

4. Michael Tonry, *Malign Neglect*, p. 64.

5. Alfred Blumstein, "Racial Disproportionality of U.S. Prison Revisited," *University of Colorado Law Review* 64(1993):743–60; but see the powerful counterargument by David Cole in *No Equal Justice: Race and Class in the American Criminal Justice System* (New York: New Press, 1999) that the functioning of the U.S. criminal justice system "affirmatively depends on inequality" and is riddled with racial double standards.

6. Thomas Bonczar and Allen Beck, "Lifetime Likelihood of Going to State or Federal Prison," *Bureau of Justice Statistics Special Report* (Washington, DC: BJS, March 1997, p. 1); for a state-by-state analysis, see Marc Maurer, "Racial Disparities in Prison Getting Worse in the 1990s," *Overcrowded Times* 8(1, February 1997): 9–13.

7. John Hagan and Ronit Dinowitzer, "Collateral Consequences of Imprisonment for Children, Communities, and Prisoners," in Michael Tonry and Joan Petersilia (Eds.), *Prisons* (Chicago: University of Chicago Press, 1999, pp. 121–62); and Jamie Fellner and Marc Mauer, *Losing the Vote: The Impact of Felony Disenfranchisement in the United States* (Washington, DC: Sentencing and Human Rights Watch, 1998).

8. "Among the groups commonly considered unassimilable, the Negro people is by far the largest. The Negroes do not, like the Japanese and the Chinese, have a politically organized nation and an accepted culture of their own outside of America to fall back upon. Unlike the Oriental, there attaches to the Negro an historical memory of slavery and inferiority. It is more difficult for them to answer prejudice with prejudice and, as the Orientals may do, to consider themselves and their history superior to the white Americans and their recent cultural achievements. The Negroes do not have these fortifications of self-respect. They are more helplessly *imprisoned* as a subordinate caste, a cast of people deemed to be lacking a cultural past and assumed to be incapable of a cultural future" (Gunnar Myrdal, *An American Dilemma: The Negro Problem and Modern Democracy* [New York: Harper Torchbook, 1944, reprinted 1962, p. 54], my emphasis).

9. The remarkable functional, structural, and cultural flexibility of slavery is amply documented in Seymour Drescher and Stanley L. Engerman, *A Historical Guide to World Slavery* (New York: Oxford University Press, 1998).

10. Woodward, *The Strange Career of Jim Crow*, and, for a highly original approach that gets to the core of the question of group (dis-)honor, Martha Rhodes, *White Women, Black Men: Illicit Sex in the 19th-Century South* (New Haven, CT: Yale University Press, 1997, esp. Chapters 7 and 8).

11. Neil R. McMillen, *Dark Journey: Black Mississippians in the Age of Jim Crow* (Urbana: University of Illinois Press, 1990, p. 126).

12. Richard Wright, *Twelve Million Black Voices* (New York: Thundermouth's Press, 1988, orig. 1941, p. 88).

13. St. Clair Drake and Horace Cayton, *Black Metropolis: A Study of Negro Life in a Northern City* (New York: Harper and Row, 1962, orig. 1945, Vol. I, pp. 112–28).

14. William M. Tuttle, Jr., *Race Riot: Chicago in the Red Summer of 1919* (New York: Atheneum, 1970, new edition University of Illinois Press, 1993); Arthur Waskow, *From Race Riot to Sit In, 1919 to the 1960s* (Garden City, NY: Doubleday, 1966); and Kerner Commission, *The Kerner Report.*

15. This was the meaning of Martin Luther King's "Freedom Campaign" in the summer of 1966 in Chicago: it sought to apply to the ghetto the techniques of collective mobilization and civil disobedience used with success in the attack on Jim Crow in the South to reveal and protest "the slow, stifling death of a kind of concentration camp life" to which blacks were condemned in the Northern metropolis (M. L. King, cited by Stephen B. Oates, *Let the Trumpet Sound: The Life of Martin Luther King* [New York: New American Library, 1982, p. 373]). The campaign to "make Chicago an open city" was swiftly crushed by a formidable combination of state repression (spearheaded by four thousand National guard troops), white mob violence, vitriolic media campaigns of denunciation by the *Chicago Tribune* and *Chicago Sun Times,* furious resistance from city hall, the real estate industry, and the courts, all with the knowing acquiescence of Congress and the White House.

16. Thomas Byrne Edsall and Mary D. Edsall, *Chain Reaction: The Impact of Race, Rights, and Taxes on American Politics* (New York: W.W. Norton, 1991); Jill Quadagno, *The Color of Welfare: How Racism Undermined the War on Poverty* (Oxford: Oxford University Press, 1994); Martin Gilens, *Why Americans Hate Welfare* (Chicago: University of Chicago Press, 1999); and Katherine Beckett and Theodore Sasson, *The Politics of Injustice* (Thousand Oaks, CA: Pine Forge, 2000, pp. 49–74).

17. It must be recalled that the carceral population of the United States had been steadily declining for nearly two decades to reach a low of about 360.000 inmates in 1973. The leading analysts of the penal question were then unanimous in predicting the imminent marginalization of the prison as an institution of social control or, in the worst-case scenario, the long-term stability of penal confinement at a historically moderate level. No one foresaw the impending quadrupling of America's incarcerated population over the ensuing twenty years.

18. For a historical recapitulation of the meanings of "ghetto" in American society and social science, leading to a diagnosis of the curious expurgation of race from a concept expressly forged to denote a mechanism of ethnoracial domination, which ties it to the changing concerns of state elites over the nexus of poverty and ethnicity in the metropolis, see Loïc Wacquant, "Gutting the Ghetto: Political Censorship and Conceptual Retrenchment in the American Debate on Urban Destitution," in Malcolm Cross and Robert Moore (eds.), *Globalisation and the New City* (Basingstoke: Macmillan, 2001).

19. Max Weber, *Economy and Society,* edited by Guenter Roth and Claus Wittich (Berkeley: University of California Press, 1978, p. 935).

20. Louis Wirth, *The Ghetto* (Chicago: University of Chicago Press, 1928, p. 32).

21. Emile Durkheim, *The Division of Labor in Society* (New York: Routledge, 1984, orig. 1893, p. 73).

22. Drake and Cayton, *Black Metropolis,* vol. II, p. xiii.

23. Describing the London Bridewell, the *Zuchthaus* of Amsterdam, and Paris's *Hôpital général,* Rusche and Kirschheimer write: "The essence of the house of correction was that it combined the principles of the poorhouse, workhouse and penal institution." Its main aim was "to make the labor power of the unwilling people socially useful" by forcing them to work under close supervision in the hope that, once released, "they would voluntarily swell the labor market" (Georg Rusche and Otto Kirscheimer, *Punishment and Social Structure* (New York: Columbia University Press, 1939, p. 42). On this point, see also Dario Melossi and Massimo Pavarini, *The Prison and the Factory: Origins of the Penitentiary System* (London: Macmillan, 1981), and Pieter Spierenburg, *The Prison Experience: Disciplinary Institutions and Their Inmates in Early Modern Europe* (New Brunswick, NJ: Rutgers University Press, 1991).

24. Claude Faugeron, "La dérive pénale," *Esprit* (215, October 1995):132–44.

25. A fuller discussion of this fateful coupling of ghetto and prison in the post–civil rights era is in Loïc Wacquant, "Deadly Symbiosis: When Ghetto and Prison Meet and Mesh," *Punishment & Society* 3(1, Winter 2001):95–134. (Also in David Garland [ed.], *Mass Imprisonment: Social Causes and Consequences* [London: Sage, 2001, pp. 82–120]).

26. David M. Oshinsky, *Worse Than Slavery: Parchman Farm and the Ordeal of Jim Crow Justice* (New York: Free Press, 1996, p. 32).

27. This is not a figure of speech: the annual mortality rate for convicts reached 16 percent in Mississippi in the 1880s, where "not a single leased convict ever lived long enough to serve a sentence of ten years or more" (Oshinsky, *Worse Than Slavery*, p. 46). Hundreds of black children, many as young as six years old, were leased by the state to the benefit of planters, businessmen, and bankers, to toil in conditions that even some patrician southerners found shameful and "a stain upon our manhood."

28. Alex Lichtenstein, *Twice the Work of Free Labor: The Political Economy of Convict Labor in the New South* (New York: Verso, 1999, p. 195).

29. Expert testimony presented to the Committees on the Judiciary and Crime of the U.S. House of Representatives during discussion of the Prison Industries Reform Act of 1998 explicitly linked welfare reform and the need to expand private prison labor.

22

Of Punishment and Crime Rates

Some Theoretical and Methodological
Consequences of Mass Incarceration

Elliott Currie

It is often said that the enormous rise in imprisonment in the United States over the past quarter-century has been one of the least debated and least planned social experiments in modern memory. As David Garland has written,

> Mass imprisonment was not a policy that was proposed, researched, costed, debated and democratically agreed. . . . Instead, America has drifted into this situation, with voters and politicians and judges and corporations willing the specific means without anyone pausing to assess the overall outcome. . . . We are just beginning to reflect upon the political and cultural meanings of this new institution, upon what it means for America to be a mass imprisonment society—a process of reflection that has begun somewhat late in the day. (2001:2–3)

But though the effort to understand the social consequences for America of mass incarceration is just beginning, it is clear that the huge rises in incarceration—heavily concentrated in low-income communities and especially communities of color—have had far-reaching and deeply troubling effects that few bothered to think about in advance. Dina Rose and Todd Clear (1998) have shown, for example, that the removal of a substantial proportion of adult residents from the neighborhoods hit hardest by mass imprisonment operates, beyond a certain point, to undercut the community's capacity for informal social control. Bruce Western (2001), Richard Freeman (1992), and others have shown that early imprisonment profoundly and adversely affects young people's chances of stable and well-paying work for years afterward, and that indeed going to prison has even more negative consequences for employment among black youth than dropping out of school does.

These findings are beginning to paint a picture that drives home the troubling long-run social and economic impacts of the massive growth in prison populations in the United States. But there are other, even less appreciated, impacts as well. In this chapter, I want to argue that mass incarceration on the American level—unprecedented in our history or that of any other country—may have complex but crucially important effects on the way we *measure* crime and, consequently, on our empirical and theoretical assessments of the dimensions and meaning of the crime problem in this and other countries.

CRIME RATES, CRIMINALITY, AND MASS IMPRISONMENT

The basic concern is this: I am increasingly convinced that the advent of mass incarceration has rendered our conventional measures of what we call the "crime rate" less and less useful, or adequate, as a way of describing the reality of criminality in America, or as a basis for understanding its roots or its remedies. And this could have important implications for public policies against crime.

To explain why I think this is a growing—and fundamental—problem, let me start with a little thought experiment. Suppose that we are public health specialists, or medical researchers and epidemiologists, rather than criminologists. And our job is to understand the dimensions of a variety of potentially preventable diseases, with the ultimate aim of both protecting the public from illness in the short run and, more crucially, learning something about the causes of illness so that we can prevent it.

Now suppose there is an epidemic of some disease—say, typhoid—in our country. Tens of thousands of people are stricken with typhoid, and many of them have to be put in hospitals. The authorities, in addition to hospitalizing great numbers of sick people, also launch various other kinds of preventive and harm-reducing measures: they give vaccinations, quarantine some people in their homes, inspect the food supply, purify the water supply, educate the public about how to avoid the kinds of settings and behaviors that put them at high risk of getting typhoid, and so on.

As public health specialists, we want to measure how bad the situation is, so that we can do a better job of dealing with it and, among other things, so we can get a sense of whether, and how much, our array of antityphoid measures is actually working. Clearly, to do this we need to measure the levels and trends of typhoid infection. So we assiduously set out to do that: but we decide, for administrative reasons, to only count those of the sick who are still walking around on the street, or in their homes—those remaining in the community—and not the ones we have put in the hospital. We continue to do this, let us suppose, even as the epidemic progresses and becomes worse and worse, to the point where we are in fact putting a significant fraction of the entire population in our hospitals.

This way of counting the sick, of course, greatly skews our sense of what is going on with this disease. To begin with, it obviously gives us a misleading underestimate of the prevalence of typhoid in our society, since it excludes from the official count not only a great many sick people, but arguably excludes the *sickest* among them—because we will have most likely hospitalized the ones who are in the worst shape. And it also gives us an oddly distorted picture of the *trajectory* of the current epidemic, and of our progress in combating it. Certainly, the numbers will unrealistically inflate our "success" against the illness, since they obscure the contrary evidence represented by the masses of ill people we have put in the hospital. Indeed if we put *enough* sick people in the hospital, it could even appear that the epidemic is waning, paradoxically enough, just when, in reality, it has gotten worse.

And then, of course, if we use these oddly curtailed figures as our guide, our assessment of the effectiveness of the various official measures we have launched to combat typhoid will be similarly distorted. Some of those efforts, at least, will look good on the surface, because we have fewer cases of typhoid—on the street. That includes the hospitalization policy itself: if we do enough of it, we will be tempted to say it has lowered the typhoid rate.

But of course it has not lowered the typhoid rate; it has merely moved the infected population from one place to another. So what appears in our official statistics as a "solution" is not really a solution at all, if what we are concerned about is the overall rate of sickness in our community. To be sure, it may be *necessary* to hospitalize those people, or at least some proportion of them, to protect the rest of the public from infection. And it may even help slow the spread of the disease. But people would look at us very strangely if, as epidemiologists, we counted it as a *solution* to the typhoid epidemic, or as evidence that our problem was less severe than it was before.

Now, in reality, no one would do this in the field of public health. No one would for a moment imagine that we could measure the prevalence of illness by counting only the unhospitalized ill—especially when the hospitalized become a larger and larger proportion of the total population of the sick. But we do something quite similar all the time, without the blink of an eye, in criminology.

What we call the "crime rate" in our conventional approach—no matter what specific techniques we use to uncover it (police reports, victim surveys, self-reports)—measures that *part* of our crime problem that is represented by those offenders who are still on the streets (or in their homes).

It does not measure the part of our crime problem that is represented by those offenders who—as in my typhoid-ridden community—we have put away in institutions in order to get them *off* the streets.

Stated so simply, that point seems obvious. But it has not affected the way we typically go about measuring the crime problem. Part of the reason for that is surely that under the conditions of imprisonment that prevail in most countries, and that prevailed for most of our own past, the point did not matter all that much, because there were far fewer offenders incarcerated. But that was before we had over two million people behind bars on any given day in the United States: before we increased the prison population sevenfold. Now that we have done that, I think it matters a great deal.

Put in another way, the problem with our conventional concept of the "crime rate" is that it measures "crime" well enough, but fails badly as a measure of *criminality*. That is, it works reasonably well as a measure of the incidence of offenses in the community, but increasingly poorly as a measure of the prevalence of offenders in our society. And in many ways, criminality is arguably the more fundamental phenomenon here, and the one we most need to know about and to measure. Not that the conventional crime rate is unimportant—it does tell us some things we want to know, and has its uses for public policy. But used by itself, it also obscures many crucial things about the crime problem in a given community, and that becomes especially problematic, as I have suggested, in communities or societies where a significant fraction of the offender population is incarcerated—and hence not only hidden from public view, but also hidden from the conventional crime statistics.

We count those offenders, of course, in the *prison* statistics. But they do not figure in the *crime* statistics. And that, I submit, may result in a misreading of our real crime problem in ways that become increasingly consequential as the level of imprisonment rises.

The problem I am pointing to here is not just that the crimes offenders commit while incarcerated are largely unrepresented in our crime statistics, though that is itself a very significant issue—especially for some kinds of crime, like rape and assault (our official rates of rape would be dramatically transformed if we adequately counted and included what happens behind bars). The problem I am talking about is both deeper and more subtle.

If what we are concerned with is the propensity of our society to produce criminals—to breed people who are violent or predatory, who hurt other people—then it makes minimal sense to count only the fraction of those people who are still at large, still on the street, in the community. But that is what the conventional crime rate measures: the activity of free offenders. In order to understand the depth and breadth of the propensity to offend in a given society, we need a measure of "criminality;" that is, the overall number of people who are either still out on the street committing crimes, or more or less safely locked away where they cannot—at least for now, and at least against the general public.

Failing to do that—to count all of the offenders, including the imprisoned—is to my mind no different than excluding the sick people in hospitals in my fictional example. And this is much more than just a semantic quibble. Without that kind of more inclusive measure, it is virtually impossible to maintain an adequate perspective on the nature, causes, and dimensions of serious crime in the United States today—or to adequately assess the impact of anticrime policies, current or proposed.

CRIME AND CRIMINALITY IN HISTORICAL AND COMPARATIVE PERSPECTIVE

The failure to distinguish between crime and criminality has consequences that are important on several levels. Let me suggest just some of them for now.

First, looking at criminality rather than the conventional crime rate gives us a very different perspective on recent trends in crime in the United States. There has been a kind of triumphalism in the public discussion about crime and punishment in recent years (though it has subsided somewhat with the leveling off of crime in the nation as a whole, and its recent rise in some jurisdictions, in the first years of the new century). At least until very recently, it was common to hear that we had "turned the corner" on crime, that crime was "on the run"—or, as a *Time* magazine cover put it in the mid-1990s, "We're finally winning the war on crime." That triumphalism about crime had implications that went far beyond the debates about crime and crime control specifically, to a much broader celebration of the thrust of contemporary social and economic policy. It suggested that we in America were doing many things right after years of having done them wrong; it suggested not only that the strategy of cracking down on crime through a vast expansion of imprisonment was working quite fabulously; but also that the broader American "model" of social organization was working splendidly as well. It suggested to some observers that we could after all fix the American crime problem without addressing the social deficits that criminologists had often said were heavily responsible for it—high levels of social inequality, extremes of poverty, widespread community disorganization, the relative absence (by comparison with other advanced industrial nations) of an effective system of social provision for vulnerable people. It accordingly bolstered the view that what criminologists had often described as "root causes" of crime were not, after all, very important.

But looking at recent crime trends through the lens of "criminality" gives us a much more complicated, and much less rosy, picture. It suggests that to an important extent we haven't really *solved* our crime problem: we've just *moved* it. We have hidden our propensity to produce criminals through the stunningly rapid expansion of the prison population. But we have not necessarily diminished that propensity, and whatever it is about our society that tends to breed predatory and violent people has not gotten much better if indeed it has gotten better at all.

And on one level, this is only common sense. I think we understand viscerally that something is very much amiss in a society that has both unusually high levels of serious violent crime *and* extraordinarily high rates of incarceration, something that is not adequately reflected in the conventional crime rate alone.

So a better understanding of how trends in our social and economic organization have affected crime requires a more inclusive measure of the real extent of criminality over time, in this country and in others. We have not put real effort into developing that kind of measure, but we could do it if we put our minds to it. Indeed, we could probably approach that measurement in several different ways.

I will not try to do that in any detail here—I am only attempting at this point to establish a general principle, and in any case there are others who are much better at this sort of methodological work than I am. But I think the empirical issues, though not exactly simple, are basically straightforward. We need a measure that combines the criminality that is represented by the masses of offenders behind bars coupled with that of offenders still in the community.

One way to arrive at that measure would be to estimate individual crime rates for various offenses for the incarcerated offenders, aggregate them, and essentially add the result to the conventional crime rate to get a measure of what, borrowing a classic sociological term, we might call the "latent" crime rate.

There have been many attempts, beginning with the efforts of Rand Corporation researchers in the early 1980s (Chaiken and Chaiken 1982; Visher 1986), to estimate the individual crime rates of incarcerated offenders—most of them designed mainly to throw some quantitative light on the incapacitative effects of incarceration for various offenses. We can use those to help us think about the magnitude of the changes in our perception of crime when we measure the prevalence of criminality rather than the conventional crime rate. Again, the reader should consider this discussion as illustrative, not definitive.

Let us consider this through the lens of robbery, a violent offense that is both frightening and often thought of as a kind of "bellwether" offense that reflects broader currents in crime in a given society. In 1999, there were roughly 162,000 inmates in state prisons sentenced for robbery. To get some handle on how much criminality those imprisoned robbers represent, we can use, for purposes of discussion, the rough self-reported figures on robbery frequency gathered from offenders in California, Texas, and Michigan in the early 1980s by Rand researchers (Chaiken and Chaiken 1982), as modified and refined in more recent work by Canela-Cacho, Blumstein, and Cohen (1997). Canela-Cacho et al. estimate that the individual robbery rate among what they call "resident inmates" (as of the late 1970s, when these inmates were initially surveyed) ranged from about 12 per year in Texas to a stunning 106 per year in Michigan, with California in the middle at about 55 robberies per year (ibid.:150). These figures are pulled upward by very high rates of robbery among a relative handful of offenders, and they are subject to a variety of biases intrinsic to self-report studies. They may also overstate the criminality of offenders who were imprisoned more recently, because there is good reason to believe that the average offending frequency of inmates falls as the level and reach of incarceration rises, and pulls in less serious offenders. But we can think of them as a very rough, illustrative, "ball park" set of estimates. (Note that in a later field study of armed robbers in St. Louis, Wright and Decker found that roughly one-fifth of their subjects reported committing more than one armed robbery a week; the number of robberies they reported committing in the past month ranged from zero to 25 [1997:14, 141–44]).

Suppose, for purposes of discussion, that we take the *lowest* of these figures as a rough guide to the overall offending frequency of the present-day population of imprisoned robbers. This means that the 162,000 robbers now in state prisons on any given day "represent" about 12.3 robberies each—for a total of just under two million. Now further suppose that of those nearly two million, a little over half—say, one million—would have been reported to police, other things equal. That gives us a fairly stunning number of what we might call "hidden" robberies. Indeed the number of "hidden" robberies is roughly two and one-half times the number of robberies actually reported in 1999, which was 409,000. Putting the two together gives us a "latent" robbery rate—including both the measured robberies and the estimate of "hidden" robberies—that is more than triple the official reported robbery rate.

Again, I make no pretense of precision in these numbers. But I would note that this way of calculating the "hidden" robberies of the imprisoned may well underestimate what I'm calling the "latent" robbery rate, for several reasons. For one thing, as Canela-Cacho et al. suggest, many robberies would also have been committed by offenders who were sentenced for something else—for drug offenses, say, or assault—but who have nothing against robbery. For another, keep in mind that the mean figure of 12 robberies a year represents the *lowest* estimate that can be derived from the early studies of self-reported offense frequency. Suppose the mean is closer to 20 robberies a year. Then the "hidden" robberies represented by the im-

prisoned robbers alone (not to mention imprisoned burglars and drug traf-
fickers) is more than 3 million, and the "latent" robbery rate dwarfs the reported rate by roughly four to one.

On the other hand, there are factors working in the other direction,
which may mean that the "latent" rate as I am constructing it overstates
the mass of "criminality" behind bars. One of them, for example, is the
effect of the aging of the inmate population, which will—other things
equal—lower the individual robbery rates we can reasonably attribute to
incarcerated robbers as a group. But on balance, I would argue that the bottom line is that we will emerge from more sophisticated calculations with
an amount of "latent" criminality that is both very large and, as the prison
population grows, greatly increasing. And we accordingly have, today, a
much bigger problem with robbery than the official robbery numbers suggest—and, by extension, of other crimes as well.

Now look at what happens to the *trends* in robbery over time, if we look
at them through the lens of latent criminality. By our official measures, robbery went up sharply in the late 1980s and into the early 1990s, and has
dropped quite significantly since. But our propensity to produce robbers
has taken a considerably different trajectory. Back in 1985 there were just
94,000 inmates in state prisons for robbery. Let us keep the same estimate
of their average rate of offending (which may be somewhat inaccurate,
since, again, the average rate may have dropped over time because of the
tendency for the hardest offenders to be the first to be locked up, meaning
that average intensity of offending may be falling as we reach deeper into
the pool of active offenders). The aggregate "latent" robberies represented
by the imprisoned robbers is thus 94,000 × 6, or 564,000. Add that to the
498,000 reported robberies that year and you get 1,062,000—versus roughly
1,400,000 in 1999. So by the "latent" measure we had well over 300,000 *more*
robberies in 1999 than in 1985. In absolute numbers, by the official measure, there was an 18 percent drop in robberies 1985–1999, but a 32 percent
increase by the latent measure. In terms of robbery *rates*, the conventional
measure gives us a drop of about 39 percent since 1985; the latent measure
shows an *increase* of about 15 percent.

Thus the "latent" robbery rate has not in fact declined at all since the
mid-1980s, though the official rate has. This suggests, among other things,
that the ballyhoo about dramatic drops in crime is somewhat misplaced.
On one level, to be sure, the official decline does reflect something of considerable importance; the citizen is less likely to be robbed on the street
than in 1985. But it does not tell us enough, and it obscures what for the social scientist may be the most important fact of all—which is that the
propensity of our social order to generate large numbers of people who,
for whatever reason, are motivated to rob other people has not improved,
and if anything seems to have worsened. (Keep in mind, too, that this has
taken place during a period that includes the longest economic boom in re-

cent history, which according to recent research reduced this kind of crime from what it would otherwise have been, net of other factors [Bernstein and Houston 2000].)

Some people, of course, would be tempted to say, so what? As long as we have gotten them off the street, why should we care about the "latent" social pathology that imprisoned offenders represent? But though that perspective may be adequate for the legislator interested mainly in reelection, it is not adequate for the criminologist—because if we leave out the criminality that is now so heavily concentrated in our prisons, we distort our understanding of the nature and causes of crime in very fundamental ways.

Consider, for example, how it might affect international comparisons of crime rates. Suppose we want to compare our crime rates with those of, say, the Swedes or the Dutch. And suppose we continue to do this the conventional way, by comparing measured crime rates for certain offenses—whether we got those rates from police statistics, victim surveys, or anywhere else. Will that kind of comparison give us an accurate picture of the real differences in criminality between these countries—in a time when our incarceration rate is in the neighborhood of ten times theirs?

Suppose we were to find that the Swedish robbery rate is getting close to ours when measured conventionally. But suppose also that we have, proportionately, ten times as many people in prison for robbery as the Swedes do. Is it really meaningful to say that the two countries have similar robbery problems?

I do not think so. And again, this is far from a quibble. If we do stick with the usual measure, there could be extremely important theoretical implications. For example, it is widely argued that there is a strong connection between extremes of economic inequality and poverty and some kinds of violent "street" crime, and also that many forms of violent crime are aggravated where there is a relative lack of strong social supports (Cullen 1994; Currie 1998). Our hypothetical comparison to Sweden would cast doubt on those links. After all, robbery is nearly as bad (in this hypothetical example) in Sweden—one of the most advanced welfare states in the world, with one of the narrowest spreads of inequality and lowest rates of poverty—as it is in the United States, with only a residual welfare state, notoriously wide inequality, and the *worst* poverty in the industrial world. Our conclusion might be that there is no connection between those social deficits and serious street crime after all—or at least not much of one.

But I think that conclusion would be enormously misleading, even if it were indeed true that the Swedish official robbery rate looked like ours. And it would be misleading primarily because it would ignore the reality that much of the criminality produced (in part) by extreme deprivation, harsh inequality, and minimal social provision in the United States had simply been removed from the reckoning by what really amounts to a sort of conceptual sleight of hand (in much the same way as the growth of mass incarceration has artificially lowered our official unemployment rate by hiding large numbers of the jobless behind bars [Western and Beckett 1999; Currie 1998]).

I think, again, that this is basically just common sense. We understand viscerally that if a country has *both* high levels of street crime *and* high levels of incarceration for street crime, then something is especially wrong there—something is especially awry in its social order—and that "something" is not adequately tapped by the simple comparison of its measured crime rate with that of other countries. If we really want to understand the depth of the crime problem in that country and therefore, understand better where crime comes from, we need a measure of criminality that encompasses both of those realities.

And though I have used a hypothetical example here, this has become more than an abstract issue. There is an increasingly widespread argument that crime in other advanced industrial countries is coming to resemble—or surpass—that in the United States (with the exception of homicide). There are many problematic aspects of this argument, not least the weakness of the data on which it is based. But most importantly, it ignores the effect of mass incarceration on our assessment of cross-national levels of criminality. And to the extent that it does so, it exaggerates the degree of international convergence in social pathology and minimizes the costs of markedly inegalitarian social arrangements.

A version of the same problem could emerge if we were studying crime across jurisdictions, or within jurisdictions, within the United States. Suppose we are trying to determine the strength of the relationships—if any—between levels of poverty or inequality and crime rates by looking at census tracts or neighborhoods across a number of large American cities. And suppose—as is in fact true—that most of the people incarcerated for street crimes come from a very concentrated set of those neighborhoods, and that the proportion of their residents who are behind bars at any given point has mounted relentlessly under the impact of ever "tougher" sentencing. This means that the current "crime rate" in those communities will surely understate the extent to which they have produced criminals. As a result, when we compare those rates with those of other, less impoverished communities, we will also understate the real differences between them—perhaps enough so that any remaining differences will fail to reach statistical significance. And we accordingly will be tempted to toss out the hypothesis of a strong link between poverty and crime—in spite of the fact that, say, 80 percent of the street criminals in prison in these states come from a relative handful of severely impoverished neighborhoods!

Again, these effects would have been much less worrisome when there was less of a divergence between crime rates and criminality rates; when our prison incarceration rate was around 100 per 100,000 versus nearly 500.

It would be less a problem in Sweden or Germany than in the United States, less a problem in Minnesota than in Louisiana. But overall, in the United States, it has arguably become a big enough problem that a different approach to the measurement of criminality has become urgent.

Keep in mind that the kind of measurement I am advocating is after all what we do when we study virtually every *other* social ill that plagues us—except for crime. Illness, again, is an obvious example. Homelessness is another. If we want a measure of the extent of homelessness, and thus of the capacity of our conventional policies to provide housing for everyone, we would not just count those of the homeless who are actually sleeping on the street; we would also count those living in shelters we have had to provide for them. And so on.

The fact that we do not measure the prevalence of criminality in some similar way as we measure other social problems is probably due less to any legitimate methodological or theoretical reason than to the political pressures that shape our discussion of crime. It is the crime on the street that concerns the legislator and most of the public; if they bring the incarcerated population into the equation at all, they are likely to view it as the solution, not as a reflection of the problem.

But for the criminologist that is not good enough, because it masks far too much that is critical in helping us to understand the roots of crime and the long-range effectiveness and consequences of strategies against it. So I urge us as a profession to set to work developing new measures of criminality that could advance our discussion of the way different social conditions and social policies affect crime. But I would argue that these concerns are not only important for criminologists but also for policymakers and the public. It *matters* to us, as a society, whether we achieve a given crime rate with or without a massive correctional complex. It matters in fiscal terms, and matters in moral and political ones.

A focus on criminality rates drives home the point that despite some welcome news on the crime front, we as a nation are still in very troubling condition. More broadly, it drives home the reality that the sort of global economic "model" that we have been celebrating—and exporting—tends to bring consequences in its wake that are far more problematic than our conventional measures indicate, or that our conventional public debates acknowledge. And it confirms the urgency of doing things differently, and better.

REFERENCES

Bernstein, Jared and Ellen Houston. 2000. *Falling Crime Rates in the 1990s: The Role of the Low-Wage Labor Market.* Washington, DC: Economic Policy Institute.
Canela-Cacho, Jose A., Alfred Blumstein, and Jacqueline Cohen. 1997. "Relation-

ship between the Offending Frequency of Imprisoned and Free Offenders." *Criminology* 35(1):133–71.

Chaiken, Jan and Marcia Chaiken. 1982. *Varieties of Criminal Behavior.* Santa Monica, CA: Rand Corporation.

Cullen, Francis T. 1994. "Social Support as an Organizing Principle for Criminology." *Justice Quarterly* 11(4):527–59.

Currie, Elliott. 1998. *Crime and Punishment in America.* New York: Metropolitan.

Freeman, Richard B. 1992. "Crime and the Employment of Disadvantaged Youth." Pp. 201–37 in *Urban Labor Markets and Job Opportunity,* edited by George Peterson and Wayne Vroman. Washington, DC: Urban Institute Press.

Garland, David. 2001. "Introduction: The Meaning of Mass Imprisonment." Pp. 1–3 in *Mass Imprisonment: Social Causes and Consequences,* edited by David Garland. London: Sage.

Rose, Dina and Todd Clear. 1998. "Incarceration, Social Capital, and Crime." *Criminology* 36(2):441–72.

Visher, Christy A. 1986. "The Rand Inmate Survey: A Reanalysis." In *Criminal Careers and "Career Criminals,"* Volume II, edited by Alfred Blumstein, Jacqueline Cohen, Jeffrey Roth, and Christy Visher. Washington, DC: National Academy Press.

Western, Bruce. 2001. "Incarceration, Unemployment, and Inequality." *Focus* 21(3): 32–36.

Western, Bruce and Katherine Beckett. 1999. "How Unregulated Is the U.S. Labor Market? The Penal System as a Labor Market Institution." *American Journal of Sociology* 104(4):1030–60.

Wright, Richard T. and Scott H. Decker. 1997. *Armed Robbers in Action.* Boston: Northeastern University Press.

Contributors

James Austin James Austin is a research professor at the George Washington University and also serves as the director of the Institute on Crime, Justice and Corrections at the university. He serves, or has recently served, as director for several U.S. Department of Justice–funded research and evaluation programs. Most recently he has assisted the Pennsylvania, Texas, and Kentucky parole boards evaluate and/or develop their parole guideline systems. He is also assisting several state prison systems revalidate their prisoner classification and risk assessment systems. Since 1999 he has served as the U.S. Department of Justice's Civil Rights Division monitor to oversee major reforms in the Georgia juvenile correctional system.

Richard A. Berk Richard A. Berk is professor in the Departments of Statistics and Sociology at UCLA and is an elected fellow of the American Statistical Association and the American Association for the Advancement of Science. His research interests center on applied research and the statistical methods by which it is best done. Recent work includes a randomized field experiment for the California Department of Corrections testing with twenty thousand inmates a new inmate classification system used to assign prisoners to different security levels.

Egon Bittner Egon Bittner received his Ph.D. in sociology from UCLA in 1961. After brief periods of teaching and research at the University of California campuses in Riverside and at the Medical School in San Francisco, he moved to Brandeis University, where he was the Harry Coplan Professor in the Social Sciences until his retirement in 1991. Most of his writings about police are contained in a volume entitled *Aspects of Police Work* (1990).

Thomas G. Blomberg Thomas G. Blomberg is Sheldon L. Messinger Professor of Criminology at the School of Criminology and Criminal Justice at Florida State University. He received his B.A., M.A, and Ph.D. degrees from the University of California at Berkeley. He has published widely in the areas of corrections and social control, education and delinquency, and evaluation research and policy. His books include *Courts and Diversion* (1979), *Juvenile Court and Community Corrections* (1984), *Punishment and Social Control* (1995), *American Penology* (2000), and *Data-Driven Juvenile Justice Education* (2001).

Alfred Blumstein Alfred Blumstein is the J. Erik Jonsson University Professor of Urban Systems and Operations Research and former Dean (from 1986 to 1993) at the Heinz School of Public Policy and Management of Carnegie Mellon University. He also directs the National Consortium on Violence Research (NCOVR). He has chaired National Academy of Sciences panels on research on Deterrent and Incapacitative Effects, on Sentencing, and on Criminal Careers. He is a Fellow of the

495

American Society of Criminology, was the 1987 recipient of the Society's Sutherland Award for "contributions to research," and was the president of the Society in
1991–92. His research over the past twenty years has covered many aspects of crim-
inal-justice phenomena and policy, including crime measurement, criminal careers,
sentencing, deterrence and incapacitation, prison populations, demographic
trends, juvenile violence, and drug enforcement policy.

Pat Carlen   Pat Carlen is Visiting Professor of Criminology at Keele University
and in 1997 was recipient of the ASC Sellin-Glueck Award for international contributions to criminology. She recently edited *Women and Punishment* (Willan 2002).

Stanley Cohen   Stanley Cohen is Martin White Professor of Sociology at the London School of Economics. He has written about criminological theory, prisons, social control, criminal justice policy, juvenile delinquency, political crime and human
rights violations. His books include: *Images of Deviance* (1971); *Folk Devils and Moral
Panics: The Making of the Mods and Rockers* (1972); *Psychological Survival: The Experience of Long-Term Imprisonment* (1973) (with Laurie Taylor); *The Manufacture of News*
(1974) (with Jock Young); *Escape Attempts* (1976) (with Laurie Taylor); *Social Control
and the State* (1983) (with Andrew Scull); *Visions of Social Control* (1985); *Against
Criminology* (1988), and *States of Denial: Knowing About Atrocities and Suffering*
(2001). In 1985 Cohen received the Sellin-Glueck award from the American Society
of Criminology and in 1998 was elected as a Fellow of the British Academy.

Elliott Currie   Elliott Currie is Visiting Professor in the School of Criminology and
Criminal Justice at Florida State University and Lecturer in Legal Studies at the
University of California, Berkeley. He is the author, among other works, of *Con-
fronting Crime: An American Challenge, Reckoning: Drugs, the Cities, and the American
Future,* and *Crime and Punishment in America.*

Malcolm M. Feeley   Malcolm M. Feeley is the Claire Clements Sanders Professor
of Law at the University of California at Berkeley, where he has taught since 1984.
Previously he held positions at the University of Wisconsin, Yale, and New York
University. He is the author of numerous books and articles including, *The Process
is the Punishment, The Policy Dilemma, Court Reform on Trial* (with Austin Sarat), and
Judicial Policy Making and the Modern State (with Edward Rubin). He also has coauthored two other articles with Jonathan Simon, "The New Penology" (1992) and
"Actuarial Justice" (1994). He is currently working on a comparative study of
women and crime in eighteenth-century Europe.

David A. Freedman   David A. Freedman is professor of statistics at the University of California, Berkeley, and a member of the American Academy of Arts and
Sciences. He has published several books and many papers in probability theory
and statistics. His current research is in the foundations of statistics and policy
analysis. He has worked as a consultant to the World Health Organization, the
Bank of Canada, the Federal Reserve Board, the Department of Commerce, and the
Department of Justice.

David Garland   David Garland is Arthur T. Vanderbilt Professor of Law and Professor of Sociology at New York University. He is a graduate of Edinburgh University and was, until 1997, Professor of Penology at Edinburgh's Centre for Law
and Society. He writes on the sociology and history of punishment, the history of

criminological ideas, and on social theory. He is the author of *Punishment and Welfare* (1985), *Punishment and Modern Society* (1990), and *The Culture of Control* (2001) and is an editor of the interdisciplinary journal *Punishment & Society.*

Rosemary Gartner   Rosemary Gartner is Director of the Centre of Criminology and Professor of Sociology at the University of Toronto. Along with her work with Candace Kruttschnitt on women's experiences of imprisonment, she is writing (with Jim Phillips) a case study of vigilantism and gender in the Pacific Northwest in the early twentieth century.

John Irwin   After serving five years in a California prison, John Irwin went to college and received his PhD. in sociology at the University of California, Berkeley, in 1968. He taught sociology and criminology at San Francisco State University for 27 years and retired in 1994. He conducted research on prisons and the criminal justice system and wrote *The Felon* (1970), *Prisons in Turmoil* (1980), *The Jail* (1985), and, with James Austin, *It's About Time* (1994). He is currently writing a new book on the contemporary prison.

James B. Jacobs   James B. Jacobs, a University of Chicago-trained lawyer/sociology is Warren E. Burger Professor of Law and Director, Center For Research in Crime and Justice, New York University. His most recent books are *Hate Crime: Criminal Law and Identity Politics* (Oxford University Press 1998), *Gotham Unbound: How New York City was Liberated from the Grip of Organized Crime* (NYU Press 1999), and *Can Gun Control Work?* (Oxford University Press 2002).

Gary Kleck   Gary Kleck is Professor of Criminology and Criminal Justice at Florida State University. His research focuses on the links between guns and violence and the deterrent effects of punishment. He is the author of four books, including *Point Blank*, which won the 1993 Michael Hindelang Award for the most outstanding contribution to criminology.

Candace Kruttschnitt   Candace Kruttschnitt is a Professor in the Department of Sociology at the University of Minnesota. She is currently writing a book with Rosemary Gartner on women's experiences of imprisonment in California in the 1960s and 1990s.

Charis E. Kubrin   Charis E. Kubrin is an Assistant Professor of Sociology and Senior Fellow at the Institute on Crime, Justice and Corrections at The George Washington University. Her research addresses neighborhood correlates of crime and violence, with an emphasis on race and violent crime. With colleagues, she has received funding from the National Science Foundation and the National Consortium on Violence Research to study racial change and victimization in Seattle neighborhoods. Her most recent work has been published in *Social Problems*, the *Journal of Research in Crime and Delinquency*, and *Homicide Studies.*

Gary T. Marx   Gary T. Marx is Professor Emeritus from Massachusetts Institute of Technology. He received his Ph.D. from the University of California at Berkeley. He has taught there, at Harvard University, and the University of Colorado, as well as Belgium, Spain, Austria, China, and other countries around the world. He is the author of *Protest and Prejudice, Undercover: Police Surveillance in America*, and co-editor of *Undercover: Police Surveillance in Comparative Perspective.* His work has appeared or been reprinted in over 250 books, monographs and periodicals and translated into many languages. He has served in an advisory capacity for many government and nonprofit organizations and on many editorial boards. Major work in progress is a book on new forms of surveillance.

David Matza   David Matza is Professor Emeritus of Sociology in the Department of Sociology at the University of California at Berkeley. He received his Ph.D. from Princeton and has been a Research Associate at the Center for the Study of Law and Society and the Institute for the Study of Social Change at the University of California at Berkeley. His books and articles include *Delinquency and Drift* and *Becoming Deviant* for which he received a Guggenheim Fellowship and was the first winner of the C. Wright Mills Award from the Society for the Study of Social Problems.

Patricia Morgan   Patricia Morgan is Associate Professor of Public Health at the University of California at Berkeley. She received her Ph.D. at the University of California, Santa Barbara, in 1978. She has published extensively in the areas of drug and alcohol, legal policy, deviance, and social problems, and directed major cross-cultural and community-based research on illicit drug use. She has received several fellowship awards, including a Fulbright, to conduct international comparative research on policy issues related to both alcohol and illicit drugs.

Raymond Paternoster   Raymond Paternoster is a Professor in the Department of Criminology and Criminal Justice at the University of Maryland. He has conducted death penalty research in the areas of juror attitudes, racial discrimination, and disproportionality. Currently, he is engaged in a comprehensive study of the workings of the death penalty in the state of Maryland.

David J. Rothman   David J. Rothman is Bernard Schoenberg Professor of Social Medicine and Director of the Center for the Study of Society and Medicine at the Columbia College of Physicians and Surgeons, and Professor of History at Columbia University. Trained in social history at Harvard University, he has explored the history and impact of caretaker and custodial institutions. His book *The Discovery of the Asylum* (1971), cowinner of the Albert J. Beveridge Prize of the American Historical Association, traced the early history of these institutions; *Conscience and Convenience* (1980) brought the story up to the present. Aldine de Gruyter has recently reissued these two works. In 1987, David Rothman received an honorary doctor of laws degree from John Jay School of Criminal Justice for this work.

Jonathan Simon   Jonathan Simon is Professor Law at the University of Miami. Simon is the author of *Poor Discipline: Parole and the Social Control of the Underclass, 1890–1990* (Chicago 1993), and the editor (with Tom Baker) of *Embracing Risk: The Changing Culture of Insurance and Responsibility* (Chicago 2002). He is currently completing a book on how crime control has reshaped American governance more generally.

Jerome H. Skolnick   Jerome H. Skolnick is the Claire Sanders Clements Dean's Chair (Jurisprudence and Social Policy) Emeritus, of the University of California, Berkeley. He currently teaches at the New York University School of Law, where he is Codirector of the Center for Research in Crime and Justice. He is former President of the American Society of Criminology and has received numerous awards for his research and writing. His books include *Society and the Legal Order, Justice Without Trial* (a recognized classic and multi-award-winning book including the C. Wright Mills Award of the Society for the Study of Social Problems), *House of Cards, The New Blue Line,* and *Above the Law: Police and The Excessive Use of Force.*

Richard Sparks   Richard Sparks is Professor of Criminology at Keele University. His main research interests lie in the sociology of imprisonment; penal politics; and public responses to crime and punishment. He is the author of *Television and the Drama of Crime* (1992) and coauthor (with Tony Bottoms and Will Hay) of *Prisons and the Problem of Order* (1996) and (with Evi Girling and Marion Smith) of *Crime and Social Change in Middle England* (2000). He has also recently coedited (with David Garland) *Criminology and Social Theory* and (with Tim Hope) *Crime, Risk and Insecurity* (2000). He is currently Editor-in-Chief of the journal *Punishment & Society.*

William Staples   William G. Staples is Professor and Chair of the Department of Sociology at the University of Kansas. He received his Ph.D. from the University of Southern California and was a Postdoctoral Fellow at UCLA. His books include *Castles of Our Conscience: Social Control and the American State, 1800–1985* (1991) and *Everyday Surveillance: Vigilance and Visibility in Postmodern Life* (2000).

Gresham M. Sykes   Gresham M. Sykes received his B.A. from Princeton University in 1950 and his Ph.D. from Northwestern University in 1953. He has taught at a number of universities in the United States, served as Executive Officer of the American Sociological Association, and retired from the University of Virginia in 1987. He is presently devoted to a career in art.

Andrew von Hirsch   Andrew von Hirsh, LL.D. is Honorary Professor of Penal Theory and Penal Law at the University of Cambridge, England, and a member of the Institute of Criminology at Cambridge. He is Director of the recently established Centre for Penal Theory and Penal Ethics at the Institute of Criminology, and also Adjunct Professor at the Law Faculty of Uppsala University, Sweden. He has published extensively on criminal sanctioning theory and practice. His books on that subject include: *Doing Justice* (1976), *Past or Futures Crimes* (1985), *Censure and Sanctions* (1993), *Criminal Deterrence and Sentence Severity* (1999). He has also written on the philosophy of criminal law, and on the ethics of crime prevention. In 1998 he received an honorary doctorate of laws from Uppsala University.

Gordon P. Waldo   Gordon P. Waldo received a B.A. in psychology from the University of North Carolina at Chapel Hill and an M.A. and Ph.D. in sociology from Ohio State University. Currently he is Professor of Criminology and Criminal Justice at Florida State University and the Program Manager of the Juvenile Justice Educational Enhancement Program. He has served as Chair of the United States Sentencing Commission's Drugs and Violence Task Force, Research Consultant to the National Research Council Panel on Rehabilitation and Deterrence, Director of the Southeastern Correctional and Criminological Research Center, Senior Research Advisor to the United States Sentencing Commission, Associate Editor of *Social Forces and Criminology,* and Academic Advisor to Mahidol University (Bangkok, Thailand) in the development of the first doctoral program in criminology in South East Asia.

Loïc Wacquant   Loïc Wacquant is Professor of Sociology and Research Fellow at the Earl Warren Legal Institute, Uniersity of California–Berkeley, and the Centre de sociologie européenne du Collège de France. He has been a visiting professor in Los Angeles, New York, Rio de Janeiro and Paris. Besides the role of carceral institutions in the management of social insecurity in advanced society and racial domination, his interests include comparative urban inequality and marginality, violence and the body, and social theory. His recent books include *Prisons of Poverty* (1999, translated in thirteen languages), *Body and Soul: Ethnographic Notes of an Apprentice Boxer* (2000, translated in six languages), *Punir les pauvres* (2002), and *Parias Urbanos* (2001), and *Deadly Symbiosis: Race and the Coming of Neoliberal Penality* (2003). He has recently completed an anthology entitled *Marcel Mauss on Exchange, Belief and Social Transformation*, and is working on an ethnography of everyday life in America's black ghetto, entitled *In the Zone*. He is cofounder and editor of the interdisciplinary journal *Ethnography*, and a regular contributor to *Le Monde díplomatique*.

Index

DATE DUE